The Princeton Review®

GED® TEST
PREMIUM PREP

32nd Edition

The Staff of The Princeton Review

PrincetonReview.com

Penguin Random House

The Princeton Review
110 East 42nd Street, 7th Floor
New York, NY 10017
princetonreview.com
penguinrandomhouse.com

Published in the United States by Penguin Random House LLC, New York.

ISBN: 979-8-217-23068-6
eBook ISBN: 979-8-217-23069-3
ISSN: 2688-1012

The material in this book is up-to-date at the time of publication. However, changes may have been instituted by the testing body in the test after this book was published.

If there are any important late-breaking developments, changes, or corrections to the materials in this book, we will post that information online in the Student Tools. Register your book and check your Student Tools to see if there are any updates posted there.

Editor: Meave Shelton
Production Editors: Emily Epstein White and Emma Parker
Production Artist: Jennifer Chapman
Content Contributors: Gina Donegan and Chris Chimera

Manufactured in the United States of America

10 9 8 7 6 5 4 3 2 1

32nd Edition

EU Contact:
Penguin Random House Ireland
32 Nassau Street
Dublin D02 YH68
https://eu-contact.penguin.ie

For customer service, please contact **editorialsupport@review.com**, and be sure to include:

- full title of the book
- ISBN
- page number

Acknowledgments

The Princeton Review would like to thank Gina Donegan and Chris Chimera for their hard work and valuable contributions to the 32nd Edition of this book.

We're also grateful to the following content experts for their contributions to previous editions: Amy Leggette, Joshua Nagel, David Stoll, Kimberly Beth Hollingsworth, Chris Chimera, Erik Kolb, Eliz Markowitz, Becky Robinson, Linda Kelley, Andy Olson, Katie Williams, Chris Hinkle, Kevin Kelly, Gina Donegan, Alexandra Wax Henkoff, Lisa Mayo, and Graham Skelhorne-Gross.

Special thanks to Adam Robinson, who conceived of and perfected the Joe Bloggs approach to standardized tests, and many of the other successful techniques used by The Princeton Review.

Finally, special thanks to Jennifer Chapman, Emily Epstein White and Emma Parker for their careful attention to every page.

Contents

Get More (Free) Content at PrincetonReview.com/prep

As easy as 1·2·3

1 Go to PrincetonReview.com/prep or scan the **QR code** and enter the following ISBN for your book: **9798217230686**

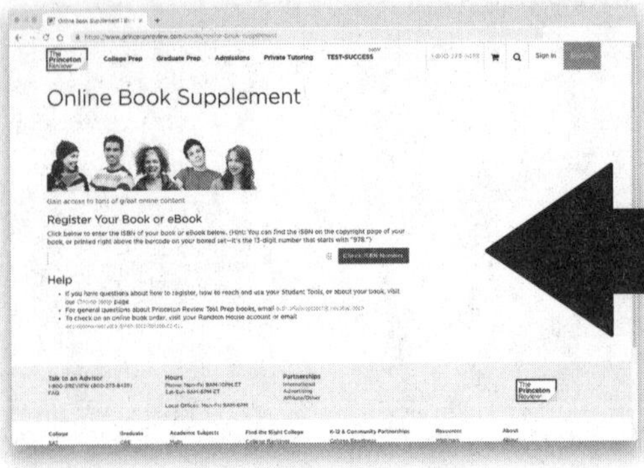

2 Answer a few simple questions to set up an exclusive Princeton Review account. *(If you already have one, you can just log in.)*

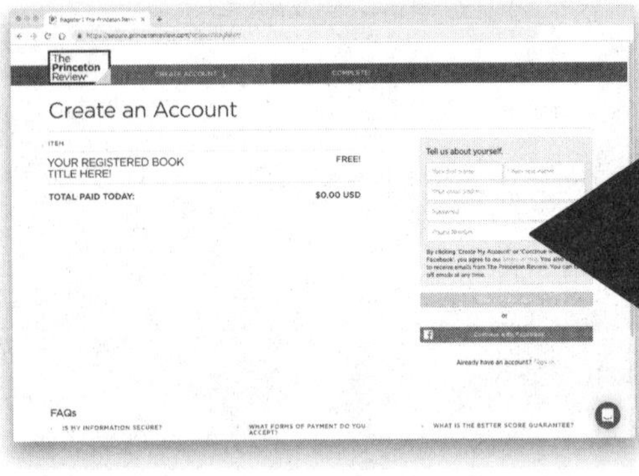

3 Enjoy access to your **FREE** content!

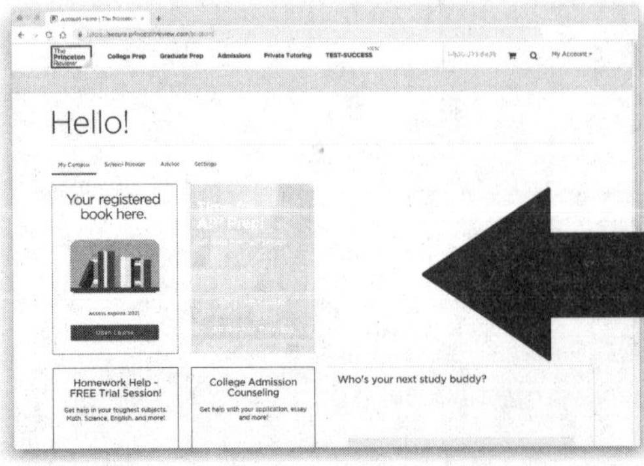

Once you've registered, you can...

- Access 3 additional full-length GED® practice tests with detailed answers and explanations (PDF)
- Supplement your prep with multiple-choice GED® practice drills in all 4 test subjects (digital)
- Get extra support for the toughest math topics with targeted drills (PDF)
- Build core skills with tutorials on reading comprehension and graphics interpretation (PDF)
- Print custom answer sheets for Practice Tests 1–4
- Check to see if there have been any corrections or updates to this edition
- Get our take on any recent or pending updates to the GED® test

Need to report a potential **content** issue?

Contact **EditorialSupport@review.com** and include:

- full title of the book
- ISBN
- page number

Need to report a **technical** issue?

Contact **TPRStudentTech@review.com** and provide:

- your full name
- email address used to register the book
- full book title and ISBN
- Operating system (Mac/PC) and browser (Chrome, Firefox, Safari, etc.)

Look For These Icons Throughout The Book

- ONLINE PRACTICE DRILLS
- ONLINE ARTICLES
- MORE GREAT BOOKS
- PROVEN TECHNIQUES
- APPLIED STRATEGIES

GED Ready®: The Official Practice Test

- With your purchase of this book, you are entitled to 20% off the price of the GED Testing Service's official GED® practice test.
- Visit **shop.gedmarketplace.com/theprincetonreview** for step-by-step instructions on how to receive this discount.

Part I
The GED® Test and You

Chapter 1
How to Use This Book to Achieve a Passing (or a College-Ready) Score

In this chapter, we'll introduce you to the resources available in this book and online, and provide you with a step-by-step plan to achieving your goals for the GED® test.

WELCOME!

You're in the right place.

If you're holding this book, you've already taken the most important step: deciding to move forward. Earning your GED® credential can open doors to college, better jobs, and new opportunities. Whatever your goals, this book is designed to help you reach them as efficiently and confidently as possible.

There's a lot of content on the GED® test. If you're at the beginning of your journey, it might feel difficult to know where to start. That's why we've built this book, including its online components, as a **complete, self-contained course**. Everything you need—content review, strategies, practice, and full-length tests—is organized into one clear system.

Your job is simple: follow the plan.

WHAT THIS BOOK INCLUDES

This book is designed to guide you step by step from your current skill level to a passing—or even College Ready—score.

Here's an overview of the resources available to you.

1. **A Diagnostic Starting Point**
   - **Practice Test 1** (page 35): a full-length GED® practice test that assesses the same skills as the official exam, using the same types of questions.
   - A **Diagnostic Answer Key** (page 116) and **detailed explanations** (page 124) that tell you:
     - what you got wrong
     - why you got it wrong
     - which subjects and specific topics to study next

   This is the **most important tool in the book** because it provides an objective measure of your current strengths and weaknesses.

2. **Complete Content Review**
   In Parts III–IX, you'll find a thorough review of the topics and skills you need to know for the four subject areas of the GED® test:
   - Reasoning Through Language Arts
   - Mathematical Reasoning
   - Social Studies
   - Science

   Each subject is divided into clear, manageable lessons, each of which includes:
   - the essential concepts you need to know (no unnecessary material)
   - example GED® questions that demonstrate how different topics are tested, along with step-by-step explanations

3. **Skill-Building Drills**
   Throughout the content review (Parts III–IX), you'll find practice questions designed to:
   - reinforce what you've learned
   - build your confidence gradually
   - help you recognize patterns on the test

4. **Strategy and Skill Support**
   As you work your way through the book, you'll also learn:
   - how to approach different question types
   - how to read passages efficiently
   - how to avoid common mistakes

5. **Additional Practice Online**
   In your online Student Tools dashboard, you'll find:
   - **Practice Tests 2, 3, and 4**, along with detailed answers and explanations (PDF)
   - 350+ GED® practice questions organized into two test-length drills per subject (digital)
   - extra practice for the most challenging math topics (PDF)

   To access your Student Tools, follow the instructions on pages viii–ix.

HOW TO USE THIS BOOK: YOUR STEP-BY-STEP PLAN

Begin by reading **Chapters 2, 3, and 4** for an overview of the GED® test, its computer-based features, and some very helpful test-taking strategies. Then, follow this plan in order. Be sure not to skip steps!

Step 1: Take Practice Test 1

STEP 1

You have the option of taking the entire GED® test in one sitting or taking individual subject tests on different days. Decide how you plan to schedule your exam and take Practice Test 1 (page 35) accordingly.

Simulate testing conditions as closely as possible:

- Time yourself, including the breaks. Sticking to the timing of the actual test will give you a clear sense of how to adjust your strategy to maximize your score in the time allotted.
- Find a window of time during which you can work without interruptions.
- Do your best, even if you're unsure. There is no penalty for wrong answers, so take your best guess and answer every question.

Then use the **Diagnostic Answer Key** (page 116) to analyze your results. This step answers the most important question: **What do you *actually* need to study?**

Step 2: Build Your Study Plan

Use your diagnostic results to:

- Identify your weak areas.
- Focus only on what needs improvement.

You do *not* need to study everything equally.

Step 3: Register Your Book Online

Follow the instructions on pages viii–ix to gain access to your **free, online Student Tools**, which include robust practice drills and full-length practice tests.

You'll use Practice Tests 2–4 later in Steps 6–8.

Step 4: Work Through Targeted Chapters

- Start with your weakest subjects.
- Read actively: take notes, pause, and reflect.
- Complete all drills in each chapter.

If a topic feels difficult:

- Slow down.
- Revisit the relevant example questions.
- Practice more before moving on. Make use of the drills in your Student Tools as well as those in this book

Step 5: Build Core Skills

If you struggle or are unfamiliar with the following skills, complete the relevant tutorials alongside your review:

- Reading and understanding passages of text: see the **Reading Comprehension tutorial** in your Student Tools.
- Reading and interpreting charts, graphs, and data: see the **Understanding Graphics tutorial** in your Student Tools.

Step 6: Take Practice Test 2

After you've completed your review:

- Revisit Chapter 4 for a refresh on test-taking strategies (optional).
- Take Practice Test 2 under timed conditions.
- Compare your performance to Practice Test 1.

First, look for the areas in which you improved, and congratulate yourself on your progress. Next, identify any remaining weak areas.

Step 7: Final Review

- Revisit challenging topics.
- Redo missed questions.
- Focus on patterns in your mistakes.
- Complete any remaining relevant questions in your online drills.

Step 8: Take Practice Tests 3 and 4

- Repeat Steps 6 and 7 as needed with your remaining practice tests.
- Feel free to focus only on the subject areas in which you are not yet 100% confident.

OPTIONAL SELF-ASSESSMENT

Use this supplementary checklist to reflect on your preparation—but note that it should *not* replace your diagnostic test results. Use it:

- after completing diagnostic Practice Test 1
- to confirm what you already suspect
- to guide additional review if needed

Check any areas where you feel unsure.

Test Skills

- ☐ Understanding question types
- ☐ Managing time effectively
- ☐ Reading passages and data

Reasoning Through Language Arts

- ☐ Reading comprehension (informational and literary)
- ☐ Grammar and sentence structure
- ☐ Writing extended responses

You'll find an even more detailed version of this self-assessment checklist in your online Student Tools (see pages viii–ix).

Mathematical Reasoning

- ☐ Basic arithmetic (fractions, percents, etc.)
- ☐ Algebra (equations, functions)
- ☐ Word problems and data interpretation
- ☐ Geometry basics

Social Studies

- ☐ U.S. history
- ☐ Civics and government
- ☐ Economics and geography

Science

- ☐ Life science
- ☐ Physical science
- ☐ Earth and space science
- ☐ Interpreting scientific data

HOW TO THINK ABOUT YOUR GOAL

Most students aim for a **passing score**, and that's a great goal! If that's your focus:

- Concentrate on reviewing unfamiliar topics and improving weak areas.
- Spend most of your time on relevant chapters and drills.

If you're aiming for a **College-Ready score**:

- Complete *all* chapters.
- Practice more extensively.
- Review more carefully.

Mindset Matters

Remember:

- You don't need to be perfect. You need to be prepared.
- Focus on progress, not perfection.
- Trust the process outlined in this book.

If you follow this plan—diagnosing your strengths and weaknesses, creating a clear study plan, and practicing consistently—you will approach the GED® test feeling confident and ready!

UNDERSTANDING THE PRACTICE TESTS IN THIS BOOK

Before you begin, it's important to understand how our practice tests compare to the official GED® test and how to use them effectively.

Paper-Based vs. Computer-Based Testing

Unlike the official GED® test, which is entirely computer-based, the practice tests in this book *and* online are paper-based, so some question formats have been adapted for pencil-and-paper use.

You'll find a **custom answer sheet** for Practice Test 1 at the very back of your book. Feel free to tear it out. There's also a printable version in your Student Tools online, along with answer sheets for Practice Tests 2–4. See pages viii–ix for details.

What this means for you:

- The interface of our paper-based tests will feel slightly different than that of the computer-based GED® test.
- The questions themselves, down to their level of difficulty, topics covered, and skills tested, are all fully representative of the questions you'll see on the GED® test.

Be sure to read the directions at the beginning of each practice test so you understand how to answer each question type.

How to Think About Your Practice Test Scores

GED Testing Service® uses a scoring system that converts your raw score into a scaled score, but this exact formula is not publicly available.

You can calculate the percentage of questions you answered correctly, and the Diagnostic Answer Key for Practice Test 1 (page 116) will help you analyze your results. However, the most important takeaway is this:

Your practice test score is a *tool for improvement,* not a final prediction! Instead of focusing on your percentage alone, focus on:

- which topics you missed
- why you missed them
- what to study next

The Best Predictor of Your GED® Score

For the most accurate measure of your readiness, **GED Ready®** is your best option. GED Ready® is the official practice test created by GED Testing Service, and it offers:

- a realistic, computer-based testing experience
- questions written by the actual test developers
- an **enhanced score report** with personalized feedback

Although GED Ready® is shorter than the full-length exam, it is the most reliable indicator of whether you're likely to pass. If you choose to include GED Ready® in your study plan, we recommend that you take it after you've completed Step 7 to confirm that you're test-ready. That way, you can use Step 8 (Practice Tests 3 and 4) to continue building proficiency in any areas in which you may need extra support.

For instructions on how to receive a 20% discount when you purchase GED Ready®, visit

shop.gedmarketplace.com/theprincetonreview

OFFICIAL GED® INFORMATION

Visit **GED Testing Service** at GED.com to find:

- test details and policies
- pricing and registration information
- free sample questions

A FINAL THOUGHT

This book gives you everything you need to prepare, but the key to success is how you use it!

- Start with diagnostic Practice Test 1.
- Focus on gaining skill in your areas of weakness.
- Practice consistently.
- Use official tools like GED Ready® to confirm your progress.

We wish you the best of luck in your studies!

Chapter 2
All About the GED® Test

This chapter provides an overview of the four GED® tests, along with information on scoring and registration.

WHAT IS THE GED® TEST?

G-E-D Spells Success!
GED graduates report high job satisfaction with employment they obtain after earning their GED. On average, they earn $200 more per week than non-high school grads.
Source: GED.com/educators-admins/program/workforce-development/

The GED® test is actually four tests that you can take in one day or over a series of days. Many people refer to it as a high school equivalency test because when you pass the test, you earn a credential that most colleges and employers recognize as the equivalent of a high school diploma.

The questions on the test come in several formats, which we'll describe in Chapter 3. The GED® test is designed to measure the skills and knowledge typically developed in high school. However, it is not a memorization test. Instead of requiring you to recall isolated facts, the test asks you to read passages, analyze information, interpret data, and apply reasoning skills. In most cases, the information you need to answer a question will be provided to you in the form of a passage, chart, graph, or diagram.

The Four GED® Tests

1. **Reasoning Through Language Arts**
   (150 minutes, approximately 51 questions)

   - Section 1 (35 minutes)
   - Section 2: One Extended Response question (45 minutes)
   - Break (10 minutes)
   - Section 3 (60 minutes)

Sections 1 and 3 will contain a mixture of grammar and reading comprehension questions. There will be six to eight reading passages with approximately six questions each and two language passages with four drop-down questions in each. The questions for the reading passages will be multiple choice or drag and drop. The reading texts will be in this approximate distribution:

Informational Texts	75%
Literature	25%

In Section 2, you'll be asked to write an extended response analyzing two passages that present different arguments on the same issue. Your task is to evaluate the arguments and determine which one is better supported, using specific evidence from the texts to support your analysis.

2. Mathematical Reasoning
(115 minutes, 46 questions)

- Part 1 (first 5 questions): calculator not allowed
- Part 2 (remaining 41 questions): calculator allowed

The Mathematical Reasoning test is divided into two parts. In the first, you will not be allowed to use a calculator. In the second, you will have access to the on-screen calculator. The test emphasizes problem-solving, with a strong focus on algebra and real-world applications. Many questions are presented as word problems, and a significant portion involve interpreting charts, graphs, and data. These questions come in several formats including multiple choice, fill in the blank, drag and drop, hot spot, and drop down. The test will encompass the following mathematical concepts:

Quantitative Problem Solving (arithmetic, averages, ratios, etc.)	45%
Algebraic Problem Solving	55%

3. Social Studies
(70 minutes, approximately 35 questions)

You will find a mixture of passages, charts, graphs, and maps. The questions will be in multiple-choice, hot-spot, drag-and-drop, and fill-in-the-blank formats. The test will cover the following areas of social studies:

Government and Civics	50%
United States History	20%
Economics	15%
Geography	15%

4. Science
(90 minutes, 1 section of approximately 34 questions)

The questions will be based on a variety of information ranging from short passages to graphs and charts. The questions will be in multiple-choice, fill-in-the-blank, drop-down, drag-and-drop, and hot-spot formats. Most questions are based on information provided in passages, charts, or graphs. Your task is to interpret that information and apply basic scientific concepts. While you are not expected to memorize detailed scientific facts, a general understanding of key principles is helpful. The questions will be about these general areas of science:

Life Science	40%
Physics and Chemistry	40%
Earth and Space Science	20%

Do You Have to Take the Test All at Once?

GED Testing Service does not require that students take the test all in one sitting. However, each state has its own rules about this. To find out what your state's policies are, visit GED.com/policies.

How Is the GED® Test Scored?

For each of the four tests, you will receive a score between 100 and 200. Because each test has a different number of available points, GED Testing Service will standardize your raw scores (or the number of questions you answered correctly for each test) through a formula to yield a score between 100 and 200.

The minimum score needed to pass any of the four subject tests on the GED® test is 145. In order to receive your completion certificate, you must achieve at least this score on each test. A higher score on one test will not make up for a lower score on another. While a passing score is sufficient to obtain your certificate, you may want to strive for a score of at least 165. Such a score entitles you to a GED® College-Ready Score, a distinction that indicates college and career readiness. And if you achieve a score of at least 175, you'll receive the GED® College Ready + Credit designation, which means that in addition to being ready to take college courses, you qualify for up to 10 hours of college credit.

Score Levels	
GED® Passing (high school equivalency)	145–164
GED® College Ready	165–174
GED® College Ready + Credit	175–200

Once you receive a passing score on a test, you do not need to retake that test. If you want to retake the test to receive a higher score, you may do so.

If you do not receive your desired score on a particular test, you can retake that test two more times without any waiting period, subject to scheduling availability. After the third attempt, you will have to wait 60 days to test again. This schedule allows for eight testing opportunities in a year, if you need that many to pass a section.

Registering for the GED® Test

The easiest way to register for the GED® test is through GED Testing Service's official website at GED.com. There, you can create an account, find testing centers, schedule your exams, and review testing policies specific to your state.

Testing is offered year-round, and you can choose to take the four subject tests on different days. Fees and policies vary by state, so be sure to check the most current information on the official website. In most states, it now costs money to take the GED® test—most states charge around $30–$40 per test subject, although some charge less and others more.

College Readiness
Over 45% of GED grads enroll in college within 3 years, and 90% re-enroll from one semester to the next.
Source: GED.com/educators-admins/program/why-ged.html

Chapter 3
The Computer-Based GED® Test: What to Expect

In this chapter, we'll introduce you to the various features and question formats that you'll encounter on the GED® test.

THE COMPUTER-BASED TESTING EXPERIENCE

The GED® test is taken on a computer, either at an official testing center or, in some cases, through online proctoring.

Taking the GED® Test at Home

If your state allows it, you can opt to take the test from home. For more information on rules, eligibility, and technical requirements, visit GED.com/take-the-ged-test-online.html.

Understanding how the testing interface works will help you feel more comfortable and confident on test day. In some cases, a question will appear on a single screen. In other cases, there will be a split screen, with a passage, chart, or other information on one side and the question on the other. At the bottom of each screen, you may click to move to the prior screen or the next screen. At the top of the screen, you will see the question number, the total number of questions in the section, and the time remaining. You can highlight text, change the foreground and background colors, and adjust the font size. You may also flag a question for later review.

For questions that require you to write, you will have access to cut, copy, and paste functions, as well as undo and redo. Where appropriate, an on-screen calculator is provided, as is a mathematical formulas sheet.

Let's now take a closer look at the specific question formats you'll encounter on the GED® test.

The Question Formats

Because the GED® test is computer-based, it includes a variety of question formats that require the use of a mouse and keyboard. While some will feel familiar, others may be new. The good news is that once you understand how each format works, they become predictable and much easier to manage.

In the following chapters, we'll go into more detail on how these question formats appear on each of the four subject tests. Right now, we'll introduce you to the look and feel of each type.

Multiple Choice

You can expect to see this question format on each of the four tests. Multiple-choice questions typically present you with a scenario and ask a question about it. There is one possible answer out of the four choices provided. In order to indicate your answer, use your mouse to click the bubble that corresponds to your answer.

Here is an example.

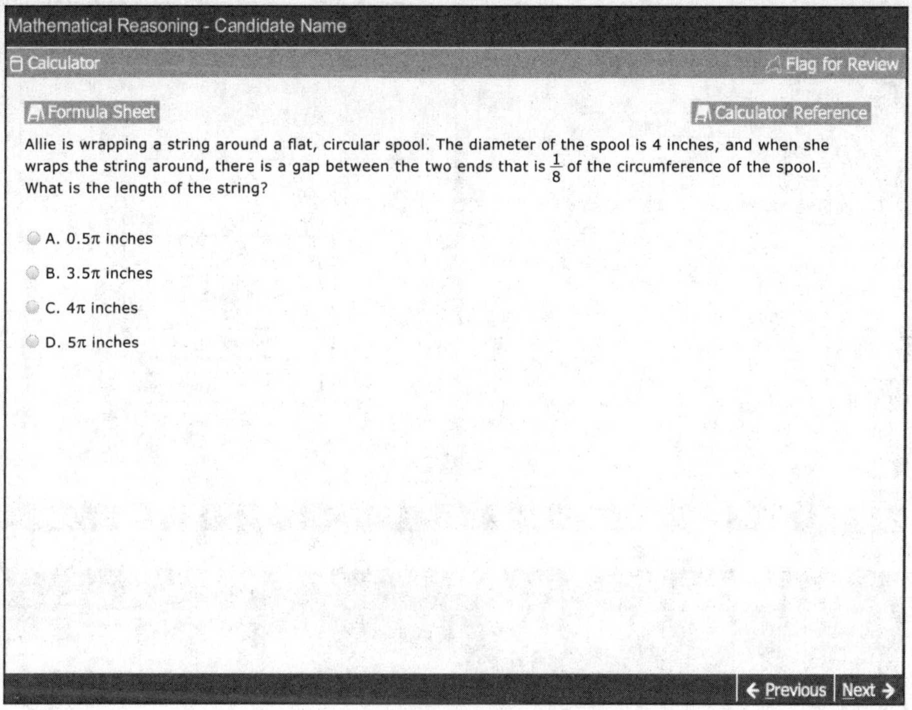

Drag and Drop

Drag-and-drop questions ask you to choose from several options and drag each option to the correct location in the question. Not only must you choose the correct options, but you must also make sure to place them in the order requested. This question format appears in each of the four tests.

Your computer screen will look similar to the following set of images. Note that in order to see the complete question, you may need to navigate between different parts of the question to view all the information (see the tabs marked "page 1" and "page 2" below).

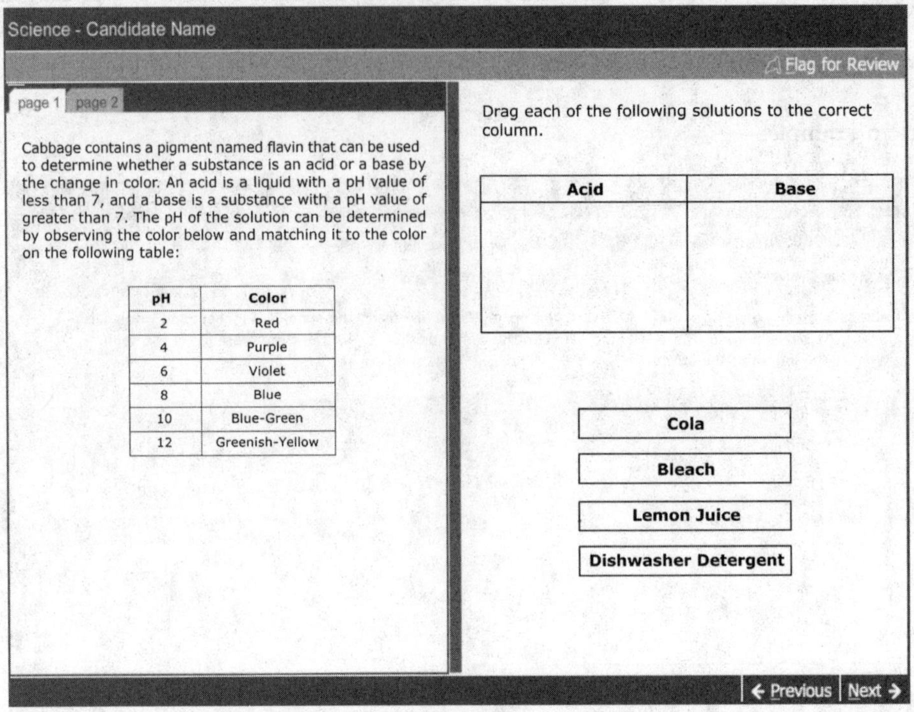

Science - Candidate Name

Flag for Review

page 1 page 2

Cabbage contains a pigment named flavin that can be used to determine whether a substance is an acid or a base by the change in color. An acid is a liquid with a pH value of less than 7, and a base is a substance with a pH value of greater than 7. The pH of the solution can be determined by observing the color below and matching it to the color on the following table:

pH	Color
2	Red
4	Purple
6	Violet
8	Blue
10	Blue-Green
12	Greenish-Yellow

Drag each of the following solutions to the correct column.

Acid	Base

Cola

Bleach

Lemon Juice

Dishwasher Detergent

← Previous Next →

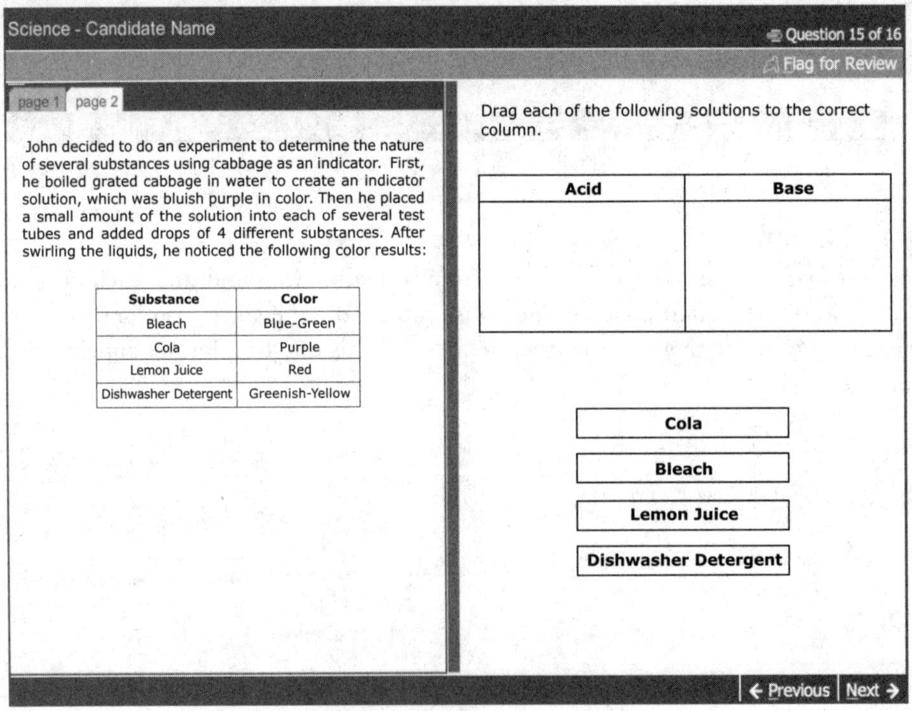

Science - Candidate Name

Question 15 of 16

Flag for Review

page 1 page 2

John decided to do an experiment to determine the nature of several substances using cabbage as an indicator. First, he boiled grated cabbage in water to create an indicator solution, which was bluish purple in color. Then he placed a small amount of the solution into each of several test tubes and added drops of 4 different substances. After swirling the liquids, he noticed the following color results:

Substance	Color
Bleach	Blue-Green
Cola	Purple
Lemon Juice	Red
Dishwasher Detergent	Greenish-Yellow

Drag each of the following solutions to the correct column.

Acid	Base

Cola

Bleach

Lemon Juice

Dishwasher Detergent

← Previous Next →

Hot Spot

Hot-spot questions appear in the Social Studies, Science, and Mathematical Reasoning tests. These questions present you with information and pose a question. In order to indicate your answer, use your mouse to click on one or several points in a chart or graph that represent possible answers.

While this type of question may seem unusual at first, it's really just a variation on multiple choice. When you have determined the answer, simply move your mouse over the area for the right answer and click. If you would like to erase a mark, click on it a second time. Some hot-spot questions require you to select a single answer, while others require multiple selections. Always read the directions carefully to determine how many answers are needed.

Here is an example.

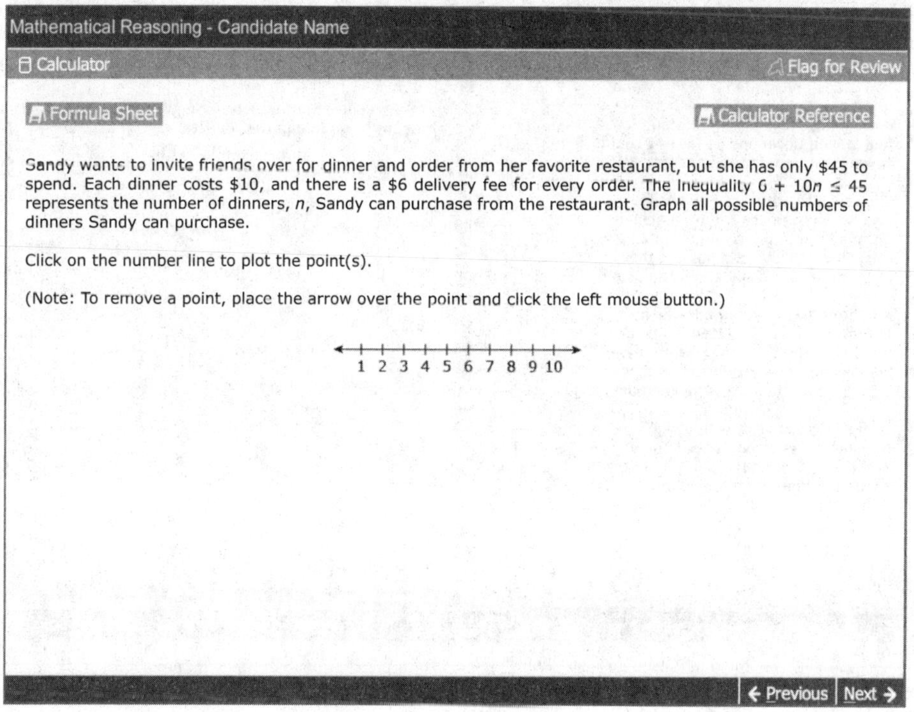

Fill in the Blank

Fill-in-the-blank questions are among the more difficult types of questions, and they may appear on multiple tests. These questions give you a set of information and ask a question. There are no answers provided, and you have to type in your own answer using your keyboard.

Because there are no answers to choose from, these questions are more difficult to guess on than multiple-choice questions. Test takers must take care to enter their answers using the correct units and rounded to the correct place. When faced with this type of question, always reread the question to be sure you are correctly following the directions in drafting your answer.

Here is an example.

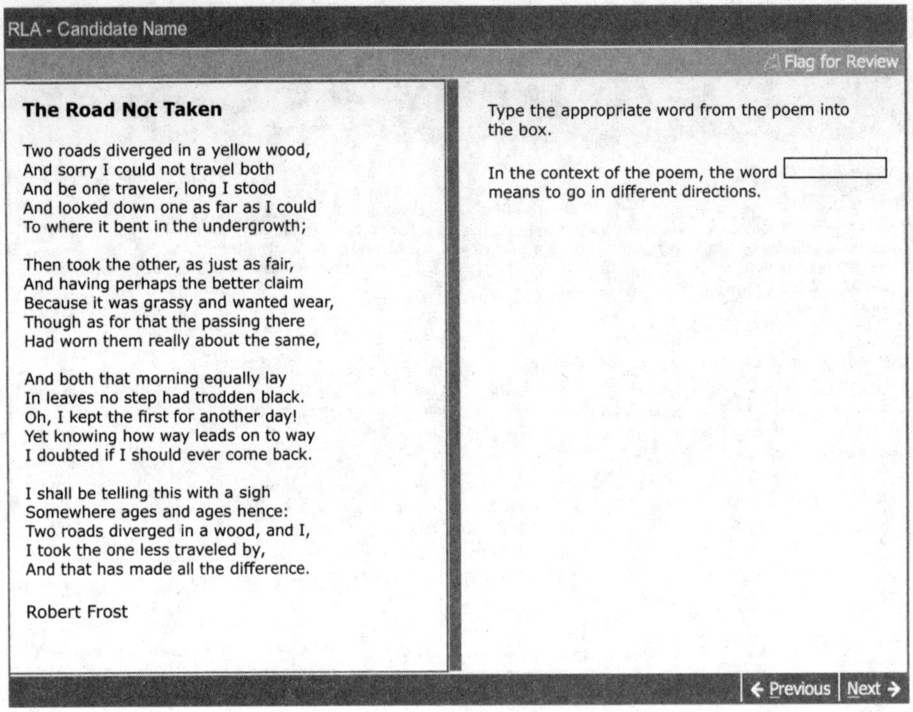

Drop Down

A drop-down question is most similar to a traditional multiple-choice question. It can appear on any of the four tests and is often used to place an answer in the context of a sentence. Use your mouse to click the arrow to the right of the box, and several answers appear in an expanded menu. To select an answer, click on your choice.

Because of their similarity to multiple-choice questions, drop-down questions should feel somewhat familiar. However, it is important to remember to open the box and see the options *before* you try the question. Doing so can greatly reduce the amount of time you spend on the question, as it reduces the number of options to consider.

Here is an example.

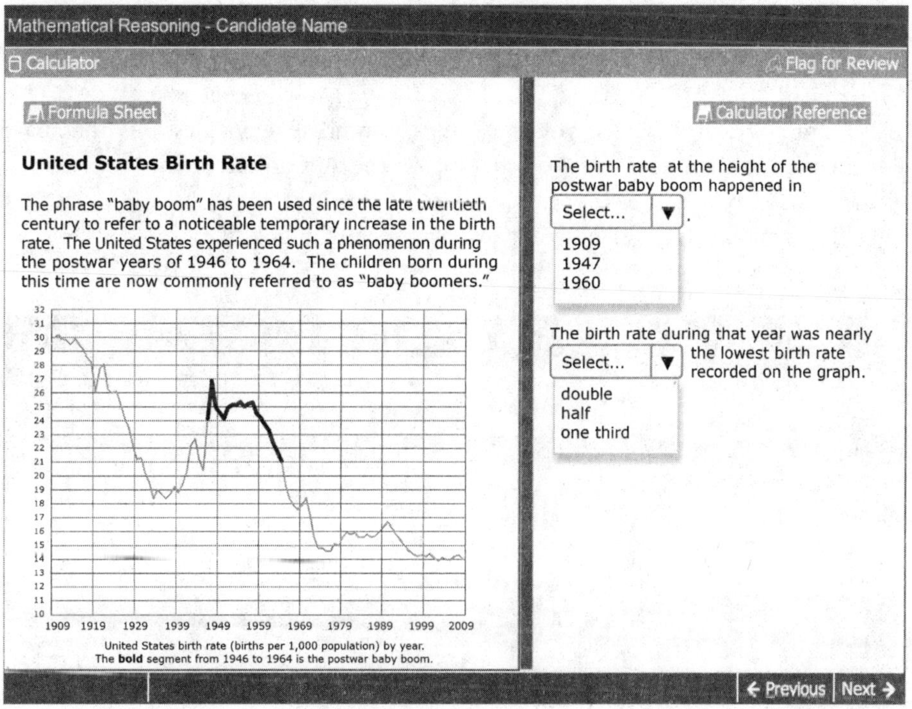

Extended Response

We will show you an example of an Extended Response question, along with more information about it, in Chapter 10.

Please note that while the test does offer some basic word-processing functions (such as cut and paste), the test does not contain many of the options test takers are used to in a word-processing program. Also, the test does not indicate when you have made a possible spelling or grammar mistake, and it does not have an autocorrect feature to fix common typos. You will need to rely on your own proofreading skills, so be sure to leave time to review your writing carefully.

Focus on the Task, Not the Format

While the formats may look different, every GED® question is testing the same core skills:

- Understanding information
- Applying reasoning
- Choosing the best answer

Don't let unfamiliar formats distract you. Focus on what the question is asking, and apply the same strategies you would use for any other question.

As mentioned earlier, please take some time to get comfortable with these question formats. Visit GED.com/educators-admins/teaching/classroom-materials.html for hands-on practice with GED Testing Service's free practice test and computer-based test tutorial.

Next, we'll show you some other features of the computer-based test, along with some tips on how to use them to best effect.

You do not need to answer questions in order. If you get stuck, flag the question and move on. Then return to it later using the review screen. This helps you manage time and avoid getting stuck on difficult questions.

The Review Screen

The review screen is one of the most powerful tools available during the test. Use it strategically to:

- quickly locate unanswered questions
- return to questions you flagged
- ensure you do not leave any questions blank

From the review screen you can quickly jump to any questions that have been marked or left unanswered by clicking on the question number.

Here's an example of what your review screen will look like:

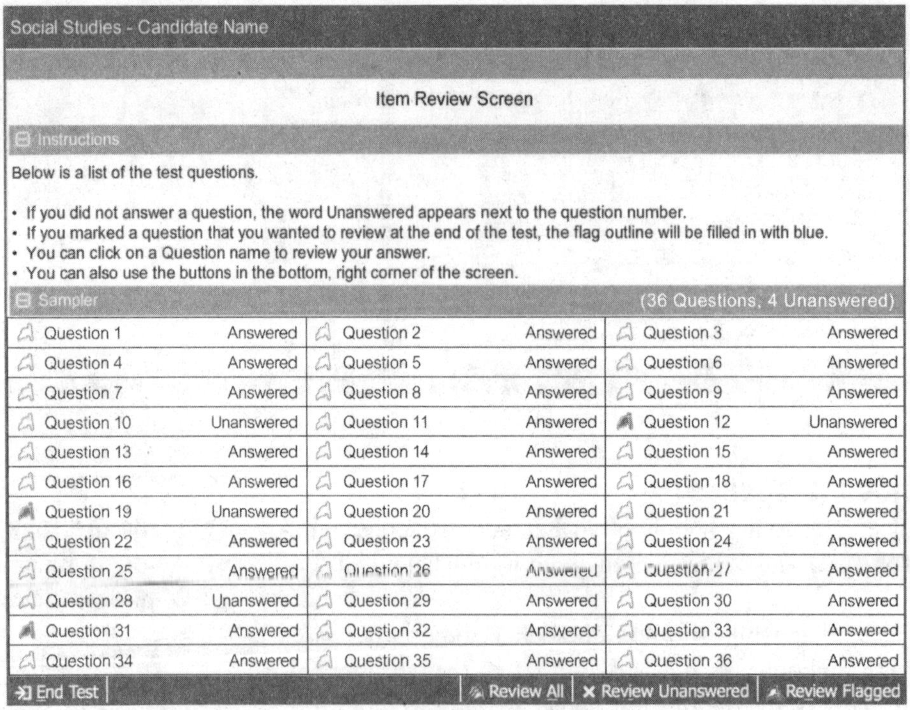
Social Studies - Candidate Name

Item Review Screen

Instructions

Below is a list of the test questions.

- If you did not answer a question, the word Unanswered appears next to the question number.
- If you marked a question that you wanted to review at the end of the test, the flag outline will be filled in with blue.
- You can click on a Question name to review your answer.
- You can also use the buttons in the bottom, right corner of the screen.

Sampler (36 Questions, 4 Unanswered)

Question 1	Answered	Question 2	Answered	Question 3	Answered
Question 4	Answered	Question 5	Answered	Question 6	Answered
Question 7	Answered	Question 8	Answered	Question 9	Answered
Question 10	Unanswered	Question 11	Answered	Question 12	Unanswered
Question 13	Answered	Question 14	Answered	Question 15	Answered
Question 16	Answered	Question 17	Answered	Question 18	Answered
Question 19	Unanswered	Question 20	Answered	Question 21	Answered
Question 22	Answered	Question 23	Answered	Question 24	Answered
Question 25	Answered	Question 26	Answered	Question 27	Answered
Question 28	Unanswered	Question 29	Answered	Question 30	Answered
Question 31	Answered	Question 32	Answered	Question 33	Answered
Question 34	Answered	Question 35	Answered	Question 36	Answered

End Test | Review All | Review Unanswered | Review Flagged

It's a good practice to leave a few minutes at the end of each section of each test to check the review screen to make sure you have answered every question or to look up questions that you marked for later review. For any question you need to answer or revisit, you can click on the question number to go directly to the question. Remember, there is no penalty for guessing on the GED® test (more on this in Chapter 4), so you have nothing to lose by answering every question.

Using Erasable Note Boards

When you take the GED® test at a testing center, you will not have access to scratch paper. Rather, you will be provided with erasable note boards and a marker for scratch work. The exact number and size may vary slightly by testing center, but you will have enough space to work through problems. If the marker runs out of ink or dries up, you may ask for a new one.

Using a note board rather than writing directly on a test booklet takes practice. Get into the habit of working with practice scratch paper from the start (assuming that you don't have access to an erasable note board at home). Developing a consistent system for organizing your work—especially for math—can save time and reduce mistakes.

We recommend that you lay out a note-board strategy as outlined in the different sections of this book. You do not need to copy most information from the screen. Instead, use your note board strategically:

- for math calculations and multi-step problems
- to organize key information when needed
- to keep track of your work clearly

For reading-based sections, you will usually work directly from the screen rather than writing everything down.

While you may use the front and back of each note board, you may have to erase work you did earlier once you've covered the entire surface of all three. A good practice is to always try to finish a problem completely before you move on to the next, to ensure you don't have to restart a problem from, well, scratch.

Your Test Results

One of the great features of a computer-based test is that you will receive your scores very quickly. In many cases, you will receive your scores within a few hours of completing each test. However, some scores (the essay, for instance) may take longer. In some cases, a test may be selected for additional review to ensure scoring accuracy. If this happens, your score may take a few business days to become available. Your scores will be available through your account on the GED Testing Service website at GED.com.

In the next chapter, we'll discuss some specific strategies to give you an advantage on the GED® test.

Chapter 4
Essential Test-Taking Strategies

In this chapter, we'll show you how to boost your score with key skills designed to maximize your performance.

Taking a standardized test involves more than knowledge. You need to approach the test with strategy and learned skills. Effective test takers adopt certain habits that help to reduce stress and increase points.

1. Answer the Easy Questions First

Depending on your specific skill set and your level of comfort with the range of difficulty on the test, some questions will be easier for you than others. It's important to remember that within each section, all of the questions (besides Extended Response) are worth approximately an equal number of points, which means that getting a difficult question wrong is not going to cost you more than missing an easy question. You also have the freedom to answer the questions in any order you like. So, to maximize your score, first answer all of the questions with which you are comfortable, and come back to the more challenging problems later. If you are running out of time, it is best to have already completed all of the "easy" problems so you can spend your remaining minutes guessing on the difficult ones.

It may feel more natural to do the problems in the order they are presented. However, you want to be able to see all of the questions in a section and know that you have worked through all of the questions you could in the time allotted. With efficient use of the flag button and review screen, discussed below, skipping questions that you consider more difficult is the best use of your time. Remember: **Skip early and skip often.**

2. Use a Note Board to Stay on Task

As we discussed in Chapter 3, you will not be provided with traditional scratch paper but with three erasable note boards and a dry-erase marker. Although you will not be able to save your work and go back to it later, that doesn't mean you shouldn't think about how to use your note boards strategically.

Keeping your hand moving while you focus on the physical task of writing is an essential way to stay focused on the test itself. If your brain has to communicate with your hand, then it is engaged and active and less likely to be distracted, which can force you to reread a question multiple times.

In addition to keeping your brain focused and on task, writing can help you to stay on target with the techniques presented in this book. Having something to write down, such as a summary of a reading passage or a math formula, may be just the push your brain needs to get it moving in the right direction. Using scratch paper, develop a note-board habit for each type of question, and stick to it!

3. Use the Flag Button and Review Screen to Get Unstuck

It is inevitable that at some point during the test, you will encounter a question that you don't understand, or one that you *think* you understand...but the answer you want isn't an option. Often, the problem is that you have misread the question or made a small calculation error. Research shows that once you have misread a question, you are likely to keep reading it in the same way, no matter how many times you try. Meanwhile the clock is ticking, and you aren't getting any closer to an answer. If you get stuck, the best thing to do is to flag the problem for review, and move on. Distracting your brain by doing other problems is often just what you need in order to come back and read the problem with fresh eyes.

At the end of the section, you will be able to use the review screen to quickly jump to any questions you have marked. Once you go back to them, you will have a better understanding of how much time you have left to deal with your marked questions. Then you can decide whether to sit down and work a problem or to simply put in a guess.

4. Pacing

Many wrong answers are the result of simply going too fast and reading too quickly. However, most test takers feel they have to rush through the "easy" problems because they won't have time on the more difficult ones. Try a few questions untimed, and you will make fewer mistakes. You'll also probably work more quickly than you think. The questions don't get harder when you add a timer, but somehow, test takers tend not to score as highly.

The trick is to take the GED® test at an even pace, recognizing when a question is more difficult and should be marked for later. Work for accuracy, because doing all the problems will not get you a higher score unless you do them correctly. Slow down and make sure that you are (a) choosing to do the questions you understand first and (b) giving them enough time, attention, and focus to answer them correctly. If you run into a question that feels like a brick wall, flag it and move on to an easier question.

The only exception to this rule is in the last few minutes of any section. This is the time to use your review screen and marked questions to ensure that you have guessed on all the questions for which that option was available.

5. Guessing and Process of Elimination (POE)

The GED® test does not penalize you for an incorrect answer; there is never any deduction for getting a question wrong. So regardless of whether you know the answer to any given problem, it is to your advantage to record an answer to every problem. Thus, guessing on problems that you don't know how to solve, or that you don't have time to work through, can actually *add* points to your score.

Pick a "Guess Letter"

If you had a one-in-four chance to win $10 (and entering didn't cost you anything), you would enter, right? The multiple-choice and drop-down questions on the GED® test are very much like that $10 chance. On any single multiple-choice question, your chance of correctly guessing is 25 percent, and on drop-down questions that chance can increase depending on the number of answer choices available. If you randomly guess a different answer for each question, those odds probably won't add up to as many points as you had hoped. However, if you

Eliminate the Out-of-Scope Answers

Q: What's the capital of Malawi?

A. Paris
B. Dukhan
C. London
D. Lilongwe

Turn the page for the answer.

choose the same answer for every multiple-choice question on which you randomly guess, you are likely to get one in four of the answers correct. Those are pretty good odds, and simply choosing a consistent "guess letter" for drop-down and multiple-choice questions can improve your score.

But what if you could increase your odds even more?

Process of Elimination (POE)

Try the following question:

1. In what year did Texas become a state?

You don't know? The good news is that the GED® test would never ask such a question. Or rather, if it did, you would be given a reading passage in which the answer could be found. The purpose of this example question is to show what you can do if you have a few extra seconds to add to your guessing.

If this were a fill-in-the-blank question, and you did not have time to read the passage, you would have to guess, but the likelihood of your getting it correct would be very small. However, using a small amount of information to guess could help you if the question was multiple choice or drop down. Now, consider the same question in multiple-choice format.

Test-Taking Tip #1
Use POE to get rid of out-of-scope answers.

1. In what year did Texas become a state?

   A. 100 B.C.
   B. 25 A.D.
   C. 1836
   D. 1990

Now the question looks a little easier, right? You know Texas became a state sometime between the 1700s and today. That eliminates (A) and (B). You are also pretty sure that it happened well before 1990, so eliminate (D) too. You didn't know the exact answer, but you did know enough to eliminate wrong answers.

You probably won't be able to narrow down the answer choices to a single one on very many questions, but you may be able to eliminate two answers, which leaves you with a fifty-fifty chance of getting the correct answer. Remember, every choice you eliminate increases your chances of guessing the correct answer.

Try one more.

2. There are 10 students in a class, and their average score on a test is 79 out of 100. If a new student is added to the class, what is the minimum score he would need to achieve in order to bring the class average up to 80 out of 100?

   A. 1
   B. 79
   C. 85
   D. 90

This problem may seem fairly complex to figure out. Don't worry if you don't know how to do averages; we will teach you all you need to know in the Mathematical Reasoning chapters. However, you can understand that if a student's score has to bring up the class average, it would have to be higher than the class average to begin with. With this information you could eliminate (A) and (B), and you would have a fifty-fifty chance of guessing the correct number, which is (D).

Test-Taking Tip #2
If you haven't figured out an answer in a minute, skip the problem and come back to it later.

6. Let It Go

No one question is that important to your score. If you read a question and aren't immediately sure how to answer it, flag it and move on. Do not spend any time beating yourself up for not knowing how to do the problem, as everyone is likely to find at least some questions they don't know how to do. If a problem is taking too much time to figure out, fill in a guess and move on. Keeping track of how many questions you think you got correct, or getting upset because you think you aren't doing well, can only impact your score negatively. Know that you have made the right decision for your overall score at every stage, and move forward to deal with the next question with confidence.

Focus on Your Strengths

Sometimes the questions on this test may seem complex and unusual, especially if you have been away from school for a long period of time. It is important to recognize the strengths that you bring to this test; they can help you to achieve the score you are looking for. Implement the six habits to take control of your testing experience. To this foundation, add the preparation and practice from the rest of this book.

Eliminate the Out-of-Scope Answers
A: The capital of Malawi is Lilongwe, but you didn't need to know that to eliminate (A) and (C).

By focusing on your strengths, you can maintain the proper perspective. The GED® test is only that—a test. It doesn't measure your worth as a human being. It measures how effectively you have acquired a few skills and how you make use of that knowledge in a timed, stressful situation. Use the test's own limitations to your advantage, and with a little hard work, you can earn your GED® test credential.

Part II
Practice Test 1

- Practice Test 1
- Practice Test 1: Diagnostic Answer Key and Explanations

Practice Tests 2, 3, and 4 can be found in your online Student Tools. See page viii for information on how to freely register and access this content.

HOW TO TAKE PRACTICE TEST 1

Depending on your needs and preferences, you have a few ways to take Practice Test 1. You can either:

1. Write directly in this book (except on the Extended Response question); or
2. Use the custom answer sheet that you'll find at the very back of the book and in your Student Tools online.

Here are some guidelines on how to answer questions for each of the GED® question formats:

- **Multiple choice:** If you are writing directly in the book, circle the letter of the answer choice you select. If you're using the answer sheet, bubble in your choice.
- **Drag and drop:** Write in the correct answer(s) in the space provided.
- **Drop down:** Circle or check your selection from the drop-down menu.
- **Fill in the blank:** Write the correct answer in the box or blank provided.
- **Hot spot:** Mark an X or dot on the graphic as indicated.
- **Extended Response:** If you'll be near a computer, we recommend typing your response for a realistic test-taking experience. Otherwise, write your response on a separate sheet of paper.

Before you begin, make sure to have the following items on hand:

- Pencils
- A notepad for scratch paper—and for writing your responses to Extended Response questions, if you will not be using a computer
- A Texas Instruments T1-30XS calculator. You may also use the online calculator at web2.0calc.com.
- A clock or watch to help you keep track of time

Good luck!

Practice Test 1

Reasoning Through Language Arts

Welcome!

Here is some information that you need to know before you start this test:

- You should not spend too much time on a question if you are not certain of the answer; answer it the best you can, and go on to the next question.
- If you are not certain of the answer to a question, you can mark your answer for review and come back to it later.
- This test has three sections.
- You have **35 minutes** to complete Section 1.
- When you finish Section 1, you may review those questions.
- You may not go back to Section 1 once you have finished your review.
- You have **45 minutes** to complete the Extended Response question in Section 2.
- After completing Section 2, you may take a **10-minute break**.
- You have **60 minutes** to complete Section 3.
- When you finish Section 3, you may review those questions.

Turn the page to begin.

GO ON TO THE NEXT PAGE

Questions 1 through 8 refer to the following passage.

Excerpt from *A Popular Schoolgirl*
by Angela Brazil

1 The Saxons were spending their summer holidays at a farm near the seaside, and for the first time in four long years the whole family was reunited. Mr. Saxon, Egbert, and Athelstane had only just been demobilized, and had hardly yet settled down to civilian life. They had joined the rest of the party at Lynstones before returning to their native town of Grovebury. The six weeks by the sea seemed a kind of oasis between the anxious period of the war that was past and gone, and the new epoch that stretched ahead in the future. To Ingred they were halcyon days. To have her father and brothers safely back, and for the family to be together in the midst of such beautiful scenery, was sufficient for utter enjoyment. She did not wish her mind to venture outside the charmed circle of the holidays. Beyond, when she thought about it all, lay a nebulous prospect, in the center of which school loomed large.

2 On this particular hot August afternoon, Ingred welcomed an excursion in the sidecar. She had not felt inclined to walk down the white path under the blazing sun to the glaring beach, but it was another matter to spin along the high road till, as the fairy tales put it, her hair whistled in the wind. Egbert was anxious to set off, so Hereward took his place on the luggage-carrier, and, after some back-firing, the three started forth. It was a glorious run over moorland country, with glimpses of the sea on the one hand, and craggy tors on the other, and round them billowy masses of heather, broken here and there by runnels of peat-stained water. If Egbert exceeded the speed-limit, he certainly had the excuse of a clear road before him; there were no hedges to hide advancing cars, neither was there any possibility of whisking round a corner to find a hay-cart blocking the way. In the course of an hour they had covered a considerable number of miles, and found themselves whirling down the tremendous hill that led to the seaside town of Chatcombe.

3 Arrived in the main street they left the motorcycle at a garage, and strolled on to the promenade, joining the crowd of holiday-makers who were sauntering along in the heat, or sitting on the benches watching the children digging in the sand below. Much to Ingred's astonishment she was suddenly hailed by her name, and, turning, found herself greeted with enthusiasm by a schoolfellow.

4 "Ingred! What a surprise!"

5 "Avis! Who'd have thought of seeing you?"

6 "Are you staying here?"

GO ON TO THE NEXT PAGE

7 "No, only over for the afternoon."

8 "We've rooms at Beach View over there. Come along and have some tea with us, and your brothers too. Yes, indeed you must! Mother will be delighted to see you all. I shan't let you say no!"

9 Borne away by her hospitable friend, Ingred presently found herself sitting on a seat in the front garden of a tall boarding-house facing the sea, and while Egbert and Hereward discussed motor-cycling with Avis's father, the two girls enjoyed a confidential chat together.

10 "Only a few days now," sighed Avis, "then we've got to leave all this and go home. How long are you staying at Lynstones, Ingred?"

11 "A fortnight more, but don't talk of going home. I want the holidays to last forever!"

12 "So do I, but they won't. School begins on the twenty-first of September. It will be rather sport to go to the new buildings at last, won't it? By the by, now the war's over, and we've all got our own again, I suppose you're going back to Rotherwood, aren't you?"

13 "I suppose so, when it's ready."

14 "But surely the Red Cross cleared out ages ago, and the whole place has been done up? I saw the paperhangers there in June."

15 "Oh, yes!" Ingred's voice was a little strained.

16 "You'll be so glad to be living there again," continued Avis. "I always envied you that lovely house. You must have hated lending it as a hospital. I expect when you're back you'll be giving all sorts of delightful parties, won't you? At least that's what the girls at school were saying."

17 "It's rather early to make plans," temporized Ingred.

18 "Oh, of course! But Jess and Francie said you'd a gorgeous floor for dancing. I do think a fancy-dress dance is about the best fun on earth. The next time I get an invitation, I'm going as a Quaker maiden, in a gray dress and the duckiest little white cap. Don't you think it would suit me? With your dark hair...I can just imagine you acting hostess in a shimmery sort of white-and-gold costume. *Do* promise to wear white-and-gold!"

19 "All right," laughed Ingred.

GO ON TO THE NEXT PAGE

20 "It's so delightful that the war's over, and we can begin to have parties again, like we used to do. Beatrice Jackson told me she should never forget that Carnival dance she went to at Rotherwood five years ago, and all the lanterns and fairy lamps. Some of the other girls talk about it yet. Hullo, that's the gong! Come indoors, and we'll have tea."

1. Which quotation from the story supports the idea that Ingred's relatives have had military experience?

   A. "Mr. Saxon, Egbert, and Athelstane had only just been demobilized, and had hardly yet settled down to civilian life."
   B. "The six weeks by the sea seemed a kind of oasis between the anxious period of the war that was past and gone, and the new epoch that stretched ahead in the future."
   C. "By the by, now the war's over, and we've all got our own again, I suppose you're going back to Rotherwood, aren't you?"
   D. "To have her father and brothers safely back, and for the family to be together in the midst of such beautiful scenery, was sufficient for utter enjoyment."

2. Which definition best matches the use of the word "native" in paragraph 1?

   A. unfamiliar or foreign
   B. occurring naturally in the environment
   C. relating to where someone was born
   D. passed down through generations

3. Read the following sentence from paragraph 2.

It was a glorious run over moorland country, with glimpses of the sea on the one hand, and craggy tors on the other, and round them billowy masses of heather, broken here and there by runnels of peat-stained water.

The detailed description of the landscape enhances the story by

   A. revealing the dangerous nature of the motorcycle trip.
   B. emphasizing Ingred's enjoyment of the experience.
   C. showing the contrast between the sea and the cliffs.
   D. introducing Egbert as a secondary character.

GO ON TO THE NEXT PAGE

4. Read the sentences from paragraph 14.

> "But surely the Red Cross cleared out ages ago, and the whole place has been done up? I saw the paper-hangers there in June."

What is the significance to Ingred of the "place" mentioned in the passage?

A. It is Ingred's family home which had been occupied by wartime personnel.
B. It is the town where Ingred lives, which has a Red Cross military hospital.
C. It is a popular ballroom that has been undergoing renovations in preparation for a dance.
D. It is one of the new buildings at Ingred's school, where she dreads returning.

5. In paragraph 15, which characteristic does the passage reveal about Ingred as she responds to Avis?

A. discomfort or unease
B. agreement
C. exhaustion
D. enthusiasm

6. Drag and drop the events into the chart to show the order in which they occur in the excerpt. (For this practice test, write the event letters in the chart.)

Order of Events

↓
↓
↓

(a) Egbert drives Ingred to the beach.

(b) Ingred is invited to tea.

(c) Avis talks about a fancy-dress dance.

(d) The Saxons unite at Lynstones.

GO ON TO THE NEXT PAGE

7. Drag and drop each word that describes Ingred into the character web. (For this practice test, write each word in the web.)

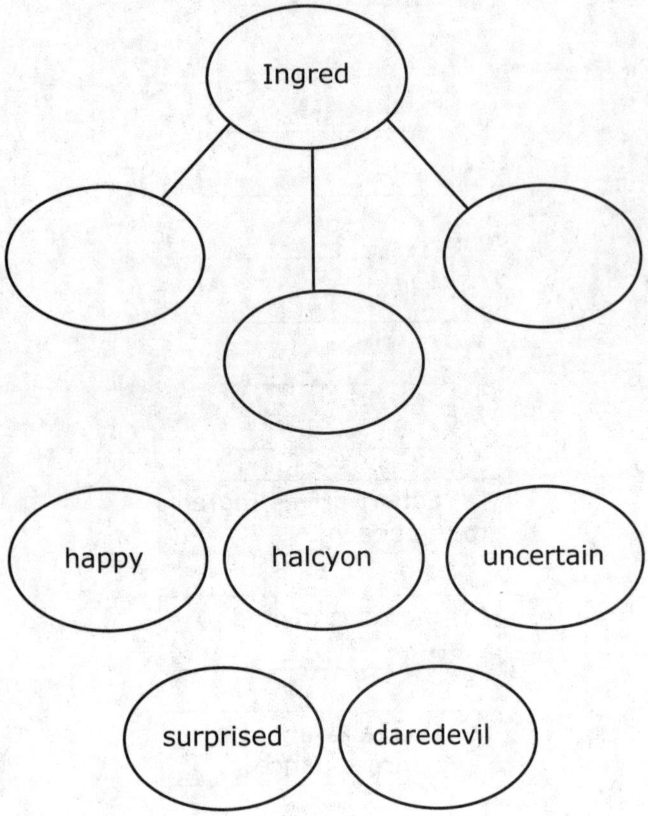

8. Based on the details in the story, what can readers predict about Avis?

A. She will be going to school with Ingred for the first time in September.
B. She will plan and host a dance after school starts.
C. She will travel to Lynstones when the afternoon is over.
D. She will return to her hometown before Ingred does.

GO ON TO THE NEXT PAGE

Questions 9 through 16 refer to the following article.

Devices and Additives to Improve Fuel Economy and Reduce Pollution—Do They Really Work?
by the U.S. Environmental Protection Agency (EPA)

Watch Out!

1 Have you seen advertisements for products that "Double Your Fuel Economy," or "Clean-up Your Car's Tailpipe Exhaust"? Be careful about these products; don't be fooled by erroneous claims.

Fuel Additives

2 Some advertisements claim that certain fuel additives have been approved by the EPA. While the EPA requires fuel additives to be "registered," the EPA does not test additives for engine efficiency, emissions benefits, or safety as part of the registration. To register an additive, manufacturers report the chemical composition and technical, marketing, and health effects information. The EPA does NOT endorse or certify fuel additives; registration with the EPA does not imply anything about the claims made by the manufacturer.

Aftermarket Devices to Improve Fuel Economy or Reduce Emissions

3 If a device has significant benefits, the manufacturer may apply for EPA testing through the Voluntary Aftermarket Retrofit Device Evaluation Program. Very few manufacturers have applied for this program in the past 10 years. Most devices tested in earlier years had a neutral or negative effect on fuel economy and/or exhaust emissions. Without this report, the EPA has no information about the safety of the device or its impact on fuel efficiency or the environment.

Popular Devices and Their Effects

- Devices that turn water into fuel: The EPA has received no credible and complete data showing fuel economy benefits from devices that split water molecules into hydrogen and oxygen gas, which is then burned with your fuel. Some devices' installation instructions include adjustments that the EPA would consider tampering. Tampering with your car's emissions control system is punishable by significant fines.

- Fuel line devices: Some devices heat, magnetize, ionize, irradiate, or add metals to the fuel lines. EPA testing of such devices has shown no substantive effect on fuel economy or exhaust emissions. Installation of devices that retard timing or adjust the air-fuel ratio of the vehicle may be considered tampering.

GO ON TO THE NEXT PAGE

- Mixture enhancers: The EPA has received no credible and complete data showing fuel economy benefits from devices that claim to increase fuel efficiency by creating aerodynamic properties or turbulence that improves the air-fuel mix prior to combustion.

Aftermarket Alternative Fuel Conversions

4 Aftermarket alternative fuel conversions are sometimes alleged to improve fuel economy and reduce pollution. However, it is difficult to re-engineer a vehicle to operate properly on a different fuel, and especially difficult to ensure that the vehicle will meet emission standards. So, before choosing a vehicle conversion, consider these factors:

- It is not the fuel alone but the integration of engine, fueling, exhaust and evaporative emission control system designs that determines how clean a vehicle will be. Vehicle conversion systems must retain a similarly integrated design and functionality to retain low emissions.
- Gaseous and alcohol fuels are less energy dense than conventional fuels, so your fuel efficiency per gallon of fuel will decrease compared to gasoline or diesel.
- Be sure to check whether your vehicle's manufacturer will honor the warranty after conversion.

If the conversion manufacturer has not followed EPA guidelines, you may be violating the tampering prohibition and/or increasing the release of harmful exhaust and evaporative emissions.

5 Therefore, thoroughly research any aftermarket part or additive before purchasing, and remember the old adage, "If it sounds too good to be true, it probably is."

Improve Your Fuel Economy
by the U.S. Department of Energy

Fuel-Saving Habits

6 There are several things you can do to obtain the best possible fuel economy and produce the lowest possible emissions.

- Avoid idling. Idling gets 0 miles per gallon and costs as much as $0.04 per minute.
- Keep tires inflated to the recommended pressure, and use the recommended grade of motor oil, which can improve fuel economy by up to 5%.
- Drive more efficiently. Each 5 MPH you drive over 60 MPH can reduce your fuel economy by 7%.

GO ON TO THE NEXT PAGE

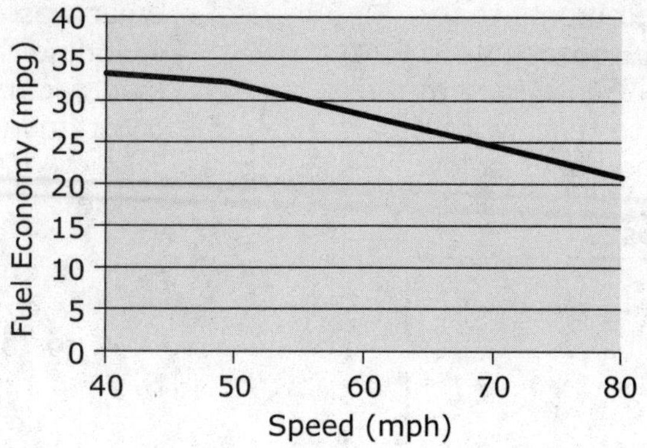

- Keep your car in shape. Fixing a car that is out of tune can improve your gas mileage by about 4%.
- Combine your trips. Many short trips taken from a cold start can use twice as much fuel as one multipurpose trip.
- Avoid carrying unneeded items. An extra 100 pounds can decrease fuel economy by 1%–2%.

Fuel-Saving Technology Highlight: Start-Stop Systems

7 An energy-saving feature is now available that can help you save fuel in stop-and-go traffic, at red lights, and in other situations where your car would normally waste fuel idling. Start-stop systems turn off the engine when a vehicle comes to a stop and automatically start it back up when the brake is released or when the accelerator or clutch is pressed. It usually takes half a second or less to restart. Until recently, these systems were mostly found on hybrid vehicles, but as of the 2014 model year, they are available on about one hundred conventional vehicle models. By turning off the engine when it's not needed, start-stop systems can improve fuel economy by around 4 to 5 percent on average. Unlike a hybrid system, which can add thousands of dollars to a vehicle's cost, a start-stop system typically adds only a few hundred dollars. A start-stop system doesn't require you to drive differently, but it may take some time for you to get used to the way the vehicle operates or feels. Most systems are robust and easy to use. If you spend significant drive time idling, a vehicle equipped with a start-stop system might just be right for you!

Sources: Adapted and abridged from *Devices and Additives to Improve Fuel Economy and Reduce Pollution—Do They Really Work?*, U.S. Environmental Protection Agency, 2012, and *Model Year 2014 Fuel Economy Guide*, U.S. Department of Energy, 2016.

GO ON TO THE NEXT PAGE

9. Drag and drop two statements that express the primary purposes of the EPA article (paragraphs 1–5) into the empty boxes. (For this practice test, write the statement letters in the boxes below.)

EPA's Purposes

(a) To promote start-stop systems as a method to increase fuel economy

(b) To list the many harmful effects that emissions can have on the environment

(c) To caution consumers about deceptive advertising

(d) To give information about the role of the EPA in evaluating fuel additives and devices

(e) To list ways to increase fuel economy

10. Which conclusion is best supported by the Department of Energy article?

A. Because of the advent of start-stop systems, other methods to improve fuel economy and reduce pollution are no longer necessary.
B. Start-stop systems offer better fuel economy benefits than aftermarket alternative fuel conversions.
C. Improving driving habits can meaningfully reduce fuel use and costs.
D. Consumers should research any devices marketed to improve fuel economy, to make sure they have been tested and endorsed by the EPA.

11. What was the author's purpose for including the sentence "Very few manufacturers have applied for this program in the past 10 years" (paragraph 3) in the Environmental Protection Agency article?

A. to emphasize that the EPA program is competitive and takes a long time to complete
B. to suggest that many manufacturers' claims lack independent verification
C. to show that only a few devices are effective enough to pass EPA testing
D. to urge more manufacturers to apply for the program, so that consumers will have better choices in the future

12. How does the chart extend the information in the article by the Department of Energy?

A. by showing that fuel economy improves 5% with every 5 MPH a driver slows down
B. by showing that reducing driving speed is more effective than vehicle maintenance
C. by illustrating the effects of more efficient driving
D. by highlighting the optimum speed for every driving condition

13. How are the two articles similar?

A. Both articles list methods to help reduce emissions.
B. Both articles discuss claims about improving fuel economy and evaluate their effectiveness.
C. Both articles use statistics to support their assertions about fuel economy.
D. Both articles describe a way to verify the claims made about a marketed device.

GO ON TO THE NEXT PAGE

14. Which idea about the effect of aftermarket fuel economy devices is included in the article by the EPA?

A. Installation of the devices might be more costly than expected.
B. The devices can improve economy 4 to 5 percent.
C. The devices are officially approved by the EPA.
D. There is no information about the safety of these devices.

15. How does the "Fuel-Saving Habits" section (paragraph 6) of the Department of Energy article relate to the "Fuel-Saving Technology Highlight" section (paragraph 7)?

A. The "Fuel-Saving Habits" section lists changes drivers can make to save fuel, while the "Fuel-Saving Technology Highlight" contradicts this list by claiming there is no need to drive differently.
B. The "Fuel-Saving Habits" list begins by cautioning against a bad driving habit; the "Fuel-Saving Technology Highlight" builds on this advice by recommending a device that automatically reduces this habit.
C. The "Fuel-Saving Habits" section implies that there are several ways to reduce fuel consumption, while the "Fuel-Saving Technology Highlight" implies that one of these ways is more effective than the others.
D. The "Fuel-Saving Habits" section focuses only on ways to operate a vehicle while the "Fuel-Saving Technology Highlight" focuses on devices that can be installed in vehicles.

16. In the Department of Energy article, what is the effect of the use of the word "robust" in paragraph 7?

A. It reassures the reader that the start-stop system is sturdy and well-made.
B. It informs the reader that the start-stop system will not be hard to drive.
C. It cautions the reader that the start-stop system is fairly bulky and may increase the weight of the car.
D. It advises the reader that the start-stop system is not expensive.

GO ON TO THE NEXT PAGE

17. The passage below is incomplete. For each "Select" option, choose the option that best improves the clarity, correctness, and overall effectiveness of the writing. (For this practice test, circle your selection.)

Macy Redizas
5366 Ardenhall Lane
Laughing Pines, NJ

Dear Ms Redizas:

As a fellow member of the Laughing Pines community, I am sending this to you with great concern for our quality of life. Surely you enjoy living in such a quiet and peaceful

Select... ▼
neighborhood, just as I do.
neighborhood. Just as I do.
neighborhood just as I do too.
neighborhood; you just as much as I do.

As it happens, in order to ensure a "quiet and peaceful" community, one sometimes must take precautions.

Select... ▼
The alarmingly increased burglary incidents, via news reports and social media posts, you must be aware of by now,
By now, via news reports and social media posts, you must be aware of the alarming increase in burglary incidents
Via news reports and social media posts you must be aware of by now, the alarming increase in burglary incidents
The alarming increase in burglary incidents you must be aware of by now, via news reports and social media posts

in our neighborhood during the past few years. While police may assert that this is an expected result of the continuing economic slump, that is no consolation to those whose homes have been targeted.

GO ON TO THE NEXT PAGE

We have decided not to meet this danger unprepared. The additional cost to double nighttime security patrols by Protect Pro will be approximately $25,000 to $30,000 annually. There are no additional funds in our budget available to cover such an unexpected, but necessary, expense. Therefore,

Select... ▼
concerning our community, as we all do
as we all were concerned about our community,
as we are all concerned about our community,
having concern about our community, as were we all,

I propose that every resident consider personally contributing to the security control budget. I am willing to spearhead this initiative with my own business. For every $2 raised in the community to cover the additional security costs, IntelliTech will donate $1 more.

Please make a donation today to support this much-needed cause for the common good. You can visit either one of our two stores and deposit your donation in the boxes provided near the front cash registers. Alternatively, if you can't make it to the store, please send a check or money order, payable to "ProtectPro Security Patrol" and mail [Select... ▼] to the address listed below.

Select... ▼
them
it
that
one

With neighborly goodwill,

Gracie Wishton

IntelliTech Design

823 Askward St.

Laughing Pines, NJ

GO ON TO THE NEXT PAGE

Extended Response Answer Guidelines

Please use the guidelines below as you answer the Extended Response question on the Reasoning Through Language Arts test. Following these guidelines as closely as possible will ensure that you provide the best response.

1. **Please note that this task must be completed in no more than 45 minutes.** However, don't rush through your response. Be sure to read through the passage(s) and the prompt. Then think about the message you want to convey in your response. **Be sure to plan your response before you begin writing.** Draft your response and revise it as needed.
2. As you read, think carefully about the **argumentation** presented in the passage(s). "Argumentation" refers to the assumptions, claims, support, reasoning, and credibility on which a position is based. Pay close attention to **how the author(s) use these strategies to convey their positions.**
3. When you write your essay, be sure to
    - **determine which position presented** in the passage(s) is **better supported** by evidence from the passage(s)
    - **explain why the position you chose is the better-supported one**
    - **remember, the better-supported position is not necessarily the position you agree with**
    - **defend your assertions with multiple pieces of evidence** from the passage(s)
    - **build your main points thoroughly**
    - **put your main points in logical order** and tie your details to your main points
    - **organize your response carefully** and consider your **audience, message, and purpose**
    - **use transitional words and phrases** to connect sentences, paragraphs, and ideas
    - **choose words carefully** to express your ideas clearly
    - **vary your sentence structure** to enhance the flow and clarity of your response
    - **reread and revise your response** to correct any errors in grammar, usage, or punctuation

GO ON TO THE NEXT PAGE

Reasoning Through Language Arts, Section 2

Instructions

Read

- On the **page 2 tab above,** you will **read two texts** presenting **different views** on the same topic.
- **Both writers argue** that **their position** on the issue is **correct.**

Plan

- **Analyze** the two texts **to determine** which writer presents the **stronger case.**
- **Develop your own argument** in which **you explain** how one position is **better supported** than the other.
- **Include** relevant and specific **evidence** from **both sources** to support your argument.

Write

- **Type** your response in the **box on the right.**
- Your response should be approximately **4 to 7 paragraphs of 3 to 7 sentences each.**
- **Remember** to allow a few minutes **to review and edit your response.**

You have up to **45 minutes** for reading, planning, writing, and editing your response.

Emissions Trading

1 "Cap-and-trade" is a market-based policy tool for controlling large amounts of harmful emissions, such as sulfur dioxide (SO_2) and nitrogen oxides (NO_x), from a group of sources. A cap-and-trade program from the Environmental Protection Agency (EPA) first sets an aggressive "cap," or maximum limit, on emissions. Businesses and industries covered by the program then receive authorizations to produce emissions in the form of emissions permits, with the total number of permits limited by the cap. Each business or industry can develop its own strategy to comply with the overall reduction requirement, including the sale or purchase (the "trade") of permits, installation of pollution controls, and implementation of efficiency measures, among other options. Businesses and industries must also completely and accurately measure and report all emissions in a timely manner to guarantee that the overall cap is met.

GO ON TO THE NEXT PAGE

Passage A: Indications That Cap-and-Trade Works

2 Under the right circumstances, cap-and-trade programs have shown strong evidence of effectiveness in many cases, providing certainty in allocations, rules, and penalties; substantial emission reductions; cost-effective, flexible compliance choices for regulated sources; complete accountability, unprecedented data quality, and public access to program data and decisions; and minimized administrative costs for industry and government. EPA's cap-and-trade programs have the force of federal and state standards behind them, including national health-based air quality standards. This ensures that local public health needs are met in conjunction with achievement of regional or national emission reductions.

3 Examples of successful cap-and-trade programs include the nationwide Acid Rain Program (ARP) and the regional NO_x Budget Trading Program in the Northeast. Additionally, EPA issued the Clean Air Interstate Rule (CAIR) on March 10, 2005, to build on the success of these programs and achieve significant additional emission reductions.

4 The programs have had measurable results:

- Since the 1990s, SO_2 emissions have dropped 40%, and according to the Pacific Research Institute, acid rain levels have dropped 65% since 1976.
- A 2017 study in the American Economic Review found that NO_x reductions due to the NO_x Budget Trading Program have led to improvements in ozone and particulate matter. The program also reduced expenditures on medicine by about $800 million annually and led to fewer premature deaths, mainly among older people.
- Ozone season NO_x emissions decreased by 43 percent between 2003 and 2008, even while energy demand remained essentially the same during the same period.
- A 2021 study found that a similar emission reduction strategy in China reduced total emissions by 16.7% and emission intensity by 9.7%.

5 Therefore, cap-and-trade has been proven to be effective in protecting human health and the environment. Successful cap-and-trade programs reward innovation, efficiency, and early action and provide strict environmental accountability without inhibiting economic growth.

GO ON TO THE NEXT PAGE

Passage B: Criticisms of Cap-and-Trade

6 Critics have several objections to cap-and-trade. Skeptical environmentalists have argued that reductions in emissions occurred due to broad trends unconnected to the program. For example, there were many other regulations that impacted emissions at the time the ARP was implemented. Therefore, the effectiveness of the emissions trading element of the ARP in reducing emissions has been questioned, since the EPA also used other regulations in conjunction with the ARP during the time period the emissions reduction took place.

7 "Carbon leakage" occurs when emissions shift from one country to another rather than decreasing overall. If one country has a strict emissions policy that raises production costs, then production may move offshore to the cheaper country with lower standards, and global emissions will not be reduced. Furthermore, cheap "offset" carbon credits are frequently available from the less developed countries, where they may be generated by local polluters at the expense of local communities.

8 Regulatory agencies run the risk of issuing too many emission credits, which can result in a very low price on emission permits. This reduces the incentive for companies to cut back their emissions, since permits are cheap. On the other hand, issuing too few permits can result in an excessively high permit price. Another issue with cap-and-trade programs has been overallocation, whereby the cap is high enough that sources of emissions do not need to reduce their emissions.

9 The price and supply of permits can result in perverse incentives. If, for example, polluting firms are given free emission permits, this may create a reason for them not to cut their emissions. A firm making large cuts in emissions could then be granted fewer emission permits in the future. This perverse incentive can be alleviated if permits are sold, rather than given, to polluters.

10 Some environmentalists argue that offsets for emission reductions are not a substitute for actual cuts in emissions, and that offsets are an excuse for business as usual, since expensive long-term changes will not be made if there is a cheaper source of carbon credits. Environmental protection will require more radical change than the modest changes driven by pollution trading schemes. These critics advocate solutions that leave most remaining fossil fuels underground.

You may take a 10-minute break before proceeding to Section 3.

GO ON TO THE NEXT PAGE

Questions 18 through 25 refer to the following passage.

Niagara
by Mark Twain

1 Niagara Falls is a most enjoyable place of resort. The hotels are excellent, and the prices not at all exorbitant. The opportunities for fishing are not surpassed in the country; in fact, they are not even equaled elsewhere. Because, in other localities, certain places in the streams are much better than others; but at Niagara one place is just as good as another, for the reason that the fish do not bite anywhere, and so there is no use in your walking five miles to fish, when you can depend on being just as unsuccessful nearer home. The advantages of this state of things have never heretofore been properly placed before the public.

2 The weather is cool in summer, and the walks and drives are all pleasant and none of them fatiguing. When you start out to "do" the Falls you first drive down about a mile, and pay a small sum for the privilege of looking down from a precipice into the narrowest part of the Niagara River. A railway "cut" through a hill would be as comely if it had the angry river tumbling and foaming through its bottom. You can descend a staircase here a hundred and fifty feet down, and stand at the edge of the water. After you have done it, you will wonder why you did it; but you will then be too late.

3 Then you drive over to Suspension Bridge, and divide your misery between the chances of smashing down two hundred feet into the river below, and the chances of having the railway-train overhead smashing down onto you. Either possibility is discomforting taken by itself, but, mixed together, they amount in the aggregate to positive unhappiness.

4 When you have examined the stupendous Horseshoe Fall till you are satisfied you cannot improve on it, you return to America by the new Suspension Bridge, and follow up the bank to where they exhibit the Cave of the Winds.

5 Here I followed instructions, and divested myself of all my clothing, and put on a waterproof jacket and overalls. This costume is picturesque, but not beautiful. A guide, similarly dressed, led the way down a flight of winding stairs, which wound and wound, and still kept on winding long after the thing ceased to be a novelty, and then terminated long before it had begun to be a pleasure. We were then well down under the precipice, but still considerably above the level of the river.

6 We now began to creep along flimsy bridges of a single plank, our persons shielded from destruction by a crazy wooden railing, to which I clung with both hands—not because I was afraid, but because I wanted to. Presently the descent became steeper and the bridge flimsier, and sprays from the American Fall began

GO ON TO THE NEXT PAGE

to rain down on us in fast increasing sheets that soon became blinding, and after that our progress was mostly in the nature of groping. Now a furious wind began to rush out from behind the waterfall, which seemed determined to sweep us from the bridge, and scatter us on the rocks and among the torrents below. I remarked that I wanted to go home; but it was too late. We were almost under the monstrous wall of water thundering down from above, and speech was in vain in the midst of such a pitiless crash of sound.

7 In another moment the guide disappeared behind the deluge, and, bewildered by the thunder, driven helplessly by the wind, and smitten by the arrowy tempest of rain, I followed. All was darkness. Such a mad storming, roaring, and bellowing of warring wind and water never crazed my ears before. I bent my head, and seemed to receive the Atlantic on my back. The world seemed going to destruction. I could not see anything, the flood poured down savagely. I raised my head, with open mouth, and the most of the American cataract went down my throat. If I had sprung a leak now I had been lost. And at this moment I discovered that the bridge had ceased, and we must trust for a foothold to the slippery and precipitous rocks. I never was so scared before and survived it. But we got through at last, and emerged into the open day, where we could stand in front of the laced and frothy and seething world of descending water, and look at it. When I saw how much of it there was, and how fearfully in earnest it was, I was sorry I had gone behind it.

18. The author's overall tone in paragraph 1 is one of

A. fearful prediction.
B. ironic contrast.
C. appreciative description.
D. satisfied recollection.

19. Read this sentence from paragraph 2.

> After you have done it, you will wonder why you did it; but you will then be too late.

Why does the author choose to conclude the paragraph with this sentence?

A. to show how important it is to arrive at the falls on time
B. to offer advice to any readers who might consider visiting Niagara Falls
C. to show the narrator's acquaintance with the motives of the reader
D. to humorously anticipate a tourist's reaction

20. Which quotation most directly contrasts with the passage's overall ironic portrayal of Niagara Falls?

A. "The weather is cool in summer, and the walks and drives are all pleasant and none of them fatiguing."
B. "You can descend a staircase here a hundred and fifty feet down, and stand at the edge of the water."
C. "Either possibility is discomforting taken by itself, but, mixed together, they amount in the aggregate to positive unhappiness."
D. "Here I followed instructions, and divested myself of all my clothing, and put on a waterproof jacket and overalls."

GO ON TO THE NEXT PAGE

21. In paragraph 6, the narrator says, "I remarked that I wanted to go home." Which characteristic does this remark reveal about the narrator?

A. homesickness
B. melancholy
C. apprehension
D. nostalgia

22. Read the following sentences from paragraph 7.

> Such a mad storming, roaring, and bellowing of warring wind and water never crazed my ears before. I bent my head, and seemed to receive the Atlantic on my back.

The description "seemed to receive the Atlantic on my back" primarily functions to

A. exaggerate the overwhelming force of the water
B. suggest the narrator has fallen into the ocean
C. compare the falls to a distant geographic location
D. emphasize the narrator's physical strength

23. Which definition best matches the use of the phrase "in earnest" in paragraph 7?

A. serious
B. vigorous
C. sincere
D. ardent

24. Drag and drop the events into the chart to show the order in which they occur in the excerpt. (For this practice test, write the event letters in the chart.)

Order of Events

↓
↓
↓

(a) Horseshoe Fall is included as a stop in the visit.

(b) The Suspension Bridge is described.

(c) The narrator mentions a view of the river.

(d) The narrator goes behind the falls.

25. Which fact can the reader infer about Niagara Falls?

A. Part of it is located outside the United States.
B. It is a good spot for fishing.
C. It is a short drive from the exhibit of the Cave of the Winds.
D. Hotels there are expensive.

GO ON TO THE NEXT PAGE

Questions 26 through 33 refer to the following article.

Excerpt from "State Lotteries"
by A. A. Milne

1 The popular argument against the State Lottery is an assertion that it will encourage the gambling spirit. The popular argument in favor of the State Lottery is an assertion that it is hypocritical to say that it will encourage the gambling spirit, because the gambling spirit is already amongst us. Having listened to a good deal of this sort of argument on both sides, I thought it would be well to look up the word "gamble" in my dictionary, and I can now tell you all about it.

2 To gamble, says my dictionary, is "to play for money in games of skill or chance." Now, to me this definition is particularly interesting, because it justifies all that I have been thinking about the gambling spirit in connection with Premium Bonds. I am against Premium Bonds, but not for the popular reason. I am against them because there is so very little of the gamble about them. And now that I have looked up "gamble" in the dictionary, I see that I was right. The "chance" element in a state lottery is obvious enough, but the "game" element is entirely absent.

3 We play for money in games of skill or chance. But it isn't only of the money we are thinking. We get pleasure out of the game. If you are only throwing dice, you are engaged in a personal struggle with another man, and you are directing the struggle to this extent, that you can call the value of the stakes, and decide whether to go on or to stop. And is there any man who, having made a fortune at Monte Carlo, will admit that he owes it entirely to chance? Will he not rather attribute it to his wonderful system, or if not to that, at any rate to his wonderful nerve, his perseverance, or his recklessness?

4 This, then, is the gambling spirit. It has its dangers, certainly, but it is not entirely an evil spirit. It is possible that the State should not encourage it, but it is not called upon to exorcise it. I am not sure that I should favor a State gamble, but my arguments against it would be much the same as my arguments against State cricket or the solemn official endowment of any other jolly game. However, I need not trouble you with those arguments now, for nothing so harmless as a State gamble has ever been suggested. Instead, we have from time to time a State lottery offered to us, and that is a very different proposition.

GO ON TO THE NEXT PAGE

5 For in a State lottery—with daily prizes of £50,000—the game (or gambling) element does not exist. Buy your £100 bond, as a thousand placards will urge you to do, and you simply take part in a cold-blooded attempt to acquire money without working for it. You can take no personal interest whatever in the manner of acquiring it. Somebody turns a handle, and perhaps your number comes out. More probably it doesn't. If it doesn't, you can call yourself a fool for having thrown away your savings; if it does—well, you have got the money.

6 Moreover, the State would be giving its official approval to the unearned fortune. In these days, when the worker is asking for a week of so many less hours and so many more shillings, the State would answer: "I can show you a better way than that. What do you say to no work at all, and £20 a week for it?" At a time when the one cry is "Production!" the State adds (behind its hand), "Buy a Premium Bond, and let the other man produce for you." After all these years in which we have been slowly progressing towards the idea of a more equitable distribution of wealth, the Government would show us the really equitable way; it would collect the savings of the many, and re-distribute them among the few. Instead of a million ten-pound citizens, we should have a thousand ten-thousand-pounders and 999,000 with nothing. That would be the official way of making the country happy and contented. But, in fact, our social and political controversies are not kept alive by such arguments as these, nor by the answers which can legitimately be made to such arguments. The case of the average man in favor of State lotteries is, quite simply, that he does not like Dr. Clifford. The case of the average man against State lotteries is equally simple; he cannot bear to be on the same side as Mr. Bottomley.

Source: Abridged and adapted from "State Lotteries," *If I May,* A. A. Milne, 1920, London: Methuen & Co Ltd.

GO ON TO THE NEXT PAGE

26. Drag and drop two statements that express Milne's purposes for writing the essay into the empty boxes. (For this practice test, write the statement letters in the boxes below.)

Milne's Purpose

(a) To propose a way to achieve a more equitable distribution of wealth

(b) To persuade the reader that playing a State Lottery isn't really gambling

(c) To analyze the dual characteristics of the definition of the word "gamble"

(d) To argue that a State Lottery should be adopted

(e) To emphasize the dangers of gambling

27. Why does the author use the phrase "behind its hand" (paragraph 6)?

A. to show that the idea of "no work at all" is shameful and should be kept discreet
B. to illustrate that the messages from the State are contradictory
C. to imply that the State functions like a human body, with hands to do its work
D. to show that gambling is illegal and conducted in secret

28. In paragraph 3, what role does the image of the gambler in Monte Carlo play in the passage?

A. It establishes Monte Carlo as a place where fortunes are made.
B. It is an example of the personal struggle with chance discussed in the previous sentence.
C. It underscores the recklessness of gambling.
D. It illustrates the aspects of gambling discussed in the previous paragraph.

29. Read this sentence from paragraph 6.

> "The case of the average man in favor of State lotteries is, quite simply, that he does not like Dr. Clifford."

What can the reader infer from this sentence?

A. Dr. Clifford is opposed to State lotteries.
B. Dr. Clifford is a supporter of State lotteries.
C. The average man is simple and unintelligent compared to Dr. Clifford.
D. The average man would not favor anything represented by Dr. Clifford.

GO ON TO THE NEXT PAGE

30. Which detail in Milne's essay supports the claim that people get pleasure out of games of skill and chance?

A. "Somebody turns a handle, and perhaps your number comes out." (paragraph 5)
B. "That would be the official way of making the country happy and contented." (paragraph 6)
C. "...it justifies all that I have been thinking about the gambling spirit..." (paragraph 2)
D. "Will he not rather attribute it to his wonderful system, or if not to that, at any rate to his wonderful nerve..." (paragraph 3)

31. What is the effect of describing the lottery as a "cold-blooded attempt" in paragraph 5?

A. It contrasts sharply with the earlier portrayal of gambling as engaging and dynamic.
B. It suggests that participants are acting without careful thought.
C. It emphasizes the legality of the lottery system.
D. It portrays the lottery as physically dangerous.

32. In paragraph 3, the author addresses the reader with direct questions. How do the questions contribute to the development of the author's essay?

A. They raise issues that will be answered in the following paragraphs.
B. They illustrate that the nature of gambling is always in question and can never be conclusively defined.
C. They inspire the reader to consider the personal characteristics of a gambler.
D. They influence the reader to agree with the author's point that "game" is essential to gambling.

33. What can the reader infer about the author's opinions regarding Premium Bonds?

A. The author would not vote in favor of them.
B. The author views them as an appropriate method for redistributing public funds.
C. The author feels that they are a prime example of gambling as defined in his dictionary.
D. The author thinks they encourage hypocrisy.

GO ON TO THE NEXT PAGE

Questions 34 through 41 refer to the following article.

Career Myths That Stop People Cold
by Olivia Crosby

1 Some career myths are less about occupations than about the working world in general. Myths like these can derail a career search and sap motivation. Here are five common myths, and realities, about careers.

2 **Myth**: There is one perfect job for me.

3 **Reality**: There are many occupations—and many jobs—that you would enjoy. Focusing on finding a single, perfect career is not only intimidating, it's limiting. If you're like most people, you will have several jobs and careers in your life, and each will have positive and negative aspects to it. Furthermore, your job preferences are apt to change over time as you gain experience, skill, and self-knowledge. Keeping your options open is a position of strength, not weakness.

4 **Myth**: I will use all of my talents and abilities in this job.

5 **Reality**: No one job uses all of your talents. And trying to find one that does will derail your job search. Learning a variety of tasks helps you to sharpen abilities that might not be needed in one job but could be invaluable in another. Especially at the start of your career, you should expect to spend time acquiring experience and skills. This is one reality about careers that, career counselors say, many new graduates fail to grasp. Counselors remind jobseekers to be patient. New workers should expect to start in entry-level positions and be willing to do routine tasks as they gain experience.

6 **Myth**: My job has to match my college major or vocational training.

7 **Reality**: You need not restrict your job search to careers related to your degree or training. Most jobs do not specify which college major is needed, even if they require that workers have a college degree. Many computer specialist positions, for example, are filled by workers whose degree is in a subject unrelated to computers. Vocational training is often more closely related to specific occupations. But even this kind of training can open the door to a wider array of jobs than people think. Consider that electrical technicians are now repairing fuel cells, for example, or that veterinary technicians become pharmaceutical sales workers. Often, technical skills are applicable to many settings—and most workers learn the specifics of an occupation on the job.

GO ON TO THE NEXT PAGE

8 **Myth**: No one will hire me because I lack experience, have low grades, have gaps in my work history, etc.

9 **Reality**: People overcome all kinds of challenges to find satisfying work. Experts say that how you handle adversity is a good indicator of your ability to persevere. Need experience? Get it! Volunteer, work in a related occupation, or focus on school projects that are relevant to your desired career. Low grades are the problem? Highlight other parts of your resume, and remember that grades usually matter only for that first job after graduation. Gaps in your work history? Overcome them with a well-designed resume that focuses on skills rather than chronology, and then get a little interviewing practice. For most entry-level jobs, employers are looking for general attributes such as communication skills, interpersonal abilities, and enthusiasm.

10 **Myth**: It's too late to change my career.

11 **Reality:** It's never too late to change careers. Workers who change careers come from many backgrounds, age groups, and situations. There's the doctor who decided she'd rather be a chef, the retiree who enrolled in college to become an accountant, the construction worker who wanted a steadier income without moving to a warmer climate. For each of these workers, the desire for job satisfaction outweighed the desire for status quo. To make the change easier, look at your past work and education to see what skills relate to the job you want. Most jobs' entry requirements are more flexible than people think. Gain needed skills with volunteer work, internships, or a class, and don't be afraid to start at the bottom to get the career you want. If you are out of school and want expert advice, consider a local One-Stop Career Center or the counseling center at a nearby school.

Source: U.S. Department of Labor, Bureau of Labor Statistics

GO ON TO THE NEXT PAGE

34. The author's tone toward the reader is one of

A. condescension.
B. reassurance.
C. intimidation.
D. satisfaction.

35. What is the author's primary purpose in writing this article?

A. to encourage readers to develop new abilities and seek new experiences
B. to caution workers against changing jobs by exposing the myths about career change
C. to showcase the types of jobs that will accept workers with low grades and work history gaps
D. to encourage job seekers to use all of their prior experience and training

36. Read this sentence from paragraph 7.

> Consider that electrical technicians are now repairing fuel cells, for example, or that veterinary technicians become pharmaceutical sales workers.

The sentence enhances the article by

A. giving examples of the types of careers readers should pursue.
B. presenting a scenario to illustrate the fact that readers should apply for jobs that match their college majors.
C. emphasizing the value and versatility of technical skills in the job market.
D. offering an example to show that skills acquired in one kind of training can be transferred to another field.

37. How does the question-and-answer structure in paragraph 9 contribute to the development of the author's argument?

A. It anticipates and directly addresses common concerns held by job seekers.
B. It introduces new problems that are resolved later in the article.
C. It highlights contradictions in common career advice.
D. It shifts the focus from general advice to specific industries.

38. Which definition best matches the use of the word "overcome" in paragraph 9?

A. overpower
B. shock
C. outlive
D. surmount

39. Read this sentence from paragraph 11.

> For each of these workers, the desire for job satisfaction outweighed the desire for status quo.

What can be inferred about the "workers" in this sentence?

A. They had all undergone a significant change in work.
B. They were concerned with staying in a familiar field.
C. They liked the status that came from professional jobs.
D. They returned to school in order to widen their career options.

GO ON TO THE NEXT PAGE

40. The author claims that prospective employees can take steps to better their odds of employment. Drag two actions that the author uses to support this claim into the boxes below. (For this practice test, write the action letters in the boxes.)

(a) Work for good grades in college to make up for lack of experience

(b) Donate your time to charitable organizations

(c) Apply for jobs within your college major to increase your odds of landing a job

(d) Carefully explain gaps in work history

(e) Anticipate questions that might arise when applying for a job

41. What can the reader infer about the article's intended audience?

A. The article is written specifically for first-time job seekers.
B. The article is written to students currently in college.
C. The article is written to help those who are uncertain about finding a job.
D. The article is written to help job seekers address gaps in their work history.

GO ON TO THE NEXT PAGE

Questions 42 through 49 refer to the following article.

Susan B. Anthony: Rebel, Crusader, Humanitarian
by Alma Lutz

1 "If Sally Ann knows more about weaving than Elijah," reasoned eleven-year-old Susan with her father, "then why don't you make her overseer?"

2 "It would never do," replied Daniel Anthony as a matter of course. "It would never do to have a woman overseer in the mill."

3 This answer did not satisfy Susan and she often thought about it. To enter the mill, to stand quietly and look about, was the best kind of entertainment, for she was fascinated by the whir of the looms, by the nimble fingers of the weavers, and by the general air of efficiency. Admiringly she watched Sally Ann Hyatt, the tall capable weaver from Vermont. When the yarn on the beam was tangled or there was something wrong with the machinery, Elijah, the overseer, always called out to Sally Ann, "I'll tend your loom, if you'll look after this." Sally Ann never failed to locate the trouble or to untangle the yarn. Yet she was never made overseer, and this continued to puzzle Susan.

4 The manufacture of cotton was a new industry, developing with great promise in the United States, when Susan B. Anthony was born on February 15, 1820, in the wide valley at the foot of Mt. Greylock, near Adams, Massachusetts. Enterprising young men like her father, Daniel Anthony, saw a potential cotton mill by the side of every rushing brook, and young women, eager to earn the first money they could call their own, were leaving the farms, for a few months at least, to work in the mills. Cotton cloth was the new sensation and the demand for it was steadily growing. Brides were proud to display a few cotton sheets instead of commonplace homespun linen.

5 When Susan was two years old, her father built a cotton factory of twenty-six looms beside the brook which ran through Grandfather Read's meadow, hauling the cotton forty miles by wagon from Troy, New York. The millworkers, most of them young girls from Vermont, boarded, as was the custom, in the home of the millowner; Susan's mother, Lucy Read Anthony, although she had three small daughters to care for, Guelma, Susan, and Hannah, boarded eleven of the millworkers with only the help of a thirteen-year-old girl who worked for her after school hours. Lucy Anthony cooked their meals on the hearth of the big kitchen fireplace, and in the large brick oven beside it

GO ON TO THE NEXT PAGE

baked crisp brown loaves of bread. In addition, washing, ironing, mending, and spinning filled her days. But she was capable and strong and was doing only what all women in this new country were expected to do. She taught her young daughters to help her, and Susan, even before she was six, was very useful; by the time she was ten she could cook a good meal and pack a dinner pail.

42. How does being told "it would never do to have a woman overseer in the mill" affect young Susan?

A. She sees the truth of the words after she watches the workers in the mill.
B. She questions her father's judgment.
C. She learns that what she is told does not always match her observations.
D. She decides to go to work in the mill to rebel against her father.

43. How do the details about Susan's home life in paragraph 5 enhance the narrative?

A. They give a portrait of the kinds of work customary for women at the time.
B. They reveal how overworked Susan's mother was because her father was away building the cotton factory.
C. They show that working at home was much harder than working in the mill.
D. They demonstrate how difficult it was to board the millworkers.

44. Which quotation from the passage supports the idea that Susan is learning skills that enhance independence?

A. "young women, eager to earn the first money they could call their own, were leaving the farms"
B. "Sally Ann never failed to locate the trouble or to untangle the yarn"
C. "she was fascinated by the whir of the looms, by the nimble fingers of the weavers, and by the general air of efficiency"
D. "by the time she was ten she could cook a good meal and pack a dinner pail"

45. In this excerpt, the overseer speaks to Sally Ann when there is trouble with the machinery. What does this action reveal about Sally Ann?

A. She is a more efficient weaver than the other women who work at the factory, which suggests that she is the best person to be overseer.
B. Her mechanical aptitude is recognized by the other workers, which suggests that she would be a competent overseer.
C. She has a habit of getting in trouble for tangling the yarn in her machinery, which confirms Susan's father's statement that she should not be overseer.
D. She enjoys being asked for help, which shows she hopes to be made overseer someday.

GO ON TO THE NEXT PAGE

46. Based on the story, what was Susan's father's attitude about the cotton mills?

A. The mills were an acceptable place for women to work.
B. The new cotton industry only had places for enterprising young men.
C. Cotton cloth made in the mills would be sure to replace homespun entirely, creating new jobs for both women and men.
D. He thought of the mills as places that proved that men were generally more efficient than women.

47. Drag and drop into the character web each word that describes Susan as she watches the mill workers. (For this practice test, write the words in the web.)

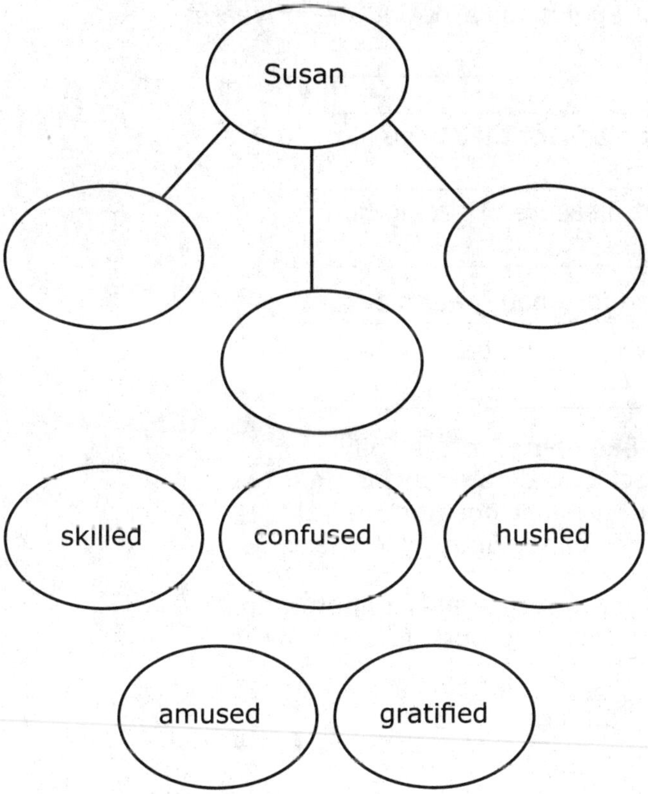

48. What can readers infer about the mill that Susan's father built?

A. It was located in Troy, New York, to take advantage of industrial development.
B. It was staffed by workers who boarded at the mill.
C. Construction on the mill was begun in 1820 in a valley.
D. It had to be located near a source of running water.

49. Based on the details in the story, what can readers tell about the women workers in Susan's father's mill?

A. Most of the weavers were qualified to become overseers.
B. For some of them, the job at the mill was their first paying job.
C. They lived on farms and traveled to their jobs in the mill.
D. They helped Susan's mother with the housework.

GO ON TO THE NEXT PAGE

50. The passage below is incomplete. For each "Select" option, choose the option that correctly completes the sentence. (For this practice test, circle your selection.)

August 25, 2010

Ms. Roberta Alvarez
Manager, Marketing Services
Zetacorp, Inc.
554 Alacor Drive
Stamford, CT 06907

Dear Ms. Alvarez:

In response to your request, I am writing to provide a letter of recommendation for Jorge Garcez who worked for me until last year. Jorge Garcez worked in my department under my direct supervision at Readywise ImageGraphics for a period of six years ending in June 2009.

Select... ▼
During that period, it is with great pleasure that I see him developing
During that period, I had the great pleasure of seeing him develop
Seeing him develop during that period, I had great pleasure
As I saw him during that period, with great pleasure, he was developing

from a paste-up assistant at the beginning, into a fully functioning Graphics Design Project Coordinator in his final two years with the company. That was the last position he held before moving on to a better career opportunity elsewhere.

Jorge is a hard-working self-starter who invariably understands exactly what a project is all about from the outset, and how to get it done

Select... ▼
quickly and effectively, during
quickly, effectively, and during
quickly and effectively. During
quick and effectively. During

his two years as Graphics Design Project Coordinator, he met every deadline, often ahead of schedule. His projects were

GO ON TO THE NEXT PAGE

rendered with the utmost quality, requiring very little revision after the first presentation. He was very budget-minded, finding creative ways to fund his team's needs within the allocated funds. Resourceful, creative, and solution-oriented, Mr. Garcez often found innovative and refreshing approaches to the challenges involved in his everyday tasks. He is flexible as a team

Select... ▼
worker, able to give guidance and step
worker. Just as able to give guidance and step
worker, just as able to give guidance and stepping
worker, just as able to give guidance as to step

back and take direction when another is leading the group.

Jorge's written and communication skills are excellent, and he was well liked by everyone on our staff. He served as a mediator on our interdepartmental committee to ensure smooth cooperation from all project levels, helping department heads communicate their needs to one another. On the interpersonal side, Mr. Garcez gets along well with all colleagues, customers, and even competitors!

When he told us, regretfully, that he was leaving to fill a new position with a larger company, we were saddened to see him leave. Still, we wished him success and happiness in his new position and endeavors.

Select... ▼
Even a year after his resignation, still, he is remembered here fondly.
A year after his resignation, even he is still remembered fondly here.
He is remembered here still fondly, even a year after his resignation.
He is still remembered fondly here, even a year after his resignation.

Therefore, I can recommend Jorge Garcez most heartily to fill any senior graphic design position you might have. I hope these details have illuminated Mr. Garcez's capabilities. If I can provide any further information, please feel free to call me at (417) 555-4495.

Sincerely,

Rita Cassat

Senior Vice President

Readywise ImageGraphics

GO ON TO THE NEXT PAGE

THIS PAGE INTENTIONALLY LEFT BLANK.

Mathematical Reasoning

Welcome!

Here is some information that you need to know before you start this test:

- You should not spend too much time on a question if you are not certain of the answer; answer it the best you can, and go on to the next question.
- If you are not certain of the answer to a question, you can mark your answer for review and come back to it later.
- You have **115 minutes** to complete this test.
- This test has two parts.
- When you finish Part 1, you may review those questions.
- You may not go back to Part 1 once you have finished your review.
- You may not use a calculator in Part 1. You may use a calculator in Part 2.

Turn the page to begin.

GO ON TO THE NEXT PAGE

Mathematics Formula Sheet

Area of a:

square	$A = s^2$
rectangle	$A = lw$
parallelogram	$A = bh$
triangle	$A = \frac{1}{2}bh$
trapezoid	$A = \frac{1}{2}h(b_1 + b_2)$
circle	$A = \pi r^2$

Perimeter of a:

square	$P = 4s$
rectangle	$P = 2l + 2w$
triangle	$P = s_1 + s_2 + s_3$
Circumference of a circle	$C = 2\pi r$ OR $C = \pi d$; $\pi \approx 3.14$

Surface Area and Volume of a:

rectangular prism	$SA = 2lw + 2lh + 2wh$	$V = lwh$
right prism	$SA = ph + 2B$	$V = Bh$
cylinder	$SA = 2\pi rh + 2\pi r^2$	$V = \pi r^2 h$
pyramid	$SA = \frac{1}{2}ps + B$	$V = \frac{1}{3}Bh$
cone	$SA = \pi rs + \pi r^2$	$V = \frac{1}{3}\pi r^2 h$
sphere	$SA = 4\pi r^2$	$V = \frac{4}{3}\pi r^3$

(p = perimeter of base B; $\pi \approx 3.14$)

Data

mean	mean is equal to the total of the values of a data set, divided by the number of elements in the data set
median	median is the middle value in an odd number of ordered values of a data set, or the mean of the two middle values in an even number of ordered values in a data set

Algebra

slope of a line	$m = \frac{y_2 - y_1}{x_2 - x_1}$
slope-intercept form of the equation of a line	$y = mx + b$
point-slope form of the equation of a line	$y - y_1 = m(x - x_1)$
standard form of a quadratic equation	$y = ax^2 + bx + c$
quadratic formula	$x = \frac{-b \pm \sqrt{b^2 - 4ac}}{2a}$
Pythagorean Theorem	$a^2 + b^2 = c^2$
simple interest	$I = Prt$ (I = interest, P = principal, r = rate, t = time)
distance formula	$d = rt$
total cost	total cost = (number of units) × (price per unit)

GO ON TO THE NEXT PAGE

Mathematical Reasoning, Part 1

You may NOT use a calculator in Part 1.

1. If $z = -3$, what is $\frac{z^3 + 2z + 3}{z^2 + 1}$?

   A. 3
   B. −1.8
   C. −3.6
   D. −3

2. Each of 4 data storage thumb drives can contain up to 3.6 hours of recorded music. If each of the thumb drives is at least half full, which of the following expressions represents the total amount of music, x, contained on all 4 thumb drives?

   A. $0 < x < 7.2$
   B. $0 < x < 14.4$
   C. $7.2 < x < 14.4$
   D. $1.8 < x < 3.6$

3. Traveling at an average speed of 58 miles per hour, Terence drives 145 miles. Three hours later, Terence makes the return trip at the same speed. How much total time elapses between Terence's original departure and final return?

   A. 2.5 hours
   B. 5 hours
   C. 5.5 hours
   D. 8 hours

4. The average temperature, in degrees Fahrenheit, in the month of July in Clark City is 4 times the average temperature in the month of February. If the average temperature in July was 82 degrees, which of the following equations could be used to determine the average temperature in February (t)?

   A. $t + 4 = \frac{82}{4}$
   B. $4t = 82$
   C. $\frac{t}{4} = 21$
   D. $4t = 21$

5. What is the greatest common factor that can reduce $\frac{84}{196}$?

   A. 7
   B. 14
   C. 28
   D. 49

GO ON TO THE NEXT PAGE

Mathematical Reasoning, Part 2

You MAY use a calculator in Part 2.

Question 6 refers to the following chart.

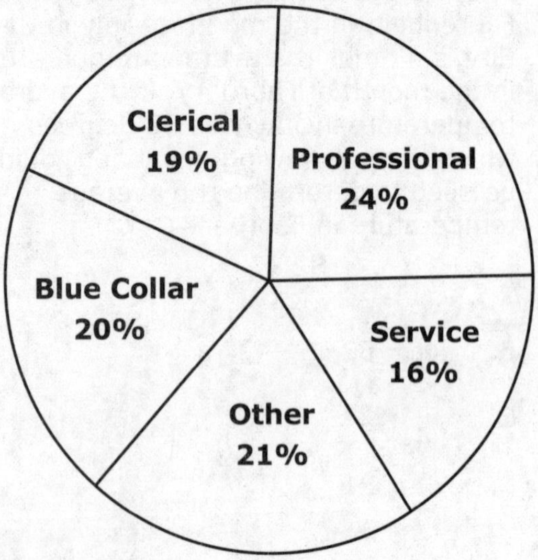

6. The figure above shows the worker distribution in a given country. If the total population of workers is 2.3 million, how many workers are employed neither in clerical nor in professional occupations?

   A. 1,311,000
   B. 1,048,800
   C. 990,000
   D. 552,000

7. Miriam and Vered buy a total of 42 stamps. Miriam bought 6 more stamps than Vered did. How many stamps did Miriam buy?

   A. 18
   B. 24
   C. 30
   D. 36

Questions 8 and 9 refer to the following number line.

8. Select the point on the number line that corresponds to the value P + S. (For this practice test, mark the point with an X.)

9. Select the point on the number line that corresponds to |Q − R| − T. (For this practice test, mark the point with an X.)

10. Solve the equation for *y*.

    $3y^2 - 12y = 10$

    A. $y = \frac{-6 \pm \sqrt{66}}{3}$

    B. $y = \frac{6 \pm \sqrt{66}}{3}$

    C. $y = \frac{-6 \pm \sqrt{6}}{3}$

    D. $y = \frac{6 \pm \sqrt{6}}{3}$

GO ON TO THE NEXT PAGE

11. A science class compares the relative strengths of two telescopic lenses. Lens X produces a magnification of 3×10^5, and Lens Y produces a magnification of 6×10^2.

Which of the following statements accurately describes the relationship between the two lenses?

A. Lens X produces a magnification 200% that of lens Y.
B. Lens X is 200 times as strong as Lens Y.
C. Lens X produces a magnification 500% that of lens Y.
D. Lens X is 500 times as strong as Lens Y.

12. If Mark can mow $\frac{2}{3}$ of a lawn in 1 hour, how many hours does it take him to mow the entire lawn?

A. $\frac{2}{3}$

B. $1\frac{1}{3}$

C. $1\frac{1}{2}$

D. 2

Question 13 refers to the diagram below.

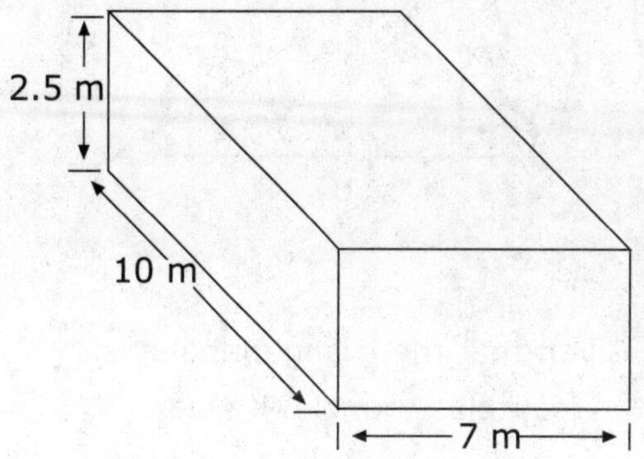

13. The dimensions of a box are shown in the diagram above. A designer wishes to paint the four larger sides of the box, leaving the smallest two sides unpainted. What will be the total surface area, in square meters, of the four sides the designer paints?

A. 175
B. 190
C. 225
D. 280

14. Evaluate $3x(x - 2a)^{-x}$, if $x = -2$ and $a = 0.5$.

☐

GO ON TO THE NEXT PAGE

Question 15 refers to the following figure.

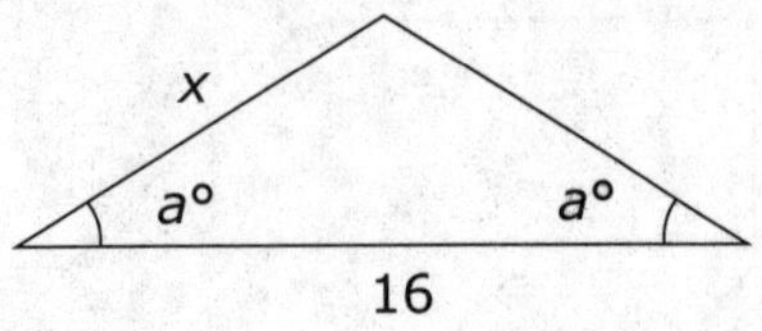

15. Given that the triangle above is an isosceles triangle, if side

x = Select... ▼, then the perimeter

9
10
13
16

of the triangle will be Select... ▼.

27
31
34
41

16. Ms. Carter decides to buy a computer system for her son. She spends $1,150 for a laptop and large monitor, $150 for a color laser printer, and $100 for an external hard drive. What would be the total cost of the system if the cost of the laptop and monitor were 10% more?

[ ]

17. Universal Products has 78 employees. If twice as many women work for Universal as men, how many women work for Universal?

A. 52
B. 42
C. 26
D. 16

18. In a study of bird migration, a researcher recorded on a certain day a total of 262 birds, consisting of 65 geese, 84 ducks, and 113 robins in the skies. Below, show a possible equation for calculating the probability that a random bird chosen from among these is NOT a duck. (For this practice test, write the numbers in the boxes below.)

$$\frac{\boxed{} + \boxed{}}{\boxed{}}$$

65

84

113

262

19. Which of the following expressions is equivalent to $2a(a - 3b^2) + a^2$?

A. $2a^2 - 6ab^2$
B. $3a^2 - 3b^2$
C. $2a(a - 3b^2)$
D. $3a(a - 2b^2)$

GO ON TO THE NEXT PAGE

Questions 20 and 21 refer to the following graph.

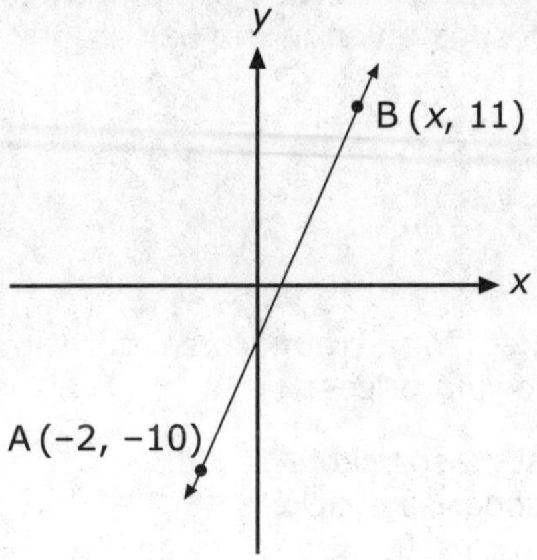

20. If the slope of the line shown is 3, then what is the *x*-coordinate of point B?

A. −5
B. −3
C. 3
D. 5

21. Given that the slope of the line is 3, what is the equation of the line?

A. $y = 3x - 3$
B. $y = 3x - 4$
C. $y = 3x - 5$
D. $y = 3x - 10$

22. The data represents scores received on the latest quiz by the students in Ms. Serrano's social studies class.

85, 92, 87, 96, 92, 87, 98, 91, 98, 87, 90, 87, 98, 92, 96

A.

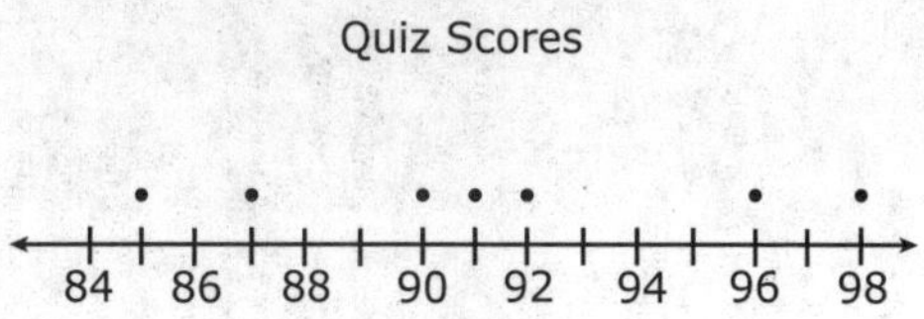

B.

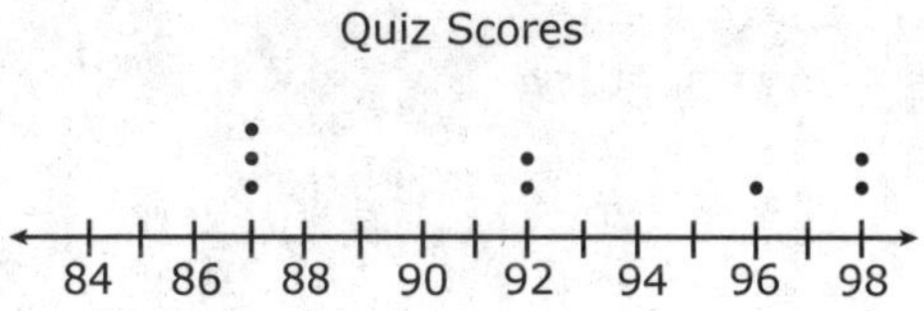

C.

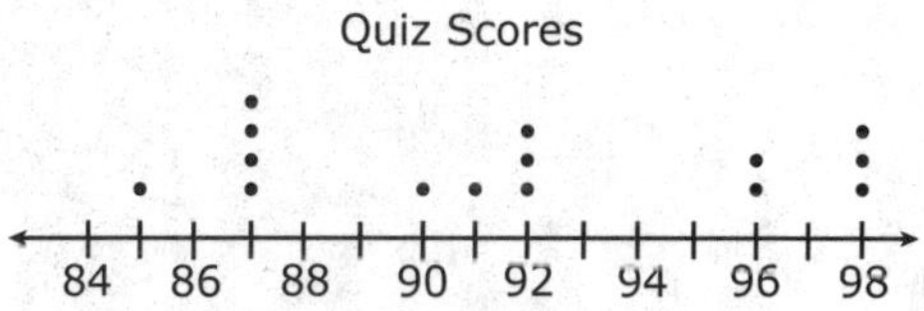

D.

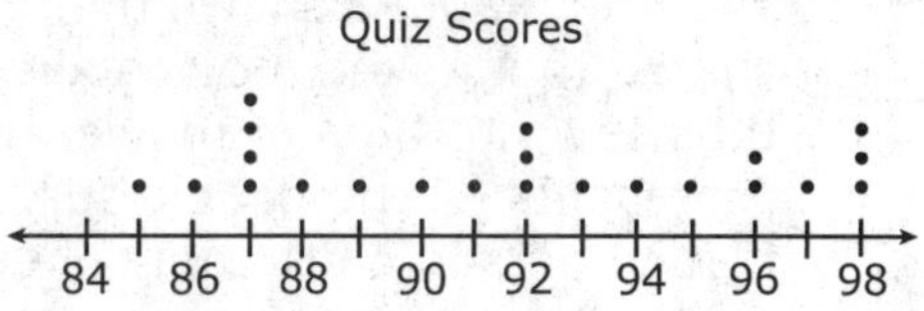

GO ON TO THE NEXT PAGE

Questions 23 and 24 refer to the following graph.

Movie Survey, by %

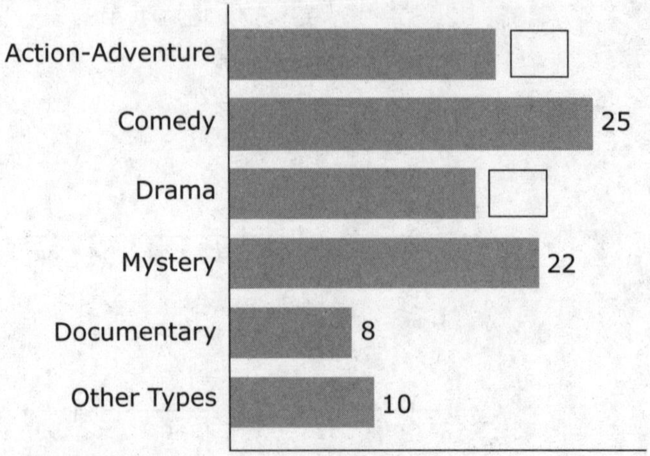

23. The graph above shows the results of a survey that asked moviegoers to choose their favorite type of movie. If the chart represents all the people surveyed and if each person chose only one type of movie, then choose two numbers below that could properly complete the graph, showing values for Action-Adventure and for Drama. (For this practice test, write the numbers in the boxes.)

Action-Adventure	**Drama**

10	15	17
18	19	25

24. Which of the following correctly represents the ratio of Comedy to Other Types, as given in the bar graph?

A. 5:2
B. 25:12
C. 2:5
D. 12:25

25. Tickets for a train trip sell for the following prices:

First-class tickets \$6.00
Second-class tickets \$3.50

Which of the following expressions represents the average ticket price for all tickets sold if the station sells 110 first-class and 172 second-class tickets?

A. $\dfrac{110 + 172}{2}$

B. $\dfrac{110(6.00) + 172(3.50)}{2}$

C. $\dfrac{(110+172) + 4.75}{110+172}$

D. $\dfrac{110(6.00) + 172(3.50)}{110 + 172}$

26. If $\dfrac{(4x + 3)^2}{2} = 72$ and $x > 0$, then $x =$

GO ON TO THE NEXT PAGE

Question 27 refers to the following diagram.

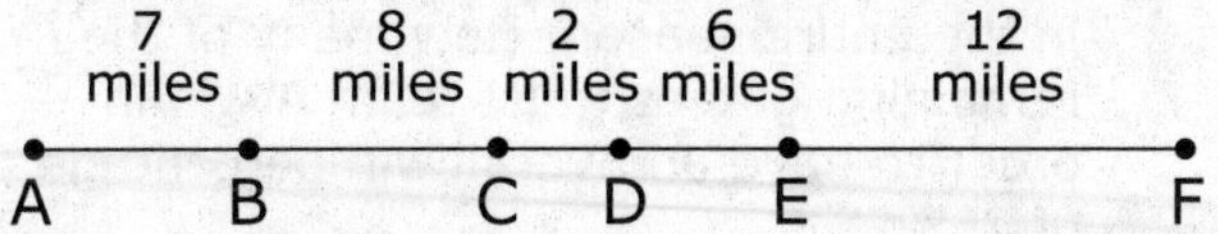

27. The towns in Maple County are located along a 35-mile section of an interstate at the points A, B, C, D, E, and F as shown in the diagram above. The Maple County Post Office is located midway between points A and E. The location of the post office is between which of the following two points?

    A. D and E
    B. C and D
    C. B and C
    D. A and B

28. The total bill for four friends eating at a restaurant (including tax) is $36.00. The friends wish to add a 20% tip and then to divide the bill evenly among the four of them. How much will each person pay?

    A. $7.20
    B. $9.00
    C. $10.80
    D. $16.20

Question 29 refers to the following coordinate plane grid.

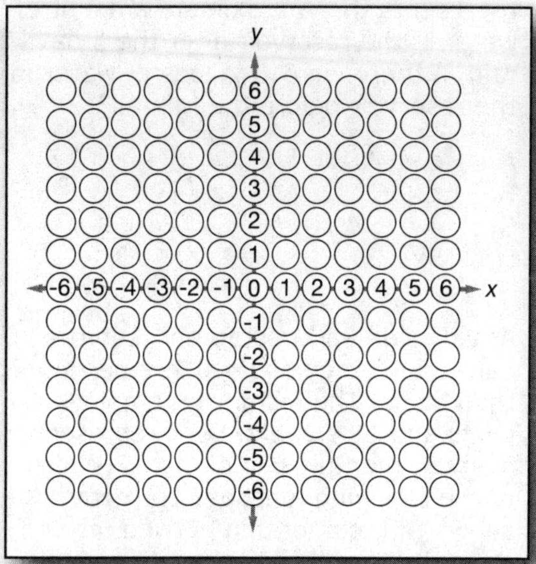

29. If the equation of a line is $y = \frac{1}{2}x + 3$, then mark on the graph the point where the line crosses the y-axis and the point where the line crosses the x-axis.

30. Makayla puts 60% of her paycheck into her savings account. If Makayla put $120 into her savings account, what was the amount of her entire paycheck?

    A. 72
    B. 180
    C. 192
    D. 200

GO ON TO THE NEXT PAGE

31. A rainfall doubled the original amount of water in a reservoir in 1 day and quadrupled the original amount in 5 days. Which of the following expressions represents the approximate amount of water in the reservoir after the 5 days of rain, if there were x gallons of water in the reservoir before the rainfall?

A. $x + 4$
B. $x + 6$
C. $4x$
D. $5x$

32. At Lakeside Park restaurant, servers earn an average of $840 less per month than chefs. The restaurant employs 4 chefs and 18 servers. Let c represent the average monthly pay of a chef. Which of the following functions correctly shows the relationship between the monthly payroll and the wages of these employees?

A. $4c + 18c - 840$
B. $4(c - 840) + 18c$
C. $22c - 840$
D. $4c + 18(c - 840)$

33. The town of Woodgreen offers billboard space along the highway. A 5 foot by 8 foot rectangular advertising space costs $140. The price ($p$) of a sign is proportional to its area. A new sign erected in the billboard space costs $336. If the new sign is 8 feet tall, then what is its length in feet?

A. 11
B. 12
C. 16
D. 42

34. Team A has won 28 of 35 games so far this season. There is a total of 44 games in the entire season. How many of the remaining games must team A win in order to have an overall win percentage of 75%?

A. 3
B. 5
C. 9
D. 33

Question 35 refers to the following diagram.

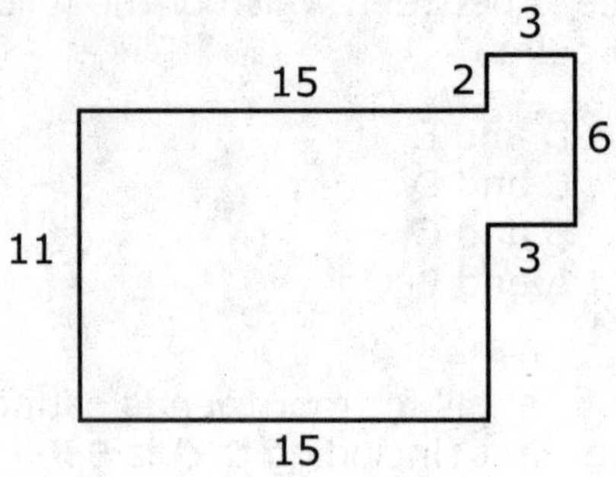

35. What is the area of the figure above?

A. 55
B. 132
C. 165
D. 183

36. A certain chest (a rectangular prism) has the following dimensions: 1.5 feet wide, 2.5 feet long, and 2 feet deep. If the chest currently holds 3 blankets that individually occupy 1 cubic foot each, then how much additional space is available in the chest?

☐ ft^3

GO ON TO THE NEXT PAGE

37. Michelle had a medical bill of \$850. After she paid the deductible of \$500, her insurance company paid 80% of the remainder. How much more of the bill did Michelle have to pay?

A. \$70
B. \$100
C. \$170
D. \$280

Questions 38 and 39 refer to the following diagram.

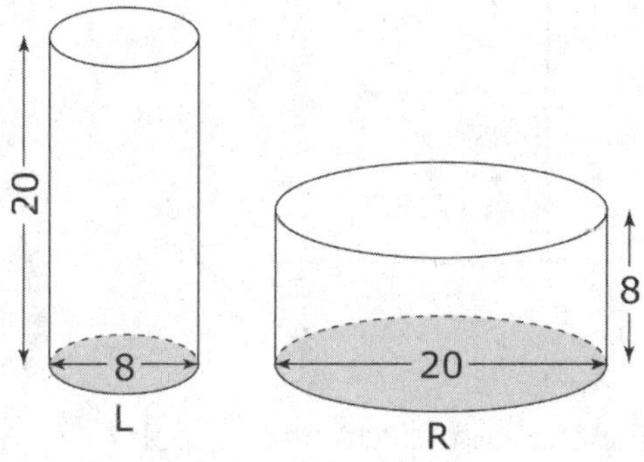

38. The volume of cylinder L is

Select...
- less than half
- slightly smaller than
- equal to
- slightly larger than
- more than twice

the volume of cylinder R.

39. If cylinder L is filled with water and then emptied into cylinder R (which was previously empty), then what will the height of the water in cylinder R be?

A. 3.2
B. 4
C. 4.6
D. 8

40. An airplane can hold 325 passengers, 30 in first class and the rest in coach. If a first-class ticket costs \$700 and a coach ticket costs \$250, then what is the minimum revenue that the airplane will gross on a flight in which exactly 3 seats remain empty?

A. \$91,900
B. \$92,650
C. \$94,000
D. \$94,750

Questions 41 and 42 refer to the following number line.

41. Let x be the distance between points A and E as shown on the number line above. Indicate where the point $\frac{x}{3}$ would appear on the number line. (For this practice test, write an X on the number line.)

42. Indicate where on the number line the point (B − C) − D would appear. (For this practice test, write an X on the number line.)

GO ON TO THE NEXT PAGE

Question 43 refers to the following diagram.

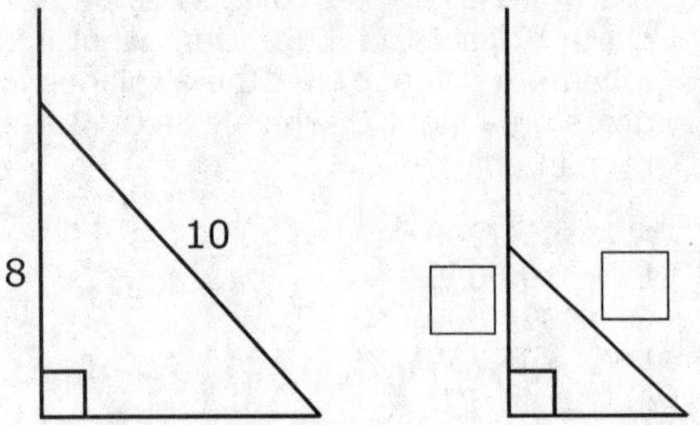

43. Two poles of different lengths are placed against a wall at identical angles, forming two similar triangles. Select two numbers from those below that give possible values for the length of the shorter pole and the height up the wall that it reaches. (For this practice test, write the numbers in the boxes above.)

4	5	6
8	11	

44. AJ was prescribed an antibiotic that must be taken as one tablet every 8 hours. Following the instructions, he took the first tablet at 2 p.m. on Monday and took the last tablet three days later, on Thursday at 2 p.m. How many tablets of antibiotic did AJ take?

45. Over an 8-year period, Katrina's $14,000 investment in the stock market increased by 180%. What was the value of her investment at the end of that period?

A. $16,520
B. $25,200
C. $39,200
D. $252,000

Question 46 refers to the following diagram.

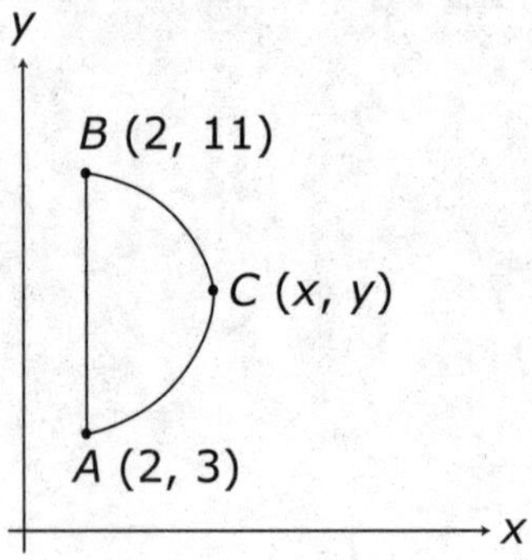

46. For the semicircle above, point *C* represents the midpoint of arc *AB*. Which of the following represent the coordinates of point *C*?

A. (6, 7)
B. (7, 7)
C. (4, 6)
D. (7, 6)

GO ON TO THE NEXT PAGE

Social Studies

Welcome!

Here is some information that you need to know before you start this test:

- You should not spend too much time on a question if you are not certain of the answer; answer it the best you can, and go on to the next question.
- If you are not certain of the answer to a question, you can mark your answer for review and come back to it later.
- You have **70 minutes** to complete this test.

Turn the page to begin.

GO ON TO THE NEXT PAGE

Questions 1 through 3 refer to the following information.

> The Department of Labor operates under the mandate that the most important capital is human capital. The Fair Labor Standards Act (FLSA), which also sets minimum wage and overtime pay standards in the private and government sectors, has specific provisions designed to protect children—the future workforce of America. Employment for minors now must conform to the following restrictions, which apply to all labor except farm labor. First, 16- or 17-year-olds may legally obtain employment as long as the job is not determined to be dangerous or ruinous to their health or well-being. Second, 14- or 15-year-olds may also work during specific hours at certain jobs as long as their employment does not negatively affect their health, schooling, or well-being. Employment of children under 14 years of age is usually prohibited. The Department of Labor has already classified 17 nonagricultural occupations as being unsuitable for minors.

1. According to the regulations described, all of the following could legally be used to deny a minor employment EXCEPT

    A. age requirements established by law.
    B. safety risks associated with the job.
    C. educational obligations of the minor.
    D. the gender of the applicant.

2. Which of the following beliefs is the basis for the regulations?

    A. Minors should judge the appropriateness of their own employment.
    B. Employment of minors must be controlled to protect them from harm.
    C. Minors should not be employed under any circumstances.
    D. School children should focus on their studies and not be burdened with jobs.

3. The most support for the passage of the FLSA likely came from

    A. factory owners.
    B. child protection agencies.
    C. workers' unions.
    D. small companies.

GO ON TO THE NEXT PAGE

Questions 4 and 5 refer to the following information.

> Most of them were disappointed in their search for gold. Many of those who failed as prospectors settled in towns such as San Francisco and Monterey. There they found jobs working for the canneries that sprang up as a result of the booming fishing industry or digging in the gold mines that others had found.

4. Which of the following best explains why the men described in the passage traveled west?

   A. to live near the ocean
   B. to start families
   C. for economic and other opportunities
   D. to escape religious persecution

5. According to the information, which of the following is a conclusion that best explains why many of those who headed west settled in coastal towns?

   A. They were able to find jobs there.
   B. There was no available land.
   C. Monterey rivers were rich in gold.
   D. The mountains were not open to settlement

Questions 6 and 7 refer to the following excerpt from the 1st Amendment to the U.S. Constitution.

> "Congress shall make no law respecting an establishment of religion, or prohibiting the free exercise thereof; or abridging the freedom of speech, or of the press; or the right of the people peaceably to assemble, and to petition the Government..."

6. Which situation would be most clearly protected by the 1st Amendment?

   A. A newspaper publishes criticism of government policies.
   B. A citizen is required to pay taxes on income.
   C. A state requires voter identification at polling places.
   D. Congress passes a law regulating business practices.

7. All of the following are guaranteed by the 1st Amendment EXCEPT

   A. the freedom to vote.
   B. the freedom of petition.
   C. the freedom of speech.
   D. the freedom of the press.

GO ON TO THE NEXT PAGE

Questions 8 through 10 refer to the following sources.

TAB 1: **Timeline of events following the end of World War II**

1945: Yalta Conference: The Allies of World War II (the USA, the USSR, Great Britain, and France) divide Germany into four occupation zones.

1947: Marshall Plan: A comprehensive program of economic assistance for the war-ravaged countries of Western Europe.

1948: Berlin Airlift: In response to Soviet Premier Joseph Stalin's attempt to block supplies to Berliners, France, Britain, and the United States launch the Berlin Airlift to supply the citizens of Berlin by air.

1949: North Atlantic Treaty Organization (NATO): Western nations unite in order to resist Communist expansion.

1955: Warsaw Pact: Soviet Union and Eastern European Communist nations unite to oppose NATO.

TAB 2:

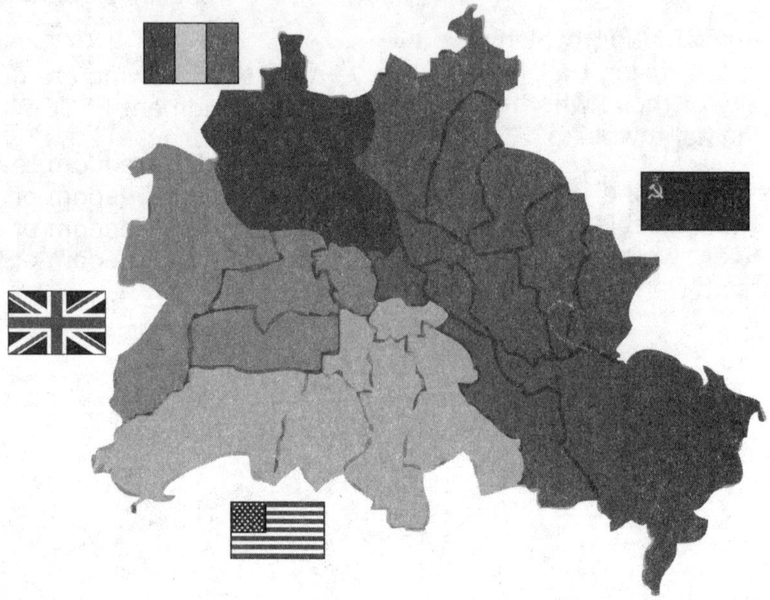

GO ON TO THE NEXT PAGE

8. Why was the Berlin Airlift necessary?

   A. Soviet forces blocked all land and water routes into West Berlin.
   B. The Marshall Plan eliminated direct supply routes to Berlin.
   C. The Yalta Conference prevented cooperation among Allied powers.
   D. NATO forces restricted access to Eastern European cities.

9. What event was a response to the formation of the North Atlantic Treaty Organization (NATO)?

   A. The Soviet Union and Eastern European countries formed the Warsaw Pact.
   B. The United States initiated the Berlin Airlift.
   C. Germany was divided into four occupation zones.
   D. The Marshall Plan provided aid to Western Europe.

10. Based on the map, which conclusion is best supported?

   A. Western Allied powers controlled geographically distinct zones of Germany after WWII.
   B. The United States controlled the largest population center in Germany.
   C. Germany was divided primarily based on economic productivity.
   D. Soviet control extended evenly across all regions of Germany.

<u>Question 11</u> refers to the following quotation.

> "Ulysses S. Grant concluded by 1863 that the very nature of a war to preserve the Union states would have the effect of changing those states and thus altering the Union."

11. Which of the following historical developments best supports Grant's conclusion?

   A. Grant had predicted a Northern triumph.
   B. In 1917, the United States entered the First World War.
   C. Women received the right to vote in 1919.
   D. The emancipation of the enslaved people affected the society of the entire nation.

12. The 24th Amendment states that "Non-payment of taxes cannot be used as a reason for denying to any citizen the right to vote for president, vice president, or a member of Congress." This amendment to the U.S. Constitution upholds which of the following common law principles?

   A. Voting rights should not depend on financial status.
   B. All citizens are required to pay taxes in order to vote.
   C. Government may limit voting rights during elections.
   D. Voting rights are determined by state governments.

GO ON TO THE NEXT PAGE

Question 13 refers to the following graph.

How Children Are Being Educated

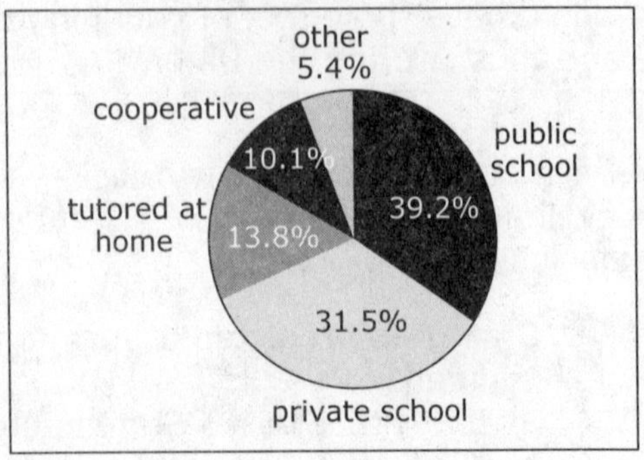

13. Which statement is supported by information in the graph?

A. Private schools provide a better education than do other types of schooling.
B. Children prefer the educational arrangements their parents have made for them.
C. Tutoring at home is the most popular method of educating children.
D. Most children attend either public or private schools.

Questions 14 and 15 refer to the following information.

> Economic systems can be classified according to the degree of government intervention and the type of control that the government exerts.
>
> A command economy is one in which the government takes a very active role. If the government chooses to use its control of the economy to redistribute all of the money equally among all of the members of society, this is a command socialist system. If the government controls the economy but allows the money to be unevenly distributed, this is known as a command capitalistic system.
>
> An economy in which the government takes no active role is known as a pure market economy. The only things that control the distribution of money in a pure market economy are market forces that no one person or organization can control.

14. Which of the following would most likely NOT occur in a pure market economy?

A. government-funded unemployment assistance
B. privately owned businesses competing freely
C. individuals seeking employment independently
D. market-driven pricing of goods and services

15. Which group would likely benefit LEAST from a shift to a socialist command economy?

A. high-income entrepreneurs with private businesses
B. unemployed individuals seeking state assistance
C. government employees in regulated industries
D. workers in low-wage labor sectors

GO ON TO THE NEXT PAGE

Question 16 refers to the following photo.

Source: Shutterstock

16. While today's car owners sometimes have difficulties, car owners in the early 20th century had to cope with quite a number of different problems.

Which of the following would have been the biggest concern for the people shown in the photo above?

A. a lack of unleaded gas, which resulted in pollution
B. a lack of seat belts and other safety features
C. a shortage of lightweight building materials, which led to much heavier cars than we have today
D. a scarcity of gas stations

Question 17 refers to the following source.

"In the spring of 1879, thousands of colored people, unable longer to endure the intolerable hardships, injustice, and suffering inflicted upon them by a class of Democrats in the South, had, in utter despair, fled panic-stricken from their homes and sought protection among strangers in a strange land. Homeless, penniless, and in rags, these poor people were thronging the wharves of Saint Louis, crowding the steamers on the Mississippi River, and in pitiable destitution throwing themselves upon the charity of Kansas. Thousands more were congregating along the banks of the Mississippi River, hailing the passing steamers, and imploring them for a passage to the land of freedom, where the rights of citizens are respected and honest toil rewarded by honest compensation. The newspapers were filled with accounts of their destitution, and the very air was burdened with the cry of distress from a class of American citizens flying from persecutions which they could no longer endure."

Report and Testimony of the Select Committee of the United States Senate to Investigate the Cause of the Removal of the Negroes from the Southern States to the Northern States, 46th Congress, 1880.

17. According to the passage, many African Americans migrated north primarily to

A. escape systemic racial oppression and economic hardship.
B. obtain land ownership opportunities in rural areas.
C. avoid military conscription in Southern states.
D. participate in industrialization campaigns.

GO ON TO THE NEXT PAGE

Question 18 refers to the following graph.

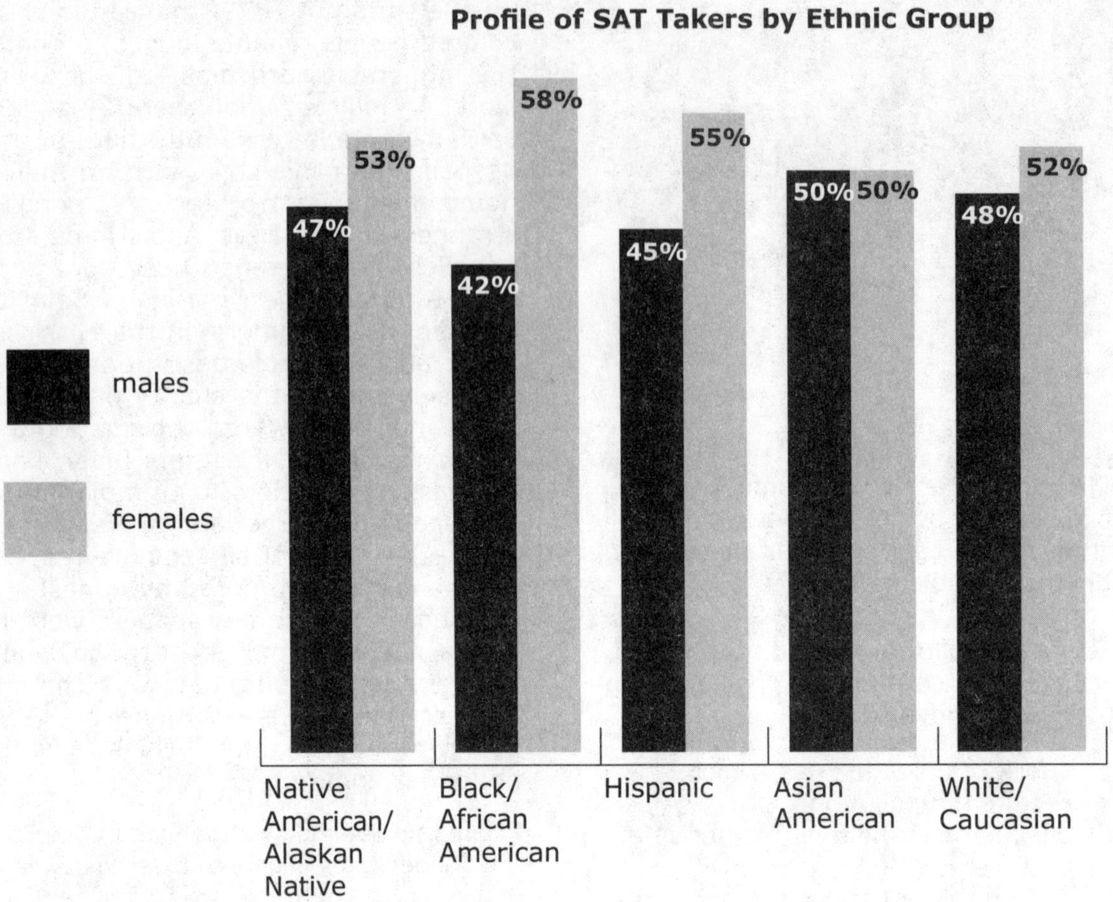

18. Which statement is clearly supported by evidence in the graph?

    A. American females perform better on the SAT than American males do.
    B. There has been a decline in the number of Asian American males taking the SAT.
    C. The number of females in general taking the SAT has increased.
    D. More females than males take the SAT.

GO ON TO THE NEXT PAGE

19. A plutocracy may be defined by the political principle of rule by the wealthy, that is, those who have accumulated wealth either through inherited property or financial success.

According to this statement, which of the following is <u>inconsistent</u> with a plutocratic form of government?

A. Citizens must abide by the decision of the select group in power.
B. Monetary interests are valued above human interests.
C. Leaders are determined by popular vote.
D. A farmer is excluded from holding office.

<u>Question 20</u> refers to the following quotation.

> "The [oil monopoly] molds public opinion in a manner creating a complete misunderstanding of the petroleum situation and influences the judgment and acts of unknowing and unwise public officials to a point where they fall to these interests of monopoly as against the welfare of the people whom they are supposed to serve."
>
> —Andrew Mellon

20. Which of the following is an opinion most likely held by the speaker above?

A. Those who profit from monopolies should not try to serve the public by running for office.
B. The interests of the people are secondary to those of public officials.
C. All should profit from the rewards gained by a monopoly.
D. Public officials should value the interests of the people they serve over the interests of any one business.

<u>Question 21</u> refers to the following paragraph.

> The U.S. government is structured with separate powers at the state and federal levels. Some political scientists have referred to this organization as a "wagon wheel," with the hub, or center, representing the federal government and the spokes representing the various state governments. This means that each state is separate, but the federal government maintains some level of centralized power.

21. Which of the following best illustrates how the "wagon wheel" analogy applies to the U.S. system of government?

A. A wagon wheel is one of four wheels needed to stabilize a wagon.
B. The hub of a wagon wheel holds in place the spokes, which strengthen the structure of the wheel.
C. A wagon wheel's hub and spokes are made of different materials.
D. A wagon wheel is created in several pieces and then assembled.

GO ON TO THE NEXT PAGE

Questions 22 through 24 refer to the following map.

Non-English-Speaking Children*

*Children aged 5 to 17 who speak another language at home and who don't speak English well or who don't speak it at all

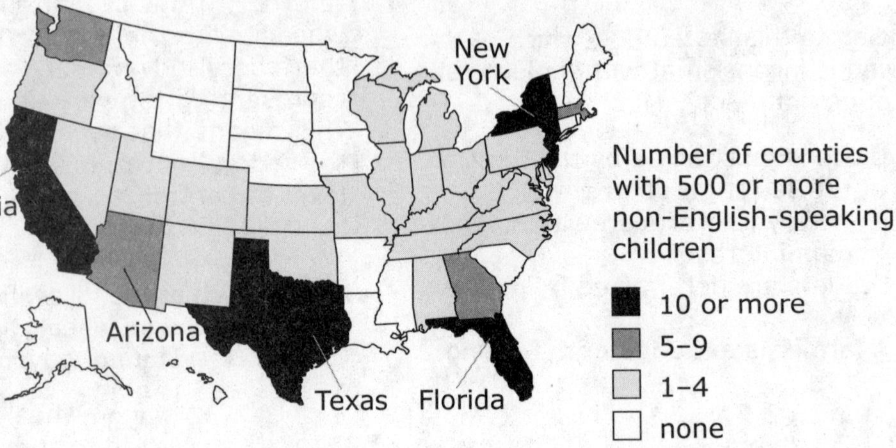

22. Which of the following best explains the distribution of non-English-speaking children shown on the map?

    A. Income taxes are lower on the coasts than in the middle of the country.
    B. Fewer children are born in states with cold climates.
    C. There are fewer English courses offered in the northern part of the United States.
    D. Recent immigrants to the United States have tended to settle in border and coastal states.

23. Which factor would have the LEAST effect upon the distribution of non-English-speaking children in the United States?

    A. migration patterns
    B. climate
    C. ESL programs
    D. immigration laws

24. Which generalization is supported by the evidence in the map?

    A. Non-English-speaking children are distributed evenly across the United States.
    B. There are more non-English-speaking children in Arizona than in California.
    C. In Texas and California, more children are unable to speak English than are able to speak English.
    D. There are fewer non-English-speaking children in the northern middle portion of the United States than in other parts of the country.

GO ON TO THE NEXT PAGE

Questions 25 through 27 refer to the following paragraph.

> The Constitution, the laws made in accordance with that Constitution, and any treaties that the United States has signed constitute the supreme law of the land, to which the judges in any state must adhere. Any state laws incompatible with this supreme law of the land are unconstitutional, and therefore null and void.

25. Which of the following is an example of the concept of supreme law?

    A. The president of the United States makes political appointments to the Supreme Court.
    B. The freedoms outlined in the Bill of Rights can't be denied by the government.
    C. The House of Representatives contains two representatives from each state.
    D. The president is elected to four-year terms.

26. Which of the following is an example of a state law that would be incompatible with the Constitution?

    A. a law that prohibits protests by a steelworkers' union
    B. a law that lowers the speed limit on a highway to 50 miles per hour
    C. a law that limits state senators to two six-year terms each
    D. legislation that requires reductions in emissions from factories

27. Which of the following is an example of a law compatible with the Constitution?

    A. legislation that prohibits the practice of certain religions
    B. a law that protects the rights of convicted criminals
    C. a law that suspends the right to trial by jury
    D. a law that prevents non-English-speakers from voting

GO ON TO THE NEXT PAGE

Questions 28 and 29 refer to the following paragraphs.

> According to several prominent professors of economics, it is impossible to be completely accurate when predicting the long-term performance of any given stock. The professors' arguments are that the various political, social, and economic pressures that affect the success of any company are constantly changing and that their combined effects are extremely unpredictable.
>
> This would explain why an amateur investor can very often do as well as a professional stock trader in long-term investments. The professors likened predicting stock performance to predicting weather patterns. Weather predictions are usually accurate up to a few days into the future, but the farther ahead the prediction, the greater the likelihood that unforeseen events render the prediction inaccurate. The same may be true of long-term stock predictions.

28. After analyzing the success of long-term stock predictions, some business professors reported that

    A. professional predictions of stock performance are usually accurate.
    B. stocks that are currently performing well will continue to do so.
    C. amateur stock investors do very poorly in long-term investments.
    D. even careful analysis of current stock performance is no guarantee of accurate long-term predictions.

29. If it is true that a company's performance is affected by many factors, one can conclude that

    A. two companies producing the same goods will perform equally well.
    B. a company's success is dependent on amateur investors.
    C. it is possible to lose money by investing in a company that has been very successful.
    D. an amateur stock investor will automatically make more money than a professional.

30. *Laissez-faire* is an economic environment in which transactions between private parties are largely free from government restrictions.

    Choose THREE characteristics that best exemplify laissez-faire economics:

    [ ]

    [ ]

    [ ]

(a) Deregulation	(d) Free Trade
(b) Labor Laws	(e) Antitrust Laws
(c) Building Codes	(f) Non-Interference

Drag and drop your choices into the three slots above. (For this practice test, write the letters of three characteristics in the slots.)

GO ON TO THE NEXT PAGE

Question 31 refers to the photo below.

Source: Photofest Archives

31. The golden age of transatlantic passenger ships was quickly coming to an end in this photo taken of six ocean liners at dock in New York City circa 1953. Which of the following events was probably the most important reason for the end of the era of crossing the Atlantic by ship?

    A. A series of highly publicized liner accidents made the public too nervous to take ships.
    B. A major war made overseas travel impossible.
    C. The advent of passenger airlines cut down the time it took to get to Europe, leaving ships outmoded.
    D. The cost of travel by boat became prohibitively expensive.

Question 32 refers to the following cartoon.

A MAN KNOWS A MAN

"Give me your hand, Comrade! We have each lost a Leg for the good cause; but, thank God, we never lost Heart."

32. This cartoon from the Civil War era depicts two veterans of the Civil War (which was fought over the emancipation of enslaved Black people) greeting each other. What is the main implication of the cartoon's caption?

    A. Shared sacrifice creates equality and mutual respect among veterans.
    B. Physical injury defines social status among soldiers.
    C. Veterans from opposing sides cannot form meaningful relationships.
    D. War experiences prevent emotional connection between individuals.

GO ON TO THE NEXT PAGE

Questions 33 through 35 refer to the following sources.

TAB 1:

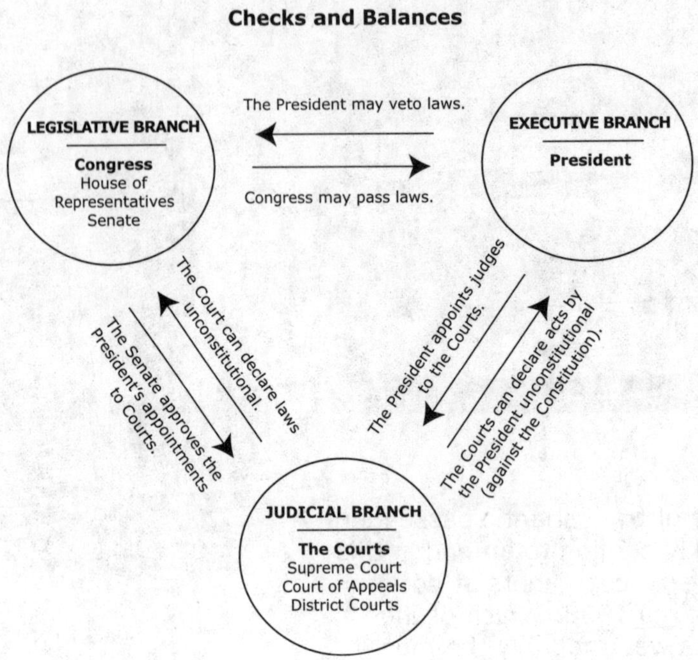

TAB 2:

"It is emphatically the province and duty of the Judicial Department [the judicial branch] to say what the law is. Those who apply the rule to particular cases must, of necessity, expound and interpret that rule. If two laws conflict with each other, the Courts must decide on the operation of each."

–Justice John Marshall, *Marbury v. Madison*, 1803

TAB 3:

"You seem to consider the judges as the ultimate arbiters of all constitutional questions; a very dangerous doctrine indeed, and one which would place us under the despotism of an oligarchy. Our judges are as honest as other men, and not more so. They have, with others, the same passions for party, for power, and the privilege of their corps.... Their power [is] the more dangerous as they are in office for life, and not responsible, as the other functionaries are, to the elective control."

–Thomas Jefferson, in response to *Marbury v. Madison*

GO ON TO THE NEXT PAGE

33. What is a primary duty of the Legislative Branch?

    A. to veto laws
    B. to pass laws
    C. to implement *Marbury v. Madison*
    D. to nominate and appoint judges to the Supreme Court

34. What was Thomas Jefferson's opinion of *Marbury v. Madison*?

    A. It balanced federal power by giving federal judges the right to override unjust laws.
    B. It conferred too much power to the Executive Branch.
    C. It made judges as honest as other men.
    D. It gave too much power to the Judicial Branch.

35. In context, what is the best substitute for the word "oligarchy"? (TAB 3)

    A. tyranny
    B. democracy
    C. passion
    D. honesty

GO ON TO THE NEXT PAGE

THIS PAGE INTENTIONALLY LEFT BLANK.

Science

Welcome!

Here is some information that you need to know before you start this test:

- You should not spend too much time on a question if you are not certain of the answer; answer it the best you can, and go on to the next question.
- If you are not certain of the answer to a question, you can mark your answer for review and come back to it later.
- You have **90 minutes** to complete this test.

Turn the page to begin.

GO ON TO THE NEXT PAGE

<u>Question 1</u> refers to the following photograph and chart.

Source: Shutterstock

Average Temperature of Various Large Bodies of Water	
Atlantic Ocean	46 degrees Fahrenheit
Arctic Ocean	36 degrees Fahrenheit
Baltic Sea	45 degrees Fahrenheit
Great Lakes of North America	44 degrees Fahrenheit
Gulf of Mexico	60 degrees Fahrenheit

1. Hurricanes such as the one pictured above gather strength as they pass over warm water. According to the chart above, over which of the following bodies of water would a hurricane gather the most strength?

   A. Baltic Sea
   B. Atlantic Ocean
   C. Arctic Ocean
   D. Gulf of Mexico

2. Blood is made up of two main elements: (1) plasma, which is largely water and proteins, and (2) the solid components of blood—red blood cells, white cells, and platelets (important for forming clots). If a patient has lost a lot of blood, that patient may receive a transfusion of "whole blood," which includes red blood cells and plasma. However, sometimes the patient needs only an increase in the *volume* of liquid in the bloodstream, in which case plasma alone may be substituted.

   A person must be tested for blood type before receiving certain kinds of transfusions because of differences in the ways that red blood cells react to one another. Under what conditions would such testing be necessary?

   A. for whole blood transfusions only
   B. for plasma transfusions only
   C. for both whole blood transfusions and plasma transfusions
   D. if the patient has not lost any blood

GO ON TO THE NEXT PAGE

Science

Questions 3 through 5 refer to the following information.

Coal is formed from the material of plants and other organisms that lived on land and whose remains were covered by mud, which later became rock. Coal is classified by carbon content.

Types of Coal

Peat	=	The remains of plants and organisms that, because they were covered in bogs, were prevented by a lack of oxygen from completely decaying. Still a porous, soft brown mass, peat has a carbon content of 52%–60%.
Lignite	=	In time, peat turns into lignite, a soft coal-like substance that is 60%–65% carbon.
Subbituminous coal	=	With more time, heat, and pressure, lignite changes into subbituminous coal, which is about 65%–75% carbon.
Bituminous coal	=	After even more heat and pressure, subbituminous coal turns into bituminous coal with a carbon level of 75%–85%.
Anthracite	=	This is bituminous coal subjected to another million years of heat and pressure. Anthracite has a carbon level of 85%–95% and will burn only at extremely high temperatures.

3. A researcher analyzes a piece of coal and finds that it is unusually dense and burns only when subjected to very intense heat. What is the lowest percentage of carbon that this coal is likely to contain?

[ ]

4. Steel is made in a process in which iron is combined with carbon at extremely high temperatures. Which of the following types of coal might be most useful in this process?

   A. peat
   B. lignite
   C. subbituminous coal
   D. anthracite

5. Drag and drop the appropriate type of coal into each box. (For this practice test, write the appropriate letter in each box.)

The type of coal most likely found closest to the surface of the earth:	The type of coal that contains the greatest amount of carbon per kilogram:

(a) Peat

(b) Lignite

(c) Bituminous coal

(d) Anthracite

GO ON TO THE NEXT PAGE

Questions 6 and 7 refer to the following information.

1 Germination is the process in which the embryonic issue inside a seed comes out of a dormant state and begins to grow into plants. Most seeds will germinate when they have moisture, oxygen, light, and the right temperature, but different seeds need different proportions of each of these ingredients. Most seeds require a temperature of between 15 degrees and 27 degrees centigrade to germinate. However, some seeds are better nurtured in other temperature ranges.

2 Oxygen should be 2–3%. Planting maple seeds in soil with course materials such as sand will help to allow for the ideal oxygen levels. The soil must also have a moisture level of above 50%. However, if the soil is too wet, the seeds could be deprived of the oxygen that they need to germinate properly. The ideal temperature for the germination of maple trees is significantly lower than the temperatures required to germinate most other types of seeds.

3 Corn seeds require a much higher oxygen level than that of maple seeds. The ideal oxygen level is comparable to that of the atmosphere. The range of temperatures needed for the germination of corn is much higher than those required by most types of seeds. Moisture levels above 35% could encourage the growth of fungus, which can halt the germination process.

6. Which of the following environments would be most suitable for the germination of corn seeds?

A. a moist, sealed container at 26 degrees centigrade
B. an arid desert plain
C. a moist, plowed field at 30 degrees centigrade
D. an environment suitable for maple seed growth

7. Based on the information in the passage, which of the following is most likely true?

A. Maple seeds can germinate in any temperature.
B. Corn is difficult to grow.
C. Water, in limited amounts, is vital to the germination process.
D. Maple seeds and corn seeds require different amounts of oxygen for germination.

GO ON TO THE NEXT PAGE

Question 8 refers to the following information.

Measles is an infectious disease that is transmitted through the air and through surfaces. Most people recover without long-term complications, but the disease is potentially deadly.

Many researchers believe that a decrease in the vaccination rate among children is linked to an increase in measles cases.

MMR Vaccination Coverage Among Kindergartners, 2020–2025

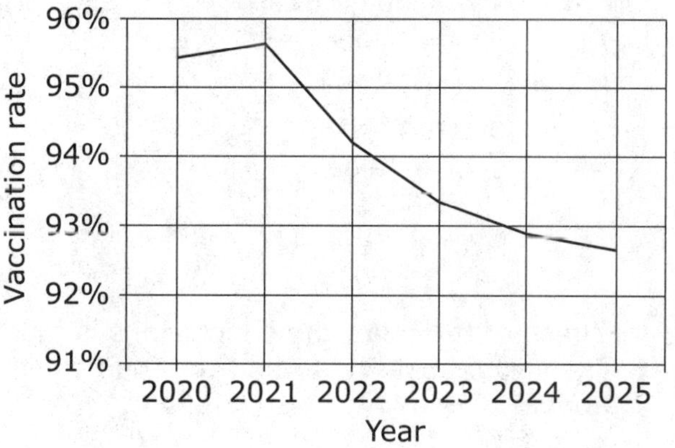

Measles Cases, 2020–2025

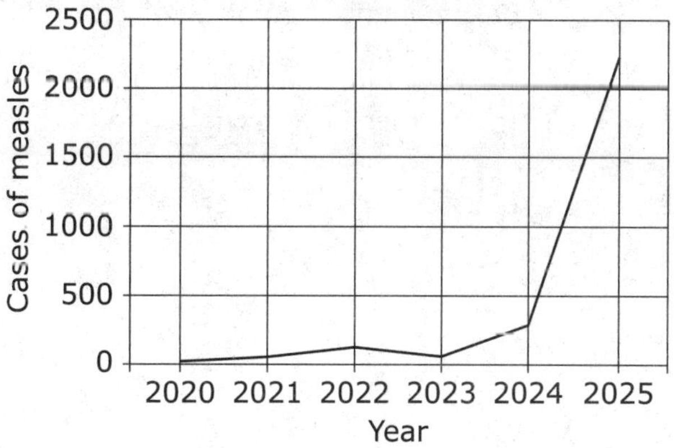

8. Why do the data support or refute the researchers' belief that a lower vaccination rate is linked to an increase in cases?

A. The data support the belief because when vaccination rates decrease the number of cases of measles decreases.
B. The data support the belief because the trend of vaccination rates decreases and the trend among measles cases increases.
C. The data refute the belief because the trend is measles cases fluctuates without a pattern as the vaccination rate decreases.
D. The data refute the belief because there is no connection between vaccination rates and measles cases.

9. During periods that are unfavorable for growth, some plants become dormant. Woody plants are protected during such periods by their bark. Perennial plants die above ground, but their roots remain alive. Annual plants die, but their seeds survive to continue the life of the species.

Which of the following would most likely be a time of year during which plants might lie dormant?

A. winter
B. spring
C. summer
D. fall

GO ON TO THE NEXT PAGE

Question 10 refers to the following diagram.

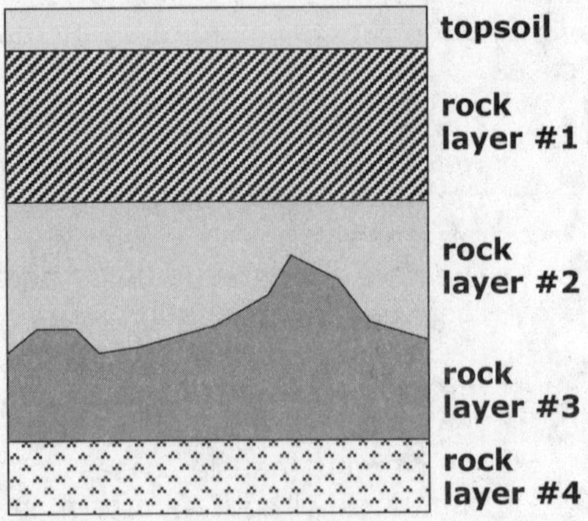

10. The diagram above shows various layers of rock that have been deposited over time. Drag and drop the rock layers into the appropriate boxes. (For this practice test, write the letters in the boxes.)

The oldest rock layer:	The newest rock layer:

(a) rock layer #1	(c) rock layer #3
(b) rock layer #2	(d) rock layer #4

Question 11 refers to the following diagram.

Food Chain

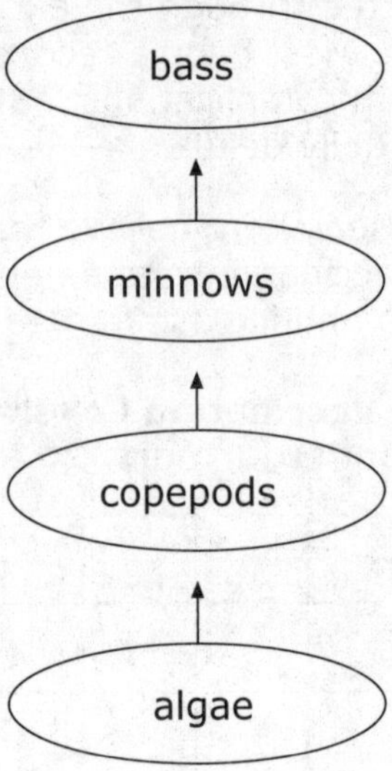

11. Which of the following conclusions is most likely to be true regarding the food chain above?

A. Bass are the only fish that eat minnows.
B. Minnows are bigger than bass.
C. Bass benefit in some ways from the existence of copepods.
D. Bass could simply "eliminate the middlemen" by eating algae.

GO ON TO THE NEXT PAGE

Question 12 refers to the following passage.

> Passive protection is a method by which organisms protect themselves from predators, not by fighting, but by their appearance, smell, or sound. Protective resemblance is a type of passive protection in which an animal's coloring mimics the natural environment, acting as a kind of camouflage. Protective mimicry is another type of passive protection in which a defenseless organism resembles a more powerful organism. Another interesting example of passive protection is the Monarch butterfly, which smells and tastes so bad to other organisms that virtually no other animal or insect will eat it.

12. Which of the following is NOT an example of passive protection?

    A. A chameleon changes its color to blend in with a leaf in order to avoid predators.
    B. The nonpoisonous scarlet kingsnake develops coloration very similar to that of the poisonous eastern coral snake.
    C. An orchid flower mimics a female insect in order to lure male insects to it so the flower can be pollinated.
    D. An edible vine adapts its leaves to match the inedible plant that it is climbing.

13. The density of seawater is 1,029 kilograms/meter^3. 1 kilogram/liter = 1,000 kilograms/meter^3. What is the density of seawater in kilograms/liter?

    You may use a calculator.

    A. 0.0001029
    B. 0.1029
    C. 1.029
    D. 1,029,000

Question 14 refers to the following scenario.

1 Researchers in a particular city theorize that decreasing the greenhouse gas emissions in that city will result in better respiratory health for its citizens. In order to test this theory, they institute two programs. The first program provides commuters with financial incentives to take public transportation, and the second program initiates a respiratory care education campaign and provides free clinics for citizens suffering from respiratory health issues.

2 During the five years after the researchers institute the two programs, greenhouse gas emissions in the city decrease by 50%, and a citywide survey reveals that cases of illness due to respiratory problems have decreased by 65%. Researchers therefore conclude that their theory was correct: Decreasing greenhouse gas emissions resulted in better respiratory health for local citizens.

14. Which of the following best shows why the researchers' conclusion is flawed?

    A. They failed to compare the city's air quality to that of any other towns, so they don't know if greenhouse gases decreased more or less than they should have.
    B. They should have tested the city's drinking water, too, since that has a greater effect on citizens' health than air quality does.
    C. Their conclusion doesn't explain the 15% difference between the decrease in greenhouse gases and the decrease in respiratory problems.
    D. They instituted two programs instead of one, so they can't be sure which is responsible for the resulting health improvements.

GO ON TO THE NEXT PAGE

15. Lobsters are crustaceans commonly found in the waters of the Atlantic Ocean off the North American coast between Maine and North Carolina. Researchers studied the weights of these creatures over a period of a few years. Some of the results are displayed in the table below.

Year	Average Weight (kg)
2005	0.43
2006	0.41
2007	0.37
2008	0.43
2009	0.38

The researchers hope to find the most commonly occurring lobster weight for the lobsters studied during the five-year period shown above. The researchers must calculate the [Select... ▼]

- average
- mode
- median
- range

of the weights, which is [Select... ▼].

- 0.04 kg
- 0.40 kg
- 0.41 kg
- 0.43 kg

You may use a calculator.

16. Amy tracks the monthly snowfall in two areas over a period of several months. One area is a region of high elevation, and the other is an area of low elevation. The table below displays her results.

Month	Area	Meters
November	low elevation	0.2
November	high elevation	0.4
December	low elevation	0.2
December	high elevation	0.8
January	low elevation	0.9
January	high elevation	1.7
February	low elevation	1.3
February	high elevation	1.8
March	low elevation	0.9
March	high elevation	1.1

What is the mean of the data shown in the table?

You may use a calculator.

[ ] meters

GO ON TO THE NEXT PAGE

17. Scientists calculate the pressure within a gas by using the following equation:

$$P = \frac{N \times k \times T}{V}$$

In the equation:

P is the pressure of the gas;
N is the number of particles in the gas;
k is a constant;
T is the temperature of the gas;
V is the volume of the gas.

If the number of particles in the gas decreases, which of the following changes will result in an increase in the pressure of the gas?

A. decreasing both the volume and the temperature of the gas
B. increasing both the volume and the temperature of the gas
C. increasing the volume and decreasing the temperature of the gas
D. decreasing the volume and increasing the temperature of the gas

18. There are four basic types of chemical reactions, as shown in the table below.

Reaction Type	**General Example**
Combination	A + B → C
Decomposition	C → A + B
Single displacement	A + BC → B + AC
Double displacement	AB + CD → AC + BD

The balanced chemical equation describing the reaction between hydrogen and fluorine is shown below.

$$H_2 + F_2 \rightarrow 2HF$$

Which of the four basic types of chemical reactions is this?

A. combination
B. decomposition
C. single displacement
D. double displacement

GO ON TO THE NEXT PAGE

Question 19 refers to the following graph.

AIDS Deaths 2011–2020

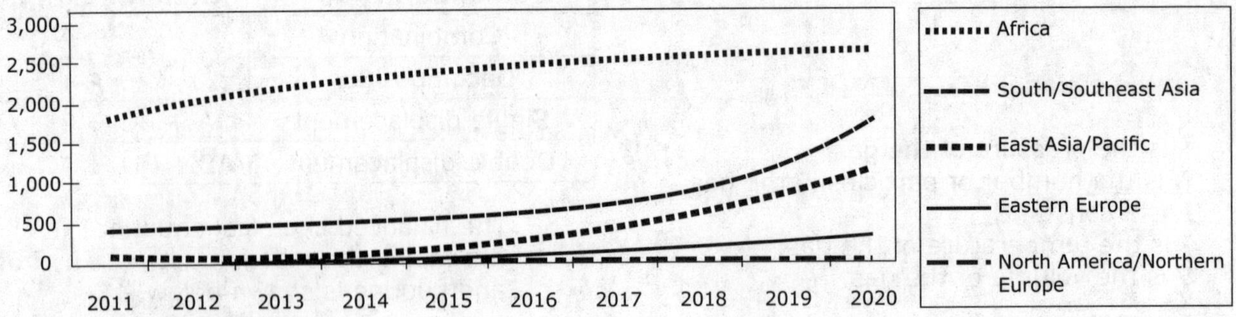

Source: World Health Organization

19. According to the chart above, which of the following regions had the largest increase in the number of AIDS deaths between 2011 and 2020?

A. Africa
B. South/Southeast Asia
C. Eastern Europe
D. North America/Northern Europe

GO ON TO THE NEXT PAGE

20. Scientists classify stars according to the following categories: O, B, A, F, G, K, M. A star's category depends upon its *spectral type*, which is determined by its temperature. The chart below shows five stars of different categories, along with their temperatures.

Star Type	Temperature (°F)
O	18,033
B	9,978
A	4,839
F	3,644
G	3,422

However, rather than measuring star temperature in degrees Fahrenheit, scientists typically measure star temperature in units of Kelvin. The conversion from Fahrenheit to Kelvin is given by the following formula:

$$K = \frac{5}{9}(°F - 32) + 273.$$

What is the approximate temperature of the A-type star in Kelvin?

You may use a calculator.

A. 2,569
B. 2,822
C. 2,929
D. 2,944

Questions 21 and 22 refer to the following graph.

Waves That Foretell Tidal Waves

Seismometer readings of earth motion from the Fault City quake reflect much larger long-period surface waves at point R1 than those from the Nicaragua quake.

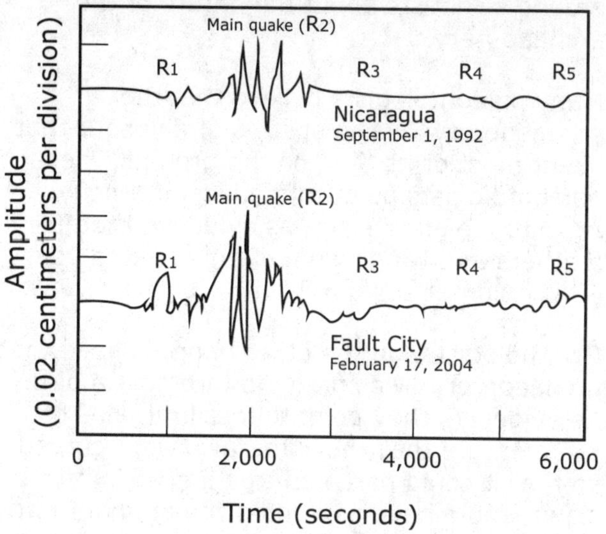

21. According to the information above, which of the following statements is true?

A. The Nicaragua main quake had a larger amplitude than did the Fault City quake.
B. The Fault City main quake had a larger amplitude than did the Nicaragua quake.
C. A seismometer was used to measure the Nicaragua quake but was not used to measure the Fault City quake.
D. The long-period surface waves at the point R1 were larger during the Nicaragua quake than during the Fault City quake.

22. Select the point on the graph that would be of the most importance in foretelling an earthquake in Nicaragua. (For this practice test, write an X on the graph.)

GO ON TO THE NEXT PAGE

Questions 23 and 24 refer to the following passage.

1 Archaeopteryx is a genus of dinosaur that lived 150 million years ago. The first fossil of the archaeopteryx was found in the form of a single feather near Solnhofen, Germany. Since its discovery, there has been a debate among scientists about the nature of the archaeopteryx.

2 Many paleontologists believe that the archaeopteryx was a species of dinosaur that spent most of its time on the ground. These paleontologists point to the lack of a bony breastbone and its size as evidence that its feathers and wings were of only limited use and could not sustain flight.

3 Ornithologists, on the other hand, believe that archaeopteryx was first and foremost a bird. As evidence, they point to fossil remains of the creature that show its claws were curved so that it could perch on tree limbs. Curved claws would have prevented the animal from walking or running quickly on the ground.

23. According to paleontologists, the archaeopteryx was incapable of

A. perching.
B. running.
C. flying.
D. walking.

24. According to the theory advanced by ornithologists, which of the following is most likely to have been a modern-day descendant of the archaeopteryx?

A. the lizard
B. the alligator
C. the crow
D. the mosquito

25. In science, work is defined as the component of force parallel to motion multiplied by displacement. One reason that individuals use ramps, rather than lifting heavy items straight up, is that using a ramp increases total displacement, but reduces the amount of force required to move an object by exactly the same amount as the increase in displacement, provided that the ramp's surface is frictionless.

According to the information in the paragraph, using a ramp with a frictionless surface will have which of the following effects?

A. The total amount of work required to move an object will decrease.
B. The total amount of work required to move an object will increase.
C. The total amount of work required to move an object will remain the same.
D. The amount of work required to move an object will initially increase, but will later decrease.

26. Below is a table listing the concentrations of chemicals found in human blood and urine.

	Albumin mg/dL	Chloride mg/dL	Glucose mg/dL	Phosphate mg/dL	Urea mg/dL
Blood	4.1	92	95	2.5	4.5
Urine	—	53	—	0.15	1.6

Based on the table above, which of the following chemicals is NOT normally found in urine?

A. albumin only
B. chloride only
C. glucose only
D. albumin and glucose

GO ON TO THE NEXT PAGE

27. In a certain forest, foxes prey on rabbits. A virus that infects only rabbits spreads through the forest, killing many rabbits.

    Which of the following is most likely to occur to the fox population?

    A. It will decrease, because the foxes will not have enough food.
    B. It will decrease, because the foxes will suffer from the virus.
    C. It will increase, because the foxes will no longer need to compete with the rabbits for food.
    D. It will increase, because the foxes will evolve to become more resistant to disease.

28. A solar eclipse is a celestial event during which the Sun appears partially or totally obstructed when viewed from a certain location on Earth. The diagram below shows a solar eclipse.

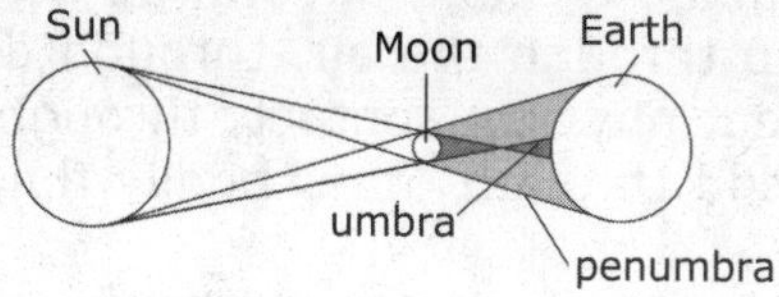

    Based on the information above, which of the following is mostly likely to be true during a solar eclipse?

    A. The entire Moon is in the penumbra, or shadow, of the Earth, so that the Moon is no longer visible from the Earth.
    B. The Moon is directly between the Sun and the Earth, thus placing certain regions of the Earth within the Moon's umbra, or deepest part of the shadow, so that the Sun's rays are not visible from those regions.
    C. Light rays from the Earth intercept those from the Sun, thus creating an umbra, or dark shadow, around the Moon so that the Sun is no longer visible from the Earth.
    D. The Sun is in the umbra, or deepest part of the shadow, cast by the Earth, and is therefore invisible from the Earth.

GO ON TO THE NEXT PAGE

Questions 29 and 30 refer to the following passage.

1 Pathogenic microbes, microorganisms that cause disease, include viruses, bacteria, fungi, and protozoa. Such microbes can invade hosts through several pathways, including through the air, through direct or indirect physical contact, through blood, and through other bodily fluids.

2 Medical researchers are currently attempting to find better treatments for microbial diseases by developing new pharmaceuticals. Currently, many doctors prescribe penicillin, which is derived from the spores of a fungus and which prevents the growth of new bacteria, to treat bacteria-induced microbial diseases, and antiviral compounds to combat viruses. However, such treatments do not always eradicate the relevant diseases, and while some microbe-induced illnesses, such as chicken pox, may not be life-threatening, others, such as Ebola, can be deadly.

29. Below is a chart of some common microbe-induced illnesses and their causes.

Illness	Cause
Common Cold	Rhinovirus
Strep Throat	Streptococcal bacterium
Athlete's Foot	Candida yeast
Malaria	Malaria protist

Which of the following is most likely treatable with penicillin?

A. common cold
B. strep throat
C. athlete's foot
D. malaria

30. Scientists typically measure speed in meters per second (m/s). However, in everyday situations, speeds are more commonly measured in miles per hour. A particular airplane travels at twice the speed of sound.

- 1 hour is equivalent to 3,600 seconds.
- The speed of sound is 343 meters per second.
- 1 mile is equivalent to 1,609 meters.

What is closest to the speed of the airplane in miles per hour?

A. 0.43
B. 21.59
C. 1,104.02
D. 1,534.87

GO ON TO THE NEXT PAGE

Questions 31 and 32 refer to the following passage.

1 Hereditary traits are encoded by genes that are located on chromosomes. Chromosomes come in pairs, and the pair of genes for a particular feature determines the characteristics of that trait. In many cases, genes exhibit a pattern called classical dominance. In such cases, the gene for a dominant trait is always expressed when present. An individual may have only a dominant gene and have two copies of that gene, or an individual may be hybrid and have one dominant gene and one recessive gene. In hybrids, the dominant gene hides the expression of the recessive gene. A recessive gene is expressed only when both copies of the gene are recessive. In literature, dominant genes are represented by capital letters, while recessive genes are represented by lowercase letters.

2 In pea plants, pea color is a hereditary trait. Green comes from a dominant gene, and yellow comes from a recessive gene, so that if a plant has one gene for green and one gene for yellow, that plant will produce green peas.

3 The following Punnett Square shows the results when two hybrid pea plants produce new plants. Punnett Squares predict the likelihood of a specific gene combination occurring. Approximately 75% of the offspring in this case are green, and the rest are yellow.

Punnett Square—Color in Pea Plants

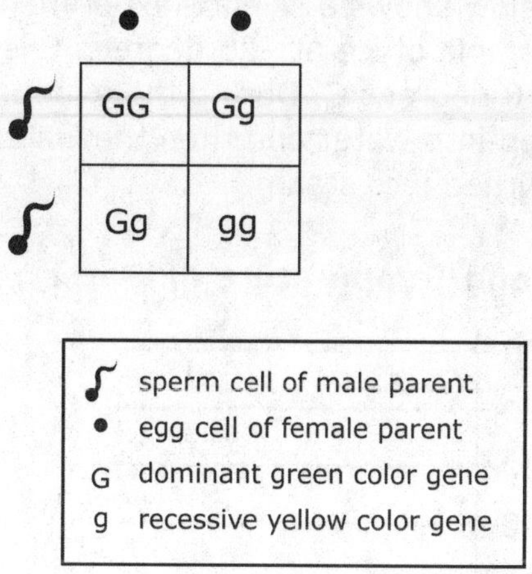

31. Which of the following is the best explanation for the results displayed in this Punnett Square?

    A. One parent plant had only the yellow gene.
    B. One parent plant had only the dominant gene.
    C. Neither parent plant had the hidden gene for yellow.
    D. Both parent plants were hybrids and carried the hidden gene for yellow.

32. Dimples result from a dominant gene, and a lack of dimples results from a recessive gene. Based on the information in the passage, which of the following will be true for an individual who is a hybrid?

    A. That individual will have dimples.
    B. That individual has an equal chance of either having or not having dimples.
    C. That individual's face will have a dimple on one side but not the other.
    D. That individual will have no dimples.

GO ON TO THE NEXT PAGE

<u>Questions 33 and 34</u> refer to the following graph.

The graph below shows a science experiment in which a sample of ice at –20 degrees C is heated to 120 degrees C. During the experiment, the ice melted into water and then the water boiled and turned into steam.

Heat and Temperature of Water

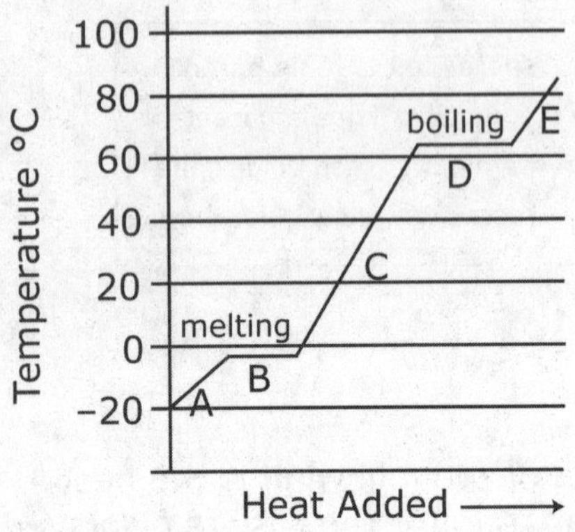

33. Based on the information presented above, which of the following statements is most accurate?

A. The temperature of the sample increased at the same rate throughout the experiment.
B. The sample remained as ice throughout most of the experiment.
C. The sample increased in temperature, then melted, then increased in temperature again, then boiled, and then increased in temperature.
D. The sample melted and increased in temperature at the same time.

34. Select the area on the graph during which the entire sample consists of liquid water. (For this practice test, write an X on the graph.)

35. Bees are insects that play an important role in any ecosystem that has flowering plants. Bees serve as primary pollinators, and enable flowering plants to reproduce. Scientists estimate that nearly one-third of the human food supply consists of plants that depend on bees for pollination.

Based on the information above, which characteristic of bees is most important to an ecosystem?

A. Bees create honey for human consumption.
B. Bees serve as pollinators.
C. Bees sting harmful insects that would otherwise eat and destroy plants.
D. Bees transfer their genes to plants.

END OF TEST

Practice Test 1: Diagnostic Answer Key and Explanations

PRACTICE TEST 1: DIAGNOSTIC ANSWER KEY

This answer key is designed to help you identify your areas of strength and weakness so you can decide how to best use your time studying. For each question, we've provided the specific chapters and sections in the book that you should review if you answered the question incorrectly. To calculate the percent of questions you answered correctly for each section, follow the three-step process below.

Note that this answer key does NOT provide a scaled score or indicate your level of preparedness to take the GED® test.

STEP 1 » Check your answers and mark any correct answers with a ✔ in the appropriate column.

Reasoning Through Language Arts, Section 1

Q #	Ans.	✔	Chapter # and Section Title	Q #	Ans.	✔	Chapter # and Section Title
1	A		**Ch. 5,** Development (of Ideas, Events, or Characters) **Ch. 7,** How Should I Read Literary Passages on the Test?, How Do the Seven Question Tasks Look in a Literary Passage?	10	C		**Ch. 7,** Putting It All Together
2	C		**Ch. 5,** Language Use **Ch. 6,** Putting It All Together	11	B		**Ch. 6,** How Should I Read Literary Passages on the Test?, Putting It All Together
3	B		**Ch. 5,** Structure **Ch. 7,** How Should I Read Literary Passages on the Test?	12	C		**Ch. 6,** Informational Passage Drill
4	A		**Ch. 5,** Structure, Development (of Ideas, Events, or Characters) **Ch. 7,** How Should I Read Literary Passages on the Test?, Putting It All Together	13	B		**Ch. 5,** Comparison (of Different Passages that Deal with Similar Topics)
5	A		**Ch. 5,** Development (of Ideas, Events, or Characters) **Ch. 7,** How Should I Read Literary Passages on the Test?, Who Are the Main Characters and What Do We Know About Them?	14	A		**Ch. 5,** Structure, Evaluation (of the Author's Argument or Reasoning) **Ch. 6,** Informational Passage Drill
6	(d), (a), (b), (c)		**Ch. 5,** Development (of Ideas, Events, or Characters) **Ch. 7,** How Do the Seven Question Tasks Look in a Literary Passage?	15	B		**Ch. 5,** Structure **Ch. 6,** How Should I Read Informational Passages on the Test?, Putting It All Together
7	Happy; Uncertain; Surprised		**Ch. 5,** Development (of Ideas, Events, or Characters) **Ch. 7,** How Should I Read Literary Passages on the Test?, Who Are the Main Characters and What Do We Know About Them?	16	A		**Ch. 5,** Language Use **Ch. 6,** Putting It All Together
8	D		**Ch. 5,** Development (of Ideas, Events, or Characters) **Ch. 7,** How Should I Read Literary Passages on the Test?, Putting It All Together	17	See explanation		**Ch. 8,** Examples of Key Areas of Language Use **Ch. 9,** How Do the Drop-Down Questions Look in a Language Passage?
9	(c), (d)		**Ch. 5,** Purpose (or Point of View) **Ch. 6,** How Do the Seven Question Tasks Look in an Informational Passage?				

Reasoning Through Language Arts, Section 2

Ch. 10, What Is the Prompt Telling Me to Do?, What Does the Prompt Mean by "Support"?, Exactly What Traits Should My Essay Demonstrate?
Ch. 11, How Do I Build My Argument?, How Do I Organize My Argument?, How Can I Improve My Writing?

Reasoning Through Language Arts, Section 3

Q #	Ans.	✔	Chapter # and Section Title	Q #	Ans.	✔	Chapter # and Section Title
18	B		**Ch. 5,** Purpose (or Point of View?) **Ch. 6,** How Do the Seven Question Tasks Look in an Informational Passage? **Ch. 7,** How Do the Seven Question Tasks Look in a Literary Passage?	28	D		**Ch. 5,** Structure **Ch. 6,** Putting It All Together **Ch. 7,** How Should I Read Literary Passages on the Test?
19	D		**Ch. 5,** Structure **Ch. 6,** Putting It All Together	29	A		**Ch. 5,** Development (of Ideas, Events or Characters) **Ch. 6,** Putting It All Together
20	A		**Ch. 5,** Structure **Ch. 6,** How Should I Read Informational Passages on the Test?, Putting It All Together	30	D		**Ch. 5,** Evaluation (of the Author's Argument or Reasoning) **Ch. 7,** Informational Passage Drill
21	C		**Ch. 5,** Development (of Ideas, Events or Characters) **Ch. 7,** How Should I Read Literary Passages on the Test?, Who Are the Main Characters and What Do We Know About Them?	31	A		**Ch. 5,** Language Use **Ch. 6,** Putting It All Together
22	A		**Ch. 5,** Structure **Ch. 6,** Putting It All Together **Ch. 7,** How Should I Read Literary Passages on the Test?	32	D		**Ch. 5,** Structure **Ch. 6,** Putting It All Together **Ch. 7,** How Should I Read Literary Passages on the Test?
23	B		**Ch. 5,** Language Use **Ch. 6,** Putting It All Together	33	A		**Ch. 5,** Purpose (or Point of View?) **Ch. 6,** How Do the Seven Question Tasks Look in an Informational Passage? **Ch. 7,** How Do the Seven Question Tasks Look in a Literary Passage?
24	(c), (b), (a), (d)		**Ch. 5,** Development (of Ideas, Events or Characters) **Ch. 6,** How Do the Seven Question Tasks Look in an Informational Passage? **Ch. 7,** How Do the Seven Question Tasks Look in a Literary Passage?	34	B		**Ch. 5,** Purpose (or Point of View?) **Ch. 6,** How Do the Seven Question Tasks Look in an Informational Passage? **Ch. 7,** How Do the Seven Question Tasks Look in a Literary Passage?
25	A		**Ch. 5,** Development (of Ideas, Events or Characters) **Ch. 6,** Putting It All Together	35	A		**Ch. 5,** Purpose (or Point of View?) **Ch. 6,** How Do the Seven Question Tasks Look in an Informational Passage? **Ch. 7,** How Do the Seven Question Tasks Look in a Literary Passage?
26	(b), (c)		**Ch. 5,** Purpose (or Point of View) **Ch. 6,** How Do the Seven Question Tasks Look in an Informational Passage?	36	D		**Ch. 5,** Structure **Ch. 6,** Putting It All Together **Ch. 7,** How Should I Read Literary Passages on the Test?
27	B		**Ch. 5,** Language Use **Ch. 6,** Putting It All Together	37	A		**Ch. 5,** Some Common Rhetorical Techniques **Ch. 6,** Putting It All Together **Ch. 7,** How Do the Seven Question Tasks Look in a Literary Text?

Reasoning Through Language Arts, Section 3 (Continued)							
Q #	Ans.	✔	Chapter # and Section Title	Q #	Ans.	✔	Chapter # and Section Title
38	D		**Ch. 5,** Language Use **Ch. 6,** Putting It All Together	45	B		**Ch. 5,** Development (of Ideas, Events or Characters) **Ch. 7,** How Should I Read Literary Passages on the Test?, Who Are the Main Characters and What Do We Know About Them?
39	A		**Ch. 5,** Development (of Ideas, Events or Characters) **Ch. 6,** How Do the Seven Question Tasks Look in an Informational Passage, Putting It All Together, Informational Passages Drill	46	A		**Ch. 5,** Development (of Ideas, Events or Characters) **Ch. 7,** How Should I Read Literary Passages on the Test?, Putting It All Together
40	(b), (e)		**Ch. 6,** How Should I Read Informational Passages on the Test?, Putting It All Together	47	Hushed, Confused, Amused		**Ch. 5,** Development (of Ideas, Events or Characters) **Ch. 7,** How Should I Read Literary Passages on the Test?, Who Are the Main Characters and What Do We Know About Them?
41	C		**Ch. 5,** Purpose (Point of View) **Ch. 6,** How Do the Seven Question Tasks Look in an Informational Passage?	48	D		**Ch. 6,** Putting It All Together, Informational Passage Drill
42	C		**Ch. 5,** Development (of Ideas, Events or Characters) **Ch. 7,** How Should I Read Literary Passages on the Test?, Who Are the Main Characters and What Do We Know About Them?	49	B		**Ch. 5,** Development (of Ideas, Events or Characters) **Ch. 7,** How Should I Read Literary Passages on the Test?, Putting It All Together
43	A		**Ch. 5,** Structure **Ch. 6,** Putting It All Together **Ch. 7,** How Should I Read Literary Passages on the Test?	50	See explanation		**Ch. 8,** Examples of Key Areas of Language Use **Ch. 9,** How Do the Drop-Down Questions Look in a Language Passage?
44	D		**Ch. 6,** Putting It All Together **Ch. 7,** How Do the Seven Question Tasks Look in a Literary Passage?				

Mathematical Reasoning							
Q #	**Ans.**	**✔**	**Chapter # and Section Title**	**Q #**	**Ans.**	**✔**	**Chapter # and Section Title**
1	D		**Ch. 15,** Simple Equations, Algebra Drill	20	D		**Ch. 16,** Graphing, Slope, Equation of a Line, Graphing Drill
2	C		**Ch. 15,** Inequalities, Algebra Drill	21	B		**Ch. 16,** Graphing, Slope, Equation of a Line, Graphing Drill
3	D		**Ch. 14,** Rate Problems, Applied Arithmetic Drill	22	C		**Ch. 14,** Charts and Graphs
4	B		**Ch. 14,** Setup problems **Ch. 15,** Translation, Algebra Drill	23	Action Adventure 18 Drama 17		**Ch. 14,** Charts and Graphs
5	C		**Ch. 13,** Factors and Multiples, Fractions	24	A		**Ch. 14,** Charts and Graphs, Ratios and Proportions
6	A		**Ch. 14,** Charts and Graphs	25	D		**Ch. 14,** Mean, Median, Mode, Range, and Weighted Mean, Setup Problems
7	B		**Ch. 13,** Basic Arithmetic Drill	26	9/4 or 2.25		**Ch. 15,** Rational Expressions, Algebra Drill
8	See explanation		**Ch. 13,** The Number Line	27	C		**Ch. 13,** Basic Arithmetic Drill
9	See explanation		**Ch. 13,** The Number Line	28	C		**Ch. 13,** Percents, Percent Word Problems, Basic Arithmetic Drill
10	B		**Ch. 15,** Quadratic Equations	29	See explanation		**Ch. 16,** Graphing, Graphing Drill, Equation of a Line
11	D		**Ch. 14,** Scientific Notation	30	D		**Ch. 13,** Percents, Percent Word Problems, Basic Arithmetic Drill
12	C		**Ch. 14,** Ratios and Proportions, Applied Arithmetic Drill	31	C		**Ch. 14,** Setup Problems
13	B		**Ch. 16,** Rectangles and Squares, Geometry Drill	32	D		**Ch. 14,** Setup Problems, **Ch. 15,** Translation, Algebra Drill
14	–54		**Ch. 14,** Radicals, Exponents and Radicals Drill	33	B		**Ch. 14,** Ratios and Proportions **Ch. 16,** Rectangles and Squares
15	9, 34		**Ch. 16,** Triangle, Geometry Drill	34	B		**Ch. 13,** Percents, Percent Word Problems, Basic Arithmetic Drill
16	1,515		**Ch. 13,** Percents, Percent Word Problems, Basic Arithmetic Drill	35	D		**Ch. 16,** Other Polygons, Geometry Drill
17	A		**Ch. 13,** Basic Arithmetic Drill	36	4.5		**Ch. 16,** Rectangles and Squares, Geometry Drill
18	See explanation		**Ch. 14,** Probability, Applied Arithmetic Drill	37	A		**Ch. 13,** Percents, Percent Word Problems, Basic Arithmetic Drill
19	D		**Ch. 13,** Computative and Distributive Properties **Ch. 14,** Exponents **Ch. 15,** Algebra Drill	38	less than half		**Ch. 16,** Circles, Spheres, Cylinders, and Cones, Geometry Drill

Mathematical Reasoning (Continued)							
Q #	Ans.	✔	Chapter # and Section Title	Q #	Ans.	✔	Chapter # and Section Title
39	A		**Ch. 16,** Circles, Spheres, Cylinders, and Cones, Geometry Drill	43	4 and 5		**Ch. 16,** Triangles
40	B		**Ch. 13,** Basic Arithmetic Drill	44	10		**Ch. 13,** Basic Arithmetic Drill
41	See explanation		**Ch. 13,** Number Line	45	C		**Ch. 13,** Percents, Percent Word Problems, Basic Arithmetic Drill
42	See explanation		**Ch. 13,** Number Line	46	A		**Ch. 16,** Circles, Graphing

Social Studies							
Q #	Ans.	✔	Chapter # and Section Title	Q #	Ans.	✔	Chapter # and Section Title
1	D		**Ch. 17,** Comprehension Questions, Application Questions **Ch. 19,** Politics in Action and Activism	12	A		**Ch. 17,** Comprehension Questions, Application Questions **Ch. 19,** Politics in Action and Activism
2	B		**Ch. 17,** Application Questions, Analysis Questions	13	D		**Ch. 17,** Application Questions, Analysis Questions, Graphic Material Questions **Ch. 20,** Economics Drill
3	C		**Ch. 17,** Application Questions, Analysis Questions **Ch. 18,** The Progressive Era	14	A		**Ch. 17,** Application Questions, Analysis Questions **Ch. 20,** Types of Economies, Markets
4	C		**Ch. 17,** Application Questions, Analysis Questions **Ch. 18,** Westward Expansion	15	A		**Ch. 17,** Application Questions, Analysis Questions **Ch. 20,** Types of Economies, Markets
5	A		**Ch. 17,** Application Questions, Analysis Questions **Ch. 18,** Westward Expansion	16	D		**Ch. 17,** Application Questions, Analysis Questions, Graphic Material Questions
6	A		**Ch. 17,** Comprehension Questions, Application Questions **Ch. 19,** The Documents That Started It All	17	A		**Ch. 17,** Application Questions, Analysis Questions **Ch. 18,** Reconstruction
7	A		**Ch. 17,** Comprehension Questions, Application Questions **Ch. 19,** The Documents That Started It All	18	D		**Ch. 17,** Application Questions, Analysis Questions, Graphic Material Questions **Ch. 20,** Statistics, Economics and Geography Drill
8	A		**Ch. 17,** Comprehension Questions, Evaluation Questions **Ch. 18,** World War II	19	C		**Ch. 17,** Application Questions, Analysis Questions **Ch. 19,** Types of Government
9	A		**Ch. 17,** Comprehension Questions, Evaluation Questions **Ch. 18,** World War II	20	D		**Ch. 17,** Analysis Questions **Ch. 20,** Markets
10	A		**Ch. 17,** Application Questions, Analysis Questions, Graphic Material Questions **Ch. 18,** World War II	21	B		**Ch. 17,** Application Questions, Analysis Questions **Ch. 19,** Constitutional Powers
11	D		**Ch. 17,** Application Questions, Analysis Questions **Ch. 18,** The Civil War	22	D		**Ch. 17,** Application Questions, Analysis Questions, Graphic Material Questions **Ch. 20,** Maps, Human Geography

Social Studies (Continued)							
Q #	Ans.	✔	Chapter # and Section Title	Q #	Ans.	✔	Chapter # and Section Title
23	B		**Ch. 17,** Application Questions, Analysis Questions, Graphic Material Questions **Ch. 20,** Maps, Human Geography	30	(a), (d), (f)		**Ch. 17,** Application Questions, Analysis Questions **Ch. 20,** Types of Economies, Production, Markets
24	D		**Ch. 17,** Application Questions, Analysis Questions, Graphic Material Questions **Ch. 20,** Maps, Human Geography	31	C		**Ch. 17,** Application Questions, Analysis Questions, Graphic Material Questions **Ch. 18,** Cold War
25	B		**Ch. 17,** Application Questions, Analysis Questions **Ch. 19,** Constitutional Powers	32	A		**Ch. 17,** Application Questions, Analysis Questions, Graphic Material Questions, The GED Test Cartoon **Ch. 18,** The Civil War
26	A		**Ch. 17,** Application Questions, Analysis Questions **Ch. 19,** Constitutional Powers	33	B		**Ch. 17,** Comprehension Questions, Application Questions **Ch. 19,** Constitutional Powers
27	B		**Ch. 17,** Application Questions, Analysis Questions **Ch. 19,** Constitutional Powers	34	D		**Ch. 17,** Comprehension Questions, Application Questions **Ch. 19,** Politics in Action and Activism
28	D		**Ch. 17,** Comprehension Questions, Application Questions **Ch. 20,** Microeconomics, Markets	35	A		**Ch. 17,** Application Questions, Analysis Questions **Ch. 19,** Types of Government
29	C		**Ch. 17,** Comprehension Questions **Ch. 20,** Markets, Economics Drill				

Science							
Q #	**Ans.**	**✔**	**Chapter # and Section Title**	**Q #**	**Ans.**	**✔**	**Chapter # and Section Title**
1	D		**Ch. 21,** Analysis Questions **Ch. 23,** Energy and Heat	19	B		**Ch. 21,** Analysis Questions **Ch. 22,** The Human Body and Health
2	A		**Ch. 21,** Comprehension Questions **Ch. 22,** The Human Body and Health	20	D		**Ch. 21,** Application Questions **Ch. 23,** Astronomy
3	85%		**Ch. 21,** Comprehension Questions **Ch. 23,** Energy and Heat, Natural Resources	21	B		**Ch. 23,** The Changing Earth
4	D		**Ch. 23,** Energy and Heat, Natural Resources	22	R1, Nicaragua		**Ch. 23,** The Changing Earth
5	Peat (a); Anthracite (d)		**Ch. 23,** Energy and Heat, Natural Resources	23	C		**Ch. 21,** Comprehension Questions **Ch. 22,** Evolution and Natural Selection
6	C		**Ch. 21,** Comprehension Questions **Ch. 22,** Plants	24	C		**Ch. 22,** Evolution and Natural Selection
7	C		**Ch. 23,** Plants	25	C		**Ch. 23,** Physical Laws, Work, and Motion
8	B		**Ch. 22,** The Scientific Method, The Human Body and Health	26	D		**Ch. 21,** Analysis Questions **Ch. 22,** The Human Body and Health
9	A		**Ch. 23,** Plants	27	A		**Ch. 22,** Ecosystems and Food Chains
10	#4 is the oldest; #1 is the newest		**Ch. 21,** Analysis Questions **Ch. 23,** Fossils	28	B		**Ch. 21,** Analysis Questions **Ch. 23,** Astronomy
11	C		**Ch. 21,** Analysis Questions **Ch. 22,** Ecosystems and Food Chains	29	B		**Ch. 21,** Analysis Questions **Ch. 22,** Bacteria and Viruses
12	C		**Ch. 22,** Evolution and Natural Selection	30	D		**Ch. 23,** Physical Laws, Work, and Motion
13	C		**Ch. 21,** Application Questions **Ch. 23,** Solids, Liquids, and Gases	31	D		**Ch. 22,** Genetics
14	D		**Ch. 22,** Scientific Method **Ch. 23,** Energy and Heat	32	A		**Ch. 22,** Genetics
15	Mode, 0.43 kg		**Ch. 21,** Application Questions	33	C		**Ch. 23,** Energy and Heat
16	0.93		**Ch. 21,** Application Questions	34	The area labeled C		**Ch. 23,** Solids, Liquids, and Gases
17	D		**Ch. 21,** Application Questions **Ch. 23,** Solids, Liquids, and Gases	35	B		**Ch. 22,** Ecosystems and Food Chains
18	A		**Ch. 21,** Analysis Questions **Ch. 23,** Chemical Reactions				

STEP 2 **Add the total number correct for each test subject. Divide Number Correct by Potential, move the decimal two places to the right, and put the results in Percent Correct.**

Test Subject	Number Correct	Potential	Percent Correct
Reasoning Through Language Arts		50	
Mathematical Reasoning		46	
Social Studies		35	
Science		35	

STEP 3 **Use the results above to customize your study plan. We recommend tackling the test subjects in order of lowest to highest percent correct. For each subject, give special attention to the chapter sections associated with your incorrect answers from Step 1.**

REASONING THROUGH LANGUAGE ARTS

Section 1

1. **A** This development question asks which sentence from the passage supports the idea that Ingred's relatives have had military experience. Since several quotations are related to the major theme of the recent war, consider what is implied as well as what is directly stated. Choice (A) is correct: It talks about "Mr. Saxon, Egbert, and Athelstane," which follows the first sentence in paragraph 1 which states that the family has been reunited; therefore, these are members of the Saxon family. Additionally, the word "demobilized" and the phrase "had hardly yet settled down to civilian life" support the idea that these members of Ingred's family had served in the war. Choices (B) and (C) are incorrect because, while they do mention that there has been a war, neither choice mentions Ingred's family. Although (D) indicates that Ingred's relatives have returned from somewhere, there is no mention of the war. The correct answer is (A).

2. **C** This language use item requires you to determine which definition of the word "native" matches its use in paragraph 1. The word is used as a part of the sentence "They had joined the rest of the party at Lynstones before returning to their native town of Grovebury." The word "returning" tells us that this is a place they have been before. Choice (A) is the opposite, so rule this out. Choice (B) is incorrect, because while there are many descriptions of the "natural" and perhaps "wild" beauty of Lynstones, "native" here refers to Grovebury, which is not described as a place in nature. The phrase suggests this is their original home, not just any town. From this context, "native town" clearly refers to the place where they originally come from; in other words, where they were born or grew up, so (C) is the best choice. Finally, (D) is incorrect, because while the Saxon family home might indeed be "inherited," there is no evidence to support this in the text. The correct answer is (C).

3. **B** This structure question asks about how the sentence describing the landscape enhances the story. The passage uses the phrase "glorious run" to emphasize Ingred's positive feelings during the trip, and paints a detailed picture of the landscape with phrases like "glimpses of the sea," "craggy," and "billowy masses." Altogether, the sense is of an appreciation of the natural scenery. Choice (A) is incorrect: While the next sentence does mention that "Egbert exceeded the speed-limit," it goes on to say, "he certainly had the excuse of a clear road before him," so the passage emphasizes that the trip is picturesque, not dangerous. Choice (B) is correct: Since the contrast between Ingred's feelings about her summer holidays versus returning to school is a main theme of this excerpt (first described in paragraph 1), the description of nature and use of "glorious" reinforces Ingred's feelings about her summer vacation home. Choice (C) is incorrect because although the quotation does describe the sea and the cliffs as having different characteristics, the difference between the sea and the cliffs is not a major theme of the story. Even though Egbert appears in this part of the narrative, the quoted description of the landscape does not reveal anything about his character or function in the story, so (D) is incorrect. The correct answer is (B).

4. **A** This structure question asks about the significance of the "place" mentioned in the quotation. The sentence included in the question says, "But surely the Red Cross cleared out ages ago," meaning that the "place" had been used by the Red Cross during the war. To find out exactly what the "place" is, look further in paragraph 12. Avis asks Ingred, "I suppose you're going back to Rotherwood, aren't you?" Since one of the major themes of the passages is Ingred's feelings about having to return to her family home as soon as the summer is over, the "going back to Rotherwood" Avis mentions must be that return to the Saxon family home. Therefore, (A) is correct. Choice (B) is incorrect because, while the passage does mention

the Red Cross, Avis is specifically referring to a house, not a town, in paragraph 16: "I always envied you that lovely house." Choice (C) is incorrect: even though the quotation mentions that the "whole place has been done up," there is no evidence that this was done to a ballroom for the purpose of a dance. Choice (D) is incorrect, because the "place" is Ingred's home, not her school. The correct answer is (A).

5. **A** This character development question asks about Ingred's character based on her response to Avis. Use the dialogue that ends with Ingred's response in paragraph 15 to get a sense of the entire exchange between the characters. When Avis asks, in paragraph 12, whether Ingred is going back to Rotherwood, Ingred gives a vague response. When Avis persists, "But surely the Red Cross cleared out ages ago," then Ingred responds, "Oh, yes!" (paragraph 15) in a voice "a little strained." Since Ingred's voice is "strained" when she discusses her return, this is consistent with previous information that Ingred enjoys her holidays and does not want to think about the time beyond summer (paragraph 1) when she will return to her family home. Therefore, (A) is correct: Ingred is uncomfortable or uneasy. Choice (B) is incorrect, because while Ingred is technically "agreeing" with Avis, the strain in her voice shows reluctance. Choice (C) is incorrect, because while "strained" does sometimes mean "exhausted," in paragraph 15 "strained" means "forced," showing that Ingred does not really want to think about her eventual return. Choice (D) is incorrect because even though Ingred says "Oh, yes!" emphatically, her inner emotion is not one of enthusiasm. The correct answer is (A).

6. This plot development item asks the reader to arrange the sequence of events in the excerpt in order in a chart. The correct order from first to last:

   1. **Event (d): The Saxons unite at Lynstones.** This occurs early in the narrative in paragraph 1: The first sentence says "the whole family was reunited," and the third sentence says "They had joined the rest of the party at Lynstones."

   2. **Event (a): Egbert drives Ingred to the beach.** Following the general description of Ingred's feelings in paragraph 1, a specific day is described in paragraph 2, during which Egbert takes Ingred for a motorcycle ride: "Egbert was anxious to set off, so Hereward took his place on the luggage-carrier, and, after some back-firing, the three started forth."

   3. **Event (b): Ingred is invited to tea.** After arriving at the seaside, Ingred meets Avis, who invites her to tea: "Come along and have some tea with us" (paragraph 8).

   4. **Event (c): Avis talks about a fancy-dress dance.** As Avis and Ingred talk, Avis becomes enthusiastic about the idea of dancing: "I do think a fancy-dress dance is about the best fun on earth" (paragraph 18).

7. This character development item asks the reader to identify three adjectives that accurately describe Ingred. The three correct adjectives:

   - **Happy.** Ingred's feelings of happiness are referenced in paragraph 1: "To have her father and brothers safely back, and for the family to be together in the midst of such beautiful scenery, was sufficient for utter enjoyment."
   - **Uncertain.** Ingred's inner thought process is highlighted with words like "nebulous" (paragraph 1) and is further suggested by the fact that her voice is "a little strained" (paragraph 15) and the fact that she says "It's rather early to make plans" when talking about her eventual return. Therefore, Ingred is uncertain about her future after she returns to her family home and to school.

- **Surprised.** Ingred is surprised to meet Avis at the seaside: "Much to Ingred's astonishment she was suddenly hailed by her name" (paragraph 3).

Of the other options, "halcyon" refers to the time period, rather than to Ingred. "Daredevil" doesn't work, since paragraph 2 makes it clear that their motorcycle trip was not dangerous.

8. **D** This development item requires making a prediction about Avis based on an overall understanding of the details that relate to her. Avis appears in the narrative in paragraphs 3–20, so use the details in these paragraphs to eliminate answers that don't conform to the passage. Choice (A) is incorrect: Avis is described as "a schoolfellow" (paragraph 3), so she has been to school with Ingred before. Choice (B) is incorrect because Avis doesn't mention hosting, but talks of Ingred possibly giving parties: "you'll be giving all sorts of delightful parties, won't you?" (paragraph 16). Eliminate (C), because it is Ingred who is visiting for the afternoon, not Avis (paragraph 7). Choice (D) is correct, because Avis sighs "only a few days now," and Ingred tells Avis she is staying "a fortnight more" (paragraphs 10–11). Even if you don't know the definition of "fortnight"—"fourteen nights," in other words, two weeks—Ingred indicates that she is staying "more" than Avis, so the correct answer is (D).

9. This item asks the reader to identify statements that express the EPA's purposes for writing its article. The two correct statements:

- **Statement (c): To caution consumers about deceptive advertising.** The EPA begins the article with a warning, "Be careful about these products" (paragraph 1) and ends the article with the old adage: "If it sounds too good to be true, it probably is" (paragraph 5).

- **Statement (d): To give information about the role of the EPA in evaluating fuel additives and devices.** Paragraph 2 informs the reader about the registration process for additives, and paragraph 3 explains the option for testing aftermarket devices to improve fuel economy. The EPA purposefully explains the process and the limitations of registration and testing to help the consumer properly evaluate any claims by manufacturers.

Of the other options, statements (a) and (e) better describe the purpose of the Department of Energy's article, while statement (b) does not describe either article.

10. **C** This question asks which answer is supported by the Department of Energy article, which covers methods of fuel economy. Choice (A) is incorrect because the article never states that other methods are replaced or "no longer necessary" because of the start-stop system. Choice (B) is incorrect because aftermarket alternative fuel conversions are mentioned only in the other article, not the Department of Energy article. Choice (C) is correct: This article is about methods of fuel economy, including better driving habits (paragraph 6). Choice (D) is incorrect because this is the main idea of the EPA article, not the Department of Energy article. The correct answer is (C).

11. **B** This structure question asks about the EPA's purpose for including a particular detail, in this case, the sentence, "Very few manufacturers have applied for this program in the past 10 years" (paragraph 3). The main idea of this passage is to warn the reader about fuel additives and devices to improve fuel economy, so consider how this detail relates to the main idea. Choice (A) is incorrect: There is no information about how long the program takes. Choice (B) is correct: Paragraph 3 goes on to say, "Without this report, the EPA has no information about the safety of the device or its impact on fuel efficiency." So the EPA cannot verify the claims of manufacturers who do not apply for the program, and consumers should be wary. Choice (C) is incorrect: This sentence in the question refers to applying for the program, not the testing that occurs later. Choice (D) is also incorrect: The tone and purpose of the EPA article is directed not at the manufacturer but at the consumer. The correct answer is (B).

12. **C** This structure question asks about how a figure relates to the overall purpose of the article by the Department of Energy, which covers methods of fuel economy. The chart illustrates the guideline about driving speed in paragraph 6: "Each 5 MPH you drive over 60 MPH can reduce your fuel economy by 7%." Choice (A) is incorrect, however, because reducing fuel economy 7% by speeding does not equate to improving fuel economy 5% by slowing down. Choice (B) is incorrect because this is a question about the role of the figure in the article, and the chart does not reflect data about vehicle maintenance. Choice (C) is correct: The chart visually illustrates the loss of fuel economy with increased speed. Finally, (D) is incorrect because the chart has no information about driving conditions. The correct answer is (C).

13. **B** This is a comparison question about the similarities in the two articles. Both articles address fuel economy, but the first article warns about devices and the second article recommends a device. Choice (A) reflects only the second passage by the Department of Energy, so this answer is incorrect. Choice (B) is correct: The EPA warns about aftermarket devices while the Department of Energy recommends the start-stop system. Again, (C) reflects only the second passage by the Department of Energy, so this answer is incorrect. Choice (D) is wrong because neither passage offers a way to verify advertisers' claims. The correct answer is (B).

14. **A** This structure question asks which specific detail is included in the EPA's article. Choice (A) is correct: Paragraph 3 warns, "Tampering with your car's emissions control system is punishable by significant fines," so there are potential hidden costs when taking these measures. Choice (B) contradicts the passage: The EPA says, "Most devices tested in earlier years had a neutral or negative effect on fuel economy" (paragraph 3). Eliminate (C), which also contradicts the passage: While the EPA registers additives (paragraph 2), it makes no similar claims about devices. Finally, (D) is too strong: Although paragraph 3 states, "Without this report, the EPA has no information about the safety of the device," it's possible that the EPA does have reports on some devices so some information is available. The correct answer is (A).

15. **B** This question asks the reader to examine the structural relationships in paragraphs 6 and 7 of the Department of Energy's article. Choice (A) is incorrect: The phrase "doesn't require you to drive differently" (paragraph 7) refers to driving with a start-stop system, not driving in general, so the parts of the article do not contradict one another. Choice (B) is correct: The first item in the list of recommended habits is to avoid idling (paragraph 6), and paragraph 7 offers a system that virtually eliminates idling. Choice (C) is incorrect because paragraph 7 does not directly compare the start-stop system to other methods that reduce fuel consumption. Finally, (D) is incorrect because the start-stop system is not installed aftermarket, but comes with new vehicles ("as of the 2014 model year, they are available on about one hundred conventional vehicle models"). The correct answer is (B).

16. **A** This language use question asks the reader to examine the effect of the use of the word "robust" in the Department of Energy's article. Paragraph 7 recommends start-stop systems. This section acknowledges "it may take some time for you to get used to" but then immediately follows with "Most systems are robust and easy to use" to reassure and persuade the reader, since "robust" means "sturdy." Therefore, (A) is correct. Choice (B) is incorrect because, even though the sentence claims the system is "easy to use," this is not the meaning of the word "robust." Choice (C) is incorrect because although another meaning of "robust" is "hefty," that does not fit the context of the paragraph. Choice (D) is incorrect because, even though paragraph 7 claims the system is "only a few hundred dollars," this is not the meaning of the word "robust." The correct answer is (A).

17. The option that correctly completes the sentence for each "Select" option:

Drop-Down Item 1: Sentence fragments and run-ons

Option 1 is correct: Appropriate punctuation (a comma) sets off the parenthetical element "just as I do" from the independent clause "Surely you enjoy living in such a quiet and peaceful neighborhood."

Option 2 is incorrect because it incorrectly uses a period, creating a sentence fragment. Option 3 removes the punctuation that sets off the parenthetical element at the end of the sentence. Option 4 treats a somewhat lengthy phrase as though it is an independent clause, separated by a semicolon. However, this phrase is actually a sentence fragment and therefore cannot be separated by a semicolon.

Drop-Down Item 2: Misplaced modifiers or illogical word order

Option 2 is correct: In this sentence, the phrase "you must be aware of" appropriately refers to "the alarming increase in burglary incidents," while "via news reports and social media posts" modifies "you must be aware." The phrases appear in an appropriate order with no dangling modifiers or unclear antecedents.

Option 1 is incorrect: In this order, the phrases appear to indicate that the "burglary incidents" are "via news reports." Option 3 is incorrect: In this option, the phrase "you must be aware of by now" seems to refer to "social media posts" and creates a sentence fragment. Option 4 is incorrect because this option presents the construction "social media posts in our neighborhood" so that it appears the social media posts (instead of the burglaries) happen in the neighborhood.

Drop-Down Item 3: Verb tense, parallelism

Option 3 is correct: This option correctly uses the present tense "are concerned" to parallel "propose" and "consider" later in the sentence.

Option 1 is incorrect: The use of "concerning" and "we all do" results in the meaning "we all do concern our community" rather than "we are all concerned about our community." Option 2 is incorrect because the past tense "were" does not match the present tense "propose" and "consider" later in the sentence. Option 4 is incorrect because the past tense "were" does not match the present tense "propose" and "consider."

Drop-Down Item 4: Pronoun usage

Option 2 is correct: The option correctly uses the singular objective pronoun case "it" to match "check or money order."

Option 1 is incorrect: The sentence is asking the reader to "send a check or a money order"—only one, not both—so a singular pronoun is required. Option 3 is incorrect: Although "that" can function as a pronoun, the word "that" refers to something specific that is clearly understood, as in "that cat (of several cats)." For "that" to work in the context, a more complete phrase like "that payment" would be required. Option 4 is incorrect for similar reasons: For "one" to work in context, the entire phrase "one of them" would be required.

Section 2: Extended Response

As noted in Chapter 10, the Extended Response essay is evaluated based on three traits. You can earn up to 2 points for each trait for a possible maximum of 6. Here, we've provided two sample responses to give you an idea of what a score of 1 and 2 looks like for each trait.

Sample Response A

The argument of whether or not cap-and-trade is beneficial is best supported by the benefits of cap-and-trade. The environment and air quality are very important and so emissions control is needed. Cap-and-trade is something that has been implemented with success and that saves lives. It is a way for the EPA to control emissions by giving businesses and industries permits.

Since nitrous oxide and sulfur dioxide are harmful it makes sense to try to control them to try to keep the air clean. The benefits argument uses studies that have shown that SO_2 emissions have dropped 40% since the 1990s, and acid rain levels have dropped 65% since 1976. Also the benefits argument mentions other countries such as China have had success with cutting emissions too. These are all good points for the benefits of cap-and-trade. If cap-and-trade was an idea that didn't work, it wouldn't have been in use for so long, starting from 1976.

The argument against cap-and-trade states that the results are brought into question because there were other regulations happening at the same time as the Acid Rain Program. They also claim that the permit process causes bad incentives because free permits mean companies might not try very hard to reduce emissions. They claim that if a company reduces emissions, then their cap might be lower next year, so a company might try not to reduce emissions. But there are no statistics to show that this would happen.

If those are the arguments that are made then people just need to rely on the actual results. Read the statistics and see how the Acid Rain Program and other programs are actually working. The EPA does a good job of making sure businesses can't pollute too much.

Trait 1—Creation of Arguments and Use of Evidence

Score: 1

The writer of this response makes an argument in favor of cap-and-trade ("The argument of whether or not cap-and-trade is beneficial is best supported by the benefits of cap-and-trade") through a somewhat unsophisticated analysis. The response contains some evidence from the source text to support the central position, but this evidence is presented as references that only summarize the source text ("The benefits argument uses studies that have shown SO_2 emissions have dropped 40% since the 1990s, and acid rain levels have dropped 65% since 1976"). There is some analysis of the issue and evaluation of the evidence for the arguments, but it is minimal ("If those are the arguments that are made then people just need to rely on the actual results" and "These are all good points for the benefits of cap-and-trade"). Overall, the writer makes an argument supported by some analysis and some evidence from the source text. Therefore, this Response A earns a score of 1 for Trait 1.

Trait 2—Development of Ideas and Organizational Structure

Score: 1

The writer establishes an organizational structure in this response by providing a comparison of the two arguments presented. In the introduction, the writer takes a position ("The argument of whether or not cap-and-trade is beneficial is best supported by the benefits of cap-and-trade"). The second paragraph addresses the benefits of cap-and-trade and shows a clear progression of ideas. In the paragraphs, main points are developed in a general sense, but the details are not as well developed. In the second paragraph, a new thought is presented about the benefits of cap-and-trade ("If cap-and-trade was an idea that didn't work, it wouldn't have been in use for so long, starting from 1976."). The third paragraph focuses on the unwelcome possibilities of cap-and-trade, summarizing the source text and offering an assessment ("They claim that if a company reduces emissions, then their cap might be lower next year, so a company might try not to reduce emissions. But there are no statistics to show that this would happen."). The conclusion is a general explanation of why the first position is better supported. The writer's word choice is sufficiently competent, and the response's tone is acceptable. Overall, the response is somewhat organized and focused, but the ideas are underdeveloped. Therefore, Response A earns a score of 1 for Trait 2.

Trait 3—Clarity and Command of Standard English Conventions

Score: 1

This brief response shows generally correct sentence structure, but without sentence variety. There is unreliable control of standard English conventions with regard to subject verb agreement ("The environment and air quality is very important") and punctuation usage. These errors do not interfere with comprehension, however, and this response is an acceptable example of draft writing. Therefore, Response A earns a score of 1 for Trait 3.

Sample Response B

There is much debate about whether cap-and-trade as a strategy for controlling emissions is effective. It is an important debate because air quality is a pressing issue today and addressing harmful emissions can possibly save lives. In this discussion of cap-and-trade, the proponents have made the better argument. They bring up several benefits to cap-and trade, including advantages to business. The pro cap-and-trade article then uses statistics to support its position. The second article from the critics' standpoint uses mostly hypothetical assertions and warnings of what might happen, with no statistical data to support the position.

In the first article, an outline of the benefits of cap-and-trade is supplied to show what makes the practice was effective—cost, accountability, and the support of federal and state standards. The first argument then provides examples of some specific successful programs: the nationwide Acid Rain Program (ARP) and the regional NO_x Budget Trading Program. The first article then cites several statistics pointing to improvements in both SO_2 and NO_x. According to the article, improvements in emissions mean saved lives, and saving lives is very strong evidence for using cap-and-trade.

The second article then calls the statistical evidence into question by pointing out that, in addition to cap-and-trade, there were other regulations in effect that impacted emissions. While the article began with a good observation here, it did not follow through. If the article had provided the exact regulations in effect, and the statistical impact on emissions, this would have been a more direct counter to the statistics presented in the previous article, and the second article may well have won the argument.

Another topic mentioned by both arguments is the cost of cap-and-trade. The first article claims that cap-and-trade provides cost-effective, flexible compliance choices for regulated sources and minimized administrative costs. This argument is supported by evidence that the program reduced expenditures on medicine by about $800 million annually. Including the information about low costs for industry and government is very important evidence for the pro-cap-and-trade side. The low costs indicate that businesses will be more likely to want to comply with this program. The second argument brings up the same point about low cost, but claims that the low cost can actually result in perverse incentives, because a low price on emission permits reduces the incentive for companies to cut back their emissions. However, the critics' argument fails for two reasons. First, the second article did not offer statistics to support this assertion. Second, the critic's argument did not consider that the program's low cost might have a positive incentive as well—encouraging companies to participate in the program at all. The point the second article was trying to make is that the negative incentives outweigh the positive ones, but the evidence is not strong enough to prove this point.

The final objection used by critics of cap-and-trade claims that expensive long-term changes will not be made if there is a cheaper source of carbon credits, and that environmental protection needs better solutions. However, the statistics provided by the pro-cap-and-trade article indicate that these programs have been in place since 1976, so the changes reported by the statistics are definitely seen in the long term. As for "better solutions," the critics' article continues to make the same faults: it does not supply any data to support the objection. It does not even offer any specific programs that would be the kind of solutions that the critics advocate. The second article does raise an interesting point about how one solution can prevent a better solution. If the critics of cap-and-trade had managed to supply some facts to prove this point, the second article would have made the better argument.

Because of the lack of supportive facts or concrete details for the arguments in the second article, it is clear that the first article contains the better researched and supported argument. The first argument supplies specific, concrete data in support of the claim that cap-and-trade is effective. If the second article were to go beyond its vague warnings and use specific data in its objections, then the second article would have a more significant impact simply because the first argument does not seem to consider the possible drawbacks of the cap-and-trade structure. In that case, article two would win the argument.

Trait 1—Creation of Arguments and Use of Evidence

Score: 2

The introduction of this essay contains a position ("In this discussion of cap-and-trade, the proponents have made the better argument") and then provides a developed explanation ("The pro cap-and-trade article then uses statistics to support its position. The second article uses mostly hypothetical assertions and warnings of what might happen, with no statistical data to support the position."). The writer reinforces this claim with an analysis of the evidence for the arguments in the source text, first focusing on the strength of the proponents' argument ("The first article then cites several statistics pointing to improvements in both SO_2 and NO_x. According to the article, improvements in emissions mean saved lives, and saving lives is very strong evidence for using cap-and-trade."). The writer then moves on to the inadequacy of the opposing argument ("While the article began with a good observation here, it did not follow through."). As further support, the writer introduces alternative interpretations of the evidence ("Second, the critic's argument did not consider that the program's low cost might have a positive incentive as well"). Finally, the writer pinpoints the critics' unsupported assertions about better solutions ("It does not even offer any specific programs that would be the kind of solutions that the critics advocate"). Overall, the response offers a well-developed, logical, and organized argument focused on the validity of the arguments in the source text. Therefore, Response B earns a score of 2 for Trait 1.

Trait 2—Development of Ideas and Organizational Structure

Score: 2

The response shows a clear structure, beginning with the importance of emissions control to frame the issue, then discussing points made by both sides of the argument, and finally concluding with an analysis. This structure permits a development of generally logical ideas that are sufficiently explored. The response establishes a clear connection between the main idea and supporting details within paragraph 2. The writer points to hypotheses about possible negative outcomes of cap-and-trade in paragraph 3 and then discusses why the claims are not supported. The writer goes on to explore the idea that the "concrete data in support of the claim that cap-and-trade is effective" outweighs the use of "vague warnings" by the opposition. The writer uses appropriate vocabulary and formal tone to express ideas, resulting in a response that is structured, focused, and developed. Therefore, Response B earns a score of 2 for Trait 2.

Trait 3—Clarity and Command of Standard English Conventions

Score: 2

This writer shows competency with several standard English rules, including subject-verb agreement, word usage, and the rules of capitalization and punctuation. The response offers a largely correct sentence structure, and the writer blends simple and complex sentences while maintaining clarity ("The second argument brings up the same point about low cost, but claims that the low cost can actually result in perverse incentives, because a low price on emission permits reduces the incentive for companies to cut back their emissions. However, this argument fails for two reasons. First, the second article did not offer statistics to support this assertion."). Transitional words and phrases are used throughout ("in that case," "however," "while"). Overall, the response indicates a strong command of the English language, and the level is appropriate for on-demand draft writing. Therefore, Response B earns a score of 2 for Trait 3.

Section 3

18. **B** This point of view question asks about the author's overall tone in paragraph 1. This paragraph begins by introducing Niagara Falls and moves on to a discussion about its "opportunities for fishing." The author states, "at Niagara one place is just as good as another, for the reason that the fish do not bite anywhere," and then goes on to say "The advantages of this state of things have never heretofore been properly placed before the public" (paragraph 1). In a discussion about opportunities for fishing, to call the fact that "the fish do not bite anywhere" an "advantage" is a strong contrast, used to convey humor through the use of paradox. Choice (A) is incorrect because the author does not express fear until later in the passage, beginning in paragraph 3. Choice (B) is correct: The author is offering a contrast to indicate irony, which is the use of language that normally signifies the opposite. Eliminate (C) because, even though the paragraph begins by calling Niagara an "enjoyable place of resort," the majority of the paragraph involves the ironic contrast. Choice (D) is incorrect; while the author may be recollecting in this narrative, there is not a particular sense of satisfaction in the discussion of Niagara's opportunities for fishing. In fact, because of the use of irony, the author's true feelings are more negative than positive. The correct answer is (B).

19. **D** This structure question asks why the author chooses to conclude paragraph 2 with that sentence. So, consider the role the sentence plays in the paragraph as a whole. Paragraph 2 relates how someone approaches the Falls: "you first drive down about a mile" and then details how to get a close look: "You can descend a staircase here a hundred and fifty feet down, and stand at the edge of the water." Therefore, the concluding sentence shows what the author thinks the tourists' feelings will be about climbing down all that way: "you will wonder why you did it; but you will then be too late" (that is, it will be too late for the tourist to take back all that effort). Choice (A) is incorrect; even though the author says "you will be too late," this refers to the effort, not the arrival at the falls. Choice (B) is incorrect because the sentence aims to estimate a tourist's reaction, not to advise future visitors. Eliminate (C) because, even though the sentence uses the second person "you," this doesn't mean that the author is personally acquainted with the reader. Choice (D) is correct: The author is humorously predicting a tourist's attitude after climbing a lengthy stairway. The correct answer is (D).

20. **A** This question asks which sentence from the passage most directly contrasts with the passage's overall ironic portrayal of Niagara Falls, so focus on the main idea, and consider what is implied as well as what is directly stated. Even though this passage begins with a positive statement about Niagara Falls: "Niagara Falls is a most enjoyable place of resort" (paragraph 1), most of the passage highlights the dangers of the Falls and the author's discomfort while being there. This negative opinion is shown throughout the passage by the use of words like "precipice" (paragraph 2), "misery" (paragraph 3), and "flimsy" (paragraph 6) and the description of the dangerous trip under the falls in paragraph 7. Therefore, (A) is correct because this sentence offers only positive qualities about the Falls, in contrast to the more negative theme. Choice (B) is incorrect, since this sentence offers only facts about the falls, with no words indicating opinion. Choice (C) is contradictory; the negative tone (shown by "discomforting" and "unhappiness") is consistent with the main idea, not contrasting with it. Choice (D) is incorrect; once again this sentence contains only factual details about the author's actions, without indications of tone. The correct answer is (A).

21. **C** This character development question asks about the author's character based on the statement "I remarked that I wanted to go home." Use the sentences that precede this statement to get a sense of the context. Immediately before the remark about wanting to go home, the author states, "Now a furious wind began to rush out from behind the waterfall, which seemed determined to sweep us from the bridge, and scatter us on the rocks and among the torrents below." So in this context, the remark about wanting to go home is a reaction to a dangerous situation. Choices (A) and (B) are incorrect because nothing in the passage

overall indicates that the author is constantly longing for home or has a depressed (melancholic) attitude. Choice (C) is correct: With the statement about wanting to go home, the author is emphasizing the feelings of apprehension—wanting to leave a dangerous situation. Choice (D) is incorrect because nothing in the passage indicates that the author is pining for an earlier era. The correct answer is (C).

22. **A** This phrase is a clear example of hyperbole, or exaggeration, (A). The narrator is not literally being hit by the entire Atlantic Ocean; instead, he uses this dramatic comparison to emphasize how powerful and intense the rushing water feels. The purpose is to help readers experience the moment by conveying the sheer force and volume of water crashing down on him. Choice (B) is too literal. The narrator is still at Niagara Falls, not in the ocean. Choice (C) is wrong since, while the Atlantic is mentioned, the goal is not comparison—it's exaggeration. Choice (D) is wrong, since the passage actually emphasizes vulnerability, not strength. The correct answer is (A).

23. **B** This language use item requires you to determine which definition of the phrase "in earnest" matches its use in paragraph 7. Each of the answer options reflects an actual definition of the phrase "in earnest," so look closely at the way the word is used in context. The word is used as a part of the phrase "how fearfully in earnest it was." The "it" refers to the "seething world of descending water" in the previous sentence. So here, "in earnest" describes the "descending water," so look for a word that would indicate "seething," which means "storming" or "furious." Choice (A) is incorrect because "serious" would not match with the violent descriptions of the waterfall found in this paragraph. Choice (B) is correct: The movement of the water is vigorous, or fast-moving. Choice (C) is incorrect because water cannot be sincere, which means true or heartfelt. Finally, (D) is incorrect because "ardent" means emotionally enthusiastic, which doesn't fit with the waterfall. The correct answer is (B).

24. This plot development item asks the reader to arrange the sequence of events in the excerpt in order in a chart. Here is the correct order from first to last:

1. **Event (c): The narrator mentions a view of the river.** This occurs in paragraph 2: "When you start out to 'do' the Falls you first drive down about a mile, and pay a small sum for the privilege of looking down from a precipice into the narrowest part of the Niagara River."

2. **Event (b): The Suspension Bridge is described.** Following the initial description of the view of the river in paragraph 2, the narrator continues the description of a trip to Niagara. The first sentence of paragraph 3 reads as follows: "Then you drive over to Suspension Bridge, and divide your misery between the chances of smashing down two hundred feet into the river below, and the chances of having the railway-train overhead smashing down onto you."

3. **Event (a): Horseshoe Fall is included as a stop in the visit.** After the description of the bridge, the author mentions Horseshoe Fall: "When you have examined the stupendous Horseshoe Fall till you are satisfied you cannot improve on it, you return to America by the new Suspension Bridge," (paragraph 4).

4. **Event (d): The narrator goes behind the falls.** The final two paragraphs describe the harrowing trip underneath the waterfall: "When I saw how much of it there was, and how fearfully in earnest it was, I was sorry I had gone behind it" (paragraph 7).

25. **A** This question asks which detail the reader can infer about Niagara Falls, so check the details in the answer choices against the information in the passage. Choice (A) is correct: Paragraph 4 states, "When you have examined the stupendous Horseshoe Fall till you are satisfied you cannot improve on it, you return to America by the new Suspension Bridge." This means that part of the Falls (the Horseshoe Fall)

is outside of the United States. Choice (B) is incorrect; this is not a good fishing resort because paragraph 1 states, "the fish do not bite anywhere." While (C) might be attractive, it is incorrect, since the Cave of the Winds is listed as a part of Niagara, and this choice would indicate that the two are separate. Choice (D) directly contradicts the passage because paragraph 1 states, "The hotels are excellent, and the prices not at all exorbitant." The correct answer is (A).

26. This item asks the reader to identify statements that express the author's purposes for writing this article. The two correct statements:

- **Statement (b): To persuade the reader that playing a State Lottery isn't really gambling.** The author begins the essay with a definition of gambling and then analyzes that definition and argues that the State Lottery doesn't fit this definition (paragraph 2).

- **Statement (c): To analyze the dual characteristics of the definition of the word "gamble."** The author analyzes the aspects of "chance" and "game" using a detailed scenario (paragraph 3).

Statements (a) and (d) are the opposite of Milne's position. As for statement (e), Milne makes only a brief reference to gambling's dangers, so it is not his purpose for his writing.

27. **B** This structure question asks why the author uses the phrase "behind its hand" (paragraph 6). This phrase comes in the context of this sentence: "At a time when the one cry is 'Production!' the State adds (behind its hand), 'Buy a Premium Bond, and let the other man produce for you.'" This sentence shows a contrast between the two actions of the state, almost a hypocrisy. Choice (A) is incorrect; this phrase doesn't refer to the "no work at all" proposition in the previous sentence. Choice (B) is correct: This phrase is part of a contrast between the two actions of the state. Choice (C) is incorrect because the analogy of the state to a human body is never made in this essay. Choice (D) is contradictory to the passage because the author has a somewhat positive, rather than negative, view of gambling (paragraph 3). The correct answer is (B).

28. **D** This structure question asks about the role that a detail—the image of the Monte Carlo gambler (paragraph 3)—plays in the passage as a whole. The author uses this image to personify the aspects of "chance" and "game" that make up the definition of "gambling" (paragraph 2). Milne provides this gambler to symbolize the human actions and ideas that comprise gambling. Therefore, (A) is wrong; the author is not trying to make a statement about Monte Carlo as a place. Choice (B) is also incorrect; while "struggle" is mentioned, it is mentioned as a part of "game," the aspect that the author is exploring. Choice (C) is contradictory to the author's tone: The author has a generally neutral to positive view of gambling, so "reckless" is too strong. Choice (D) is correct: The image of the gambler is there to complete the picture begun with the definition of gambling. The correct answer is (D).

29. **A** This structure question asks about what inference can be made from the sentence. The author asserts, "The case of the average man in favor of State lotteries is, quite simply, that he does not like Dr. Clifford" (paragraph 6). The author implies that favoring lotteries is not based on logic but instead on personal dislike for Dr. Clifford. If the average man in favor of lotteries does not like the doctor (or his views), then it follows that the man is in favor of lotteries, simply because the doctor is not. Therefore, (A) is correct and (B) is wrong. Choice (C) is incorrect because intelligence is not addressed in the essay. Choice (D) is far too broad an assertion to make based on that one sentence—there's no evidence that the average man would not favor anything represented by the doctor. The correct answer is (A).

30. **D** This evaluation question asks about which detail supports the claim that people get pleasure out of games of skill and chance (paragraph 3). Immediately following this claim, the author draws out the scenario of the gambler in Monte Carlo. Choice (A) is incorrect because it is the bland description of the State Lottery.

Choice (B) is incorrect; although it refers to making the country "contented" (paragraph 6), it doesn't refer back to getting pleasure out of a game of chance. Choice (C) is incorrect; this quote (paragraph 2) just refers to the author's consideration of the definition of "gambling." Therefore, (D) is correct—the repeated use of "wonderful" indicates the gambler's elation. The correct answer is (D).

31. **A** Earlier in the passage, the author describes gambling as something involving skill, excitement, and personal engagement—a "game." By calling the lottery a "cold-blooded attempt," the author shifts the tone dramatically. The phrase suggests something mechanical, emotionless, and lacking human involvement. This contrast reinforces the author's argument that a state lottery is not real gambling, because it lacks the active, engaging qualities of a game. Choice (B) is somewhat plausible, but this is not the main effect; the focus is on the nature of the lottery, not the players. Choice (C) is wrong, since "cold-blooded" has nothing to do with legality. Choice (D) is too literal. The phrase is figurative, not about physical harm. The correct answer is (A).

32. **D** This development question asks about how the author's use of direct questions in paragraph 3 contributes to the author's essay. Paragraph 3 states, "And is there any man who, having made a fortune at Monte Carlo, will admit that he owes it entirely to chance? Will he not rather attribute it to his wonderful system, or if not to that, at any rate to his wonderful nerve…?" These questions to the reader are rhetorical, designed to encourage thinking about the topic and convince the reader of the author's perspective on gambling. Choice (A) is incorrect because there are no answers to these rhetorical questions. Choice (B) is contradictory to the passage, since the essay begins with a definition. Choice (C) is incorrect because the personality of the gambler is not under discussion. Choice (D) is correct—the questions cause the reader to consider the "game" or pleasure of gambling. The correct answer is (D).

33. **A** This question asks about the author's opinions regarding Premium Bonds. The author declares, "I am against Premium Bonds, but not for the popular reason. I am against them because there is so very little of the gamble about them" (paragraph 2). Thus, (A) is correct. Choice (B) is wrong because the author's tone when discussing the redistribution of funds (paragraph 6) is definitely satirical: "Instead of a million ten-pound citizens, we should have a thousand ten-thousand-pounders and 999,000 with nothing. That would be the official way of making the country happy." Choice (C) is contradictory because the author feels that Premium Bonds "have so very little of the gamble about them." Choice (D) is incorrect because the author mentions "hypocritical" in paragraph 1 as the views of others, not his own view. The correct answer is (A).

34. **B** This point of view question asks about the author's tone toward the reader, so examine the passage for tone indicators. In several places the author gives opinions and addresses the reader directly: "There are many occupations—and many jobs— that you would enjoy" (paragraph 3), "You need not restrict your job search to careers related to your degree" paragraph (7), and "It's never too late to change careers" (paragraph 11). Overall, the author offers encouragement to the reader or job seeker. Choice (A) is incorrect because "condescension" means talking down to someone, which is not what the author is doing. Choice (B) is correct: The author is offering information to reassure and help job seekers. Choice (C) is incorrect because the author is not trying to intimidate the reader. Choice (D) is incorrect because "satisfaction" expresses a concern with the self. However, this author is concerned primarily with the reader. The correct answer is (B).

35. **A** This question asks about the author's primary purpose in writing the article. The author's identification as part of the Department of Labor suggests that the author is familiar with the realities of the working world, and paragraph 3 asserts "There are many occupations—and many jobs—that you would enjoy."

The final paragraph, paragraph 11, states, "It's never too late to change careers." Therefore, the author is trying to help people persist in a job search despite temporary setbacks. Choice (A) is correct because the author emphasizes "keeping your options open" (paragraph 3) and "learning a variety of tasks helps you to sharpen abilities" (paragraph 5). Eliminate (B) because the author's tone is encouraging, not cautionary. Choice (C) is incorrect because, while the article mentions low grades and work history gaps, it does not mention the specific types of jobs that accept people with these limitations. Choice (D) contradicts the passage: Paragraph 5 states, "no one job uses all your talents."

36. **D** This structure question asks how this sentence relates to the article as a whole. The sentence is "Consider that electrical technicians are now repairing fuel cells, for example, or that veterinary technicians become pharmaceutical sales workers." This sentence appears in the context of a paragraph that begins with "You need not restrict your job search to careers related to your degree" (paragraph 7). Therefore, the sentence in question offers support for that topic sentence. Choice (A) is incorrect: While the sentence does present examples of specific careers, the author is not advocating that readers pursue these careers. Eliminate (B) because it contradicts the topic sentence of the paragraph. Choice (C) may seem attractive because the last sentence of paragraph 7 reads "Often, technical skills are applicable to many settings." However, the purpose of paragraph 7 is to address the flexibility of skills in general, not just technical skills, so (D) is correct.

37. **A** In paragraph 9, the author raises common worries (lack of experience, low grades, gaps in work history) then immediately provides solutions to each one. This question-and-answer structure mirrors the internal doubts many readers have and directly responds to them. This technique strengthens the argument by making the advice feel practical and relevant, reassuring readers that their concerns are normal and manageable, and guiding readers toward action. Choice (B) is wrong, since the problems are addressed immediately, not later. Choice (C) is incorrect, since the passage does not focus on contradictions, but on solutions. Finally, (D) is wrong because the advice remains general and broadly applicable. The correct answer is (A).

38. **D** This language use item requires you to determine which definition of the word "overcome" matches its use in paragraph 9. Each of the answer options reflects an actual definition of the word "overcome," so look closely at the way the word is used in context. The word is used as a part of this sentence: "People overcome all kinds of challenges to find satisfying work," which is connected to the later phrase "how you handle adversity." So here, the word "overcome" is used to mean "rise above" the challenges or the adversity. Choice (A) is incorrect because "overpower" means to "defeat in physical contest" or "overwhelm the senses"; neither makes sense with "challenges." Choice (B) is also incorrect because "shock the challenges" would not make sense either. Choice (C) might seem attractive because of the phrase "a good indicator of your ability to persevere"; however, "People outlive all kinds of challenges" would not make sense in a paragraph advising job seekers to assertively handle adversity. Choice (D) is correct: "surmount" means "rise above." The correct answer is (D).

39. **A** This question asks you to make an inference about the "workers" mentioned in the quotation. To answer this question, refer to the paragraph mentioned and read beyond the sentence to find out more about the "workers." The topic sentence of paragraph 11 is "It's never too late to change careers" followed by examples of workers who move into very different fields. Therefore, (A) is correct. Choice (B) contradicts the passage, which states, "For each of these workers, the desire for job satisfaction outweighed the desire for status quo." Eliminate (C) because "status quo" means current state, not prestige. Choice (D) is incorrect because the workers in the example did not all return to school—only one did. The correct answer is (A).

40. This item asks the reader to choose two examples the author uses to support the claim that prospective employees can take steps to better their odds of employment. The two correct answers are as follows:

- **Action (b): Donate your time to charitable organizations.** In paragraph 11, the author recommends "Gain needed skills with volunteer work."

- **Action (e): Anticipate questions that might arise when applying for a job.** The author also advises to "get a little interviewing practice." (paragraph 9).

Action (a) is incorrect, since the author's advice is not aimed at those currently in college. Eliminate Action (c) since Paragraph 7 specifically states the opposite. Action (d) is incorrect since "carefully explaining" is not the author's advice for addressing such gaps.

41. **C** This is a purpose question about the author's intended audience, so use the main idea from the passage as a starting point. This author is concerned with correcting "career myths" so that these myths won't "derail a career search and sap motivation" (paragraph 1). Therefore, the author is addressing job seekers who might be affected or "derailed" by these myths. Choices (A) and (B) are incorrect: There is nothing in the article to indicate that the information is targeted specifically at "first-time job seekers" or college students. Choice (C) is correct: The article addresses myths that cause people to doubt their ability to get a job (paragraphs 8 and 10). Choice (D) is incorrect because addressing work history gaps is just one detail in the passage, not the purpose of the whole article. The correct answer is (C).

42. **C** This character development question asks specifically how her father's words affect young Susan. After the sentence, "It would never do to have a woman overseer in the mill" (paragraph 2), the very next sentence conveys Susan's reaction: "This answer did not satisfy Susan and she often thought about it" (paragraph 3). Choice (A) is incorrect: As she watched the mill workers, the fact that women weren't overseers "continued to puzzle Susan" (paragraph 3). Eliminate (B) because, while Susan questions her father *before* being told "it would never do to have a woman overseer" (paragraph 2), there is no indication that Susan questions her father's judgment *after* being told this. Choice (C) is correct: Susan sees that her father's words do not match what she observes happening in the mill. Choice (D) is incorrect because nothing in this excerpt indicates that Susan goes to work in the mill or rebels against her father. The correct answer is (C).

43. **A** This structure question asks about how the details about Susan's home life enhance the narrative, so connect these details to the main idea. The main idea of the passage is about the kinds of work considered appropriate for women. The description starts with the second sentence of paragraph 5, indicated by "in the home of the millowner." At home, Susan's mother cared for three daughters and eleven boarders, and her days were filled with cooking, washing, ironing, mending, and spinning. Then the passage states, "But she was capable and strong and was doing only what all women in this new country were expected to do." So, the description of Susan's home life shows both her mother's capabilities and the enormous workload women were expected to handle. Therefore, (A) is correct. Choice (B) is incorrect because the passage does not indicate that Susan's father is absent; rather, her mother's workload is depicted as a typical number of daily duties. Choice (C) is incorrect because the housework and the millwork are not compared in the passage. Even though boarding the millworkers is part of Susan's mother's work, it is only one part of it, not the primary reason to give all the details of home life. Therefore, eliminate (D). The correct answer is (A).

44. **D** This evaluation question asks which sentence from the passage supports the idea that Susan is learning skills that enhance independence. Since several answers contain quotations related to the major themes of women's work or independence, consider what is implied as well as what is directly stated. Choices (A) and (B) are incorrect since these sentences refer to the women who work in the mills, not Susan. Choice (C) is incorrect; even though this quotation describes Susan, she is only observing other workers, not

learning skills. Choice (D) is correct: It is part of the sentence that states, "Susan, even before she was six, was very useful" (paragraph 5), so this quotation highlights Susan's ability to care for herself and do grown-up work. The correct answer is (D).

45. **B** This development question asks about the character of Sally Ann as shown through the overseer's actions. The reference is located in paragraph 3: "When the yarn on the beam was tangled or there was something wrong with the machinery, Elijah, the overseer, always called out to Sally Ann." The passage goes on to say "Sally Ann never failed to locate the trouble or to untangle the yarn." This shows that Sally Ann's mechanical ability was known and relied upon. Choice (A) is incorrect because the overseer is not relying upon Sally Ann's weaving abilities in these sentences, nor does the passage indicate that she is a more efficient weaver than the other women. Choice (B) is correct: The overseer (another worker) recognizes her mechanical ability. Choice (C) is somewhat contradictory since Sally Ann is the person who untangles the yarn. Choice (D) can be eliminated because there is no information about Sally Ann's hopes or whether she enjoys being asked for help. The correct answer is (B).

46. **A** This question asks about Susan's father's attitude about the cotton mills. Susan's father's point of view is a major theme of the passage: He has definite ideas about the women who work in his mills. Since the cotton mills are discussed throughout most of the excerpt, use the passage to either confirm or eliminate answers based on details in the choices. That the mills were an acceptable place for women to work is not directly stated in the passage but is strongly implied by the fact that Susan's father employs women weavers, so keep (A) and eliminate (B), since that answer directly contradicts the fact that Susan's father employed women. Choice (C) can be eliminated because, even though the passage states, "Brides were proud to display a few cotton sheets instead of commonplace homespun linen" (paragraph 4), there is no indication in the passage that Susan's father felt cotton would replace homespun entirely. Eliminate (D) because even though paragraph 3 states the mill had a "general air of efficiency," there is no indication that Susan's father considered men generally more efficient than women. The correct answer is (A).

47. This character development item asks the reader to identify three adjectives that accurately describe Susan as she watches the mill workers. This scene is found in paragraph 3. Here are the three correct adjectives:

- **Hushed.** The second sentence in paragraph 3 states, "to stand quietly and look about," when describing Susan's experience of the mill, so she is quiet as she watches.
- **Confused.** The last sentence of paragraph 3 reveals that as Susan observes Sally Ann doing a task the overseer can't, the fact that Sally Ann isn't an overseer herself "continued to puzzle Susan."
- **Amused.** The mill is described as "the best kind of entertainment" from Susan's point of view, and paragraph 3 states that Susan was "fascinated."

Eliminate "skilled," since that better describes Sally Ann than it does young Susan. And Susan is not "gratified" because we are told that she is instead "not satisfied" by the attitudes toward women workers, and "puzzled" by their treatment.

48. **D** This question asks about the mill that Susan's father built. Since different details about cotton mills are discussed in paragraphs 3, 4, and 5, use the passage to either confirm or eliminate answers based on details in the choices. Choice (A) is incorrect: The first sentence of paragraph 5 directly states that cotton had to be brought *from* Troy to the mill, a distance of 40 miles. Choice (B) is incorrect because paragraph 5 states that the workers boarded at the home of the millowner, not the mill. Eliminate (C) because the passage states that Susan was born in 1820 (paragraph 4) and Susan's father built the mill when she was two years old (paragraph 5). Choice (D) is correct: Paragraph 5 states that Susan's father's mill was built

beside a brook, and paragraph 4 states that "men like her father, Daniel Anthony, saw a potential cotton mill by the side of every rushing brook," implying that a source of running water is necessary for a mill. The correct answer is (D).

49. **B** This development question asks about the women workers in Susan's father's mill. The women mill workers are depicted at work in paragraph 3, their backgrounds are discussed in paragraph 4, and their living conditions are mentioned in paragraph 5. Choice (A) is incorrect because only Sally Ann is presented as a worker possibly qualified to be overseer—there is no information about the others. Choice (B) is correct: It accurately summarizes the sentence in paragraph 4: "young women, eager to earn the first money they could call their own, were leaving the farms, for a few months at least, to work in the mills." Choice (C) directly contradicts the passage, which states in paragraph 5 that the workers lived at the home of the millowner. Eliminate (D) because Susan's mother wasn't helped by the mill workers but by "a thirteen-year-old girl who worked for her after school hours," (paragraph 5). The correct answer is (B).

50. The option that correctly completes the sentence for each "Select" option is as follows:

Drop-Down Item 1: Verb tense and misplaced modifier/illogical word order

Option 2 is correct: In this sentence, the verb "had" (the simple past tense of "have") is used appropriately in a sentence that refers to a period in the past.

Option 1 is incorrect, because the present tense "I see him developing" does not fit in this sentence about "a period of six years ending in June 2009." Past tense is needed here. Option 3 is incorrect: This option results in illogical construction: "I had great pleasure from a paste-up assistant at the beginning, into a fully functioning Graphics Design Project Coordinator." Option 4 is incorrect, because this option results in ambiguous construction that could be read "with great pleasure, he was developing" instead of "As I saw him, with great pleasure."

Drop-Down Item 2: Parallelism and run-ons

Option 3 is correct: This option correctly divides two independent clauses with a period and keeps the items in the list in parallel adverbial form: "quickly and effectively."

Option 1 is incorrect: A comma is too weak to divide the two independent clauses and so this option results in a comma splice, aka a type of run-on sentence. Option 2 incorrectly merges "quickly, effectively, and during" into a list form, resulting in a comma splice as the two independent clauses are connected with a comma. Option 4 is incorrect because the items in the list (connected by "and") are not parallel: "quick" is an adjective and doesn't match the adverb "effectively."

Drop-Down Item 3: Parallelism

Option 4 is correct: This option keeps the structure parallel by pairing an infinitive with an infinitive in a comparison structure: "just as able to give guidance as to step."

Option 1 is incorrect because it results in the construction "able to give guidance and step back and take direction," which is awkward wording and should be avoided. A list of three items should be written "give guidance, step back, and take direction." Option 2 is incorrect, because the dependent clause is separated from the rest of the sentence with a period, forming the sentence fragment "Just as able to give guidance and step back and take direction when another is leading the group." Option 3 is incorrect because the construction "to give guidance and stepping" is not parallel, as it pairs an infinitive with a gerund.

Drop-Down Item 4: Misplaced modifiers or illogical word order

Option 4 is correct: In this sentence, the words "still" and "fondly" are correctly placed next to "remembered," which they both modify. The word "even" is placed next to "a year" to emphasize the time period, so that the sense of "still remembered" matches "even a year."

Option 1 is incorrect: In this order, the placement of the word "fondly" makes it appear to modify the word "here" when it should modify "remembered." Option 2 is incorrect: In this option, the placement of the word "even" makes it appear to modify "he," resulting in the phrase "even he" which distinguishes a person from other people. However, since no other people are the subject of discussion, "even he" is unnecessary and confusing. The word "even" should modify "year," to distinguish a time period. Option 3 is incorrect: The placement of the word "still" seems to modify "fondly" when it should modify "remembered" so that the emphasis on time in "still remembered" would match "even a year."

MATHEMATICAL REASONING

Part 1

1. **D** Replace every z with –3 and solve the equation. Remember that when you square a negative number, it becomes positive, but when you cube a negative number, it stays negative. So,

$$\frac{z^3 + 2z + 3}{z^2 + 1} = \frac{(-3)^3 + 2(-3) + 3}{(-3)^2 + 1} = \frac{(-27) + (-6) + 3}{9 + 1} = \frac{-30}{10} = -3$$

2. **C** The question tells us that each thumb drive is at least half full. So we need to know how much the thumb drives will hold if they're half full, which will be our lower limit. Then, we need to know how much they'll hold if they're totally full, and that will be our upper limit. For one thumb drive to be half full, we divide the total (3.6 hours) by 2, and get 1.8 hours. Since there are four thumb drives, multiply 1.8 by 4 and get 7.2 hours. For a thumb drive to be full it would hold 3.6 hours, so we multiply that by 4, giving 14.4 hours. So, the lower limit is 7.2 hours, and the upper limit is 14.4 hours. Choice (C) gives this expression. If you got (D), you did the right things but got an expression for just one thumb drive, rather than all four.

3. **D** The total time must include the trip there, the 3 hours in between, and the trip back. To calculate the time for the trip there (2.5 hours), divide 145 by 58. The trip back is also 2.5 hours, so for total time add 2.5 + 2.5 + 3.

4. **B** The July temperature should equal four times the February temperature, so $4t$ (remember that t represents the February temperature) is equal to 82. If you chose (C) or (D), you solved for the February temperature and got 21 and incorrectly made that a part of the equation. Note that the question asks for the equation, not the solution.

5. **C** The question asks for the greatest common factor that can reduce $\frac{84}{196}$. Find the factors of 84 and 196. The factors of 84 are 1, 2, 3, 4, 6, 7, 12, 14, 21, 28, 42, and 84. The factors of 196 are 1, 2, 4, 7, 14, 28, 49, 98, and 196. The greatest common factor is 28, so the correct answer is (C).

Part 2

6. **A** The total number of workers employed in neither clerical nor professional jobs is equal to the total number of workers (2,300,000) minus the number of clerical workers (19% of 2,300,000 = 437,000) minus the number of professional workers (24% of 2,300,000 = 552,000). If you answered (C), you found the total workers in those two professions but forgot to subtract it from the total workforce.

7. **B** This question can be solved algebraically or by plugging in answer choices for Miriam and seeing which number works. To solve algebraically, set Vered's stamps equal to $m - 6$. Now, $m + m - 6 = 2m - 6 = 42$. Solving, $m = 24$.

8. 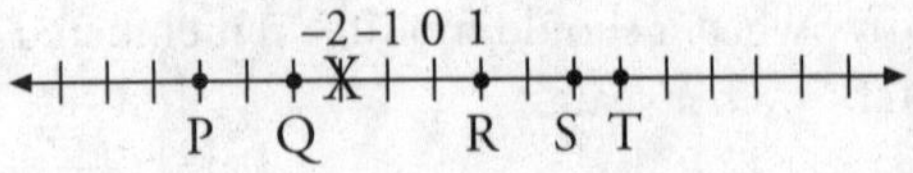

Since point P is at −5 and point S is at 3, P + S = −2.

9. 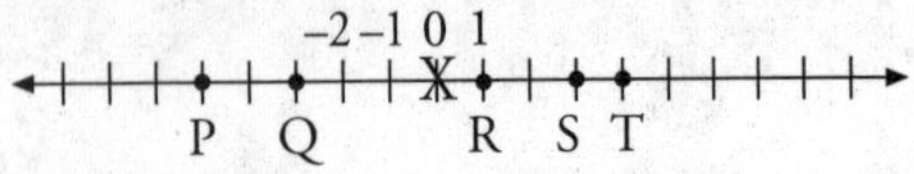

Since point Q is at −3, point R is at 1, and point T is at 4, $|Q - R| - T = |(-3) - 1| - 4 = |-4| - 4 = 4 - 4 = 0$. Don't forget to do the operation inside the absolute value sign before applying the absolute value.

10. **B** The question asks you to solve a quadratic equation. Use the form of the answer choices as a clue that you'll need to use the quadratic formula rather than factor. The quadratic formula is as follows:

$$x = \frac{-b \pm \sqrt{b^2 - 4ac}}{2a}$$

To use the quadratic formula, you'll need to get the equation in the form $ax^2 + bx + c = 0$. The given equation is already close to that form. Just subtract 10 from both sides to get $3y^2 - 12y - 10 = 0$, so $a = 3$, $b = -12$, and $c = -10$. Put these values into the quadratic formula to get:

$$x = \frac{-(-12) \pm \sqrt{(-12)^2 - 4(3)(-10)}}{2(3)}$$

$$x = \frac{12 \pm \sqrt{144 + 120}}{6}$$

$$x = \frac{12 \pm \sqrt{264}}{6}$$

This doesn't quite match any of the answer choices. However, you simplify the root by pulling out the perfect square factor 4.

$$x = \frac{12 \pm \sqrt{4 \times 66}}{6}$$

$$x = \frac{12 \pm \sqrt{4}\sqrt{66}}{6}$$

$$x = \frac{12 \pm 2\sqrt{66}}{6}$$

Finally, factor and cancel a 2 from the numerator and denominator:

$$x = \frac{2\left(6 \pm \sqrt{66}\right)}{2(3)}$$

$$x = \frac{6 \pm \sqrt{66}}{3}$$

This matches (B).

11. **D** Each answer choice describes a relationship in which lens X is stronger than lens Y, so to find out *how many* times stronger it is, divide the strength of lens X by the strength of lens Y. $3 \times 10^5 \div 6 \times 10^2 = 300{,}000 \div 600 = 500$. If you chose (C), remember that 500% of a number is equivalent to multiplying by 5, not by 500. If you chose (A) or (B), you probably divided 6 by 3 instead of 3 by 6.

12. **C** One good way to solve this equation is with ratios. Mark's rate of mowing, which is equal to the amount mowed divided by time, remains constant. So $\frac{\frac{2}{3}\ lawn}{1\ hour} = \frac{1\ lawn}{x\ hours}$. Solve this equation using cross multiplication to determine that $\frac{2}{3}x = 1$. Divide both sides by $\frac{2}{3}$ to get $x = \frac{3}{2}$, or $1\frac{1}{2}$.

13. **B** The smallest sides are the ones that are 2.5 m by 7 m (the front and back sides, in the image). We'll ignore them and find the areas of the larger sides. For the left and right sides, 2.5×10 gives us 25 square meters, which we then multiply by two (since there are two of these sides). That's 50 square meters. For the top and bottom sides, 7×10 gives 70, and then multiply by two again to get both sides. That's 140 + 50, which is 190 square meters.

14. **-54**

First substitute the values of x and a into the equation and then solve, being careful about order of operations. $3x(x - 2a)^{-x} = 3(-2)(-2 - 2 \times (.5))^2 = (-6)(-2 - 1)^2 = (-6)(-3)^2 = (-6) \times 9 = -54$, if $x = -2$ and $a = 0.5$.

15. **9, 34**

The task here is to find a value in the first pull-down menu that will give a perimeter found in the second pull-down menu. Just start plugging in values from the first menu until you get a perimeter that is in the second menu. If $x = 9$, then perimeter $= 9 + 9 + 16 = 34$.

16. **1,515**

The laser printer and hard drive do not change price, so they will still cost \$150 and \$100, respectively. The price of the laptop and monitor, however, goes up 10%, so calculate 10% of \$1,150 and add that to the previous price. So now the laptop and monitor costs \$1,150 + \$115 = \$1,265. The total bill therefore would be \$1,275 + \$150 + \$100 = \$1,515.

17. **A** This is a trickier algebra problem, but Backsolving makes it easier. Always start with a middle answer choice, such as (C). Say there are 26 women at Universal. If there were twice as many women as men, that means there would be 13 men. Altogether, there are *supposed* to be 78 employees, but your numbers add up to only 39. Could (C) be the right answer? Nope, too small. You need a bigger number. Move

up to (B) and say there are 42 women, which means there would be 21 men. You're supposed to get 78 employees, but 42 + 21 equals only 53 employees. Still too small. That must mean the correct answer is (A). If you did use algebra, you would set it up as

$$\text{men } (m) + \text{women } (w) = \text{total } (78)$$

and since there are twice as many women as men, replace the w with $2m$, giving you

$$m + 2m = 78$$

Combine like terms:

$$3m = 78$$

And divide to get $m = 26$, which is the number of men. Since we're asked about women, we need twice as many, so that's 52. (Now you can see why Backsolving is so convenient!)

18. $\mathbf{\frac{65 + 113}{262}}$ or $\mathbf{\frac{113 + 65}{262}}$

Probability questions always ask for a part divided by a whole. To calculate the probability that a random bird is NOT a duck, you need to divide the total number of non-ducks by the total number of birds. The total number of non-ducks is equal to the number of geese (65) plus the number of robins (113).

19. **D** This question tests distribution. First, distribute the term outside the parentheses to both of the terms inside the parentheses,

$$2a(a - 3b^2) + a^2 = 2a^2 - 6ab^2 + a^2$$

and then combine like terms and simplify.

$$2a^2 - 6ab^2 + a^2 = 3a^2 - 6ab^2$$

But this is not an answer choice. Notice that both terms now are divisible by $3a$, so you can get (D) by factoring out the $3a$. If you chose (A), you forgot to add the a^2. If you chose (B), you did not distribute the $2a$. You may also try plugging in for values of a and b in the original equation and checking the answer choices to see which is equivalent.

20. **D** A slope of 3 means that the line goes up 3 steps for every 1 step to the right. So, we can just count 3 up for every 1 to the right. We start at (–2, –10), and go one to the right (on the x-axis) and three up (on the y-axis), which puts us at (–1, –7). Another "one over, three up" and we're at (0, –4), then (1, –1), then (2, 2), then (3, 5), then (4, 8), then (5, 11). So, our x-coordinate is 5.

21. **B** Now we need the y-intercept of the line, which is the point at which it crosses the y-axis. The y-axis is located at $x = 0$, so we can find this the same way we found the answer to Question 20 (above). In fact, we already found it when we were solving Question 20. Our line passed through (0, –4), so our y-intercept is –4.

22. **C** The question asks for a dot plot to represent the data provided. In a dot plot, there is one dot above the number on the number line for each instance of that number in the data. In the data, there is one 85, so there should be one dot above 85. There are four 87's, so there should be four dots above 87. There is one 90, so there should be one dot above 90. There is one 91, so there should be one dot above 91. There are three 92's, so there should be three dots above 92. There are two 96's, so there should be two dots above 96. Finally, there are three 98's, so there should be three dots above 98. No other numbers should have a dot above them. The only graph that matches is (C).

23. **Action-Adventure 18, Drama 17.** The total of the values on the chart must add up to 100%, since the chart represents all the people surveyed. The current values add up to 65. Subtract this from 100 to get 35, which should be the sum of the missing numbers. Looking at the length of the bars on the chart, you can see that 10 is much too small and that 25 is too large. Try numbers until you find two that add up to 35. The only options are 17 and 18. Since Action-Adventure is a longer bar than Drama, place the 18 by Action-Adventure and the 17 by Drama.

24. **A** The ratio of Comedy to Other Types is 25:10, but this is not one of the answer choices. You must reduce the ratio just as you reduce a fraction. Divide both 25 and 10 by 5 and you get 5:2.

25. **D** The question asks for an average price, so you need to divide the total price of the tickets by the total number of tickets. The total price of the first-class tickets is 110(6.00), the total price of the second-class tickets is 172(3.50), and the total number of tickets is 110 + 172.

26. $\mathbf{\frac{9}{4}}$ or **2.25**

Be careful about order of operations. First multiply both sides by 2 to eliminate the fraction. So $(4x + 3)^2 = 144$. Take the square root of both sides. That gives us two equations, $4x + 3 = 12$, AND $4x + 3 = -12$ [since 12^2 and $(-12)^2$ both equal 144]. Solve each separately.

$$4x + 3 = 12, \text{ so } 4x = 9, \text{ so } x = \frac{9}{4} \text{ or } 2.25$$

and

$$4x + 3 = -12, \text{ so } 4x = -15, \text{ so } x = -\frac{15}{4}, \text{ or } -3.75$$

We are told that $x > 0$, so we want the positive answer.

27. **C** The post office is located halfway between points A and E. Using the diagram, we can calculate that the distance between A and E is 23 miles. Therefore, the post office is located 11.5 miles from A and 11.5 miles from E, right in the middle. Start at point A and go 11.5 miles to the right. You will be between B and C.

28. **C** First add the tip to the given bill, so multiply \$36 by 20% and then add \$36. So the total bill is \$43.20. Now divide this by 4.

29.

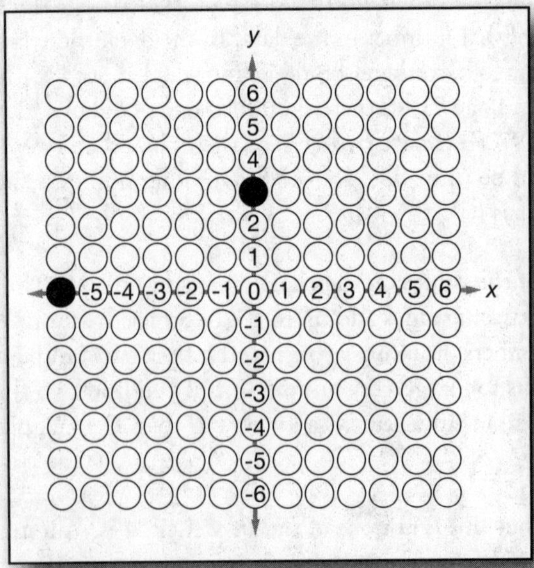

Remember that when a point lies on the *y*-axis, that means the *x*-coordinate is 0, and when a point lies on the *x*-axis, the *y*-coordinate is 0. Given the equation, $y = \frac{1}{2}x + 3$, when *x* is 0, then *y* is 3: $y = \frac{1}{2}(0) + 3$, or $y = 0 + 3$. So mark the point (0, 3) on the *y*-axis. Then set $y = 0$ in the equation and solve for *x*. $\frac{1}{2}x + 3 = 0$, so $\frac{1}{2}x = -3$, and $x = -6$. So mark point (–6, 0) on the *x*-axis.

30. **D** The classic mistake here is to find 60 percent of \$120, or \$72. However, the \$120 is 60 percent of Makayla's entire paycheck. In other words, you need to find 60 percent of a number we don't know yet, and set that equal to \$120. Since \$120 is 60 percent of the paycheck, this means that $120 = \frac{60}{100}x$. Multiply both sides by 100 to get $12{,}000 = 60x$. Then divide both sides by 60 to get 200. The answer is (D).

31. **C** In this problem, there was more information given than you really needed. After one day, the amount of water in the reservoir had doubled from its original amount. After five days, the amount of water had quadrupled from its original amount. If all we need to know is how much water there was after *five* days, the fact that it doubled after the *first* day is irrelevant. If *x* represents the original amount, the correct answer is 4*x*.

32. **D** There are 4 chefs, and each one averages *c* per month. There are 18 servers, and each one averages \$840 less than the chefs' wages (*c*). Subtract \$840 from *c* and multiply that by 18 servers. Add the totals of the two groups to get the monthly payroll.

33. **B** First find the area of the sign for which you know the price. Area = length × width = 5 ft × 8 ft = 40 ft^2. Make x the area of the new sign and calculate it using a ratio of area to price. $\frac{40 \text{ ft}^2}{\$140} = \frac{x}{\$336}$. Cross-multiply and solve for $x = 96$. So the area of the large sign is 96 ft^2. Now divide area by height (8) to get the length = 12 ft.

34. **B** Since the total number of games team A will play is 44, take 75% of 44 to calculate the total number of games that team A must win. 75% of 44 is 33 games, so that is their target. So far team A has won 28 games, so they need to win an additional 5 games.

35. **D** In order to find the area of a more complicated figure, divide the figure into more manageable shapes. Here if you draw in the dotted line shown, you will have two rectangles. The area of the larger rectangle is 15 × 11 = 165. The area of the smaller rectangle is 3 × 6 = 18. So the area of the whole figure is 165 + 18 = 183.

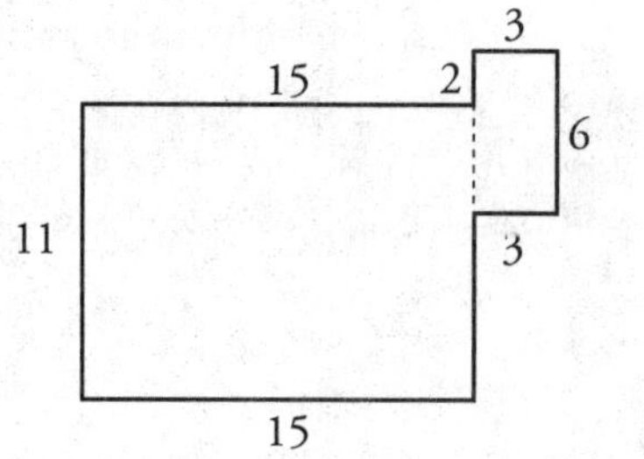

36. **4.5**

To find the empty space, find the volume of the entire chest by multiplying the three dimensions (length, width, depth): 2.5 × 1.5 × 2 = 7.5 cubic feet. Then subtract the size of the blankets (3 total cubic feet, since 3 blankets) to get 4.5 cubic feet of empty space.

37. **A** After Michelle paid the deductible of $500, there was $350 remaining. The insurance company paid 80% of that, so $350 × 0.8 = $280. Michelle had to pay the remaining $70 ($350 – $280 = $70).

38. The volume of cylinder L is **[less than half]** the volume of cylinder R.

Use the formula for the volume of a cylinder to calculate the volume for each cylinder. Although the numbers in both cylinders (8 and 20) are the same, the volumes are not equal. The reason is that the formula for volume requires that the radius of a cylinder be squared. Therefore, the radius has a greater effect on volume than height does. As a result, the volume of the cylinder with the larger radius (the one with the diameter of 20) has a greater volume. Volume of cylinder L = $\pi r^2 h = \pi 4^2 \times 20 = 320\pi$. Volume of cylinder R = $\pi 10^2 \times 8 = 800\pi$. So, the volume of cylinder L is less than half the volume of cylinder R.

39. **A** First calculate the volume for cylinder L. (You have already done this for Question 38.)

$V = \pi r^2 h$

$V = \pi 4^2 20$

$V = 320\pi$

So this is the volume of the water poured into cylinder R. The water in cylinder R now forms a cylinder that comes part of the way up the side of cylinder R. To determine the height, use the volume equation again:

$V = \pi r^2 h$

$320\pi = \pi 10^2 h$

$320\pi = 100\pi h$

Divide both sides by 100π, and h (the height of the water) = 3.2.

40. **B** To calculate the minimum revenue, consider which empty seats will cost the airline the most money. Three empty first-class seats will reduce the total revenue much more than three empty coach seats. So calculate the total income from (30 – 3) = 27 first-class passengers and (325 – 30) = 295 coach passengers. So Total minimum revenue = (27 × \$700) + (295 × \$250) = \$18,900 + \$73,750 = \$92,650, which is (B).

41.

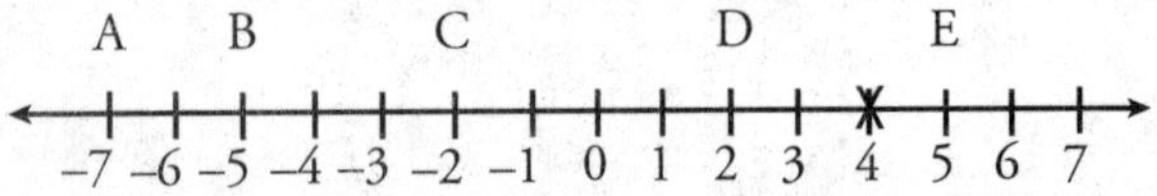

The distance between two points on a number line is found either by counting the steps between the two points, or by subtracting (and distance is always positive). So 5 – (–7) = 12. $\frac{1}{3} \times 12 = 4$, so you should mark 4 on the number line.

42.

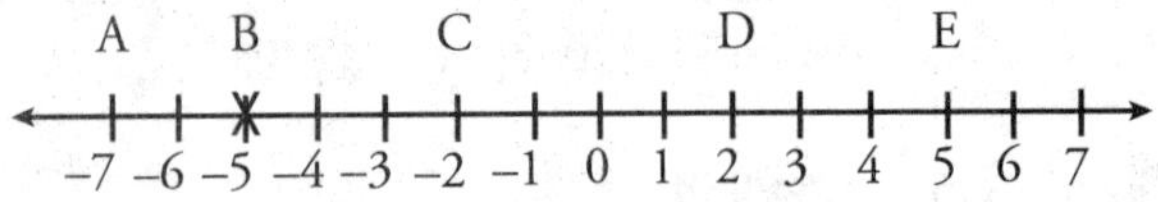

Insert the values from the number line into the expression and solve. ((–5) – (–2)) – 2 = (–3) – 2 = –5. Remember that subtracting a negative number will move to the right on a number line and subtracting a positive number will move to the left.

43.

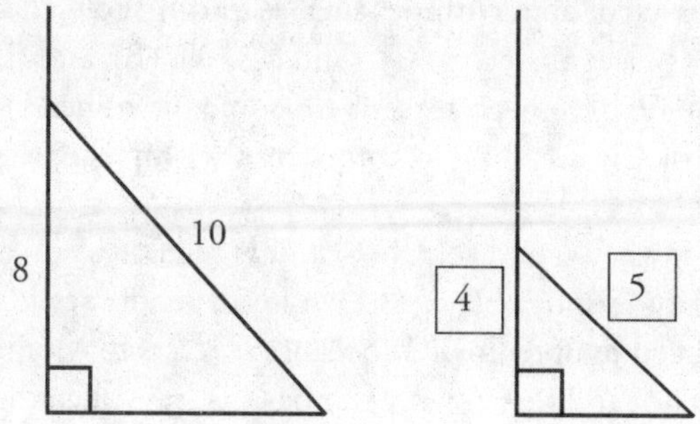

When two triangles are similar, respective sides must have the same proportion. So in this case, the ratio of the height to the length must be 8:10. Look for two numbers among those available that give the same ratio. 4 and 5 are the only possibilities. Note that $\frac{8}{10}$ reduces to $\frac{4}{5}$.

44. **10** Count 'em up! On Monday, AJ took 2 tablets: one at 2 p.m. and then one 8 hours later at 10 p.m. On Tuesday and Wednesday, he took 3 tablets a day, at 6 a.m., 2 p.m., and 10 p.m. On Thursday, he took 2 tablets: one at 6 a.m. and the last one at 2 p.m. 2 + 3 + 3 + 2 = 10 tablets.

45. **C** Notice that the question says Katrina's investment *increased* by 180%. That means that the difference between the new value and the old is equal to 180% of \$14,000. 180% of \$14,000 = 1.8 × \$14,000 = \$25,200. Add this to the original (\$14,000) to get \$39,200—the current value of her investment.

46. **A** Diameter *AB* has length 8 (subtract the *y* values: 11 – 3), so the radius of the circle is 4. Since *AB* is a semicircle, the center of the circle must be directly between points *A* and *B* at point (2, 7). Point *C*, then, must be directly to the right of the center, since it is the midpoint of the arc. Therefore, its *x*-coordinate will also be 6 and (add the radius 4 to the *x* value) its *y*-coordinate will be 7.

SOCIAL STUDIES

1. **D** The passage explains employment restrictions based on (A), age (14–17 rules); (B), job safety; and (C), educational obligations, but never mentions (D), gender, as a hiring factor. The correct answer is (D).

2. **B** Choice (A) says that it should be up to minors to decide when and whether they want to take a job—but the passage says this is decided by the Department of Labor, so you can eliminate this one. Choice (C) says minors can't work under any circumstances, which directly contradicts the entire passage, so you can eliminate this one too. Choice (D) is saying the same thing as (C) using different words. The correct answer, which sums up the reason for the need for regulations, is (B).

3. **C** Who would be most likely to support the passage of the FLSA, including its regulations to protect children? Factory owners *may* be kindhearted, but then again, there have been a lot of factory owners who have exploited child labor—so eliminate (A). Child protection agencies would seem very likely to protect children; let's hold onto (B) while we look at the other choices. Workers' unions might well also support regulations to protect children, so let's hold onto (C) as well. Small companies *might* be kindhearted too, but we don't know that they will be, so eliminate (D). We have two choices left: (B) and (C). Which is better? The clue is in the passage's description of the FLSA. Along with provisions designed to protect children, the FLSA also sets minimum wage and overtime pay standards—all of which are supported by workers' unions. The correct answer is (C).

4. **C** The passage says that the young men went west in search of opportunities such as finding gold and striking it rich. Which of the answer choices says that? The correct answer is (C). Choices (A), (B), and (D) didn't appear in the passage itself—and while these all *might* have been reasons for someone to head west, the correct answer to a GED® Reading passage is almost always going to come from within the passage.

5. **A** The only reference to towns in the passage comes in the second sentence, and it refers to San Francisco and Monterey. The next sentence reads, "There they found jobs...." So why did people settle in those towns? The correct answer is (A). You might have been tempted by (C) because it refers to Monterey and the gold to be found there—but by the time they got to these towns, the passage says that the settlers had given up on being prospectors and just needed jobs. Choices (B) and (D) contain information not found in the passage itself.

6. **A** The First Amendment protects fundamental civil liberties, including freedom of speech and freedom of the press. This means individuals and organizations have the right to express opinions and publish information (even if it criticizes the government) without government censorship or punishment. Choice (A) is correct because a newspaper criticizing government policies is a direct example of freedom of the press, which is explicitly protected by the First Amendment. Choice (B) is incorrect because requiring citizens to pay taxes is an exercise of government fiscal authority under the Constitution; it is unrelated to First Amendment protections. Choice (C) is incorrect because voter identification laws relate to election regulation and voting procedures, not free speech or press freedoms protected by the First Amendment. Choice (D) is incorrect because Congress regulating business practices falls under its constitutional powers (such as interstate commerce), not First Amendment protections.

7. **A** The 1st Amendment does not guarantee the right to vote. Rather it makes five guarantees: those listed in (B) through (D), along with the freedom of assembly and the freedom of religion.

8. **A** The Berlin Airlift was a response to the Soviet blockade of access routes into West Berlin. Choice (A) is correct; this blockade directly caused the airlift. The Marshall Plan, (B), provided aid but did not block routes. The Yalta Conference, (C), did not directly cause the crisis. And NATO, (D), did not restrict access to Eastern Europe.

9. **A** According to the timeline, the Warsaw Pact was created after the formation of NATO. All remaining answers include events that happened before NATO.

10. **A** The map shows Germany divided into separate occupation zones after WWII. Choice (A) is correct. This directly reflects postwar division by Allied powers. Choice (B) is incorrect; population centers were not the key division factor. Choice (C) is incorrect; division was political and military, not economic productivity. Choice (D) is also incorrect; Soviet control was concentrated in the east, not evenly spread.

11. **D** In the passage, Grant says that the Civil War would change the nation as a whole. Which historical development best supports that? The triumph by one side in a civil war isn't an example of how the country was changed by the war. Eliminate (A). The entry of the United States into World War I does not seem to be directly related to the Civil War either. Eliminate (B). Women winning the right to vote also doesn't seem like a direct result of the Civil War. Eliminate (C). The correct answer is (D). The Civil War was waged to free the enslaved Black people—which profoundly changed the entire nation.

12. **A** The 24th Amendment to the U.S. Constitution (1964) eliminated the use of poll taxes in federal elections. Poll taxes were fees required to vote, which effectively prevented many low-income citizens—especially African Americans in the South—from exercising their voting rights. This amendment supports the constitutional principle that the right to vote cannot be limited by a person's ability to pay money,

reinforcing the idea of equal political participation. Choice (B) is incorrect because the 24th Amendment does not require citizens to pay taxes to vote. Instead, it removes a financial barrier to voting. Choice (C) is incorrect because the amendment does not give the government power to limit voting rights during elections. It actually restricts government from imposing financial barriers. Choice (D) is incorrect because the amendment applies at the federal constitutional level, meaning it overrides states. It does not leave voting rights determination solely to state governments.

13. **D** Before you turn to the question, make sure that you understand the pie chart. The title says that it is about how children are being educated. It says that 39.2 percent are being educated in public school, 31.5 percent are being educated in private school, and the rest of the children are being educated in other ways. Which statement is supported by the information in the pie chart? Choices (A) and (B) imply value judgments that are not supported by the chart. Who knows which is better, or which ones the children prefer? Choice (C) contradicts what we can see from the chart. If tutoring at home were the most popular method, it would have the largest percentage of kids doing it. The correct answer is (D).

14. **A** A pure market economy has no government intervention, so programs like unemployment assistance would not exist; (A) is correct. Choice (B) is wrong since private competition is a core feature of markets. Choice (C) is wrong since independent job seeking occurs in all systems. Choice (D) is incorrect since market pricing is fundamental to market economies.

15. **A** A socialist command economy reduces private ownership and redistributes wealth. Choice (A) is correct since entrepreneurs would lose autonomy, profit incentives, and possibly ownership. Choice (B) is not the best choice since unemployed individuals may benefit from redistribution. Eliminate (C) since government employees are typically stable or expanded. Also eliminate (D) since laborers may benefit from wage equalization or protections.

16. **D** As you study the photograph, you will probably notice two things: (1) The car in the photo is quite old, and (2) it isn't working. The people in this old photograph are pushing the car instead of riding in it. The question itself says that while today we sometimes have difficulties with cars, the people back then had to deal with other kinds of problems. What was it? Does it seem as if the people in that photo are concerned about pollution? We didn't think so. Are they concerned about seat belts? Not when most of them are pushing the car. Are they concerned about heavy cars? Now, we're getting warmer. If you were pushing a car, you would probably want it to be as light as possible. But let's read the last answer choice before we pick: Could the people in the photo be concerned with a shortage of gas stations? Aha! This answer gets to the heart of *why* they are pushing the car in the first place: It is out of gas. The correct answer to this question is (D).

17. **A** The passage describes "hardships," "injustice," "suffering," and "persecution." Choice (A) is correct; it captures both racial and economic motivations. Choice (B) is not supported; land ownership is not mentioned. Likewise, military conscription, (C), is not referenced. Industrialization campaigns, (D), are unrelated to the passage.

18. **D** Read the graph carefully before looking at the questions. We see bars representing males and females who take the SAT, broken down by ethnic group. From this graph, we can see that in all but one group, more females than males take the SAT. The one group in which this does not appear to be true is that of Asian Americans. Looking at the answers, (A) makes a claim not supported by the graph. We are not given any information about how males and females perform on the test—just about how many took it. Choices (B) and (C) make statements of fact not supported by the graph. We have no idea whether numbers are declining or increasing from year to year. This graph is of a single snapshot in time. The correct answer is (D): According to the chart, clearly more females than males take the SAT.

19. **C** The question is basically asking, "Which of the following is NOT an example of a plutocratic government?" The best answer is (C), in which the leaders are elected by popular vote. In a plutocracy, the leaders are chosen because they are the wealthiest citizens. This means that there is no vote. All the other choices reflect situations that could occur in a plutocracy.

20. **D** You don't have to know anything about Andrew Mellon to realize that, in this statement at least, he is on the side of the people. He writes that "unwise" public officials "fall to these interests of monopoly as against the welfare of the people of whom they are supposed to serve." So we are looking for an answer choice that is sympathetic to the people and critical of officials who lose sight of the people's welfare. Choice (A) seems possible at first, but goes too far: Mellon doesn't suggest that public officials who profit from a monopoly shouldn't run for office. Choice (B) is wrong because it sides with the public officials over the interests of the people. Choice (C) goes too far, because Mellon never says the profits of monopolies should be shared by all. This leaves us with (D), which is a simple restatement of what Mellon says in the passage.

21. **B** The passage compares the relationship between the federal and state governments to that between the hub and spokes of a wagon wheel. This is called an analogy (which means a comparison between two things to help you understand one of them better). You have to find an answer choice that illustrates the analogy. Choice (A) is no good because, in the analogy, the entire government is represented by one wheel. What purpose would three other wheels serve? This might have been a good analogy if we were talking about four separate countries, each with its own wagon wheel helping to support the world-wagon—but that's a different analogy. Choice (B) basically restates the analogy—and is the correct answer. Choices (C) and (D) extend the analogy in meaningless ways.

22. **D** The map of the United States shows which areas have a high number of non-English-speaking children. You'll notice that the highest concentrations tend to be on the outside edges of the country, not the interior. Question 22 asks you to pick the best geographic explanation for the areas that have the highest numbers of non-English-speaking children. Choice (B) is irrelevant because we aren't concerned with the total number of children in the country—only the children who can't speak English. Choice (C) is irrelevant because, according to the map, some of the heaviest areas of non-English-speaking kids are in the north, such as New York and Washington. Choice (A) seems possible at first because lower income taxes might attract new immigrants, but then again, wouldn't they attract just about everyone? Let's hold onto this as we look at (D). If recent immigrants settled in border and coastal states, wouldn't that be a pretty logical explanation for why these areas contain the most non-English-speaking kids? Choice (D) is a much better choice than (A).

23. **B** All of the answer choices would have an effect on the distribution of these kids EXCEPT (B), climate. In general, new immigrants would seem to make decisions based more on the availability of ESL programs, immigration laws, social services, and even migration patterns (where immigrants have gone before) than on climate. One of the states with the largest number of non-English speakers (according to the chart) is New York (which has a colder climate), while others include California and Florida, with warmer climates.

24. **D** To answer this question, you have to consider each answer choice in turn. Are non-English-speaking children evenly distributed across the entire country? The map says no. Eliminate (A). Are there more of these kids in Arizona than in California? No, according to the map, California has the highest level of counties with at least 500 non-English-speaking kids. Arizona has between five and nine counties with 500 or more non-English-speaking children, but not as many as California, so we can eliminate (B). And while Texas and California *do* have the highest levels of kids who don't speak English, could that really mean that they have more kids who can't speak English than kids who *can*? The map does not show information that compares these two groups of children, so eliminate (C). The correct answer is (D) because it best reflects what the map tells us: In the middle states in the north of the United States, there are fewer non-English-speaking children.

25. **B** The passage tells us that the Constitution and other laws "made in accordance" with the Constitution can't be set aside by judges or any other laws. So, which is an example of this? The correct answer is (B), which says that the Bill of Rights (the first 10 amendments of the Constitution) can't be denied by any arm of the government. Choices (A), (C), and (D) are all irrelevant to this concept.

26. **A** Lowering the speed limit, limiting senators to two terms, and reducing pollution—none of these deprives people of their constitutional rights. However, prohibiting protests by a union takes away a fundamental right guaranteed by the Constitution: the right to free speech. Thus, the correct answer is (A).

27. **B** Freedom of religion is a fundamental right guaranteed by the Constitution—so we can eliminate (A). A right to a trial by jury is also guaranteed by the Constitution—so we can eliminate (C). The right to vote is also guaranteed to citizens by the Constitution—so we can probably eliminate (D), because even if they don't speak English, people can be citizens. The correct answer is (B).

28. **D** The passage states that the economics professors say there are too many factors to be able to make long-term stock-market predictions. Choice (D) accurately restates that idea. Choices (A), (B), and (C) all make statements that contradict the passage.

29. **C** Because so many different factors can affect stock prices, there can be no guarantee that two companies producing the same goods will do equally well—so we can eliminate (A). While amateur investors are mentioned in the passage, their behavior is not the most important factor in a stock's success—so eliminate (B). The passage says that amateurs may do as well as professional stock traders, but it does not say that they will do better—so we can eliminate (D). The correct answer must be (C), because past success does not ensure future performance—a concept always mentioned in stock prospectuses, but often forgotten in practice.

30. Since laissez-faire economics is free from government restrictions, labor laws, building codes, and antitrust laws would all be incorrect choices. **Deregulation, (a); free trade, (d); and non-interference, (f),** all imply a lack of government oversight in business.

31. **C** What caused the end of the era of transatlantic ship-crossings? Do you think it was a series of accidents, a major war that disrupted routes, or the cost of travel by boat? Nope, it was something much more basic—the airplane, which made the trip across the ocean so much more quickly. The correct answer is (C).

32. **A** The cartoon shows two injured veterans joking and bonding over shared experiences. The caption emphasizes mutual respect despite injury. Choice (A) is correct; it captures the message of unity through sacrifice. Choice (B) misreads the tone (not about hierarchy of injury). Choice (C) is the opposite of what is shown; they are connecting. And (D) is too broad and not supported by the caption's emphasis on camaraderie.

33. **B** The flowchart indicates that Congress is responsible for passing laws. They do not veto; that is the president's role. TAB 2 indicates that the Judicial Branch gained power in *Marbury v. Madison*, so eliminate (C). Choice (D) is tempting, but there is no indication that the Congress nominates judges. The president does this.

34. **D** In TAB 3, Jefferson states that "judges as the ultimate arbiters of all constitutional questions" is "a very dangerous doctrine." He made this statement in response to *Marbury v. Madison*. The quote also indicates that "their power is…dangerous." This matches best with (D). Choices (A) and (C) are too positive in tone to match with the Jefferson quote. Choice (B) is close, but *Marbury v. Madison* pertains to the Judicial Branch, not the Executive Branch.

35. **A** Jefferson is using negative language, such as "dangerous." The only negative word in these answers is "tyranny." It is not a literal definition of "oligarchy," but is the only word that captures the spirit of Jefferson's opinion regarding *Marbury v. Madison.*

SCIENCE

1. **D** The question states that hurricanes gather strength over warm water, so a hurricane should gather the most strength over the warmest body of water. Since the Gulf of Mexico has the highest average temperature of the bodies of water listed, the correct answer is (D).

2. **A** According to the passage, patients must receive tests for blood type before certain kinds of transfusions because of the ways in which different red blood cells interact with each other. Therefore, blood type tests must be necessary only when there is going to be an exchange of red blood cells. Since the passage states that whole blood transfusions involve both red blood cells and plasma, blood type tests must be necessary before whole blood transfusions. Since plasma transfusions do not involve red blood cells, you can eliminate (B) and (C). The passage states that patients may receive transfusions when they have lost a lot of blood, not when they have not lost any blood. Therefore, (D) is not supported by the passage and is incorrect. Thus, (A) is the best answer.

3. **85%**

According to the information given, coal turns into anthracite only after the coal has been subjected to heat and pressure for more than a million years. Thus, this type of coal is likely very dense, or hard. Additionally, the passage indicates that anthracite burns only when subjected to very high temperatures. Thus, the question most likely describes anthracite, which is 85–95% carbon, so the lowest level of carbon the coal is likely to contain is 85%.

4. **D** According to the question, steel is formed when iron combines with carbon at very high temperatures. Since you need carbon to form steel, you likely do not want all of the carbon to burn up before it combines with the iron. Additionally, the form of coal that contains the highest percentage of carbon is likely to be the most effective for this process. Since anthracite burns only at very high temperatures, and contains the highest percentage of carbon of the coals listed, the correct answer is (D).

5. **Peat, (a); Anthracite, (d).** Peat turns into lignite, which in turn becomes subbituminous coal, which in turn becomes bituminous coal, which in turn becomes anthracite. Notice that these changes require both heat and pressure, which would result from the coal being farther and farther underground. Additionally, anthracite is millions of years old, and therefore is likely to become covered by layers of earth over the centuries. Therefore, peat is likely to be closest to the surface. According to the chart, the coal with the highest level of carbon is anthracite.

6. **C** According to the passage, seeds need moisture and oxygen. Additionally, while most seeds require temperatures between 15 and 27 degrees centigrade, corn seeds require even higher temperatures. Therefore, the correct answer must involve temperatures higher than 27 degrees centigrade. Eliminate (A). Since "arid" means "without moisture," corn seeds likely will not germinate in an arid environment, so (B) is not the credited answer. Choice (C) mentions an environment that is moist, has plenty of oxygen, and is warmer than 27 degrees centigrade, so (C) is the correct answer. Since the passage states that maple trees can germinate in temperatures lower than 15 to 27 degrees centigrade, an environment that is suitable for maple trees will not necessarily be suitable for corn seeds. Thus, (D) is incorrect.

7. **C** According to the passage, maple seeds can germinate in low temperatures. However, that does not necessarily mean that they can germinate in any temperature; there may still be temperatures that are either too high or too low for them to germinate. Thus, (A) is incorrect. The passage does state that corn seeds require temperatures higher than 27 degrees centigrade in order to grow, but that does not necessarily mean that corn is difficult to grow. Therefore, (B) is incorrect. The passage states that "most seeds will germinate when they have moisture." So, some water is necessary for the germination process. Choice (C) is supported by the passage and is the credited answer. The passage states that maple seeds and corn seeds germinate in different temperatures, but does not mention the respective amounts of oxygen that they require. Choice (D) is not supported by the passage and is therefore incorrect.

8. **B** According to the passage, many researchers believe that a decrease in the vaccination rate among children is linked to an increase in measles cases. The first graph indicates that the vaccination rate for the MMR vaccine among kindergartners declined overall from 2000 to 2005. The second graph indicates that the cases of measles increased overall during the same period. This is consistent with the researchers' belief, so eliminate (C) and (D). This same information is inconsistent with the reason provided in (A), so eliminate that choice as well. The correct answer is (B).

9. **A** The passage states that plants lie dormant during periods that are unfavorable for growth. Winter is generally the season least favorable for growth, so the correct answer is (A).

10. **#4 is the oldest; #1 is the newest.** Unless volcanic activity has occurred, the oldest rock layers are the ones located deepest within the ground. Therefore, rock layer #4, the deepest, is the oldest rock layer, and rock layer #1, the shallowest, is the newest rock layer.

11. **C** According to the information in the food chain, bass do eat minnows. However, the food chain does not provide any information as to whether any other fish also eat minnows. Since minnows may have more than one predator, (A) is not supported by the information in the food chain. The food chain begins with microscopic algae and ends with the much larger bass. In general, the living things on the food chain seem to be ordered from smallest to largest. Since bass are higher on the food chain than minnows, bass are likely larger than minnows, rather than the other way around. Therefore, you can eliminate (B). Bass eat minnows, which in turn eat copepods. Therefore, if there were no copepods, minnows would have fewer food options and would likely suffer. In turn, bass would suffer since they would have fewer minnows to consume. Choice (C) is supported by the information in the food chain and is the credited answer. Since bass may derive benefits from minnows that they could not derive from algae, there is no evidence that (D) is true.

12. **C** While the orchid is an example of mimicry, it is not passive protection, since the orchid is not protecting itself from predation, but instead trying to achieve a different goal.

13. **C** You can solve this by setting up a proportion:

$$\frac{1\,\text{kg/liter}}{1{,}000\,\text{kg/meter}^3} = \frac{x\,\text{kg/liter}}{1{,}029\,\text{kg/meter}^3}$$

Then, cross-multiply and divide to find *x*, the unknown representing the density of seawater: 1.029 kg/liter. Therefore, the correct answer is (C).

14. **D** According to the scientific method, experiments should test only one variable in order to reach a conclusion about that variable. In this study, the researchers did two things instead of just one: they created incentives to decrease pollution and also created free clinics. Therefore, they don't know which is responsible for the health improvements. Choice (D) best describes this. Other answer choices do not address this flaw.

15. **Mode, 0.43 kg.** The mode is defined as the most commonly occurring number, so in this case the researchers would need to find the mode of the weights. Since the weight 0.43 kg occurs most frequently in the list, the correct answer to the second question is 0.43 kg.

16. **0.93**

To find the mean of a list of numbers, add up all of the numbers and then divide by the number of items that you have. 0.2 + 0.4 + 0.2 + 0.8 + 0.9 + 1.7 + 1.3 + 1.8 + 0.9 + 1.1 = 9.3. You have 10 numbers, so divide this result by ten: 9.3 ÷ 10 = 0.93.

17. **D** Decreasing the volume of the gas will make the denominator of the fraction smaller, and will contribute toward making the fraction as a whole larger. However, decreasing the temperature of the gas will make the numerator smaller, and will contribute toward making the fraction as a whole smaller. Therefore, decreasing both the volume and the temperature of the gas will not necessarily increase the pressure within the gas, and you can eliminate (A). Increasing the volume of the gas will make the denominator of the fraction larger, and will therefore make the fraction as a whole smaller, so you can eliminate both (B) and (C). Decreasing the volume of the gas will make the denominator smaller, and will thus make the fraction as a whole larger. Increasing the temperature of the gas will make the numerator of the fraction larger, and will thus make the fraction as a whole larger. Thus, only (D) will cause an increase in the pressure within the gas.

18. **A** According to the table, a combination occurs when A + B → C. Note that this matches the reaction described in the equation. In this case, H_2 = A, F_2 = B, and 2HF = C. All of the other types of reactions have additions on the right sides of the equations, so (B), (C), and (D) are incorrect. The credited answer is (A).

19. **B** Use the chart and estimate. According to the chart, the number of AIDS deaths in 2011 in Africa was approximately 1,800, and was approximately 2,500 in 2020. Therefore, the increase in AIDS deaths in Africa between the two years was about 2,500 – 1,800 = 700. The number of AIDS deaths in 2011 in South/Southeast Asia was approximately 500, and was approximately 1,500 in 2020. Therefore, the increase in AIDS deaths in South/Southeast Asia between the two years was about 1,500 – 500 = 1,000. Eliminate (A), since (B) gives you a larger answer. The number of AIDS deaths in 2011 in Eastern Europe was approximately 0, and was approximately 250 in 2020. Therefore, the increase in AIDS deaths in Eastern Europe between the two years was about 250. Eliminate (C). Finally, the number of AIDS deaths in North America/Northern Europe was approximately 0 in 2011, and was just slightly more than 0 in 2020, so you can eliminate (D). The correct answer is (B).

20. **D** The A-type star has a temperature of 4,839 degrees Fahrenheit, so substitute 4,839 into the formula in place of °F. You then have $K = \frac{5}{9}(4{,}839 - 32) + 273$. Simplify inside the parentheses first to get $K = \frac{5}{9}(4{,}807) + 273$. Multiply the $\frac{5}{9}$ and the 4,807 so that you have $K \approx 2{,}670.55 + 273$. Finally, add to get $K \approx 2{,}943.55$. The correct answer is (D).

21. **B** Amplitude is a measure of the difference between the middle height of a wave and the height at the top (or bottom) of a wave. If you look at the two waves, you will see that the distance from the middle height to the top of the Fault City wave is much greater than the distance from the middle height to the top of

the Nicaragua wave. Therefore, the Fault City wave had a much greater amplitude. You can eliminate (A), and the correct answer is (B). The information in the caption indicates that a seismometer was used to measure the Fault City quake, so (C) is incorrect. Finally, the long-period surface waves at point R1 were larger during the Fault City quake than during the Nicaragua quake, so (D) is incorrect.

22. **R1, Nicaragua.** Since you're looking for a point that would allow you to identify signs of an earthquake before the earthquake actually occurred, you need a point before the earthquake. Points R2, R3, R4, and R5 are all located on the timeline at points after the earthquake. Only point R1 is before the earthquake, and is a point at which signs of seismic activity actually occur.

23. **C** The passage mentions that ornithologists have observed that the archaeopteryx could perch on tree limbs, but does not state whether paleontologists agree with this observation. Eliminate (A). According to the passage, ornithologists believe that the archaeopteryx could not run quickly, but again the passage does not state whether paleontologists agree with this view, so (B) is not the credited answer. Paragraph 1 indicates that paleontologists believe that the archaeopteryx "could not sustain flight." Thus, (C) is supported by the passage and is the correct answer. Paragraph 2 states that ornithologists believe that the archaeopteryx may not have been able to walk quickly, but the passage does not state whether paleontologists agree with this view, so (D) is incorrect.

24. **C** According to ornithologists, the "archaeopteryx was first and foremost a bird." Of the animals listed in the answer choices, only the crow is a bird. Therefore, the correct answer is (C).

25. **C** According to the information in the paragraph, work is equal to force multiplied by displacement. The paragraph also states that if you use a ramp to move an object rather than lifting the object straight up, then the amount of force required decreases, while displacement increases by exactly the same amount that the force decreases. Thus, the net product of force times displacement should not change. The correct answer is therefore (C).

26. **D** Look at the chart, and read horizontally across the row for urine. Note that the columns for both albumin and glucose have dashes for entries, signaling that neither is generally present in urine. Therefore, the correct answer is (D), albumin and glucose.

27. **A** The passage states that the foxes prey on rabbits, so if there are fewer rabbits in the forest, the fox population will suffer because one of its food sources will be depleted. Choice (A) is therefore supported by the passage and is the correct answer. The passage indicates that the virus infects only rabbits, so you can eliminate (B). Since the foxes rely on the rabbits for food, the foxes are not in competition with the rabbits for food, so you can eliminate (C). Finally, because the virus infects only rabbits, the foxes are unlikely to evolve to become more resistant to disease under these circumstances, so (D) is not the credited answer.

28. **B** According to the introductory sentence, a solar eclipse occurs when the Sun cannot be seen from the Earth. Choice (A) claims that a solar eclipse occurs when the Moon is no longer visible from the Earth, so you can eliminate (A). Based on the information in the figure, a solar eclipse occurs when the Moon is situated directly between the Earth and the Sun. Note that in the figure, parts of the Earth are in the umbra, or deepest part of the shadow, of the Moon. Since this is the situation that (B) describes, (B) is the correct answer. If light rays intercept one another, the resulting light would likely be brighter, rather than darker, so (C) is not the credited answer. The figure shows that the Earth, not the Sun, is in the Moon's umbra, so you can eliminate (D).

29. **B** According to the passage, penicillin prevents the growth of new bacteria. Therefore, the correct answer should involve an illness caused by bacteria. The chart indicates that streptococcal bacteria cause strep throat. Therefore, penicillin is likely to be an effective treatment for strep throat.

30. **D** The airplane travels at twice the speed of sound. The speed of sound is given as 343 meters per second, so the speed of the airplane is $2 \times 343 = 686$ meters per second. The question asks for the speed in miles per hour. First, convert meters into miles by setting up the following proportion:

$$\frac{1 \text{ mile}}{1{,}609 \text{ meters}} = \frac{x \text{ miles}}{686 \text{ meters}}$$

Then, cross-multiply and divide to find x, to get 0.426 miles. Now convert 1 second into hours:

$$\frac{1 \text{ hour}}{3{,}600 \text{ seconds}} = \frac{y \text{ hours}}{1 \text{ second}}$$

Cross-multiply and divide to find y to get 0.000278. Finally divide the miles and the hours to get $\frac{0.426}{0.000278} = 1{,}532.37$. The closest answer is (D).

31. **D** According to the passage, both plants were green and were hybrids, so you can eliminate (A), (B), and (C), leaving only (D). If both parents carry a hidden yellow gene, then some of the offspring may be yellow (genotype gg), so the passage supports (D).

32. **A** The passage states that in hybrids the dominant gene hides the expression of the recessive gene. Therefore, an individual who has both the dominant gene for dimples and the recessive gene for a lack of dimples will have dimples. The correct answer is (A). Choices (B) and (C) do not accurately reflect dominant and recessive traits, while (D) misstates the passage's information.

33. **C** According to the graph, the temperature increases, then remains constant while the sample melts, then increases, then stays constant while the sample boils, and then increases. Since this is the scenario that (C) describes, the correct answer is (C). Note that a horizontal line means that the variable on the y-axis, in this case, temperature, is not changing.

34. **The area labeled C** represents the sample at the point when it is between melting and boiling. Such a sample would be liquid, so if you selected a point near C, then you selected the correct region of the graph. Before the sample melted, it would be entirely solid, so the region of the graph near A would not represent a time during which the sample would be liquid. During melting, some of the sample would be solid and some of the sample would be liquid, so the region of the graph near B would not represent a time during which the sample would be liquid. During boiling, some of the sample would be liquid and some of the sample would be gas, so the region of the graph near D would not represent a time during which the sample would be liquid. After boiling, the sample would be entirely gas, so the region of the graph near E would also not represent a time during which the sample would be liquid.

35. **B** The passage states that bees are important because they pollinate flowering plants, so (B) is supported by the passage. While (A) describes another role of bees, that role is not mentioned in the passage. Choices (C) and (D) do not describe actions that bees take, and are therefore both incorrect.

Part III
Reasoning Through Language Arts: Reading

Chapter 5
Reading Overview

At 150 minutes, Reasoning Through Language Arts (RLA) is the longest of the four GED® subject tests, combining 95 minutes of Reading and Language, a 10-minute break, and the 45-minute Extended Response (essay) section. We'll talk about the language questions and Extended Response section in upcoming chapters. For now, let's look at Reading, which will take up most of your time in this section.

Need some extra help with reading comprehension? Register your book online to download our Reading Comprehension supplement from your Student Tools! See pages viii–ix for details.

You're more likely to encounter informational (nonfiction) texts than literary passages, which is good news if you've ever had to struggle with complex literary language and ideas while the clock ticks. Only 25 percent of the reading passages will be literary; 75 percent will be informational material, which tends to be more straightforward, with concrete language and clearer presentation.

RLA AND THE REAL WORLD

The focus on informational material reflects the GED® test's emphasis on the skills required for a career or college. Employees in every industry and at all levels are expected to respond appropriately to the information they receive, and college students need to work with large volumes of information. That's why the reading passages and questions, with their emphasis on informational material, are considered so important in predicting readiness for a career or for college.

Therefore, the Reading section is all about critical thinking and active reading—analyzing and questioning the passage as you go through it instead of just passively absorbing what it says. You'll see six to eight passages of up to 900 words each, and you will need to show that you not only understand the material, but that you can *do* something with it—summarize it, find reasoning flaws in it, or make inferences from it, for example. (We'll get into that in more detail when we discuss the types of questions you can expect.)

Taking this test gives you a chance to develop and demonstrate critical thinking and analytical skills for potential employers or college admissions officers. The strategies you'll discover as you work through this book will help you prepare, so you'll walk into the testing center knowing what to expect and feeling confident in your abilities.

Most of the reading passages are nonfiction texts taken from the real world of the workplace and academia.

WHAT KIND OF READING PASSAGES ARE ON THE RLA TEST?

The passages span a range of difficulty (more good news), starting with the type of material that would be appropriate for a student just entering high school. (Some are set at the high school graduation level.) And the topics have been chosen to appeal to the majority of test takers, so there's a good chance you'll find most of the passages interesting to read.

What are they about? Well, informational passages could cover a broad range of topics, as long as they're nonfiction. Readings are drawn from both the workplace and the academic worlds; they could be from ads or letters for customers, and from speeches, manuals, or government documents, for example. A literary passage will tell a good story, with vivid characters and a strong narrative line.

WHAT KINDS OF QUESTIONS ARE ON THE TEST?

The GED® test is very systematic about the reading skills it assesses, following a detailed set of criteria called the Common Core State Standards (CCSS). So what? So now we know what reading skills the test writers are looking for, which determines the passages they select and the questions they ask.

In fact, there are seven of these reading standards, each with a dizzying array of subsections. Only some subsections will appear on different versions of the test, but you can bet that each of the seven main standards will show up somewhere. And that, in turn, tells us the seven main question tasks you can expect.

> **Where Are the Answers?**
> They're in the reading passages, although they may not always be obvious. You're expected to use your critical thinking skills, analyze the text, dig beneath the surface, and make inferences. Don't draw on your own knowledge and experience; they could lead you astray. Rely only on the information in the passages.

The questions will appear in two formats. Most will be multiple choice, with four choices. As always, Process of Elimination is your friend with multiple-choice questions. If you start by looking for what's clearly *wrong*, you should find you can eliminate a couple of the choices, and then look for the *right* answer in the other two—or, worst case, *guess* at which one is right. By using Process of Elimination to get rid of two of the four choices, you've just increased your chances of making a correct guess to 50 percent instead of the original 25 percent.

The computer-based test also presents you with drag-and-drop questions, in which you could be asked to arrange events in the proper order, or sort out which of two authors made which statements. Your options will be mixed up, and you'll need to "drag" them, one at a time, to a chart full of empty boxes and "drop" them into the correct positions on the chart. There will be only one or two drag-and-drop questions per passage, and you might find they're kind of fun to do—a nice break from the multiple-choice questions that predominate. (See Chapter 3 for an illustration of what a drag-and-drop question looks like.)

Most questions are worth one point, but some might be worth two (such as the example mentioned in the previous paragraph, in which you need to match statements to one of two different authors), so the number of questions per passage isn't set in stone. You can expect a total of about 48 questions spread across six to eight passages.

Question Tasks

The seven main reading skills the test writers are assessing lead to seven main question tasks.

1. Main Idea or Theme
2. Development (of Ideas, Events, or Characters)
3. Language Use
4. Structure
5. Purpose (or Point of View)
6. Evaluation (of the Author's Argument or Reasoning)
7. Comparison (of Different Passages that Deal with Similar Topics)

You'll notice there's no plain old "comprehension" question task in that list. Comprehension is a given on the GED® test—you need to understand the passage before you can do any of the things the questions will ask you to do with it. Download and read the supplemental tutorial on reading comprehension, if you need to.

A question's format (multiple choice or drag and drop) will NOT tell you what task it's asking you to perform.

One last tip about the questions: Read each one carefully to make sure you understand what it's asking you to do. It's important not to confuse the question's task with its format. Just because the last drag-and-drop question was a development task asking you to arrange events in the proper sequence, for example, doesn't mean the next one is. It could be a comparison question asking you to sort out which of two authors said what, or a purpose question asking you to choose the words that most accurately describe the author's point of view.

Let's take a closer look at what each question task is asking you to do with the passage. In the next two chapters, we'll work through examples of informational and literary passages with the seven question tasks.

Main Idea or Theme

This is what we like to call a "helicopter question," because it asks you to take the 10,000-foot view of the passage (or perhaps of one or more paragraphs in it). This is not about details or writing techniques, but about the big picture. When you look out the helicopter window and see all the details and writing techniques below, what overall main idea or theme do they convey?

In **main idea** questions, look at the forest, not the trees.

The question will probably then ask you to *do* something with that big-picture overview you've gained—identify the details that support it, for instance, or draw a conclusion by stitching together the main ideas of a few different paragraphs. Whatever task the question sets, your first step is to get a clear view of that main idea or theme.

Development (of Ideas, Events, or Characters)

The key to development questions is that the passage starts at Point A and ends up at Point B. You need to follow the route the author takes to get there.

For some tasks, think of driving to a destination, passing different landmarks along the way. This works for such tasks as arranging events in the proper order (a classic "drag-and-drop" assignment). For other questions, think of a jumble of building blocks (Point A), and piling them carefully on top of each other to construct a tall tower (Point B). This type of task might ask how a particular character contributes to the progression of the plot in a literary passage, or what you can infer about that character from the separate details the author has given. Other development questions might ask you how the author's ideas are connected (cause and effect? problem and solution?), or how the context chosen for an informational passage influences its meaning.

In **development** questions, follow the author's route from Point A to Point B.

It's all about getting from Point A to Point B, whether that involves encountering things one after another as you travel through the passage, or seeing how one thing builds upon something that came before it, or figuring out how the separate elements connect to create the whole.

Language Use

You'll come across some unfamiliar words in Reading passages, and Language Use questions ask you to figure out an unfamiliar word's meaning from its context. The words won't be obscure technical terms that only a specialist, such as an economist or a master electrician, would know. They'll be words that aren't specific to any particular field of study—words such as "specificity" and "formulate" (in informational material) or "unabashedly" and "faltered" (in literary passages). Look at what the context is telling you, try substituting a word you know for the unfamiliar word, and see whether it makes sense. Here's an example.

In **language use** questions, figure out the word's meaning from the context.

> Although the mayor and town council were initially ardent supporters of a new public library building, their position faltered when the cost estimates started coming in.

What does the context tell you about "ardent" and "faltered"? Well, the cost estimates were apparently higher than expected, causing local officials to reconsider. If you guessed from that a meaning of "enthusiastic" or "passionate" for "ardent" and "weakened" for "faltered," you'd be right. You can read more about guessing a word's meaning from its context in the Reading Comprehension supplement.

Language use questions might go further, too, and ask you what impact the author's word choice has on the tone or the meaning of the passage. For example, someone who offers to "assist you in reaching out to a competent attorney" is setting a more formal tone than someone who offers to "help you find a good lawyer."

In **structure** questions, ask yourself, "Why is it there?"

Structure

Structure questions could ask what a particular part of the passage adds to the author's purpose or to the development of the author's ideas. In other words, why is it there? That's the question to ask yourself with structure questions. Why did the author put a particular description or instruction, sentence or paragraph in the passage, and why does it appear where it does?

Hunting for transitional or signal words will be a big help here. What are those? They're words that indicate a change (or transition)—perhaps from one opinion to another—or that signal a relationship—perhaps between two statements. Consider the following example:

> I prefer living in a big city because there are so many things to do. *On the other hand,* (change to the opposite point of view) a small town offers warmth and a sense of community that big cities lack.

> Frosty-Man air conditioners are the most energy-efficient units on the market. *In addition,* (signal that the author is going to build upon a previous point), with an average lifespan of 15 years, they are the most reliable.

Some Common Transition and Signal Words

Changing course:
- alternatively
- however
- nevertheless
- on the other hand
- otherwise

Adding:
- also
- in addition
- furthermore
- moreover
- not only...but also

Reaching a conclusion:
- accordingly
- as a result
- consequently
- on the whole
- therefore

In the first example above, the transition to the opposite opinion reveals something important about the character making the statements—they may be indecisive or confused or perhaps weak. In the second case, the author is strengthening the goal of promoting Frosty-Man air conditioners by building a list of their advantages. Transition and signal words help give the reader a smoother ride through the author's points.

Purpose (or Point of View)

Here's another helicopter question. From 10,000 feet above the passage, looking at what all of the details and descriptions and sections add up to as a whole, for what purpose did the author write this passage? Did the author want to persuade readers to do something? Educate them? Entertain them? Defend a position against someone who has publicly attacked it?

A related question asks about the author's point of view. Overall, is the author positive about the subject of the passage? Critical? Neutral? Nailing down the point of view can add another dimension to the author's purpose. For instance, if the purpose seems to be to persuade readers to join a local ski club, but the tone seems neutral about the health benefits of skiing and the author strongly cautions readers about the risks of injury, you've got to wonder if promoting the ski club is really the purpose of this piece.

There could even be a deeper, more subtle purpose underlying the obvious surface goal, or perhaps the purpose is not even explicitly stated. That doesn't mean the author's point of view and purpose are difficult to figure out, though, if you just use your critical thinking skills.

Take a look at this brief excerpt, for instance:

Excerpt from *A Narrative of the Life of Frederick Douglass, An American Slave,* by Frederick Douglass, 1845

I was utterly astonished at her goodness. I scarcely knew how to behave towards her. She was entirely unlike any other white woman I had ever seen. I could not approach her as I was accustomed to approach other white ladies. My early instruction was all out of place. The crouching servility, usually so acceptable a quality in a slave, did not answer when manifested toward her. Her favor was not gained by it; she seemed to be disturbed by it.

Even from these few sentences it's pretty clear that the author's purpose, on the surface, is to describe an event in his life, while "crouching servility" gives a clue that his unstated purpose and point of view are critical of slavery.

Besides simply asking you to identify the author's purpose or point of view, these questions might ask what rhetorical techniques the author uses to achieve their purpose more effectively. What are rhetorical techniques? They're simply tools that writers use, like hammers or wrenches, to get the job done better.

In **purpose** questions, ask yourself, "What did the author want to accomplish by writing this?"

One common rhetorical technique is analogy—comparing something to another thing that will be more familiar to readers, in order to help them understand the author's point and increase the chance that they will agree with it. For instance, the passage might explain that "a Hemi engine is more powerful than a flathead engine because the Hemi is designed to minimize heat loss and unburned fuel, in much the same way as a toaster oven is more energy efficient than a full sized oven." Because most people are familiar with toaster ovens and full-sized ovens, this comparison helps the reader to see the relationship between Hemi engines and flathead engines.

Another common rhetorical technique is repetition. Think of the last ad you saw for a new car. How many times, in how many different ways, did the ad tell you that you would be powerful, free, safe, and environmentally responsible if only you would buy this car?

If you wanted to be an extremist, you could find ridiculously long lists of obscure rhetorical techniques (paraprosdokian, anyone?). The GED® test, however, is not extremist. The test writers expect you to recognize only a few of the most commonly used rhetorical techniques, and you can often guess a technique's name just by looking at what it does. Try this one:

In your SnoSqual parka, you'll enjoy unmatched protection from the cold, unrivaled flexibility for your gear, and unsurpassed style on the slopes.

Paraprosdokian, in case you're curious, is a rhetorical technique in which a familiar phrase gets an unexpected ending—for instance, "Discretion is the better part of making a serious mistake." It can be useful for waking up bored readers.

Now the question:

Apply the Strategy
You can use Process of Elimination to answer this question.

1. The writer creates a positive image and desire for a SnoSqual parka through the use of

   A. alliteration.
   B. parallelism.
   C. hyperbole.
   D. repetition.

Remember Process of Elimination, or POE? You can get rid of "repetition"—the sentence doesn't say the same thing over and over. Check out "Some Common Rhetorical Techniques" in the box below, and you'll see that "alliteration" and "hyperbole" are eliminated. So "parallelism" is left, and indeed that's the technique the author uses.

Some Common Rhetorical Techniques

Alliteration: creating rhythm through repeating initial consonant sounds. Example: "The *store's spectacular sales season* yielded enormous profits."

Analogy: enhancing readers' understanding by comparing two things that have similar features. Example: "A jet pump *works much like a drinking straw* in a glass of soda."

Hyperbole: exaggerating a statement to make a point. Example: "I've tried *a million* different ways to open the file you sent, but it's broken."

Metaphor: describing something by saying it's the same as an otherwise unrelated thing. Example: "The empty *highway was a ribbon* stretching over the distant mountains."

Parallelism: stringing together phrases or sentences with similar structures. Example: "*First push the power button, then select fan mode, and finally select the fan speed.*"

Qualifying Statement: toning down what sounds like an extreme statement. Example: "That's the worst lasagna I've ever eaten—*since I had Aunt Mabel's lasagna last week*, that is."

Repetition: stating the same thing in different ways to emphasize a point. Example: "A snow shovel with a curved handle *puts less strain on your back*. It *makes shoveling easier* and *minimizes the risk of injury*."

Simile: adding impact to a description by comparing one thing to another unrelated thing using the word "like" or "as." Example: "His stare was *as cold as ice*."

Understatement: making something sound less significant than it really is to achieve an effect. Example: "The country has a *minor* trade deficit of $3 trillion."

You could also have chosen "parallelism" based simply on what the author's description does: it presents the SnoSqual parka's three advantages (warmth, flexibility, and style) in parallel structures (each starting with an "un-" description and ending with a phrase, such as "from the cold," that puts the advantage in context). The end result is a product claim that sounds organized, trustworthy, and appealing, and would advance the author's purpose of making readers want this coat.

Evaluation (of the Author's Argument or Reasoning)

Yes, you, the GED® test taker, get to evaluate whether the author has done a thorough, reliable, persuasive job of making their case. How's that for giving you power and letting you show off your critical thinking skills?

Evaluation questions ask you to judge the author's evidence, reasoning, or assumptions.

To begin, of course, you need to travel through the passage to create a map of the argument as the author moves from Point A to Point B to Point C to arrive at a final conclusion. Only then will you be able to do what the questions ask you to do with that argument. For evaluation questions, those tasks generally fall into three categories.

First, you could be asked to evaluate the evidence the author uses to support claims. Is the evidence trustworthy—the opinion of a well-known expert in the field, perhaps, or the results of a professional research study? Is the evidence directly applicable to the claim, or does it sound good but really not have much to do with the author's point? Does the author provide *enough* evidence to support a claim, or perhaps no evidence at all?

Second, the question might ask you to evaluate whether the author's reasoning is sound. Here you're looking for what are called logical fallacies—major flaws in reasoning that may not be apparent until you really think about it. Like rhetorical techniques, logical fallacies come in a long list of creatively named types. In this case, the GED® test writers won't expect you to know those names, but they will expect you to recognize faulty reasoning when you see it.

One logical fallacy you might find familiar is called the slippery slope. Politicians often use it to gain support for their positions by generating fear. For example, "If we allow the Bank of Broad River to refuse loans to any company that hasn't been profitable for the past 10 years, pretty soon all of the banks will be refusing those loans and small business in the state will collapse." The first act is the beginning of a snowballing slide down toward destruction. But wait a minute—who

Some Common Logical Fallacies

Slippery Slope—In an attempt to persuade people to do (or not to do) something, this technique claims the result of inaction (or action) will be widespread disaster, but doesn't provide evidence to support that conclusion. Wars have been started this way: "If we don't stop this dictator now, he'll take over every country in the whole region."

Straw Man—This technique exaggerates or misstates an opponent's argument so it's easy to knock it down. For instance, "Advocates of compact fluorescent light bulbs want us all to die from mercury poisoning in order to save energy."

Appeal to Emotion—In appealing for donations, a charity often tells heartbreaking stories of the people it has helped. But do these emotional appeals perhaps hide the fact that the organization is paying its executive director a huge salary, or that it uses half of the money it raises to pay for more fundraising campaigns?

Ad Hominem—If you can't refute the opponent's argument, attack the opponent. An ad hominem fallacy might concede that a prominent scientist's latest published theory "seems to sound promising, but don't forget that this is the author who was suspected of plagiarizing other researchers' work a few years ago."

To explore more logical fallacies, take a look at the Purdue University Online Writing Lab (OWL) at owl.purdue.edu/owl/general_writing/academic_writing/logic_in_argumentative_writing/fallacies.html.

said any other banks would adopt the same policy? What evidence does the author provide to support that claim? The chain of reasoning from one bank's change in policy to the annihilation of small business in the entire state is unreliable.

Third, you might need to dig out the assumptions behind the author's argument and judge whether they're valid. For instance, say a candidate for mayor is trying to persuade voters to support her because her top priority is expanding the mass transit system to reduce traffic gridlock. What are the underlying assumptions? She's presuming that most voters use mass transit or that they even care about it enough to fund it with their tax dollars. She's thinking they would choose mass transit as a solution instead of adding traffic lanes or a new bypass highway. In a large, sprawling city where many businesses and shopping areas are miles away and constructing long rail or subway lines could be very expensive, her assumptions might not be valid. She could just have lost a large group of potential supporters.

Comparison (of Different Passages That Deal with Similar Topics)

In comparison questions, you're looking for what's different and why. Those differences will fall into three broad categories.

First, the two readings could present the same information in different formats. Think, for instance, of a computer blog's feature article about a new tablet and the technical spec sheet for that same product on the manufacturer's website. Both pieces probably include such information as processor speed and memory size, but the two formats will present it in quite different ways. Why? Think about the purposes, audiences, and tone of the two pieces. The article aims to interest a more general audience—readers who are perhaps just investigating tablet brands—and will have a more casual tone. The spec sheet, on the other hand, is designed to give detailed technical information to more knowledgeable readers who are seriously considering a purchase, and will have a neutral, objective tone to inspire confidence in the accuracy of the information.

Second, the two pieces might treat a similar topic differently because they were written in different eras, when writing styles and cultural values differed. Consider, for example, these two quotes about education:

> "I know no safe depository of the ultimate powers of the society but the people themselves; and if we think them not enlightened enough to exercise their control with a wholesome discretion, the remedy is not to take it from them, but to inform their discretion by education."
>
> —Thomas Jefferson

> "What does education often do? It makes a straight-cut ditch of a free, meandering brook."
>
> —Henry David Thoreau

Comparison questions ask about the differences between passages with separate formats, styles, or biases.

Jefferson, one of the Founders, writes in the lengthy, complex, formal sentence structure of his era and his status, at a time when the young democracy was defining itself and establishing its legitimacy. In plain language, he's saying that ordinary people are the only safe source of power and if you don't think they'd exercise it wisely, then educate them to do it. Thoreau, on the other hand, writes with the simplicity of a naturalist during the American Romantic era and sees manufactured institutions, including education, as threats to nature. Even if you weren't familiar with these two authors or the times in which they wrote, you would be able to see the differences in their writing styles and in the values they consider important. The questions will target those more general differences.

The third and trickiest type of comparison questions will present opposing viewpoints on a topic and ask you to delve down to see how the arguments rely on different interpretations of the same facts, or how they emphasize different evidence that supports their positions. Look for authors with rigid opinions who select evidence to support conclusions they've already reached. For example, fracking (or hydraulic fracturing) is a topic for which there is a lot of information—from the shale gas industry on one side and environmental groups on the other. An author could easily construct a strong pro or con argument just by selecting the right research results or expert statements. The GED® test question could expect you to detect that type of bias.

OUR APPROACH

In the next two chapters, we'll look at informational and literary reading passages in more detail, with examples to help you develop strategies for tackling different question tasks. Then, we'll give you a drill for each kind of passage to try on your own.

Chapter 6 Informational Passages

In this chapter, we'll look at informational texts and then guide you through active reading strategies to help you crack the questions.

Think about it—what do you spend more time reading and listening to in a typical day? News reports, advertisements, political speeches and similar nonfiction material, or literary stories? Nonfiction, right? Life is filled with informational material that you need to deal with in some way (even if only to decide to tune it out), so that's what the GED® test emphasizes. In fact, 75 percent of the six to eight reading passages are classified as informational.

The critical thinking and active reading skills you'll gain in preparing for the reading passages will help you sort through the informational material that fills your life outside the test too. With those skills, you'll learn to question, identify flaws in reasoning, recognize a legitimate argument when you see it, and in short, become a wiser, more discriminating consumer of information.

Use critical thinking skills with the information that fills your own life too.

WHAT KIND OF INFORMATIONAL PASSAGES ARE ON THE TEST?

How about an article explaining how wind turbines work? Or a speech from a company's president outlining the great opportunities for growth—and profit—that lie ahead? Or perhaps the results of a study on which foods are the best choices for good cholesterol?

Since the GED® test aims to measure readiness for career and college, subjects can be drawn from both the workplace and the academic worlds. That's a pretty big target, and indeed, the range of real-world subjects is broad.

From the workplace, you could see letters or ads aimed at customers, corporate policy statements, executive speeches, or community announcements about events the company is sponsoring. From the academic world, subjects focus on science (especially energy, human health, and living systems) and on social studies. Those social studies subjects are built around what's called The Great American Conversation, which includes documents created when the United States was founded as well as later discussions about American citizenship and culture. There, you might see editorials or essays, speeches, biographies, letters written by famous people, government documents, court decisions, or contemporary articles.

Informational texts come from the real world of the workplace and from the fields of science and social studies.

Readings could be in the public domain, which means they're old enough that any copyright has expired and they sport the long sentences and flowery language characteristic of earlier styles of writing. The older writing style means that you'll have to apply a fair amount of critical thinking in order to get what the author is saying.

Try this Great American Conversation excerpt, for instance:

Excerpt from *A Defense of the Constitution of Government of the United States of America,* by John Adams, 1786

> If we should extend our candor so far as to own, that the majority of men are generally under the dominion of benevolence and good intentions, yet, it must be confessed, that a vast majority frequently transgress; and, what is more directly to the point, not only a majority, but almost all, confine their benevolence to their families, relations, personal friends, parish, village, city, county, province, and that very few, indeed, extend it impartially to the whole community.

That's how people wrote back in 1786. Once you break this long sentence into pieces, skip over the parts that don't make a direct statement, and substitute simpler words in the parts that do, you end up with a pretty straightforward summary: "Even if we say that most men mean well, we have to admit that almost all of them limit their kindness to the people around them." The context should help you take a good guess at the meaning of words that may not be familiar, such as "candor," "benevolence," and "transgress," as well as the unusual meaning of "own." After you've tossed out the extra words and phrases, though, the only one of these words really needed for your straightforward summary is "benevolence," and the pairing of that word with "good intentions" makes its meaning fairly obvious.

What you won't see among the informational readings are objective, neutral passages that simply describe or explain something, such as you'd find in an encyclopedia or a product instruction manual. The GED® test's informational passages are more complex than that. They will have a "voice"—an author with a specific point of view and purpose. The author might be trying to persuade readers to boycott a particular company, for instance, or the author may be giving a speech criticizing a new government policy. These passages will draw on your analytical and critical thinking skills to discover not only the author's purpose but also what techniques the author uses to support a position, what assumptions the author has made, and whether the argument is logical and sound.

Informational passages are written by an author who has a specific purpose and point of view.

HOW SHOULD I READ INFORMATIONAL PASSAGES ON THE TEST?

First, keep your mind actively engaged with the passage and second, think critically instead of simply accepting the passage at face value.

While you may not have time for full-blown active reading strategies, you'll still need to use them (and your note boards) to some extent in order to seize control of the passage and make it give you what you need, instead of letting the passage run the show. You're on a mission—you have questions to answer in a limited amount of time—and passively absorbing (or worse, skimming through) the passage will only force you to keep going back and rereading it.

Active Reading
Using your **note boards** can remind you to read actively and help you take control of the passage.

How do you read actively? In a nutshell, keep asking questions and looking for specific things as you go through the passage. Hunt for the flaws and gaps that weaken an argument; recognize the structured support and smooth organization that strengthen it. When you read each section or paragraph, summarize quickly, in your own words, what it's saying.

You'll need to do a lot of this in your head—that's about all you have time for—but you can scribble a couple of words to capture a main idea, or a one-word-per-line list of what happens first, second, and so on. You won't need to get far into the passage before you'll know what's important. For many people, just writing something down helps them remember, even if they don't look at their note board again, and searching for words that would be important enough to jot down can force you into active reading mode. You can try using this technique with the drills and practice tests in this book to see how much it helps you.

Questions to Ask As You Read Informational Passages

- What does the author want readers to do or to think after they read this?
- Who is the intended audience?
- What is the author's main point?
- How, and how well, is the main point supported?
- Does the author have an obvious bias or point of view?
- What assumptions does the author make?
- What is the author's tone?
- Is the author's reasoning logical?
- Is the piece complete, or does it leave unanswered questions?
- Are the language and sentence structure appropriate for the audience and for the time in which the author was writing?

Answering those questions as you read will put you in command of just about any informational piece, whether it's from a workplace or an academic context. Then you can start cracking the questions.

PUTTING IT ALL TOGETHER

Let's go through a couple of examples that will help you practice reading actively and approaching the different question tasks.

The following CD review appeared in the pages of *Soul Blues* magazine

1 Even by genre standards, Texas bluesman Sam "Lightnin" Hopkins released a stupefying amount of material during his lengthy career. As a guitar player, he was never what one would call a perfectionist: few of his recordings are free of off-notes or mis-fretted chords, and he had no compunction about putting out version after version of the same song, either under the same or different titles.

2 For such reasons, many fans feel that Hopkins is better served by "Best of" compilations than by individual albums. But how is one to choose which tracks to include on a compilation CD, when there is such a surfeit of material? How can one select the best, say, "Mojo Hand," when there are 30-odd recordings of it floating around? Seemingly every time he sat down to record, he'd do another run through "Mojo Hand." Every time he recorded the song he played it a little differently: each has its recommendations, each its shortcomings. And every one of those takes has been released at some point over the years.

3 Since so many versions of the song were released, none sold appreciably better than the others—making "popular acclaim" a moot point. No particular recording can be called a "Greatest Hit," even though the song itself is probably his best-known composition.

4 So, when it's time to put out another "Lightnin" Hopkins compilation CD, that means it's time to decide upon a "Mojo Hand" to include on it.

5 It would seem that all the intrepid compiler can do is choose one version of "Mojo Hand" that is just as good as (although admittedly no better than) many others...and then do the same for "Katie Mac," and again for "Lightnin's Boogie," and on and on... thus rendering any purported "Best of" album less representative of Sam "Lightnin" Hopkins than of the person putting it together.

6 So it is with this most recent album: the song titles are there, and a fan finds few surprises among them. But do you need *this* album? Do you need these particular versions, culled from various sessions spanning five decades? Do you need yet another "Lightnin" Hopkins CD titled—you guessed it—MOJO HAND?

Before we tackle some questions, let's look at how to read this passage actively by asking yourself questions as you go through it. To train yourself in the active reading techniques you'll need for the test, note your answers on some scratch paper (or at least *think* of your answer) before you read the ones below the questions.

What does the author want readers to do or to think after they read this? The overall impression, by the time you reach the end of the review, is summed up in the question, "do you need *this* album?" (paragraph 6). The author wants readers to understand that, if they already have a selection of "Lightnin" Hopkins's huge roster of albums, they probably don't need this one too.

Who is the intended audience? You can tell by the casual tone, lack of musical terminology (except for "mis-fretted chords" in paragraph 1), and absence of background information on the singer or the songs mentioned, that the reviewer is writing for people who are probably not professional musicians but who are familiar with Hopkins's work.

What is the author's main point? That's in the references to how many versions of a song Hopkins habitually recorded, and in the conclusion that so many versions make "any purported 'Best of' album less representative of Sam 'Lightnin' Hopkins than of the person putting it together" (paragraph 5).

How, and how well, is the main point supported? The difficulty of compiling a truly representative "Best of" album is well supported. The author says that Hopkins "had no compunction about putting out version after version of the same song" (paragraph 1) and that "each [version] has its recommendations, each its shortcomings" (paragraph 2). There is no objective yardstick for selecting what to include, leading to subjective decisions by the person making the selections.

Does the author have an obvious bias or point of view? The author clearly thinks Hopkins was sloppy in creating his body of work—"few of his recordings are free of off-notes or mis-fretted chords, and he had no compunction about putting out version after version of the same song" (paragraph 1).

What assumptions does the author make? The lack of background information about the artist and the songs mentioned reveals an assumption that readers are already familiar with Hopkins's work.

What is the author's tone? You can tell from opinions such as "never what one would call a perfectionist" (paragraph 1) and "all the intrepid compiler can do is choose one version of 'Mojo Hand' that is just as good as (although admittedly no better than) many others" (paragraph 5) that the author is critical of both the singer's careless approach and the objective of creating a "Best of" compilation.

Is the author's reasoning logical? Yes; the author builds a logical chain of reasoning from too many versions of a song, with none standing out as superior, to a compilation that relies on the subjective opinions of an unknown compiler and is therefore of questionable value in representing the best of an artist's work.

Is the piece complete, or does it leave unanswered questions? Since the author places so much weight on the person selecting which version of each song to include, it would be helpful to know who actually made the compilation. Was it someone who had followed Hopkins's career for a long time? Someone who is well versed in that genre of music?

Are the language and sentence structure appropriate for the audience and for the time in which the author was writing? Yes, the language is appropriate for an educated audience, whose members are well versed in this genre of music but are not professional musicians. The sentence structure is contemporary and varied, making the piece interesting to read.

Now that you've got a good sense of what the author is trying to achieve and how they went about reaching that destination, let's look at a few questions. Try to select each answer yourself, using the insight you gained from the active reading questions, before you read the explanation below the choices.

1. The questions in the final paragraph are intended to make the reader

   A. wonder if compilation CDs serve any purpose.
   B. realize that Hopkins was less talented than many listeners believe.
   C. see that this compilation CD may not be a necessary addition to a Hopkins collection.
   D. understand that nobody can predict which version of a song will sell the most copies.

Apply the Strategy
Reading actively can help you to answer this question.

Here's How to Crack It

You got the answer to this structure question (Why is it there?) from the very first active reading question (What does the author want readers to do or to think?) that you asked yourself as you read through the passage. The author wants them to think (C). The last paragraph reinforces the reasons given earlier in the passage: With so many versions of a song, all of about equal value, why would someone need these particular, subjectively chosen versions?

Choice (A) is too broad (the passage is talking only about Hopkins's work); (B) is inaccurate (Hopkins is described as careless, not untalented); and (D) is beside the point (the compilation is being done from an existing body of work, so no prediction is involved, and it is supposed to include the best, not necessarily the best selling).

2. The writer describes the compiler (paragraph 5) as being

   A. misguided.
   B. intelligent.
   C. artistic.
   D. adventurous.

Here's How to Crack It

This language use question is asking you to figure out the meaning of "intrepid" from the context. You've discovered from your active reading that we're not told anything about the compiler's credentials for making selections, and that choosing from a long list of roughly equal versions is, at best, a subjective gamble. Process of Elimination gets rid of (A) (the compiler is not following a wrong path by making a compilation, but just has to make a judgment call when doing so) and of (B) and (C) (intelligence and artistic talent wouldn't help when all of the versions have about the same value). That leaves (D) as the correct answer, and indeed, an adventurous spirit would be useful in taking that subjective gamble with track after track.

3. The author implies that "Katie Mae"

   A. exists in multiple versions.
   B. is better than "Lightnin's Boogie."
   C. was recorded after "Mojo Hand."
   D. has been overshadowed by Hopkins's other songs.

Here's How to Crack It

At its heart, this is a development question. You know from your active reading that this song isn't the main focus of the passage. So what is the author saying about it and how does that contribute to the development of the main point? The answer, as always, is right in the passage. "Katie Mae" is yet another instance of having to choose one version "that is just as good as (although admittedly no better than) many others" (paragraph 5). It's a building block in constructing the main point about any Hopkins compilation representing the compiler, not the singer. So (A) is the only answer that is supported in the passage.

4. The author implies that "Lightnin" Hopkins's body of musical works

   A. is larger than that of any other blues musician.
   B. is filled with too many mistakes for any of the recordings to be considered good.
   C. resists easy song selection processes.
   D. cannot be represented on a compilation CD.

Here's How to Crack It

This question takes the main point, which you've already identified in your active reading questions, and then asks you to take it a step further to figure out what it implies about Hopkins's work. For this question, you'd follow the main point to (C): the many and roughly equal versions of the same songs make selection difficult, leading to a compilation that is more representative of the person doing the selecting than it is of the singer's work. The author never says (or implies) (A), (B), or (D); they are all too extreme for the statements made in the passage.

How Do the Seven Question Tasks Look in an Informational Passage?

Now that we've seen how the active reading questions can help you take control of a passage and answer questions about it, let's go through an example in which we can focus on the seven question tasks in action.

"The Wild West," from *The Life of Abraham Lincoln*
by Henry Ketcham

1 At the beginning of the twentieth century there is, strictly speaking, no frontier to the United States. At the beginning of the nineteenth century, the larger part of the country was frontier. In any portion of the country to-day, in the remotest villages and hamlets, on the enormous farms of the Dakotas or the vast ranches of California, one is certain to find some, if not many, of the modern appliances of civilization such as were not dreamed of one hundred years ago. Aladdin himself could not have commanded the glowing terms to write the prospectus of the closing years of the nineteenth century. So, too, it requires an extraordinary effort of the imagination to conceive of the condition of things in the opening years of that century.

2 The first quarter of the century closed with the year 1825. At that date Lincoln was nearly seventeen years old. The deepest impressions of life are apt to be received very early, and it is certain that the influences which are felt previous to seventeen years of age have much to do with the formation of the character. If, then, we go back to the period named, we can tell with sufficient accuracy what were the circumstances of Lincoln's early life. Though we cannot precisely tell what he had, we can confidently name many things, things which in this day we class as the necessities of life, which he had to do without, for the simple reason that they had not then been invented or discovered.

3 In the first place, we must bear in mind that he lived in the woods. The West of that day was not wild in the sense of being wicked, criminal, ruffian. Morally, and possibly intellectually, the people of that region would compare with the rest of the country of that day or of this day. There was little schooling and no literary training. But the woodsman has an education of his own. The region was wild in the sense that it was almost uninhabited and untilled. The forests, extending from the mountains in the East to the prairies in the West, were almost unbroken and were the abode of wild birds and wild beasts. Bears, deer, wild-cats, raccoons, wild turkeys, wild pigeons, wild ducks and similar creatures abounded on every land.

4 Consider now the sparseness of the population. Kentucky has an area of 40,000 square miles. One year after Lincoln's birth, the total population was 406,511, or an average of ten persons—say less than two families—to the square mile. Indiana has an area of 36,350 square miles. In 1810 its total population was 24,520, or an average of one person to one and one-half square miles; in 1820 it contained 147,173 inhabitants, or about four to the square mile; in 1825 the population was about 245,000, or less than seven to the square mile.

5 The capital city, Indianapolis, which is to-day of surpassing beauty, was not built nor thought of when the boy Lincoln moved into the State.

6 Illinois, with its more than 56,000 square miles of territory, harbored in 1810 only 12,282 people; in 1820, only 55,211, or less than one to the square mile; while in 1825 its population had grown a trifle over 100,000 or less than two to the square mile.

7 It will thus be seen that up to his youth, Lincoln dwelt only in the wildest of the wild woods, where the animals from the chipmunk to the bear were much more numerous, and probably more at home, than man.

8 There were few roads of any kind, and certainly none that could be called good. For the mud of Indiana and Illinois is very deep and very tenacious. There were good saddle-horses, a sufficient number of oxen, and carts that were rude and awkward. No locomotives, no bicycles, no automobiles. The first railway in Indiana was constructed in 1847, and it was, to say the least, a very primitive affair. As to carriages, there may have been some, but a good carriage would be only a waste on those roads and in that forest.

9 The only pen was the goose-quill, and the ink was home-made. Paper was scarce, expensive, and, while of good material, poorly made. Newspapers were unknown in that virgin forest, and books were like angels' visits, few and far between.

10 There were scythes and sickles, but of a grade that would not be salable to-day at any price. There were no self-binding harvesters, no mowing machines. There were no sewing or knitting machines, though there were needles of both kinds. In the woods thorns were used for pins.

11 Guns were flint-locks, tinder-boxes were used until the manufacture of the friction match. Artificial light came chiefly from the open fireplace, though the tallow dip was known and there were some housewives who had time to make them and the disposition to use them. Illumination by means of molded candles, oil, gas, electricity, came later. That was long before the days of the telegraph.

12 In that locality there were no mills for weaving cotton, linen, or woolen fabrics. All spinning was done by means of the hand loom, and the common fabric of the region was linsey-woolsey, made of linen and woolen mixed, and usually not dyed.

13 Antiseptics were unknown, and a severe surgical operation was practically certain death to the patient. Nor was there ether, chloroform, or cocaine for the relief of pain.

14 As to food, wild game was abundant, but the kitchen garden was not developed and there were no importations. No oranges, lemons, bananas. No canned goods. Crusts of rye bread were browned, ground, and boiled; this was coffee. Herbs of the woods were dried and steeped; this was tea. The root of the sassafras furnished a different kind of tea, a substitute for the India and Ceylon teas now popular. Slippery elm bark soaked in cold water sufficed for lemonade. The milk-house, when there was one, was built over a spring when that was possible, and the milk vessels were kept carefully covered to keep out snakes and other creatures that like milk.

15 Whisky was almost universally used. Indeed, in spite of the constitutional "sixteen-to-one," it was locally used as the standard of value. The luxury of quinine, which came to be in general use throughout that entire region, was of later date.

16 These details are few and meager. It is not easy for us, in the midst of the luxuries, comforts, and necessities of a later civilization, to realize the conditions of western life previous to 1825. But the situation must be understood if one is to know the life of the boy Lincoln.

17 Imagine this boy. Begin at the top and look down him—a long look, for he was tall and gaunt. His cap in winter was of coon-skin, with the tail of the animal hanging down behind. In summer he wore a misshapen straw hat with no hat-band. His shirt was of linsey-woolsey, above described, and was of no color whatever,

unless you call it "the color of dirt." His breeches were of deer-skin with the hair outside. In dry weather these were what you please, but when wet they hugged the skin with a clammy embrace, and the victim might sigh in vain for sanitary underwear. These breeches were held up by one suspender. The hunting shirt was likewise of deer-skin. The stockings—there weren't any stockings. The shoes were cow-hide, though moccasins made by his mother were substituted in dry weather. There was usually a space of several inches between the breeches and the shoes, exposing a tanned and bluish skin. For about half the year he went barefoot.

18 There were schools, primitive and inadequate, indeed, as we shall presently see, but "the little red schoolhouse on the hill," with the stars and stripes floating proudly above it, was not of that day. There were itinerant preachers who went from one locality to another, holding "revival meetings." But church buildings were rare and, to say the least, not of artistic design. There were no regular means of travel, and even the "star route" of the post-office department was slow in reaching those secluded communities.

19 Into such circumstances and conditions Lincoln was born and grew into manhood.

Source: "Chapter I. The Wild West," *The Life of Abraham Lincoln.* Henry Ketcham, 1901.

1. Based on the passage, how would the author most likely account for the strength of character in a person who grew up in poverty?

   A. A person's childhood has little to no determining influence on their character.
   B. Coping with limited means as a child can strengthen a person's character.
   C. Strength of character is the result of parenting and family relationships.
   D. Enjoying luxuries as a child can weaken a person's character.

Here's a two-part main idea question. First you need to determine which main idea (for the entire passage? for a section of it?) is relevant to the question. Then you need to do something with that main idea. In this case, the question asks you to speculate about how a main idea would apply to a new situation.

Here's How to Crack It

A good way to approach this type of question is to start by eliminating answer choices that have nothing to do with any of the main ideas in the passage. If you used active reading techniques, you should have identified the main idea of each section of the passage as you were going through it, so you should already have a list (either in your head or else jotted down in a few key words).

The passage discusses limited means of everyday life—not luxuries—and makes several statements implying that these circumstances account for the development of character. So (A) and (D) can be eliminated. We can be sure about (B) by eliminating (C), since that choice discusses parenting, while the passage doesn't have any main ideas about family relationships. The correct answer, then, is (B), which expresses the author's claim about rough circumstances in childhood and development of character.

2. One reason the author brings up the conveniences of his own time is to

   A. show that not much has changed since the days of Lincoln's youth.
   B. illustrate the effects of industrial development.
   C. prompt the reader to imagine the lived experiences of young Lincoln.
   D. establish the historical timeline of Lincoln's life.

This development question concerns the overall way in which the author connects, develops, and organizes his ideas.

Here's How to Crack It

You need to look at a development question in the context of the passage as a whole. In this case, why does the author mention the modern "comforts" known in his time when he is describing the conditions of Lincoln's early life? He emphasizes how much development has taken place since the days of "the wild west," from household products to city and state populations. But why is this so important to grasp—and in such detail? Reflecting on the present allows the author to explain this.

The passage says that basic things and familiar marks of civilization were "not dreamed of" in Lincoln's time (paragraph 1), so (A) is clearly not the answer. Also note how (A) uses extreme language—"nothing has changed"—which is usually a suspect answer choice in a GED® question.

There is also no description in the passage to support (B). When the author refers to developments, he is not describing in any detail, and he is not presenting any "effects," other than inventions becoming "necessities of life" (paragraph 2). No dates are given for inventions or for Lincoln's life, as we would see for a historical timeline, so (D) does not fit.

That leaves (C), which we can confirm as the author's *stated* reason; he says that "it requires an extraordinary effort of the imagination to conceive of the condition of things" that Lincoln experienced in his time. And since it's so hard for the reader to shed what they know and imagine the past, the author supplies as much detail as possible.

3. In paragraph 3, when describing the environment in which Lincoln grew up, the author uses the word "wild" numerous times. What implications of the word "wild" apply to Lincoln's home region? Drag the most accurate answers into the empty boxes below. (For this example, letters have been added to each answer choice to clarify the explanation that follows.)

(a) barbaric
(b) uncultivated
(c) vicious
(d) natural
(e) neglected
(f) free

In this language use question, you'll need to consider the context of the passage as a whole to determine why the author chose to use a particular word.

Here's How to Crack It

Think about the main idea the author conveys about conditions of Lincoln's everyday life and character. He is not describing the people of the region at that time as "barbaric" (a); in fact, he explicitly says that they were *not* less "morally" or "intellectually" developed. He does mention the learning or education of people who live in the woods, like young Lincoln, but in terms of closeness to the land, which is "uncultivated" (b) and "natural" (d).

That leaves one remaining answer to fill in the third slot. Although the author uses the word "wild" to refer to animals, this meaning does not apply to the description of the region and its character. We can then rule out "vicious" (c). But what about the other meaning of "wild" describing animals as "free" (f)? Living on land unconstrained by development is key to Lincoln's character, according to this author's account, so this meaning of "free" does apply to the region's way of life. Finally, we can leave out "neglected," since this meaning of "wild" implies a failure or lapse in attention or care. To recap, the answers in the box should be (b), (d), and (f).

4. What primary function does the physical description of Lincoln as a boy (paragraph 17) serve in the passage?

   A. to express ridicule toward the subject of the passage
   B. to introduce contrast in the author's depiction
   C. to visualize Lincoln in the setting of his development
   D. to reinforce the author's credibility with researched facts

Here's a structure question: Why did the author insert a whole paragraph of physical description of Lincoln as a boy? What do these details add to achieving the purpose of the passage?

Here's How to Crack It

A good way to approach this type of question is to ask yourself what the passage would be like without the elements identified in the question (the physical description, in this case). If you've practiced active reading techniques (asking yourself about the author's audience, main point, purpose, and so forth) as you worked through the passage, you should have a good idea of what the author is trying to achieve. Could he do it as effectively without the physical description? Why not?

Remember that this passage is the opening chapter of a biography, and it was written for an audience living in a different time than the subject. So the author's purpose here is to connect his very detailed description of this past era with his overall subject: the story of Lincoln's growth from a boy to historical leader. The physical description in paragraph 17 calls the appearance of young Lincoln, fully in his historical context, into the reader's mind. Choice (C) stands out as the most fitting answer.

To support this choice, we can quickly reason through the others, (A), (B), and (D): there is no ridicule or making fun of Lincoln in the author's language; there is no contrast between Lincoln's physical description and the picture created by the entire passage (the opposite, in fact); and there are no more researched facts in this paragraph than in the passage as a whole.

5. What is the relationship between the author's point of view and his purpose?

   A. The point of view is aligned with the author's purpose.
   B. A different point of view would advance his purpose more effectively.
   C. His point of view changes at different points in the passage.
   D. The purpose and point of view work against each other.

This purpose/point of view question demands a "big picture" analysis of the passage as a whole.

Here's How to Crack It

First, consider that the passage is a chapter of a biography entitled *The Life of Abraham Lincoln.* In a biography of a well-known historical person, the author's purpose is to give an account of the subject's life, most often beginning, as with this chapter, by detailing the conditions of childhood.

The point of view of the author remains consistent throughout the passage. He's steady in conveying the importance of understanding his subject. He's also measured in how much can be known about the distant era he's presenting, but confident in his purpose of getting the reader to imagine. Choice (A)—the purpose and point of view are aligned—describes the passage as a whole.

We can be sure about this choice by eliminating the others: (C) is incorrect because it deals with only half of the question. It ignores purpose and how that relates to these changing points of view. Choices (B) and (D) say essentially the same thing: the author's point of view and purpose are not working together, which is not correct.

6. As the passage describes state and city populations (paragraphs 4–6), the underlying assumption is that

   A. the number of people per square mile increased since Lincoln's youth.
   B. census data about populations is not accurate.
   C. there are too many people living in the Midwestern U.S.
   D. the reader will relate positively to the development of the city.

This evaluation question requires you to identify the assumptions underlying a topic.

Here's How to Crack It

First, you need to locate the topic that the question is asking about, and then consider the viewpoint that may come across in statements of that topic. In paragraphs 4 and 6, the author is citing population data to show that the number of people per square mile has increased over time; these are *facts*, so we know that (A) cannot be an answer to the question about the author's assumption. We can also eliminate (B), because why would the author cite all of this data if he thought it was inaccurate? That leaves (C) and (D) to consider. There are no statements to suggest any opinions about there being "too many people," but we *can* locate the author's view of the city, expressed as if it is shared by his audience: "The capital city, Indianapolis, which is to-day of surpassing beauty" (paragraph 5). Choice (D) is the correct answer.

Now, assume that the passage is paired with the following brief excerpt.

Rocky Flats: From Hazard to Haven

1 On the site of what was once a highly contaminated nuclear weapons production facility, the Rocky Flats National Wildlife Refuge is committed to protecting endangered species. Visitors can now hike, take guided nature tours, cycle, or horseback-ride along a year-round trail system. The grand-scale cleanup, initially estimated at $37 billion over 60–70 years, was completed within 10 years for just $7 billion.

2 But just how safe is this former weapons plant site? The debate revolves around the concerns of thousands of nearby homeowners who claim that residual plutonium and other toxins put their health at risk.

7. Drag and drop the concept or theme evident in each passage under the correct passage on the chart. (For this example, letters have been added to each answer choice to clarify the explanation that follows.)

The Wild West	Rocky Flats

(a) environmental risks
(b) influence of material conditions
(c) characteristics of people living in a particular region
(d) consequences of changes to an area

This comparison question requires you to grasp and analyze the major themes of two works that deal with similar topics.

Here's How to Crack It

Four empty boxes, four answer choices. There are no "extra" alternatives to eliminate as a starting point. In a case like this, the best approach is simply to look at each concept or theme in turn and decide which of the two readings best exhibits that trait. If you're not sure about one choice, skip it and see whether there's an empty box left for it at the end.

Both passages discuss environment, but only "Rocky Flats" presents dangers as "risks," so we can move (a) into the right column. Both passages also deal with a physical place, its features, and the impact of these conditions, but the words "material" and "influence" in (b) align with the theme and purpose of the "Wild West" chapter of Lincoln's biography. This goes for (c) as well; although both passages concern the "people living in a particular region," only the "Wild West" text presents information about their "characteristics." That leaves (d) for "Rocky Flats," and we can confirm that the main idea of this passage is about "consequences" to developments in a specific area. To recap: (b) and (c) belong on the left, (a) and (d) on the right.

Informational Passage Drill

Over to you now. Ask yourself the active reading questions as you go through this passage, and make sure your critical thinking skills are in gear. Then try the questions, using your knowledge of the seven question tasks. (The order of those tasks is mixed up in this drill, as it will be in the test.) You can check your answers and reasoning in Part IX: Answer Key to Drills.

Companies use statements of Corporate Social Responsibility (CSR) to explain the values and principles that govern the way they do business, and to make a public commitment to follow them. These documents typically have high-level support from management and the board of directors, and are made available to all stakeholders, from employees to investors, customers to government regulators.

Pine Trail Timber—Statement of Corporate Social Responsibility

1 In carrying out our mission to supply the residential construction industry with the highest quality products from sustainably managed sources, Pine Trail Timber adheres to the following commitments to its stakeholders, to the communities in which it does business, and to the environment.

Responsibility to Stakeholders

2 Our stakeholders place their trust in us, and we work every day to merit that trust by aligning our interests with theirs.

3 All employees deserve a safe, supportive work setting, and the opportunity to achieve their full potential. We stress safety training, prohibit any type of discrimination or harassment, and support employees' efforts to enhance their job-related skills. In return, we expect our employees and officers to devote themselves to fulfilling our commitments to other stakeholders.

4 Investors have a right to expect transparency, sound corporate governance, and a fair return on their investments. We pride ourselves on full disclosure, adherence to the most rigid standards of ethical oversight, and a track record of profitable operations, as our rising stock chart and uninterrupted five-year series of dividend increases show.

5 Our valued customers are entitled to exceptional value and service. Our product innovation and wise management of resources ensure that they receive both.

6 Our suppliers rely on us for fair dealing in specifying our requirements and in meeting our obligations. We consider our suppliers to be our partners—when we succeed, they succeed.

7 We meet the expectations of government and industry regulators by complying with all applicable laws of the countries in which we carry out our business operations, and cooperating in all authorized investigations.

8 We fulfill our duty to the media and the public through providing timely information about any events that might have an impact beyond our operations, and making senior spokespeople available on request.

Support for Local Communities

9 We aim to enhance our host communities. Our presence provides training and jobs, and contributes to the local economy.

10 In the field and in our processing facilities, we recognize the impact our activities may have on local groups. We strive for open communication in order to build relationships, and create opportunities for consultation to foster understanding of our plans.

11 In urban centers where we have administrative operations, we match charitable donations made by our employees and run programs that give employees a block of time off work to volunteer with local organizations. Pine Trail Timber routinely forms one of the largest volunteer groups in the annual Arbor Day activities in several countries, planting trees and teaching other participants how to care for them.

Respect for the Environment

12 We recognize that our current and future success depends on the wise use of renewable resources. We value our reputation as a conscientious steward of the lands that furnish our products.

13 All of our production and processing operations worldwide are certified by the Forest Stewardship Council (FSC) as meeting its rigorous standards for responsible resource management. The FSC certification assures our stakeholders and host communities of independent verification of our operations.

14 Through constant process innovation, we aim to make the least possible use of non-renewable resources in our production.

15 We strive to leave the smallest possible footprint and, where necessary, carry out prompt and thorough remediation. After we finish our operations in an area but before we leave, we ensure that the land is returned to a state where it can produce abundant crops, offer a welcoming home for wildlife, and provide outdoor enjoyment for local residents.

We're Listening

16 If you have any questions or comments about our Corporate Social Responsibility commitments, we invite you to contact Mr. Joseph d'Argill, our Chairman and Chief Executive Officer.

1. The CSR statement specifies that employees are expected to "devote themselves to fulfilling our commitments to other stakeholders" (paragraph 3) because
   A. the authors of the CSR statement are worried that they can't take responsibility themselves for the promises they're making.
   B. the authors know that stakeholders will usually be dealing with lower-level employees instead of with the senior executives and board members who created the CSR statement.
   C. the authors want to exert additional influence on employees through this public statement that stakeholders can expect everyone who works for Pine Trail Timber to fulfill these commitments.
   D. employees work in many different locations and countries, far from the home office where the senior executives and directors behind the statement work.

2. When the company refers to "obligations" (paragraph 6), it means
   A. its responsibilities as a good corporate citizen.
   B. burdens it must bear.
   C. its duties.
   D. money it owes.

<u>Question 3</u> refers to the following table.

Number of employees	**North America**	**Central America**	**Africa**	**Southeast Asia**
In production jobs	54,200	17,054	3,214	9,875
In remediation jobs	1,210 [2.2%]	651 [3.8%]	55 [1.7%]	62 [0.6%]
Earned safety certification	11,254 [20.8%]	1,675 [9.8%]	424 [13.2%]	681 [6.9%]
On worker safety committees	325 [0.6%]	153 [0.9%]	107 [3.3%]	31 [0.3%]
Designated as safety representatives	22 [0.04%]	103 [0.6%]	28 [0.9%]	3 [0.03%]
Refused dangerous work	318 [0.59%]	122 [0.72%]	116 [3.6%]	19 [0.02%]

3. Compare the figures in the table above to the overall company image portrayed in the CSR statement. From the answer choices below, identify the *most significant* similarity or difference in topics covered by *both* of the two sources. (Assume the percentages shown in the table are correct; you do not need to calculate them.)

   A. The table suggests the safety and remediation commitments made in the CSR statement apply unevenly to different geographic locations.

   B. The table reinforces the extensive worldwide operations suggested in the text statement.

   C. The table reveals that workers have more control over their safety than the text statement says.

   D. The table confirms the CSR statement's commitment to restoring the land after the company's work there is complete.

4. The authors wrote and published this CSR statement because

   A. government regulations require them to do it.

   B. they want to present a public image of Pine Trail Timber as a responsible, ethical, trustworthy company.

   C. all of their competitors in the forestry industry have one.

   D. they want to explain the company's mission.

5. Decide whether the claims below are supported in Pine Trail Timber's CSR statement or whether the company makes the claim without providing support for it. Drag each claim to the appropriate column in the chart.

(For this drill, write the letter next to each claim in the appropriate column.)

Claim Is Supported	Claim Is Not Supported

(a) We manage resources responsibly.

(b) We consult with local residents.

(c) We take responsibility for the claims made in this CSR statement.

(d) We put the safety of our employees first.

(e) We provide exceptional customer service.

(f) We run a profitable business.

6. Considering the overall theme of the CSR statement, what conclusion can you draw from the last two paragraphs in the "Responsibility to Stakeholders" section (paragraphs 7–8)?

A. The company sometimes fails in its goals of being a trustworthy steward and improving the areas in which it has operations.
B. Responsibilities to regulators and to the public are considered less important than responsibilities to employees and other stakeholders.
C. The company fosters close relationships with governments and the media.
D. There is a strong sense of responsibility to stakeholders who are not directly involved with the company's business operations.

7. What is the most significant contribution made by the mention of Arbor Day (paragraph 11) to the company image portrayed in the CSR statement?

A. It reinforces the global nature of the company's operations, since Arbor Day is celebrated in many different countries.
B. It supports the company's claim of giving employees time off work to volunteer for charitable activities.
C. It would help attract potential employees who want to preserve the environment.
D. It demonstrates the company's wise use of resources, since participation in Arbor Day would replace some of the trees the company takes in its harvesting operations.

Chapter 7
Literary Passages

In this chapter, we'll move on to fictional texts and how to crack questions about them.

Literary passages should keep your interest up if you prefer the world of fiction to informational material. The literary selections are more fanciful, imaginative, and for some people, easier to read. On the other hand, though, fictional passages leave a lot more scope for complexity—flashbacks, dream sequences, raving mad narrators, multiple layers of meaning—and can challenge your active reading and critical thinking skills more than informational passages drawn from the real world.

WHAT KIND OF LITERARY PASSAGES ARE ON THE TEST?

From the modern era or from an older time, with lots of dialogue or with paragraphs of lengthy descriptions—you could find it all in the literary selections. These passages don't fall into clear categories as the informational passages do. What the literary selections have in common is good storytelling—a strong plot line and well-developed characters—and the use of literary elements such as imagery and rich language. Beyond that, though, you could encounter just about any topic or type of literature.

These passages run between 450 and 900 words, like the informational passages, and make up roughly one-quarter of the reading tasks. Like the informational passages, they may represent earlier eras when different styles of writing—such as the long, intricate sentences of Victorian novels—were common. Take a look at this one, for instance:

Excerpt from *The Pickwick Papers*, by Charles Dickens, 1837

They had no sooner arrived at this point, than a most violent and startling knocking was heard at the door; it was not an ordinary double-knock, but a constant and uninterrupted succession of the loudest single raps, as if the knocker were endowed with the perpetual motion, or the person outside had forgotten to leave off.

Yes, that's all one sentence and yes, essentially it just says "someone kept banging on the door." Early Victorian writers were not known for getting straight to the point, though, and this lengthy description adds vivid images of sight and sound that a modern version would lack. So while literary passages can indeed be filled with complex layers of meaning, they can also (as in this example) convey rather basic information in a wordy, flowery style, in keeping with the writer's era. The active reading technique of summarizing in your own words will help you see the difference between real complexity and writing styles that may look complex but really aren't.

> Even though literary passages tell interesting stories, you still need to read them actively and think critically about them on the test.

Greater length can also lead to more complexity, though. Now there's room for things like flashbacks, for knocking events out of sequence, or for different levels of meaning. (For instance, when is a house a place to live and when does it symbolize a particular culture's claim to a stretch of land?)

Consider this brief excerpt, drawn from a literary source that is classified at a level appropriate for grades 9 and 10:

Excerpt from *Candide, Or The Optimist*
by Voltaire

1 The French captain soon saw that the captain of the victorious vessel was a Spaniard, and that the other was a Dutch pirate, and the very same one who had robbed Candide. The immense plunder which this villain had amassed, was buried with him in the sea, and out of the whole only one sheep was saved.

2 "You see," said Candide to Martin, "that crime is sometimes punished. This rogue of a Dutch skipper has met with the fate he deserved."

3 "Yes," said Martin; "but why should the passengers be doomed also to destruction? God has punished the knave, and the devil has drowned the rest."

Excerpt from *Candide, Or The Optimist*, by F.A.M. de Voltaire. Translated by H. Morley. 1888 (1759), George Routledge and Sons, Ltd.

Even from this short exchange, you can guess that something more is going on than the simple sinking of a ship in battle. There are indications of much broader concepts of justice, retribution, and good and evil. You can expect layers of meaning like that in many of the literary passages.

HOW SHOULD I READ LITERARY PASSAGES ON THE TEST?

You can't just relax and soak up a story the way you can when you're reading a novel for entertainment. You're taking a test and need to seize control and shake the right answers out of the passage. That means active reading again. The questions to ask yourself as you go through the passage will be different than they were for informational texts, though.

Questions to Ask as You Read Literary Passages

- What's happening?
- Who are the main characters?
- Who is telling the story?
- What is the setting?
- What is the mood?
- Who is the intended audience?

PUTTING IT ALL TOGETHER

Let's work through a couple of examples that will help you practice reading actively and approaching the different question tasks in literary passages.

Excerpt from *The Moonstone*
by William "Wilkie" Collins

1 "I'm afraid Rosanna is sly. It looks as if she had determined to get to that place you and I have just come from, without leaving any marks on the sand to trace her by. Shall we say that she walked through the water from this point till she got to that ledge of rocks behind us, and came back the same way, and then took to the beach again where those two heel marks are still left? Yes, we'll say that. It seems to fit in with my notion that she had something under her cloak, when she left the cottage. No! not something to destroy—for, in that case, where would have been the need of all these precautions to prevent my tracing the place at which her walk ended? Something to hide is, I think, the better guess of the two. Perhaps, if we go on to the cottage, we may find out what that something is?"

2 At this proposal, my detective-fever suddenly cooled. "You don't want me," I said. "What good can I do?"....

3 "If I go alone to the cottage, the people's tongues will be tied at the first question I put to them. If I go with you, I go introduced by a justly respected neighbour, and a flow of conversation is the necessary result. It strikes me in that light; how does it strike you?"

4 Not having an answer of the needful smartness as ready as I could have wished, I tried to gain time by asking him what cottage he wanted to go to....

5 On the Sergeant describing the place, I recognised it as a cottage inhabited by a fisherman named Yolland, with his wife and two grown-up children, a son and a daughter.... Rosanna's acquaintance with them had begun by means of the daughter, [Lucy, who had] a misshapen foot....[The two girls with deformities] had, I suppose, a kind of fellow-feeling for each other.... The fact of Sergeant Cuff having traced the girl to THEIR cottage, set the matter of my helping his inquiries in quite a new light. Rosanna had merely gone where she was in the habit of going; and to show that she had been in company with the fisherman and his family was as good as to prove that she had been innocently occupied so far, at any rate. It would be doing the girl a service, therefore, instead of an injury, if I allowed myself to be convinced by Sergeant Cuff's logic....

6 Good Mrs. Yolland received us alone in her kitchen. When she heard that Sergeant Cuff was a celebrated character in London, she clapped a bottle of Dutch gin and a couple of clean pipes on the table, and stared as if she could never see enough of him.

7 I sat quiet in a corner, waiting to hear how the Sergeant would find his way to the subject of Rosanna Spearman. His usual roundabout manner of going to work proved, on this occasion, to be more roundabout than ever. How he managed it is more than I could tell at the time, and more than I can tell now. But this is certain, he began with the Royal Family, the Primitive Methodists, and the price of fish; and he got from that (in his dismal, underground way) to the loss of the Moonstone, the spitefulness of our first house-maid, and the hard behaviour of the women-servants generally towards Rosanna Spearman. Having reached his subject in this fashion, he described himself as making his inquiries about the lost Diamond, partly with a view to find it, and partly for the purpose of clearing Rosanna from the unjust suspicions of her enemies in the house. In about a quarter of an hour from the time when we entered the kitchen, good Mrs. Yolland was persuaded that she was talking to Rosanna's best friend, and was pressing Sergeant Cuff to comfort his stomach and revive his spirits out of the Dutch bottle....

8 The great Cuff showed a wonderful patience; trying his luck drearily this way and that way, and firing shot after shot, as it were, at random, on the chance of hitting the mark. Everything to Rosanna's credit, nothing to Rosanna's prejudice—that was how it ended, try as he might; with Mrs. Yolland talking nineteen to the dozen, and placing the most entire confidence in him. His last effort was made, when we had looked at our watches, and had got on our legs previous to taking leave.

9 "I shall now wish you good-night, ma'am," says the Sergeant. "And I shall only say, at parting, that Rosanna Spearman has a sincere well-wisher in myself, your obedient servant. But, oh dear me! she will never get on in her present place; and my advice to her is—leave it."

10 "Bless your heart alive! she is GOING to leave it!" cries Mrs. Yolland....

11 Rosanna Spearman going to leave us! I pricked up my ears at that. It seemed strange, to say the least of it, that she should have given no warning, in the first place, to my lady or to me. A certain doubt came up in my mind whether Sergeant Cuff's last random shot might not have hit the mark. I began to question whether my share in the proceedings was quite as harmless a one as I had thought it. It might be all in the way of the Sergeant's business to mystify an honest woman by wrapping her round in a

> network of lies... Beginning to smell mischief in the air, I tried to take Sergeant Cuff out. He sat down again instantly, and asked for a little drop of comfort out of the Dutch bottle. Mrs. Yolland sat down opposite to him, and gave him his nip. I went on to the door, excessively uncomfortable, and said I thought I must bid them good-night—and yet I didn't go.

This passage is complex in its character development, its layers of appearance and reality, and its unstated implications. Did you pick up those characteristics as you were reading through it? Let's explore the active reading questions for literary passages to find some clues to what's going on under the surface. To sharpen your active reading skills, note your answer on some scratch paper (or at least think of your answer) before you read the one below each question.

Summarize in your own words by answering the classic news questions: who, what, when, where, why, and how?

What's happening? Imagine that you are reading a book, and your friend asks you what the book is about. You wouldn't just start reading aloud to your friend; instead, you'd probably describe the action and characters. In other words, you'd give your friend a summary of the text. If you can summarize a GED® Reading passage in your own words—ideally as you're reading it, not just after—then you're in control.

How do you summarize? A good place to start is to answer as many as possible of the classic news reporter questions: who, what, when, where, why, and how? In this passage, a detective is tracking a girl. He talks the narrator into accompanying him to the fisherman's cottage where he traced the girl. The detective talks to the fisherman's wife and drinks some Dutch gin. He and the narrator start to leave and then return.

So there's not a lot of action in the passage. However, the excerpt is rich in layers. One person's view of what's going on isn't the same as another's. What appears on the surface differs from the reality beneath, particularly when it comes to motivation. The detective is sure the girl has a stolen diamond, but he tells the narrator that a visit to the cottage could help him discover what the girl might have hidden under her cloak. The narrator sees through Cuff's "roundabout manner" (paragraph 7) of trying to get information from Mrs. Yolland, but later wonders whether the sergeant has duped him, too, into doing Rosanna "an injury" instead of "a service" (paragraph 5) by introducing him. Cuff wants to find Rosanna and the diamond, the narrator wants to prove that Rosanna had been "innocently occupied" (paragraph 5), and Mrs. Yolland thinks she is "talking to Rosanna's best friend" (paragraph 7). The answers to some of the classic news questions will differ markedly depending on which character is in focus.

Who are the main characters, and what do we know about them? There are four main characters in this passage, although only three are present.

Mrs. Yolland is a humble fisherman's wife, completely incapable of seeing through Cuff's subtle tactics. A simple and "honest woman" (paragraph 11), she is overwhelmed by the visit from a "celebrated character in London" (paragraph 6) and reassured by the presence of a "respected neighbour" (paragraph 3), so she speaks openly, "placing the most entire confidence" (paragraph 8) in the detective. She even reveals to the narrator that Rosanna was planning to leave his house.

The narrator seems more perceptive than Mrs. Yolland, but even he is no match for Cuff. He doesn't want to go to the cottage because his "detective-fever suddenly cooled" (paragraph 2). Then, however, he allows himself to be persuaded when he learns it's Yolland's cottage, where Rosanna was "in the habit of going," proving that she "had been innocently occupied" (paragraph 5). He recognizes the detective's "roundabout manner" in questioning Mrs. Yolland, but admits that "how he managed it is more than I could tell" (paragraph 7). In addition, the narrator had no idea that Rosanna was planning to leave his house, even though she worked there and he presumably saw her every day. He suspects that Cuff might have deceived him: "I began to question whether my share in the proceedings was quite as harmless a one as I had thought it" (paragraph 11). He senses "mischief in the air" (paragraph 11) and tries to get Cuff to leave, but ends up staying with the sergeant and Mrs. Yolland. The narrator seems unaware and not in control when manipulative tactics and subterfuge are directed at him.

Sergeant Cuff is an expert at reading the other characters and manipulating them to achieve his own ends. He wins Mrs. Yolland's confidence and convinces her that his aim is "clearing Rosanna from the unjust suspicions of her enemies in the house" (paragraph 7). He enlists the narrator's help by giving him an opportunity to prove that Rosanna "had been innocently occupied" (paragraph 5). He is also a skilled reader of evidence, figuring out how Rosanna had moved on the beach to conceal her path.

We only learn about Rosanna through the statements and actions of other characters, yet she is the force that sets the entire passage in motion. She is described as having a deformity (paragraph 5), a servant in the narrator's house, and persecuted by other women servants. Except for the Yolland family, she is alone. She is also devious, planning to leave without telling her employers. Beyond that, Rosanna is an enigma. Would she be capable of stealing a diamond and outwitting Sergeant Cuff? She may be "sly" (paragraph 1), but couldn't fool him with her attempts to avoid being traced on the beach. Why was she preparing to leave in secret? Where would she be able to go? We can't answer those questions from the information in the passage.

Three other characters are simply mentioned: Yolland, the fisherman, his adult son and adult daughter, Lucy, who seems to be Rosanna's only friend.

Who is telling the story? A story can be told by either a first-person narrator (an "I" narrator who is a character in the story) or a third-person narrator (a narrator who is not a character in the story, using "he/she/they," but not "I"). They could be as objective as an unbiased third-person narrator, or they could be highly biased or just plain crazy too. You need to pay close attention to what they reveal about themselves in order to judge whether you can take the story they're telling at face value.

First-person ("I") narrators may not be reliable or objective in telling their stories.

In this case, the narrator can see through Cuff's "usual roundabout manner" (paragraph 7) of questioning someone. However, as we saw in the analysis of his character, he's not particularly reliable or perceptive concerning tactics that are directed at him.

What is the setting? Sometimes the setting (place and time) can add a lot to your grasp of the passage, and sometimes it doesn't reveal much. In this passage, the places—the deserted beach, the fisherman's cottage—reinforce the distance between the celebrated London detective and the other characters. Cuff is in an alien environment, but is still functioning very effectively, revealing his skill. The narrator and Mrs. Yolland are on home ground, but Cuff still manages to get what he wants from both of them.

What is the mood? There is a murky, mysterious mood to this passage that complements the plot line of a clever detective trying to penetrate appearances and discover the truth. Cuff's method of "[mystifying] an honest woman by wrapping her round in a network of lies" (paragraph 11), and the narrator's suspicion that Cuff has outsmarted him, add a negative tone. Does the detective's goal justify his rather devious methods?

In other passages, the mood could be lighthearted or neutral; it could add a lot to your understanding of the passage, or it might not be very helpful. It all depends on the passage.

Who is the intended audience? You might not be able to guess from the passage; it's not as easy with literary texts as it is with informational pieces. If you can get a picture of the intended audience, though, you'll have another layer of insight into the passage. Perhaps it's intended for young readers. That would explain fairly black-and-white characters and straightforward action. Or perhaps it's intended for readers of detective and mystery fiction, as this example is. That's your clue that the undertones you may have sensed in this passage are, in fact, real; these readers would expect and be looking for them.

Now that active reading has given you a firmer grip on the passage, let's tackle a few questions. Try to choose the answer yourself, using the insight gained from the active reading questions, before you read the explanation below the choices.

---

1. What main function does Lucy serve in the passage?

   A. She increases the reader's sympathy for Mrs. Yolland.

   B. She helps create a picture of a "balanced" family.

   C. She makes the reader feel more negatively toward Sergeant Cuff.

   D. She reinforces the impression that Rosanna is alone and vulnerable.

Here's How to Crack It

Here's a structure question as it applies to a literary passage. Lucy isn't present in the excerpt; she's mentioned only briefly. Why? What main purpose does that brief mention serve?

The narrator explains that Rosanna knew the Yolland family through Lucy. That's not one of the answer choices for Lucy's function, though. The fact that Mrs. Yolland has a daughter with a "misshapen foot" (paragraph 5) might add to the sympathy readers feel because of the way Cuff is manipulating her (A). However, the question asks for the main purpose. Is there a stronger choice?

You can guess that there probably is from the fact that the author concentrates his description of Lucy on Rosanna, not on Mrs. Yolland. Both girls have "deformities" and "a kind of fellow-feeling for each other" (paragraph 5). Contrast this with "the hard behaviour of the women-servants generally towards Rosanna" (paragraph 7). Lucy is the only one to whom Rosanna feels a connection. Her colleagues reject and persecute her. That leads to (D), reinforcing the impression of Rosanna as alone (except for Lucy) and vulnerable.

Choice (C) is incorrect because it refers to essentially the same thing as (A). If readers feel sympathy for Mrs. Yolland because of Cuff's behavior toward her, then they would also feel negative sentiments toward Cuff. Again, (D) is a stronger choice. Choice (B) is also incorrect. It's too vague. What does a "balanced" family (presumably a son and a daughter) add to the passage?

2. Does the narrator's account of Sergeant Cuff's questioning of Mrs. Yolland support Cuff's contention that he is "making his inquiries about the lost Diamond...partly for the purpose of clearing Rosanna" (paragraph 7)?

   A. Yes. While he is talking to Mrs. Yolland, Cuff refers to "the hard behaviour of the women-servants generally towards Rosanna" and to the "unjust suspicions of her [Rosanna's] enemies in the house" (paragraph 7), suggesting he wants to help Rosanna.
   B. No. The narrator says that Cuff is "wrapping her [Mrs. Yolland] round in a network of lies" (paragraph 11), implying that Cuff's stated purpose can't be believed.
   C. Yes. The narrator agrees to accompany Cuff to the Yollands' cottage because that allows Cuff to be "introduced by a justly respected neighbour, and a flow of conversation is the necessary result" (paragraph 3). Cuff wants Mrs. Yolland to feel comfortable talking to him.
   D. No. The narrator says Cuff was "firing shot after shot, as it were, at random, on the chance of hitting the mark" (paragraph 8), suggesting that Cuff's questions had a hostile, destructive quality.

Here's How to Crack It

This is an evaluation question as it applies to a literary passage. Here you're evaluating whether the narrator's account of the questioning is consistent with the motive Cuff explains to Mrs. Yolland.

Too much in the narrator's description contradicts the two "yes" choices, so those can be eliminated. The detective's references to Rosanna's enemies (A) are part of his tactic of convincing Mrs. Yolland that "she was talking to Rosanna's best friend" (paragraph 7). And Cuff could just as easily want Mrs. Yolland to open up to him (C) out of a desire to accuse Rosanna as out of a desire to clear her.

That leaves the two "no" choices. Which one provides a more direct answer to the question? Choice (D) has merit. The narrator's descriptions of "firing shot after shot" and "hitting the mark" do suggest hostility rather than goodwill. However, (B) is a more direct answer, and is therefore the correct choice. The narrator's account describes Cuff's questioning as a "network of lies," and therefore does not support Cuff's stated motive, which would also be a lie.

3. When the narrator says Mrs. Yolland was "talking nineteen to the dozen" (paragraph 8), he is referring to her

A. refusal to let Cuff get a word in.
B. attempts to evade Sergeant Cuff's questions.
C. unrealistically positive comments about Rosanna.
D. meaningless chatter about irrelevant topics.

Here's How to Crack It

The passages on the GED® test are often in the public domain, which means they have an older style of writing (such as very long sentences) and terms that aren't familiar to modern readers. (*The Moonstone* was written in 1868.) That's true of both the informational and the literary selections. Language-use questions such as this one will help you develop skills in using context to guess the meaning of an unfamiliar word or term. These questions force you to delve deeper into the passage and understand it more thoroughly (instead of simply skipping over the part you can't figure out). In some cases, they'll help you expand your vocabulary too.

Since this is a literary passage, first ask yourself what's going on when that term is used. Sergeant Cuff is getting nowhere in his attempts to wring some information about Rosanna and the diamond from Mrs. Yolland. He needs—and is exercising—"wonderful patience," firing random questions at her "on the chance of hitting the mark," but all he's hearing is "everything to Rosanna's credit, nothing to Rosanna's prejudice" (paragraph 8). Moreover, Mrs. Yolland is "talking nineteen to the dozen" (paragraph 8).

Process of Elimination (looking for clearly wrong answers and eliminating those first) is an efficient approach when you're really not sure. Mrs. Yolland is talking about a relevant topic (Rosanna), which eliminates (D). The narrator says she's an "honest woman," in contrast to Cuff's "network of lies" (paragraph 11), which gets rid of (C). She places her "entire confidence" (paragraph 8) in the detective, and has been persuaded that he is "Rosanna's best friend" (paragraph 7), so she wouldn't be trying to evade his questions, eliminating (B). Now only (A) is left. Does it make sense? Yes. Mrs. Yolland feels safe talking to Cuff, and is excited about the visit from this celebrated man. As the greater weight of nineteen compared to a dozen suggests, she's talking practically nonstop, outweighing his conversation and making it difficult for him to launch even his random-shot questions.

4. Why does the passage begin with Sergeant Cuff's efforts to trace Rosanna's movements on the beach?
   A. Cuff needs to find out where Rosanna went before he can find the diamond.
   B. The tracking episode shows how clever Rosanna is.
   C. It helps Cuff determine whether Rosanna was carrying something to destroy or something to hide.
   D. Cuff's reasoning while tracking Rosanna illustrates his ability to understand people.

Here's How to Crack It

You could encounter two types of development questions with a literary passage: plot development and character development. Often the two types overlap, such as when the development of a character also advances the plot, or when a development in the plot also reveals more about a character.

The event described in the question falls into that last category. In terms of the plot, Cuff is able to figure out where Rosanna went and decide to go there too. That development in the plot also reveals something new about his character. He shows that he can read people well enough to understand what Rosanna did to try to hide her tracks, and why. That same character trait is put to use again later on in the passage, when he convinces the narrator to accompany him to the cottage and when he gets Mrs. Yolland to reveal that Rosanna is planning to leave.

Now you need to decide which answer choice provides the closest match. Choice (A) is incorrect because it deals only with plot development. It ignores the aspect of Cuff's character that is revealed by his reasoning as he follows Rosanna's movements. If Rosanna were that clever, Cuff wouldn't have been able to track her, so (B) is incorrect. Choice (C) is too narrow. Cuff wants to figure out where Rosanna went, too, not simply what she was carrying. That leaves (D) as the correct answer. The part of the plot that occurs on the beach also provides a way to develop Cuff's character as someone with a keen ability to understand people and get what he wants from them.

How Do the Seven Question Tasks Look in a Literary Passage?

Now that we've seen how the active reading questions can help you get a better grip on a literary passage, let's go through an example in which we can focus on the seven question tasks in action.

Excerpt from *Tom Sawyer*
by Mark Twain, 1876

1 Tom did play hookey, and he had a very good time. He got back home barely in season to help Jim saw next-day's wood and split the kindlings before supper—at least he was there in time to tell his adventures to Jim while Jim did three-fourths of the work. Tom's younger brother (or rather half-brother) Sid was already through with his part of the work (picking up chips), for he was a quiet boy, and had no adventurous, troublesome ways.

2 While Tom was eating his supper, and stealing sugar as opportunity offered, Aunt Polly asked him questions that were full of guile, and very deep—for she wanted to trap him into damaging revealments. Like many other simple-hearted souls, it was her pet vanity to believe she was endowed with a talent for dark and mysterious diplomacy, and she loved to contemplate her most transparent devices as marvels of low cunning. Said she:

3 "Tom, it was middling warm in school, warn't it?"

4 "Yes'm."

5 "Powerful warm, warn't it?"

6 "Yes'm."

7 "Didn't you want to go in a-swimming, Tom?"

8 A bit of a scare shot through Tom—a touch of uncomfortable suspicion. He searched Aunt Polly's face, but it told him nothing. So he said:

9 "No'm—well, not very much."

10 The old lady reached out her hand and felt Tom's shirt, and said:

11 "But you ain't too warm now, though." And it flattered her to reflect that she had discovered that the shirt was dry without anybody knowing that that was what she had in her mind. But in spite of her, Tom knew where the wind lay, now. So he forestalled what might be the next move:

12 "Some of us pumped on our heads—mine's damp yet. See?"

13 Aunt Polly was vexed to think she had overlooked that bit of circumstantial evidence, and missed a trick. Then she had a new inspiration:

14 "Tom, you didn't have to undo your shirt collar where I sewed it, to pump on your head, did you? Unbutton your jacket!"

15 The trouble vanished out of Tom's face. He opened his jacket. His shirt collar was securely sewed.

16 "Bother! Well, go 'long with you. I'd made sure you'd played hookey and been a-swimming. But I forgive ye, Tom. I reckon you're a kind of a singed cat, as the saying is—better'n you look. *This* time."

17 She was half sorry her sagacity had miscarried, and half glad that Tom had stumbled into obedient conduct for once.

18 But Sidney said:

19 "Well, now, if I didn't think you sewed his collar with white thread, but it's black."

20 "Why, I did sew it with white! Tom!"

21 But Tom did not wait for the rest. As he went out at the door he said:

22 "Siddy, I'll lick you for that."

23 In a safe place Tom examined two large needles which were thrust into the lapels of his jacket, and had thread bound about them—one needle carried white thread and the other black. He said: "She'd never noticed if it hadn't been for Sid. Confound it! sometimes she sews it with white, and sometimes she sews it with black. I wish to geeminy she'd stick to one or t'other—I can't keep the run of 'em. But I bet you I'll lam Sid for that. I'll learn him!"

1. The main theme of this passage is

   A. the contrast between Tom's personality and Sid's.
   B. the conflict between chores (work) and school on the one hand, and avoiding those duties on the other.
   C. the contrast between the choices Tom can make and the choices Jim has.
   D. the struggle between Tom and Aunt Polly to outwit each other.

Here's How to Crack It

Several subjects run through this passage, but we're looking for the overall big-picture theme to answer this question. Choices (A) and (B) are certainly present, but they're not central to the entire passage. Tom does seem to have more options than Jim—Tom can go to school or go swimming, but Jim has to prepare wood and do most of the work as he listens to Tom talk about his day. Jim isn't at supper with Aunt Polly and the other two boys, either. Again, though, (C) doesn't filter through the entire passage.

After eliminating those sub-themes, (D) emerges as the main theme. It's evident right from the beginning (Tom playing "hookey" [paragraph 1] in defiance of Aunt Polly) to the end (Tom feeling outfoxed by Aunt Polly's habit of switching thread colors).

2. What was Aunt Polly's aim in questioning Tom?

   A. She hoped to start an argument between Tom and Sid.
   B. She wanted to practice using the diplomatic skills she believed she possessed.
   C. She wanted to get Tom to admit that he'd gone swimming instead of going to school.
   D. She was trying to exert her authority over him.

Here's How to Crack It

This question examines the development of the plot. Let's use Process of Elimination to get rid of the incorrect answers first. Aunt Polly made no attempt to draw Sid into the conversation, so (A) is gone. Her supposed diplomatic skills were a means to an end; simply practicing them was not her objective, so (B) is out too. Now we're left with (C) and (D): Was Aunt Polly trying to achieve a specific victory (C) or establish her authority in general (D)?

The narrator says that "Aunt Polly asked him [Tom] questions that were full of guile, and very deep—for she wanted to trap him into damaging revealments" (paragraph 2). That pretty well takes us to (C) as the correct answer, but just to make sure, we need to figure out what on earth "revealments" means.

The passage was written almost a century and a half ago, and Aunt Polly is from a particular geographic region and economic class (as indicated by the references to the heat and to family members doing their own sewing and wood-chopping), so her use of language seems unusual to modern readers throughout the dialogue. The narrator's choice of an odd word such as "revealments" isn't too surprising in the context of the way Aunt Polly speaks. Combined with "trap" and "damaging," the word points to its root, "reveal," indicating she is questioning Tom in order to get him to disclose something he wants to hide. We learn later what that is, when she says, "I'd made sure you'd played hookey and been a-swimming." So, (C) is correct.

3. What does Aunt Polly regret when she feels "her sagacity had miscarried" (paragraph 17)?

    A. that she had wrongly accused Tom
    B. that she hadn't taken him to school herself, to make sure he went
    C. that Tom apparently hadn't played hookey after all
    D. that her cunning had failed her

Here's How to Crack It

Here's a challenging language use question in the context of a passage that displays unusual language throughout. First, look at the context. The next part of that sentence eliminates (C): Aunt Polly says she is "half glad" (paragraph 17) that Tom apparently had gone to school, so that's not what she regrets. If he went to school after all, there would be no need for her to take him there herself, so (B) is out too.

Now we're left with (A) and (D), which are different in a subtle way. Is Aunt Polly sorry about making this specific false accusation (A), or is she sorry that her cunning (which led her try to make Tom admit the accusation was true) had failed (D)? The description of Aunt Polly in paragraph 2 points to (D). She believes she has a "talent for dark and mysterious diplomacy" (paragraph 2) and sees her attempts to display it as "marvels of low cunning" (paragraph 2). She tried using those powers to get Tom to admit he'd played hookey, and when it seemed he'd really been at school, she's troubled by the failure of her talents. That's (D). Her cunning (sagacity) had failed to achieve her intended purpose (it had miscarried).

4. What main function does the character of Sid serve in the passage?

    A. He acts as a counterweight to Tom.
    B. He is an example of the type of boy Aunt Polly prefers to Tom.
    C. He introduces another source of tension in Tom's life, in addition to Aunt Polly.
    D. His status in the family suggests that Tom isn't a full member.

Here's How to Crack It

This is a structure question as it applies to a literary passage: Why is Sid there? He doesn't appear very much in the passage, but when he does (with the observation about the thread color), his impact is significant.

The passage doesn't give us enough information to know whether (D) is correct. Sid is Tom's half-brother, and their caregiver is Tom's aunt, but we don't know whether Aunt Polly is Sid's mother. There are suggestions that (B) might not be true. Sid is quiet, with "no adventurous, troublesome ways" (paragraph 1). Aunt Polly seems to enjoy Tom's adventurous spirit in a way, though—it gives her an opportunity to try to outwit him—and Sid's comment about the black thread ends her ability to be "half glad that Tom had stumbled into obedient conduct for once" (paragraph 17). So let's eliminate (B).

Sid does fulfill the functions described in both (A) and (C): He is the opposite of Tom (A) and seems determined to get Tom into trouble (C). Which is the *main* function, though? Choice (A) is too general: Sid could be acting as an opposite balancing force to any aspect(s) of Tom's character. Choice (C) is the correct answer because it reflects the tension between Tom and Aunt Polly. That tension runs throughout the dialogue, and Sid reignites it from left field when he pops up with the thread comment.

5. For what purpose did the author use a dialogue between Aunt Polly and Tom instead of simply describing the conflict over going to school?

   A. so readers could get to know the characters more directly
   B. to convey the type of language used in that time period and geographic area
   C. because he does a better job of writing dialogue than he does of writing narrative descriptions
   D. because the literary style in the author's time favored dialogue

Here's How to Crack It

Here's a purpose question as it applies to a literary passage. In this case, we're trying to discover the author's purpose in choosing to tell the story the way he did.

Again, let's use Process of Elimination to get rid of the wrong answers. Choice (B) is too general. If that were the author's purpose, he could have done the same thing elsewhere besides the dialogue. Indeed, he uses the same type of language in narrative sections. Choice (C) isn't as silly as it might sound. If there were an obvious difference in skill between the narrative and the dialogue sections, it could be true. However, there isn't in this passage. Choice (D) would take you beyond the passage if it were true, and you need to stay within the boundaries of the passage to find the right answer.

So we're left with (A). Instead of having the narrator describe the conflict, which would be one step removed from the characters involved, the author lets the characters speak for themselves, putting readers more directly in touch with them.

6. Does the author's account of the exchange between Aunt Polly and Tom support the idea that they seem about equally matched?

   A. No. The author describes the talents and cunning Aunt Polly believes she can put to use in dealing with Tom, but Tom is just a disobedient boy with no special abilities.
   B. Yes. Tom senses immediately what Aunt Polly is trying to find out, and "forestalled what might be the next move" (paragraph 11) by explaining his wet hair without being asked.
   C. Yes. Tom gets Jim to do most of the wood splitting, so he would be a match for Aunt Polly's attempts to get him to admit to playing hookey.
   D. No. Until Sid intervenes with his observation about the thread color, Tom is the clear winner.

Here's How to Crack It

This is an evaluation question as it applies to literary passages. The author obviously wants to portray Tom and Aunt Polly as pretty well equally matched in their ongoing contests. (Aunt Polly's concession of defeat "*this* time" [paragraph 16] suggests a series of exchanges like this, where she doesn't always win.) Has the author done a credible job of it, though?

Tom seems to have a natural ability to anticipate Aunt Polly's moves and head them off (when he sewed his shirt collar again after swimming, for instance). That eliminates (A). Tom won only "*this* time" (paragraph 16), not *every* time, which eliminates (D).

That leaves us with two choices that say yes, the author has done a credible job of presenting Aunt Polly and Tom as about equally matched, but for different reasons. The only one that pits Tom directly against Aunt Polly in a contest of wills is (B), which is the correct answer. Just because Tom can outwit Jim, as (C) claims, doesn't make him a match for Aunt Polly.

7. In this passage, both Aunt Polly and Sid are Tom's adversaries. But when it comes to the contest of wills with Tom, their approaches differ. Drag the descriptions of their approaches to the correct columns, depending on whether Aunt Polly or Sid displays that attitude.

Aunt Polly	**Sid**

- mystifying
- a game
- a source of mixed emotions
- serious
- a test of wills
- a risk

Here's How to Crack It

This comparison question asks you to dig deeper into the relationships among the characters, based on what the passage tells you. If you find the descriptions and statements surrounding Aunt Polly's attempt to get Tom to admit to playing hookey (or better yet, if you jotted a word or two down as you were actively reading the passage), you'll see that the second, third, and fifth descriptions apply to her approach to the contest with Tom. She treats it as a bit of a game and as a test of her powers of "dark and mysterious diplomacy" (paragraph 2) against Tom's deceptive ways. It's also a source of conflicting emotions for her, though, since she's half upset that her powers failed and half glad that Tom wasn't deceiving her for once.

There are no "left over" descriptions in this question, so the other three must apply to Sid. Indeed, his deliberate attempt to get Tom into trouble by mentioning the thread color is both mystifying and a risk, since he likely knows from past experience that Tom will make good on his threat to "lick you for that" (paragraph 22). There's a serious quality to his confrontation with Tom too: He doesn't take part in the game-like contest of wills between Tom and Aunt Polly, but just calmly reignites the dispute when it seems as if Tom has won.

Literary Passage Drill

Now it's your turn. Ask yourself the active reading questions as you go through this passage, and use your critical thinking skills. Then try the questions, using your knowledge of the seven question tasks. (All seven are represented in the questions below, to give you a chance to try each task on your own. However, the order of the tasks is mixed up.) You can check your answers in Part IX: Answer Key to Drills.

Excerpt from *The Leopard Man's Story*
by Jack London, 1903

1 He was the Leopard Man, but he did not look it. His business in life, whereby he lived, was to appear in a cage of performing leopards before vast audiences, and to thrill those audiences by certain exhibitions of nerve for which his employers rewarded him on a scale commensurate with the thrills he produced.

2 As I say, he did not look it. He was narrow-hipped, narrow-shouldered, and anaemic, while he seemed not so much oppressed by gloom as by a sweet and gentle sadness, the weight of which was as sweetly and gently borne. For an hour I had been trying to get a story out of him, but he appeared to lack imagination. To him there was no romance in his gorgeous career, no deeds of daring, no thrills—nothing but a gray sameness and infinite boredom.

3 Lions? Oh, yes! he had fought with them. It was nothing. All you had to do was to stay sober. Anybody could whip a lion to a standstill with an ordinary stick. He had fought one for half an hour once. Just hit him on the nose every time he rushed, and when he got artful and rushed with his head down, why, the thing to do was to stick out your leg. When he grabbed at the leg you drew it back and hit him on the nose again. That was all.

4 With the far-away look in his eyes and his soft flow of words he showed me his scars. There were many of them, and one recent one where a tigress had reached for his shoulder and gone down to the bone. I could see the neatly mended rents in the coat he had on. His right arm, from the elbow down, looked as though it had gone through a threshing machine, what of the ravage wrought by claws and fangs. But it was nothing, he said, only the old wounds bothered him somewhat when rainy weather came on.

5 Suddenly his face brightened with a recollection, for he was really as anxious to give me a story as I was to get it.

6 "He was a little, thin, sawed-off, sword-swallowing and juggling Frenchman. De Ville, he called himself, and he had a nice wife. She did trapeze work and used to dive from under the roof into a net, turning over once on the way as nice as you please.

7 "De Ville had a quick temper, as quick as his hand, and his hand was as quick as the paw of a tiger. The word went around to watch out for De Ville, and no one dared be more than barely civil to his wife. And she was a sly bit of baggage, too, only all the performers were afraid of De Ville.

8 "But there was one man, Wallace, who was afraid of nothing. He was the lion-tamer, and he had the trick of putting his head into the lion's mouth. He'd put it into the mouths of any of them, though he preferred Augustus, a big, good-natured beast who could always be depended upon.

9 "As I was saying, Wallace—'King' Wallace we called him—was afraid of nothing alive or dead. He was a king and no mistake.

10 "Madame de Ville looked at King Wallace and King Wallace looked at her, while De Ville looked at them darkly. We warned Wallace, but it was no use. He laughed at us, as he laughed at De Ville.

11 "But I saw a glitter in De Ville's eyes which I had seen often in the eyes of wild beasts, and I went out of my way to give Wallace a final warning. He laughed, but he did not look so much in Madame de Ville's direction after that.

12 "Several months passed by. Nothing had happened and I was beginning to think it all a scare over nothing. We were West by that time, showing in 'Frisco. It was during the afternoon performance, and the big tent was filled with women and children.

13 "Passing by one of the dressing tents I glanced in through a hole in the canvas: in front of me was King Wallace, in tights, waiting for his turn to go on with his cage of performing lions. I noticed De Ville staring at Wallace with undisguised hatred. Wallace and the rest were all too busy to notice this or what followed.

14 "But I saw it through the hole in the canvas. De Ville drew his handkerchief from his pocket, made as though to mop the sweat from his face with it (it was a hot day), and at the same time walked past Wallace's back. The look troubled me at the time, for not only did I see hatred in it, but I saw triumph as well.

15 "'De Ville will bear watching,' I said to myself, and I really breathed easier when I saw him go out the entrance to the circus grounds. A few minutes later I was in the big tent. King Wallace was doing his turn and holding the audience spellbound. He was in a particularly vicious mood, and he kept the lions stirred up till they were all snarling, that is, all of them except old Augustus, and he was just too fat and lazy and old to get stirred up over anything.

16 "Finally Wallace cracked the old lion's knees with his whip and got him into position. Old Augustus, blinking good-naturedly, opened his mouth and in popped Wallace's head. Then the jaws came together, *crunch*, just like that."

17 The Leopard Man smiled in a sweetly wistful fashion, and the far-away look came into his eyes.

18 "And that was the end of King Wallace," he went on in his sad, low voice. "After the excitement cooled down I watched my chance and bent over and smelled Wallace's head. Then I sneezed."

19 "It...it was...?" I queried with halting eagerness.

20 "Snuff—that De Ville dropped on his hair in the dressing tent. Old Augustus never meant to do it. He only sneezed."

1. The overall structure of this passage most closely resembles which of the following shapes?

   A. an inverted pyramid
   B. a maze
   C. a frame within a frame
   D. a spiral

2. Why does the author give such a lengthy description of the Leopard Man's attitude toward the work he does?

   A. to show that any profession can get boring after a while
   B. to reveal how aging can affect someone's enthusiasm for life
   C. to highlight the contrast between the Leopard Man and Wallace
   D. to reflect one of the main ideas in the story that the Leopard Man tells

3. When the narrator speaks of "the ravage wrought by claws and fangs" (paragraph 4), he is referring to

   A. the result of performing with leopards throughout the Leopard Man's career.
   B. the Leopard Man's advancing age.
   C. the damage caused by the big cats the Leopard Man fights.
   D. the Leopard Man's lack of excitement about his career.

4. Compare the Leopard Man's attitude toward De Ville with Wallace's. Which of the following statements is true?

   A. Both the Leopard Man and Wallace let their guard down.
   B. The Leopard Man believed warnings were needed; Wallace completely ignored warnings.
   C. Wallace underestimated De Ville; the Leopard Man did not.
   D. Wallace thought his physical strength made him invincible; the Leopard Man knew that De Ville's cleverness was more dangerous than physical strength.

5. Drag and drop the events into the chart in the order in which they occur in the passage. Not all of the events below actually take place, so you will have some left over.

(For this drill, write the event letters in the chart.)

Order of Events

(a) Wallace stops looking at De Ville's wife.

(b) The Leopard Man watches De Ville walk behind Wallace.

(c) Wallace notices the hatred in De Ville's stare.

(d) De Ville's wife looks at Wallace.

(e) Augustus sneezes.

(f) Wallace tries to talk to De Ville to defuse the tension.

(g) Several people in the circus warn Wallace about De Ville.

(h) De Ville tells the Leopard Man that he intends to get revenge on Wallace.

6. Which event in the passage has the *weakest* support from the other descriptions and events in the passage?

A. the Leopard Man repeatedly warning Wallace about De Ville
B. De Ville waiting so long for revenge when the cause of his anger had stopped
C. Wallace not being afraid of De Ville
D. Augustus biting off Wallace's head

7. The moral of this passage is

A. brains are better than brawn.
B. don't try to fight nature.
C. never underestimate your opponent.
D. the grass is never greener.

Part IV
Reasoning Through Language Arts: Language

Chapter 8
Language Overview

What would you think of an employer who posted a job ad full of obvious grammar mistakes? Does that sound like someone who might mess up your paycheck too? Or how about a political candidate who dropped off a "vote for me" flyer filled with spelling errors? Is that someone you would trust to be careful with your tax dollars?

Proper use of the English language isn't just about grammar or punctuation—it's also about clarity and credibility. It's about getting your message across and inspiring confidence in the skill and accuracy people can expect from you. If you don't care whether your résumé is written clearly and correctly, why should an employer spend time figuring out what it says? If you don't bother putting proper sentences together on a loan application, why would the lender trust you to make the effort to repay it on time?

Get your message across and inspire trust by using language correctly.

Your language use can reveal a lot about yourself; you want it to make the best impression.

HOW DOES THE GED® TEST MEASURE LANGUAGE USE?

You're about to explore one of the two ways the GED® test evaluates your language skills: the Language assessment. It consists of two passages, each containing four places where you need to select from four possible ways to complete a sentence correctly. Those two passages could be mixed in with the reading passages or they might appear at the end. Either way, you will have 95 minutes to do the six to eight reading passages and two language passages, before the 10-minute break.

Since the GED® test aims at skills that demonstrate readiness for a career or college, the language passages are drawn from the real world: workplace documents, professional communications, and messages to consumers. You might see business letters or emails, flyers, advertisements, or employee notices. Like the reading texts, these passages reflect different high school levels. They're shorter (350–450 words) and less complex than the reading passages, though, to allow you to focus on the language issues.

Why are there only two language passages? It's because part of your essay score in the Extended Response section is based on language use, too, so your language skills are being tested in both editing tasks (that's this section of the test) and in writing.

WHAT WILL I NEED TO KNOW ABOUT LANGUAGE?

The GED® Language assessment targets eight areas of language use that have been identified as the most important for a career or college. Don't panic when you see the list below, though—in the next chapter, you'll learn how the question format on the GED® test makes it easier to reach the correct answer.

Language Skills on the GED® Test

- **Word choice**: avoiding words that are often confused or used in a nonstandard way
- **Agreement**: of subject and verb, of noun and pronoun
- **Pronoun use:** clear antecedents, correct case
- **Modifiers:** correctly placed
- **Joining thoughts:** proper coordination, subordination, and parallel construction
- **Sentence construction:** avoiding wordiness, run-on sentences, and fragments
- **Logic and clarity:** effective use of words and phrases that mark a clear path for the reader
- **Punctuation and capitalization**

You don't even need to know the names of any of these areas of language use, either. For the Language assessment, you simply need to be able to recognize when something is wrong—for whatever reason—and when it's correct. Looking at the eight target areas simply shows you what kind of errors you can expect to see on the test so you can eliminate them more quickly from the four answer choices.

Of course, you'll also be expected to know how to express your ideas clearly and concisely when you write an essay for the Extended Response section. (See Chapter 11 on page 253.) Reviewing the language skills covered in this chapter can help you improve your Extended Response score, too, because part of the essay is evaluated on how well you demonstrate these skills.

Examples of the Key Areas of Language Use

First let's look at some brief examples of what those eight language targets look like in practice. Then in the next chapter, we'll explain how the GED® question format will help you find the right answer. This chapter isn't a complete grammar review—there are plenty of thorough grammar textbooks and reliable online grammar resources already. Instead, it's a brief refresher to help you recognize if there is a key area in which you know you have difficulty, so you can focus on that aspect of language use when you're preparing for the test.

Word Choice

Some words are commonly confused or easily used in a nonstandard way, especially when you're working under time pressure. Here are some examples:

> *They're* (contraction for "they are") putting *their* (possessive) coats over *there* (location).
>
> The *effects* (noun) of climate change will *affect* (verb, action) us all.

Other Commonly Confused Words

accept/except
allusion/illusion
cite/site
complement/compliment
fewer/less
ensure/insure
principal/principle
stationary/stationery
whose/who's

Other Nonstandard Uses

anyway (not "anyways")
couldn't care less (not "could care less")
a couple of (versus the informal "a couple")
regardless (not "irregardless")
supposed to (not "suppose to")
would have (not "would of")

It's (contraction for "it is") amazing how quickly the tree shed *its* (possessive) leaves when *it's* (contraction for "it is") still so warm at night.

That report is due on Friday. If you submit it *then* (a point in time), the boss will be more willing to consider a raise *than* (a comparison) if you hand it in late. If you're even later *than* (a comparison) Steve usually is, *then* ("in that case") you can probably forget about any raise this year.

You should *try to see* ("to see" is the infinitive form of the verb "see") him before he leaves (not "*try and see*...," which is a nonstandard, incorrect use).

You're the best one to make a list of the words that you sometimes confuse or use incorrectly. Research them in a good grammar book or online resource before the test, so you can choose the correct words with confidence, in spite of the time pressure.

Agreement

Subject-verb agreement is fairly straightforward: If the subject is singular, so is the verb. Here are some examples:

> John *learns* quickly.
>
> Beth and Marc *learn* (plural, now there are two subjects) more slowly.
>
> Neither Sam nor Anita *learns* (singular again, because we're dealing with only one singular subject at a time) much at all.
>
> The entire class, which will be going on a camping trip this weekend, *is learning* (singular because "class" is singular; don't get tripped up by the words stuffed in between the subject and the verb) how to read a compass.

Noun-pronoun agreement is a common difficulty, though. Try this one:

> The company released _______ quarterly results before the board members announced _______ intention to raise the dividend.

The first answer is "its" because "company" is singular. The second is a plural pronoun, "their," because we're talking about more than one board member. If the sentence said "...before the board of directors announced...," the pronoun would again be "its" because "board" is singular. "Board" is the subject; "of directors" is simply a phrase that describes it.

Another common error occurs when people try to avoid using "his or her":

Each student should buy _______ own books.

If you said "their," the GED® test still considers that to be an error. The credited answer will be "his or her" own books because we don't know the gender of the student. The student is singular, though, so the pronoun must be singular too. If you find "his or her" awkward or noninclusive, you can avoid using it by making the subject plural: *Students* should buy *their* own books.

Pronoun Use

There are a couple of flavors of correct pronoun use on the GED® test. The first is that every pronoun must have a clear antecedent (the noun that the pronoun is replacing). Things can get rather confusing when it's difficult to figure out which noun should be paired with the pronoun. Consider the following example:

Jorge asked Tony whether he had found his wallet yet.

Well, whose wallet is missing? Has Tony been searching for his own wallet, or had he offered to find Jorge's wallet for him? The antecedent of "his" (Jorge or Tony) isn't clear.

The other aspect of pronoun use is correct case. The old comedy line "*Whom* shall I say is calling?" is actually incorrect. Reword the sentence "I shall say whom is calling," and it becomes apparent that the correct version would be "I shall say *who* is calling," because "who" is the subject of the verb "is calling." (Similarly, it would be correct to write, "I should say she is calling," using the subject "she.") On the other hand, in another phrase—"To *whom* am I speaking?"—the pronoun "whom" is in the objective case, because it is the object of the preposition "to."

Modifiers

A modifier describes a noun, as in "the golf ball *that went into the sand trap.*" It's not the golf ball in the caddy's hand or the one at the bottom of the water feature; it's the one in the sand trap. The problem arises if a modifier is misplaced—not clearly beside the noun it's (there's that "it is" contraction again) modifying. That can make things confusing for the reader. Take a look at this example:

The delivery man left a package at the door *that looked as if it had been used as a football by the night crew.*

Just what was the night crew kicking around here—the door or the package? To fix this confusing sentence, you could either omit "at the door" (after all, where else would he leave it?) or else start a new sentence ("The beaten-up package looked as if...").

That's called a misplaced modifier—it's placed too far away from what it's describing. Just as confusing is the dangling modifier. That occurs when a sentence starts with a modifier but the thing that comes right after it is not, in fact, what the modifier is describing. The modifier just dangles there at the beginning of the sentence without being attached to anything sensible.

> Put **modifiers** near the noun they describe in order to avoid confusion.

Here's an example:

> *Determined to cut the budget, salaries* were lowered by 12 percent after the new governor took office.

So the salaries are determined to cut the budget? No; those words must be describing the new governor, not the salaries:

> *Determined to cut the budget, the new governor* lowered salaries by 12 percent after she took office.

Joining Thoughts

There are two sides to this coin. The first is parallel construction, and you can see it most easily in bulleted lists. To guide the reader smoothly through the list, each bullet point should be built the same way. Try to figure out which bullet point needs to be changed in this example:

When you go on the wilderness survival course, you'll learn

- how to start a camp fire
- how to canoe
- tree climbing
- how to hunt

There are three "how to" bullets and one oddball "...ing," which needs to be changed to "how to climb trees" in order to make the structure of the bullets the same, or parallel.

The second aspect of joining thoughts is coordination and subordination. What's the difference? Well, in coordination, the two thoughts are equally important; in subordination, one is more important than the other. The choice of coordination or subordination—and the choice of which thought is subordinated—can have a profound impact on the meaning.

Build them the same (parallel). Build them equal (coordination). Build them unequal (subordination).

Take a look at two brief statements that someone might be including in a cover letter for a job application:

I have no paid work experience in marketing.

I chaired the volunteer marketing committee for a charity.

Coordinating those two thoughts (using "and") would just plain confuse the employer:

> I have no paid work experience in marketing, and I chaired the volunteer marketing committee for a charity.

What is this applicant trying to tell the employer? By coordinating the two facts, the applicant is presenting them as equal in importance. It seems as if the statements on either side of the "and" are fighting each other, though. Now see what a different impression you can create by subordinating each of those statements:

> Although I chaired the volunteer marketing committee for a charity, I have no paid work experience in marketing.

What does the employer see and remember? "No paid work experience in marketing." Now consider this sentence:

> Although I have no paid work experience in marketing, I chaired the volunteer marketing committee for a charity.

Now what does the employer see and remember? This applicant is being honest about his lack of paid experience, but he's downplaying it by subordinating it (with "although"), and highlighting his volunteer leadership experience instead.

Sentence Construction

Here we're looking at three things: wordiness, run-on sentences, and sentence fragments. All three can torpedo a clear, concise expression of your ideas.

Let's start with wordiness. Here's part of a letter from a cellist who blew her audition for the local symphony orchestra:

> I hope you will reconsider and think again about giving me another chance to audition. I was extremely tired and nervous that day because I hadn't slept much the night before. I was too anxious and excited to sleep. If you'll just give me another chance, I'll show you how well I can play because I won't be as nervous the second time.

Now how's that for saying the same thing several times in slightly different ways? That's wordiness, and it puts readers to sleep. Say it once, say it concisely, and move on.

Run-on sentences also make good sleeping potions:

> Ingrid might make a good addition to the volleyball team, I guess, except that she hasn't been playing for very long and she doesn't have a car, someone else would always have to take her to out-of-town games and besides, she never has any money so she couldn't go out with us after the games, maybe we shouldn't ask her to join the team after all.

There are several separate sentences in that monster run-on, and that's how they should be presented.

Watch out, too, for complete thoughts that are being held together only by commas, like this:

> Industries are using less coal, natural gas is often the replacement of choice.

There should be a period after "coal" and a new sentence starting with "Natural" or, if the writer *really* wants to stress the connection between the two ideas, a semicolon after "coal." A comma never connects two complete thoughts.

Sentence Sins
Wordiness, Run-ons: There's too much stuffed inside. Fragments: It's not all there.

Sentence fragments are the opposite of run-ons: Instead of having too much in them, fragments aren't all there. A complete sentence needs a subject and a verb, at minimum, and it must stand on its own. Fragments don't have both a subject and verb (sometimes they don't even have either one), and they need something else added before they can stand alone.

The conductor ran. (That's a complete sentence.) Being cold and wet from the howling storm that threatened the train's very survival. (That's not—there is no subject associated with the verb "being.")

Logic and Clarity

Communication that is clear and logical is easy for the reader to follow. It guides the reader with transition and signal words that indicate a change in direction, perhaps, or a more detailed explanation of a point just made. The skilled use of these road signs allows the reader to concentrate on the writer's argument instead of struggling to figure out exactly what that argument is. See how easy you find it to read this example:

> Deep water drilling promises to unlock rich sources of untapped energy. There are environmental concerns. A major storm could damage a drilling rig, leading to an oil leak that would threaten the surrounding ecosystem.

Now see how much more sense that example makes if you simply add "however" before the second sentence and "for example" before the third, telling the reader that you're changing direction and then that you're going to elaborate on a point.

For a list of common transition and signal words, see page 166 in Chapter 5.

Punctuation and Capitalization

Every sentence must begin with a capital letter and conclude with end punctuation (a period, a question mark, or an exclamation point). Capitalize the names of specific people, places, national holidays, months, days of the week, and titles when used with a person's name (Dr. O'Reilly). Read the answer choices carefully, though. Don't let time pressure trick you into missing the lower case "t" on "tuesday." The GED® Language assessment could very well have a question like that because the ability to take in and process information carefully is very much part of readiness for a career or college.

In addition to those general punctuation and capitalization rules, the GED® test focuses on three specific punctuation items. One is the correct use of an apostrophe in possessives. "The banker*'s* bonus" (apostrophe "s" if the noun is singular: the bonus of the banker) and "the boys' skateboards" ("s" apostrophe if the noun is plural and ends in "s": the skateboards of the boys) are fairly straightforward cases. How about "the people's choice," though? Even though there are a lot of individuals in that noun, "people" doesn't end in an "s"; therefore, the possessive form is apostrophe "s," just as if the noun were singular. Another special case is possessive pronouns (such as hers, theirs, and its), which do not have apostrophes.

A second focus is the use of commas in a series or in apposition (we'll explain that one):

> She stopped off at the grocery store for bread, eggs, milk, and cheese. (That's a series of three or more items separated by commas.)

> Wheeling General, the largest employer in town, is building another new plant next year. (That's apposition: "Wheeling General" and "the largest employer in town" both refer to the same thing and share the same function in the sentence—both work as the subject. "The largest employer in town" is *in apposition* to "Wheeling General" and needs commas around it.)

The third punctuation item the GED® test highlights is punctuation between clauses. An independent clause stands alone (it could be a separate sentence); a dependent clause doesn't (it depends on the independent clause for its existence). You need a comma between two independent clauses that are joined by a word such as "but" or "and" (a coordinating conjunction):

> Fire destroyed six houses on the street, but the corner store suffered only minor damage.

You also need a comma when a dependent clause comes before an independent clause, but not when it comes after:

> Even though fire destroyed six houses on the street (the dependent clause; it needs a comma because it comes first), the corner store suffered only minor damage (the independent clause).

> The corner store suffered only minor damage (the independent clause; no comma because the dependent clause comes after it) even though fire destroyed six houses on the street.

There are other rules for comma use in English, but the ones we've noted are the ones that GED Testing Service prefers to test.

OUR APPROACH

Now that you've learned to recognize the types of language mistakes you could see on the test, you're well on the way to using Process of Elimination to narrow down the choices. Remember that it's often easier to eliminate what's obviously wrong than it is to start by searching for what's right. In the next chapter, we'll see how the question format can help you get even closer to the right answer, and give you some practice with passages and questions.

Chapter 9
Language Questions

In this chapter, you'll learn how the format of the language questions can help you find the answers more easily.

Sometimes it's easier to figure out what you don't want than what you do. Shopping for a car or a place to live can be like that—you hate the transmission shift or the neighborhood, but couldn't explain exactly why or describe what would make you happier instead.

So it is with the language questions: only in this case, getting rid of what's clearly wrong should, ideally, leave you with what's right. You don't need to know exactly *why* an answer is wrong—perhaps it just sounds odd—but as long as you can find and eliminate at least a couple of those incorrect choices, you're closer to the right answer.

WHAT KIND OF QUESTIONS ARE ON THE TEST?

Now that we've reviewed the key language use skills that are targeted on the test (see Chapter 8 on page 221), let's see how the questions make it easier to find the right answers. The language questions are all drop-down items within a passage. There will be a big gap in a sentence, with the word "Select" in the gap. When you click on it, a menu of four possible answers drops down. Click on an answer from that list and poof!—magically it appears where the gap was. (See page 23 in Chapter 3 for an illustration of a drop-down question.)

Drop-down questions let you see your chosen answer in the context of the passage.

There are two good things about that type of question: One, you get to see your answer within the context of a passage right away, and two, there *has* to be one correct choice within the options given. It's much easier to judge whether an answer seems right in the context of a passage than it is in an isolated sentence.

What Strategies Should I Use to Answer the Questions?

The wrong answers represent common errors in any of the eight language use areas covered in Chapter 8. You don't need to remember the names of the errors or how to fix them, although reviewing the list will help you learn to recognize them more quickly. All you need to do is use Process of Elimination to identify the wrong choices, click on the one remaining, and verify that it is correct when read in the context of the passage.

You do need to be careful when you're reading the choices, though, because they can be very close to each other in wording, and time pressure can trip you up. Would you notice the difference between these two answer choices on a test?

"...your poor customer service and having high costs. if you..."
"...your poor customer service and high costs. If you..."

Read Carefully. One comma or capital letter can make the difference between a right and a wrong answer.

The first one lacks parallel structure in the last two items on a list, and is missing a capital letter at the beginning of the next sentence. If you were skimming the answer choices quickly, though, the two seem close. Those are the kinds of tricky differences the test writers can and do throw at you.

A good approach is to compare the choices that are left after you've eliminated those that are clearly wrong. Is one answer missing a capital letter where it should have one? Does one have an extra word, such as "although," that turns a complete sentence into a fragment? The difference between a right and a wrong answer can be that small.

After you've made your final choices, check your answers in the context of the passage. Context can be a huge help in showing you whether you've made the right decision.

How Do the Drop-Down Questions Look in a Language Passage?

Here's an example of a typical GED® language passage. It's a flyer that a candidate for mayor is using to introduce herself to voters, and it needs some help. Try to select the correct answers yourself, circling them with a pencil, before you read the explanations that follow the passage. The wording for the passage instructions is the same as the wording you'll see on the test.

Review the language use errors in Chapter 8 so you can spot wrong answers more quickly.

The passage below is incomplete. Navigate to each "Select..." button and choose the option that correctly completes the sentence.

A Mayor for the Rest of Us!

Sybil Simbalah lives in a neighborhood like yours. She grew up here, and has watched this city change from a family-friendly place into a sprawl of uncontrolled urban development, fueled by your tax dollars and pouring profits into the pockets of corrupt elected officials and their buddies in business and industry.

During four years on the city council and, before that,

Select... ▼
six years on the school board, Sybil has fought
six earlier years on the school board. Sybil has fought
six years on the school board where Sybil has fought
on the school board for six years, Sybil has fought

tirelessly and courageously for family values. She gathered enough support to defeat the ill-conceived expansion of the freeway through town, and

Select... ▼
helped them stop the demolition
helped local residents stop demolishing plans
helped local residents stop the city council when they wanted to plan the destruction and demolition
helped local residents stop the planned demolition

of a beautiful 100-year-old library building. She has fought every proposed rate hike for mass transit and, on the school board, defeated a plan to cut back after-school programs.

Select... ▼
Sybil understands because she has a degree in urban planning
Sybils urban planning degree makes her understand proper planning and
With her degree in urban planning, Sybil understands
Although her degree is in urban planning, Sybil understands

what makes a city welcoming, healthy, and livable. She is always ready to hear from the people she represents, and consults with her constituents before she votes on any major project.

Sybil lives in a century-old house with her husband, three children, and three dogs. She chairs the symphony's community engagement committee,

Select... ▼
is a hospital board member and a fund raiser for the food bank a couple days a month.
sits on the hospital board, and raises funds for the food bank.
while also volunteering for the hospital board and helps them raise funds at the food bank.
works for the Hospital Board and is a food bank fund raiser.

Sybil Simbalah knows what the residents of this city need.

- Reliable electricity
- Safe drinking water
- Affordable mass transit
- Parks and playgrounds
- A new team in charge at city hall

As long as the current city officials run the show, their cronies in industry and big business will continue getting the contracts—and the kickbacks for massive projects we can't afford and don't need.

You can end corruption in city hall and stop big business and industry from dictating where your tax dollars go.

It's time to capture city hall—for the rest of us!

On November 13, take back control of your city and vote Sybil Simbalah for mayor!

To join Sybil's team of eager volunteers or contribute to Sybil's campaign, contact her campaign office at

- 531-3115
- gosybil@mayor.com
- mayorsybil.com
- 1395 Baker Lane, Unit 43

We'd love to hear from you or meet you!

Now let's go through the process for finding the errors and choosing the correct answers to complete the four sentences.

Apply the Strategy
Use POE on Language questions like the ones in this passage!

In the first set of drop-down answers, the first choice is correct. Read on to see how you could have eliminated the other three (all of which contain errors in the key language skills) and arrived at this one through Process of Elimination.

> During four years on the city council and, before that, six years on the school board, Sybil has fought tirelessly and courageously for family values.

The second choice (below) is redundant—"before that" and "earlier" say the same thing. More importantly, the period after "board" creates a fragment; the first "sentence" is not actually a complete sentence. That's why you need to read the answer choices very carefully.

> During four years on the city council and, before that, six earlier years on the school board. Sybil has fought tirelessly and courageously for family values.

The addition of "where" in the choice below makes the sentence into a fragment instead of a complete sentence. Here, only one word separates this choice from the correct answer.

> During four years on the city council and, before that, six years on the school board where Sybil has fought tirelessly and courageously for family values.

The fourth choice (below) lacks parallel construction.

> During four years on the city council and, before that, on the school board for six years, Sybil has fought tirelessly and courageously for family values.

In the second set of drop-down answers, the first choice is wrong because it has an unclear antecedent. (See page 225 in Chapter 8 for an explanation of antecedent.) Who is "them"?

> She gathered enough support to defeat the ill-conceived expansion of the freeway through town, and helped them stop the demolition of a beautiful 100-year-old library building.

The next choice (below) has awkward, unclear wording that would confuse a reader. Is "demolishing" a verb or an adjective here? Are the residents demolishing (a verb) plans, or are they stopping plans that describe demolishing (an adjective)?

> She gathered enough support to defeat the ill-conceived expansion of the freeway through town, and helped local residents stop demolishing plans of a beautiful 100-year-old library building.

Now where do we start listing the problems with the third choice below? There's a noun-pronoun agreement problem ("city council" is singular, so "when *it* wanted...), it's wordy (what's the difference between the "destruction" and the "demolition" of a building?), and it's just plain longer than it needs to be.

> She gathered enough support to defeat the ill-conceived expansion of the freeway through town, and helped local residents stop the city council when they wanted to plan the destruction and demolition of a beautiful 100-year-old library building.

The one below (the fourth choice) is the one you want. Now it's clear whom (objective case—remember that one from Chapter 8?) Sybil helped and what she helped them do.

> She gathered enough support to defeat the ill-conceived expansion of the freeway through town, and helped local residents stop the planned demolition of a beautiful 100-year-old library building.

In the third drop-down question, the first choice is wrong because it breaks up the independent clause ("Sybil understands what makes...") with a dependent clause ("because she has a degree in urban planning"). The dependent clause should begin this particular sentence, followed by a comma (remember that from Chapter 8?) before the independent clause.

> Sybil understands because she has a degree in urban planning what makes a city welcoming, healthy, and livable.

Aside from the fact that the second choice (below) is wordy (one would hope an urban planning degree would lead to an understanding of proper planning), the lack of an apostrophe on the possessive ("Sybil's") eliminates this version. You can see how carefully you need to read the choices when just one missing apostrophe means a wrong answer.

> Sybils urban planning degree makes her understand proper planning and what makes a city welcoming, healthy, and livable.

After you eliminate the first two choices because of the errors in them, you come to the third choice (below), which is the correct one.

> With her degree in urban planning, Sybil understands what makes a city welcoming, healthy, and livable.

Now why would anyone subordinate the urban planning degree with "although"? The degree *explains* Sybil's understanding of a healthy city. This improper subordination in the fourth choice makes it sound as if her understanding is in spite of the degree, not because of it.

> Although her degree is in urban planning, Sybil understands what makes a city welcoming, healthy, and livable.

In the final set of drop-down answers, the first choice (below) might have been the one you eliminated first. The structure in this list of volunteer activities isn't parallel, and it uses the more colloquial "couple days a month" instead of the standard "couple *of* days a month." It's not clear whether the "couple of days" applies only to the food bank or to all three volunteer activities, either. Specifying the small amount of time Sybil devotes to volunteer activities also undercuts the image of extensive community involvement that she's trying to present.

> She chairs the symphony's community engagement committee, is a hospital board member and a fund raiser for the food bank a couple days a month.

The second option is the correct one. The structure of the three descriptions of Sybil's volunteer activity is parallel (each one begins with a verb) and there are no other errors.

> She chairs the symphony's community engagement committee, sits on the hospital board, and raises funds for the food bank.

Need More Help with Language?
Check out *Grammar Smart,* by the Staff of The Princeton Review.

This third choice was likely your second throw-away. The structure of the three volunteer activity descriptions isn't even close to parallel, and it's not clear who "them" is referring to.

She chairs the symphony's community engagement committee, while also volunteering for the hospital board and helps them raise funds at the food bank.

In addition to the lack of parallelism in the three volunteer activities, the fourth choice (below) has a capitalization problem. There is no reason to capitalize "Hospital Board" when the symphony committee and the food bank are not capitalized.

She chairs the symphony's community engagement committee, works for the Hospital Board and is a food bank fund raiser.

Language Drill

Now you try a language passage on your own, circling your selections. Review the eight language use areas from Chapter 8 before you start; the errors you see will be in those eight areas. Remember to read the answer choices carefully, too, so you won't miss a small difference between a wrong answer and one that's correct. You can check your answers in Part IX: Answer Key to Drills.

The passage below is incomplete. Navigate to each "Select..." button and choose the option that correctly completes the sentence.

Subject: Request to restructure loan

Dear Ms. Mertz:

Thank you again for your time during our phone conversation this morning. As requested, I am sending this email to confirm my request for a restructuring of my small business loan.

I would appreciate an additional six months to pay, and a 0.25 percent reduction in the interest rate. If you are unable to approve both requests, then the additional six months would be my priority.

Economic conditions have deteriorated since I first applied for a loan, unfortunately, with the result that I need to request this restructuring. My customers are spending more of their food dollars on groceries and less on restaurant meals. The harsh winter kept people at home more

Select... ▼
this year, which meant even less customers, even on weekends.
since the beginning of the winter, which meant fewer customers, even on weekends.
this year, too, meaning even fewer Customers, even on weekends.
this year, too, which meant fewer customers, even on weekends.

You asked what efforts I've made to increase revenue by attracting new customers. Let me assure you that I have tried a variety of things during the past year. For example, I advertised in the local media, offering a special "new customer" discount.

Select... ▼
Participating in a local trade fair, the recent "Home Grown Goodness" food exhibition. I sponsored
I participated in a local trade fair, the recent "Home Grown Goodness" food exhibition, and sponsored
I participated in a local trade fair the recent "Home Grown Goodness" food exhibition and sponsored
I participated in a local trade fair, the recent "Home Grown Goodness" food exhibition, and we were also sponsoring

a booth for a local charity at the fall fair. Hoping to attract new business from the surrounding communities, I promoted my restaurant through coupons and worked with a well-known insurance company to host special group dinners for its top salespeople in the region.

In spite of my efforts, however, any increase in customers is more than offset by the increase in my costs. Food is getting more and more expensive, and leasing and insurance costs are rising at a rate far greater than inflation. I changed the menu and laid off some staff in an attempt to reduce expenses. I have a small restaurant, though, and I can carry cost-cutting only so far before it starts to have a negative impact on my ability to keep my remaining customers happy.

Until the economy improves and people feel more comfortable spending on restaurant meals, I'm not sure what else I can do.

Select... ▼
I would, of course, welcome any suggestions you can offer.
Although I would, of course, welcome any suggestions you can offer.
Welcoming any suggestions you can offer, you may have some other ideas for me.
Since I don't have any other ideas, I would, of course, welcome any suggestions you can offer but I believe I've already tried every possible way to cut costs and raise revenue so I'm not sure you could present any new ideas.

I realize you probably have several customers asking for the same type of loan relief as I am requesting.

Select... ▼
However, I hope that my excellent credit record and their long business relationship with me
I hope that my excellent credit record and my long business relationship of doing business with your bank
However, I hope that my excellent credit record and my long business relationship with your bank
However, I hope that my excellent credit record and I have a long business relationship with your bank which

would make me eligible for special consideration. I look forward to a favorable response after you have a chance to consult your manager.

Kind regards,

J. Enrico Flavino

Part V
Reasoning Through Language Arts: Extended Response

Chapter 10
Extended Response Overview

If any part of the Reasoning Through Language Arts (RLA) test could make prospective test takers gasp and rethink their plan, it would be the Extended Response section.

You can relax, though. No, *really*—relax. With the strategies you'll discover in this book, you'll have a process and a plan for tackling the Extended Response, so you won't have to waste time figuring out your approach on test day. You'll know exactly what to write about and where to start, and you'll gain some good tips for improving your writing too.

WHAT IS THE EXTENDED RESPONSE TASK?

First we're going to look at *what* you're doing for the Extended Response section. Then, in the next chapter, we'll look at some strategies for *how* to do it.

You'll tackle the 45-minute Extended Response question right after the 10-minute break that follows the first reading and language section. The prompt will include two passages arguing opposite sides of a real-world "hot button" issue such as oil pipelines or the minimum wage. The passages could come in different formats (for example, an employee memo and a magazine article). The authors might also be quite different—a professional teacher and a concerned parent, for instance.

Choose the passage on which you feel you could do the best job. There is no "right" or "wrong" passage.

Your task is to explain which passage provides better support for the position it argues. The passages have been chosen so the support they provide is roughly equal. There is no "right" or "wrong" passage. In other words, you could argue effectively that either one of the passages provides better support. As you read through them, you might find that one type of support is more familiar to you, or that you feel more comfortable with one format. Choose the passage for which you feel you could build a stronger argument.

What Will You See on Your Screen?

The Extended Response screen was recently reformatted to provided clearer instructions and a more user-friendly interface for typing your answer. It has three main components.

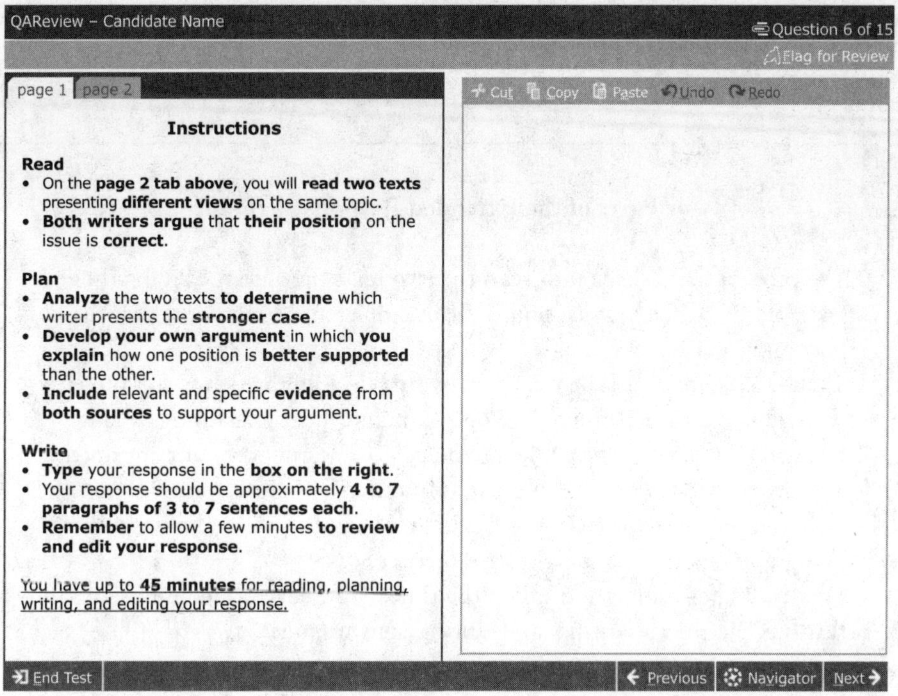

1. The **prompt** (also known as the instructions) describes your task and appears on the left side of the screen on the "page 1" tab. It has four parts, which we'll describe next.

2. The **passages** themselves appear on the "page 2" tab. Make sure to read both passages. Together they will be about 650 words.

   The paragraphs are numbered consecutively so when you're writing, you'll be able to find points that you've already noted more quickly. If the first passage ends with paragraph 5, then the second passage will begin with paragraph 6.

3. The third part of the Extended Response screen is a **text box** occupying the right half of the screen. As you type your response, a scroll bar will appear on the right-hand side to let you review your essay.

   There are no spelling or grammar checkers. You can cut, copy, and paste within the text box, but you can't copy text from the passage and paste it into your essay.

What Is the Prompt Telling Me to Do?

While the passages on page 2 will vary, the instructions on page 1 will always have the same four components.

Four Parts of the Extended Response Prompt

1. The prompt first asks you to **read** the two texts on the page 2 tab. These texts present different views on the same topic, and both argue that their position is correct.
2. Then it asks you to **plan** your essay by first deciding which writer presents the stronger case, and then developing an argument explaining WHY. Determine what specific evidence you can use to support your argument.
3. Next, **write** your response. Note that in order for your response to count, it should be approximately 4 to 7 paragraphs in length, and each of these paragraphs should contain 3 to 7 sentences.
4. Finally, it ends with a note about the time: "You have up to 45 minutes for reading, planning, writing, and editing your response."

Here are some important tips to keep in mind about the task that's described in the prompt.

Write about which author's argument is better supported, not about the topic of the authors' arguments.

- **Take a step back from the topic.** Two authors are making opposing cases about an issue. Your mission is to look at *how* they make their cases, not at the cases themselves. Focus on the *support* provided by the two authors, not on the topic they're discussing. If, for example, you think burning coal is a major cause of climate change and air pollution, but you feel that the passage promoting clean coal has better support for its position, then your essay will explain how the clean coal passage is better supported. It won't discuss the issue of burning coal. Your grade will be lowered if your essay strays far from support to the topic itself. (We'll explain later on how the essay is graded.)
- **Stick to the passages.** That's where you'll find the support. If you bring in your own opinions or knowledge about an issue, you run the risk of wandering into an essay about the topic instead of an essay about how the two authors make their cases.
- **Back up your points with evidence from the passages.** For instance, perhaps you feel that one passage provides stronger support because it mentions specific studies and experts instead of simply making vague claims. Your essay should refer to those specific details.
- **There are no right or wrong answers.** If you can make a credible case that one side of the argument provides better support, and back that up with evidence from the passages, then your position will not be considered wrong.

What Does the Prompt Mean by "Support"?

Support can take several forms, which we'll outline below. You might also find it helpful to review the section on evaluation questions in the reading part of the test (page 169 in Chapter 5), because that's exactly what you're doing here—evaluating the evidence, reasoning, and assumptions of two authors to argue that one has provided better support for their position.

Evaluate each author's evidence, reasoning, and assumptions, just as you did for evaluation questions in the reading passages.

Support Through Evidence

The most obvious type of support would be evidence—examples or other details that the author provides, or authorities the author cites. Elements such as those can add a lot of weight to an argument. Consider this example:

> The polar bear population is threatened.

versus

> A 2006 study revealed that the skull size and body weight of adult male polar bears in the Southern Beaufort Sea population had decreased during the past 20 years. Fewer cubs were surviving too. Scientists saw both measures as symptoms of stress, and a repeat of the warning signs noticed earlier in the polar bears of Western Hudson Bay. There, the population subsequently fell from about 1,200 in 1987 to about 950 bears 17 years later.

Clearly the second claim provides stronger support for this specific point. It outlines specific research studies, years, symptoms, and numbers; and it builds its case on the findings of scientists, who are the authorities in the field.

Support through evidence can be a bit less clear cut too. For instance, suppose one side of the argument makes only one major claim, but backs up that claim thoroughly with evidence from professional research studies and the opinions of acknowledged experts in the field. The other side gives four reasons for its position instead of one, but doesn't offer as much support for any of them. Which one is stronger? There are no right or wrong answers, as long as you can build a credible argument and support it from the passages. In this case, you would choose the side for which you can do a better job of explaining why the support for that position is stronger. Another test taker might choose the opposite side, and that's fine, as long as each of you can explain what makes your side's support better.

When you're looking at evidence-based support, watch for adequacy and relevance too. Does the author provide enough credible evidence in comparison to the other passage, and is that evidence relevant to the claim the author is making?

Support Through Reasoning

This support issue is more subtle than evidence-based support. Is the author's chain of reasoning sound and logical? Or do you detect a logical fallacy? (See page 169 in Chapter 5.) Do the author's claims *seem* well supported by evidence, but when you follow the path from claim to conclusion, does it go seriously off course?

Suppose, for example, an author claims that purple loosestrife, an invasive plant species, is harming natural wetlands in the area by discouraging wildlife and beating out native plants in the competition for nourishment and space. Studies done during the past three years show the retreat of native species and the alarming spread of purple loosestrife, backing up this claim. So far, so good. But then the author says that this means that the town authorities should begin a program of spraying toxic chemicals on wetlands in order to eliminate the invasive plant. The author is making a big leap: going from saying that there's a problem (and presenting evidence) to insisting on a drastic solution (without evidence for the solution being a good one). What happens to the remaining native plants if toxic chemicals are sprayed? And what about the wildlife in the area? The claim looks good, the evidence looks good, but the reasoning leading from the claim to the extreme solution is flawed. Because of its faulty reasoning, the author's position is not well supported.

Support Through Assumptions

Another subtle support issue involves the author's assumptions. Are they valid, considering the likely audience? All the evidence and logical reasoning in the world doesn't make a well-supported argument if the assumptions on which it's based don't make sense. Consider, for instance, an author who wants to add life to a new suburb filled with young families. The writer argues that $20 should be added to each property tax bill to fund facilities for a Wednesday morning fruit and vegetable market in the local park. The piece includes compelling evidence of the health benefits of eating fresh fruits and vegetables, and the wisdom of buying produce grown "close to home." What's wrong with this argument? The author is assuming that there will be enough customers on a Wednesday morning (the traditional market day) to make the project a good business proposition for vendors. What about the suburban adults who have day jobs and their kids who are in school? The invalid assumption drains support from the author's position.

HOW IS THE EXTENDED RESPONSE GRADED?

The Extended Response task pulls together the critical thinking, active reading, analytical, and language skills you'll also use in the reading and language sections of the RLA test. As in other sections, the aim is to allow test takers to demonstrate the skills required for college or a career.

The Extended Response task draws on the critical thinking, active reading, analytical, and language skills you acquired for the reading and language sections of the test.

In the Extended Response section, you'll be graded on how well you can:

- understand and analyze the two source passages
- evaluate the argumentation in those passages
- create a written argument in your own words, supported by evidence drawn from the passages

One bit of good news: Because you have only 45 minutes to plan, write, and edit the essay, it's considered an "on-demand draft" and is not expected to be completely free of errors.

Exactly What Traits Should My Essay Demonstrate?

Your essay is scored on three separate rubrics. Each one covers a trait that should be evident in your essay.

Creation of Arguments and Use of Evidence

This trait looks at two aspects of your essay: how well you build an argument for your position about which passage is better supported, and how well you incorporate evidence drawn from the passages. We'll give you some practice Extended Response questions in the next chapter. The following questions will help you evaluate your own practice essays for this trait:

- Did you establish a purpose that's connected to the task in the prompt? In other words, is it clear that your purpose is to explain why one passage is better supported than the other (instead of discussing the topic of the two passages)?
- Did you make clear claims?
- Did you explain why the evidence you're taking from the passages is important (instead of simply plunking it into your essay without any commentary)?
- Have you demonstrated that you can distinguish between supported and unsupported claims in the passages?
- Have you shown that you can evaluate the credibility of the support the authors use?
- Have you spotted any faulty reasoning in an author's argument?
- Are you making reasonable inferences about the assumptions underlying the authors' arguments?

Development of Ideas and Organizational Structure

Now that you've shown you can create a solid argument for your position, we're moving on to how well you develop and organize that argument. Here are some questions to ask yourself about your practice essays:

- Did you explain how your ideas are relevant to the task, or did you just fire off ideas without elaborating on them?
- Is there a logical progression to your ideas, or do they jump around all over the place? (You might find it helpful to review the transition and signal words on page 166 in Chapter 5.)
- Is there a clear connection between your main points and the details that elaborate on them? (In the next chapter, you'll learn more about connecting main points and accompanying details.)
- Do the style and tone of your essay demonstrate an awareness of your audience and purpose? (Do you use complete sentences most of the time, instead of bullet lists? Is the language appropriate, or is it filled with slang and inappropriate short forms?)
- Did your organizational structure contribute to conveying your message and purpose? (We'll talk about organizing your argument in the next chapter.)

Clarity and Command of Standard English Conventions

There's just one question to ask yourself for this trait: Did you follow all eight of the language skills described in Chapter 8? The editing questions in the Language assessment were the first part of testing you on the elements of language use that are considered most important for a career or college. The writing task in the Extended Response section is the second part.

Is the Essay Graded by Computer?

Yes—and the good news about this is that you won't have to wait weeks for your results. In fact, the scoring is done almost immediately. Scoring by computer (instead of tying up a bunch of human graders) also allows for giving you specific feedback on your essay performance as part of the score report.

You might be wondering how a computer (actually, it's called an automated scoring engine) could ever do an accurate job of assessing your unique, original essay. The test writers spent months teaching it, feeding it the scores awarded by human graders to an extensive range of sample essays so it would learn the characteristics of, say, a high score on the trait of "development of ideas and organizational structure." If the scoring engine doesn't recognize something about an essay (one that's unusually short, for instance, or that uses uncharacteristically sophisticated vocabulary), it kicks the essay out to a human grader. However, the test writers are confident that the engine will score at least 95 percent of the essays accurately.

OUR APPROACH

Now that you understand the Extended Response task and the traits you need to demonstrate in your essay—that's the "what"—we'll move on in the next chapter to the process for building and organizing your argument—the "how." We'll walk you through that process, using some examples and then give you one to try on your own. Along the way, you'll pick up some tips for improving your writing in any type of task too.

Chapter 11
Extended Response Writing

In this chapter, we'll guide you through the process of assembling and organizing points for your argument and writing the essay. Then we'll give you some practice.

Anyone can learn to write an essay. Yes, anyone. You need a plan to follow (which we'll give you in this chapter) and confidence (which will increase as you get more practice writing and evaluating your own work).

You can use our method to help you analyze the arguments you encounter in everyday life beyond the test too. Try it the next time you get a message from someone urging you to buy something or do something. Switch into active reading (or active listening) mode right away and start looking for the main arguments and how well they're supported. You'll soon know whether you should consider the request or not.

HOW DO I BUILD MY ARGUMENT?

From studying the prompt (the test writers call it "unpacking the prompt"), you know what you need to do:

1. Analyze the arguments in the two passages to decide which author you think provides stronger support.
2. Write your own argument about which one is better supported, using evidence from the passages.
3. Be objective; consider the support, not the topic.
4. Do it in 45 minutes.

First, we'll define each author's argument using our active reading skills. Remember active reading from Chapter 5? In active reading, you summarize and ask questions as you read, forcing the passage to give you what you need from it. And during this process, you should also start assembling the points and evidence for your argument.

Let's try active reading with a brief example. *While you are reading* the following excerpt (not after you're done), determine the author's argument and the support he provides for it, and note them briefly on your scratch paper. You'll likely find it helpful to make a quick chart for yourself, such as this one:

Argument	Support

Excerpt from *The New Freedom*
by Woodrow Wilson

For indeed, if you stop to think about it, nothing could be a greater departure from original Americanism, from faith in the ability of a confident, resourceful, and independent people, than the discouraging doctrine that somebody has got to provide prosperity for the rest of us. And yet that is exactly the doctrine on which the government of the United States has been conducted lately. Who have been consulted when important measures of government, like tariff acts, and currency acts, and railroad acts, were under consideration? The people whom the tariff chiefly affects, the people for whom the currency is supposed to exist, the people who pay the duties and ride on the railroads? Oh, no! What do they know about such matters! The gentlemen whose ideas have been sought are the big manufacturers, the bankers, and the heads of the great railroad combinations. The masters of the government of the United States are the combined capitalists and manufacturers of the United States.

That was published in 1913 so yes, the sentences are a bit long, but we can still define the author's main points. Your chart might look like the one below:

Argument	Support
U.S. government is being run by leaders of business and finance instead of by the people, as originally intended (paragraph 1)	Three examples: tariff, currency, and railroad acts (paragraph 1)

Apply the Strategy
Use active reading and scratch paper (or your note boards on test day) to boil the passage down to the evidence you need for your essay.

On the test, of course, you'll be working with several paragraphs in each passage, so you would also note the number of the paragraph that contains each point so you can find it again quickly. And since you're under a strict time limit, your chart would contain short forms and abbreviations that are meaningful to you. You should note all three of the types of support outlined in Chapter 10, too: evidence, reasoning, and assumptions. (See pages 249–250.)

What's the value of this chart? It boils an article, or a news release, or a letter—any of the different types of documents you might encounter in a passage—down to one common bare-bones list of the arguments and support points you need for your essay. It saves you the time of rereading and clicking from tab to tab just to find something again. And it gives you a clear picture of the support in each passage, making it easier to decide which one you think provides better support. That's the topic of your essay, after all.

Later on in this chapter, we'll give you some examples that will let you practice active reading and boiling the passages down into argument/support charts.

HOW DO I ORGANIZE MY ARGUMENT?

You've read both passages actively, and now you've got a couple of quick charts listing the authors' arguments and the support for those arguments. You can make a clear case for which author provides better support for their position. In other words, you have the main points that you want your essay to hit. Now what?

Let's work through an example of how you would organize and develop your essay. Suppose one of the two passages on the test is a letter to the editor from a local consumers' group complaining about the large, unexplained car insurance rate increase imposed on drivers in that city. The other is a response from a local association of insurance brokers arguing that, after three years of flat rates, an increase was overdue.

The Essay Template

The Beginning

- Introductory paragraph
  - Attention-getter
  - Thesis statement
  - Big picture list of evidence that proves the thesis statement

The Middle

- One paragraph for each piece of evidence that proves the thesis statement
  - Topic sentence
  - Evidence from the passages
  - Explanation of how the evidence supports the thesis statement

The End

- Restatement of the thesis in different words
- Reminder of the pieces of evidence that prove the thesis

The Essay Template

First, let's look at the template—or framework—for the essay. We'll discuss the pieces in more detail later, but first we need a picture of what the whole structure looks like.

In 45 minutes, you won't be able to produce a polished essay. Even the test writers regard this as an "on-demand draft" and expect that it will contain some errors. However, if you have a concept of how an ideal essay would be structured, you'll have a plan for where to start and what to write in the limited time available.

The essay has a beginning, a middle, and an end. Well of course, you may say. However, it isn't quite as simple as it sounds. The essay has a *specific* beginning, middle, and end. You might be familiar with the classic advice given to people who have to make a speech: "Tell them what you're going to tell them, tell them, tell them what you told them." That's a pretty good outline of the beginning, middle, and end of the essay too.

The Beginning

This is the first paragraph, which sets expectations about what readers will find in the rest of the essay. It has three components.

The Attention-Getter Ideally, the first paragraph begins with an attention-getter—something that would make a human reader want to see what's in the rest of your essay. Although you don't have a human reader for the GED® Extended Response, an attention-getter will still get your essay off to a strong start for the robo-reader. Remember, everything it knows, it learned from human graders.

What would capture a reader's attention?

- You could begin with a question—for example, "Why have car insurance rates gone up so much?"
- You could start with what's called the "startling fact"—for instance, "The average U.S. driver pays about $900 in car insurance premiums." (You can probably find a good startling fact candidate in the two Extended Response passages.)
- You could open with a quotation (if one pops into your head without spending time thinking of one). It doesn't have to be a direct quote, using the exact words of whoever said it. You could paraphrase it instead. For example, a paraphrase such as "Abraham Lincoln claimed that it was impossible to fool everyone all of the time" would avoid trying to remember Lincoln's exact words. In this example, you'd need to add a sentence tying that quote to the passages: "However, in its letter to the editor, the consumers' group complains that car insurers seem to be trying to do just that—fool all of their customers into accepting unexplained rate hikes."

The essay begins with a three-part paragraph.

- An attention-getter, which makes the reader want to keep going
- A thesis statement, which outlines what the essay will prove
- A big picture outline of the arguments that prove the thesis statement

If you can't think of an attention-getter quickly, then you could simply begin with a statement about the two passages: "Rising car insurance premiums are drawing complaints from consumers and forcing the industry to defend itself, as these two passages reveal." This leads readers into the essay rather than hitting them over the head right at the start, and it's a much stronger opening than "This essay will discuss..." or "The subject of this essay is...."

You're not writing about car insurance premiums, though; you're writing about which side (consumers or brokers) makes the stronger case in the passages. The thesis statement, which we'll discuss next, makes the topic of your essay clear.

The Thesis Statement After the attention-getter comes the thesis statement, which makes the claim that you intend to prove in the rest of your essay. In this case, the claim is that passage X provides the stronger support for its position. The thesis statement might read as follows:

> "In the dispute between drivers and insurance brokers, the consumers' group provides stronger evidence for its position that the steep rise in car insurance premiums is both unfair and unnecessary."

Depending on your attention-getter, you might need to add some type of transition sentence to tie that first sentence to the thesis statement.

Although it's called a statement, the thesis can be more than one sentence long. It should be specific: The example above mentions the two sides, the subject of the dispute, and the stronger side's position. It should also cover *only* what you will support with evidence in your essay.

The Big Picture Arguments Finally, the first paragraph ends with a high-level list of the evidence that supports your thesis statement and which you'll explain in detail in the middle paragraphs. You've already got a list of this evidence (the authors' arguments in the chart you made up during your active reading of the passages). Sticking with the car insurance topic, let's say you found three pieces of evidence that make the "stronger" side's support better. You would finish the introductory paragraph by listing those three arguments:

> "As the consumers' group points out, insurance companies made record profits last year, while the average driver had to cope with a 10 percent increase in gas prices but only a one percent rise in wages."

The Middle

In the next few paragraphs (likely the same number as the number of points you outlined in the "big picture arguments" part of the first paragraph), you'll provide evidence to support each argument that proves your thesis. Be sure to explain *why* or *how* it proves your thesis. Remember, too, that you need to incorporate some evidence from the less-supported passage. Deal with one point per paragraph, and start each paragraph with a topic sentence.

The Topic Sentence The topic sentence is just what it says—a sentence that introduces the topic of the paragraph. Like transition and signal words (see page 166 in Chapter 5), it guides the reader through your essay and demonstrates your skill in organizing and developing your argument, traits on which you'll be graded. It does not give details about the topic (such as dollar amounts or dates or specific examples). Those come later in the paragraph.

Let's take the example of the consumers' first argument in the car insurance case. They say that car insurance companies already made record profits last year. Read the paragraph below and see how you think it flows, not counting the bracketed words, which are just our own notes and would not be in the actual essay. Remember that it would be the next paragraph after the introductory paragraph.

> The consumers' argument that the car insurance industry recorded $10 billion in profits last year, more than any year in the past decade, proves that the insurance companies don't really need extra money. The brokers' position [here we're drawing in some evidence from the less-supported passage too] is much weaker because it doesn't address the industry's financial success. Three years of flat premiums do not justify raising prices, as the brokers argue, when the insurance companies have already made so much money.

The essay writer just jumped into that first argument. Now see how much more smoothly this writer glides into the argument by using a topic sentence before getting into specific details such as $10 billion in profits.

> The consumer group refutes the brokers' claim about cash-poor insurance companies. The consumers' argument that the car insurance industry recorded $10 billion in profits last year....

The next paragraph (the third one) could then begin with a topic sentence introducing the consumers' second argument and making a smooth transition to the new point.

> On the other hand [this signals a transition], the consumers argue, they are already paying more to drive.

Following that topic sentence, you would provide details about this second argument (the 10 percent increase in gas prices), and point out what makes it stronger (likely the brokers ignored the issue).

The fourth paragraph would repeat this formula with the third argument, which says consumers' wages haven't increased enough to cover the extra driving costs they already face.

The Evidence The rest of each middle paragraph will give details about the "relevant and specific" (as the prompt says) piece of evidence you're explaining in that particular paragraph. Again, this information is in the chart you made during the active reading phase. So, continuing on from the topic sentence, you'll:

- describe the author's argument and the support they provide for that argument in the passage; remember to be specific
- explain why that evidence proves your thesis that one passage has the better support (in other words, explain why it's relevant)

> Be specific. If the passage says the price of cabbages fell by two percent, use that product and figure. Don't be vague and say the price of vegetables is lower.

Here's the complete paragraph describing the consumer group's first argument, with notes pointing out what function each part of the paragraph performs.

> The consumer group refutes the brokers' claim about cash-poor insurance companies [the topic sentence]. The consumers' argument that the car insurance industry recorded $10 billion in profits last year, more than any year in the past decade, [the argument and support for it] proves that the insurance companies don't really need extra money [how this argument proves the thesis that the consumers' case has better support]. The brokers' position is much weaker because it doesn't address the industry's financial success [evidence brought in from the other passage]. Three years of flat premiums do not justify raising prices, as the brokers argue, when the insurance companies have already made so much money [how this argument is weaker, which again proves the thesis that the consumers' case has better support].

Quoting and Paraphrasing Evidence How you incorporate evidence into your essay is important. You can't quote directly from the passage unless you put the author's words in quotation marks. Without the quotation marks, it's called plagiarism. In many colleges, that earns you a mark on your record the first time and expulsion the second. Adults have lost established careers when their decades-old acts of plagiarism were exposed. It's important to start building the habit now of correctly including sources.

How do you include evidence from the passages, then? Most of the time, the answer is paraphrase—rephrase the evidence in your own words. For example, let's say the brokers' passage contains the following argument and support for the argument:

> Insurance companies report little or no increase in average premiums during the past three years. However, claims payouts have risen, on average, by three percent in each of those years.

Try rephrasing that in your own words.

Did you end up with something like "The brokers argue that premium revenue has remained flat for three years, while claims expenses have kept increasing"?

Next, you need to explain *why* that paraphrased piece of evidence is important to your thesis.

> The brokers weaken their own case by mentioning rising claims costs but failing to acknowledge the other side of the story: the record profits that more than cover the insurance companies' higher claims payouts.

When should you use a direct quote (in quotation marks)?

- When the passage author's exact words are important for proving your thesis
- When the author phrases an idea in such a unique way that a paraphrase wouldn't convey its true meaning accurately

Both cases will be rare in the passages you're likely to encounter in the Extended Response section, so you should usually count on paraphrasing your evidence. You should also be sure to mention which side of the debate offered the evidence you're using.

Paraphrasing Exercise Imagine the following statements are made in a passage. Try paraphrasing them so you can use them as evidence in your essay. Some possible paraphrases are below the list of statements.

1. A landmark study conducted in Antarctica found that penguins were thriving despite the evidence of the toll taken by climate change on other facets of the environment.
2. In its report, the commission concluded, "We should all learn from the experiences of First Nations people, who are trying to strike a balance between their traditional customs and the change demanded by industrial development."
3. Although fish farming increases the supply of fish, there is alarming evidence that it lowers the quality.

There is no one "correct" paraphrase. An acceptable paraphrase should be in your own words and should convey the content of the original statement accurately. Below are some possible ways to paraphrase these statements.

1. Penguins in Antarctica are flourishing, according to a pioneering study, even though climate change is causing environmental damage elsewhere on the continent.
2. The commission's report highlighted the lessons to be learned from the conflict between the growth of new industries and the traditional way of life for First Nations.
3. Evidence suggests that fish farms lead to higher production but lower quality.

The End

Ideally, the final paragraph concludes your argument by restating your thesis *in different words,* and reminding readers of the arguments that prove your thesis. Your final paragraph will be stronger if you simply say it and avoid starting with "In conclusion,..."

> Because it considers both consumers and the insurance industry, and backs up its claims with actual figures, the consumer group's letter to the editor provides the better support. (This topic sentence introduces the main arguments and restates the thesis.) The group draws a strong contrast between the industry's record profits on the one hand and, on the other, a 10 percent increase in drivers' fuel costs that must be financed with only a one percent average increase in wages. The brokers' weak argument that a premium increase is overdue, and their failure to consider consumers' financial hardship, make their position the weaker of the two. (These sentences remind readers of the main arguments in the passages.)

The Five-Paragraph Essay

This is the classic template. You might even remember it from earlier years in school. The first paragraph is the introduction (the beginning described earlier). Along with the attention-getter and the thesis statement, it gives three high-level reasons why the thesis statement is true.

Each of the next three paragraphs provides details about one of those three reasons. The second paragraph begins with a topic sentence covering the first reason you mentioned, and explains details about it. The third paragraph does the same for the second reason, and the fourth paragraph for the third reason. Those paragraphs are the middle described above.

The fifth paragraph is the conclusion (the end). It wraps up the thesis statement and the details from the middle section, and concludes your argument neatly. It doesn't simply restate the introduction, though, because by now you've added details that put meat on the bare bones of the introduction.

Of course, your essay doesn't have to be exactly five paragraphs. You might have four reasons for your thesis statement, or only two. There might be six reasons, but two of them are so weak they're not worth discussing. There is an expectation that the essay will be four to seven paragraphs in length, of three to seven sentences each, but that's the only guideline the test writers give.

Prewriting

The template above gives you an organizational structure into which you can pour your essay (remember, organization is one of the traits on which you'll be graded) and a plan to follow in developing your argument about which passage has stronger support.

> You'll save time and write a better essay if you spend five minutes planning.

The template also explains why you don't just jump in and start writing. Your essay will sound like you just jumped in and started writing. For a coherent, persuasive essay that responds to the prompt, "hangs together" well, and gets a high score, you first need to plan it. That's where prewriting comes in.

Understanding your task through upfront thinking and planning has a tremendous impact on the quality of the final product (your Extended Response, in this case). As one of the world's great minds said,

> "If I had an hour to solve a problem I'd spend 55 minutes thinking about the problem and 5 minutes thinking about solutions."
>
> —Albert Einstein

We're certainly not advocating that you spend more than 90 percent of the time thinking about the task in the prompt, but do spend five minutes or so thinking about why one passage provides stronger support, and planning the order in which you'll discuss the evidence from the passages. Use a note board to jot down any ideas you have for a strong opening paragraph and conclusion. Write a number beside each point in your argument/support chart to remind yourself which claim you want to cover first, second, and so on. You can cross off each one as you finish discussing it, so you'll see the progress you're making.

Taking a few of your 45 minutes to plan will save you from getting 40 minutes into writing and realizing you're badly off track. It will also leave you a couple of minutes at the end to review your essay so you can improve it and fix errors. (There are no spelling or grammar checkers for the Extended Response section, so you're on your own.)

Your goal with prewriting is to have the whole essay essentially done—in your head, in thin air, on your note boards, wherever. It's just not written down yet, and that's all you need to do with the next 30 or so minutes, leaving yourself a couple of minutes at the end to review and improve what you've written.

Dividing Up Your Time

5 minutes—Actively reading the two passages, noting the main arguments and supporting points on the chart
5 minutes—Prewriting
32 minutes—Writing
3 minutes—Reviewing and improving the essay

45 minutes

HOW CAN I IMPROVE MY WRITING?

You already encountered several ways to improve your writing: the eight areas of language use targeted on the GED® test (see page 223 in Chapter 8) and the use of a topic sentence to begin each paragraph (see page 258 in this chapter).

Here are two more tips to make your writing stronger, more interesting, and easier to read.

Use Active Verbs

As the name implies, with an active verb, the subject is performing the action. With a passive verb, the subject is passive; the action is being done to it. Take a look at these stripped-down examples:

> John closed the door. (That's an active verb. The subject, John, is doing the closing.)

> The door was closed by John. (That's passive. The subject, the door, is getting the action done to it.)

Recognizing active and passive verbs gets a bit more complicated when phrases and clauses enter the picture:

> Tired, cold, and hungry from their frightening adventure in the dark woods, the *three boys began devising a plan* to return home without attracting the attention of anyone in the house. (That's active—the wayward boys are devising the plan.)

> Although the antique mahogany piano weighed a ton and would have sold for a fortune, *it was unloaded* from the moving van quickly and carelessly, in complete defiance of its great value. (Here's a passive verb—the subject, the piano, is receiving the action of being unloaded.)

There are a few cases in which you might want to use a passive verb. Let's say the owner of the small company where you work forgot to pay the computer service contract fee last month, leading the service company to cancel its contract. What do you tell Sofia in accounting when she asks why she can't get her computer fixed? Do you say, "Our idiot boss forgot to pay the computer service invoice last month"? (That's an active verb, by the way—the subject is doing the forgetting.) No, not likely. You might say something like, "The bill wasn't paid on time last month." That's passive—the subject is the one getting acted upon (in this case, not being paid). By using a passive verb, you can focus on the action and avoid blaming the one who carried out that action (the boss).

Cases in which a passive verb is a better choice are rare, though. Your writing will be stronger and more interesting to read if you use active verbs most of the time.

Active Verb Exercise

Try turning the passive verbs in the following sentences into active verbs. You'll find answers below. After you've finished, compare the active and passive versions. Notice how much stronger and easier to read the active version is.

1. An umbrella was purchased by Juanita because of the weather forecast for several days of rain.
2. Since it was clearly dying, the tree was felled by city maintenance workers.
3. After receiving a prize for the best children's book of the year, the author was honored at a lavish reception given by the local literary society.
4. The house was renovated during the winter by electricians, plumbers, and painters.

Here are some possible answers:

1. Juanita bought an umbrella because the weather forecast called for several days of rain.
2. City maintenance workers felled the tree because it was clearly dying.
3. The local literary society held a lavish reception to honor the author of the best children's book of the year.
4. Electricians, plumbers, and painters renovated the house during the winter.

Use Variety in Sentence Length and Structure

How many paragraphs like the one below could you read?

> Carrots are a root vegetable. Carrots are healthy. Carrots contain beta-carotene. Beta-carotene is an antioxidant. Carrots have Vitamin A. Vitamin A is good for vision.

Are you tired of those short, choppy sentences yet? They're all the same structure and all about the same length. They soon become boring, and they make the topic they're describing sound boring too.

Look what happens when you combine these short sentences in different ways, though. Now the subject is interesting and the writing is more engaging.

> Carrots, a root vegetable, are healthy because they contain the antioxidant beta-carotene. They also have Vitamin A, which is good for vision.
>
> Carrots are loaded with beta-carotene, an antioxidant. This root vegetable is also healthy because it contains Vitamin A, a vision-boosting nutrient.
>
> Carrots, a member of the root vegetable family, provide the vision and health benefits of Vitamin A and the antioxidant beta-carotene.
>
> Health and vision benefits come from carrots, a root vegetable, because of the beta-carotene (an antioxidant) and Vitamin A they provide.

As those examples show, you can combine short sentences into more interesting structures in several ways.

- By coordinating or subordinating thoughts from two or more sentences (see pages 226–227 in Chapter 8)
- By using phrases ("Carrots, a member *of the root vegetable family,...*")
- By using a series of words ("...beta-carotene and Vitamin A")
- By using compound subjects or verbs ("*Health and vision benefits* come from carrots...")

Sentence Variety Exercise

Try your hand at combining the following short sentences into more varied structures. See how many different solutions you can create. One possible answer is below the short sentences.

> The house was painted white. The house was old. The paint was faded. The stairs were crooked. The porch floor had a hole. Some windows were broken. The house was empty. The house was not welcoming.

There are many possible ways to combine those sentences into a more interesting description of the house. Here's just one way:

> The old house, with its faded white paint and broken windows, stood empty. Its crooked stairs and unsafe porch floor made it seem unwelcoming.

HOW DO I IMPROVE MY COMPLETED ESSAY?

Because you planned your essay before you started writing, you should have about three minutes left to review it. The test writers don't expect a perfect job in 45 minutes (*they* probably couldn't do a perfect job in 45 minutes, either). However, you should use the extra time to improve your essay as much as you can, revising and editing it as you read through it.

Revising

When you revise your work, you're making changes to the content. No, you won't have much time to do this, but you can check to make sure that you've supported each of your arguments with evidence drawn from the passages, and that you've explained how the evidence proves your thesis (that one passage is better supported than the other). If you notice a statement that seems unclear, see whether there's a better way to say what you intended.

Editing

Editing involves simply correcting language and spelling errors, without changing the content of your essay. Watch for the eight language use points explained in Chapter 8. (See page 223.) Remember, too, that you can't rely on spelling or grammar checkers in the test.

Reminder: the test has no spelling or grammar checkers.

PUTTING IT ALL TOGETHER

Let's use a fairly straightforward example to work through the process of building and organizing an argument. The first passage is a flyer for a seminar at which modern urban cave dwellers can learn about the Paleo diet, the diet of the hunter-gatherers who roamed the earth before the birth of agriculture and the domestication of livestock. The second is a warning notice on the bulletin board of a sports medicine clinic that has many patients who do CrossFit training, a program that recommends the Paleo diet.

Remember, these passages will appear on the page 2 tab on the left side of your screen.

Use active reading to extract the authors' arguments and support as you read, and note them in a chart. Then plan, write, and review your essay. Use the questions listed in Chapter 10 (see page 251) to assess your own work. Then read the suggestions at the end of this example.

Passage A

Are you living in an unheated, unlit basement cave but still eating like it's the 21st century?

1 Embrace the Paleo diet and harmonize your lifestyle!

What is the Paleo diet?

2 It's a way of eating that's close to that of Paleolithic humans. It means eating the foods that our bodies evolved to consume.

3 The Paleo diet eliminates all foods that were not available in Paleolithic times. It avoids many staples of the modern American diet, such as grains, dairy, high-fat meats, starchy vegetables, legumes, sugars, salty foods, and processed foods. It includes foods that are as similar as possible to foods available to Paleolithic humans. That means grass-fed beef and free-range bison instead of the corn-fed meat readily available at most grocery stores.

What makes it good for you?

4
- By eliminating legumes, grains, and processed foods, the Paleo diet results in a healthy weight loss for most people. In a study of 14 participants, those who followed a strict Paleo diet lost an average of five pounds after three weeks on the program.
- Debilitating diseases such as cancer, arthritis, multiple sclerosis, and diabetes are a modern problem, brought on partly by cultivated crops. These illnesses were unknown in Paleolithic times, when people ate a diet rich in meat and in the berries, fruits, and nuts that grew naturally around them.

- The Paleo diet is "clean." It doesn't contain additives, preservatives, or chemicals that have been linked to lower energy levels and problems focusing on detailed tasks. The plant nutrients in the Paleo diet have significant anti-inflammatory benefits, and the higher red meat intake leads to an increase in iron. Followers find they can accomplish more in their day.

- The Paleo diet promotes a natural rotation of nutrients in harmony with the seasons and the landscape. By eating only what would have been available in a particular season and location, people following the Paleo diet avoid overworking their digestive systems with out-of-sync foods, such as fresh oranges in the depths of the Wisconsin winter.

Want to learn more?

5 Join us for a free seminar to

- see the Paleo diet creator, Dr. Loren Cordain, on video as he explains the theory and benefits of eating the Paleolithic way

- hear real-life stories from fans who will never go back to a modern diet

- sample some Paleo staples

Tuesday night at 7:30 p.m.
Charming Gulf District School auditorium
at the corner of Relling & 184th St

Don't just live like our ancestors—eat like them too!

Passage B

6 The medical staff at Sutton Sports Medical Centre cautions patients about the harmful effects of the Paleo diet, which many of you are following.

7 The potential risks include:

8 **Nutritional imbalance**—Even with a very long list of allowed foods, the Paleo diet does not provide guidance on a balanced approach to nutrition. It also does not guarantee that people following the plan get enough of certain nutrients that are necessary to optimal health.

9 **Weight gain**—Because many of the allowed foods (such as nuts) are very high in calories, some people may find that following the Paleo diet actually causes weight gain instead of the rapid weight loss promised by the program. For instance, calorie consumption becomes a problem if a person eats five pounds of nuts in the course of one day.

10 **Suboptimal athletic performance**—The diet is restrictive in carbohydrates, which may be inadequate for athletes who use carbohydrates as a source of energy when exercising. Athletes need between three to six grams of carbs per pound of body weight per day; this is very difficult to achieve when consuming only the foods allowed by the Paleo diet. Thus, athletes may be faced with suboptimal performance.

11 **Bone and heart problems**—Removing all dairy products from your diet can cause a significant decrease in calcium and Vitamin D. A reduction in these essential nutrients can be harmful to bone health. In addition, the diet's focus on red meat can cause heart problems; a 2012 study confirmed that red meat consumption is associated with an increased risk of cardiovascular disease.

12 The clinic's resident nutritionist, Dr. Arpad Geuin, is available to create a diet plan customized to your nutritional needs and athletic goals.

Here's How to Crack It

Follow the steps we've explained.

1. Build your argument, using active reading to extract evidence (the authors' arguments and how they support those arguments), and note them on a chart.
2. Decide on your thesis (which passage is best supported).
3. Plan how you will organize the evidence.
4. Fill in the essay template to write your essay.
5. Review and improve your work.

Building the Argument

This example makes it easy to find the arguments each side uses to make its case. In most of the passages you'll encounter in the Extended Response section, the arguments will be "buried" in text paragraphs instead of clearly laid out in bullet points.

The charts you filled in during your active reading might look like the ones below. (Of course, given the limited time you have on the test, yours would contain a lot of short forms and abbreviations.)

Pro side (flyer):

Argument	Support
weight loss (paragraph 4)	study (paragraph 4)
no modern illnesses (paragraph 4)	unknown in Paleolithic times (paragraph 4)
followers get more done (paragraph 4)	more energy, better focus (paragraph 4)
followers don't overwork digestive systems (paragraph 4)	natural rotation of nutrients (paragraph 4)

Con side (warning):

Argument	Support
nutritional imbalance (paragraph 8)	no guidance on balanced nutrition (paragraph 8)
weight gain (paragraph 9)	nuts example (paragraph 9)
lower athletic performance (paragraph 10)	amount of carbs needed (paragraph 10)
bone and heart problems (paragraph 11)	red meat study (paragraph 11)

Now you have a bare bones list of the evidence you need. Each side presents four arguments, all of them supported. Two of the arguments are contradictory (weight loss/weight gain). Which passage is better supported?

Choosing Your Thesis

Although an effective argument can be created for either passage, for this example let's say you choose the warning. You might choose this one because it cites one study (as the flyer does), but also gives specific figures (the nuts and carbs) for two other arguments. Its author is familiar enough with the diet to know that it doesn't include advice on balanced nutrition. (Showing an understanding of the other side's position boosts credibility.) The warning's support is more specific and credible than the support offered in the flyer too. In two cases, the flyer supports arguments with only the vague experiences of unidentified "followers" of the diet.

The strongest reason for choosing the warning side, though, could lie in the authors and their purposes. The flyer's author is trying to promote a seminar, and is making the assumption that urban cave dwellers want to eat like the real thing—not necessarily a valid assumption. The promotional tone of the flyer and the benefits offered (free food samples, video) undercut the credibility of the "pro" side's argument. The warning's author, on the other hand, has the credibility of being a medical professional. This author's purpose is to prevent the clinic's patients from damaging their health with a harmful diet, and the underlying assumption that patients are concerned about their health is valid.

Organizing Your Argument

From the chart, you can see that you'll end up with a six-paragraph essay: the introduction (the beginning), one paragraph for each of the four arguments (the middle), and a conclusion (the end).

You have two choices for the order in which you'd discuss the arguments. You could stick with the order in which they're listed in the better-supported passage you've chosen (the warning), or else start with the warning's strongest argument (either the heart issue, which is supported with a specific study, or else the low athletic performance, which would be important to the warning's audience). Here, too, there is no right or wrong answer; choose the order you think you could do the best job of covering in the middle four paragraphs. Remember to start each paragraph with a topic sentence and use transitions (such as "in addition" or "furthermore") to guide readers smoothly through your discussion of the four pieces of evidence.

Writing the Essay

Now you've got everything you need to write your essay. You have your thesis (that the warning provides the best support), the evidence that supports your thesis (the arguments from the chart), and the template to follow in presenting your points. So let's get started on the writing.

The Introduction This example would work well with a question attention-getter:

> Should modern urban cave dwellers and athletes be eating like Paleolithic people?

Then you would tie that question to the topic of your essay, state your thesis, and give the big picture outline of the arguments:

> The promoter of a Paleo diet seminar thinks they should. However, a sports medicine clinic's warning about the diet's nutritional, health, and athletic dangers is better supported than the arguments in favor of eating like our ancient ancestors.

The Middle Here you'd give the evidence from the passage (one argument per paragraph), and explain why it proves your thesis that the case against the Paleo diet is better supported.

For instance, if you're following the order used by the better-supported side, you would begin with the evidence about nutritional imbalance, which is supported by a medical professional's familiarity with the Paleo diet and its lack of guidance about nutrition. You could also point out the weakness of the corresponding argument from the seminar promoter: The vague statements about a natural rotation of nutrients and not overworking the digestive system aren't credible from someone who isn't a professional nutritionist.

The next three paragraphs would deal with the next three arguments, always explaining how each one contributes to proving your thesis that the warning is better supported.

The End Here you would restate your thesis in different words, and remind readers of the main pieces of evidence that prove your thesis. This concluding paragraph might say something like this:

> Based on the credibility of the medical professional who wrote the warning and the specific support for the arguments given, the case against the Paleo diet is better supported. Detailed figures back up the arguments about health dangers (weight gain and cardiovascular problems) as well as the argument about lower athletic performance. This author has also made the effort to learn about the Paleo diet, and has noted its failure to provide nutritional guidance. The seminar promoter, on the other hand, cites only one study and is clearly trying to entice people to attend by mentioning the goodies that will be available.

Reviewing Your Work

Now, while you're practicing, you have time to ask yourself the questions listed in Chapter 10 (see page 251) to assess your own work. During the test, of course, you won't. Then, you'll simply be reviewing your essay to revise it (is something not clear? is there a better way to say it?) and edit it (correcting grammar and spelling errors).

Online Practice Drills
For extra practice with Reasoning Through Language Arts topics, register your book online to access two digital RLA drills in your Student Tools.

Extended Response Drills

Now *you* try building and organizing your argument and writing an essay on your own. There are two Extended Response tasks below. (Remember, the more practice you get, the better you'll become at writing these essays.)

The first task, about electric vehicles, will give you some experience digging evidence out of the text paragraphs in two very different types of documents. The second, about antibiotics in farm animal feed, provides an example of unequally weighted evidence (one main argument on one side, several on the other). Depending on your opinion about this issue, it might also allow you to exercise the discipline of arguing for a position with which you don't agree.

Use active reading to extract the authors' arguments and support as you read, and note them in a chart. Then plan, write, and review your essay. Use the questions listed in Chapter 10 (see page 251) to assess your own work. Then read the suggestions in Part IX: Answer Key to Drills.

Instructions

Read

- On the **page 2 tab above,** you will **read two texts** presenting **different views** on the same topic.
- **Both writers argue** that **their position** on the issue is **correct.**

Plan

- **Analyze** the two texts **to determine** which writer presents the **stronger case.**
- **Develop your own argument** in which **you explain** how one position is **better supported** than the other.
- **Include** relevant and specific **evidence** from **both sources** to support your argument.

Write

- **Type** your response in the **box on the right.**
- Your response should be approximately **4 to 7 paragraphs of 3 to 7 sentences each.**
- **Remember** to allow a few minutes **to review and edit your response.**

You have up to **45 minutes** for reading, planning, writing, and editing your response.

Electric Vehicles

Below are two passages: a government document about the benefits of electric vehicles and a letter from a father to his daughter, urging her not to buy an electric car because of the dangers.

Passage A

The following document uses these short forms (or acronyms) in discussing different types of vehicles powered by electricity: EV (electric vehicle), HEV (hybrid electric vehicle), and PHEV (plug-in hybrid electric vehicle).

Benefits and Considerations of Electricity as a Vehicle Fuel

1 All forms of energy vehicles can help improve fuel economy, lower fuel costs, and reduce emissions.

Energy Security

2 The United States became a net exporter of petroleum in 2020 with exports surpassing imports, although imports of 7.86 million barrels per day remained an important part of balancing supply and demand for domestic and international markets. Overall, the transportation sector accounts for approximately 30% of total U.S. energy needs and 70% of U.S. petroleum consumption.

3 Using more energy-efficient vehicles like hybrid and electric vehicles supports the U.S. economy and helps diversify the U.S. transportation fleet. The multiple fuel sources used to generate electricity results in a more secure energy source for the electrified portion of the transportation sector. All of this adds to our nation's energy security.

Fuel Economy

4 Hybrid electric vehicles (HEVs) typically use less fuel than similar conventional vehicles. Both plug-in hybrid electric vehicles (PHEVs) and all-electric vehicles are capable of being powered solely by electricity.

5 Electric vehicles can reduce fuel costs dramatically because of the high efficiency of electric-drive components. Because all-electric vehicles and PHEVs rely in whole or part on electric power, their fuel economy is measured differently than that of conventional vehicles. Miles per gallon of gasoline equivalent (MPGe) and kilowatt-hours (kWh) per 100 miles are common metrics. Depending on how they are driven, today's light-duty all-electric vehicles (or PHEVs in electric mode) can exceed 130 MPGe and can drive 100 miles consuming only 25–40 kWh.

Infrastructure Availability

6 All-electric vehicles and PHEVs have the benefit of flexible charging because the electric grid is near most locations where people park. To safely deliver energy from the electric grid to a vehicle's battery, a charging station, sometimes referred to as electric vehicle supply equipment (EVSE), is needed. Drivers can charge overnight at a residence, as well as at multi-family housing, the workplace, or a public charging station when available. PHEVs have added flexibility because they can also refuel with gasoline or diesel (or possibly other fuels in the future) when necessary.

7 Public charging stations are not as ubiquitous as gas stations. Charging equipment manufacturers, automakers, utilities, Clean Cities coalitions, municipalities, and government agencies are rapidly establishing a national network of public charging stations. The number of publicly accessible charging stations reached more than 41,000 in 2021, offering more than 100,000 places to charge.

Costs

8 Although energy costs for electric vehicles are generally lower than for similar conventional vehicles, purchase prices can be significantly higher. Prices are likely to equalize with conventional vehicles, as production volumes increase and battery technologies continue to mature. Also, initial costs can be offset by fuel cost savings, a federal tax credit, and state and utility incentives.

Emissions

9 Hybrid and plug-in electric vehicles can have significant emissions benefits over conventional vehicles. All-electric vehicles produce zero tailpipe emissions, and PHEVs produce no tailpipe emissions when operating in all-electric mode. HEV emissions benefits vary by vehicle model and type of hybrid power system.

Source: Office of Energy Efficiency and Renewable Energy (EERE), U.S. Department of Energy (Abridged)

Passage B

10 My dear Melissa:

11 I'm so proud of you for completing your dental technician course and graduating with such exceptional grades!

12 As promised when you first returned to school, I'm transferring enough money to your account to allow you to buy a reasonably priced new car. You deserve this reward for your perseverance and hard work.

13 The choice of car is up to you. However, I know you want to "live green" and I'm concerned you might be thinking of an electric vehicle. If you are, I want to urge you to buy a regular gasoline-powered car instead. Your safety is very important to me, and there are just too many dangers with an electric vehicle.

14 First, you could find yourself stranded on a dark highway in the middle of nowhere. Electric cars have such a limited range (an average of about 250 miles) and even a state as big as Texas has only about 2,000 charging stations. Assuming you can find a public charging post when you need one, a charge can take hours if it's not a rapid-charge station. I have visions of you hanging around some station alone at night for up to eight hours.

15 Second, parts and repairs for electric cars are much more expensive. And the batteries need to be replaced after about five years, at a cost of thousands of dollars. That's on top of the initial price of the car, which can be as much as twice the cost of a gasoline-powered car.

16 Third, electric cars are not as environmentally friendly as you might think. Making the batteries requires the mining of rare-earth minerals such as lithium and cobalt, the supplies of which could not possibly support all the electric vehicles that people might want to purchase in the future. What's the difference between drilling for oil and mining for lithium?

17 And finally, I've been seeing news reports of a few electric vehicles catching on fire while they're just sitting in the owner's garage or driveway. No one seems to know what causes them to ignite, but I don't want to be worrying about you every night asleep in your ground-floor apartment while your car is burning away just outside.

18 I hope you enjoy your well-deserved reward, and that you'll use it wisely and choose a gasoline-powered car.

19 Your loving father.

Antibiotics in Farm Animal Feed

Below are two passages: a government media release about a voluntary ban on antibiotics in farm animal feed, and a posting on a farmers' online forum warning about the negative effects such a ban would have on farmers, consumers, and the economy. (The instructions for this drill are the same as those for the previous drill; for a refresher, see page 272.)

Passage A

1 The Food and Drug Administration (FDA) is implementing a voluntary plan with industry to phase out the use of certain antibiotics for enhanced food production.

2 Antibiotics are added to the animal feed or drinking water of cattle, hogs, poultry, and other food-producing animals to help them gain weight faster or use less food to gain weight.

3 Because all uses of antimicrobial drugs, in both humans and animals, contribute to the development of antimicrobial resistance, it is important to use these drugs only when medically necessary. Governments around the world consider antimicrobial-resistant bacteria a major threat to public health. Illnesses caused by drug-resistant strains of bacteria are more likely to be potentially fatal when the medicines used to treat them are rendered less effective.

4 FDA is working to address the use of "medically important" antibiotics in food-producing animals for production uses, such as to enhance growth or improve feed efficiency. These drugs are deemed important because they are also used to treat human disease and might not work if the bacteria they target become resistant to the drugs' effects.

5 "We need to be selective about the drugs we use in animals and when we use them," says William Flynn, DVM, MS, deputy director for science policy at FDA's Center for Veterinary Medicine (CVM). "Antimicrobial resistance may not be completely preventable, but we need to do what we can to slow it down."

6 Once manufacturers voluntarily make these changes, the affected products can then be used only in food-producing animals to treat, prevent, or control disease under the order of or by prescription from a licensed veterinarian.

7 Bacteria evolve to survive threats to their existence. In both humans and animals, even appropriate therapeutic uses of antibiotics can promote the development of drug-resistant bacteria. When such bacteria enter the food supply, they can be transferred to the people who eat food from the treated animal.

Why Voluntary?

8 Flynn explains that the final guidance document made participation voluntary because it is the fastest, most efficient way to make these changes. FDA has been working with associations that include those representing drug companies, the feed industry, producers of beef, pork, and turkey, as well as veterinarians and consumer groups.

Source: U.S. Food and Drug Administration (Abridged)

Passage B

The following posting appeared on the FairToFarmers.org forum.

Ban the FDA's Antibiotic Ban!

9 The FDA is banning the use of antibiotics in animal feed. Food producers will be barred from adding antibiotics to feed or water unless an animal is sick and threatens the health of the rest of the herd or flock. Even then, a veterinarian's order will be required.

10 The FDA fails to realize that the regular use of antibiotics *prevents* disease, and prevention is much cheaper than curing an illness that has taken root on the farm. Antibiotics not only maintain animal health; they also promote faster growth, and therefore faster time to market. In addition, antibiotics lead to more efficient growth, since less feed is required to reach the desired weight.

11 The FDA's reasoning is that antibiotic use in food animals *might* contribute to the development of antibiotic-resistant "superbugs." Scientific studies have so far been inconclusive, and some point to doctors overprescribing antibiotics for human patients as the cause, together with unsafe food handling practices by consumers. The FDA made the ban voluntary for the present; but if the scientific evidence were clear, the ban would have been mandatory right away.

12 European countries that have banned antibiotics in animal feed have not seen a decline in antibiotic-resistant diseases, but they have seen a significant increase in meat and poultry prices and a reduction in export sales. Food animals take several days longer to reach the desired weight and consume more feed before they do, increasing farmers' costs.

13 Each American farmer today feeds an average of 155 people, *six times* more than in 1960. Advances in agricultural practices, including the regular use of antibiotics in animal feed, have made that possible. Without antibiotics, American farmers will not be able to meet the food needs of a growing population.

14 Do people want enough food? Do they want affordable food? Do politicians want a thriving agricultural economy? Then we must end this voluntary ban on antibiotics in animal feed while we still can, before it becomes mandatory.

15 Add your voice to the petition to ban the FDA's ban on antibiotics in animal feed. Simply click on the button below. The petition will be delivered to the FDA when we have 100,000 signatures.

Petition to Ban the FDA Ban on Antibiotics in Animal Feed

Part VI
Mathematical Reasoning

Chapter 12
Mathematical Reasoning Overview

If the GED® Mathematical Reasoning test covered all the math topics taught in high school, it would be an overwhelming test. Fortunately, it doesn't, and it isn't. The GED® test writers concentrate on a few areas very heavily, which means that by reading the chapters that follow and doing the exercises we provide, you should be able to score very well—even if you've always hated math.

What's on the Test

The Mathematical Reasoning test contains 46 questions to be answered in 115 minutes, which gives you two and a half minutes for each question. The areas covered in the Mathematical Reasoning test are as follows:

Quantitative Problem Solving with Rational Numbers	25%
Quantitative Problem Solving in Measurement	20%
Algebraic Problem Solving with Expressions and Equations	30%
Algebraic Problem Solving with Graphs and Functions	25%

What Isn't on the Test

There is no calculus or even precalculus. No logs, no proofs, no imaginary numbers. To make things even easier, the Mathematical Reasoning test provides a list of formulas that you can reference, just in case you don't remember how to find the volume of a cylinder, for example.

To Calculate, or Not to Calculate?

The 46-question Mathematical Reasoning test is broken up into two parts. In the first part, you will have 5 questions and you *will not* be allowed to use a calculator. You *must* submit your answers to these 5 questions before moving on to the rest of the test. In the second part, you will have 41 questions and you *will* be allowed to use a calculator.

You may think that the second section (in which you can use a calculator) would be easier than the first, but there's one hitch: You can't take your *own* calculator. You must use the on-screen calculator that is automatically available: the Texas Instruments TI-30XS, shown below.

You will be provided on-screen instructions for using the calculator. However, it is vital that you become familiar with this particular model ahead of time. Why spend your valuable test time learning how to use the calculator when that time could be better spent actually solving the questions? We strongly recommend that you buy (or borrow) this specific calculator and practice with it for several weeks before the test. It is available in most office supply stores or online for about $20–$25. Additionally, check out GED Testing Service's helpful TI-30XS Calculator Reference Sheet at GED.com/content/dam/websites/ged/post/calculator-sheet.pdf.

There are two major features of the Texas Instruments TI-30XS that can be pretty confusing. They are the arrow keys and the green "2nd" key.

The arrow keys (located at the top right) can be used to move within a function on the screen or to exit a function and return to the main expression you are calculating. You will use the arrow keys to input fractions, mixed numbers, or numbers in scientific notation.

Pushing the "2nd" key (located at the top left) before another key accesses the function that is written above the key, similarly to the way the "Shift" key works on a computer keyboard. You will use this to input mixed numbers and to calculate roots and percentages.

The Calculator is Color Coded!
The GREEN "2nd" key accesses the functions written in GREEN above the other calculator keys.

Let's take a look at how you would input the mixed number $12\frac{1}{2}$:

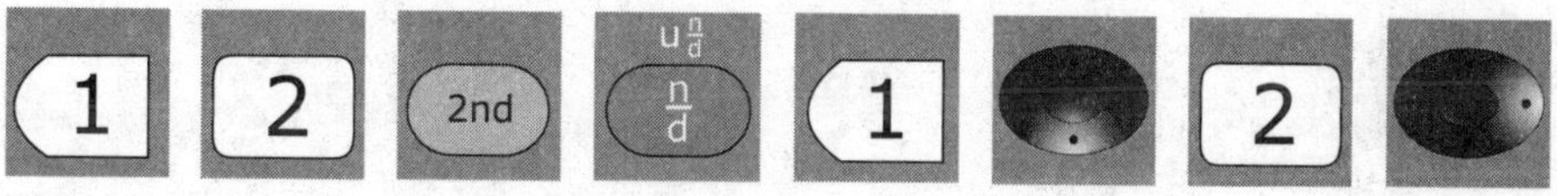

You can see why we are telling you to get the calculator in advance and become familiar with it.

Will All the Math Questions Be Multiple Choice?

At least 50 percent of the Mathematical Reasoning test is multiple choice. But both Parts 1 and 2 could include question formats such as fill in the blank, drag and drop, hot spot, or drop down. You should have already seen what these look like in Chapter 3 of this book. If not, take the time to review that chapter now.

Ballparking

We've already introduced you to the concept of POE in Part I of this book, and we've explained that there's no guessing penalty on the GED® test. On the Mathematical Reasoning test, you can use POE to eliminate any out-of-scope answer choices, leaving just the answers that make sense. This is what we call **Ballparking,** and it is especially useful for answering those difficult questions that you may not know how to solve!

Ballparking is a guessing strategy that can help you eliminate "out of the ballpark" answers.

In school, you may once have encountered a problem on a math test that looked like this:

1. This month, 1,500 new members joined a particular health club. The club's goal for this month was 2,000 new members. What percentage of the club's goal was achieved?

If you weren't sure how to solve this fill-in-the-blank problem during that test, you were pretty much out of luck. It certainly wouldn't have made sense to guess, would it? For example, if you had closed your eyes and picked a number at random ("...uh, 14!"), the chances that you would happen to pick the right answer would have been pretty slim. (By the way, if you aren't sure how to do this problem right now, don't worry. We'll cover percentages in Chapter 13.)

But most of the problems on the GED® test are NOT the fill-in-the-blank types. Most questions are in the multiple-choice format. Here's how that question would look on the GED® test:

1. This month, 1,500 new members joined a particular health club. The club's goal for this month was 2,000 new members. What percentage of the club's goal was achieved?

   A. 75%
   B. 82%
   C. 112%
   D. 150%

You may be saying, "Big deal. Same problem." But, in fact, this is not the same problem at all. If you happened to spot this question on the real GED® test and still didn't know how to do it, you would have an enormous advantage because you no longer have to guess completely at random. In the multiple-choice question format, there are only four possibilities, and *one* of them has to be right. Just by guessing among the four answer choices, you have a 25 percent chance of answering the question correctly.

We can do even better than that. Fortunately, it turns out that many answer choices to Mathematical Reasoning questions aren't reasonable at all. In fact, some of them are pretty crazy. Let's just think about that problem above. The health club's goal was 2,000 new memberships, but they actually got only 1,500 new memberships. Did they reach their goal? No way. Putting this in the language of percentages, let's restate the question: Did they reach 100 percent of their goal? The answer is still no.

Apply the Strategy
By taking a step back from a problem, you can often eliminate at least one or two answer choices.

Obviously, the correct answer to this problem must be *less* than 100 percent. Even if you are unsure about how to calculate the exact percentage, you can look over the answer choices and often rule out several that just don't make sense in the given situation. Look at (D), 150%. This answer implies that not only did the club meet its goal, it exceeded it as well. Forget (D). Look at (C), 112%. Again, this is just way off from what's possible. The correct answer must be less than 100%. Both of these answers are way out of the ballpark.

We have eliminated two answer choices. This means the correct answer to this question is either (A) or (B). All of a sudden, your odds of getting this question correct are much better. You now have a fifty-fifty chance of being right. Pick one. If you picked (A), you just got the question correct.

Even if you picked (B) and got the question wrong, there are probably more questions that you can ballpark. Let's say you have two questions that you don't know how to solve, but you can ballpark. You probably get both of them narrowed down to two possible answers (as we just did). Thus, in each question, you are down to a fifty-fifty guess. What would be the results if you were to guess on both of them? The odds say you're going to get one of them wrong (maybe you picked (B) for this question). That's a shame, but after all, there's no guessing penalty, and more to the point, you didn't know how to do the question anyway, so you're no worse off than you were before. However, the odds also say that you're going to get the other one *right*! And that's not bad, considering you had no idea how to do that question either.

Don't know how to "do" a question?
Try Ballparking and then guess!

Okay, let's say you know exactly how to do a problem. Should you bother to ballpark it first? Definitely. You might be the greatest mathematician in the world ordinarily, but if you're taking all four GED® tests on the same day, you might find it hard to think straight by the time you get to Mathematical Reasoning. Or you may be rushing to finish a question and make a mistake that you would never normally make. You can prevent lots of careless errors by stepping back from a math problem and saying,

> *Wait a minute. Before I even start multiplying or dividing, which answers don't make sense?*

Once you've eliminated the crazy answer choices, then you can start solving the problem. And if your calculations happen to lead you, mistakenly, to one of those out-of-scope answer choices —well, you'll know you just made a mistake, and you'll be able to figure out what went wrong.

You'll find that once you start looking at GED® problems in this way, you'll spot many opportunities to ballpark. This is because the test writers construct their incorrect answer choices not to be reasonable but to anticipate common errors that test takers make when they're in a hurry.

You can ballpark on many question types:
- multiple choice
- drop down
- drag and drop

Partial Answers

One of the most common errors that the GED® test knows that test takers make is not reading the math question carefully enough, and therefore solving only some of what the question requires. Such a mistake can lead you to wrongly choose a *partial answer* (even though you may be on the right track). Let's look at another multiple-choice problem.

1. Eric buys a coat from an online retailer. The coat costs $140, plus an $8 shipping charge and a $2 handling fee. If there is a 10% sales tax on the entire amount, what would be the <u>total</u> cost of buying the coat?

   A. $135
   B. $150
   C. $160
   D. $165

Like many problems on the Mathematical Reasoning test, this requires several steps. What is the first thing you would do if you were actually buying this coat? We add up the costs we have so far.

the coat	$140
shipping	$8
handling	+ $2
	$150

We are already up to $150, and we haven't even added in the tax yet. Do you see any answer choices we can cross out? If you said (A) and (B), you are right on the money. The correct answer must be *greater* than $150, which means there are only two possibilities left: (C) and (D). Look at that—we just created another fifty-fifty chance of guessing the correct answer.

Slow Down for "Traps"

GED® test writers love to leave "trap" answers for you—such as an answer that subtracts two numbers instead of adding them. Watch out for these traps by working the problem carefully, which may mean you need to SLOW DOWN. It is better to take your time and answer one question correctly than to hurriedly answer two questions incorrectly.

Why did the test writers choose two answers that didn't make sense? Because they wanted to include some answers that many test takers are likely to pick by mistake. For example, let's say that you were doing this problem, and you got to the point we have already reached: You added up the numbers and got $150. If you were anxious, or in a hurry (as most test takers are), you might look at the answer choices, see (B), $150, figure that you must be done, and click the bubble for (B) on the screen. However, this number is only a *partial* answer to the question.

To find the correct answer to this question—(D), $165—requires you to do three separate calculations. First, add up the cost of the coat and the postage and handling. Check. Second, calculate the tax. To compute this, you find 10 percent of $150, which turns out to be $15 (Don't worry if you weren't sure how to find 10 percent of 150. We'll show you how in a later chapter.) Third, add the tax to the previous total. If a test taker chose (B), $150, it was not because he made a mistake in his calculations. The answer to step one of this problem is $150. And if a test taker chose (A), $135, it was because he accidentally subtracted the tax instead of adding it.

On the GED® test, you will frequently find partial answers lurking in wait for you. To avoid getting taken in by one of these, you have to read the problem very carefully the first time and then read it again just as carefully right before you select your answer.

Because the test writers employ partial answers so often on the Mathematical Reasoning test, you can actually use the partial answers as clues to help you find the final answer. For example, working on a two-step problem, you may find that the answer to the first step of the problem is also one of the answer choices. This is a good sign. It means you are on the right track. If the answer to your first step is *close* to one of the answer choices, but just a little off, you might try redoing the calculation to see if you made a mistake.

Using Graphics to Ballpark

Anywhere from one-third to one-half of the questions on the Mathematical Reasoning test refer to "graphic material": drawings of geometric figures, graphs, and charts. Whenever you see a diagram on the Mathematical Reasoning test, you have the single most efficient way to ballpark that you could possibly imagine: You can just *measure* the diagrams. We know it's bizarre, but it's true.

For extra help reading charts and graphs, download our Understanding Graphics supplement from your Student Tools, free when you register your book online! See pages viii–ix for details.

Here's a typical drag-and-drop geometry problem:

Question 1 refers to the following diagram.

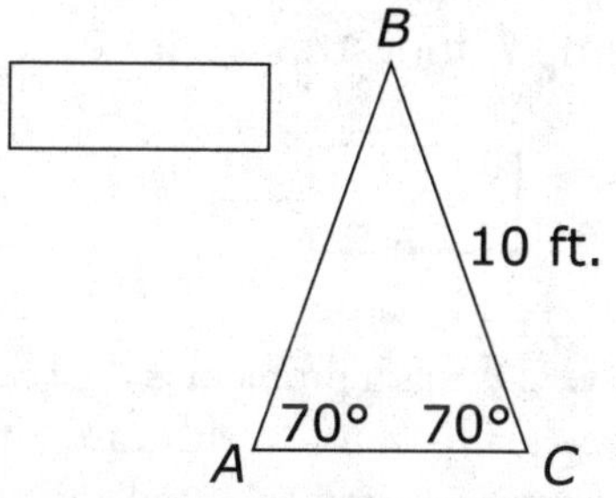

1. If angle A and angle C both equal 70°, then what is the length, in feet, of side AB? Click on the number you want to select and drag it into the box.

3 ft.	7 ft.	9 ft.
10 ft.	12 ft.	15 ft.

Don't worry if you don't remember the geometric principle involved in solving this problem (the properties of an isosceles triangle). We'll review geometry in Chapter 16.

The question is, how long is side *AB*? Let's find out. Simply take any straight edge you can find, and carefully measure side *BC*, which the diagram says is 10 feet long. Mark the length of side *BC* along the edge of one of the erasable note boards that is provided to you for the duration of the test. Now all you have to do is compare that length to side *AB*. If it's a lot bigger, you can get rid of any choices less than 10. If it's a lot smaller, you can get rid of any choices greater than 10.

If you measured our diagram correctly, you probably noticed that side *AB* appears to be exactly the same size as side *BC*. So is the correct answer 10 feet? Well, in fact it is. However, because the GED® drawings are drawn only *roughly* to scale, you wouldn't know for sure that the answer is exactly 10 feet unless you knew the geometric reasoning behind the problem. Going by the diagram alone, you could only have gotten the answer down to either 9 feet or 10 feet. Between these two, it would have been too close to call. However, you could be pretty certain that the answer was *not* 3 feet, 7 feet, 12 feet, or 15 feet.

The Red Herring

On every Mathematical Reasoning test, there will be several problems that give you more information than you actually need. We call this extra information the "red herring." Here's an example of a fill-in-the-blank question type:

Sounds Fishy to Me
A "red herring" is an expression in which a clue or piece of information is intended to be misleading or distracting from the actual question. Distractor answers are common on standardized tests like the GED® test.

1. This year, $\frac{3}{4}$ of the employees at Acme made contributions to a voluntary retirement fund. Last year, only $\frac{2}{3}$ of the employees contributed. If there are now 2,100 employees, how many contributed to the voluntary retirement fund this year?

The most important part of any GED® math problem is the last line, which is where the test writers tell you what they really want. In this case, they want the number of employees who contributed to their retirement fund *this year*. In this problem, the only year you care about is this year. To answer the question, you have to find out from the problem what fraction of the total employees contributed this year, and then multiply that fraction by the total number of employees. (If you aren't sure how to find a fractional part of a number, don't worry. We'll show you how in Chapter 13.)

Look at the problem and ask yourself, "Is there any information that is not about this year?" Well, as a matter of fact, there is. The second sentence, "Last year, only $\frac{2}{3}$ of the employees contributed," has nothing to do with what the question asks. The GED® test writers threw that sentence in to see whether it would trick you. It was a red herring.

To answer this question, we need to take $\frac{3}{4}$ of 2,100. The correct answer is 1,575.

Taking the Mathematical Reasoning Test

When you click to begin the Mathematical Reasoning test, you will probably begin with question 1, then do question 2, and then do question 3, and so on. This is a fine strategy as long as you are prepared to be flexible. Every year, we hear stories from test takers who got stuck on some early problem—let's say it was question 3. They just couldn't get it. They read it and read it again. They tried solving it one way and then another. But some people have orderly minds, and *darn it,* they aren't going to go on to question 4 until they get question 3. After 10 minutes, when they finally give up and go on to number 4, they are thoroughly rattled, jittery, and very angry at themselves for wasting so much time.

The lesson here?

Don't Get Stubborn

There are always going to be problems that, for whatever reason, you just can't get. It might be a mental block, or maybe you never learned a particular type of problem, or maybe the question was simply written so confusingly that it is impossible for you to understand. No matter how easy you think the problem ought to be, don't let yourself get hung up on it! Even if you can't do the very *first* problem, there are 45 others waiting for you, and you will find that many of them are pretty easy.

First Pass, Second Pass

Of course, it isn't necessary to solve every problem to do very well, and in fact, you will see that by skipping the problems you don't know how to do, you can actually increase your score. Here's how.

The Two-Pass System can help to save you time and lock in those points!

We recommend that you take the Mathematical Reasoning test in two passes. On your first pass, you'll begin at the beginning and do every problem that comes easily to you. If you read a question and know just what to do, then it is a first-pass problem. However, if you read a problem and have no idea of how to solve it, then you should click the "Flag for Review" icon in the upper right corner and move on. You have not skipped this problem forever. You are merely saving it for later, after you've locked in all the easy points.

First pass: Do the ones you KNOW you can get.

When you finish your first pass, a "Question Review" screen will show you which questions you flagged along the way. Now you can take a second look. Sometimes, when you read a problem again, you'll immediately see what was unclear to you the first time, and you'll know just what to do. Other times you may not be sure, but you'll be able to eliminate several answer choices by Ballparking. And sometimes, of course, you will just say, "Yuck!" and answer with your best guess. Remember, you should NEVER leave a question unanswered on the GED® test. Right before you submit the Mathematical Reasoning test, make sure that the status for every question number (even the flagged ones) is "answered."

Second pass: Go back over your flagged questions.

Chapter 13
Basic Arithmetic

This chapter reviews basic math terminology and definitions including the number line, positive and negative numbers, digits, rounding, multiplying and dividing, using the order of operations, fractions, decimals, and percents.

The arithmetic on the Mathematical Reasoning test is not necessarily the arithmetic you learned in school. The folks who write the test are striving to make GED® math more relevant to real life. Consequently, you won't find any questions on the more theoretical aspects of arithmetic—properties of integers, for example. Nor will there be any questions about prime numbers, imaginary numbers, or any of the other terms that generally go under the name "axioms and fundamentals." Instead, the test focuses on practical math. Several of the questions will be word problems that try to evoke situations you might find in everyday life.

In this chapter, we're going to show you all the basic arithmetic topics that come up on the Mathematical Reasoning test. With each topic, we'll first show you the concept behind the topic, then illustrate it with typical examples, and finally give you a small drill so you can practice the concept on your own. At the end of the entire chapter, there will be a big drill in GED® test format, including all the concepts we've shown you. The purpose of this is to give you some practice recognizing the different types of questions when they are all mixed together—as they are on the real GED® test. In the next chapter, we'll cover *applied* arithmetic topics in just the same way.

Here are the basic arithmetic concepts that appear on the GED® test:

- The number line
- Rounding
- Operations with positive and negative numbers
- Order of operations
- Commutative and distributive properties
- Fractions
- Decimals
- Percents

THE NUMBER LINE

The number line is a visual way of understanding positive and negative numbers in relation to one another.

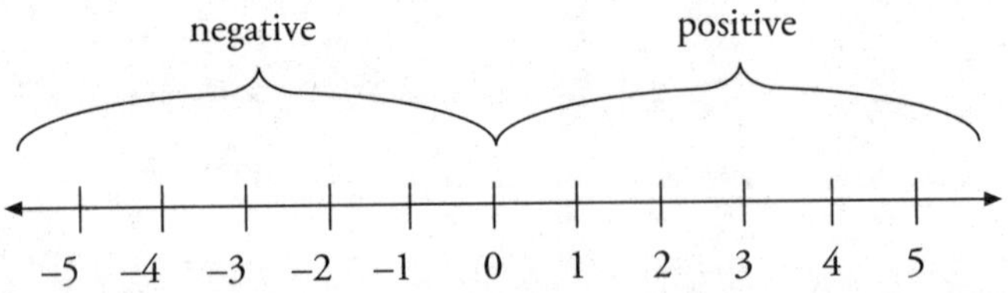

As you can see on the number line above, positive numbers are to the right of the zero; negative numbers are to the left of zero.

Negative numbers are marked with a negative (–) sign in front, while positive numbers are not marked (it's just assumed that they are positive). Zero is the crossover point between positive and negative numbers, so think of zero itself as neutral—neither positive nor negative.

Note that positive numbers get bigger as they move away from zero to the right. Negative numbers get smaller in value as they move away from zero to the left. (The more negative a number, the smaller the value, and the further to the left of zero it falls on the number line.)

For example, –3 is smaller than –1. A number line can extend infinitely to the left or right, but the number lines on the GED® test generally look like the example on the previous page, with a fairly small number of position points. Let's try identifying some points on the number line.

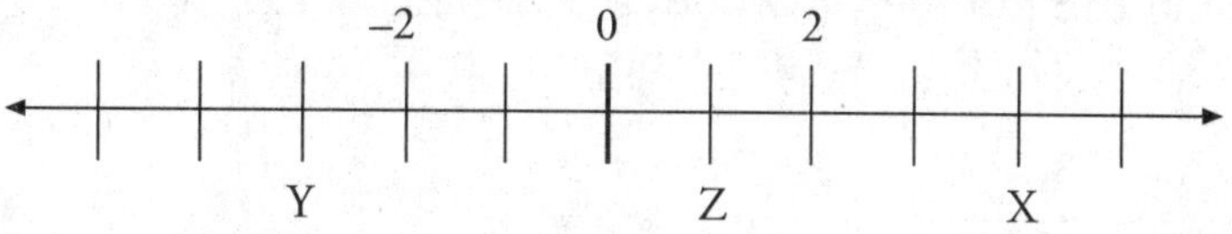

Find point X on the number line. What number does point X represent? If you said 4, you were absolutely right. How about points Y and Z? If you said –3 and 1, you were right again. Here's how a number line problem would look on the GED® test:

Question 1 refers to the following number line.

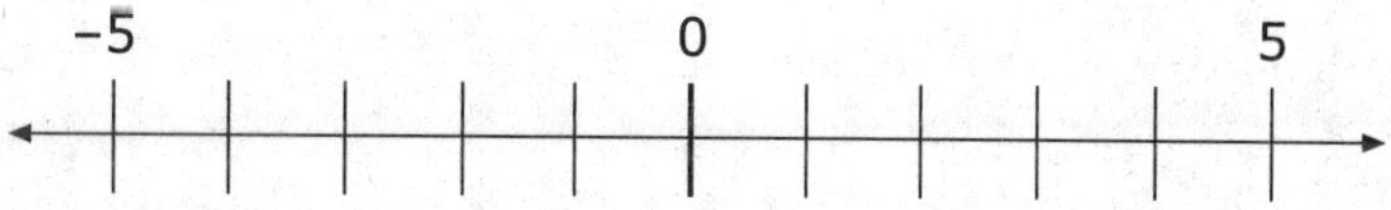

1. Which point represents the number -3?

   Click on the number line to plot a point.

Here's How to Crack It

Generally, the only thing that's difficult in a number line problem is orienting yourself. The best place to begin is to find 0. Did you find it? Now, determine the scale. Count the number of spaces between 0 and 5. There are five. Therefore, each space represents 1. Now, in which direction do you move for negative numbers? To the left. And how many places to the left do you count from 0? Three. Mark your point there (or click the cursor on the real GED® Mathematical Reasoning test) and you're done!

Here's a slightly more difficult number line problem:

Question 2 refers to the following diagram.

2. On the number line above, AB = BC = CD. If AD = 12, then what is the length of AB?

   A. 3
   B. 4
   C. 5
   D. 8

When a question asks for the *length* or *distance*, the answer MUST be positive.

Here's How to Crack It

In this problem, there is no way to orient yourself because neither the diagram nor the problem identifies a specific point on the number line. Instead, this problem is concerned with the *lengths* of segments on the line. On the GED® test, lengths are always positive, never negative. In this case, the only actual length you are given is AD, which equals 12. Let's look at the other information in the problem. If AB = BC = CD, then these segments break up AD into three equal parts. Because the whole is 12, what is the length of a single part? Divide the total length 12 by the 3 equal segments to find that the length of AB is 4, and the answer is (B).

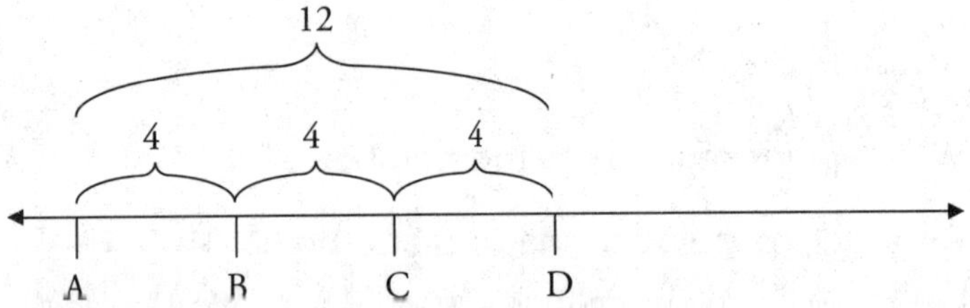

The *absolute value* of a number is the distance from the number to zero on a number line. Since absolute value measures distance (or length), it is always a nonnegative number. To write the absolute value of a number, you place the number in between two vertical lines. For example, you would write the absolute value of –5 as |–5|. How far from zero is –5 on the number line? –5 is five steps from 0, so |–5| = 5. The absolute value of a number will always be positive (or zero).

Sometimes number line problems will ask you about the midpoint of a line segment. A **midpoint** is simply the place halfway between either end of the line segment. A GED® problem might look like this:

<u>Question 3</u> refers to the following diagram.

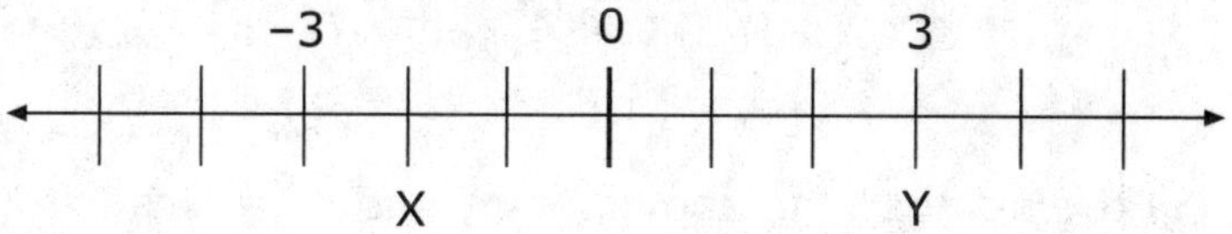

3. If point X on the line above represents –2 and point Y on the line represents 3, then the midpoint of segment XY would be between which two numbers?

   A. –2 and –1
   B. –1 and 0
   C. 0 and 1
   D. 1 and 2

Here's How to Crack It

This time, there are concrete numbers marked on the number line, so take a second to get oriented. Now, the midpoint of XY is the point exactly halfway between point X and point Y. Count the number of spaces between X and Y. Did you get 5? Good. What is half of 5? Half of 5 is $2\frac{1}{2}$. So all you have to do is count over $2\frac{1}{2}$ to the right of point X or $2\frac{1}{2}$ to the left of point Y. In either case, the midpoint is between 0 and 1, and the correct answer is (C).

Number Line Drill

You can check your answers in Part IX: Answer Key to Drills.

Questions 1 through 3 refer to the diagram below.

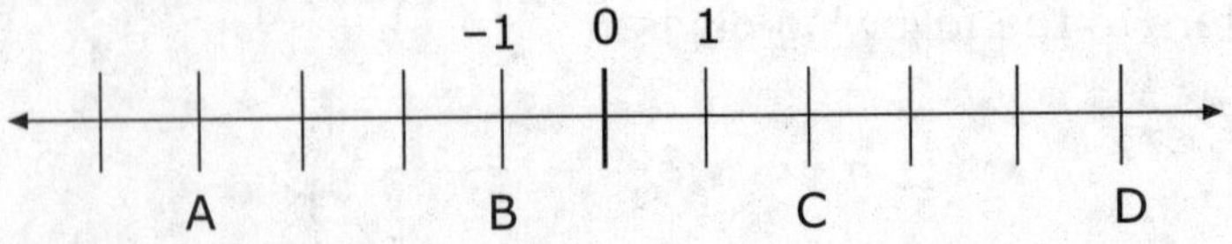

1. On the number line above, point A is

   Select... ▼ point B.
   - greater than
   - equal to
   - less than

2. On the number line above, what is the distance from point A to point B?

   A. -4
   B. -3
   C. 3
   D. 4

3. If a new point E was to be added to the number line exactly halfway between points A and D, where would it be located?

   A. between points -3 and -2
   B. at point 0
   C. between points 0 and 1
   D. at point 2

Digits

All numbers are made up of digits, and the place of each digit in a number determines its value. For example, the number 6,342 has four digits: 6, 3, 4, and 2. In this number, the 6 represents the value 6,000 (6 thousand, not 6). The 6 is in the thousands place. What about the other digits? The 3 is in the hundreds place. The 4 is in the tens place. And the 2 is in the ones place.

Let's look at a number that is less than 1. The number 0.57 has a 0 in the ones place. Behind the decimal, there are two non-zero digits: 5 and 7. In this case, the 5 is in the tenths place. The 7 is in the hundredths place. The digits in places to the right of a decimal get smaller in value as they move away from zero.

Let's put these digits together on one number and identify the place values of each digit:

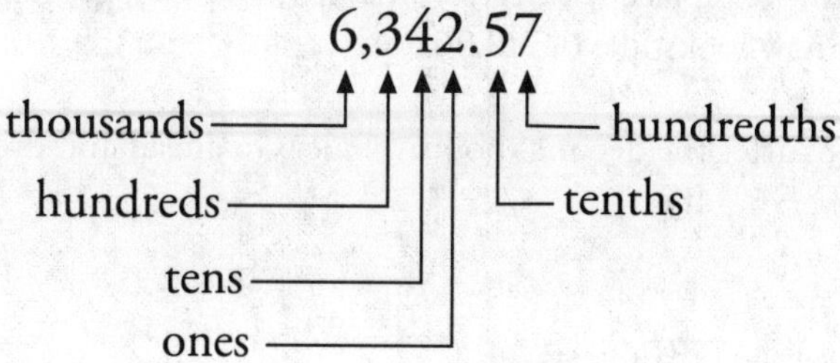

Digit Quiz
Q: Which of these numbers has more digits?
(1) 37.5
(2) 342

Turn the page for the answer.

ROUNDING TO THE NEAREST WHATEVER

The GED® test writers sometimes ask you to round a number. The problem might read, "To the nearest thousand, how many…" or "What number to the nearest tenth…."

Whether you round to the nearest thousand or the nearest tenth, the process is exactly the same. Let's begin by rounding to the nearest dollar. If you have up to $1.49, then to the nearest dollar you have $1. If you have $1.50 or more, then to the nearest dollar you have $2.

Exactly the same principles hold true when you round any type of number.

1. Identify the place you are rounding to.
   - For example, let's round 6,342.57 to the nearest ten.
   - Which digit is in the tens place? The 4 is in the tens place.

   Since we are rounding to the tens place, draw a number line that counts by tens:

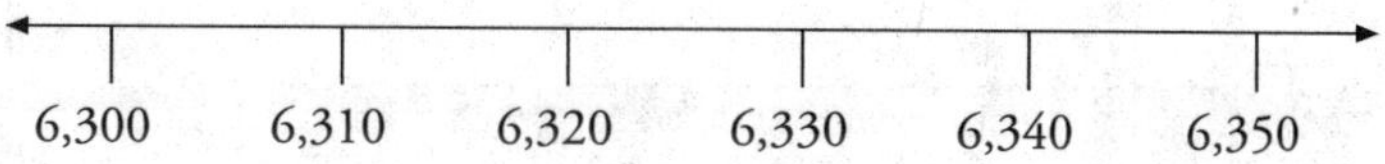

2. Look at the digit that comes *after* the place you are rounding to—this number is your decision-maker. In our example number, 6,342.57, what is the digit after 4? The next digit is 2.
   - If that digit is 0, 1, 2, 3, or 4, you will round down to the tens place you have. (Keep the 4.)
   - If that digit is 5, 6, 7, 8, or 9, round up to the next tens place. (Change the 4 to a 5.)

   Let's look at this on the number line. Make a mark where the original number lies.

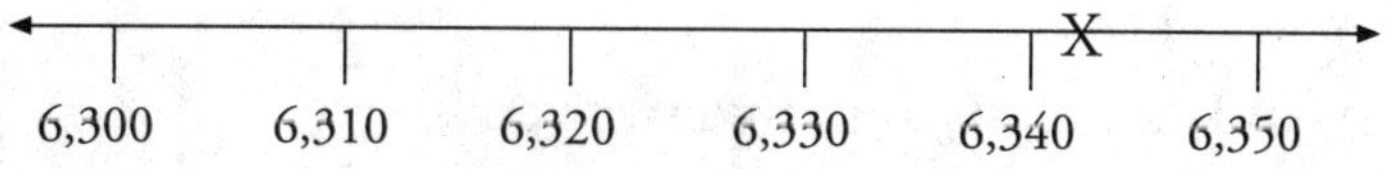

   Is it closer to 6,340 or to 6,350? In this case, it is closer to the smaller amount, 6,340.

3. Replace any digits after the rounding place with zeros.
   - Which digits will we replace with zeros? The 2, 5, and 7 all get replaced.
   - So our number now looks like 6,340.00.

Do we need the zeros after the decimal point? Nope. Go ahead and drop those off to get the final answer: 6,340.

Here's how this might look on the GED® test.

1. You buy a loaf of bread for $2.99, deli meat for $3.65, and sliced cheese for $4.49. To the nearest dollar, how much will you owe at checkout?

$ [ ]

Here's How to Crack It

There are two steps to the problem. The first step is to add up the items you will be purchasing. $2.99 + $3.65 + $4.49 = $11.13. Great—now don't forget about Step 2! The problem asks for the total "to the nearest dollar." So Step 2 is to round. Which is the dollars place? If you aren't sure, try saying the number out loud: "Eleven *dollars* and thirteen cents." So we have 11 dollars plus 13 cents more. Now look at the first digit after the dollars place, which is 1. Since this is less than 5, we do not round up. The correct answer is $11.

Rounding Drill

You can check your answers in Part IX: Answer Key to Drills.

1. To the nearest thousand, what is 3,400?
2. To the nearest tenth, what is 3.46?
3. To the nearest hundred, what is 565?
4. What is $432.70 to the nearest dollar?
5. What is 4.80 to the nearest hundredth?

ADDING AND SUBTRACTING POSITIVE AND NEGATIVE NUMBERS

Let's look at that number line one more time.

Digit Quiz

A: Both have the same number of digits: 3.

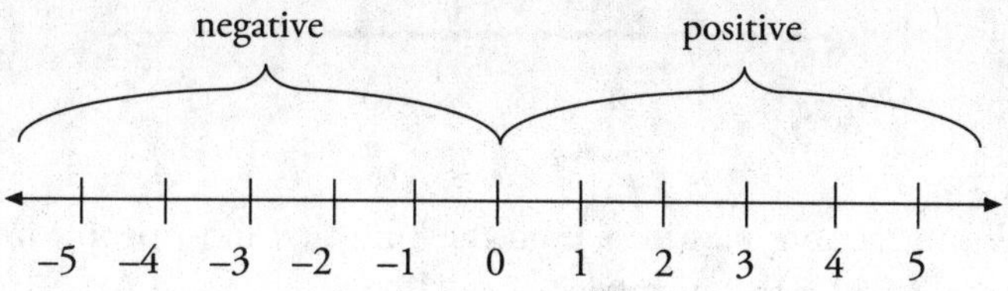

Many people have trouble adding and subtracting negative numbers. The number line helps us perform these operations effectively. First, let's look at adding. For example, (–2) + 6.

To add any two numbers, begin by locating the first number on the number line.

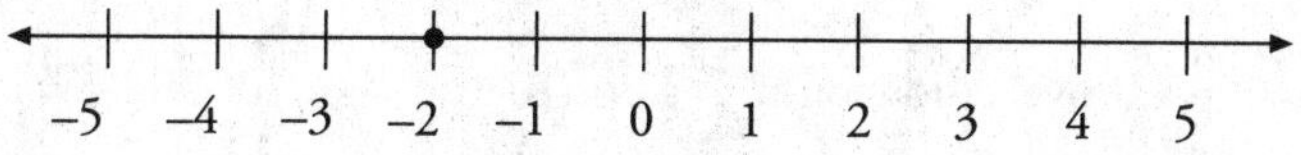

The absolute value of the second number tells us how many steps we'll move. |6| = 6, so we'll move six steps.

If that second number is positive, we'll move that many steps to the right. If it's negative, we'll move that many steps to the left. The number 6 is positive, so we'll move six steps to the right from (–2).

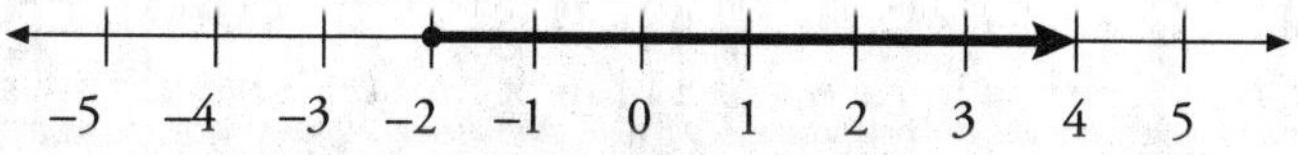

So, we see that (–2) + 6 = 4.

This method works whether you are adding two positives, a positive and a negative, or two negative numbers!

Using the same method, we can see that 7 + (–5) = 2, and (–3) + (–5) = (–8).

The process of subtracting positive and negative numbers is also pretty straightforward if we consider one thing: subtracting is the same as adding the opposite. Did you notice, in our example above, that 7 + (–5) is the same as 7 – 5? That's an illustration of this very idea.

Whenever you have a subtraction question, you can change it to an addition (of the opposite) question, and solve it as we did above. This is very helpful when you are subtracting with negative numbers. Here's how it works:

$$4 - 7 =$$

Let's rewrite this, so instead of *subtracting,* we're *adding* the *opposite.*

4 – 7 is the same as 4 + (–7). Now we've got an addition question, so we'll use our addition method, and see that 4 + (–7) = (–3).

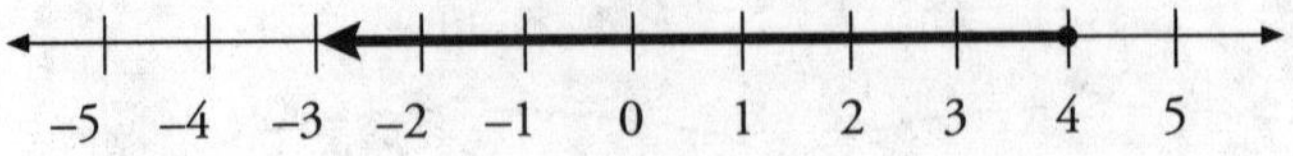

This method works on all subtraction questions, even the kind that most people find the trickiest: subtracting a negative. Consider this example:

$$(-11) - (-7) =$$

This is perplexing at first. So many minuses! But let's rewrite it so we're *adding* the *opposite.* Instead of subtracting –7, we'll add the opposite of –7, which is positive seven. So, (–11) – (–7) = (–11) + 7. Make sure that you keep the sign on the first number the same!

Use your addition steps above, and count 7 steps to the right of –11. Where do you land? On –4.

$$(-11) - (-7) = (-11) + 7 = (-4)$$

It might take a little time and practice to perfect these adding and subtracting processes, but it's worth the time and energy. These processes work no matter what the numbers are.

MULTIPLYING POSITIVE AND NEGATIVE NUMBERS

Multiplication is actually just the process of adding a number several times. For example, to multiply 4 by 3, you are actually just adding 4 three separate times:

$$4 \times 3 = 4 + 4 + 4 = 12$$

or adding 3 four separate times:

$$3 \times 4 = 3 + 3 + 3 + 3 = 12$$

To multiply 5 by 2, you are actually just adding 5 two separate times:

$$5 \times 2 = 5 + 5 = 10$$

or adding 2 five separate times:

$$2 \times 5 = 2 + 2 + 2 + 2 + 2 = 10$$

Of course, it's a lot quicker to use the multiplication (times) tables. We just wanted to remind you of the theory behind multiplication. If your times tables are a little rusty, don't worry. You're going to get lots of opportunity to practice over the next three chapters.

There are four rules regarding the multiplication of positive and negative numbers.

Multiplying and Dividing: Is My Answer Positive or Negative?
SAME sign? The answer will be POSITIVE. DIFFERENT signs? The answer will be NEGATIVE.

positive × positive = positive $2 \times 3 = 6$

positive × negative = negative $2 \times -3 = -6$

negative × positive = negative $-2 \times 3 = -6$

negative × negative = positive $-2 \times -3 = 6$

A simple way to apply these rules when you are multiplying is to remember: negative makes your answer negative; two negatives make a positive. We have provided the following multiplication table for you to fill in to refresh your memory.

	1	2	3	4	5	6	7	8	9
1									
2									
3									
4									
5									
6									
7									
8									
9									

DIVIDING POSITIVE AND NEGATIVE NUMBERS

Division is actually the opposite of multiplication. If we multiply 2 by 3, we get 6. If we divide 6 by 2, we are actually asking what number times 2 equals 6?

$6 \div 2 = 3$. You can also write this as $\frac{6}{2}$ or $2\overline{)6}$.

The same four rules of multiplication apply to the division of positive and negative numbers.

That Wacky Zero!
Any number × 0 = 0
Any number ÷ 0 = undefined
0 ÷ any number = 0

positive ÷ positive = positive	**6 ÷ 2 = 3**
positive ÷ negative = negative	**6 ÷ –2 = –3**
negative ÷ positive = negative	**–6 ÷ 2 = –3**
negative ÷ negative = positive	**–6 ÷ –2 = 3**

Adding, Subtracting, Multiplying, and Dividing Positive and Negative Numbers Drill

Do these problems first on your own. Then, on a separate piece of paper, do them again using your calculator.

You can check your answers in Part IX: Answer Key to Drills.

1. 5 + (–3) =
2. (–4) + (–7) =
3. (6 × 3) =
4. (–2)(6) =
5. (–3) – (2) + (6) =
6. 10 ÷ 2 =
7. (–5)(–2) =
8. –21 ÷ –7 =
9. 12 ÷ –3 =
10. –12 ÷ 3 =

ABSOLUTE VALUES

Remember the number line from earlier in the chapter.

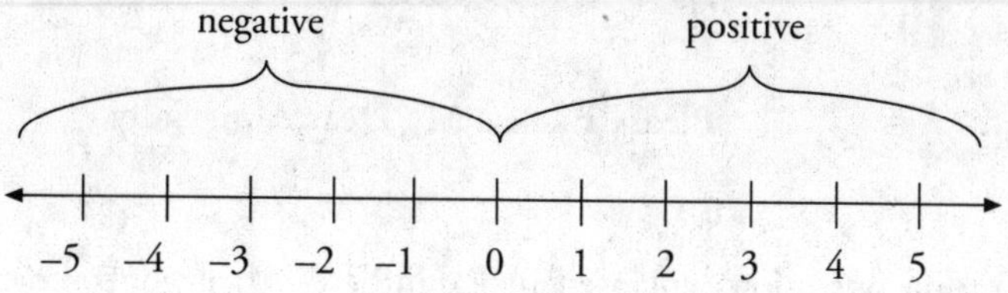

Let's look at the numbers 5 and –5. What do they have in common? Remember that positive and negative numbers are defined based on their relationship to 0. Positive numbers are to the right of 0, and negative numbers are to the left of 0. In particular, the number 5 is five units to the right of 0, and the number –5 is five units to the left of 0. Even though they are in different positions on the number line, both are the same *distance from the number 0. In math, this is said to mean that they have the same absolute value.* Since both 5 and –5 are five away from 0, both have an absolute value of 5. In an equation or an expression, the absolute value is represented by two vertical lines: | |. Therefore, it can be written that $|5| = |-5| = 5$.

Although, by definition, the absolute value refers to distance from 0, it can be used to express the distance from any other number. Consider $|4 - 1|$ and $|-2 - 1|$. One way of thinking about this is by taking the difference and then taking the absolute value of the result as below.

$$|4 - 1| = |3| = 3$$

$$|-2 - 1| = |-3| = 3$$

Another way of thinking about this is by considering the distance on the number line to both 4 and –2 from 1. Both quantities above are equal to 3 because both 4 and –2 are three units from 1 on the number line: –2 is three units to the left and 4 is three units to the right.

Absolute Values Drill

You can check your answers in Part IX: Answer Key to Drills.

1. $|4| =$

2. $|-7| =$

3. $|6 - 2| =$

4. $|3 - 5| =$

5. $|x| = 10, x =$

6. $|y - 9| = 5, y =$

ORDER OF OPERATIONS

In a problem that involves several different operations, the operations must be performed in a particular order. There's an easy way to remember the order of operations:

Tip: Remember the acronym PEMDAS for the correct order of operations!

Please **E**xcuse **M**y **D**ear **A**unt **S**ally

First, you do operations enclosed in **P**arentheses; then you take care of **E**xponents; then you **M**ultiply or **D**ivide (in the order that they appear); finally, you **A**dd or **S**ubtract (also in the order that they appear). We're going to save exponents for the next chapter, but let's try out PEMDAS with a couple of problems.

$$((-5)+4)\left(\frac{8}{2}\right)+4=$$

Let's walk through the steps in order according to PEMDAS. There are **P**arentheses, so we will start with those. We want to find the parentheses that are holding an operation inside. (The parentheses around –5 are just keeping the sign with the number 5 to show that it is negative.)

So we start with: (–5) + 4 = (–1)

Then we can deal with what is inside the next set of parentheses: the improper fraction $\frac{8}{2}$ can be simplified by dividing. 8 divided by 2 gives us 4.

Let's rewrite the equation to keep track of what we have now:

$$(-1)(4) + 4 =$$

We've done all operations inside parentheses, so now what's next? **M**ultiply or **D**ivide. When you see a number right next to a set of parentheses without an operation sign inside—that means multiply!

PEMDAS Quiz

Q: 3(7 – [5 – 3]) = ?

Turn the page for the answer.

Here we have: (–1) × (4)

What happens when we multiply and the signs are different like this (negative and positive)? One negative makes your answer negative, so that gives us (–4).

Next, we are going to **Add** –4 + 4, and this gives us our answer: 0.

How about this one?

$$(3)+\left(\frac{8}{2}\right)(4-5)+1=$$

Same process: let's look for any **P**arentheses holding an operation inside: first, $\left(\frac{8}{2}\right)$ can be simplified as (4) and (4 – 5) = (–1). Now we can rewrite what we have as (3) + (4)(–1) + 1 so that we can see what is next.

There are numbers in parentheses that are directly next to each other, so this means we **M**ultiply them together:

$$(4)(-1) = -4$$

All that is left to do is **A**dd from left to right: 3 + (–4) + 1 = –1 + 1 = 0

You would not get the same answer (that is, the correct answers to both!) without following the order of operations.

Using Your Calculator on Order of Operations

During Part 2 of the Math test, you will be provided with an on-screen Texas Instruments TI-30XS calculator, which automatically knows the order of operations. As long as you enter the equation correctly, it will give you the correct answer every time. But entering the equation correctly can be painstaking work. For example, in the operation above, you would enter 3, hit the "plus" key, then the "left parenthesis" key, then 8, then the "division" key followed by the 2, then the "right parenthesis" key, then the "multiplication" key, then the "left parenthesis" key, then the 4 followed by the "minus" key, then the 5, then the "right parenthesis" key, then the "plus" key, then the 1 key, and finally the "enter" key.

Many students find that they can do this faster on paper.

COMMUTATIVE AND DISTRIBUTIVE PROPERTIES

The Commutative Property: When you add a string of numbers, you can add them in any order. You can also move numbers around as you like when you multiply them together.

4 + 5 + 8 is the same as 8 + 5 + 4 is the same as 5 + 8 + 4.

$6 \times 7 \times 9$ is the same as $9 \times 7 \times 6$ is the same as $7 \times 6 \times 9$.

> The Commutative Property works ONLY with addition and multiplication. It does NOT apply to subtraction or division.

The Distributive Property: The GED® test writers will sometimes use an equation that can be written in two different ways. They do this to see whether you understand what the equation really means, and whether you can spot when it is in your interest to change the equation into its other form.

Often, a given equation can be written in a different form by multiplying or dividing across several numbers. We do this by applying the distributive property. Let's look at an example of when we can distribute multiplication to rewrite an equation:

$$6(a + 2) = 4a$$

We cannot add what is inside the parentheses, but we can multiply the 6 and $(a + 2)$. When we do this, we distribute the multiplication across both terms inside parentheses, so that we get this: $6a + 12 = 4a$. Now we can actually solve this equation!

Be careful when there are any negative numbers involved, as in the following equation:

$$-5(b + 1) = 8$$

You also distribute the negative when you multiply, so here we would get $-5b - 5 = 8$. (Remember: one negative makes your product negative!)

In formula terms, applying the distributive property looks like this:

$$a(b + c) = ab + ac$$

and

$$a(b - c) = ab - ac$$

Example: $3(4 + 2) = 3(4) + 3(2) = 18$

Example: $3(4 - 2) = 3(4) - 3(2) = 6$

If a problem gives you information in the format $a(b + c)$, with the number a "factored" out, you should distribute the multiplication: $ab + ac$.

If the information is given in the distributed form $ab + ac$, you should factor it: $a(b + c)$.

Take the following example:

$$\frac{1}{2}(5)+\frac{1}{2}(3)=$$

Finding $\frac{1}{2}$ of 5 and $\frac{1}{2}$ of 3 is a bit troublesome because the answers do not work out to be whole numbers. It isn't that you can't find half of an odd number if you have to (or at least you *will* be able to, after our review of fractions later in this chapter), but why do more work than necessary?

Look at what would happen if we changed this distributed equation into its factored form instead:

$$\frac{1}{2}(5+3)=$$

Isn't that a lot easier? One half of 8 equals 4. Always be on the lookout for chances to do less work on the GED® test. It's a long, tiring test, and you need to conserve your strength. Now, try this one.

PEMDAS Quiz
A: Remember to do inner parentheses first. The answer is 15.

1. If $3X + 3Y = 21$, then what is the value of $X + Y$?

   A. 3
   B. 6
   C. 7
   D. Not enough information is given.

Here's How to Crack It

Everyone's first impulse on a problem like this is to pick (D), not enough information is given. After all, there are two different variables (X and Y), so unless we know what both variables are, how can we figure out the problem?

The answer is the distributive property. You may not have noticed that the equation in the problem above was in one of the formats we were just looking at: $ab + ac$, otherwise known as the distributive form. Therefore, before we give up hope, let's try putting the equation into its mirror-image format: $a(b + c)$, otherwise known as its factored form.

$$3X + 3Y = 3(X + Y) = 21$$

Hmm. You want to know what $(X + Y)$ equals. Well, three *times* $(X + Y)$ equals 21. Three times what number equals 21? That's right, 7, and the correct answer to this question is (C).

A number directly in front of a parenthesis implies multiplication. To enter 2(5 + 3), first enter 2, then the "multiplication" key, then "left parenthesis," then 5 "plus" 3, then "right parenthesis."

Order of Operations and Commutative and Distributive Properties Drill

Do these problems first on your own. Then on a separate piece of paper, do them again using your calculator.

You can check your answers in Part IX: Answer Key to Drills.

1. $5(3 - 4) + 2 =$

2. $7 \times 2 \times 3 =$

3. $3(3 - 1 - 2) + 6(2 - 4) =$

4. $8(4[3 - 5]) =$

5. $\frac{1}{4}(3) + \frac{1}{4}(9) =$

ABSOLUTE VALUE AND PEMDAS

Remember that the absolute value of a number is its distance from zero. On a number line, this is how many steps away from zero the number is, whether those are steps to the right (positive number) or steps to the left (negative number). The symbol for absolute value is bars on either side of the number (or numbers), like this: $|9|$

Since 9 is nine steps from zero, $|9| = 9$.

Likewise, $|-9| = 9$, because –9 is also nine steps from zero. That it's nine steps in the opposite direction does not affect the absolute value. Finding the absolute value of a single number is as simple as dropping the negative sign, if there is one, from the number inside the bars.

However, if there are multiple numbers and one or more operations inside the bars, you need to do the indicated operations (according to PEMDAS) until you have just one number as a result, and then take the absolute value of that one resulting number. For example,

$$|-3 + 2| =$$

We add the numbers together, keeping the absolute value bars around them,

$$|-3 + 2| = |-1|$$

And then find the absolute value of that resulting number,

$$|-1| = 1$$

And that's our answer. If you have other numbers and operations outside the absolute value bars, then find the absolute value you need before combining that absolute value with the rest of the question.

$$10 + |4 \times (-2)| = 10 + |-8| = 10 + 8 = 18$$

In this way, absolute value works something like parentheses, since you need to calculate what's inside and find the absolute value of that before moving on to the rest of the question.

FACTORS AND MULTIPLES

Factors are numbers that divide *evenly* into a given number. For example, what are the factors of 6?

$$6 \div 1 = 6,\ 6 \div 2 = 3,\ 6 \div 3 = 2, \text{ and } 6 \div 6 = 1.$$

When 6 is divided by 1, 2, 3, or 6, the result is a whole number; therefore, the numbers 1, 2, 3, and 6 are factors of 6. However, when 6 is divided by 4 or 5, the result is a decimal. Therefore, 4 and 5 are not factors of 6. Notice also that the factors of 6 (1, 2, 3, and 6) are all ways to *multiply* two numbers to get 6: $1 \times 6 = 6$, $2 \times 3 = 6$, $3 \times 2 = 6$, and $6 \times 1 = 6$. Let's look at an example.

1. Which of the following is a list of all the factors of 18?

   A. 1 and 18
   B. 1, 3, 6, and 24
   C. 1, 2, 3, 6, 9, and 18
   D. 1, 2, 3, 4, 6, 9, 12, and 18

Here's How to Crack It

To find the factors of a number, start with the two obvious factors. The number 1 is a factor of every number as is the number itself. Therefore, 1 and 18 are factors of 18. Now work upward from 1. Is 2 a factor of 18? Since $18 \div 2 = 9$, 2 is a factor and so is 9. Is 3 a factor of 18? Since $18 \div 3 = 6$, 3 is a factor and so is 6. Is 4 a factor of 18? Since $18 \div 4$ is a decimal, it is not. Is 5 a factor of 18? Since $18 \div 5$ is a decimal, it is not. Is 6 a factor of 18? Remember that 6 is already on the list since $18 \div 3 = 6$. When you get to a number that's already on the list, you have all the factors. Therefore, the complete list is 1, 2, 3, 6, 9, and 18. The correct answer is (C).

One concept that is important to factors is that of the *greatest common factor* (GCF), which is just what it sounds like: the largest factor that two numbers have in common. The GCF will be the largest number that divides evenly into both numbers. Consider the numbers 24 and 40. To find the GCF of 24 and 40, find the factors of both numbers. Find the factors of 24 and 40 in pairs as in the problem above. The factors of 24 are 1 and 24, 2 and 12, 3 and 8, and 4 and 6. The factors of 40 are 1 and 40, 2 and 20, 4 and 10, and 5 and 8. The common factors of 24 and 40 are the numbers that are in both lists (regardless of what pairs they're in). The common factors of 24 and 40 are 1, 2, 4, and 8. The GCF is simply the greatest number of the list of common factors. In this case, the GCF is 8. Let's look at another example.

2. What is the greatest common factor of 15 and 28?
   A. 1
   B. 3
   C. 4
   D. 15

Here's How to Crack It

Find the factors of each number. The factors of 15 are 1, 3, 5, and 15. The factors of 28 are 1, 2, 4, 7, 14, and 28. The only number that is a factor of both 15 and 28 is 1. Therefore, the GCF of 15 and 28 is 1. The correct answer is (A).

The concept of a factor goes hand in hand with the concept of a multiple. Instead of seeing how you can divide a number (its factors), you see how you can multiply a number to find its multiples. A multiple is a number for which a given number is a factor. Since 1, 2, 3, and 6 are factors of 6, 6 is a multiple of 1, 2, 3, and 6. To find the multiples of a given number, take the number and multiply it by other whole numbers. For example, $6 \times 1 = 6$, $6 \times 2 = 12$, $6 \times 3 = 18$, $6 \times 4 = 24$, and $6 \times 5 = 30$, so 6, 12, 18, 24, and 30 are all multiples of 6. Notice that 6 is both a factor and a multiple of itself. This is the case for every number. Also, since 1 is a factor of every number, every number is a multiple of 1.

Another way to think of multiples is as "counting by" a number. To "count by 6," start with 6 and keep adding 6. Since $6 + 6 = 12$, then 12 is a multiple of 6. Since $12 + 6$ is 18, then 18 is a multiple of 6. Since $18 + 6 = 24$, then 24 is a multiple of 6. Since there is no limit to the number of times you can add 6, there is no limit to the multiples of 6 or of any other number.

An important concept involving multiples is *least common multiple* (LCM). For any two numbers, a common multiple is simply a number that is a multiple of both. Consider the numbers 4 and 6. Some of the multiples of 4 are 4, 8, 12, 16, 20, 24, 28, 32, 36, and 40. Some of the multiples of 6 are 6, 12, 18, 24, 30, 36, 42, 48, 54, and 60. Therefore, some of the common multiples of 4 and 6 are 12, 24, 36, and 48. The LCM is the smallest number on the list of common multiples. In this case, the LCM of 4 and 6 is 12. Let's look at another example.

3. What is the least common multiple of 15 and 25?
   A. 1
   B. 5
   C. 75
   D. 150

Here's How to Crack It

To find the LCM of two numbers, list the multiples of one number and stop when one is also a multiple of the other. In this case, find the multiples of 15 by counting by 15 and stopping when one is a multiple of 25. Counting by 15, the multiples of 15 are 15, 30, 45, 60, 75, 90, 105, 120, 135, 150, etc. The numbers 15, 30, 45, and 60 are not multiples of 25, so none of them is the LCM. However, $75 = 25 \times 3$, so 75 is a common multiple. Since none of the lesser multiples of 15 is a common multiple, 75 must be the least common multiple. The correct answer is (C).

Factors and Multiples Drill

You can check your answers in Part IX: Answer Key to Drills.

1. List the factors of 36.
2. List the factors of 43.
3. List the factors of 80.
4. List the first 10 positive multiples of 7.
5. List the first 10 positive multiples of 9.
6. What is the greatest common factor of 32 and 80?
7. What is the least common multiple of 7 and 9?
8. What is greatest common factor of 24 and 48?
9. What is the least common multiple of 24 and 48?

FRACTIONS

A fraction is part of a whole. We write a fraction as $\frac{(PART)}{(WHOLE)}$, in which the top number is the number of parts we are referring to and the bottom number is the total number of parts that make up one whole.

Take a look at the pie below:

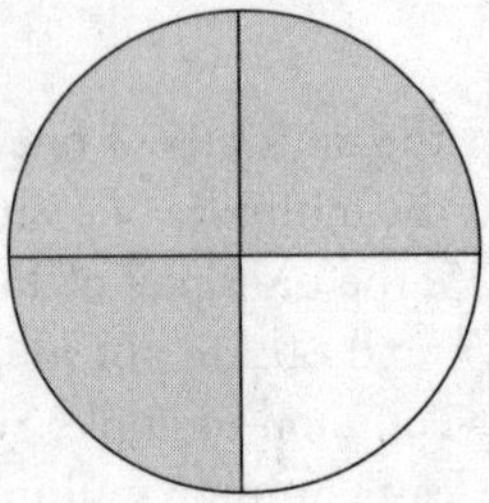

This pie has been divided into four equal pieces. Three of the four pieces are shaded. If we wanted to express the part of the pie that is shaded, we would say that $\frac{3}{4}$ of the pie is shaded. If we wanted to express the part of the pie that is not shaded, we would say that $\frac{1}{4}$ of the pie is not shaded.

A fraction is always a part over a whole.

$$\frac{1}{2} \quad \frac{\text{(PART)}}{\text{(WHOLE)}}$$

In the fraction $\frac{1}{2}$, we have one part out of a total of two equal parts.

In the fraction $\frac{3}{7}$, we have three parts out of a total of seven equal parts.

Another way to think of a fraction is as just another kind of division. The expression $\frac{1}{2}$ means 1 divided by 2. The fraction $\frac{x}{y}$ is nothing more than x divided by y. A fraction is made up of a numerator and a denominator. The **numerator** is on top; the **denominator** is on the bottom. When a number can be written as a fraction in which both the numerator and denominator are integers (numbers with no fraction or decimal part), then the number is called a **rational number.**

$$\frac{1}{2} \quad \frac{\text{numerator}}{\text{denominator}}$$

In math, a number cannot be divided by 0. Therefore, anytime the denominator of a fraction is 0, the fraction is undefined.

Reducing (Simplifying) Fractions

Every fraction can be expressed in many different ways:

$$\frac{1}{2} = \frac{2}{4} = \frac{3}{6} = \frac{4}{8} \ldots \text{ and so on.}$$

Each of these fractions means the same thing: a half portion of a whole. Fractions often need to be reduced or rewritten in their simplest form. We do this when we divide both the top and bottom of a fraction by the same factor. For example, both the numerator and the denominator of $\frac{2}{4}$ can be divided by 2, which reduces the fraction to $\frac{1}{2}$. With larger fractions, it may save time to find the largest number that will divide evenly into both numbers, also known as the greatest common factor (GCF). You can still reduce a fraction using any common (shared) factor, but you will probably have to reduce several times. Using the GCF guarantees that you will have to reduce only once! So how can you find the GCF of your numerator and denominator? Look at the factors of each. Let's take the fraction $\frac{8}{12}$. What are the different ways to make 8? $1 \times 8 = 8$ and $2 \times 4 = 8$.

So the factors of 8 are 1, 2, 4, and 8.

Now, what are the different ways to make 12?

$1 \times 12 = 12$, $2 \times 6 = 12$, and $3 \times 4 = 12$.

The factors of 12 are 1, 2, 3, 4, 6, and 12.

To find our GCF, we compare these two lists. What is the largest number that occurs in both? That's right—4 is your GCF. Now divide both your numerator and denominator by 4 and you have the simplest (most reduced) form of your fraction.

$$\frac{8}{12} = \frac{8 \div 4}{12 \div 4} = \frac{2}{3}$$

Whenever your answer to a math question is a fraction, make sure to reduce the fraction to its simplest form. The multiple-choice answers that are fractions will virtually always be fractions in their simplest (most reduced) form.

Reducing Fractions Drill

Reduce the following fractions to their simplest forms. You can check your answers in Part IX: Answer Key to Drills.

1. $\frac{9}{12}$

2. $\frac{11}{33}$

3. $\frac{14}{35}$

4. $\frac{4}{9}$

5. $\frac{15}{8}$

Comparing Fractions

Sometimes a problem will involve deciding which of two fractions is bigger.

Which is bigger, $\frac{2}{5}$ or $\frac{4}{5}$? Think of these as parts of a pie. Which is bigger, two parts out of five, or four parts out of five? The fraction $\frac{4}{5}$ is clearly bigger. In this case, it was easy to tell because both fractions had the same whole: the same denominator.

It's more complicated when the fractions have different denominators. Which is bigger, $\frac{2}{3}$ or $\frac{3}{7}$? To decide, we need to rewrite the two fractions so that they have the same denominator. How do you decide what your new denominator should be? It's called the *least common denominator* (*LCD*), and is the smallest number that all of your denominators can divide into. How do you find the LCD? Start by listing the multiples of each denominator. Let's find the LCD of 3 and 7. What are the multiples of 3?

Count by threes: 3, 6, 9, 12, 15, 18, 21, 24, 27, 30, 33, 36, 39, 42,....

Don't go on forever; just write down a few and if you need to add more later on you can. Now what are the multiples of 7?

Count by sevens: 7, 14, 21, 28, 35, 42, 49,....

Do we have a number that is common to both of these lists? Yes—21 and 42 appear in both lists. But which number is the smaller of the two? The smaller number, 21, is our LCD.

Now we'll rewrite our two original fractions so they have the same denominator. We'll change the denominator of $\frac{2}{3}$ into the number 21. To get 3 to equal 21, we have to multiply it by 7. Because we want an equivalent fraction, anything we do to the denominator, we have to do to the numerator, so we also have to multiply the numerator by 7.

$$\frac{2 \times 7}{3 \times 7} = \frac{14}{21}$$

The fraction $\frac{14}{21}$ still has the same value as $\frac{2}{3}$ (it would reduce to $\frac{2}{3}$) because we multiplied the fraction by $\frac{7}{7}$, or one.

Let's change the denominator of $\frac{3}{7}$ into 21 as well.

$$\frac{3 \times 3}{7 \times 3} = \frac{9}{21}$$

The fraction $\frac{9}{21}$ still has the same value as $\frac{3}{7}$ (it would reduce to $\frac{3}{7}$) because we multiplied the fraction by $\frac{3}{3}$, or one.

Now we can compare the two fractions. Which is bigger, $\frac{14}{21}$ or $\frac{9}{21}$? Clearly $\frac{14}{21}$ (or $\frac{2}{3}$) is bigger than $\frac{9}{21}$ (or $\frac{3}{7}$).

Let's do it again. Which is bigger, $\frac{2}{3}$ or $\frac{3}{5}$?

First we look at the two denominators, 3 and 5.

The multiples of 3 are 3, 6, 9, 12, 15, 18, 21,....

And the multiples of 5 are 5, 10, 15, 20, 25,....

This time, the least common denominator is 15.

$$\frac{2}{3} \qquad \frac{3}{5}$$

$$\frac{2}{3}\times\frac{5}{5}=\frac{10}{15} \qquad \frac{3}{5}\times\frac{3}{3}=\frac{9}{15}$$

So $\frac{2}{3}$ is bigger than $\frac{3}{5}$.

Using Your Calculator on Fraction Problems

We have found that a calculator is only of limited use on fraction problems. However, it can make comparing fractions very easy: simply divide the numerator by the denominator of each fraction and pick the bigger number. If you need your answer in fraction format, the Texas Instruments TI-30XS has a convenient button called the answer toggle. It looks like ◀ ▶ and is located at the bottom right, just above the enter button. Pressing this button will change a decimal answer into a fraction (or root). If you enter an expression as a fraction, using the $\frac{n}{d}$ button, the answer will be automatically given as a fraction. And if you need to change that answer into a decimal, you can press the answer toggle button, ◀ ▶, to do so.

Tip: Save yourself time by using the Bowtie!

The Bowtie

The Bowtie is a shortcut that finds a common denominator and converts the numerators for you. Let's compare the last two fractions again. First, we get the common denominator by multiplying the two denominators together:

$$\frac{2}{3} \quad \frac{3}{5} = \frac{\ }{15}$$

Then, we get the new numerators by multiplying using the bowtie-shaped pattern shown below:

$$\textcircled{10}\ \frac{2}{3} \times \frac{3}{5}\ \textcircled{9} = \frac{\ }{15}$$

Finally, compare the fractions. Once again, we see that $\frac{10}{15}$ (or $\frac{2}{3}$) is bigger than $\frac{9}{15}$ (or $\frac{3}{5}$).

Adding and Subtracting Fractions

Whenever you add or subtract fractions, you need the fractions to have a common denominator. You can use the LCD method that we looked at to compare fractions, or you can use the Bowtie method, but you must somehow rewrite the fractions in the problem so that they have a common denominator before you add or subtract.

Let's use the Bowtie to add $\frac{2}{5}$ and $\frac{1}{4}$.

$$\frac{2}{5} + \frac{1}{4} =$$

$$(8)\ \frac{2}{5} \times \frac{1}{4}\ (5) = \frac{8+5}{20} = \frac{13}{20}$$

Let's use the Bowtie to subtract $\frac{2}{3}$ from $\frac{5}{6}$.

$$\frac{5}{6} - \frac{2}{3} =$$

$$(15)\ \frac{5}{6} \times \frac{2}{3}\ (12) = \frac{15-12}{18} = \frac{3}{18} = \frac{1}{6}$$

Fraction Quiz

Q: Which is bigger, $\frac{8}{9}$ or $\frac{7}{8}$?

Turn the page for the answer.

Adding and Subtracting Fractions Drill

You can check your answers in Part IX: Answer Key to Drills.

1. Which is bigger, $\frac{4}{5}$ or $\frac{5}{7}$?

2. $\frac{4}{5} + \frac{4}{7} = ?$

3. $\frac{2}{3} - \frac{1}{4} = ?$

4. $\frac{1}{3} + \frac{1}{6} + \frac{1}{18} = ?$

5. $\frac{2}{7} - \frac{1}{3} = ?$

Multiplying and Dividing Fractions

To multiply fractions, line them up and multiply straight across.

$$\frac{5}{6} \times \frac{4}{5} = \frac{20}{30} = \frac{2}{3}$$

Was there anything we could have canceled or reduced *before* we multiplied? You betcha. We could cancel the 5 on top and the 5 on the bottom. What's left is $\frac{4}{6}$, which reduces to $\frac{2}{3}$.

Sometimes people think they can cancel or reduce in the same fashion *across an equals sign.* Consider this example:

$$\frac{\cancel{5}x}{6} = \frac{4}{\cancel{5}} \text{ No!}$$

Fraction Quiz

A: Use the Bowtie! The fraction $\frac{8}{9}$ is bigger than $\frac{7}{8}$.

You *cannot* cancel the 5s in this case, or reduce the $\frac{4}{6}$. When there is an equals sign, you have to cross-multiply, which you will see more of in Chapter 14.

To divide one fraction by another, just flip the second fraction and multiply.

$$\frac{2}{3} \div \frac{3}{4} \text{ is the same thing as } \frac{2}{3} \times \frac{4}{3} = \frac{8}{9}.$$

Reciprocal Fact

Dividing by 4 is the same as multiplying by $\frac{1}{4}$: we divide a whole into 4 equal parts (denominator) and then take 1 (numerator).

You may see this same operation written like this:

$$\frac{\frac{2}{3}}{\frac{3}{4}}$$

Since every fraction is the numerator divided by the denominator, this is the same as $\frac{2}{3}$ divided by $\frac{3}{4}$. So, just flip the second fraction and multiply as usual.

Try the next example.

$$\frac{6}{\frac{2}{3}}$$

Here we are dividing a whole number by a fraction. To do this, first we need to write that whole number 6 as a fraction. We can write any whole number as a fraction by putting it over 1. So think of 6 as $\frac{6}{1}$, and do the same thing.

$$\frac{6}{1} \div \frac{2}{3} = \frac{6}{1} \times \frac{3}{2} = \frac{18}{2} = 9$$

Converting to Fractions

A whole number, such as 8, can always be expressed as a fraction by making that number the numerator and 1 the denominator: $8 = \frac{8}{1}$.

Sometimes the GED® test gives you numbers that are mixtures of whole numbers and fractions, for example, $3\frac{1}{2}$. These numbers are called mixed fractions (or mixed numbers). It is often easier to work with these numbers by converting them completely into fractions. Here's how you do it: Because the fraction is expressed in halves, let's convert the whole number into halves as well: $3 = \frac{6}{2}$. Now just add the $\frac{1}{2}$ to the $\frac{6}{2}$. You get $\frac{7}{2}$.

Fractions like $\frac{7}{2}$ are called **improper fractions,** because the numerator is larger than the denominator. Despite the name, though, there is nothing wrong with improper fractions. They are much easier to do any operation with than mixed numbers are, so whenever you have to add, subtract, multiply, or divide with mixed numbers, change them to improper fractions.

There is also a shortcut for converting mixed fractions. Multiply the denominator by the whole number, and then add the numerator. This number becomes your new numerator, and you keep the original denominator.

$$3\frac{1}{2} = \frac{3 \times 2 + 1}{2} = \frac{7}{2}$$

Multiplying, Dividing, and Converting Fractions Drill

You can check your answers in Part IX: Answer Key to Drills.

1. $\frac{4}{5} \times \frac{3}{8} =$

2. $\frac{9}{10} \div \frac{3}{5} =$

3. $\frac{\frac{2}{9}}{\frac{12}{10}} =$

4. $\frac{2}{3} \times \frac{3}{4} \times \frac{4}{5} =$

5. $1\frac{1}{3} \times \frac{3}{8} =$

Fraction Word Problems

Now let's try some fraction problems in the GED® test format.

1. If $\frac{1}{2}$ of a group of students say their favorite leisure activity is swimming, and $\frac{1}{3}$ of the group say their favorite leisure activity is tennis, what fraction of the group prefers neither swimming nor tennis?

   A. $\frac{1}{8}$

   B. $\frac{1}{6}$

   C. $\frac{1}{2}$

   D. $\frac{5}{6}$

Here's How to Crack It

Test takers are often intimidated by word problems, but you should realize that beneath all those words lies a simple math problem.

Before you even read it, there should be one thing you notice right away: There are fractions in the problem. That can mean only one thing. This is a fraction problem.

On the GED® test, the only things you are ever asked to do with fractions is add them, subtract them, multiply them, divide them, or compare them—and you've just learned how to do all those things, if you didn't know them already.

Let's read the problem. Half of the students like swimming. One-third like playing tennis. Basically, the question is, who's left? After we take away the students who like swimming and tennis, what fraction of the students remains?

Before you do any work at all, let's see if we can *ballpark* a little. If we add $\frac{1}{2}$ and $\frac{1}{3}$ together, that's quite a lot. There can't be too much of the whole left over. So do any of the answer choices strike you as unlikely? Choices (C) and (D) are clearly out of the ballpark because they are much too large. Let's eliminate both of them and now actually solve the problem.

First, let's use the Bowtie to add up the parts of the whole that we know about.

$$\frac{1}{2} \times \frac{1}{3} = \frac{3+2}{6} = \frac{5}{6}$$

So $\frac{5}{6}$ of the students like either swimming or tennis. Now the big question: What part of the whole remains? If the whole is $\frac{6}{6}$, subtract $\frac{5}{6}$ from that, and you're left with $\frac{1}{6}$, making the correct answer (B). Note that (D), $\frac{5}{6}$, was a *partial* answer. It was there for people who were in a hurry and thought they were done when they finished adding $\frac{1}{2}$ and $\frac{1}{3}$. However, if you read the question carefully and ballparked this problem first, there was no way you were going to fall for that trap. You already knew it was a crazy answer.

Here's another example:

2. It takes $1\frac{1}{4}$ hours for a factory worker to assemble one television set. How many television sets can be assembled in $17\frac{1}{2}$ hours?

Here's How to Crack It

Again, at first glance, you may feel intimidated by all the words in this problem, but don't let it fool you. This one's easy.

As we said earlier, whenever you see mixed numbers, you probably should change them into improper fractions before you do any calculations.

$$1\frac{1}{4} = \frac{5}{4}$$

$$17\frac{1}{2} = \frac{35}{2}$$

It takes $\frac{5}{4}$ of an hour to make one TV. How many sets can you make in $\frac{35}{2}$ hours? We want to know how many $\frac{5}{4}$s go into $\frac{35}{2}$, and that just means division.

$$\frac{35}{2} \div \frac{5}{4} = \frac{35}{2} \times \frac{4}{5}$$

Let's do some canceling.

$$\frac{\cancel{35}}{2} \times \frac{4}{\cancel{5}} = \frac{7}{\cancel{2}} \times \frac{\cancel{4}}{1} = \frac{7}{1} \times \frac{2}{1} = 14$$

The correct answer is 14.

Fraction Word Problem Drill

You can check your answers in Part IX: Answer Key to Drills.

1. In the town of Arkville, a total of 80 people came in to be tested for Lyme disease. Half of them were found to have the disease. Of those who did not have the disease when first tested, one-quarter later developed it. What fraction of the original 80 people got Lyme disease?

   A. $\frac{1}{4}$

   B. $\frac{1}{2}$

   C. $\frac{5}{8}$

   D. $\frac{3}{4}$

2. A pie company baked 100 pies in July, as shown in the table below. In August, the company increased production by $\frac{1}{10}$. In September, the pie company again increased production by $\frac{1}{10}$. Determine the number of pies baked in the months of August and September.

   Click on the numbers you want to select and drag them into the table. (For this drill, write the numbers in the table.)

Month	Number of Pies
July	100
August	
September	

101	102	110
112	120	121

3. According to a company survey, $\frac{1}{3}$ of the workers take public transportation to get to work, $\frac{2}{5}$ drive cars to work, and the remainder walk to work. What fraction of the workers walk to work?

DECIMALS

Fractions can also be expressed as decimals and vice versa. You probably know the decimal equivalent of certain fractions by heart (for example, $\frac{1}{2}$ = 0.5), but you may not know how to convert a fraction into a decimal.

As we said earlier, one way to think of a fraction is just as a division problem.

$$\frac{1}{2} = 1 \div 2 = 2\overline{)1.0}\quad (.5)$$

$$\frac{3}{4} = 3 \div 4 = 4\overline{)3.00}\quad (.75)$$

You can also convert any decimal into a fraction. The first digit to the right of the decimal is the tenths place. The second digit to the right of the decimal is the hundredths place. Consider these examples:

$$0.5 = \frac{5}{10} = \frac{1}{2}$$

$$0.75 = \frac{75}{100} = \frac{3}{4}$$

Adding and Subtracting Decimals

Calculating with decimals, unlike calculating with fractions, is almost always faster on the calculator. However, because you won't have the calculator during the first part of the test, it makes sense to practice these both ways. To add or subtract decimals, all you have to do is line up the decimal points and then add or subtract, just as you would any two whole numbers.

$$\begin{array}{r} 2.5 \\ +\,9.3 \\ \hline 11.8 \end{array} \qquad \begin{array}{r} 10.3 \\ -\,6.4 \\ \hline 3.9 \end{array} \qquad \begin{array}{r} 1.423 \\ +\,2.620 \\ \hline 4.043 \end{array} \qquad \begin{array}{r} 3.92 \\ +\,2.61 \\ \hline 6.53 \end{array}$$

If you're adding or subtracting one number that has fewer digits than another, it helps to add zeros to fill out the decimal places. For example, to subtract 3.26 from 8.4, adding a zero to 8.4 makes the problem easier to see:

$$\begin{array}{r} 8.40 \\ -\,3.26 \\ \hline 5.14 \end{array}$$

Here, the zero helps you see that you are subtracting 26 hundredths from 40 hundredths. Filling in with a zero like this will prevent you from making the common mistake of just bringing a digit down into your answer.

Multiplying Decimals

The best way to multiply decimals is to ignore the decimal points entirely until after you've performed the multiplication. For example, let's multiply 4.3 by 0.5. We'll start by multiplying 43 by 5:

$$\begin{array}{r} 43 \\ \times\,5 \\ \hline 215 \end{array}$$

Now count the total number of digits to the right of the decimal points in the two original numbers you were multiplying. In this case, there were a total of two digits to the right of the decimal points. Therefore, this is the number of digits there should be to the right of the decimal point in your final product. The answer is 2.15. Let's do another.

$$\begin{array}{r} 5.6 \\ \times 0.03 \\ \hline \end{array} \qquad \begin{array}{r} 56 \\ \times\;\;3 \\ \hline 168 \end{array}$$

There is a total of three digits to the right of the decimal points in the original numbers, so after multiplying, we place the decimal so that there are three digits to the right in the answer as well. The answer in this case is 0.168.

Dividing Decimals

The best way to divide decimals is first to convert the number you are dividing *by* (in math terminology, the **divisor**) into a whole number. You do this simply by moving the decimal point to the right as many places as necessary. This works as long as you remember to move the decimal point in the number that you are *dividing* (in math terminology, the **dividend**) the same number of spaces.

For example, to divide 12 by 0.6, set it up the way you would an ordinary division problem:

$$0.6\overline{)12}$$

To make 0.6 (the divisor) a whole number, you simply move the decimal point over one place to the right. You must also move the decimal one place to the right in the dividend. Remember that for any whole number, you can add a decimal and as many zeros as you want after it. So here, we think of whole number 12 as 12.0, and this allows us to move the decimal one place to the right. Now the operation looks like this:

$$6\overline{)120} \qquad \begin{array}{r} 20 \\ 6\overline{)120} \end{array}$$

Decimals Drill

Do these problems first on your own. Then, on a separate piece of paper, do them again using your calculator.

You can check your answers in Part IX: Answer Key to Drills.

1. $1.34 + 5.72 =$

2. $7.6 - 3.24 =$

3. $3.4 \times 2.41 =$

4. $6.4 \div 0.002 =$

5. $32 \div 0.8 =$

PERCENTS

Percent means "per 100" or how many out of a hundred. So a percent is really just a fraction with 100 as the denominator.

$$25\% = \frac{25}{100} \qquad 50\% = \frac{50}{100} \qquad 32\% = \frac{32}{100}$$

Decimal/Percentage Dictionary
0.01 = 1%
0.1 = 10%
1.0 = 100%

Like any fraction, a percentage can be converted to a decimal and vice versa. Percentage/decimal conversion is even easier than converting a normal fraction because both percentages and decimals are almost invariably *already* being expressed in hundredths.

$$25\% = \frac{25}{100} = 0.25 \qquad 0.50 = \frac{50}{100} = 50\%$$

To convert a regular fraction into a percent, you can first convert the fraction to a decimal, which, as we just said, is very close to a percentage already. Here are a few examples:

$$\frac{2}{5} = 5\overline{)2.0}^{\,0.4} = 0.4 = 0.40 = 40\%$$

$$\frac{12}{20} = 20\overline{)12.0}^{\,0.6} = 0.6 = 0.60 = 60\%$$

$$\frac{2}{3} = 3\overline{)2.000}^{\,0.666} = 0.666666\ldots \approx 66.67\%$$

$$\begin{array}{r} 18 \\ \hline 20 \\ 18 \\ \hline 20 \end{array}$$

In that last example, you'll notice that no matter how many places you carry that division to, you will always get a remainder. The fraction $\frac{2}{3}$ produces a decimal that goes on forever. However, if we are going to round to the nearest percent, then it's 67%.

There are some fractions, decimals, and percentages that come up so often that it's worth memorizing them. We've filled in some for you. Practice your conversions on a separate piece of paper to fill in the remaining boxes. Check your work with a calculator afterward.

Fraction	Decimal	Percent
		1%
$\frac{1}{50}$		
	0.05	
$\frac{1}{10}$		
		11.11%
	0.2	
$\frac{2}{9}$		
		25%
$\frac{1}{3}$		
$\frac{2}{5}$		
		44.44%
	0.5	
$\frac{5}{9}$		
		60%
$\frac{2}{3}$		
	0.75	
$\frac{7}{9}$		
		80%
$\frac{8}{9}$		
	1	

Most percent problems on the Mathematical Reasoning test ask you to find a percentage of a larger number. Here's an example:

1. If 10% of the 3,400 people who entered a sweepstakes won a prize, how many people did NOT win a prize?

   A. 34
   B. 340
   C. 3,060
   D. 3,366

We'll come back to this problem in a minute. But first, we want to show you…

Old-Fashioned Percents

Here's the way you probably learned percents: A percentage is just a fraction with 100 in the denominator, and the word *of* always means *multiply* in math. So when the GED® test asks you to find 20 percent of 400, it can be written this way:

$$\frac{20}{100} \times \frac{400}{1} = ?$$

Now you could do some canceling.

$$\frac{20}{\underset{1}{\cancel{100}}} \times \frac{\overset{4}{\cancel{400}}}{1} - 80$$

While this method will get you the right answer, it can be a long and tedious process when the numbers don't work out as nicely as the ones we chose for this example. But don't worry because you are about to learn a more efficient way to approach these problems.

The Princeton Review Percents

We have a fast, foolproof method for finding percents. This method involves almost no written calculation at all. You can thank us later.

To find 20 percent of a number, multiply the number by 0.20. To find 35 percent of a number, multiply the number by 0.35. To find 5 percent of a number, multiply the number by 0.05.

Ballparking Percent Quiz

Q: Roughly speaking, what's 10 percent of 305?

Turn the page for the answer.

To find 10 percent of any number, all you have to do is move the decimal point of that number over one place to the left.

10% of 4 = 0.4
10% of 30 = 3
10% of 520 = 52
10% of 21 = 2.1

Now, here's the great part. Ten percent of 30 = 3, right? So how much is 20% of 30? That's easy. It's twice as much as 10 percent, or 6. Here are a few examples:

What is 20% of 520?
10% of 520 = 52, so 20% of 520 = 2 × 52 = 104.

What is 20% of 4?
10% of 4 = 0.4, so 20% of 4 = 2 × 0.4 = 0.8.

What is 30% of 600?
10% of 600 = 60, so 30% of 600 = 3 × 60 = 180.

What is 40% of 500?
10% of 500 = 50, so 40% of 500 = 4 × 50 = 200.

This takes care of a lot of GED® problems right here, but there are some GED® problems that will ask you to find amounts like 15 percent or 27 percent. How do you do this?

To find 1 percent of any number, all you have to do is move the decimal point of that number over *two* places to the left.

1% of 4 = 0.04
1% of 30 = 0.3
1% of 520 = 5.2
1% of 21 = 0.21

In just the same way we found 20 percent by doubling 10 percent, we can now find 2 percent by doubling 1 percent.

What is 2% of 500?
1% of 500 = 5, so 2% of 500 = 2 × 5 = 10.

What is 3% of 60?
1% of 60 = 0.6, so 3% of 60 = 3 × 0.6 = 1.8.

Now, here's the *really* great part. We can combine these two techniques to find any percentage the test writers can invent.

Let's find 23% of 600.

Well, 10% of 600 = 60.
So 20% of 600 = 2 × 60 = 120.
And 1% of 600 = 6, so 3% of 600 = 18.

So what is 23% of 600?
20% of 600 = 120
3% of 600 = 18
120 + 18 = 138

Most students find that with a little practice, they can do this process in their heads or with minimal scratch work. Which is faster: using this method or using a calculator? Why don't you try it both ways on the following drill?

Ballparking Percent Quiz
A: Roughly speaking, 10 percent of 305 is about 30.

Percents Drill

Do these problems on your own. Then, on another piece of paper, do them again using your calculator.

You can check your answers in Part IX: Answer Key to Drills.

1. Find 20% of 83.
2. Find 30% of 15.
3. Find 40% of 720.
4. Find 3% of 70.
5. Find 5% of 180.
6. Find 23% of 500.
7. Find 15% of 98.
8. What is 35% of 140?
9. What is 50% of 62?
10. What is 25% of 144?

(Hint: On the last two problems, remember that 50% = $\frac{1}{2}$ and 25% = $\frac{1}{4}$.)

PERCENT WORD PROBLEMS

Now, let's go back to the first percentage problem we showed you.

Outta Here!

In the following question, find the answers that are out of the ballpark.

Q: Barry Bonds hits three home runs of lengths 375 feet, 380 feet, and 400 feet. What was the average length of his home runs?

A. 385 feet
B. 405 feet
C. 420 feet
D. 1,155 feet

Turn the page for the answer.

1. If 10% of the 3,400 people who entered a sweepstakes won a prize, how many people did NOT win a prize?

A. 34
B. 340
C. 3,060
D. 3,366

Here's How to Crack It

The first thing you see is "10% of 3,400." At this point, figuring out 10 percent of anything should be second nature to you. Using either Old-Fashioned Percents or The Princeton Review Percents method, we find that 10 percent of 3,400 is 340. But are you done?

Reread the last line of the question. It asks you how many people did *not* win a prize. You need to take one more step. The total number of people who entered the sweepstakes was 3,400. You now know that 340 of them won a prize. So how many people didn't? All you have to do is subtract the winners from the entire group. What you're left with is the number of losers: 3,400 – 340 = 3,060. The correct answer is (C).

If you were really thinking, you could have saved yourself a step by realizing that if 10 percent won, then 90 percent didn't. You could simply have multiplied 340 (10 percent) by 9 to get 3,060 in one step.

Could you have ballparked this problem? Sure. A careful reading of the question would have told you that the number of people you were looking for was the number who did not win. Because only 10 percent won, you were looking for a large percentage of the people who entered. Which answers didn't make sense? Choice (A) was ridiculously small. Choice (B) was a partial answer for those who forgot that they were looking for the losers, not the winners. It was easy to pick (B) from a math standpoint, but impossible to pick if you were Ballparking.

Here's another example:

2. A DVD player is on sale for 20% off its normal price of \$400. If the sales tax is 5%, what is the cost of the DVD player?

Here's How to Crack It

This question requires two separate operations. First, let's find the sale price of the DVD player.

What is 20% of 400?

10% of $400 = 40$

20% of $400 = 2 \times 40 = 80$

So if the DVD player has been marked down by \$80, the sale price is \$400 – \$80 = \$320.

Now let's find the sales tax. Here's the tricky part: Is the sales tax the original \$400 or on the sale price of \$320? That's right—it is on the sale price.

What is 5% of \$320?

10% of $320 = 32$

5% of $320 = \frac{1}{2} \times 32 = 16$

So what's the final price?

$$\begin{array}{r} \$320 \\ +\ \$16 \\ \hline \$336 \end{array}$$

Backward Percents

Sometimes the test writers will ask you a percentage problem backward.

Outta Here!

A: Choice (D), 1,155, is WAY out of the ballpark—it's the sum of all three numbers in the question. So are (B) and (C) because the average length can't be bigger than the largest number being averaged. The correct answer is (A).

3. If a mailing of 15,000 letters resulted in 3,750 responses, what was the percentage of responses to the mailing?

   A. 20%
   B. 25%
   C. 30%
   D. 35%

Here's How to Crack It

Your old teacher from high school, a gleam in her eye, would be telling you to set up an equation—but there's a much simpler way. Let's use POE to get rid of wrong answers.

Start with (A), 20%, and (C), 30%. Both of these are multiples of 10%, and we already know a great trick to find that! Take the 15,000 letters and move the decimal over one place to the left to get 10% = 1,500. Multiply by three to find 30% = 4,500. That's too big! Now multiply 1,500 by two to get 20% = 3,000. This isn't big enough.

Do we need to calculate an exact amount for (B), 25%, and (D), 35%? No! If 20% is too small, and 30% is too big, we know our answer must be somewhere in between. The correct answer must be (B), 25%.

Percent Word Problems Drill

You can check your answers in Part IX: Answer Key to Drills.

1. An investor is deciding between two different investments, X and Y. Investment X is a one-year certificate of deposit that pays 8% in interest, into which the investor would deposit $650. Investment Y is a high-yield savings account that pays 3% in interest, into which the investor would deposit $1,500.

   After one year, the amount earned by investment X will be Select... ▼ the amount earned by investment Y.

Select...
greater than
less than
the same as

2. Janice sells household products door to door. If she must pay her supplier 60% of the money that she takes in, how much would she keep for herself if she took in $1,200?

   A. $720.00
   B. $560.50
   C. $480.00
   D. Not enough information is given.

3. A student furnishing his first apartment goes shopping and buys a bed for $120, a sofa for $635, and a lamp for $74. If the sales tax is 9%, how much did the student pay in total for the furniture?

   $ ☐

4. Carmen owns a computer store and had $6,750 in sales this May. The year before, she had $8,437.50 in sales in May. If Carmen had a profit of $5,400 this May, what percent of her sales were profits?

   A. 36%
   B. 60%
   C. 64%
   D. 80%

"Standardized" Means Predictable

The nice thing about any standardized test is that each one is very similar to the one before. This means that after you have gone through this book, completed our practice tests, and perhaps taken GED Ready®: The Official Practice Test, you will have seen every type of problem and topic that the test could possibly throw at you at least three or four times each. The GED® test presents percent problems exactly the same way each time. Number line problems employ the same ideas year after year.

This means that it's important for you to remember the problems you've already completed. Math questions that you do in this book should be added to a mental file. Then, when a problem just like one of them surfaces on the real GED® test, instead of staring at it perplexedly, you'll be saying, "Ah, what an interesting variation on that decimal problem I studied last week."

PUTTING IT ALL TOGETHER

Now that you've seen the basics of arithmetic one topic at a time, we're going to give you a drill that mixes up all the different problems we've discussed so far. Often, the toughest part of the Mathematical Reasoning test is recognizing what kind of problem you are facing.

As we said in Chapter 12, the last line of a question is usually the key to understanding the entire question. Read the question carefully—you may need to slow down—to ensure you don't fall for any tricks or traps along the way. And if you are unsure of an answer, flag the question to come back to later with a fresh perspective.

Basic Arithmetic Drill

You can check your answers in Part IX: Answer Key to Drills.

1. Which of the following have the same value as $\frac{3}{5}$? Click on the numbers you want to select and drag them into the boxes. (For this drill, write the numbers in the boxes.)

$$\square = \frac{3}{5} = \square$$

6%	1.7	$\frac{9}{15}$	0.6	3%
0.9	$\frac{5}{3}$	$\frac{9}{10}$	20%	

2. Darius goes out to lunch and receives a bill listing a subtotal of $14.65 and tax of $1.47. Darius leaves a 20% tip on the total amount. The amount he tips is Select... ▼ the amount of tax charged.
   - greater than
   - less than
   - equal to

3. If a boat takes 2 hours to travel 30 miles, how long will it take to travel 72 miles?

   A. 1.2 hours
   B. 4.0 hours
   C. 4.8 hours
   D. 6.0 hours

4. Tatiana did $\frac{1}{4}$ of her homework on Tuesday and $\frac{1}{5}$ of her homework on Wednesday. What fraction of her homework remains to be done?

   A. $\frac{9}{20}$
   B. $\frac{11}{20}$
   C. $\frac{7}{9}$
   D. $\frac{19}{20}$

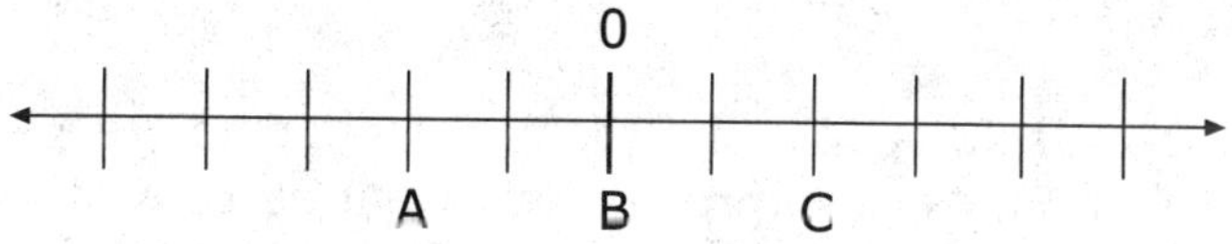

5. In the figure above, point B represents the number 0. If the midpoint of segment AB is at point −2 on the number line and the midpoint of BC is at point 2 on the number line, then which point represents the midpoint of segment AC?

   Click on the number line to plot the point. (For this drill, plot the point by marking an X on the number line.)

6. You are working out a one-year payment plan for a new bicycle. The bicycle costs \$275. Tax on the purchase is 11%. You will make 12 equal payments and do not owe any additional interest. How much is each payment, to the nearest dollar?

A. \$20.00
B. \$23.00
C. \$25.00
D. \$30.00

7. If $5R - 5S = 35$, then what is the value of $R - S$?

A. 5
B. 6
C. 7
D. Not enough information is given.

8. $5(2 - 4 + 1) + \frac{2}{3}(7 - 1) = ?$

9. If 30 people in a room of 70 people are smokers, approximately what percent of the people in the room are smokers?

A. 23%
B. 30%
C. 43%
D. 57%

10. A bankrupt company agrees to pay its creditors 80% of what they are actually owed. If the company pays \$9,600, what did they originally owe?

A. \$7,680
B. \$8,000
C. \$11,520
D. \$12,000

11. Click on the numbers below and drag them into the boxes that represent the appropriate places on the number line. (For this drill, simply write the numbers in the boxes.)

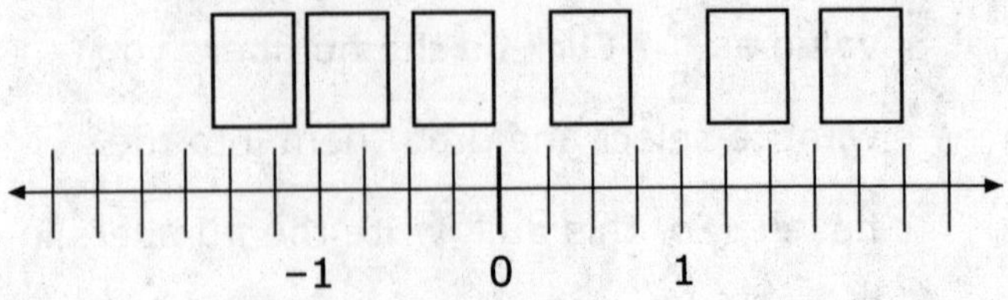

2	0.5	$-\frac{4}{3}$
−0.8	$-\frac{1}{4}$	$\frac{11}{8}$

12. $14 - |6 - (-5)| \times 3 = ?$

A. −19
B. 9
C. 47
D 75

13. Which of the following represents the sum of the factors of 14?

A. 9
B. 10
C. 23
D. 24

14. Which of the following is NOT a multiple of 4?

A. 4
B. 12
C. 34
D. 68

Chapter 14
Applied Arithmetic

In this chapter, we go over more arithmetic problems involving setup problems, averages, ratios and proportions, rate problems, charts and graphs, exponents, radicals, scientific notation, probability, and counting.

Now we're going to show you some additional arithmetic concepts that build on the ideas you've already learned in the last chapter. As in that chapter, we'll introduce a concept first and then give you some sample GED® questions followed by a short drill. At the end of the chapter, you'll find a big drill that mixes and matches all the different concepts. These are the subjects we'll cover.

- Setup problems
- Mean, median, mode, range, and weighted mean
- Ratios and proportions
- Rate problems
- Charts and graphs
- Exponents and square roots
- Scientific notation
- Probability
- Counting

SETUP PROBLEMS

Wouldn't it be interesting if a test question asked you to do the entire setup of a problem, but didn't want you to actually solve it? In fact, if you go on to college, you will find that this is often exactly what college math tests are like. College professors are much more interested in seeing *how you think* than how careful you are with your addition and subtraction.

Here's an example:

1. Jim started a business selling mattresses. He sold 12 standard mattresses and 7 deluxe mattresses last week. Which expression below represents how many dollars he took in last week if the standard mattress costs $100 and the deluxe costs $160?

   A. 12(100) + 7(100)
   B. 12(160) + 7(100)
   C. 12(100) + 7(160)
   D. 12(160) + 7(160)

Here's How to Crack It

To find out the total price, you have to multiply the number of standard mattresses by the price of a standard mattress, and the number of deluxe mattresses by the price of a deluxe mattress. There were 12 standards at \$100 each, so that's 12(100). There were seven deluxes at \$160 each, so that's 7(160). Altogether that's 12(100) + 7(160). The correct answer is (C).

Take Your Time...

Try not to be in too much of a rush on setup problems. The answer choices are all close variations of one another, and it's easy to pick the wrong one if you're in a hurry. In addition, sometimes the GED® test writers may not have written their equation in quite the same way that you did. For example, in this problem, you might have written *your* equation starting with the expensive mattresses—7(160) + 12(100)—in which case, if you looked through the answer choices quickly, you might have thought *your* answer wasn't there. So be prepared to be flexible as you look at the answer choices on a setup problem. You may have to add the numbers in a different order or convert a fraction to a decimal.

...But Not Too Much Time

Some test takers actually *solve* setup problems; they find the correct answer (even though the problem does not require it) and then find the answer choice that adds up to the same number they calculated. We think this generally takes a little too much time. However, if there's one problem that you're really not sure of, you can check the expression you wrote by solving the problem and then making sure that the answer you chose agrees with the number you calculated.

Here's another setup problem, this time about percentages:

---

2. Mr. James goes into an investment with two partners. Together the three of them put a total of \$30,000 into an investment that pays annual interest of 12%. At the end of the year, the three people share the interest evenly. How much did Mr. James receive in interest?

A. $\frac{30{,}000 \times 12}{3}$

B. $\frac{30{,}000 \times 0.12}{3}$

C. $\frac{30{,}000 \times 3}{12}$

D. $\frac{30{,}000 \times 3}{0.12}$

Here's How to Crack It

Mr. James and his two partners share the interest evenly. If this were a normal problem, first you would find 12% of $30,000, and then you would figure out Mr. James's share. If you want to, you can do the problem this way—actually solve it and then figure out the numeric value of each of the answer choices, one by one, until you find the one that matches your solution. Unfortunately, as we said, this can take some time.

Rather than solving this problem, it may be better to set it up as if you were *going* to solve it using a traditional equation. When we first discussed percents in Chapter 13, we said that the word *of* always means *multiply*. If we want to find 12% of $30,000, we could write that in two ways:

$$\frac{12}{100} \times 30{,}000 \text{ or } 0.12 \times 30{,}000$$

They both mean the same thing.

Whatever this number is—and remember, in this problem, you don't need to know what it is—it represents the entire amount of interest. The problem is asking for only Mr. James's share. Because all three investors share the interest evenly, you have to divide the entire amount by 3.

$$\frac{0.12 \times 30{,}000}{3}$$

The correct answer is (B).

Setup Quiz

Q: Which two setups below are identical?

(A) 40($1.25) + 25($0.90)
(B) 25($0.90) + 40($1.25)
(C) (40 + 25)($1.25 + $0.90)

Turn the page for the answer.

Setup Drill

You can check your answers in Part IX: Answer Key to Drills.

1. Sam works 8 hours per day, 6 days a week, delivering flowers. If he earns $20 per hour, how much, in dollars, does he make in 4 weeks?

A. $8 \times 6 \times 4 \times 20$
B. $8 \times 6 \times 20$
C. $[4(8) + 4(6)]20$
D. $5.50 \times 8 + 20 \times 4$

2. This year, the price of a particular model of car went up 4% from last year's price of $12,000. Which of the following represents the new price?

A. 0.04($12,000)

B. 0.04($12,000) + $12,000

C. $\frac{\$12{,}000}{0.04} + \$12{,}000$

D. 0.96($12,000) + $12,000

MEAN, MEDIAN, MODE, RANGE, AND WEIGHTED MEAN

The **mean,** or **average,** is a single number that represents the central value of a set of numbers. In spite of its name, a mean problem is almost always pretty gentle and easy. To find the *mean* of several different numbers, first add them up, and then divide the sum of the numbers by the actual number of items that you added. For example, to find the average of 5, 10, and 15, first add the three numbers:

$$\begin{array}{r} 5 \\ +10 \\ \underline{+15} \\ 30 \end{array}$$

Then, because there are three items being added, divide the sum of the numbers by three:

$$\begin{array}{r} 10 \\ 3\overline{)30} \end{array}$$

That's it. The mean (average) of 5, 10, and 15 is 10. Let's try a problem like some you'll see on the GED® test.

Setup Quiz
A: (A) 40($1.25) + 25($0.90) is the same as (B) 25($0.90) + 40($1.25).

1. A realtor hires a plumber to make x repairs. The plumber bills the realtor $1,450 in total. Which expression determines the average cost of each repair?

A. $1{,}450x$

B. $1{,}450 + x$

C. $\dfrac{1{,}450}{x}$

D. $\dfrac{x}{1{,}450}$

Here's How to Crack It

This problem is different from the above example in two ways. First, there is no actual number of repairs. Instead, that number is represented by a variable, *x;* second, in this problem you don't have to add up the individual elements (i.e., the cost of *each* of the individual repairs) because it has already been done for you.

In spite of these differences, this is still an average problem, and we can solve it using the average formula:

$$\frac{\text{sum of all items}}{\text{number of items}} = \text{average}$$

Okay, let's start by adding the elements to get the sum of all the elements—oh, wait, the elements have *already* been added. The total cost of all the repairs is $1,450. All that's left to do is divide the total cost ($1,450) by the number of repair jobs—oh, wait, there is no precise number. Well, you do at least have a variable representing this number, so divide by the variable:

$$\frac{1{,}450}{x}$$

The correct answer is (C).

The *median* of a set of ordered numbers (that is, numbers in ascending order) is the number right in the middle. For example, the median of 3, 16, and 17 is 16. The median of 139, 234, 326, 327, and 328 is 326.

The median is usually different from the mean. Let's take the numbers 2, 3, and 10. The mean of these numbers is $\frac{2+3+10}{3}$, or 5, but the median is simply the middle number, or 3.

If you are asked to find the median of a set of numbers that is not in ascending order, first put the numbers in ascending order, and then take the middle number. For example, the median of 3, 7, and 6 would be 6.

What if there is no middle number? Take the following list of numbers:

4, 8, 10, 20

This time, two numbers are sharing the middle. In cases like this (in which there is an even number of items), take the mean of the two middle numbers. This time, the median is 9.

How do median problems look on the Mathematical Reasoning test?

2. Priya played 4 Starmaster games at a video arcade. Her scores were 125, 135, 120, and 140.

Click on the numbers you want to select and drag them into the boxes.

What was her mean (average) score? ☐

What was her median score? ☐

120	125	128	130

130	135	140

Ballparking Averages
The average of a string of numbers has to be less than the biggest number and more than the smallest number.

Here's How to Crack It

As soon as you see the words *mean* and *average,* you know just what to do: Add the items together, and divide by the number of items—in this case, 4.

$$\begin{array}{r} 120 \\ 125 \\ 135 \\ +\ 140 \\ \hline 520 \end{array}$$

$$4\overline{)520}\ = 130$$

The correct answer to the first question is 130.

To find the *median,* you must first order the numbers from least to greatest: 120, 125, 135, 140. What number is in the middle? There are two numbers in the middle, 125 and 135, which means you must take the *mean* of those two. Find the sum, 125 + 135 = 260, and then divide by two, 260 ÷ 2 = 130.

The correct answer to the second question is also 130!

The *mode* of a set of numbers is the number that appears the most often. For example, the mode of 1, 4, 4, 5, 5, 5, 8 is 5. The number 4 occurs twice, but the number 5 occurs three times, so 5 occurs the *most* in this list.

Sometimes there is more than one mode. Let's look at another example set: 2, 5, 9, 2, 4, 1, 8, and 5. First you should order the numbers from least to greatest: 1, 2, 2, 4, 5, 5, 8, 9. Now it is much easier to see which numbers repeat. Both 2 and 5 occur twice, and no number occurs more than twice. So, both 2 and 5 are the modes.

Try it out on this problem:

---

3. If there were 24 traffic summonses issued in September, 45 in October, 24 in November, and 39 in December, what was the mode number of summonses issued over the four months?

Here's How to Crack It

First, put the numbers in ascending order: 24, 24, 39, 45. Now, do any numbers appear more than once? That's right—the correct answer is 24.

The *range* of a set of numbers is the distance between the smallest value and the largest value. For example, look at the following set: 2, 5, 6, 8, 99. The largest value is 99 and the smallest value is 2, so the range is 99 – 2 = 97. As with the mean, median, and mode, be sure your numbers are in ascending order before subtracting!

See whether you can solve the following GED® range question.

Jill's Work Week

	Number of Hours Worked	Hourly Pay
Monday	6	$15.00
Tuesday	5	$15.00
Wednesday	8	$12.50
Thursday	7	$12.50
Friday	4	$15.00

4. Jill gets paid different rates for working on different projects. She worked on one project Monday, Tuesday, and Friday of last week, and worked on the second project on Wednesday and Thursday of last week. Her hours spent working and pay rates are shown in the table above. What was the range of Jill's daily earnings last week?

   A. $2.50
   B. $20.00
   C. $37.50
   D. $40.00

Here's How to Crack It

This question asks about Jill's daily earnings. Do you know how much she earned each day? No, but you can find out. Multiply the number of hours worked each day by the hourly rate for that day to find Jill's daily earnings.

On Monday, Jill earned 6 × \$15.00 = \$90.00.

On Tuesday, Jill earned 5 × \$15.00 = \$75.00.

On Wednesday, Jill earned 8 × \$12.50 = \$100.00.

On Thursday, Jill earned 7 × \$12.50 = \$87.50.

On Friday, Jill earned 4 × \$15.00 = \$60.00.

Therefore, the greatest daily earning was \$100.00 on Wednesday and the least was \$60.00 on Friday.

To calculate the range, we need to find the distance, or difference, between those two values. So we subtract \$100.00 – \$60.00 = \$40.00. The correct answer must be (D).

The *weighted mean* is used when the numbers in a set are not all equally important. Those with more importance are given more *weight* when calculating the mean, or average. Here's how.

Let's say there are 4 tests in total for a certain class: Exam A, the Midterm Exam, Exam B, and the Final Exam. Exams A and B may be worth only 20% each of your final grade, while the Midterm and Final Exams may each be worth 30% of your final grade. You happen to score the following on each:

Exam A—95
Midterm Exam—90
Exam B—92
Final Exam—87

To calculate your final grade for the class, you can't *just* take the mean (average), since the Midterm and Final exams have more weight than Exams A and B. So you must find the weighted mean. Start by writing the weights next to each corresponding item.

Exam A—95	20%
Midterm Exam—90	30%
Exam B—92	20%
Final Exam—87	30%

Now multiply each score by its weight and write that new value off to the right.

Exam A—95	→	20%	=	1,900
Midterm Exam—90	→	30%	=	2,700
Exam B—92	→	20%	=	1,840
Final Exam—87	→	30%	=	2,610

Add up both the final column and the weights column.

Exam A—95	→	20%	=	1,900
Midterm Exam—90	→	30%	=	2,700
Exam B—92	→	20%	=	1,840
Final Exam—87	→	+ 30%	=	+ 2,610
		100%		9,050

Now divide the total value by the total of the weights to get the weighted average:

$$100\overline{)9050}\quad 90.5$$

Your final grade in the class would be 90.5.

In summary, you can calculate the weighted mean by following these steps:

1. Multiply your values by their respective weights.
2. Add all your weights together and all your new values together.
3. Divide the total new value by the total weight.

Try another weighted mean problem.

5. Juwon is the best player on his basketball team. During the first 8 weeks of the season, he scored on 65% of his attempts. For the following 4 weeks, Juwon scored on only 32% of his attempts. During the final 4 weeks of playoffs, Juwon practiced more and scored on 74% of his attempts. If Juwon made the same number of attempts each game, then what percent of his attempts during the entire season did he score?

   A. 57%
   B. 59%
   C. 63%
   D. 67%

Here's How to Crack It

This may not seem like a weighted mean problem at first, but look closer. The percentages given throughout the season represent Juwon's *average* scoring over those periods. So in order to find his percentage for the entire season, you must combine the 65 percent, 32 percent, and 74 percent. Notice that if you calculate just the mean (average) of 65, 32, and 74, you get (A), 57 percent. This is a trap!

Each percentage represents a portion of the season—65 percent for 8 weeks, 32 percent for 4 weeks, and 74 percent for 4 weeks. First multiply these percentages by the length of time over which they occurred.

$$65 \times 8 = 520$$
$$32 \times 4 = 128$$
$$74 \times 4 = 296$$

Since the question asks about the entire season, find the total number of weeks and the total of the new weighted values.

$$8 + 4 + 4 = 16$$
$$520 + 128 + 296 = 944$$

Now divide the total weighted value by the total number of weeks.

$$16\overline{)944} = 59$$

The correct answer is (B).

Mean, Median, Mode, Range, and Weighted Mean Drill

You can check your answers in Part IX: Answer Key to Drills.

Do these problems on your own. Then, on another piece of paper, do them again using your calculator.

1. A consumer group buys one identical radio at each of 14 different stores. If the mean (average) price per radio is $23.40, how much did the consumer group spend for all the radios?

$ ______

2. The data below represents the scores students achieved on a test.

92, 85, 86, 92, 86, 89

Complete the line plot to display the data. Click on the X and drag it onto the graph as many times as necessary. (For this drill, simply mark the Xs on the line plot.)

Student Test Scores

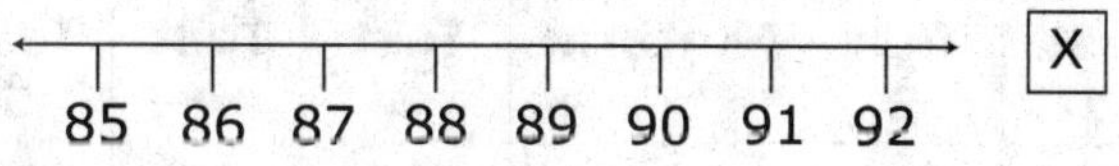

3. What is the range of weekly business expenses of a sewing supply shop over a three-week period if $65.00, $73.23, and $35.77 were the weekly expense totals for the three weeks?

   A. $8.23
   B. $29.23
   C. $37.46
   D. $58.00

Ice Cream Cones Sold at the Store "Cone Central" Over 5 Consecutive Days

Monday	Tuesday	Wednesday	Thursday	Friday
105	80	95	110	205

4. What is the mean (average) number of ice cream cones sold at the store "Cone Central" during the period shown in the table above?

   A. 95
   B. 105
   C. 110
   D. 119

5. What is the median number of ice cream cones sold at the store "Cone Central" during the period shown in the graph above?

A. 95
B. 105
C. 110
D. 119

6. Olivia is calculating her grade in math class. Her scores for the class are recorded in the table below.

	Test 1	Test 2	Midterm	Test 3	Test 4	Test 5	Final
Scores	83	95	84	93	84	92	90

The five in-class tests each account for 10% of her final grade, while the midterm and final exams account for 25% each. What is Olivia's grade in math class, rounded to the nearest percent?

A. 84%
B. 87%
C. 88%
D. 89%

RATIOS AND PROPORTIONS

As we said earlier, a fraction can express the same relationship (part-to-whole) with larger or smaller numbers. For example, $\frac{1}{2} = \frac{2}{4} = \frac{3}{6}$.... A ratio or proportion problem merely asks you to express a particular relationship in a form that looks and behaves like a fraction. Here's an example:

1. A map uses a scale in which 1 inch = 200 miles. If the distance between two cities measures 5 inches on the map, how many miles separate the two cities?

A. 1,000
B. 800
C. 600
D. 400

Here's How to Crack It

Let's talk about this problem in terms of inches per mile, which can be expressed as follows:

$$\frac{1 \text{ inch}}{200 \text{ miles}}$$

This is actually a ratio, which is a way of writing a part-to-part comparison. A ratio is very similar to a fraction, and has many of the same properties that a fraction does. Like a fraction, a ratio can be expressed in an infinite number of different equivalent ratios. For example, it could equal a ratio with a numerator of 5:

$$\frac{1 \text{ inch}}{200 \text{ miles}} = \frac{5 \text{ inches}}{?}$$

You have just set up a proportion, which is two equivalent ratios. One inch represents 200 miles, so five inches represents…you don't know yet. Instead of "?" put an x in its place, to represent the number you don't know yet. To find out how many miles are represented by five inches, cross-multiply the denominator of the left-hand ratio with the numerator of the right, and then the denominator of the right-hand ratio with the numerator of the left:

$$\frac{1 \text{ inch}}{200 \text{ miles}} \times \frac{5 \text{ inches}}{x \text{ miles}} \qquad 1{,}000 = 1x$$

And $x = 1{,}000$ miles. To check this, you can stick this number into the proportion you just wrote:

$$\frac{1 \text{ inch}}{200 \text{ miles}} = \frac{5 \text{ inches}}{1{,}000 \text{ miles}}$$

Does $\frac{5}{1{,}000}$ reduce to $\frac{1}{200}$? You bet. The correct answer is (A).

Let's do another:

2. If Janira can finish her work assignment in half an hour, what part of it can she finish in 20 minutes?

A. $\frac{1}{6}$

B. $\frac{1}{3}$

C. $\frac{2}{3}$

D. $\frac{3}{4}$

Here's How to Crack It

First of all, did you notice that this is the same type of problem as the one we did above? Janira can do one job in a half hour, so how much can she do in 20 minutes? To solve this, set up a proportion.

To make your job easier, you should use the same time measurement throughout the problem, so instead of talking about half an hour, permanently convert that to 30 minutes. Now, on to the proportion.

$$\frac{1 \text{ job}}{30 \text{ minutes}} = \frac{x \text{ (part of the job)}}{20 \text{ minutes}}$$

As you did before, cross-multiply.

$$\frac{1 \text{ job}}{30 \text{ minutes}} = \frac{x \text{ (part of the job)}}{20 \text{ minutes}} \qquad 30x = 20 \qquad x = \frac{20}{30} \text{ or } \frac{2}{3}$$

The correct answer is (C).

Could you have done some Ballparking here? Of course! If the whole job takes 30 minutes, obviously 20 minutes is time to do more than half the job. Both (A) and (B) are less than half and can be eliminated right away. In fact, you might even have noticed that 20 minutes out of

30 minutes was $\frac{2}{3}$ without even setting up the proportion. But it's always a good idea to do the work, just to make sure.

Ratios and Proportions Drill

You can check your answers in Part IX: Answer Key to Drills.

1. If a shrub 5 feet tall casts a 2-foot shadow, how tall, in feet, is a tree standing next to the shrub that casts a 10-foot shadow at the same moment?

   A. 50
   B. 25
   C. 20
   D. 13

2. Two songwriting collaborators decide that they will share profits in a song in a ratio of 3 parts for the lyric writer to 2 parts for the music writer. If the music writer gets $2,500, how much does the lyric writer receive?

   A. $2,500
   B. $3,750
   C. $5,000
   D. $7,500

3. A particular lawn requires 6 bags of fertilizer. A lawn next door requires 4 bags of fertilizer. How big, in square feet, is the lawn next door?

   A. 10
   B. 24
   C. 50
   D. Not enough information is given.

RATE PROBLEMS

It's easy to spot rate problems: They almost always use the word "per" in the question.

Rate Problem Quiz
Q: How do you spot an $R \times T = D$ problem?

Turn the page for the answer.

You may not think so, but you already know the formula to solve every rate problem. Don't believe us? Let's say you drive in a car for 2 hours at 50 miles per hour. How far have you traveled? That's right: 100 miles. Fifty miles per hour is the *rate* at which you traveled, 2 hours is the *time* it took you to travel, and 100 miles is the *distance* you traveled.

The formula looks like this:

$$\begin{array}{ccc} \text{Rate} \times & \text{Time} = & \text{Distance} \\ 50 & 2 & 100 \end{array}$$

Or like this:

$$\text{Rate} = \frac{\text{Distance}}{\text{Time}}$$

Both equations are the same, as you will see in Chapter 15, Algebra. Memorizing this formula can save you a headache later on when you aren't sure whether to divide or multiply. Let's try two problems.

---

1. A train traveled at a speed of 120 kilometers per hour for $2\frac{1}{2}$ hours. How many kilometers did the train travel?

   A. 300
   B. 280
   C. 240
   D. 200

Here's How to Crack It

As soon as you see the words "kilometers *per* hour" and "hours," you should immediately be writing down $R \times T = D$ on your scratch paper, even before you finish reading the problem. Now all you'll have to do is plug in, or substitute, the numbers from the problem:

$$R \times T = D$$

$$120 \times 2\frac{1}{2} = ?$$

Multiplying $120 \times 2\frac{1}{2}$, you get 300, which is (A).

Could you have ballparked this question? Sure. If the train is traveling at 120 kilometers per hour, then in one hour it must have traveled 120 kilometers. Since your train has been traveling for more than two hours, it must have traveled more than 240 kilometers. Eliminate (C) and (D).

Here's another example:

2. Flying at 400 miles per hour, approximately how long will it take for a plane to travel between two cities that are 2,600 miles apart?

   A. between 4 and 5 hours
   B. between 5 and 6 hours
   C. between 6 and 7 hours
   D. between 7 and 8 hours

Here's How to Crack It

Again, after reading the first line, you should have been reaching for your scratch paper to write down $R \times T = D$. Plug in the numbers the problem gives you.

$$R \times T = D$$

$$400 \times ? = 2{,}600$$

Ballpark a little first, before you solve this. The answer choices give you some clues as to what this missing number T should be. Start with (A). If T were 4 hours, given that the rate is 400, what would the distance be? $4 \times 400 = 1{,}600$. You need a larger T if you want the distance to be 2,600. Now if T were 5 hours, $5 \times 400 = 2{,}000$. That's still not large enough. Let's try 6 hours: $6 \times 400 = 2{,}400$. Well, you're getting closer. How about 7 hours? $7 \times 400 = 2{,}800$. Now this is too big. The correct time must be between 6 and 7 hours.

How do you calculate this problem the traditional way? Solve for the missing T. If $R \times T = D$, then $T = \frac{D}{R} = \frac{2{,}600}{400} = 6.5$ hours. The correct answer is (C).

Rate Problems Drill

You can check your answers in Part IX: Answer Key to Drills.

1. If a man runs 12 miles in 3 hours, what is his rate in miles per hour?

2. A glacier is moving at a rate of 4 feet per year. At this rate, how many years will it take the glacier to travel one mile?
(1 mile = 5,280 feet)

A. 920
B. 1,100
C. 1,320
D. 1,540

Rate Problem Quiz
A: It will use the word "per" in the question.

3. Marie drives from her home to the supermarket 10 miles away and then drives back home after shopping. If it takes her two hours for the entire trip, including one hour spent shopping in the supermarket, what was her average speed, in miles per hour, driving to and from the supermarket?

A. 5
B. 10
C. 15
D. 20

SCALE AND UNIT CONVERSION

Sometimes you will be asked to find the scale on which something is drawn. The easiest way to find the scale is to set up a proportion, which you already know how to do! Let's see how this might be introduced to a problem.

1. Emi builds a toothpick model of a bridge for a school project. The real bridge is 1,650 feet long and 134 feet high. Emi's model bridge is only 8 inches high. Find the scale that Emi uses for her model bridge. Then determine the approximate length, in inches, of her model bridge shown in the drawing below.

Click on the numbers you want to select and drag them into the boxes.

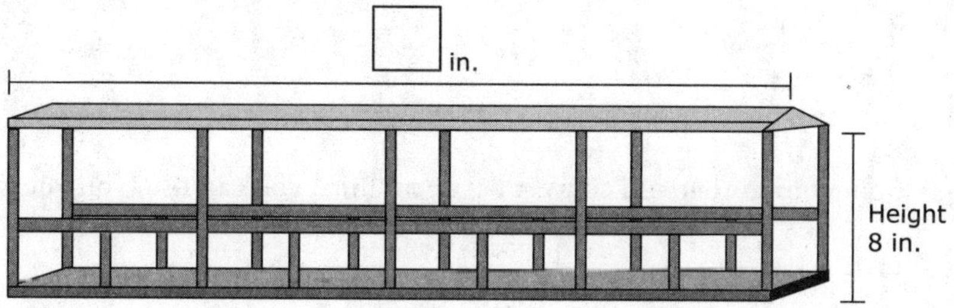

Scale: ☐ ft. = 1 in.

8	$10\frac{10}{11}$	12	$12\frac{1}{3}$	
$16\frac{3}{4}$	$17\frac{7}{8}$	$98\frac{1}{2}$	195	$206\frac{1}{4}$

Here's How to Crack It

The dimensions of the bridge will remain proportional to each other as they shrink down to the scale of Emi's model, meaning that the height and length of the bridge will change by the same factor (both are divided by the same number).

So we can set up a proportion (equal ratios) to find what the length should be:

Heights		**Lengths**
$\frac{8\text{ in.}}{134\text{ ft.}}$	=	$\frac{x}{1{,}650\text{ ft.}}$

Now cross-multiply to get

$$1{,}650 \times 8 = 134x$$

The length of the model bridge must be approximately 98.5, or $98\frac{1}{2}$ inches.

Now we can use what we know about the relationship between heights (real bridge to model bridge) to find the scale, or the actual size represented by 1 inch of the model. Set up the proportion to determine the number of feet represented by 1 inch of the model:

$$\frac{8 \text{ in.}}{134 \text{ ft.}} = \frac{1 \text{ in.}}{y}$$

Now cross-multiply to get

$$134 \times 1 = 8y$$

The scale must be 16.75, or $16\frac{3}{4}$.

Similarly, if a question requires that you convert between units, you can use (you guessed it!) a proportion.

Take a look:

2. A football coach makes his players run two laps around the football field to warm up before practice. If the field is 120 yards long and 160 feet wide, how many miles do the players run to warm up? (Hint: There are 3 feet in a yard and 5,280 feet in a mile.)

   A. 0.1
   B. 0.2
   C. 0.4
   D. 0.5

Here's How to Crack It

This problem uses three different units of measurement—feet, yards, and miles. Yikes! Before you do any major calculations, try to get all of the numbers in the same unit. You start with 120 *yards* and 160 *feet*. Which one will be easier to work with? Feet. So convert 120 yards:

$$\frac{120 \text{ yards}}{x} = \frac{1 \text{ yard}}{3 \text{ feet}}$$

$$120 \times 3 = 1x$$

$$360 = x$$

Now you know that the football field is 360 feet long, and the width is already in feet. How far is one lap around the field? The 360 feet and 160 feet are only one length and one width, but a lap consists of running two lengths and two widths. You could add all four measurements: 360 + 160 + 360 + 160 = 1,040. Or you can add the single length and single width, and then multiply by two:

$$360 + 160 = 520$$
$$520 \times 2 = 1{,}040$$

Either way will result in the same answer. You know how far one lap around the field is, but the question asks for two laps. Double the answer: 1,040 × 2 = 2,080. You're not done yet! All of the answer choices are in *miles*. Convert 2,080 feet to miles:

$$\frac{2{,}080 \text{ feet}}{x} = \frac{5{,}280 \text{ feet}}{1 \text{ mile}}$$
$$2{,}080 \times 1 = 5{,}280x$$

Then divide 2,080 by 5,280 to find the answer in miles: 2,080 ÷ 5,280 ≈ 0.4 miles, or (C).

You can also use common sense to help in converting units. You have 120 yards and want to convert to feet. There are 3 feet in a yard. Since you are converting to a smaller unit, *multiply* 120 by 3 to find the answer.

Let's look at converting 2,080 feet to miles. There are 5,280 feet in a mile. Are miles a bigger or smaller unit than feet? They are bigger, so you will *divide* 2,080 by 5,280.

Scale and Unit Conversion Drill

You can check your answers in Part IX: Answer Key to Drills.

1. A man who weighs 200 pounds goes on a diet and loses 16% of his body weight. How much weight, in ounces, did he lose? (Hint: 1 pound = 16 ounces.)

   A. 2
   B. 32
   C. 200
   D. 512

2. A cookie recipe that makes 24 cookies calls for the following ingredients:

$2\frac{3}{4}$ c. flour	$1\frac{1}{3}$ c. sugar	$\frac{3}{4}$ c. butter
1 egg	$3\frac{1}{2}$ t. baking powder	$1\frac{1}{2}$ t. vanilla extract

Brenda is hosting a party and will have a total of 16 people in attendance, including herself. She wants to make one large batch of cookies to accommodate everyone. If each person will eat three cookies, what are the new amounts that Brenda must measure for each ingredient?

Click on the numbers you want to select and drag them into the boxes. (For this drill, write the numbers in the boxes.)

☐ c. flour	☐ c. sugar	☐ c. butter
☐ egg	☐ t. baking powder	☐ t. vanilla extract

$1\frac{1}{4}$	$1\frac{1}{2}$	2	3	$2\frac{2}{3}$	$2\frac{1}{2}$
$4\frac{1}{4}$	5	$5\frac{1}{4}$	$5\frac{1}{2}$	6	7

CHARTS AND GRAPHS

Some test takers are scared by charts and graphs. If you count yourself among them, we recommend that you review our "Understanding Graphics" supplement, which you can download online once you register your book. Roughly one-third to one-half of the Mathematical Reasoning test questions include a graphic of some sort. This can be a figure, a chart, a graph, a table, or a data plot. One great thing about the graphics is that they are roughly drawn to scale, so you can always ballpark. Math test graphics may cover any of the concepts included in this book, from the number line and percentages to the slope and equation of a line. Let's start with a common type of graph: the bar graph.

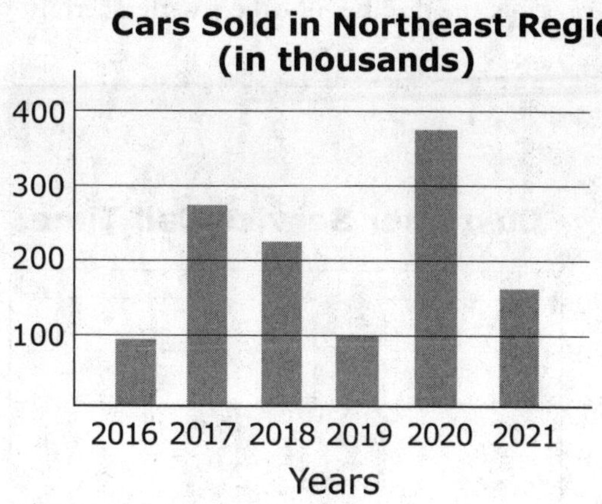

1. In the figure above, by approximately how much did sales of cars increase from 2019 to 2020?

   A. 100,000
   B. 200,000
   C. 260,000
   D. 360,000

Here's How to Crack It

If you've read the "Understanding Graphics" supplement, you know that you should always take a moment to read the title of the graph and study the two variables. You are looking at the number of cars sold in a particular region, broken down *by year*. The number of cars is expressed *in thousands*.

For more on reading graphs, charts, tables, and more, download our free "Understanding Graphics" tutorial from your online Student Tools. See pages viii–ix for details.

In 2019, according to the graph, 100,000 cars were sold. In 2020, more than 300,000 were sold. How many more? It's difficult to say exactly because the scale on the left is marked only every 100,000 cars, but it looks to be a little more than half the distance between the markings, or about 70,000 more. So the total 2020 figure is about 370,000. The question wants to know the increase from 2019 to 2020. How do you get that? Subtract. Roughly 370,000 minus 100,000 is roughly 270,000. Is this close to any of the answers? Yes. The correct answer is (C).

In effect, this was officially sanctioned Ballparking. There was no way to get the precise answer mathematically. The GED® test writers expected you to use your eyes and estimate in order to get the right answer.

Similar to a bar graph, a histogram uses bars of different lengths to represent data. But instead of showing the counts for different categories, a histogram groups data into ranges. In the example below, each bar represents the number of callers with a certain wait time:

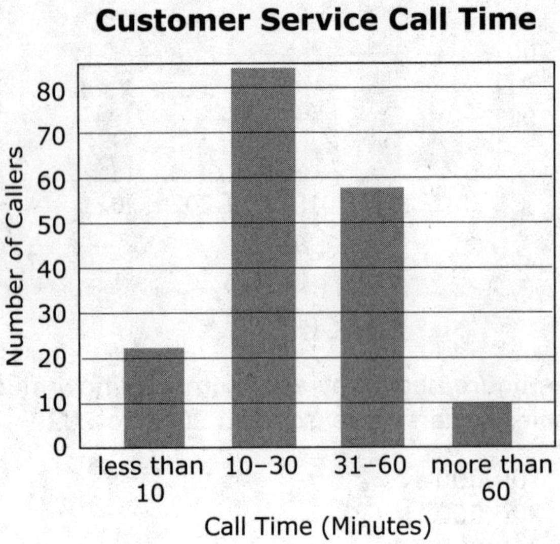

2. Based on the histogram above, which of the following statements is accurate?

A. Most callers waited less than 10 minutes.
B. Most callers waited less than 30 minutes.
C. Most callers waited more than 30 minutes.
D. Most callers waited more than 60 minutes.

Here's How to Crack It

Read over each statement to see which bar (or bars) the range corresponds to. "Less than 10 minutes," (A), and "more than 60 minutes," (D), are both shorter bars on the histogram. "Less than 30 minutes," (B), should make you pause; this range includes both "10–30" and "less than 10." Those bars combined are pretty large. The same goes for "more than 30 minutes," (C): this range includes both "31–60" and "more than 60." Add those bars together, and compare to the other combined range. "Less than 30 minutes" is larger, so this range includes most callers. The correct answer is (B).

Like the bars on a histogram, the dots on a dot plot show frequencies. Instead of ranges, the columns of a dot plot represent specific numbers. Count the dots in a column to know how many times a number was counted in the data set. You can compare the heights of stacked dots. Look at how the dot plot below shows numbers of children per household, and then try the question.

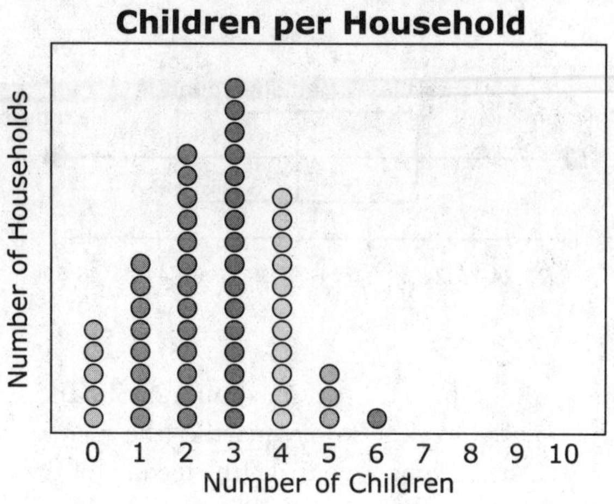

3. Which of the following could be inferred from the dot plot above?

   A. There are more households with 8 children than households with no children.
   B. There are more households with fewer than 2 children than households with 3 children.
   C. There are more households with 4 children than households with 1 child.
   D. There are more households with more than 5 children than households with no children.

Here's How to Crack It

For this type of question asking you to infer from a graphic, you can check each statement against the data to see which one is true. There are 5 dots in the "0" children column and no dots for "8" children, so (A) cannot be true. For (B), we have to combine dots for the range "fewer than 2 children," which includes "1" child and "0" children. (Be careful not to include the "2" column—2 children is NOT fewer than 2 children.) The dots for "3" children still make a taller column, so (B) is also not true. There are more dots in the "4" children column than in the "1" child column, so (C) is our answer. And we can be confident, since with this problem, it was easy to eyeball the heights of the columns, but just to be sure, we can quickly eliminate (D): there are more dots in the "0" children column than in all columns more than "5" combined.

Another way to show how numbers are distributed in a data set is a box plot. A box plot shows the spread of data over 5 data points: minimum, maximum, median (middle number), and the middle numbers of each half made by the median. These 5 points, when drawn as a box over a number line, divide the data into 4 parts or "quartiles." This sounds complicated, but it's pretty simple to identify these parts of a basic box plot.

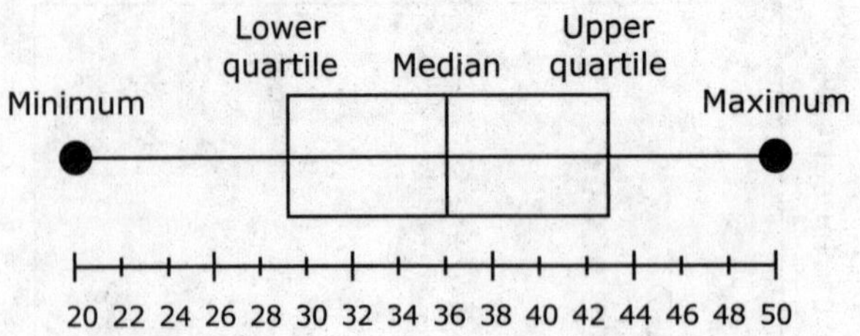

The data set ranges from a minimum of 20 to a maximum of 50. The median (the line drawn down the middle of the box) is 36. The lower quartile (the median of the numbers from minimum to median) is 29. And the upper quartile (the median of the numbers from median to maximum) is 43.

4. Based on the box plot above, which of the following can we infer about the data set?

   A. The number that occurred the most times is 36.
   B. The smallest number in the data set is 29.
   C. Most numbers in the data set are in the upper quartile.
   D. Most numbers in the data set are greater than 32.

Here's How to Crack It

Box plots do not show us the most frequent number, so (A) cannot be inferred. The smallest number in the data set is the minimum, which is 20. Choice (B) is not correct. The upper quartile is one of the four parts that a box plot divides the data into, so only $\frac{1}{4}$ or 25% of the numbers can be in this quartile (or in any quartile). Choice (C) doesn't make sense either. That leaves us with (D), which is true: 32 is smaller than the median, so most numbers in the set (more than half) are greater than 32. Choice (D) is the correct answer.

You should be able to "read" any of these graphs and data plots just by recognizing which type they are. You'll also come across problems with graphics that are just graphics. Let's look at an example:

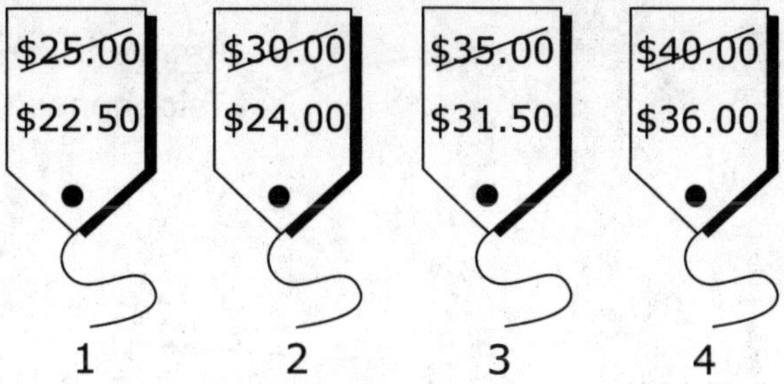

5. A man is searching through a bin of shirts that are on sale, some for 10% off and some for 20% off. Which sales tag above has been reduced by 20%?

   A. 1
   B. 2
   C. 3
   D. 4

Here's How to Crack It

In spite of the fact that there is a graphic that goes with it, this is just a percent problem. The question asks you to identify the tag that has been reduced by 20 percent. Begin with the first tag. It started at $25.00 and has been reduced to $22.50. Take away 20 percent from 25 and see whether you get 22.50. If you do, it's the answer. If you don't, you can throw it back in the bin and try another. Twenty percent of $25.00 is $5.00, so the reduced price ought to be $20.00 if this were the correct answer. It isn't, so you can eliminate (A). Go to the next tag: It started at $30.00 and has been reduced to $24.00. What is 20 percent of 30? That's right: 6. If you take away the $6, you are left with $24.00. Bingo! The answer is (B).

Charts and Graphs Drill

You can check your answers in Part IX: Answer Key to Drills.

Types of Telephones in Use

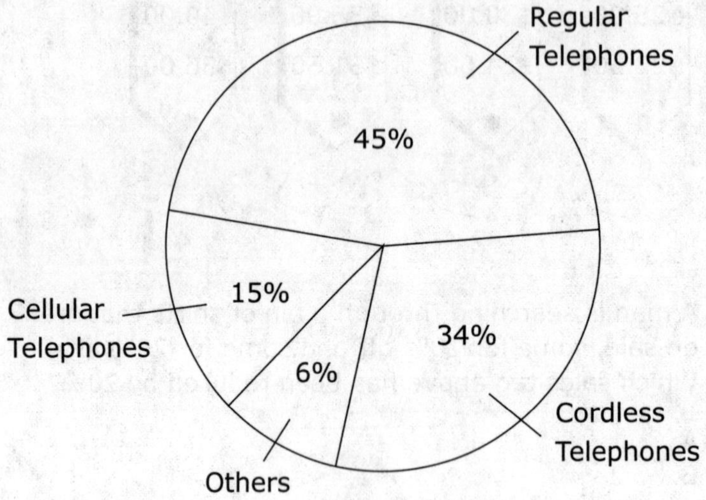

1. In the figure above, the number of regular telephones in use is how many times the number of cellular phones?

   A. 2.5
   B. 3
   C. 4
   D. 7.5

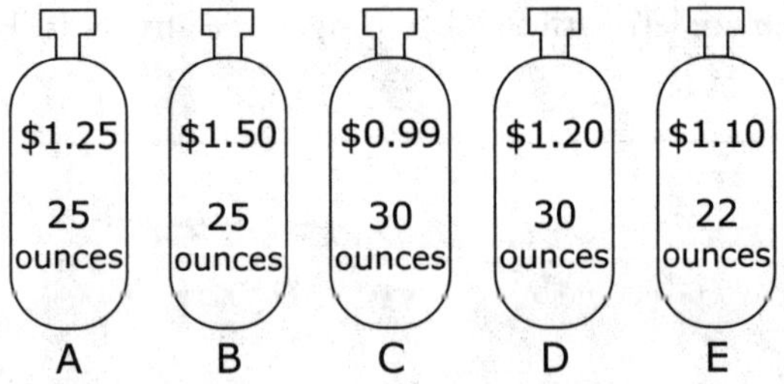

2. Each of the bottles in the figure above contains different amounts of cola at different prices. Which bottle represents the cheapest price per ounce?

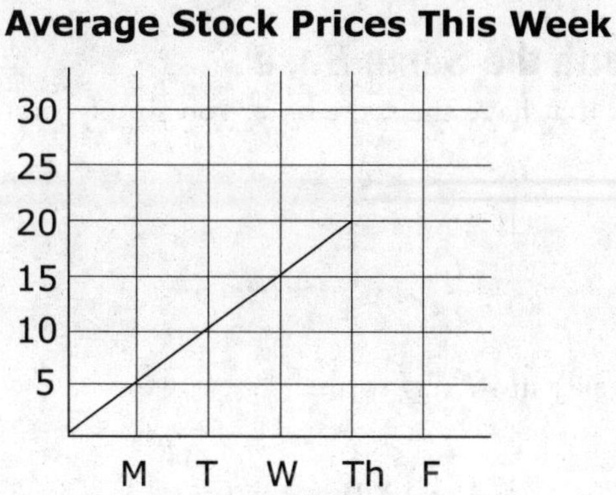

3. The price of a particular stock has been increasing at the same rate each day for the first four days of the week, as shown in the graph above. If the increase continues at its present rate, what should the price be on Friday?

A. 20
B. 25
C. 30
D. Not enough information is given.

EXPONENTS

An exponent is shorthand for multiplication. The expression $4 \times 4 \times 4 \times 4 \times 4$ can also be written as 4^5, because the 4 is being multiplied 5 times. This is expressed as "4 to the fifth power." The large number (4) is called the **base,** and the little number (5) is called the **exponent.**

Although there aren't very many exponent questions on the GED® test, there are a few rules that you should remember.

Multiplying Numbers with the Same Base

When you multiply numbers that have the same base, you simply add the exponents.

$$6^2 \times 6^3 = 6^{(2+3)} = 6^5$$

Why is this true? Let's write this out in long form:

$$6^2 = 6 \times 6 \qquad 6^3 = 6 \times 6 \times 6$$

$$\text{so, } 6^2 \times 6^3 = 6 \times 6 \times 6 \times 6 \times 6 \text{ or } 6^5$$

Dividing Numbers with the Same Base

When you divide numbers that have the same base, you simply subtract the bottom exponent from the top exponent.

$$\frac{6^3}{6^2} = 6^{3-2} = 6^1 = 6$$

Why is this true? Let's write it out in long form:

$$\frac{6^3}{6^2} = \frac{6 \times 6 \times 6}{6 \times 6} = \frac{6}{1} = 6$$

Raising a Number with an Exponent to Another Exponent

When you raise a number with an exponent to another exponent, multiply the exponents.

$$(6^2)^3 = 6^{2 \times 3} = 6^6$$

Why is this true? Let's write this out in long form:

$$(6^2)^3 = 6^2 \times 6^2 \times 6^2 = (6 \times 6) \times (6 \times 6) \times (6 \times 6) = 6^6$$

The Zero Power

It may seem strange, but any number to the zero power is 1.

$$4^0 = 1 \quad x^0 = 1$$

The First Power

Anything to the first power equals that number.

$$4^1 = 4$$
$$(-3)^1 = -3$$

But Watch Out For...

There are several operations that seem like they ought to work with exponents but don't.

Does $x^2 + x^3 = x^5$? NO!!
Does $x^4 - x^2 = x^2$? NO!!!

Does $\frac{x^2 + y^3 + z^4}{x^2 + y^3} = z^4$? NO!!!!

In fact, none of these three expressions can be reduced.

Exponent Facts

$5^0 = 1$
$5^1 = 5$
$5^2 = 25$
If $x^2 = 25$, then $x = 5$ or -5.

You would expect that raising a number to a power would increase that number, and usually it does, but there are exceptions.

- If you raise a positive fraction of less than 1 to a power, the fraction gets smaller.

$$\left(\frac{1}{2}\right)^2 = \frac{1^2}{2^2} = \frac{1}{4}$$

- If you raise a negative number to an odd power, the number gets smaller.

$$(-3)^3 = (-3)(-3)(-3) = -27$$

(Remember –27 is smaller than –3.)

- If you raise a negative number to an even power, the number becomes positive and is larger than the original number.

$$(-3)^2 = (-3)(-3) = 9$$

Exponent problems on the GED® test tend to be pretty basic.

1. 3^3 equals which of the following values?

   A. 9×9
   B. 3×3
   C. 3×9
   D. 1^{27}

Here's How to Crack It

The expression 3^3 equals 27. All you have to do is find the answer choice that also equals 27. You got it. The correct answer is (C).

RADICALS

The **square root** of a positive number *x* is the number that, when squared (multiplied by itself), equals *x*.

To find the square root of a number on your TI-30XS, first press the "2nd" key, then the "x^2" key, enter the number, and then press the right arrow key.

For example:

- The square root of 16 equals 4 because 4 × 4 = 16.
- The square root of 9 equals 3 because 3 × 3 = 9.
- The square root of 4 equals 2 because 2 × 2 = 4.

The symbol for a square root is $\sqrt{\ }$, also called a radical.

$$\sqrt{16} = 4$$

$$\sqrt{9} = 3$$

Most numbers do not have a whole number square root. For example, there is no whole number whose value is $\sqrt{13}$. But we can say that $\sqrt{13}$ is *between* 3 and 4.

Here's an example:

Radical Facts

$\sqrt{4} = 2$

$\sqrt{1} = 1$

If $x = 4$, then $\sqrt{x}$ = positive 2.

1. The square root of 7 is between which of the following pairs of numbers?

A. 2 and 3
B. 3 and 4
C. 4.5 and 5.5
D. 9 and 10

Here's How to Crack It

There is no whole number square root of 7, so see what numbers it is between that do have whole number square roots. The expression $\sqrt{9}$ is the next biggest number that comes out evenly: $\sqrt{9} = 3$. The expression $\sqrt{4}$ is the next smallest number that comes out evenly: $\sqrt{4} = 2$. Thus, the square root of 7 is between 2 and 3. The correct answer is (A).

Sometimes a question will ask for the square root of a fraction. To do this, take the square roots of the numerator and denominator separately. For example, to determine $\sqrt{\frac{9}{4}}$, start with the fact that $\sqrt{\frac{9}{4}} = \frac{\sqrt{9}}{\sqrt{4}}$. Since $\sqrt{9} = 3$ and $\sqrt{4} = 2$, $\sqrt{\frac{9}{4}} = \frac{\sqrt{9}}{\sqrt{4}} = \frac{3}{2}$. Let's look at another example.

2. What is $\sqrt{0.25}$?

   A. 0.005
   B. 0.05
   C. 0.5
   D. 5

Take 0.25 and convert it to a fraction: $0.25 = \frac{0.25}{1.00} = \frac{25}{100} = \frac{1}{4}$. Since $0.25 = \frac{1}{4}$, $\sqrt{0.25} = \sqrt{\frac{1}{4}} = \frac{\sqrt{1}}{\sqrt{4}} = \frac{1}{2}$. Since the answer choices are decimals, convert $\frac{1}{2}$ into a decimal: $2\overline{)1.0}$ = 0.5. The correct answer is (C).

Exponents and roots are two related concepts. In fact, a root can be expressed as an exponent. This exponent will be a fraction, and its numerator and denominator will tell you how to set up a root or radical. Let's take an example:

$$4^{\frac{1}{2}}$$

The base (4) is the number that goes inside the root sign. The bottom number of the fractional exponent (2) tells us that this is a square root, and the top number (1) becomes the exponent of the base, so we would have: $\sqrt{4^1}$ which is the same as $\sqrt{4} = 2$.

You can turn any fractional exponent into a radical:

$$\text{base}^{\text{numerator (exponent)/denominator (root)}}$$

Let's try to write a square root as an exponent (as a base with an exponent that is a fraction). $\sqrt{2}$ can be rewritten as a base to a fractional power by taking the 2 as the base, 1 as the numerator, and 2 as the denominator (because this is a regular square root):

$$2^{\frac{1}{2}}$$

You might also see radicals that are *not* square roots—for example, $\sqrt[3]{8}$ is asking for the number that when cubed (multiplied by itself 3 times) equals 8. $\sqrt[3]{8} = 2$ because $2 \times 2 \times 2 = 8$.

How would we write this cube root as a fraction? Same thing: the number inside the root sign (8) becomes the base with an exponent of $\frac{1}{3}$ because this is a cube root: $\sqrt[3]{8} = 8^{\frac{1}{3}}$.

See whether you can apply this to a problem with a different fractional exponent:

3. What is the value of $9^{\frac{3}{2}}$?

A. 3
B. 9
C. 27
D. 81

Here's How to Crack It

The only difference with this fractional exponent is that the numerator is not 1. The base (9) goes inside the root, the denominator (2) tells us that this is a square root, so we have $\sqrt{9}$. The numerator (3) tells us to cube it (or multiply it by itself 3 times), like this: $\sqrt{9} \times \sqrt{9} \times \sqrt{9} = 3 \times 3 \times 3 = 27$. So, (C) is the correct answer. (Note that the square root of 9^3 yields exactly the same result. It doesn't matter how you order the arithmetic!)

Exponents and Radicals Drill

You can check your answers in Part IX: Answer Key to Drills.

1. Which of the following values is equal to 2^3?

A. $(2 + 2)^2$
B. $2^2 + 2$
C. 4^2
D. $2(2^2)$

2. $3^3 + 2^2 = ?$

3. What is the value of $\sqrt{16} - \sqrt{4}$?

   A. 2^2

   B. $\sqrt{12}$

   C. $16^2 + 4^2$

   D. $\sqrt{4}$

4. Which of the following is equal to $(0.04)^{\frac{5}{2}}$?

   A. 0.00032
   B. 0.0032
   C. 0.032
   D. 0.32

SCIENTIFIC NOTATION

Scientific notation combines your knowledge of decimals and your knowledge of exponents to allow you to express very large numbers without endless strings of zeros. Take the number 3,200,000,000. Numbers like this can be difficult to read and even more difficult to add or subtract. Here is the same number in scientific notation:

$$3.2 \times 10^9$$

How do you expand this out to its full size? Let's start with an easier example.

$$3.2 \times 10^2$$

All you have to do to simplify this expression is move the decimal point over to the right by the same number as the power of 10. In this case, two places.

$$3.2 \times 10^2 = 320$$
$$3.2 \times 10^3 = 3{,}200$$
$$3.2 \times 10^4 = 32{,}000$$

How do you contract a big number into scientific notation? Just perform the same process in reverse. Let's take 4,750,000. In scientific notation, the decimal is always immediately to the right of the first digit (1 to 9). So, if you wanted to express this large number as 4.75 to the *n*th power of 10, what would the *n*th power be? On the large number, put your pencil point where you want the decimal to be (in this case, between the digit 4 and the digit 7), and now count the number of places you have to move the pencil to the *right* to get to the end of the number. Did you move your pencil 6 places? You are now a certified scientific notationalist.

$$4{,}750{,}000 = 4.75 \times 10^6$$

Let's try a problem.

1. Which of the following expresses the number 5.6×10^4?

A. 0.00056
B. 5,600
C. 56,000
D. 560,000

Here's How to Crack It
On a piece of scratch paper, write down 5.6 with some space to the right of it. Now, take your pencil, and move the tip of the pencil over four times, like this:

5.6

Fill in the 0s. The correct answer is (C).

Probability Quiz
Q: If there is one probability question on your 46-question Mathematical Reasoning test, what's the probability that the first question on the test will be a probability question?

Turn the page for the answer.

PROBABILITY

If you flip a coin, what are the odds that it's going to come out tails? If you said anything but "$\frac{1}{2}$," "1 out of 2," or "fifty-fifty," then there's a poker game we'd like to invite you to next Thursday.

To figure out the probability that something is going to happen, you take the number of chances that the thing could happen and compare that to the *total* number of possible outcomes of *all* kinds. For example, let's take that coin we just mentioned. If you toss the coin once, how many chances are there on this *one* toss that it will be heads? One chance. And how many total possible outcomes are there? There are two possible outcomes—heads or tails. Therefore, you have a 1 out of 2, $\frac{1}{2}$, or fifty-fifty chance of seeing tails.

On the GED® test, probabilities are generally expressed as fractions because they are part-to-whole relationships. The number of possibilities that *one* thing could happen is the numerator (part). The number of *total* possibilities is the denominator (whole).

Let's try a problem.

1. 9 workers decide to draw straws to see who will be the one to stay late and clean up. If there are 9 straws, 8 long and 1 short, what is the probability that Anthony, who goes first, will draw the short straw?

A. $\frac{1}{18}$

B. $\frac{1}{9}$

C. $\frac{1}{8}$

D. $\frac{8}{9}$

Here's How to Crack It

To solve any GED® probability problem, you have to find the number of chances that a particular thing could happen (in this case, there is only one short straw, so Anthony has only one chance of picking a short straw). This is your numerator. Then you have to find the total number of outcomes of *any* kind (in this case, the total number of straws is 9). This is your denominator. The correct answer to this question is (B).

Let's try another.

2. If a box of chocolates contains 3 caramels, 3 nut clusters, and 5 raspberry creams, which of the following fractions represents the chance of picking a caramel on the first try?

A. $\frac{1}{11}$

B. $\frac{1}{3}$

C. $\frac{3}{11}$

D. $\frac{5}{11}$

Probability Quiz
A: 1 out of 46

Here's How to Crack It

As before, figure out the number of possible ways to pick a caramel. There are three caramels, so there are three possibilities for picking one. That becomes your numerator.

Now, you need the total number of possibilities of any kind. There is a total of 11 chocolates, so that becomes your denominator. The correct answer is $\frac{3}{11}$, or (C).

Suppose you want to know the probability of flipping a coin and landing on heads 3 times in a row. This is a compound event because more than one event must happen for your favorable outcome here.

To calculate compound probability, you find the simple probability of each event as if they were happening separately. Then you multiply these fractions:

> Compound probability = (probability of first event) × (probability of second event)...

Note that in this situation, the outcome of one event does not affect the outcome of the next, so this is all that you have to do! All you may be asked to find on the GED® test is the probability of independent events like these.

We know that the simple probability of flipping heads is $\frac{1}{2}$, so the compound probability of landing on heads 3 times in a row is

$$\frac{1}{2} \times \frac{1}{2} \times \frac{1}{2}$$

Multiply fractions as usual: across the top, then across the bottom. One-eighth ($\frac{1}{8}$) is the compound probability of these 3 events happening together.

Notice that the fraction gets smaller when you multiply (which makes sense because the likelihood of 3 events happening together is less than the likelihood of just one!).

Let's try a problem:

3. Stan has a spinner with 6 sections of equal parts, each a different color: purple, red, blue, green, yellow, and orange. If he spins twice, what is the probability that it will land on red then yellow?

A. $\frac{1}{6}$

B. $\frac{1}{12}$

C. $\frac{1}{36}$

D. $\frac{2}{12}$

Here's How to Crack It

First we find the simple probability of the first spin landing on red. That's 1 out of 6, so $\frac{1}{6}$. The probability of spinning yellow is the same: $\frac{1}{6}$. So to find the compound probability, we multiply these two fractions together: $\frac{1}{6} \times \frac{1}{6} = \frac{1}{36}$.

Now try another one:

4. Ana borrows Stan's spinner and gives it two spins. What is the probability that she will land on green only once, and on the first spin?

A. $\frac{1}{6}$

B. $\frac{1}{12}$

C. $\frac{5}{36}$

D. 0

Here's How to Crack It

First, let's define the two events that must happen for our favorable outcome: the first spin is green, and the second spin is NOT green (it is any one of the other 5 colors). The simple probability of the first event (spinning green) is 1 out of 6, or $\frac{1}{6}$. The second event (spinning NOT green) has 5 chances out of 6, or $\frac{5}{6}$. Now we multiply these two fractions together: $\frac{1}{6} \times \frac{5}{6} = \frac{5}{36}$.

Scientific Notation and Probability Drill

You can check your answers in Part IX: Answer Key to Drills.

1. A painting has three lights illuminating it, each with an output of 2,550 lumens. What is the total amount of light illuminating the painting, in lumens, expressed in scientific notation?

   A. 51.0×10^4
   B. 76.5×10^3
   C. 7.65×10^3
   D. 5.1×10^3

2. Taraneh's closet has no light. Taraneh owns 2 blue dresses, 1 green dress, 1 purple dress, and 2 black dresses. What is the probability that she will pick a blue dress?

   A. $\frac{1}{4}$
   B. $\frac{1}{3}$
   C. $\frac{1}{6}$
   D. $\frac{1}{2}$

3. Which of the following is equivalent to $(3.4 \times 10^3) + (4.1 \times 10^4)$?

A. 750,000
B. 444,000
C. 75,000
D. 44,400

COMBINATIONS AND PERMUTATIONS

On some GED® questions, you will have to determine the number of possible choices that you can make in a given situation. If you're choosing what to have for lunch and are offered either a sandwich, soup, or a salad, how many choices would you have? That's right: 3. However, the GED® test is not likely to ask questions like this. The GED® test is more likely to ask questions that require you to determine the total number of options when making multiple choices. Let's look at an example below.

1. The manager of a department store has to hire a new cashier, a new salesperson, and a new shift supervisor. If there are 3 applicants for cashier, 8 applicants for salesperson, and 5 applicants for shift supervisor, and no applicant applies for more than one position, how many different ways can the manager hire one person for each of the three positions?

A. 17
B. 20
C. 60
D. 120

Here's How to Crack It

The manager needs to hire people to fill three positions. The question tells you that no applicant applies for more than one position. This means that there is a completely different pool of applicants for each position. When there is a different source for each choice, treat each choice independently. Draw a slot for each position as below.

________ ________ ________
Cashier Salesperson Shift Supervisor

Now, for each position, fill in the number of possible applicants as below.

3	8	5
Cashier	Salesperson	Shift Supervisor

Now, multiply each of the three numbers to get $3 \times 8 \times 5 = 120$. The correct answer is (D).

Sometimes, however, you'll be working with the same source of items for each choice that you're making. In some of these examples, the order will matter but not in others. If the order doesn't matter, mathematicians call it a **combination;** if order does matter, it's called a **permutation**. The method you use to solve questions in which there is one source and order matters is actually very similar to that for questions in which there are multiple sources. This is common in questions that ask about arrangements or filling different positions. Let's look at one below.

2. A DJ has enough time to play four more songs at a school dance. If she has seven different songs available to choose from, how many different orderings of songs can she choose?

   A. 22
   B. 35
   C. 840
   D. 2,401

Here's How to Crack It

The DJ needs to choose four songs. Just as before, draw a slot for each position as below.

______ ______ ______ ______

Now, for each song, fill in the number of possible choices. For the first song, there are seven choices. For the second song, there are six choices remaining (since you already used one song as the first selection). For the third song, there are five choices remaining (since you already used two songs). For the fourth song, there are four choices remaining (since you already used three songs). Fill this in as below.

7	6	5	4

Now, multiply each of the three numbers to get $7 \times 6 \times 5 \times 4 = 840$. The correct answer is (C).

In other cases, though, the order will not matter. This means there will be fewer possibilities than cases in which order does matter. In these cases, you will follow the same method as when order matters but with an extra step to reduce the number of possibilities. This is common when questions ask about teams or committees. Look at an example below.

3. A DJ is choosing four new records to add to his collection. If he is in a store that has seven different records available to choose from, how many different groups of records can he choose?

A. 22
B. 35
C. 840
D. 2,401

Here's How to Crack It

This looks similar to the previous question, and it is but with a key difference. The DJ needs to choose four records. Just as before, draw a slot for each position as below.

_____ _____ _____ _____

Now, for each record, fill in the number of possible choices. For the first record, there are seven choices. For the second record, there are six choices remaining (since you already used one record as the first selection). For the third record, there are five choices remaining (since you already used two records). For the fourth record, there are four choices remaining (since you already used three records). Fill this in as below.

$\underline{\quad 7 \quad}$ $\underline{\quad 6 \quad}$ $\underline{\quad 5 \quad}$ $\underline{\quad 4 \quad}$

So far, it is the same as the previous question. The difference is that since each record will simply either be purchased or not purchased, the order doesn't matter. When this is the case, you want to divide by the number of possible orderings of each set of 4. This is 4 × 3 × 2 × 1. Divide the numbers above by this to get the following:

$$\frac{7}{4} \times \frac{6}{3} \times \frac{5}{2} \times \frac{4}{1}$$

Reduce these fractions before you multiply them. The 6 in the numerator can cancel with the 3 and 2 in the denominator and the 4 in the numerator can cancel with the 4 in denominator to get the following:

$$\frac{7}{1} \times \frac{1}{1} \times \frac{5}{1} \times \frac{1}{1}$$

Now, multiply what remains to get 7 × 5 = 35. The correct answer is (B).

Combinations and Permutations Drill

You can check your answers in Part IX: Answer Key to Drills.

1. A deli offers a made-to-order sandwich to its customers. Customers can choose one type of bread, one type of meat, one type of cheese, and one type of lettuce. If the deli has four types of bread, five types of meat, eight types of cheeses, and three types of lettuce, how many different types of sandwiches can a customer order?

   A. 20
   B. 120
   C. 240
   D. 480

2. A school president is choosing three cabinet members to appoint: a vice president, a secretary, and a treasurer. If she has eight candidates to choose from, each of whom can serve any cabinet position, how many possible cabinets can the president appoint?

   A. 21
   B. 56
   C. 336
   D. 512

3. A teacher is selecting students for a trivia bowl team. If there are nine interested students and a trivia bowl team consists of three players, how many different teams can the teacher select?

   A. 24
   B. 84
   C. 252
   D. 504

PUTTING IT ALL TOGETHER

Now that you've seen the basics of applied arithmetic one topic at a time, we're going to give you a drill that mixes up all the different applied arithmetic concepts we've discussed in this chapter. This drill will help to reveal whether you're having trouble recognizing individual types of problems, as we discussed in the last chapter. Some people are fine once they know that a question is about probabilities or percents, for example, but they have trouble spotting the key words that should tell them what type of problem they're dealing with. As you do this drill, make it a point to identify each question before you start calculating:

"This is an average question."
"That is a rate problem."
"This one is an exponent question."

Applied Arithmetic Drill

You can check your answers in Part IX: Answer Key to Drills.

1. Darryl puts $5,000 into an insured bank account that pays simple interest of 8%. How much interest will he earn in 2 years?

   A. 2[0.08(5,000)]

   B. $\frac{0.08(5{,}000)}{2}$

   C. 2[0.92(5,000)]

   D. 2[1.08(5,000)]

2. If Laverne walks steadily at a rate of 5 kilometers per hour, how many hours will it take her to walk 17.5 kilometers?

   A. $1\frac{3}{4}$

   B. $3\frac{1}{2}$

   C. 52

   D. $87\frac{1}{2}$

Computer Preferences

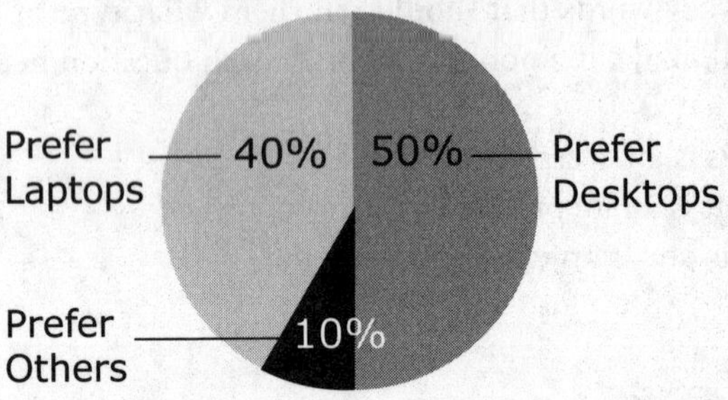

3. The figure above shows the results of a survey of a group of 200 professionals who were asked what type of computer they preferred. How many more people prefer desktop computers than prefer laptop computers?

   A. 5
   B. 10
   C. 15
   D. 20

4. There is a total of four tests in Xiaojue's history class. She earned 94, 88, and 85 on the first three. What score does Xiaojue need on the fourth test to pass the class with an average of 90 (the equivalent of an A)?

   A. 89
   B. 90
   C. 91
   D. 93

5. Which of the following is equal to $5^2 - \sqrt{9}$?

A. 2^{11}

B. $3^2 + \sqrt{25}$

C. $2(2^3) + 6$

D. $2^3 + 3^2$

6. Which of the following is the closest approximation of $\sqrt{10}$?

A. 2
B. 3
C. 5
D. 100

7. Michael calls a taxi to pick him up at his house. He knows that the taxi company has 1 limousine, 2 sedans, 3 vans, and 1 compact. What is the probability that he will ride in a sedan?

8. A set contains the following five numbers: 12, 4, 8, 16, 23. What is the median of the set?

9. Sheila works in a factory for $14.50 per hour for any hours up to 40. After 40 hours, she is paid an overtime rate that is one and a half times her regular pay. If Sheila worked 43 hours last week, which expression below shows how much she earned?

A. 40(14.50) + 3(1.5)
B. 40(14.50) + 3(1.5)(14.50)
C. 43(1.5)(14.50)
D. 43(14.50)

10. If one cell is 2.3×10^4 microns wide and another cell is 3.2×10^4 microns wide, then one cell is how much bigger than the other in microns?

A. 0.9
B. 11.0
C. 110.0
D. 9,000.0

11. Barb has five television shows she would like to watch. She has enough time to watch three of them today, and must decide in what order she will watch them. How many different orderings of the three shows she watches today can Barb choose?

A. 10
B. 30
C. 60
D. 120

12. Which of the following is the value of

$$\frac{(2^{12})(2^5)(\sqrt{5})^4}{(2^{16})(5^3)}?$$

A. $\frac{2}{5}$

B. 4

C. 10

D. 20

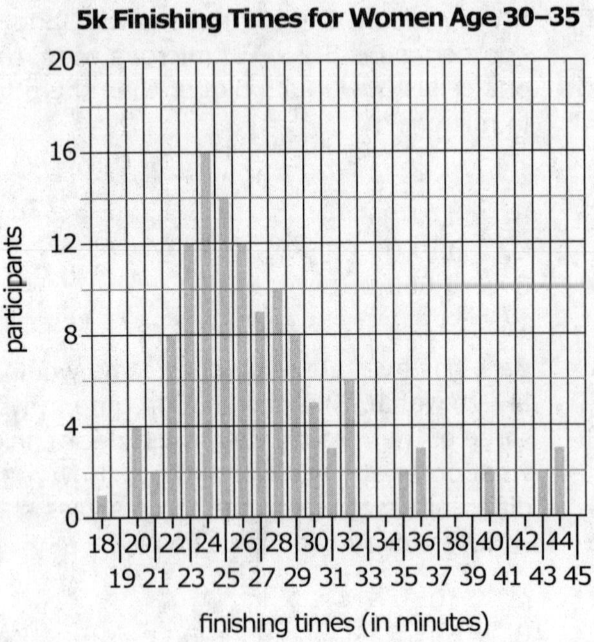

13. Based on the histogram above, which of the following statements is accurate?

A. The top 5 runners all finished in under 20 minutes.

B. Most runners finished in between 22 and 29 minutes.

C. More runners finished in under 24 minutes than over 24 minutes.

D. The finishing time for the final runner was 45 minutes.

14. Kaori and Vitor are playing a game with different-sided dice, one die with 6 sides and another with 8 sides. What is the probability that they roll a 2 on the 6-sided die and on the 8-sided die?

A. $\frac{1}{4}$

B. $\frac{1}{14}$

C. $\frac{1}{36}$

D. $\frac{1}{48}$

Chapter 15
Algebra

In this chapter, we introduce the basics of algebra—plus we'll show you powerful techniques that make certain types of difficult algebra questions really easy.

Algebra accounts for slightly more than half of the GED® Mathematical Reasoning test. Most people just don't like algebra, and they never did. Well, we have some good news for you.

You don't always need to use algebra to solve the algebra problems.

In just a few pages, we'll show you a great technique that will allow you to do some of the tougher algebra problems without writing equations. However, let's begin by going over the basics of the easy "solving for x"-type of GED® problems.

SIMPLE EQUATIONS

If you've completed the first two math chapters, then you've already been solving simple equations, also known as equalities. Every time you set up a proportion or an average formula, you were using algebra. Here is the most basic type of algebra equation:

1. If $2x - 14 = 10$, then $x = ?$

   A. 5
   B. 12
   C. 15
   D. 22

The GED® test writers use some variation of this problem on practically every test. To find the answer to this question, we must "solve for x," which simply means getting x all by itself on one side of the equals sign, and everything else on the other side. The x is already on the left-hand side of the equals sign in this equation, so let's try to move the *other* numbers on the left side over to the right side.

First, let's tackle the number that is not attached to the x: the number 14 that is subtracted from $2x$. To make this *subtraction* of 14 disappear, we must *add* 14 to the left side. This is the concept of inverse operations, because adding is the inverse (opposite) of subtracting. Now, we want both sides to remain equal, so we must then add 14 to the *right* side of the equation as well, since that's what we did to the left side.

$$\begin{array}{r} 2x-14=10 \\ +\quad 14\quad 14 \\ \hline 2x-0\ =24 \end{array}$$

As long as you do the exact same thing (make the same change) on BOTH sides of an equation, the equation is still true: both sides of the equals sign are still equal to each other. So now, the equation looks like this:

$$2x = 24$$

Now, tackle the number 2, which is being multiplied by x. To make this *multiplication* of 2 disappear, you must *divide* by 2 on the left side, since dividing is the inverse of multiplying. As before, you want to avoid unbalancing the equation, so also divide by 2 on the right side.

$$\frac{2x}{2} = \frac{24}{2}$$

As long as you multiply or divide your number on *both* sides of the equation, the equation stays proportionately the same. At this point, you can cancel the 2s on the left side and reduce the fraction on the right side as shown:

$$\frac{\cancel{2}x}{\cancel{2}} = \frac{\overset{12}{\cancel{24}}}{\cancel{2}} \quad \text{so } x = 12$$

The correct answer to this question is (B).

Whatever you do to the left side of an equation, you MUST do to the right side as well.

Another kind of algebraic-equation question that comes up fairly often on the GED® test looks like this:

2. Given the formula $2a = 3b(c - 4)$, find a if $b = 5$ and $c = 6$.

   A. 30
   B. 23
   C. 15
   D. 9

Here's How to Crack It

These problems give you an equation and values for two of the three variables. All you have to do is plug the values for the two variables you know into the equation and then solve for the third.

Start by writing the equation on your scratch paper, substituting 5 for *b* and 6 for *c*. It should look like this:

$$2a = (3 \times 5)(6 - 4)$$
$$2a = (15)(2)$$
$$2a = 30$$

If you were in a hurry, you might now pick (A), 30, but the problem asks for the value of *a*, not 2*a*. To solve for *a*, you must divide both sides by 2. The correct answer is 15, or (C).

Simple Equation Drill

You can check your answers in Part IX: Answer Key to Drills.

1. If $2x - 5 = 11$, then $x =$

   A. 32
   B. 12
   C. 8
   D. 3

2. If $3x + 6 = 51$, then $x =$

   [ ]

3. Evaluate $3x^2 - 4y$, if $x = 2$ and $y = 3$.

   A. 24
   B. 6
   C. 0
   D. -6

INEQUALITIES

While an equality, or equation, allows you to solve for x and get one answer, an inequality has a range of answers. For example, in the inequality $x > 5$, we know that x must be greater than 5, but there are an infinite number of values that x could be. Thus, an inequality defines a range of values for the variable without giving you one specific value. Here are the symbols for inequalities:

$>$	greater than
$<$	less than
$\geq$	greater than or equal to
$\leq$	less than or equal to

One way to keep these symbols straight is to remember that the inequality sign always points to the smaller value. An inequality is solved in exactly the same way as an equality. Let's use the same example we used at the beginning of the chapter, with one small change.

1. If $2x - 14 > 10$, then which of the following expressions gives all the possible values of x?

A. $x > 5$
B. $x > 12$
C. $x < 15$
D. $x < 22$

Here's How to Crack It

Pretend it's just a normal equality. This is what your work should look like:

$$\begin{array}{r} 2x-14>10 \\ +\ \ 14\ \ \ 14 \\ \hline 2x-0\ >24 \end{array}$$

$$\frac{2x}{2} > \frac{24}{2}$$

So, the correct answer is (B), $x > 12$.

The only difference between solving an inequality and solving an equality occurs when you have to multiply or divide by a negative number.

> Solving an inequality is just like solving an equality EXCEPT when multiplying or dividing by a negative number. In this case, reverse the inequality sign.

2. If $-3x + 6 < 18$, then which of the following expressions gives all the possible values of x?

A. $x < 2$
B. $x < -4$
C. $x > 2$
D. $x > -4$

Here's How to Crack It

Until the very last step, this will be just like solving an equality. This is what the work should look like right up until that last step:

$$\begin{array}{rcr} -3x+6 & < & 18 \\ -6 & & -6 \\ \hline -3x & < & 12 \end{array}$$

Now comes the tricky part. Remember how multiplying or dividing by a negative number changes the sign of your answer? Well, this is why when you multiply or divide an inequality by a negative number, we have to change the direction of the inequality sign (that is, from > to <, or from < to >).

In this case, to get x alone on the left side of the equation, you're going to divide both sides by –3.

$$\frac{-3x}{-3} < \frac{12}{-3}$$

But the moment you divide by a negative number, the sign flips over.

$$x > -4$$

So, the correct answer to this question is (D).

Take a look at a typical GED® inequality below.

3. For which value of x below is the inequality $4x > 3$ true?

A. -4

B. 0

C. $\frac{3}{4}$

D. 1

Here's How to Crack It

You want to isolate x on one side of the equation, so get rid of the 4 by dividing both sides by 4.

$$\frac{4x}{4} > \frac{3}{4}$$

So $x > \frac{3}{4}$. When you look at the answer choices, you may be tempted to choose (C), $\frac{3}{4}$. However, read the question again. "For which value of x below is the inequality...true?" In other words, which of the answer choices is within the range of values expressed by the inequality $x > \frac{3}{4}$? Is –4 greater than $\frac{3}{4}$? No. Is 0 greater than $\frac{3}{4}$? No. Is $\frac{3}{4}$ *greater* than $\frac{3}{4}$? No. Is 1 greater than $\frac{3}{4}$? Yes! The correct answer is (D).

Since the solution of an inequality is a range of numbers, we can graph this solution on a number line to show which numbers are included in the range. You just need to pay attention to the direction of the inequality sign (> or <) and whether "equal to" is an option (as in ≥ or ≤) or not. Let's see what this looks like with a couple of examples.

The solution $x > -4$ means x can be any number greater than –4. On a number line, this would include all numbers to the right of –4. Since –4 is NOT greater than –4, and our sign does not include the "equal to" option, we will not include –4 in our graph. We mark this with an open circle at the point –4. And we draw an arrow extending infinitely to the right to include all numbers greater than –4 as possible solutions. (Notice that the arrow points in the same direction as the > sign!)

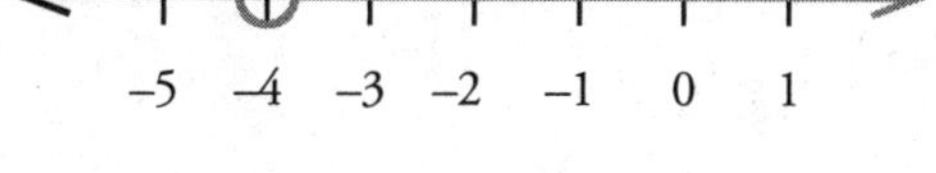

Let's try one with a different inequality sign: $x \leq 3$. This means that the solution of the inequality can be any number less than or equal to 3. Since "equal to" is an option here, we include 3 in our graph. We mark this with a filled-in circle at point 3. And we draw an arrow extending infinitely to the left to include all numbers less than 3 as possible solutions. (Notice that the arrow points in the same direction as the ≤ sign!)

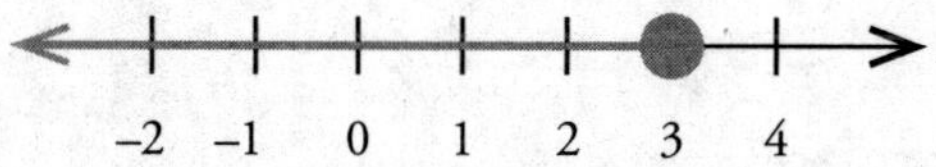

Now try reading an inequality graph to answer a multiple-choice test question:

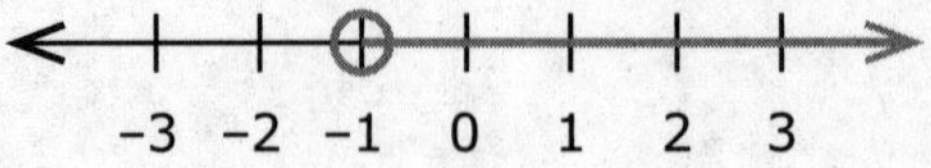

4. The graph above shows the solution of an inequality as all possible values of x. Which of the following is NOT a possible value of x?

A. 6
B. 1
C. 0
D. −1

Here's How to Crack It

The arrow clearly includes 1 and 0, so you can eliminate (B) and (C) right away. You also know that the arrow extends infinitely to the right, including numbers like 6 that are beyond the scope of the graph we can see. Choice (A) is ruled out, leaving (D), which we can confirm as correct by noting the open circle at point –1; this means that –1 cannot be a solution to the inequality. Choice (D) is the correct answer.

Inequalities Drill

You can check your answers in Part IX: Answer Key to Drills.

1. Frida is not allowed on the roller coaster because she is under the minimum age of 5. Which of the following inequalities expresses all the ages that *are* allowed on the roller coaster?

   A. $x < 5$
   B. $x > 5$
   C. $x \geq 5$
   D. $x > -5$

2. If $5x + 3 < 28$, then which of the following expressions gives all the possible values of x?

   A. $x < 5$
   B. $x < -5$
   C. $x > 0$
   D. $x > 5$

3. If m is the positive number 4, which of the following inequalities contains the number m?

   A. $x < 3$
   B. $x > 7$
   C. $2x > 6$
   D. $3x \leq -6$

Work backward from the answer choices to see which one solves the problem.

BACKSOLVING

You've seen throughout this book that POE—Process of Elimination—can be a very important tool in answering difficult multiple-choice GED® questions. **Backsolving** is the ultimate extension of POE. Let's look again at the very first example from this chapter.

1. If $2x - 14 = 10$, then $x = ?$

   A. 5
   B. 12
   C. 15
   D. 22

The traditional way to solve this problem is to use algebra to "solve for *x*." In fact, this problem is pretty easy, and you will probably want to do it the traditional way (which we just showed you above).

However, there is another way to do this problem, and we're going to show it to you because this same way can be used to solve many more difficult algebra problems that appear on the Mathematical Reasoning test.

The correct answer is staring you in the face. The problem asks for the value of *x* and then presents you with four possible answers. In other words, one of those four possibilities is the number you're looking for.

Well, since one of these four answers is correct, why not try plugging each of them back into the question until we find the one that works?

We'll start with (C). Let's suppose for a moment that 15 is the correct answer and plug it into the question.

$$2(15) - 14 = 10$$

Is this true? No! $30 - 14 = 16$. We've just proven that (C) is wrong.

But we've done something even better than that. Choice (C) is not just wrong—it's too big. Do we need to check (D), 22, which is even bigger than (C)?

Just by trying out (C), we eliminated any answers that were bigger. On the Mathematical Reasoning test, multiple-choice math answers are always listed in ascending or descending order. Therefore, every time you try substituting one of the middle answer choices—(B) or (C)—back into the problem, you will eliminate at least one other answer immediately. If the number you get is too big, you can get rid of any choices that are even bigger. If the number you get is too small, you can get rid of any choices that are even smaller.

The only two possibilities left are (A) and (B). Let's try (B).

$$2(12) - 14 = 10$$

Is this true? When we substitute 12 into the equation, we get exactly the correct answer: 24 – 14 = 10. Therefore, the answer to this problem is (B).

This technique is called Backsolving, and while it is probably unnecessary on a simple equation such as this, it will prove quite valuable on tougher questions. The method is always exactly the same: Start with one of the middle numbers. Plug it into the equation in the problem. If it makes the equation work, then you're done; you have the right answer. If the number is too big, eliminate any choices that are bigger, and zero in on the remaining choices. Try one of them. If it's still too big, then the answer must be the remaining choice. Pick it, and move on.

Let's try this technique on some more difficult problems.

Apply the Strategy
Use Backsolving to answer questions like this one.

2. The 8 passengers on a small plane have paid a total of $900 for the flight. If an economy ticket costs $100 and a first-class ticket costs $200, how many first-class tickets were bought?

   A. 5
   B. 4
   C. 2
   D. 1

Here's How to Crack It

At first glance, this may not seem to resemble the equation problem we just finished. This is a word problem, for one thing, and there doesn't seem to be an equation in the problem at all.

In fact, the words of this problem actually contain an equation. The difficulty is that it's pretty tricky to translate these words into math. The correct equation that will solve this problem is

$$200x + [100(8 - x)] = 900$$

But if you don't think you could have come up with this, don't spend any time kicking the ground because you can solve this algebra problem *without* algebra.

Backsolve! One of those four answers must be correct, so try putting one of them into the problem and see what happens. Which choice do you want to start with? Choice (B) works because it's in the middle. If (B) is too big, you can eliminate the choice that is even bigger. If (B) is too small, you can eliminate the choices that are even smaller. If (B) is just right, then you can go on to the next problem because you'll be done.

Choice (B) says that four passengers flew first class. And because there was a total of eight passengers, that means that four passengers flew economy class.

$$4 \times \$200 = \$800$$

$$4 \times \$100 = \$400$$

Backsolving Quiz

Q: With which answer choice do you start when you backsolve?

Turn the page for the answer.

If this is the correct answer, the total dollar amount should add up to the total given in the problem: $900. Does it? No, it's way too big. Which choices can you then eliminate? That's right: Cross off (A) and (B). The only remaining possibilities are (C) and (D). We'll try (C) next.

Choice (C) says that two passengers flew first class. And because there were a total of eight passengers, that means that six passengers flew economy class.

$$2 \times \$200 = \$400$$

$$6 \times \$100 = \$600$$

If this is the correct answer, the total dollar amount should add up to the total given in the problem: $900. Does it? No, but you're getting warmer; $1,000 is a lot closer to $900 than you were before.

You know the answer is *not* (A), (B), or (C). Can you guess what the correct answer to this problem is?

Just to be sure, check (D). Choice (D) says that one passenger flew first class. And because there were a total of eight passengers, that means that seven passengers flew economy class.

$$1 \times \$200 = \$200$$

$$7 \times \$100 = \$700$$

Does this add up to $900? You bet. The correct answer to this tough algebra word problem is (D).

Can You Use This Technique on *Every* GED® Problem?

No. Many problems on the GED® test cannot be backsolved because their answer choices contain variables or formulas or because the correct answer choice is the final result of a calculation rather than a missing ingredient in an equation. And, of course, it is impossible to work backward from the answer choices when there are no answer choices. Generally, each GED® test contains as many as three or four problems that can be backsolved. These are frequently considered some of the hardest problems on the test because they involve algebra. Of course, if you backsolve, these problems are actually kind of easy.

When to Backsolve

You can backsolve if:

1) there are numbers in the answer choices.
2) the last line of the question asks a simple question.
3) the only other way to solve the problem is to use algebra.

How Do You Spot a Backsolve Problem?

Problems that can be backsolved have several characteristics. First, they must be multiple choice; the answer choices are invariably made up of simple numbers (such as 16, 27, or 5) rather than formulas or variables. In addition, the last lines of the problems ask straightforward questions (such as "How many of the workers are women?" or "How many tickets were bought originally?").

Most important, the best way to spot a backsolve problem is to recognize that the only other way to solve that particular problem—the *traditional* way—would be to write an algebraic equation. If you need to write an algebraic equation, then you could backsolve instead.

Let's try another:

3. Forty-two people have signed up for the little league annual dinner. If there are twice as many children as adults signed up, how many children are signed up?

   A. 14
   B. 20
   C. 28
   D. 32

Here's How to Crack It

Is this a Backsolving problem? It certainly has all the earmarks: It is a multiple-choice question, the last line asks a straightforward question, and the answers are simple numbers rather than variables or equations. Most important, the only other way to do this problem would be to write an algebraic equation. And by the way, if you came up with the equation ($x + 2x = 42$), you could *still* get the wrong answer because when you solve for x, you get 14—which happens to be (A). Unfortunately, the variable x in this equation represents the number of *adults*, not the number of children. In this problem, you could have written a perfectly good equation and still have gotten the problem wrong.

Try Backsolving instead. The question asks how many children have signed up for the dinner. One of the answer choices has to be right. Why not start with (B), 20? The problem tells you that there are twice as many children as adults, so if there are 20 children, how many adults can there be? That's right: 10. If you add the number of children and the number of adults, you are supposed to get the same total number of people as there are in the problem (42 people). Do you? No, you have only 30. Choice (B) is not just the wrong answer—it is too small. So you can eliminate any choices that are smaller than (B), which means (A) bites the dust as well.

The answer is either (C) or (D). Let's try (C), 28. If there are 28 children and there are twice as many children as adults, that means that there are 14 adults. If you add 28 and 14, you are supposed to get 42. Do you? Yes! The correct answer to this difficult algebra question is (C).

Backsolving Drill

You can check your answers in Part IX: Answer Key to Drills.

1. Two physical therapists have a total of 16 patients to see in one day. Onome has to see 2 more patients than Lewis. How many patients will Onome see?

   A. 9
   B. 7
   C. 5
   D. 3

2. Which of the values of *m* below would make the inequality $3m < 12$ true?

   A. 7
   B. 6
   C. 4
   D. 2

3. If there are 4 times as many women as men employed by the Ace Insurance Company, then how many of the 75 workers are women?

   A. 75
   B. 60
   C. 45
   D. 15

4. If the tax on a $45.00 restaurant check is $4.05, what is the tax rate?

A. 8%
B. 9%
C. 10%
D. 11%

5. If $2x - 7 = 3$, then $x =$

A. 2
B. 3
C. 4
D. 5

Backsolving Quiz
A: One of the middle ones. That way, if it isn't right, you can tell whether to go up or down.

TRANSLATION

Math itself is a kind of language that can be translated into English. For example, when you see 3 + 4 = 7, you automatically translate the symbols on the page into English (three plus four equals seven). A small number of Mathematical Reasoning problems will ask you to do the reverse: translate a word problem from English into algebra. These problems are easy to spot, for the answer choices always contain variables. Here's an example:

1. Marjorie makes an investment and doubles her money. If she ends up with $480, which equation below could be used to discover the amount of her original investment of x dollars?

A. $\frac{x}{2} = 480$

B. $x - 2 = 480$

C. $x + 2 = 480$

D. $2x = 480$

To translate a problem from English to math, you need to know what some English terms mean in math. Here are the terms that come up on the GED® test.

GED® Term	What It Means	Example
of	multiply	"$\frac{1}{5}$ of the 30 women" (translated: $\frac{1}{5} \times 30$)
percent	over 100	"40 percent" (translated: $\frac{40}{100}$)
double	times 2	"is double the original amount, x" (translated: $2x$)
triple	times 3	"is triple the original amount, x" (translated: $3x$)
more than	add	"…three more than m" (translated: $m + 3$)
less than	subtract	"…three less than n" (translated: $n - 3$)
is, are	equals	"The number of boys is five more than the number of girls" (translated: $b = g + 5$)

The key to any translation problem is its variable. The variable (x, y, z, or whatever) is always defined for you by the GED® test writers. For example, in the previous problem, the variable represents the original amount of money Marjorie had before the investment. In a translation problem, you have to figure out what to do to this variable to get the final outcome of the problem. Let's look at Marjorie's question again.

1. Marjorie makes an investment and doubles her money. If she ends up with $480, which equation below could be used to discover the amount of her original investment of x dollars?

A. $\frac{x}{2} = 480$

B. $x - 2 = 480$

C. $x + 2 = 480$

D. $2x = 480$

Math/English Dictionary

- "is" means "="
- "of" means "×"
- "more than" means "+"
- "less than" means "–"

Here's How to Crack It

The gist of the problem is this: Marjorie put her nest egg into an investment that doubled her money.

You need to express this in mathematical terms, and the key, as always, is the variable. In this case, the variable x represents the money Marjorie had *before* she invested. The \$480 represents the money she had *after* she invested. Mathematically, what do you have to do to x in order to double it? That's right: $2x$. (If you aren't sure of this or any other translation we talk about in the next couple of problems, just look it up on the chart on the previous page.) And after it was doubled, how much money did she have? That's right: \$480. The equation should read:

$$2x = 480$$

The correct answer is (D).

Let's try another one.

---

2. Isabela is three years less than twice the age of her brother Hector. If h represents Hector's age, which expression shows Isabela's age?

   A. $h - 3$
   B. $3 - 2h$
   C. $2h - 3$
   D. $3h - 2$

Here's How to Crack It

The variable h represents Hector's age. What can you do to h in order to get Isabela's age? Let's translate. She is *three years less than* (which we know from the chart above means "– 3") *twice Hector's age* (which we know means "$2h$").

When you see "three years less than," leave some space and put – 3 as below.

$$\_\_\_\_\_\_\_\_ - 3$$

Then fill this space with whatever follows "than": in this case "twice the age of her brother Hector." Since Hector's age is h and "twice" means two times something, this is $2h$. Fill this into the space to get:

$$2h - 3$$

The correct answer is (C).

Sometimes, the GED® test writers will require you to translate information in a word problem into a system of equations. Let's look at an example.

3. A coffee shop sells only large and small lattes. It sells large lattes for $2.50 and small lattes for $1.75. If a group of friends goes into the coffee shop and buys 5 lattes for a total of $10.25, which of the following systems of equations could be used to determine the number of large lattes, *L*, and the number of small lattes, *S*, that the group of friends bought?

A. $L + S = 5$
$2.50L + 1.75S = 10.25$

B. $L + S = 5$
$1.75L + 2.50S = 10.25$

C. $L + S = 10.25$
$1.75L + 2.50S = 5$

D. $L + S = 10.25$
$2.50L + 1.75S = 5$

Here's How to Crack It

The question tells you that L and S represent the number of large and small lattes bought, respectively. A total of 5 lattes were bought. "Total" translates to addition, so $L + S = 5$. Eliminate any choice that doesn't include this equation. Eliminate (C) and (D). The total cost is $10.25, so the sum of the cost of the large lattes and the cost of the small lattes is $10.25. Each large latte costs $2.50, so the cost of L large lattes is $2.50L$. Each small latte costs 1.75, so the cost of S small lattes is $1.75S$. Therefore, $2.50S + 1.75S = 10.25$. Eliminate any choice that doesn't include this equation, so eliminate (B). The correct answer is (A).

Translation Drill

You can check your answers in Part IX: Answer Key to Drills.

1. Madison weighs 5 pounds more than her younger brother Mason. If Mason's weight is represented by x, what is an expression for the *combined* weight of the two children?

   A. $x + 5$
   B. $2(x + 5)$
   C. $2x + 5$
   D. $2(x) + 2(5)$

2. The number of rabbits at a zoo doubled in 2000 and rose to five times the original number by the end of 2001. If the original number of rabbits is represented by m, then how many rabbits did the zoo have by the end of 2001?

   A. $2m$
   B. $5m$
   C. $7m$
   D. $10m$

3. Frank is two years more than three times the age of Tyler. If x represents Tyler's age, which expression shows Frank's age?

   A. $x + 2$
   B. $2x - 3$
   C. $3x + 2$
   D. $3x - 2$

4. Alexis is playing a game in which blue chips are worth 5 points and red chips are worth 3 points. If Alexis has 9 chips for a total of 21 points and the game has no other color chips, then

   A. $B + R = 21$
   $5B + 3R = 9$

   B. $B + R = 21$
   $3B + 5R = 9$

   C. $B + R = 9$
   $5B + 3R = 21$

   D. $B + R = 9$
   $3B + 5R = 21$

Online Practice Drills
For extra practice on the trickiest math topics, including translation, check out the Targeted Math Drills in your Student Tools.

POLYNOMIALS

A **polynomial** is an expression that has multiple terms. These terms can include combinations of variables, numbers, and exponents. On the GED® test, you may be asked to simplify a polynomial by combining like terms or to rewrite a polynomial by factoring it. We will start with simplifying a polynomial.

$$4a - 2b + 2c + a + 8b - 3c^2 = ?$$

First, identify the terms that share the same variable(s). There are six terms in the above expression; each is separated from the others by a + or a – sign.

$$\textcircled{4a} - 2b + 2c + \textcircled{a} + 8b - 3c^2$$

The terms $4a$ and a share the same variable, so combine the two to get $5a$.

$$5a - \textcircled{2b} + 2c + \textcircled{8b} - 3c^2$$

Now let's combine the terms $-2b$ and $8b$ to get $6b$.

$$5a + 6b + 2c - 3c^2$$

The only terms left to combine are $2c$ and $-3c^2$. However, even though both $2c$ and $-3c^2$ have the same variable c, the different exponents mean that these are not like terms, so the two CANNOT be combined. The simplified version of the original polynomial looks like this (simplified from 6 terms down to 4):

$$5a + 6b + 2c - 3c^2$$

Here is another example of simplifying a polynomial:

---

1. Which expression below is equivalent to $2x^2 + 8y - x + 3y - 13$?

   A. $x^2 + 11y - 13$
   B. $x^2 - 2y$
   C. $2x^3 + 11y - 13$
   D. $2x^2 - x + 11y - 13$

Here's How to Crack It

The first term contains the variable x^2; are there any other terms that also contain an x^2? No. Leave it and move on to the following term, $8y$. There is another term that also contains the y variable, $3y$. Add the two to get the new y term: $11y$.

Look at the third term, $-x$. Are there any other x terms? No. What about the final term, -13? It does not have a variable, so it cannot be combined with any other variable terms. Leave that one as well.

The correct answer is (D).

Adding and Subtracting Polynomials

Adding and subtracting polynomials simply means combining the like terms.

2. $(3z^2 - 12z + 7) + (-5z^2 + z + 6) =$

   A. $-2z^2 - 11z + 13$
   B. $8z^2 - 11z + 13$
   C. $-2z^2 - 13z + 13$
   D. $8z^2 - 13z + 13$

Here's How to Crack It

Since the polynomials are being added together, simply ignore the parentheses and rewrite like this: $3z^2 - 12z + 7 - 5z^2 + z + 6$. Remember that adding a negative is the same as subtracting. Now combine like terms.

$$3z^2 - 5z^2 = -2z^2$$
$$-12z + z = -11z$$
$$7 + 6 = 13$$

The result is $-2z^2 - 11z + 13$, which is (A).

Subtracting polynomials is the same, except you have to be careful with the negatives.

3. $(-10b^2 + 6b + 2) - (-4b + 1) =$

   A. $-10b^2 + 2b + 1$
   B. $-10b^2 + 10b + 3$
   C. $-10b^2 + 2b + 3$
   D. $-10b^2 + 10b + 1$

Here's How to Crack It

Again rewrite without the parentheses, but this time the negative must be distributed to every term in the second set of parentheses. Remember that two negatives equal a positive. This looks like $-10b^2 + 6b + 2 + 4b - 1$. Now combine like terms to get $-10b^2 + 10b + 1$, which is (D).

Multiplying, Factoring, and Dividing Polynomials

Multiplying polynomials relates to the distributive law from Chapter 13. Remember that

$$a(b + c) = ab + ac \text{ and } a(b - c) = ab - ac$$

The same principle applies to polynomials. Consider $(x + 2)(x^2 + 3x - 5)$. The $(x + 2)$ factor distributes to each term of the $(x^2 + 3x - 5)$ factor to get $(x + 2)(x^2) + (x + 2)(3x) - (x + 2)(5)$. Now apply the distributive law again to each of the resulting terms. Distribute (x^2) in $(x + 2)(x^2)$ to get $(x)(x^2) + (2)(x^2) = x^3 + 2x^2$. Distribute $(3x)$ in $(x + 2)(3x)$ to get $(x)(3x) + (2)(3x) = 3x^2 + 6x$. Distribute (5) in $(x + 2)(5)$ to get $(x)(5) + (2)(5) = 5x + 10$. Thus, $(x + 2)(x^2) + (x + 2)(3x) - (x + 2)(5) = (x^3 + 2x^2) + (3x^2 + 6x) - (5x + 10)$. Now the problem becomes one of polynomial addition and subtraction. Combine like terms to simplify: $(x^3 + 2x^2) + (3x^2 + 6x) - (5x + 10) = x^3 + 2x^2 + 3x^2 + 6x - 5x - 10 = x^3 + 5x^2 + x - 10$. Let's look at an example.

Tip: Remember the acronym FOIL when multiplying binomials.

4. $(x + y)(x - y) = ?$

A. $2x - 2y$
B. $x^2 - y^2$
C. $x^2 + 2xy + y^2$
D. $x^2 - 2xy + y^2$

Here's How to Crack It

In the case of multiplying binomials (i.e., polynomials with only two terms), there is a shortcut method. This method is called **FOIL (Firsts, Outers, Inners, Lasts).** Multiply the FIRST term of each factor by each other: $(x)(x) = x^2$. Then multiply the OUTERMOST terms together: $(x)(-y) = -xy$. Next, multiply the INNERMOST terms together: $(y)(x) = xy$. Finally, multiply the LAST terms by each other: $(y)(-y) = -y^2$. Combine the results of these four steps to create the polynomial expression and then simplify: $x^2 - xy + xy - y^2 = x^2 - y^2$. The correct answer is (B).

A polynomial expression can be factored by identifying terms that share factors. For example, let's factor this expression:

$$3x + 15$$

The term $3x$ factors into 3 times x and the term 15 factors into 3 times 5. Do these two terms share a factor? They both can be factored by 3.

$$(3)(x) + (3)(5) =$$
$$3(x + 5)$$

Now let's try a longer polynomial expression:

5. Which of the following is equivalent to the expression $5x - 10 + x^2 - 2x$?

A. $(5 + x)(x - 2)$
B. $(5 - x)(x + 2)$
C. $2(x + 5)$
D. $5(x^2 - 2)$

Here's How to Crack It

Look at the first two terms, $5x$ and -10. They share the factor 5. The last two terms, x^2 and $-2x$, also share a factor, x. Rewrite these two pairs.

$$5x - 10 + x^2 - 2x =$$
$$(5)(x) - (5)(2) + (x)(x) - (2)(x) =$$
$$5(x - 2) + x(x - 2)$$

Now you see yet another factor appear, $(x - 2)$. Rewrite the expression again.

$$5(x - 2) + x(x - 2) =$$
$$(x - 2)(5 + x)$$

The answer is (A). You can also check your answer by using FOIL to arrive at the original polynomial.

Factoring is the key to dividing polynomials. Look at $\frac{x^2 + 5x}{3x + 15}$. Factor x from both terms in the numerator to get $x(x + 5)$, and factor 3 from both terms in the denominator to get $3(x + 5)$. In the resulting fraction, $\frac{x(x+5)}{3(x+5)}$, cancel $(x + 5)$ to get $\frac{x}{3}$.

Now let's look at a more complex example.

6. Which of the following expressions is equivalent to

$$\frac{x^2 - 7x - 2x + 14}{x^3 + 2x^2 - 3x - 2x^2 - 4x + 6}?$$

A. $\frac{(x+2)}{(x^2+2x+3)}$

B. $\frac{(x-7)}{(x^2-2x+3)}$

C. $\frac{(x-2)}{(x^2+2x-3)}$

D. $\frac{(x-7)}{(x^2+2x-3)}$

Here's How to Crack It

Start by factoring the numerator. Factor the x from $(x^2 - 7x)$ to get $x(x - 7)$ and -2 from $(-2x + 14)$ to get $-2(x - 7)$, leaving a numerator of $x(x - 7) - 2(x - 7)$. Now factor $(x - 7)$ to get $(x - 2)(x - 7)$. Now factor the denominator. Factor x from $(x^3 + 2x^2 - 3x)$ to get $x(x^2 + 2x - 3)$ and -2 from $-2x^2 - 4x + 6$ to get $-2(x^2 + 2x - 3)$, leaving a denominator of $x(x^2 + 2x - 3) - 2(x^2 + 2x - 3) = (x - 2)(x^2 + 2x - 3)$.

From the resulting fraction, $\frac{(x-2)(x-7)}{(x-2)(x^2+2x-3)}$, cancel $(x - 2)$ to get $\frac{(x-7)}{(x^2+2x-3)}$. The correct answer is (D).

Remember the Translation lesson from earlier in the chapter? Sometimes the GED® test will include polynomial word problems. The basic rules of translating still apply to polynomials. For example, if a question were to refer to the sum of the cube of x and the square of the difference between x and 3, what would be the result? Remember that *sum* refers to addition. What is added? The first term is *the cube of x*. Since *cube* refers to raising a number to the third power, the first term is x^3. The second term is the *square of the difference between x and 3*. Break this term into pieces. The *difference between x and 3* is $(x - 3)$. The word *square* refers to raising an expression to the second power, so the second term is $(x - 3)^2$. Therefore, the entire expression is $x^3 + (x - 3)^2$. Let's look at another example.

7. When an object is stationary and begins to move at a constant acceleration, the square of the velocity is twice the product of the acceleration and the distance traveled. If an object travels at a constant acceleration of 10 m/s² for 45 m, what is its velocity, in meters per second?

   A. 30
   B. 90
   C. 450
   D. 900

Here's How to Crack It

First translate the statement: *the square of the velocity is twice the product of the acceleration and the distance traveled.* Let the velocity be represented by v, the acceleration be represented by a, and the distance be represented by d. Translate this one piece at a time. First, *the square of the velocity* translates to v^2. The word *is* translates to =. The word *twice* translates to 2 times whatever follows. What follows is *the product of the acceleration and the distance traveled.* Since *product* translates to multiplication, this translates to $a \times d$. *Twice* this is $2ad$. Therefore, the statement translates to $v^2 = 2ad$. The question states that $a = 10$ and $d = 45$, so plug in these values to get $v^2 = 2(10)(45)$, so $v^2 = 900$. Take the square root of both sides to get $v = 30$. The correct answer is (A).

Polynomial Drill

You can check your answers in Part IX: Answer Key to Drills.

1. What is the sum of $5x + 2y + x - 3y$?

   A. $6x - y$
   B. $6x + y$
   C. $5x^2 - 6y^2$
   D. $4x - y$

2. Which of the following is a factor of $x^2 - 4x + 3x - 12$?

   A. $(x + 4)$
   B. $(x - 4)$
   C. $(x - 3)$
   D. $(x - 2)$

3. Which of the following is equivalent to $\frac{1}{4}x^2 + \frac{2}{4}x - \frac{2}{3}x - \frac{4}{3}$?

   A. $\left(\frac{1}{4}x + \frac{2}{3}\right)(x+2)$
   B. $\left(\frac{1}{4}x - \frac{2}{3}\right)(x+2)$
   C. $\left(\frac{1}{4}x + \frac{2}{3}\right)(x-2)$
   D. $\left(\frac{1}{4}x - \frac{2}{3}\right)(x-2)$

4. Which of the following is equivalent to $(x^2 + 2x + 8)(x - 4)$?

   A. $x^2 + 2x + 32$
   B. $x^2 + 3x + 4$
   C. $x^3 - 2x^2 - 32$
   D. $x^3 + 6x^2 + 16x + 32$

5. In a certain card game, a deck has cards with integers labeled 1 through 10, and each player has two cards. A player's score is determined by taking the sum of the squares of the numbers on the two cards. If the numbers on Jennifer's two cards have a product of 24 and a sum of 11, what is her score?

A. 52
B. 73
C. 148
D. Not enough information is given.

QUADRATIC EQUATIONS

A quadratic expression is a polynomial in which the highest exponent is 2. Some quadratic equations are fairly simple. For example, look at this equation:

$$x^2 = 36$$

This question can be solved by using the inspection method. The inspection method simply involves taking the square roots of both sides. The square root of x^2 is x and the square root of 36 is 6. However, the answer is not as simple as $x = 6$. It is true that $6^2 = 36$, so $x = 6$ is *one of* the solutions to the equation. However, remember the lesson on multiplying negatives. The product of two negatives is positive. Therefore, $(-6)^2 = (-6)(-6) = +36$, so $x = -6$ is also a solution to this equation. Quadratic equations will often have two solutions. When an equation is in the form $x^2 = a$, the inspection method will yield the solutions $x = \pm\sqrt{a}$.

However, other quadratic equations will be more difficult to solve: in particular, ones that have not only an x^2 but also an x term. We already discussed this type of quadratic (although not by name) in the polynomial multiplication lesson. These expressions are often the result of using the FOIL method. Let's look at an example.

1. Which of the following is equal to $x^2 + 6x + 8$?

A. $(x + 2)(x + 1)$
B. $(x - 3)(x + 4)$
C. $(x + 1)(x - 3)$
D. $(x + 4)(x + 2)$

Here's How to Crack It

You now know how to FOIL, so you can use the answer choices and FOIL each one to see which one gets the expression that is given. To save some time, though, notice that the number by itself must be 8. The number by itself is represented in the LAST step of FOIL. By multiplying just the LAST numbers in the parentheses, you can see that the LAST term in (A) is going to be 2, in (B) is –12, in (C) is –3, and in (D) is 8. Since (D) is the only one that is 8, it must be the correct answer. If you use FOIL on (D), you multiply the FIRST terms (x and x) to get x^2, multiply the OUTSIDE terms (x and 2) to get $2x$, multiply the INSIDE terms (4 and x) to get $4x$, and multiply the LAST terms (4 and 2) to get 8. The result is $x^2 + 2x + 4x + 8 = x^2 + 6x + 8$.

Factoring

Another way to get the answer to the previous question is by factoring. Factoring is the opposite of using FOIL. It takes a quadratic like the ones you've just seen, and puts it into the two sets of parentheses. Let's take a look at $x^2 + 6x + 8$ again. To factor it, draw two sets of parentheses:

$$(\quad)(\quad)$$

The first two terms will usually be x and x. You might sometimes have a number before one or both of them, but in this case there isn't a number before the x^2 so they are both just x.

$$(x\quad)(x\quad)$$

Now you need to figure out what the numbers are. The term without a variable in this quadratic is 8. When you FOIL, you get this number by multiplying the "last" terms in the parentheses, so the two numbers in this case must multiply together to equal 8. Think about what has a product of 8: 1×8 or 2×4. As you saw before, you find the second term in the quadratic, the x, with the "outside" and "inside" terms that are added together after being multiplied. So the two numbers must add or subtract to equal 6 since that is the number before the x in the second term of this quadratic. The numbers 1 and 8 cannot add or subtract to equal 6, but 2 and 4 can if they are added. Thus, the parentheses look like this:

$$(x + 2)(x + 4)$$

You can and should always use FOIL to check that your factors multiply together to equal what you started with.

Let's try an example that involves negatives.

$$x^2 - 4x - 12$$

Start with the parentheses and x in each one:

$$(x\quad)(x\quad)$$

Now list the factors of 12: 1×12, 2×6, and 3×4. Ask yourself which one could add or subtract to equal –4. Keep in mind that since they multiply to equal –12, one will be positive and one will be negative because two positives or two negatives multiply together to equal a positive. The only two that could add or subtract to equal –4 are 2 and 6.

$$(x \quad 2)(x \quad 6)$$

Now determine which is positive and which is negative. If it is +6 and –2, the sum will be positive 4. It needs to be –4, so that will be –6 and +2. The quadratic factored is as follows:

$$(x + 2)(x - 6)$$

One type of question you may see involves an equation, not just an expression like the previous examples. You may have to factor a quadratic and also solve for *x*. If you use the same example, the problem might look like this:

2. Consider this equation: $x^2 - 4x - 12 = 0$

What is the positive solution in the equation above?

Here's How to Crack It

Finding the solution to an equation that looks like this always requires factoring first. We've already done this above and determined that it was $(x + 2)(x - 6) = 0$. Don't forget to write the "= 0" part at the end. Notice now that we have two binomials multiplied together that equal 0. How could this equal 0? Well, a product equals 0 if either of the two factors equals 0, so if the first or the second binomial equaled 0, the whole thing would equal 0. Set the first binomial equal to 0: $x + 2 = 0$. Now subtract 2 from both sides to get $x = -2$. This is one solution. Now set the second binomial equal to 0: $x - 6 = 0$. Add 6 to both sides to get $x = 6$. The two solutions are $x = -2$ and $x = 6$. It is common for quadratic equations to have two solutions as this one does. In this case, the question asks for the positive solution, so you enter 6. You may also see a multiple-choice question that asks for both solutions, or it may even ask for something like the sum or the product of the solutions. Regardless, the method is the same.

Note: If the equation doesn't equal 0 but does involve an x^2 term and an x term like the polynomials we've seen in this section, be sure to subtract everything from the right side so it equals 0 if you use the factor method.

Completing the Square

There are other methods that can be used to solve a quadratic. One is called completing the square. Consider this quadratic equation:

$$x^2 - 6x + 9 = 0$$

Using the factor method, you need to find a pair of numbers with a sum of –6 and a product of 9. These are –3 and –3, so the equation factors to $(x - 3)(x - 3) = 0$. Notice that the two factors are the same, so this equation can be rewritten as $(x - 3)^2 = 0$. This looks similar to an equation that can be solved using the inspection method. Take the square root of both sides to get $x - 3 = 0$. (Remember that ±0 is the same as 0.) Add three to both sides to get $x = 3$. Now, consider instead this equation:

$$x^2 - 6x + 9 = 4$$

Again, you can factor the left side to get $(x - 3)^2 = 4$. Take the square root of both sides to get $x - 3 = \pm 2$. Consider both $x - 3 = 2$ and $x - 3 = -2$. In $x - 3 = 2$, add three to both sides to get $x = 5$. In $x - 3 = -2$, add three to both sides to get $x = 1$. Therefore, the two solutions are $x = 1$ and $x = 5$.

This method can be used only when one side of the equation factors into a perfect square. A quadratic expression in the form $x^2 + bx + c$ is a perfect square if $c = \left(\frac{b}{2}\right)^2$. (In the case above, $b = -6$, so $\frac{b}{2} = \frac{-6}{2} = -3$ and $\left(\frac{b}{2}\right)^2 = (-3)^2 = 9 = c$.) But what if an equation doesn't have a perfect square? Let's look at an example.

---

3. If $x^2 + 4x - 8 = 13$, what are the possible values of x?

–7	–5	–3	–1
1	3	5	7

Here's How to Crack It

On the left side of the equation, the coefficient on the x term is 4. $\left(\frac{4}{2}\right)^2 = 4$, so this is not a perfect square. However, you can manipulate the equation to get a perfect square. If you add 12 to both sides, you get $x^2 + 4x + 4 = 25$. Now, the left side is a perfect square. Factor the left side to get $(x + 2)^2 = 25$. Take the square root of both sides to get $x + 2 = \pm 5$. If $x + 2 = 5$, subtract two from both sides to get $x = 3$. If $x + 2 = -5$, subtract two from both sides to get $x = -7$. The correct answers are 3 and –7.

Quadratic Formula

On other equations, it will be more difficult to factor or complete the equation. For example,

$$3x^2 + 9x - 10 = 0$$

There is no simple way to solve this equation for x by finding factors or by completing the square. However, there is a fall-back plan for quadratics that will work no matter how easy or difficult the equation is. This fall-back plan is called the *quadratic formula*. For an equation in the form $ax^2 + bx + c = 0$, $x = \frac{-b \pm \sqrt{b^2 - 4ac}}{2a}$. In the case above, $a = 3$, $b = 9$, and $c = -10$, so $x = \frac{-9 \pm \sqrt{9^2 - 4(3)(-10)}}{2(3)} = \frac{-9 \pm \sqrt{201}}{6}$.

Let's look at another example.

4. Solve the equation for x.

$$2x^2 - 5x = 4$$

A. $x = 8$ and $x = -1$

B. $x = -8$ and $x = 1$

C. $x = \frac{5 \pm \sqrt{57}}{2}$

D. $x = \frac{5 \pm \sqrt{57}}{4}$

Here's How to Crack It

Use the answer choices as a hint that this may be difficult to factor. Use the quadratic equation: $x = \frac{-b \pm \sqrt{b^2 - 4ac}}{2a}$. However, to use this, the equation must be in the form $ax^2 + bx + c = 0$.

Subtract 4 from both sides to get $2x^2 - 5x - 4 = 0$, so $a = 2$, $b = -5$, and $c = -4$. Thus, $x = \frac{-(-5) \pm \sqrt{(-5)^2 - 4(2)(-4)}}{2(2)} = \frac{5 \pm \sqrt{57}}{4}$. The correct answer is (D).

Quadratic Equations Drill

You can check your answers in Part IX: Answer Key to Drills.

1. Which of the following are the solutions to the equation $x^2 - 7x + 12 = 0$?

   A. $x = 3$ and $x = 4$
   B. $x = 6$ and $x = 2$
   C. $x = -6$ and $x = -2$
   D. $x = -3$ and $x = -4$

2. Which of the following equations has the same solutions as $x^2 - 10x + 16 = 0$?

   A. $(x - 5)^2 = 4$
   B. $(x - 5)^2 = 9$
   C. $(x + 5)^2 = 9$
   D. $(x + 5)^2 = 4$

3. Which of the following are the solutions to the equation $x^2 - 8x + 5 = 0$?

   A. $x = \frac{-8 \pm \sqrt{44}}{2}$
   B. $x = \frac{-8 \pm \sqrt{84}}{2}$
   C. $x = \frac{8 \pm \sqrt{84}}{2}$
   D. $x = \frac{8 \pm \sqrt{44}}{2}$

RATIONAL EXPRESSIONS

Rational expressions are fractions made up of polynomials. Because a rational expression is just a type of fraction, the same rules for adding, subtracting, multiplying, and diving fractions still apply.

Addition and Subtraction

Remember adding and subtracting fractions from Chapter 13? There were two methods: Bowtie and common denominator. When you're working with polynomials rather than numbers, the Bowtie may be too cumbersome of a method. However, common denominator works well. Let's look at an example:

1. Which of the following is equivalent to $\frac{x-2}{x} + \frac{2x+3}{2}$?

A. $\frac{2x^2 + 5x - 4}{2x}$

B. $\frac{2x^2 + x - 6}{2x}$

C. $\frac{2x^2 - 6}{x + 2}$

D. $\frac{3x - 5}{x + 2}$

Here's How to Crack It

Find the common denominator for the two fractions. The denominators are x and 2. Since these don't have any common factors, the common denominator is the product $2x$. Multiply the first fraction by $\frac{2}{2}$ and multiply the second by $\frac{x}{x}$. For the first fraction, $\frac{x-2}{x} \times \frac{2}{2} = \frac{2(x-2)}{2x} = \frac{2x-4}{2x}$. For the second, $\frac{2x+3}{2} \times \frac{x}{x} = \frac{x(2x+3)}{2x} = \frac{2x^2+3x}{2x}$. Since the denominators are now the same, add the numerators to get $\frac{(2x-4)+(2x^2+3x)}{2x}$. Combine like terms in the numerator to get $\frac{2x^2+5x-4}{2x}$. The correct answer is (A).

In the case above, the least common denominator is simply the product of the two denominators. That won't always be the case.

2. Which of the following is equivalent to $\frac{3x}{x^2 - 4} - \frac{5x^2 + 3x}{x^2 - 4x + 4}$?

A. $\frac{-5x^2}{4x - 8}$

B. $\frac{-2x^2 - 3x}{x^2 - 4x + 4}$

C. $\frac{5x^3 + 11x^2}{x^3 - 2x^2 - 4x + 8}$

D. $\frac{5x^3 - 10x^2 - 12x}{x^3 - 2x^2 - 4x + 8}$

Here's How to Crack It

The denominators are factorable polynomials, so it's possible that they have common factors. In the first fraction, $(x^2 - 4)$ factors to $(x - 2)(x + 2)$. In the second fraction, $(x^2 - 4x + 4)$ factors to $(x - 2)^2$. Since both denominators have a factor of $(x - 2)$, it is only necessary to multiply the first fraction by $\frac{x-2}{x-2}$ and the second by $\frac{x+2}{x+2}$. In the first fraction $\frac{3x}{x^2-4} \times \frac{x-2}{x-2} = \frac{3x(x-2)}{(x^2-4)(x-2)} = \frac{3x^2-6x}{x^3-2x^2-4x+8}$. In the second, $\frac{5x^2+3x}{x^2-4x+4} \times \frac{x+2}{x+2} = \frac{(5x^2+3x)(x+2)}{(x^2-4x+4)(x+2)} = \frac{5x^3+13x^2+6x}{x^3-2x^2-4x+8}$. Now that the denominators are the same, subtract the numerators to get $\frac{(3x^2-6x)-(5x^3+13x^2+6x)}{x^3-2x^2-4x+8} = \frac{-5x^3-10x^2-12x}{x^3-2x^2-4x+8}$.

The correct answer is (D).

Multiplication and Division

Once again, the rules for multiplying and dividing rational expressions are the same as those for multiplying and dividing fractions. When multiplying rational expressions, there is no need to worry about a common denominator. Just line them up and multiply straight across.

3. Which of the following is equivalent to $\frac{x-3}{x+2} \times \frac{x+4}{x-8}$?

A. $\frac{2x+1}{2x-6}$

B. $\frac{x^2-11x+24}{x^2+8x+8}$

C. $\frac{x^2+x-12}{x^2-6x-16}$

D. $\frac{x^2+7x+12}{x^2-6x-16}$

Here's How to Crack It

Multiply straight across: Multiply the numerator of the first fraction by the numerator of the second and multiply the denominator of the first fraction by the denominator of the second. For the numerators, $(x-3)(x+4) = x^2 + x - 12$. For the denominators, $(x+2)(x-8) = x^2 - 6x - 16$. Therefore, the product of the fractions is $\frac{x^2+x-12}{x^2-6x-16}$. The correct answer is (C).

For dividing rational expressions, invert the second fraction and multiply.

4. Which of the following is equivalent to

$$\frac{x^2 - 6x + 9}{2x^2 + 10x - 48} \div \frac{x^2 - 7x + 12}{x^2 + 8x}?$$

A. $\frac{x}{2x - 4}$

B. $\frac{x}{2x - 8}$

C. $\frac{x - 4}{2x}$

D. $\frac{x^2 - 3x}{2x - 8}$

Here's How to Crack It

You're dividing fractions, so flip the second and multiply to get $\frac{x^2 - 6x + 9}{2x^2 + 10x - 48} \times \frac{x^2 + 8x}{x^2 - 7x + 12}$.

This looks painful to multiply, but remember that you can reduce fractions by common factors when you multiply. You can do the same for rational expressions. Factor each polynomial. For the numerator of the first fraction, $x^2 - 6x + 9$ factors to $(x - 3)^2$. For the denominator of the first fraction, first notice that 2 is a common factor of all three terms. Therefore, you can factor a 2 to get $2(x^2 + 5x - 24)$. Factor the polynomial inside the parentheses to get $2(x - 3)(x + 8)$. For the numerator of the second fraction, $x^2 + 8x$ factors to $x(x + 8)$. For the denominator of the second fraction, $x^2 - 7x + 12$ factors to $(x - 4)(x - 3)$. Therefore, the product becomes $\frac{(x - 3)^2}{2(x - 3)(x + 8)} \times \frac{x(x + 8)}{(x - 4)(x - 3)}$. Now reduce the fractions. The first fraction can be reduced by $(x - 3)$ to get $\frac{(x - 3)}{2(x + 8)} \times \frac{x(x + 8)}{(x - 4)(x - 3)}$.

Remember that before you multiply, you can reduce fractions diagonally. Therefore, you can cancel a factor of $(x - 3)$ and a factor of $(x + 8)$ to get $\frac{1}{2} \times \frac{x}{(x-4)}$. Multiply straight across to get $\frac{x}{2(x-4)} = \frac{x}{2x-8}$. The correct answer is (B).

As you learned from the Translation lesson earlier in this chapter, sometimes you will have to rewrite a given description as an expression, using numbers and math symbols.

Let's practice doing this with rational expressions. The only difference is that our expressions will be fractions, so pay extra attention to the words that indicate what goes on the top and what goes on the bottom. For example, "the ratio of a number squared plus one and the product of five and that number minus the ratio of the number squared minus one and the product of two and that number"—so many words, but we can break them down into phrases.

First, we'll call the number x and start working on one ratio at a time. In the first ratio, the number is squared, x^2, plus 1: $x^2 + 1$. This is the top of the first ratio, and on the bottom, the "product" of 5 and that number, so simply $5x$. Next it says "minus" another ratio. This time, it's "the number squared minus one" or $x^2 - 1$ on top, and on the bottom, "the product of two and that number," $2x$. Now we can put it all together as a rational expression:

$$\frac{x^2+1}{5x} - \frac{x^2-1}{2x}$$

Let's try this out with a question that has answer choices:

---

5. Which of the following expressions is equivalent to this sum: the ratio of a number minus three and that number times two plus the ratio of a number minus five and that number squared?

A. $\frac{x-3}{2x} + \frac{x-5}{x^2}$

B. $\frac{x-3}{2x} - \frac{x-1}{x^2}$

C. $\frac{2x-8}{x^2}$

D. $(x-3)(2x)(x^2-1)(2x)$

Here's How to Crack It

This is actually a good problem for applying your POE skills. You know from the word "sum" in the question that you are going to be adding, and the word "ratio" tells you that these are going to be fractions. Notice that one of the answer options has a subtraction sign between fractions, so you can eliminate (B) right away. Choice (C) is a single fraction, so it can also be ruled out because it does not contain two ratios. Another answer option does not involve ratios at all, so you can rule out (D) as well. That leaves you with (A) as the correct answer without even translating! You can still double check by reading out the verbal phrases and matching them with the rational expression.

Rational Expressions Drill

You can check your answers in Part IX: Answer Key to Drills.

1. Which of the following is equivalent to

$$\frac{3}{x^2 - 2x - 8} - \frac{2}{x-4}?$$

A. $\frac{1}{x^2 - 3x + 4}$

B. $\frac{5}{x^2 - x - 12}$

C. $\frac{-2x - 1}{x^2 - 2x - 8}$

D. $\frac{2x + 7}{x^2 - 2x - 8}$

2. Which of the following is equivalent to

$$\frac{3x - 9}{x^2 - 6x + 9} \div \frac{x^2 + 8x + 15}{x^2 - 9}?$$

A. $\frac{3}{x+5}$

B. $\frac{1}{x-3}$

C. $\frac{3x + 15}{x^2 - 6x + 9}$

D. $\frac{3x^3 + 81}{x^4 - 48x^2 + 135}$

SIMULTANEOUS EQUATIONS

Solving a simple one-variable equation like $3x - 10 = 11$ can be done with the method described earlier. However, what if you were given the equation $3x - 10 = y$ and were asked to come up with a specific value for x? This would be impossible. Different values for y will result in different values for x. However, what if you were also given a second equation like $4x - 17 = y$? Although neither equation on its own can determine a value for x, the two of them together can, using a method called the substitution method. Since both equations are isolated for y, set

$$3x - 10 = 4x - 17$$

Subtract $3x$ from both sides to get

$$-10 = x - 17$$

Add 17 to both sides to get

$$7 = x$$

Need the value of y? Just substitute $x = 7$ into one of the above equations to get

$$y = 4(7) - 17 = 28 - 17 = 11$$

Look at an example.

1. If $3x + 6y = 30$ and $2x + 5y = 26$, choose two numbers below that are possible values of x and y.

$x =$	

$y =$	

−6
−2
6

−2
1
6

Here's How to Crack It

There are two equations and two variables. Isolate one of the variables in one of the equations. Take $3x + 6y = 30$ and isolate x. Subtract $6y$ from both sides to get $3x = 30 - 6y$. Divide both sides by 3 to get $x = 10 - 2y$. Now you have an expression for x. Substitute this expression for x into the other equation. $2x + 5y = 26$ becomes $2(10 - 2y) + 5y = 26$. Distribute 2 to get $20 - 4y + 5y = 26$. Combine like terms to get $20 + y = 26$. Subtract 20 from both sides to get $y = 6$. Now, to get x, substitute this value of y into one of the equations. Try the second one. $2x + 5y = 26$ becomes $2x + 5(6) = 26$ and $2x + 30 = 26$. Subtract 30 from both sides to get $2x = -4$. Divide both sides by 2 to get $x = -2$. Therefore, select -2 for x and 6 for y.

There is another method for solving this type of problem, called the linear combination method. Let's use the equations from the previous question. Stack the two equations as below.

$$3x + 6y = 30$$
$$2x + 5y = 26$$

To do this method, the first thing you want to do is make sure the coefficients on one of the variables are the same in both equations. In this case, you can multiply the first equation by 2 and the second equation by 3 to get

$$6x + 12y = 60$$
$$6x + 15y = 78$$

Now, the coefficients on the *x* variable are the same. Next, subtract the two equations by subtracting the lined-up terms to get

$$\begin{aligned} 6x + 12y &= 60 \\ -(6x + 15y &= 78) \\ -3y &= -18 \end{aligned}$$

Divide both sides by –3 to get $y = 6$. To get the value of *x*, substitute this value into one the original equations to get $x = -2$, just as before.

Try another example.

2. If $4x - 3y = 15$ and $5x = 12 - 3y$, what is the value of x?

A. -3
B. −1
C. 1
D. 3

Here's How to Crack It

To solve this using the linear combination method, first get both equations in the same form. To do this, add $3y$ to both sides of the second equation to get $5x + 3y = 12$. Now line up the two equations to get

$$4x - 3y = 15$$
$$5x + 3y = 12$$

Notice that the coefficients on the *y*s are negations of each other. In this case, you can just add the two equations to get

$$\begin{array}{r} 4x - 3y = 15 \\ +\underline{(5x + 3y = 12)} \\ 9x \quad\quad = 27 \end{array}$$

Divide both sides by 9 to get $x = 3$. The correct answer is (D).

Simultaneous Equations Drill

You can check your answers in Part IX: Answer Key to Drills.

1. If $x = 2y + 5$ and $x = 3y - 6$, what is the value of x?

   A. 11
   B. 22
   C. 27
   D. 33

2. If $3x + 4y = -5$ and $-2x - 5y = 8$, what is the value of y?

   A. −2
   B. 1
   C. 3
   D. 7

3. At a certain fruit stand, apples cost 25 cents and bananas cost 30 cents. If Bill buys a total of 8 apples and bananas for $2.15, how many bananas did Bill buy?

   A. 3
   B. 4
   C. 5
   D. 6

FUNCTIONS

Sometimes the GED® test will ask you about relations. A relation is an association between two variables: an input variable called the domain and an output variable called the range. The relations that the GED® test will be most interested in are called functions. Functions are relations in which each member of the domain corresponds to a unique member of the range. Look at the two relations below.

x	y
0	3
2	7
6	5
2	1

x	y
2	4
0	1
7	4
3	8

Are these relations functions? When a relation in is table notation, the domain is the variable on the left, in this case x, and the range is the variable on the right, in this case y. For the table on the left above, a member of the domain, 2, goes to two different members of the range, 7 and 1. Therefore, this is not a function. However, in the relation on the right, each member of the domain corresponds with only one member of the range, so this is a function. Does it matter that 2 and 7 from the domain correspond with 4 from the range? No. Each member of the domain has to correspond with a unique member of the range, but each member of the range need not correspond with a unique member of the domain.

Relations can also be put into graphical form.

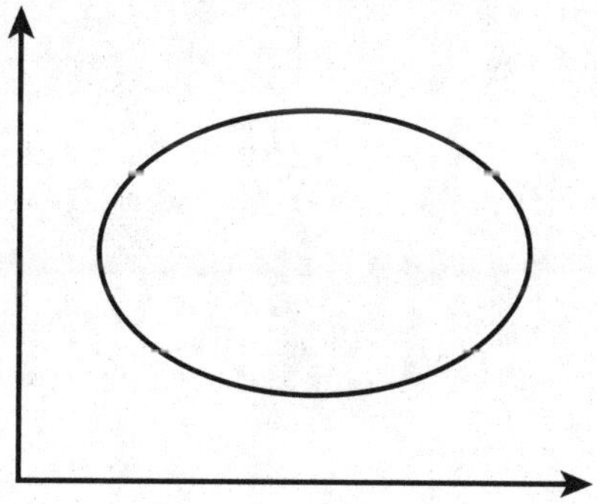

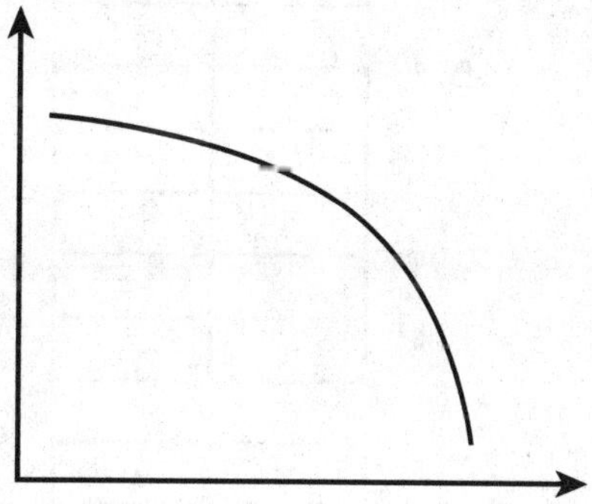

In the graphical form of a relation, the horizontal axis represents the domain and the vertical axis represents the range. (You'll see more about graphic functions in the next chapter.) Are these two relations functions? To determine this, use what is called the vertical line test. Since, in a function, every member of the domain corresponds with a unique member of the range, any vertical line drawn on the graph will hit the curve at only one point. If any vertical line touches the curve at more than one point, the relation is not a function. For the graph on the left, multiple vertical lines can be drawn that will touch the curve at more than one point. Therefore, this is not a function. However, for the graph on the right, any vertical line drawn will touch the curve at only one point. Therefore, this relation is a function. This can be seen in the following graphs.

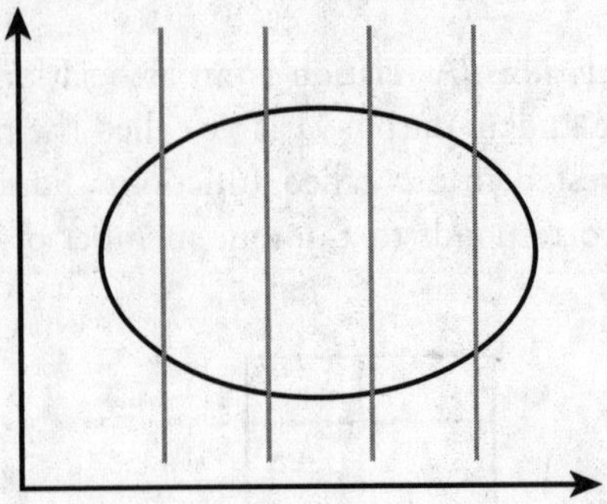

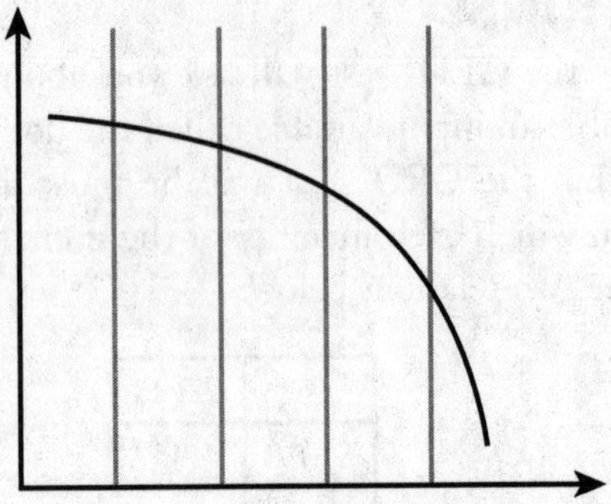

Sometimes the GED® test writers will test your ability to determine whether a relation is a function. Let's look at an example.

1. Which of the relations below represents a function?

A.

x	y
1	2
5	6
3	2
1	1

B.

x	y
−1	6
4	1
2	4
4	−3

C.

x	y
−2	−4
3	−3
8	−3
5	−5

D.

x	y
3	−2
−5	3
2	−4
2	7

Here's How to Crack It

In order for a relation to be a function, each member of the domain must correspond with a unique member of the range. Check for any repeated x values in the domain of each table. In (A), 1 from the domain corresponds with 2 and 1 in the range, so this is not a function. Eliminate (A). In (B), 4 from the domain corresponds with 1 and –3 in the range, so this is not a function. Eliminate (B). In (C), each element of the domain corresponds with only one element from the range. Keep this choice. In (D), 2 from the domain corresponds with –4 and 7 in the range, so this is not a function. Eliminate (D). The correct answer is (C).

Now let's look at a graphical example.

2. Which of the following graphs does NOT represent a function?

A.

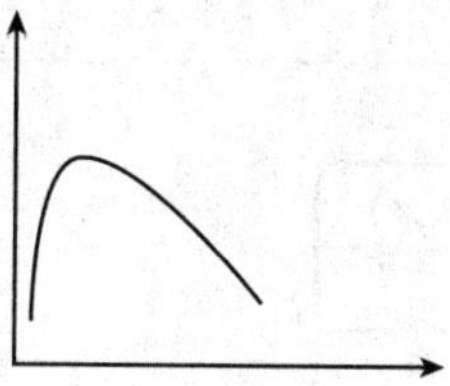

B.

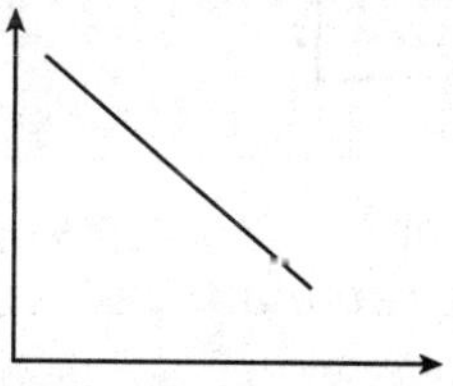

C.

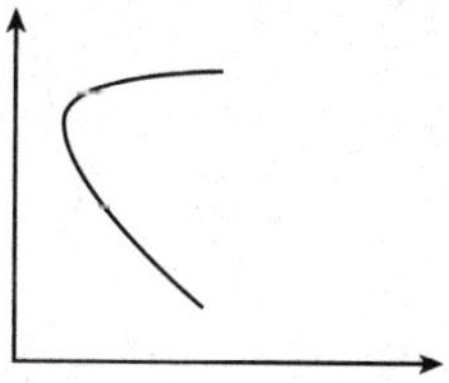

D.

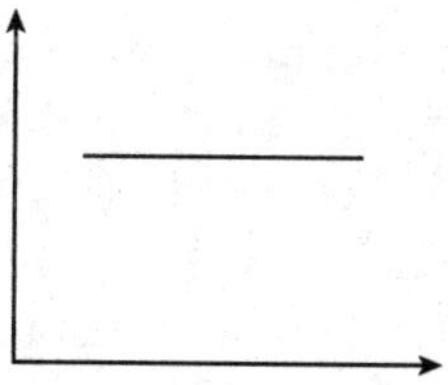

Here's How to Crack It

Since the question is asking whether graphs represent functions, use the vertical line test. In (A), no vertical line can be drawn that will touch the curve more than once. This represents a function. In (B), no vertical line can be drawn that will touch the curve more than once. This represents a function. In (C), several vertical lines can be drawn that will touch the curve more than once. This does not represent a function. In (D), no vertical line can be drawn that will touch the curve more than once. This represents a function. The only graph that does not represent a function is (C), so the correct answer is (C).

Another way to represent a function is using function notation. This is commonly $f(x)$, though a function could be represented with any letter other than f as well. $f(x)$ can be stated as "f of x," "the function of x," or "f as a function of x." For example, look at the function $f(x) = x^2 + 5x$. If you were asked for the value of $f(3)$, you would take the number inside the parentheses—3, in this case—and plug it in for each appearance of x in the definition of the function. So $f(3) = 3^2 + 5 \times 3 = 9 + 15 = 24$. If you need $f(4)$, do the same thing. $f(4) = 4^2 + 5 \times 4 = 16 + 20 = 36$. Let's look at an example.

x	$g(x)$
1	2
2	6
3	10
4	14

3. Which of the following functions could represent the function described in the table above?

A. $g(x) = 2x$
B. $g(x) = 3x - 1$
C. $g(x) = 4x - 2$
D. $g(x) = 2x + 4$

Here's How to Crack It

For a question like this, use POE extensively. Start with the first row of the table, which says that $g(1) = 2$. Go through the answer choices and eliminate any choice for which $g(1)$ does not equal 2. In (A), $g(1) = 2 \times 1 = 2$, so keep this choice. In (B), $g(1) = 3 \times 1 - 1 = 2$, so keep this choice. In (C), $g(1) = 4 \times 1 - 2 = 2$, so keep this choice. In (D), $g(1) = 2 \times 1 + 4 = 6$, so eliminate this choice. Now look at the next row, which says that $g(2) = 6$, and go through the answer choices, eliminating any choice for which $g(2)$ does not equal 6. In (A), $g(2) = 2 \times 2 = 4$, so eliminate this choice. In (B), $g(2) = 3 \times 2 - 1 = 5$, so eliminate this choice. In (C), $g(2) = 4 \times 2 - 2 = 6$, so keep this choice, which is the only remaining choice. The correct answer is (C).

Some GED® questions will combine functions with translating. Let's look at an example.

4. A certain fruit stand sells only bananas. The fruit stand earns a profit of five dollars less than 3 dollars for each banana it sells. Which of the following is a function representing the stand's profits, p, as a function of the number of bananas sold, b?

A. $p(b) = 5b - 3$
B. $p(b) = -2b$
C. $p(b) = 5 - 3b$
D. $p(b) = 3b - 5$

Here's How to Crack It

Translate the information in the question into an equation. The profit is p as a function of b, which is written as $p(b)$. The profit is equal to "five dollars less than 3 dollars for each banana it sells." When you see "five dollars less than," leave some space and write ______ – 5. Then fill that space with whatever follows "than": in this case "3 dollars for each banana it sells." Since this translates to $3b$, the function becomes $p(b) = 3b - 5$. The correct answer is (D).

Functions Drill

You can check your answers in Part IX: Answer Key to Drills.

x	$h(x)$
3	−1
5	4
3	y
−2	−6

1. For which of the following values of y does $h(x)$ represent a function?

A. −6
B. −1
C. 3
D. 4

2. If $g(x) = x^2 - 6x + 9$, which of the following is equal to $g(5)$?

   A. 2
   B. 4
   C. 5
   D. 9

3. Which of the following represents the statement, "The function of x is three times 4 more than the square of x"?

   A. $f(x) = 3(x^2 + 4)$
   B. $f(x) = 3x^2 + 4$
   C. $f(x) = 3(x + 4)^2$
   D. $f(x) = [3(x - 4)]^2$

PUTTING IT ALL TOGETHER

Now that you've seen all the elements of algebra separately, we'd like you to try a drill in which they are all mixed together. This will give you practice in recognizing the different types of problems so that you can zero in on exactly which technique you need to solve them quickly. Pay particular attention to spotting Backsolving questions, which our students find takes a bit of practice.

Algebra Drill

You can check your answers in Part IX: Answer Key to Drills.

1. If $5x + 9 = 44$, then $x =$

   A. 12
   B. 10
   C. 7
   D. 6

2. Laura has $4 more than three times the amount of money Steven has. If x represents the amount of money Steven has, which expression shows how much money Laura has?

   A. $3x + 4$
   B. $3x - 4$
   C. $4x + 3$
   D. $x + 4(3)$

3. Evaluate $5x^2 - 4y$, if $x = 3$ and $y = 4$.

4. The Oakdale Preschool accepts 4-year-olds and 5-year-olds and has a total of 63 students. If the school has 7 more 4-year-olds than 5-year-olds, then how many of the children are 4 years old?

   A. 14
   B. 28
   C. 35
   D. 42

5. If $3m + 7 < 28$, then which of the following expressions gives all the possible values of m?

   A. $m < 9$
   B. $m < 7$
   C. $m > -5$
   D. $m > -7$

6. What is the sum of $2(x + y) + 3x + 2y$?

   A. $5x + 3y$
   B. $6x + 3y$
   C. $6x + 4y$
   D. $5x + 4y$

7. If $p = 4$, which of the following inequalities contains the number p?

   A. $x < 4$
   B. $x > 5$
   C. $2x < 3$
   D. $x < 5$

8. If 36 of the 120 workers in a factory work overtime, what percentage of the workers work overtime?

   A. 10%
   B. 20%
   C. 30%
   D. 40%

9. Multiply.

$$(4x - 8)(x + 2)$$

A. $4x^2 - 16$
B. $-4x + 2$
C. $4x^2 + 16x - 16$
D. $5x - 6$

10. Lucas is 4 years older than Erica, and Erica is 5 years younger than Max. If the sum of their ages is 69, how old is Lucas?

A. 18
B. 20
C. 24
D. 25

11. If $3x + 2 = -2y$ and $-x + 3y = -14$, what is the value of y ?

A. -4
B. -2
C. 2
D. 4

x	$f(x)$
-2	
1	3
	19

12. If the table above represents the function $f(x) = 2x^2 + 1$, select possible values to complete the table.

5	17
-3	19
9	-1

13. If $\frac{-2x+8}{x^2-3x-10} \times \frac{x^2-x-20}{x^2-16} = x+5$, which of following is a possible value of x ?

A. -4
B. -2
C. 3
D. 5

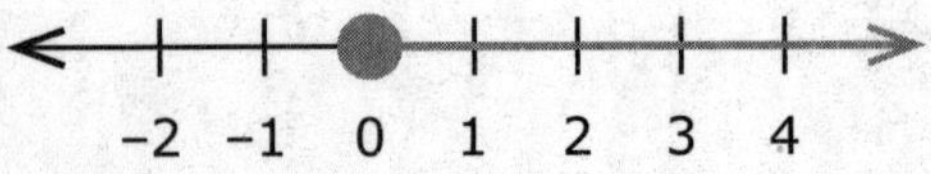

14. For which of the following inequalities does the graph above show all values for x?

A. $x < 4$
B. $x > 0$
C. $x \geq 0$
D. $x > -2$

Chapter 16 Geometry

In this chapter, we'll cover all the geometry you need to know for the Mathematical Reasoning test—including lines and angles, triangles, rectangles, circles, volume, and graphing.

The good news is that the geometry on the GED® test covers only a fraction of what is covered in high school. Even if you never took geometry, you can learn everything you need to get the GED® geometry questions right just by reading this chapter and doing the exercises that follow.

Measuring Diagrams

One reason GED® geometry isn't too tough is that the diagrams are always roughly drawn to scale. As we showed you in our introduction to the Mathematical Reasoning test, this means that anytime there's a diagram, you always have a wonderful, concrete way to ballpark the problem. As we cover each of the geometry topics in this chapter, we'll show you how to measure the different types of diagrams.

What If There Is No Diagram?

If a geometry problem doesn't come with a diagram, then you should immediately draw your own. Believe us, it's a lot tougher to solve a geometry problem if you can't see it. Take a few seconds to sketch the information provided for you in the question, and if possible, try to draw your figure to scale so you'll have some idea of which answer choices are out of the ballpark.

Geometry Diagrams
If there's a diagram, use your eyes to estimate what the answer ought to be. If there's no diagram, draw one yourself.

The Formula List

On each GED® Mathematical Reasoning question, there is a clickable button to a list of many of the mathematical formulas you may need during the test. Here you will find the volume of a cube, the surface area of a pyramid, and the Pythagorean Theorem (don't worry if you don't know what that is yet).

You need to know the formulas for area and perimeter before taking the test—they will not be provided to you! You will be much more confident if you walk into the test room with these formulas already memorized and even more confident if you have practiced using the formulas on our two practice tests and the drills in this chapter.

Everything You Need to Know About GED® Geometry

Here are the geometry topics that are tested on the Mathematical Reasoning test:

- Lines and angles
- Rectangles and squares
- Triangles and pyramids
- Circles and spheres
- Cones and cylinders
- Perimeter and area
- Surface area and volume
- Setup geometry
- Graphing points and functions
- Slope and the *y*-intercept

As in the previous chapters, we'll first cover a concept, then give you examples of how this concept is used on the GED® test, and then give you a short drill. At the end of the chapter, there will be a larger drill that covers all the geometry topics together.

LINES AND ANGLES

Here is a line:

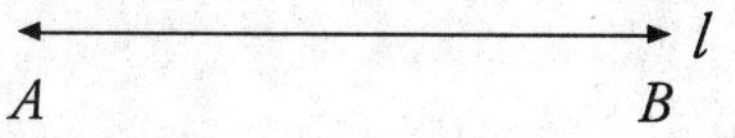

This particular line is labeled *l*, and like all lines, it extends forever to the left and to the right. *A* and *B* are points on the line, and the portion of the line between them, which has length *AB*, is called line segment *AB*.

How many degrees does a line contain? If the second hand on the face of a watch moves from 12 all the way around to 12 again, it has gone 360 degrees. A straight line drawn on the face of that watch from 12 straight down to 6 cuts the face of the watch in half: All straight lines create an angle of 180 degrees.

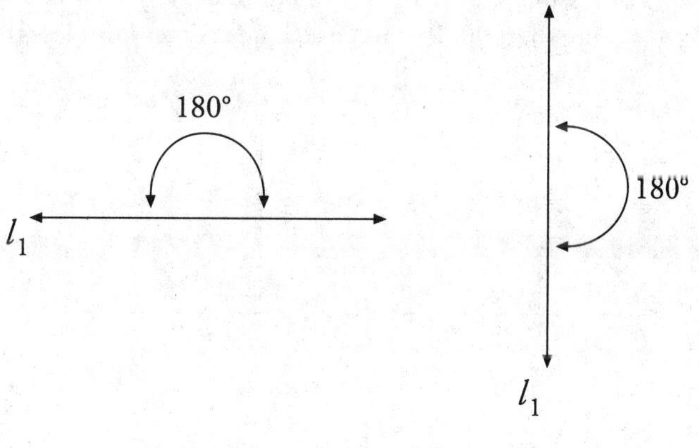

If that line is cut by another line, it divides that 180 degrees into two angles whose measures together add up to 180 degrees.

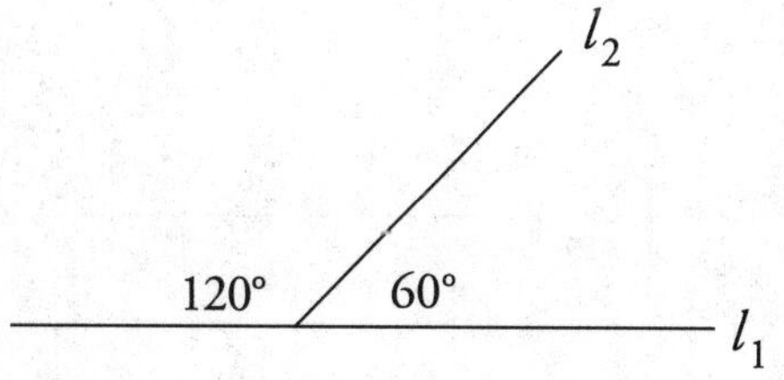

Perpendicular Lines

If the two lines cut across each other in such a way that they form two angles of 90 degrees each, then the two lines are called **perpendicular.** A 90-degree angle is also known as a **right angle.** On GED® diagrams, this is sometimes indicated by a little box drawn into the corner of the angles.

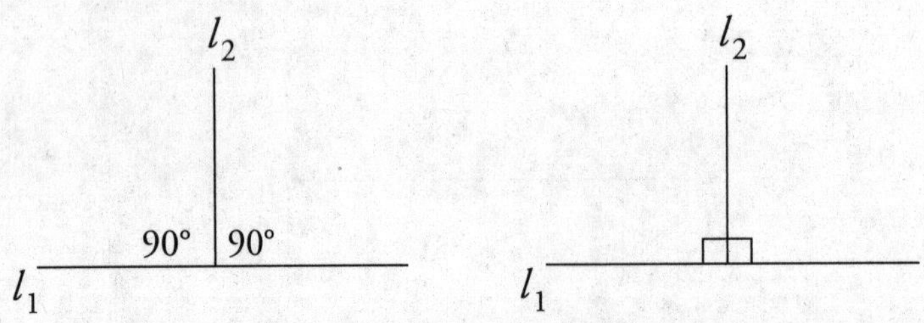

Using a Right Angle as a Measuring Tool

Whenever you see any angle on the Mathematical Reasoning test, it helps to compare it in your mind to a 90-degree angle. Take angle *A* below. Is it bigger or smaller than the 90-degree angle? If it's bigger, then you can eliminate any answer choices that say that the measure of angle *A* is less than 90. If it is smaller, then you can eliminate any answer choices that say that the measure of angle *A* is more than 90. In this case, angle *A* measures less than 90 degrees.

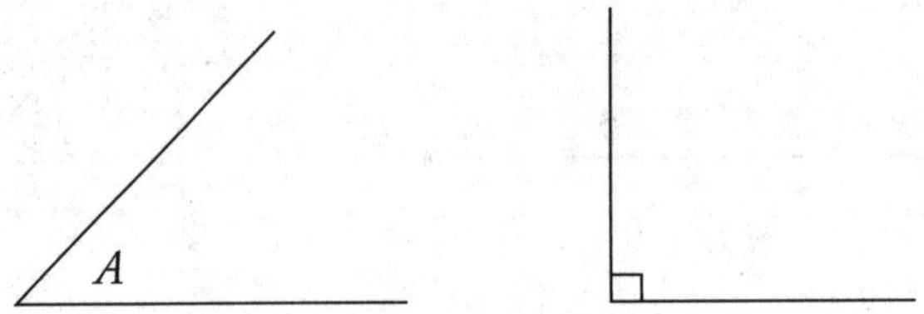

Parallel Lines

If two lines are drawn so that they could extend into infinity without ever meeting, these lines are considered **parallel.** The two lines below are an example of parallel lines.

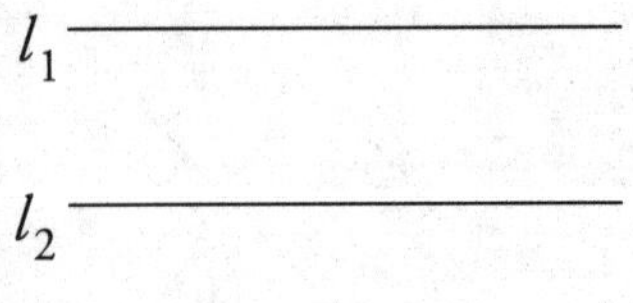

Lines and Angles Drill

You can check your answers in Part IX: Answer Key to Drills.

Determine the measure of angle x in each of the diagrams below.

(1)

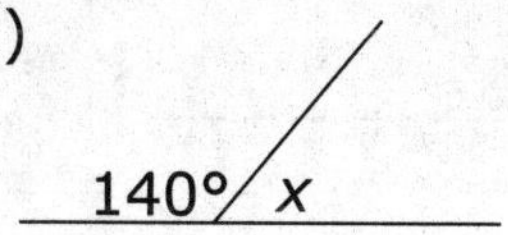

(2)

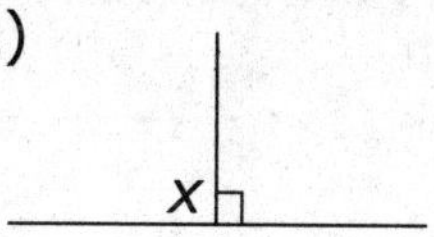

(3)

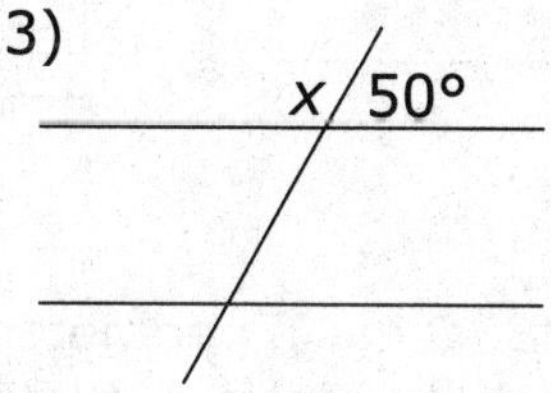

RECTANGLES AND SQUARES

A rectangle is an object with 4 sides that make 4 angles, each measuring 90 degrees.

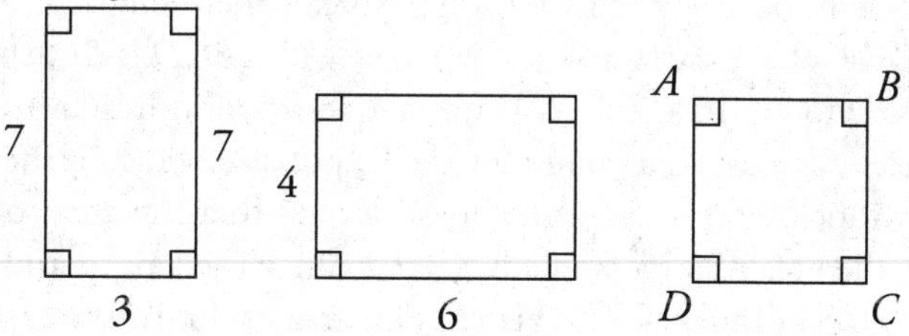

Rectangle A Rectangle B Rectangle C

The area of a rectangle is found by multiplying its length (l) by its width (w). The area of rectangle A is 7×3, or 21. The area of rectangle B is 4×6, or 24.

The lengths of the opposite sides of a rectangle are always equal to each other. For example, in rectangle C, side *AB* has the same length as side *DC*, and side *AD* has the same length as *BC*. To find the perimeter of a rectangle, you simply add the four sides together. The perimeter of rectangle A is 20 (7 + 3 + 7 + 3). The perimeter of rectangle B is also 20 (4 + 6 + 4 + 6).

A square is a rectangle whose four sides all happen to have the same length. The area of a square can still be found by multiplying length by width, but because the length and width in a square are the *same*, you can also say that the area of a square equals the length of the side squared.

Square Rectangle Quiz

Q: Is a rectangle always a square, or is a square always a rectangle?

Turn the page for the answer.

Let's look at an example:

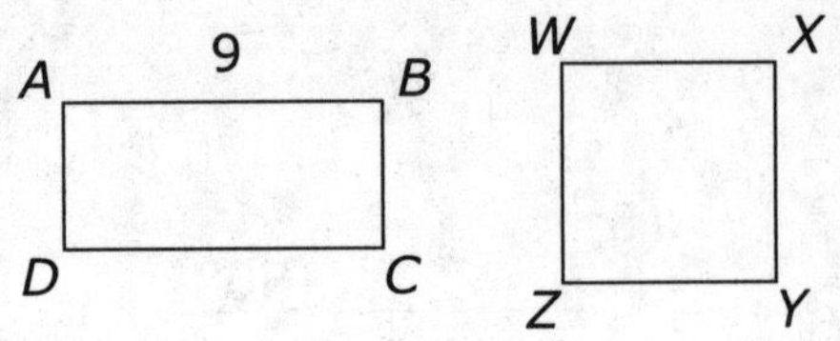

1. If rectangle *ABCD* has a perimeter of 26 and an area equal to that of square *WXYZ*, what is the length of segment $\overline{XY}$?

   A. 4
   B. 6
   C. 13
   D. 36

Here's How to Crack It

First, get clear on what the question is asking: the length of segment *XY* is the side length of the square *WXYZ*. Since opposite sides in a rectangle are equal, side $\overline{DC}$ is also 9. Sides $\overline{AD}$ and $\overline{BC}$ are still unknown, but they must be equal, so call their length *x*. Since the perimeter is the sum of the lengths of the sides and the perimeter of *ABCD* is 26, then $9 + 9 + x + x = 26$. Simplify the left side to get $18 + 2x = 26$. Subtract 18 from both sides to get $2x = 8$. Divide both sides by 2 to get $x = 4$. Now that you know the length and width of the rectangle, you can find its area, which will help you because the question says that the areas of the rectangle and the square are equal. The area of a rectangle is $A = lw$. Since the length and width are 9 and 4, respectively, $A = (9)(4) = 36$. Thus, *WXYZ* also has an area of 36. In the case of a square, since all four sides are equal, use the simplified version of $A = lw$, which is $A = s^2$. In this case, since the area of the square is 36, $36 = s^2$. Take the square root of both sides to get $6 = s$. The question asks for the length of segment $\overline{XY}$, which is one of the sides of the square, so its length is 6. The correct answer is (B).

While area is always a two-dimensional measurement of flat objects on a page, volume is a three-dimensional measurement. Imagine a square metal lunch box. The volume of the box would represent how much space there is inside.

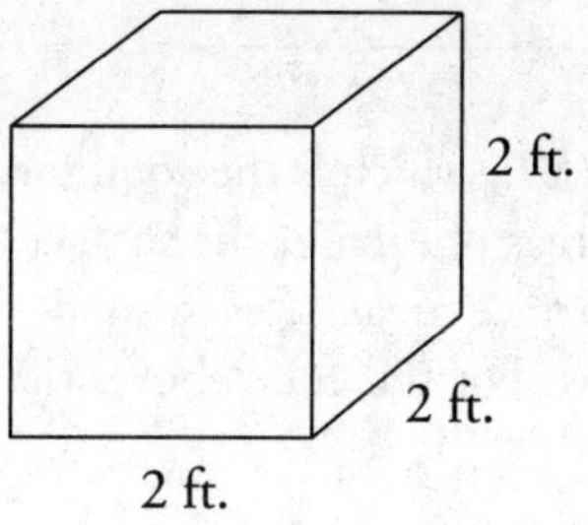

A cube

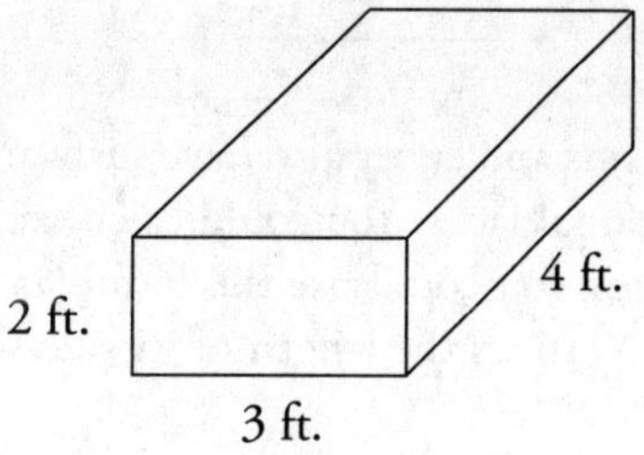

A rectangular prism

Both images shown above are rectangular prisms. A cube, however, is a specific type of rectangular prism for which all three measurements (length, width, and height) are the same.

To find the volume of any rectangular prism, use this formula: length × width × height. For the rectangular prism shown above on the right, the volume is 2 × 3 × 4, or 24 cubic feet.

To find the volume of a cube, you can either use that same formula or you can simply cube the length of one side, since all three measurements are the same. (If you remember, the area of a square is the length of its side squared.) For the cube on the left, the volume is 2^3, or 8 cubic feet.

Here's how this might look on the Mathematical Reasoning test:

2. If Maya wants to fill a rectangular pool with water, approximately how many cubic feet of water will she need if the pool's dimensions are 10 feet wide by 12 feet long by 5 feet deep?

   A. 1,200
   B. 600
   C. 300
   D. 150

Here's How to Crack It

The key words in this problem are *volume* and *rectangular.* As soon as you see these words, you should know just what to do. The volume of a rectangular solid is length × width × height. In this case, that means 12 × 10 × 5 = 600. The correct answer is (B).

Rectangular prisms and cubes also have surface area (*SA*), which is the combined areas of all of the two-dimensional faces. You could calculate the areas of each of the six faces, and then add all six together, or you could use the formulas for surface areas of each solid. For a cube, the formula is *SA* = 6 times the length of its side squared. For the cube above, the surface area is 6×2^2, or 24 square feet.

For a rectangular prism, the surface area is 2 times the length × width, plus 2 times the length × height, plus 2 times the width × height. For the rectangular prism above, that would give us (2 × 2 × 3) + (2 × 3 × 4) + (2 × 2 × 4) = 12 + 24 + 16, or 52 square feet.

Let's look at how you might apply surface area in an example:

A gift is wrapped in a rectangular box. The dimensions of the box are 4 inches high, 10 inches long, and 8 inches wide. What is the surface area of the box?

First, get clear on what values you know from the problem: $h = 4$, $l = 10$, $w = 8$.

Now we can plug these values in place of the variables in the formula for surface area of a rectangular prism:

$SA = 2(lw) + 2(wh) + 2(lh)$

$= 2(10)(8) + 2(8)(4) + 2(10)(4)$

$= 2(80) + 2(32) + 2(40)$

$= 160 + 64 + 80$

= 304 square inches

Suppose you are *given* the volume or surface area, and you need to find a missing dimension. In a problem like this, you would just work backward. Let's say you know a cube has a volume of 64 cubic inches. What is its side length? Take the volume, which is s^3, and find its cube root: $\sqrt[3]{64} = 4$ because 4 × 4 × 4 = 64. Your answer would be 4 inches.

Let's try a different one:

The surface area of a rectangular prism is 400 square yards. Its length is 15 yards and its height is 5 yards. What is its width?

Work backward from the formula for surface area of a rectangular prism; plug in the values you know from the problem, and then solve for w (width).

$SA = 2lw + 2wh + 2lh$

Substitute what you know: $SA = 400$, $l = 15$, $h = 5$

$400 = 2(15)w + 2w(5) + 2(15)(5)$

$400 = 30w + 10w + 150$

$400 = 40w + 150$

$250 = 40w$

$w = 6.25$ yards

Let's try a volume problem as a multiple-choice question:

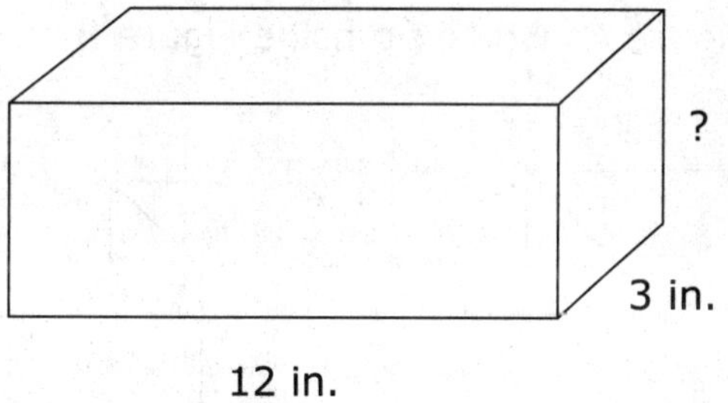

3. If the volume of this box is 252 cubic inches, what is its height?

A. 2
B. 7
C. 8
D. 12

Here's How to Crack It

You can rule out answers just by looking at the figure in this one (2 and 12 are too small and too large, respectively, to make any sense), and then test the two remaining answers to see whether they work in the volume formula to get 252. Because 12 × 7 × 3 does equal 252, you have found your answer, (B).

Square Rectangle Quiz

A: A square is always a rectangle. But a rectangle doesn't have to be a square.

Rectangles and Squares Drill

You can check your answers in Part IX: Answer Key to Drills.

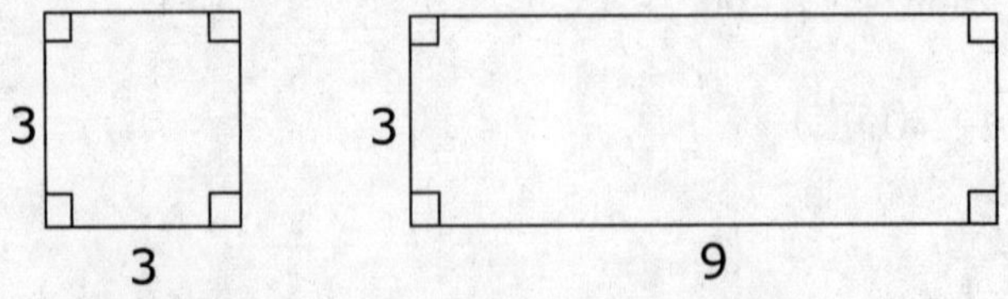

Figure A Figure B

Answer questions 1–5 based on the two figures above.

1. Identify Figure A.
2. Identify Figure B.
3. What is the area of Figure A?
4. What is the perimeter of Figure B?
5. How many Figure As would fit inside Figure B?

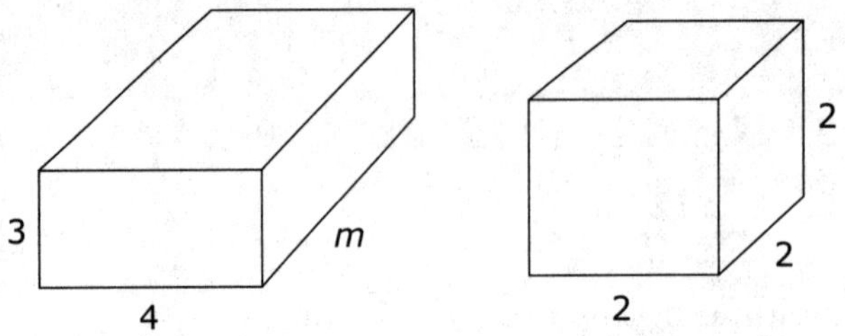

Figure A Figure B

Answer questions 6 and 7 based on the two figures above.

6. If the volume of Figure A is 60 cubic feet, then what is the length of segment *m*?
7. Figure B is a tank in the shape of a cube. If this tank is to be filled halfway to capacity, how many cubic units will be in the tank?

8. Chen plans to wallpaper a rectangular room with the dimensions 10 feet by 12 feet by 9 feet high. If there are no windows, and only one door measuring 2 feet by 7 feet, and she does not wallpaper the ceiling or floor, approximately how much will it cost to wallpaper the room?

   A. $395
   B. $400
   C. $412
   D. Not enough information is given.

TRIANGLES AND PYRAMIDS

A **triangle** is a geometric figure with three sides. The three angles inside a triangle always add up to 180 degrees, no matter how the triangle is drawn.

Triangle Facts

- The number of degrees in a triangle always adds up to 180°.
- An isosceles triangle has two equal sides and two equal angles.
- An equilateral triangle has three equal sides and three equal angles.

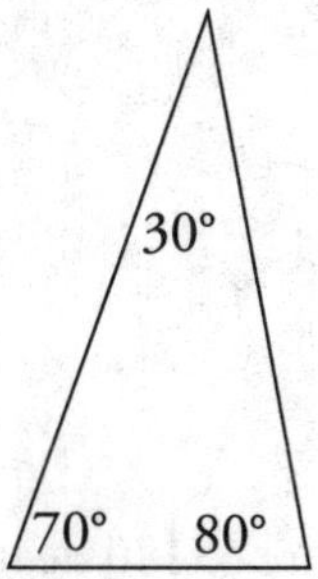

Triangle A

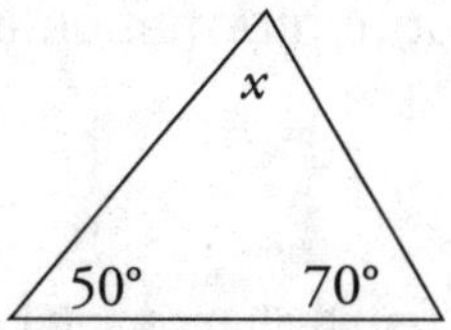

Triangle B

In triangle A, if you add up the measures of the three angles, you will notice that they add up to a total of 180 degrees. In triangle B, in order for the same thing to be true, how many degrees does the measure of angle x have to be? To find this out, add up the measures of the other two angles ($50 + 70 = 120$), and then subtract this from 180 ($180 - 120 = 60$).

Let's see how this would look on the GED® test.

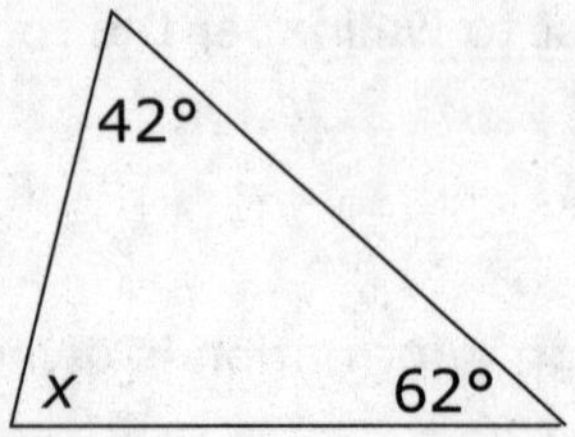

1. In the figure above, the triangle has three internal angles. One angle measures 42 degrees. Another angle measures 62 degrees. How many degrees does the third angle measure?

A. 104
B. 76
C. 52
D. Not enough information is given.

Here's How to Crack It

The three interior angles of *every* triangle have a total measure of 180 degrees. If the GED® test writers give you the measures of two out of the three angles, then you can find the measure of the third. Add up the two measures whose values you know (42 + 62 = 104). Now, just subtract the sum of the two measures from 180 (180 – 104 = 76). The correct answer to this question is (B).

Could you have *ballparked*? Of course. Look at the angle with the missing measure in the figure. Is it greater than or less than 90 degrees? Obviously it's a bit less, so we can eliminate (A). Now, compare it with the 62-degree angle directly across from it. Is it larger or smaller than 62 degrees? Come to think of it, it's a little bit larger, isn't it? This lets us eliminate (C) as well.

The test writers have certain favorite triangles that they use over and over again on the tests. These are the **isosceles** triangle and the **right** triangle.

The Isosceles Triangle

There are two important things to know about an isosceles triangle: First, it has two equal sides; second, the angles opposite those sides turn out to be equal as well.

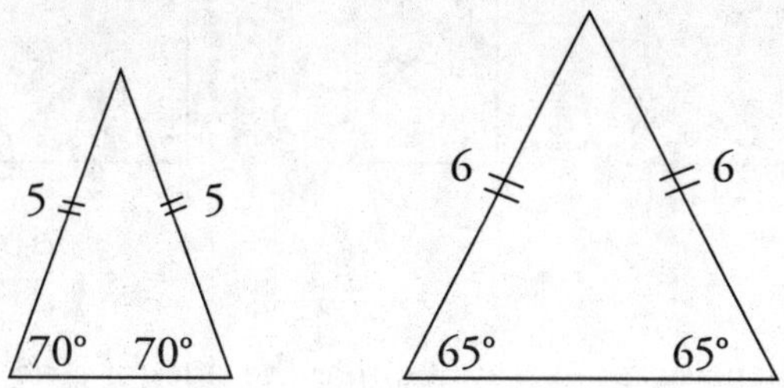

Generally, the test writers will tell you one of these two important things and then ask you to supply the other. Here's an example:

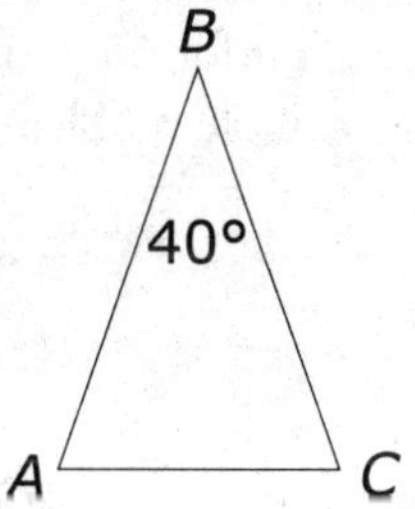

2. In the triangle above, if $AB = BC$, then what is the measure, in degrees, of angle A?

Here's How to Crack It

If the length of side AB equals the length of side BC, then the two angles opposite those sides (angles A and C) must have equal measures as well. Although the problem doesn't mention it, this is in fact an isosceles triangle because of its two equal sides. First, find out the value of angle A's measure plus angle C's measure. The entire triangle has 180 degrees in it. If you subtract the measure of angle B (40 degrees) from the total measure of the triangle's angles, that leaves 140 degrees. Now, remember that the measures of angle A and angle C are equal to each other. How do you get the measure of angle A alone? Divide by 2. The correct answer to this question is 70 degrees.

The Right Triangle

A right triangle contains one angle that measures 90 degrees.

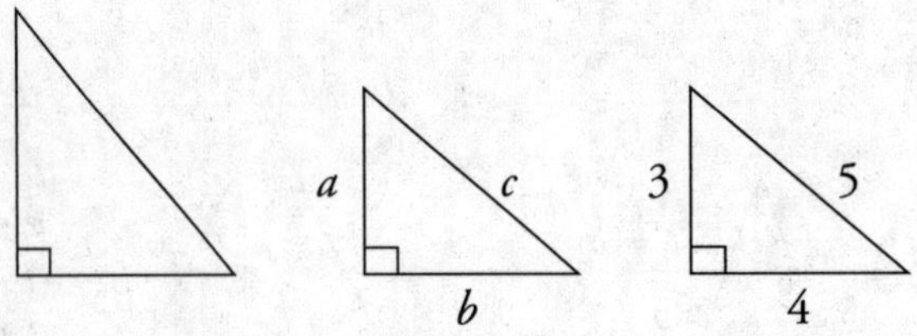

Pythagoras, a Greek mathematician, discovered that the sides of a right triangle always have a particular relationship, which can be expressed by the formula $a^2 + b^2 = c^2$, in which a and b are the lengths of the two shorter sides of the triangle, and c is the length of the longest side, opposite the 90-degree angle. This longest side is called the **hypotenuse**.

The most common right triangle on the Mathematical Reasoning test is a triangle whose side lengths are in a ratio of 3-4-5 (shown above). Let's see whether Pythagoras knew what he was talking about, by trying out his theorem with the 3-4-5 triangle. According to the formula, $3^2 + 4^2$ should equal 5^2. Does it? Yes! 9 + 16 does equal 25. The Pythagorean formula is provided on the Mathematical Reasoning test along with all the other formulas, and you may need it for other right triangles. But you won't need it for the writers' favorite, the 3-4-5 triangle, since that one you can just remember. Here's a sample problem:

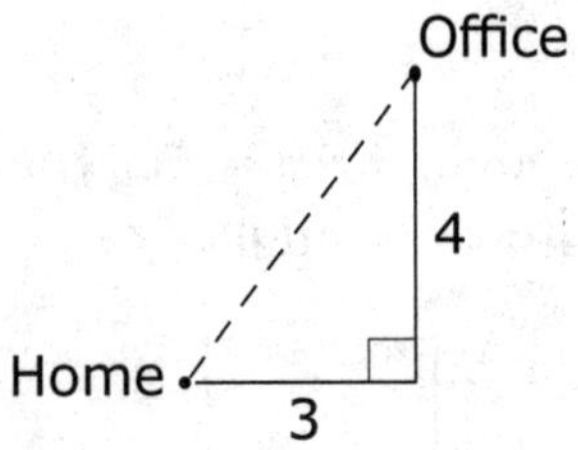

3. To get to her office, Joohee must drive due east for 3 miles and then due north for 4 miles, as shown in the figure above. If she could drive directly from her home to her office, how many miles would that route be if Joohee traveled in a straight line?

   A. 2
   B. 3
   C. 5
   D. 6

Here's How to Crack It

The shortcut from her office to her home forms the hypotenuse of a right triangle, as the diagram shows. One side of the triangle is 3; the other side is 4. Do you need to plug these numbers into the Pythagorean Theorem? Not if you memorized the 3-4-5 triangle. The correct answer to this question is (C).

The Perimeter of a Triangle

The perimeter is the distance around the outside edge of any two-dimensional object. The perimeter of a triangle is the sum of the lengths of the three sides. What was the perimeter of the triangle in that last problem? 3 + 4 + 5 = 12.

The Area of a Triangle

The formula for the area of a triangle is

$$\frac{1}{2}(\text{base} \times \text{height}) \text{ or } \frac{(\text{base} \times \text{height})}{2}$$

where the base equals the length of the bottom side of the triangle, and the height equals the length of a perpendicular segment from the base of the triangle to the triangle's highest point.

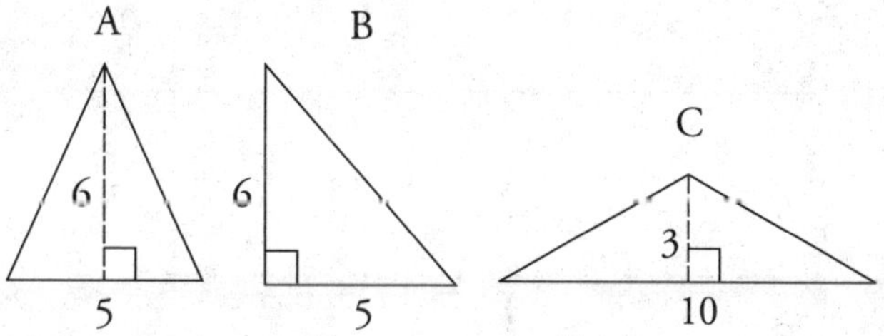

- In triangle A, the base equals 5, and the height equals 6, so the area is $\frac{1}{2}(5 \times 6)$, or 15.
- In triangle B, the base and height again equal 5 and 6, and the area of the triangle is again 15. However, note that because this is a right triangle, the height in this case is also the side of the triangle.
- In triangle C, the base equals 10, and the height equals 3, so the area is $\frac{1}{2}(10 \times 3)$, or 15.

Triangle Quiz
Q: What's the area of a triangle with base 3 and height 6?

Turn the page for the answer.

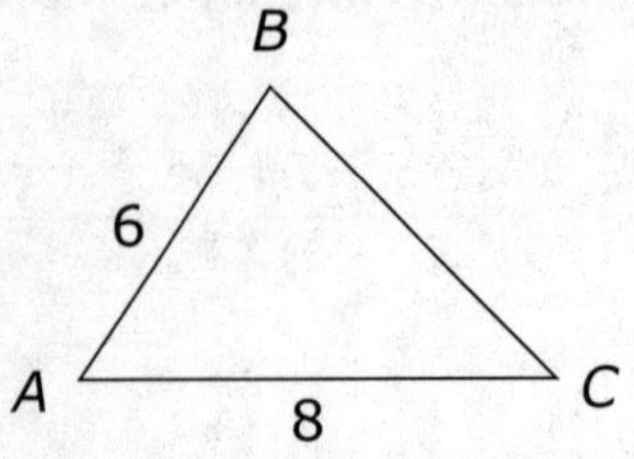

4. What is the area of the triangle above?

A. 7
B. 24
C. 48
D. Not enough information is given.

Here's How to Crack It

To find the area of a triangle, you need the base and the height. In this triangle, you know the base (8) but not the height. The number 6 is simply the length of one of the other sides of this triangle and would have been the height only if this were a right triangle with angle *A* equal to 90 degrees. Therefore, the correct answer to this question is (D), Not enough information is given.

Let's look at another one.

5. If a triangle has an area of 24 and a height of 8, what is the length of the base?

A. 1.5
B. 3
C. 6
D. 12

Here's How to Crack It

The question gives the area of a triangle. The formula for area of a triangle is $A = \frac{1}{2}bh$. The question states that the area is 24 and the height is 8, so plug these into the formula to get $24 = \frac{1}{2}b(8)$. Simplify the right side (by multiplying $\frac{1}{2} \times 8$) to get $24 = 4b$. Divide both sides by 4 to get $b = 6$. The correct answer is (C).

Pyramids

A **pyramid** is a three-dimensional shape made of triangular sides that sit atop a two-dimensional base. On the GED® test, this base will typically be a rectangle, so there will be four triangular sides.

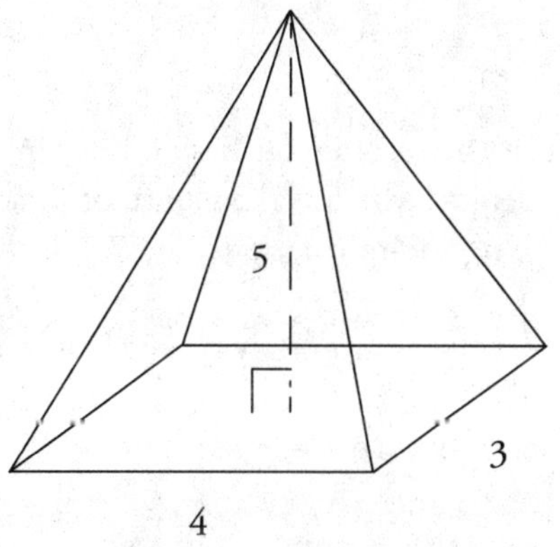

To find the volume of a pyramid, you must first find the area of the rectangular base, B, and the height, h, from the base to the top of the pyramid. The volume is the amount of space *inside* the shape. The formula for the volume of a pyramid is

$$V = \frac{1}{3}Bh$$

In the above example, the volume would be

$$V = \frac{1}{3}(3 \times 4)(5) = 20.$$

The area of the base, B, is $3 \times 4 = 12$. After that point, simply plug in values for the variables in the equation.

Triangle Quiz

A: $\frac{1}{2}(3 \times 6) = 9$

To find the surface area (*SA*), you will need the perimeter, *p*, of the base, and the slant height, *s* (the distance from the base to the apex along a lateral face) of a side of the pyramid. The surface area essentially adds up the areas of each face of the pyramid, including the base, *B*.

$$SA = \frac{1}{2}ps + B$$

Again, let's try this formula out with an example:

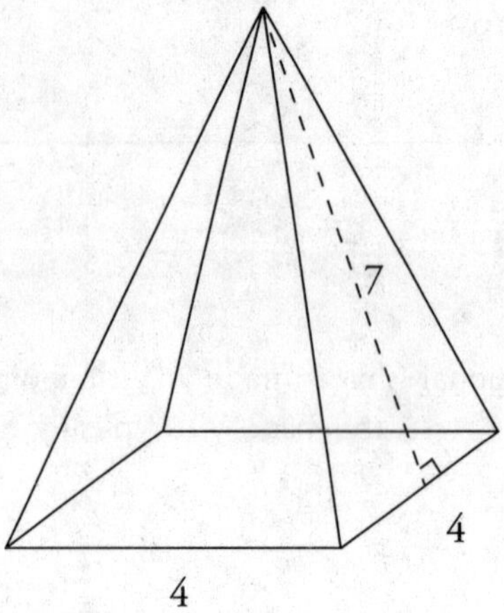

First, let's find *p*, the perimeter of the rectangular base, by adding up its 4 sides: 4 + 4 + 4 + 4 = 16. We also know *s*, the slant height, which is the length of the dotted line segment going up the side face from the base to the top point (the apex): *s* = 7.

Finding *B* (the area of base) is as simple as multiplying the length and width of the rectangle:

$$4 \times 4 = 16$$

So now we can plug these values into the formula as follows:

$$SA = \frac{1}{2}(16)(7) + (4 \times 4)$$

$$SA = 56 + 16 = 72$$

Don't worry about memorizing these formulas—they will be provided to you on the formulas page when you take the GED® test. Just familiarize yourself with them so that you know how to use them.

Triangles and Pyramids Drill

You can check your answers in Part IX: Answer Key to Drills.

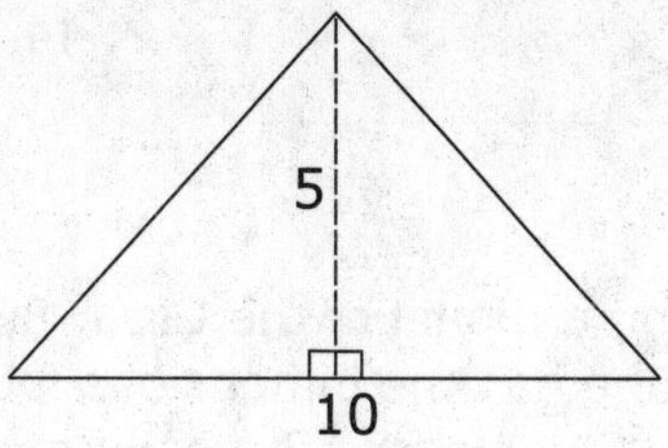

1. Marcus is constructing a triangular garden as shown above. If the base of the garden is 10 feet long and the perpendicular distance from the base to the top corner of the garden is 5 feet, then what is the area of the garden, in square feet?

   A. 50
   B. 25
   C. 15
   D. Not enough information is given.

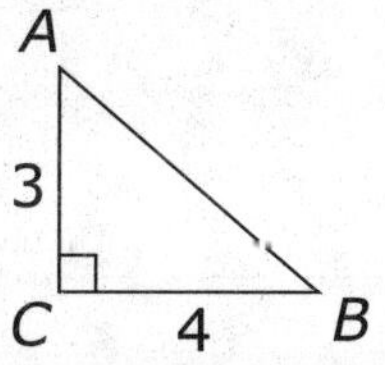

2. The distance from point *A* to point *B* is how much longer than the distance from point *A* to point *C*?

3. If a triangle has interior angles of 27 degrees and 53 degrees, then what is the measurement, in degrees, of the third angle?

   A. 26
   B. 80
   C. 100
   D. 154

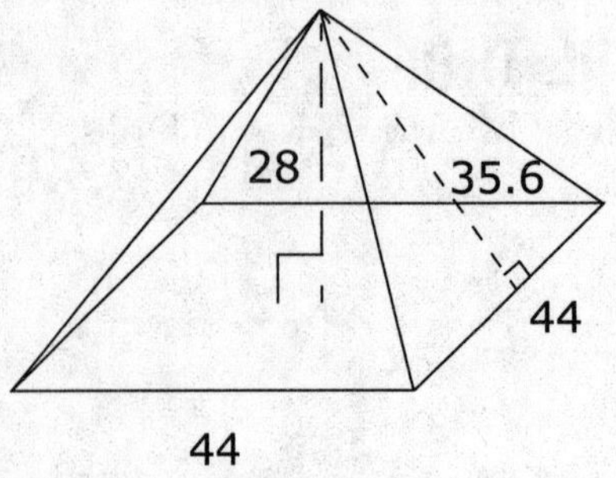

4. Sara is making a model of the Great Pyramid for math class. She has the dimensions labeled on the drawing above, in inches. The paint she plans to use on the outside of the model says that 1 can will cover 1,296 square inches. How many cans will Sara need to paint all the surfaces of her model pyramid?

A. 1
B. 2
C. 3
D. 4

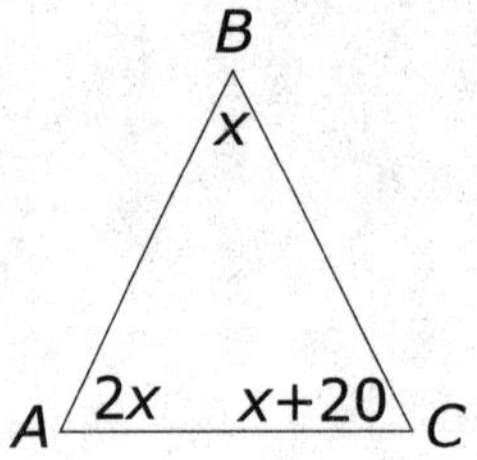

5. In triangle *ABC* above, the measures of the angles are shown in terms of *x*. What is the measure, in degrees, of angle *A*?

A. 40
B. 45
C. 70
D. 80

6. A pyramid with a square base has a volume of 320 and a height of 15. What is the perimeter of the base?

A. 8
B. 16
C. 32
D. 64

OTHER POLYGONS

A polygon is a closed figure made up of line segments. Squares, rectangles, and triangles are all examples of polygons. Although those are the most common types of polygons on the GED® test, other polygons will also appear on the test. Pentagons (five-sided polygons), hexagons (six-sided polygons), heptagons (seven-sided polygons), octagons (eight-sided polygons), and other polygons can appear on the GED® test. A **regular polygon** is one in which the lengths of all sides are equal, and the measures of all angles are equal. Squares and equilateral triangles are examples of regular polygons.

One concept tested on other polygons is perimeter. Luckily, determining perimeter on less common polygons is not very different from determining perimeter on the more common ones. Either way, the perimeter is just the sum of the lengths of the sides. Let's look at an example.

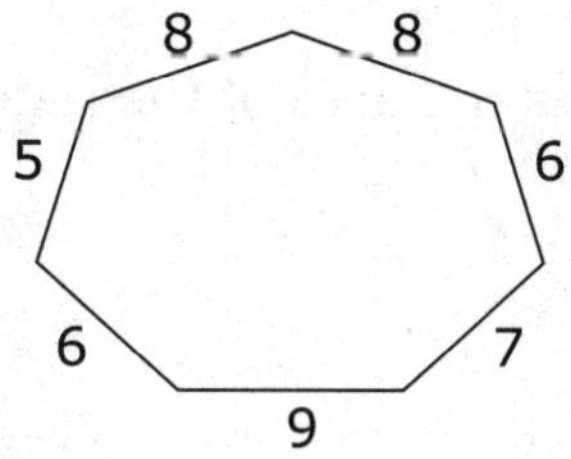

1. What is the perimeter of the polygon above?

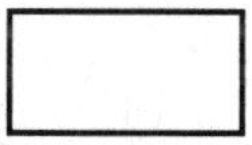

Here's How to Crack It

To find the perimeter, add the length of each of the sides. In this case, the perimeter is 8 + 8 + 6 + 7 + 9 + 6 + 5 = 49. The correct answer is 49.

Other times, you may need to find the area. At such times, you will be provided with the area formula.

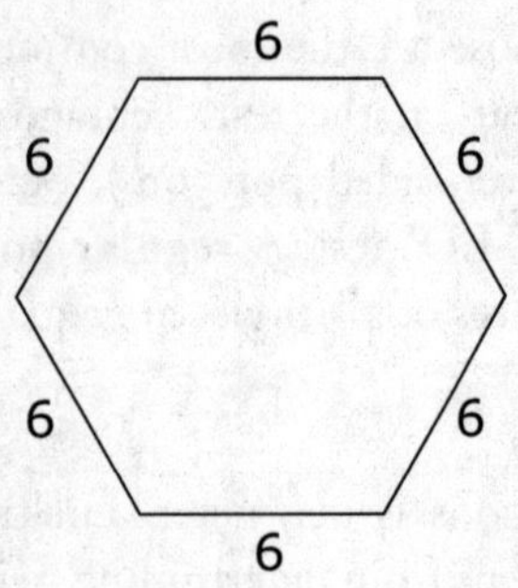

2. The area of a regular hexagon can be found with the formula $A = \frac{3\sqrt{3}}{2}s^2$, where s is the length of the side. What is the area of the regular hexagon shown above?

A. $18\sqrt{3}$
B. $27\sqrt{3}$
C. $54\sqrt{3}$
D. $108\sqrt{3}$

Here's How to Crack It

The question gives a formula for the volume in terms of the side of the hexagon. The figure gives you that the side is 6, so plug this in for s to get $A = \frac{3\sqrt{3}}{2}(6)^2 = \frac{3\sqrt{3}}{2}(36) = \frac{108\sqrt{3}}{2} = 54\sqrt{3}$.

The correct answer is (C).

Other Polygons Drill

You can check your answers in Part IX: Answer Key to Drills.

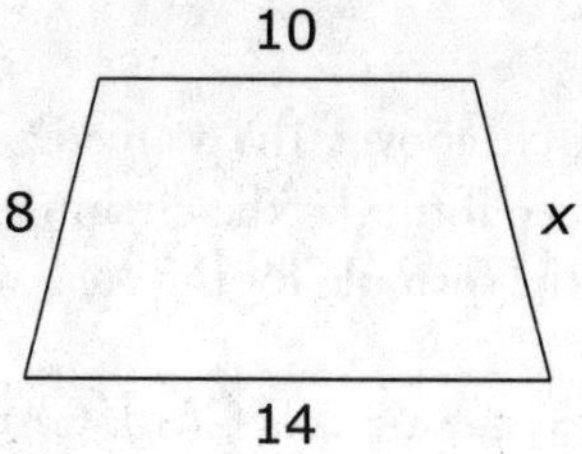

1. The figure above has a perimeter of 40. What is the value of x ?

   A. 4
   B. 8
   C. 16
   D. 72

2. A regular octagon has a perimeter of 56. If the area of a regular octagon can be found using the formula $A = 2\left(1+\sqrt{2}\right)s^2$, where s is the length of the side of the octagon, what is the area of the octagon?

   A. $49 + 49\sqrt{2}$
   B. $98 + 49\sqrt{2}$
   C. $49 + 98\sqrt{2}$
   D. $98 + 98\sqrt{2}$

CIRCLES, SPHERES, CYLINDERS, AND CONES

The distance from the center of a circle to any point on the circle is called the **radius.** The distance from one side of a circle through the center of the circle to the other side is called the **diameter.** The diameter of a circle is always equal to twice the radius. In the circle below, the radius is equal to 3, so the diameter is 2 × 3, or 6.

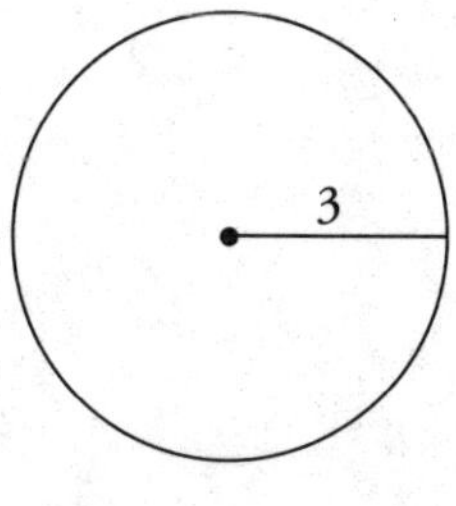

The **circumference** of a circle is the distance all the way around the outside edge of the circle. In other words, circumference is the name for a circle's perimeter. The formula for the circumference of a circle is πd, where d is the diameter of the circle, and π is a number with the approximate value of 3.14, or 22/7. A long time ago, mathematicians discovered that this number, when multiplied by the diameter, gave the value for a circle's circumference. The area of a circle is given by the formula πr^2.

What is the circumference of the circle above? The diameter of this circle is twice the radius, or 6. Therefore, using the circumference formula, the circumference of this circle is 6π. What is the area of the circle above? Using the formula for the area, we get $\pi 3^2$, or 9π.

One concept that is helpful on circle questions is CArd. CArd stands for Circumference, Area, radius, and diameter. If you know of one these, you can determine the other three. Look at the table below. In each row, there is one piece of the CArd puzzle. Fill in the other three.

Circumference	Area	radius	diameter
πd	πr^2	$\frac{d}{2}$	$2r$

C	***A***	***r***	***d***
		4	
	25π		
12π			
			18
		1	
π			

In the first row, $r = 4$. Therefore, $d = 2r = 8$, $C = \pi d = 8\pi$, and $A = \pi r^2 = 16\pi$.

In the second row, $A = 25\pi$. Since $A = \pi r^2$, $r = 5$, $d = 2r = 10$, and $C = \pi d = 10\pi$.

In the third row, $C = 12\pi$. Since $C = \pi d$, $d = 12$, $r = \frac{d}{2} = 6$, and $A = \pi r^2 = 36\pi$.

In the fourth row, $d = 18$. Therefore, $C = \pi d = 18\pi$, $r = \frac{d}{2} = 9$, and $A = \pi r^2 = 81\pi$.

In the fifth row, $r = 1$, so $d = 2r = 2$, $C = \pi d = 2\pi$, and $A = \pi r^2 = \pi$. (Remember that $1^2 = 1$ and $1\pi = \pi$.)

In the last row, $C = \pi$. Since $C = \pi d$, $d = 1$, $r = \frac{d}{2} = \frac{1}{2}$, and $A = \pi r^2 = \pi\left(\frac{1}{2}\right)^2 = \frac{1}{4}\pi = \frac{\pi}{4}$.

With more practice, you'll be able to fill out CArd nearly instantaneously. Therefore, it can be a good habit to fill it out as routine anytime you're given one piece of CArd. You won't always need all four pieces. However, it will often take longer to figure which pieces you need than it will take you to figure out all four pieces. CArd can actually be a time-saver in the long run!

Spheres

Many objects, such as basketballs and baseballs, are spherical.

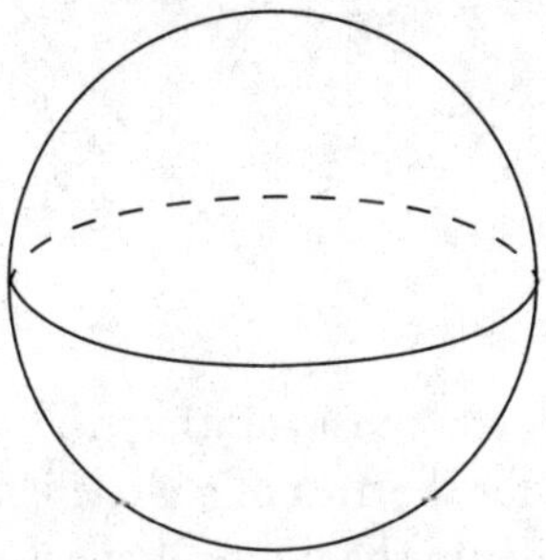

A **sphere** has a radius, r, and a diameter just like a circle. To find the volume of a sphere, use this formula (which is also provided on the formula page when you take the GED® test):

$$V = \frac{4}{3}\pi r^3$$

To find the surface area of a sphere, use this formula:

$$SA = 4\pi r^2$$

You need only the radius in order to find both the volume and the surface area.

Let's apply these formulas to find the volume and surface area of the sphere described below:

A globe has a diameter of 30 centimeters.

First, remember that you need the radius of a sphere to calculate volume and surface area, so you will be working with half the diameter: $r = 15$ cm.

Volume: $V = \frac{4}{3}\pi(15)^3 \approx (1.33)(3.14)(3{,}375) \approx 14{,}094.675 \text{ cm}^3$

Surface area: $SA = 4\pi(15)^2 \approx 4(3.14)(225) \approx 2{,}826 \text{ cm}^2$

Cylinders

A cylinder is essentially a circle with a third dimension (height or depth). Take a look at the following figure:

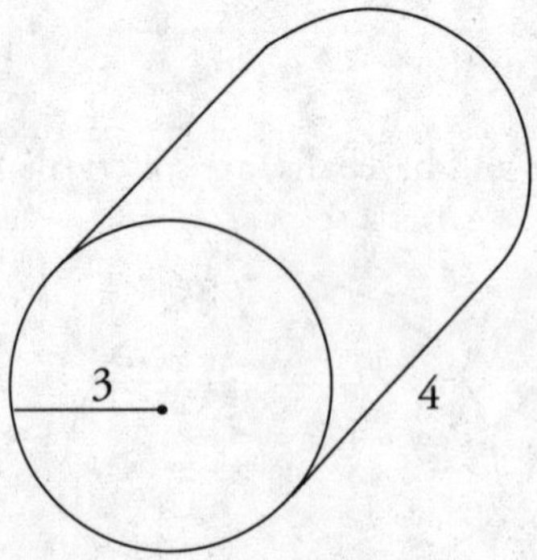

To find the volume of any cylinder, you must multiply the area of the circle at one end of the cylinder by its height. The formula for the area of a circle is πr^2. So the volume of a cylinder is $\pi r^2 h$. Thus, the volume of the cylinder in the figure above is $\pi 3^2(4)$, or 36π.

The surface area of a cylinder can be found by taking $2\pi rh + 2\pi r^2$. In the example above, the surface area would be 42π.

Again, all of these equations are provided to you on the formulas page when you take the test.

Cones

A **cone** has a circular base that has a radius, r. The height, h, is measured from the center of the circle to the tip of the cone.

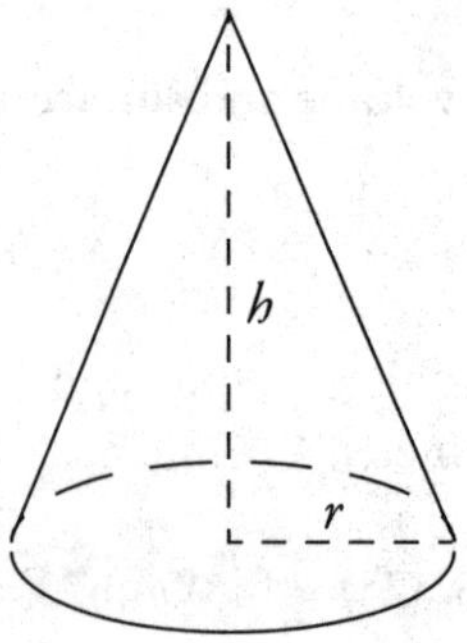

The volume of a cone can be found by using this formula:

$$V = \frac{1}{3}\pi r^2 h$$

And the formula for surface area looks like this:

$$SA = \pi rs + \pi r^2$$

where s is the slant height, or the length from the outer edge of the base to the tip of the cone.

Practice applying the formulas by calculating the volume and the surface area of the cone below. Be careful when choosing the height (*h*) and the slant height (*s*)!

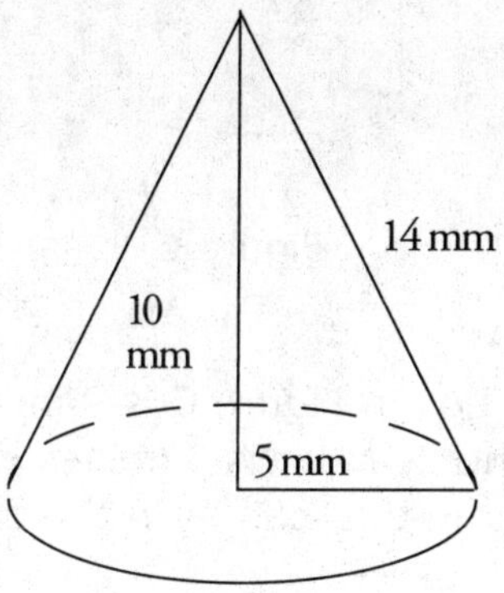

Volume: $\frac{1}{3}\pi(5)^2(10) = \frac{1}{3}\pi(250) \approx 83.3\pi \approx 261.7 \text{ mm}^3$

Surface Area: $\pi(5)(14) + \pi(5)^2 = 70\pi + 25\pi = 95\pi \approx 298.3 \text{ mm}^2$

Circles, Spheres, Cylinders, and Cones Drill

You can check your answers in Part IX: Answer Key to Drills.

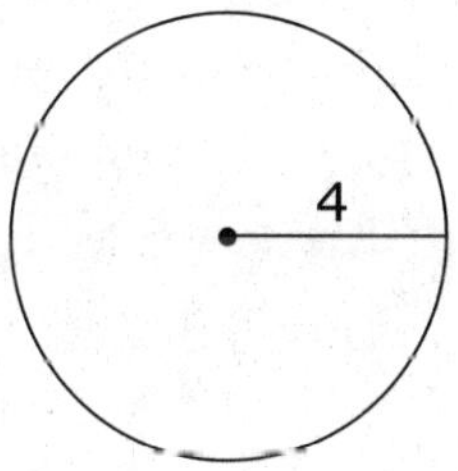

Using the figure above, answer the following questions.

1. What is the radius of this circle?
2. What is the diameter?
3. What is the circumference of this circle?
4. What is the area of this circle?

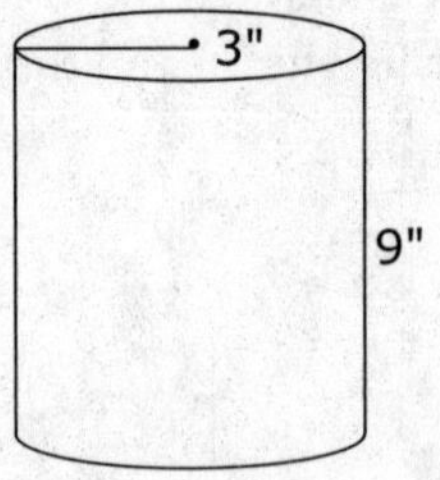

Figure C

5. The cylindrical box in Figure C is 9 inches tall. If the radius of the cylinder is 3 inches, what is the maximum volume that can fit in the box?

6. The diameter of a rubber ball is 4 inches. What is the total surface area of the ball?

A. 16π
B. 64π
C. 128π
D. 144π

7. If a cone has a volume of 100π and a circular base with an area of 25π, what is its height?

A. 4
B. 8
C. 12
D. 24

8. A sphere has a volume of 36π, what is the length of the diameter?

A. 3
B. 6
C. 9
D. 12

COMPOSITE 3-D FIGURES

Sometimes geometry problems combine 3-D objects into one composite figure. All you have to do is recognize the shapes that you know how to deal with, find the measurement you're asked to find for each one, and then add them together.

Take this example of a composite figure:

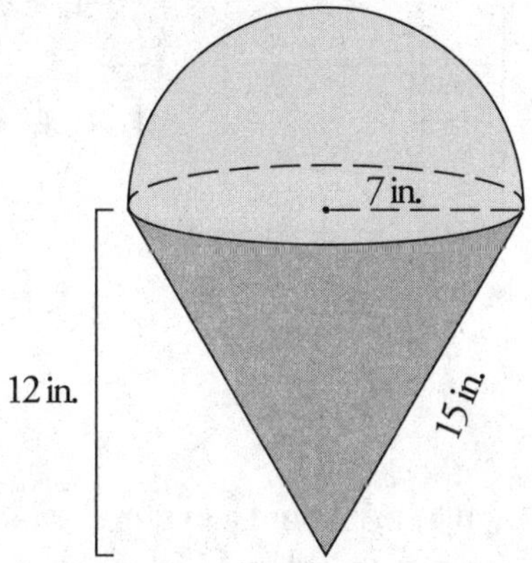

What shapes do you see combined here? One cone with a half sphere on top.

To find the volume of the composite figure, you would find the volume of each object, and then simply add them together.

Cone: $V = \frac{1}{3}\pi(7)^2(12) = 196\pi$

Sphere: $V = \frac{4}{3}\pi(7)^3 \approx 457.3\pi$

Half sphere $\approx 228.7\pi$

Cone + half sphere $\approx 196\pi + 228.7\pi = 424.7\pi = 424.7 \times 3.14$ or $\approx 1{,}333.56$ in.^{3}

For surface area, the approach is the same, but you need to look out for any surfaces that are shared between objects. Let's look at this example:

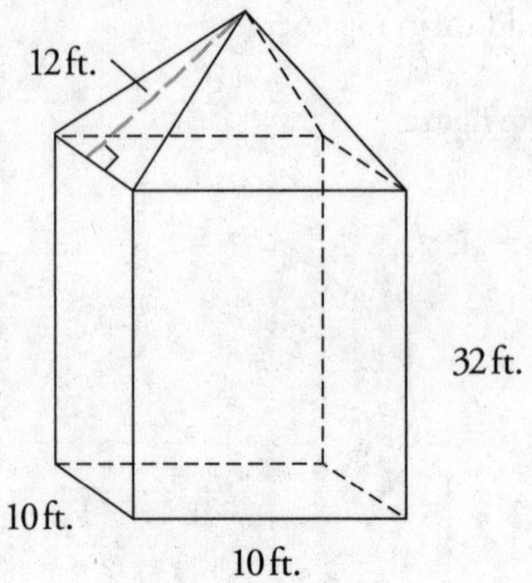

This figure is made up of a rectangular prism and a pyramid on top. If you work out the surface area formulas for each object separately, you would include the surface that they share between them twice. You would then have to remove this area twice because it is on the interior of the composite figure, not the surface. So in this case, it is actually easier to add up the areas of each surface of the figure:

4 Rectangular sides: $lw = (32)(10) = 320 \times 4 = 1{,}280$

1 Square base: $s^2 = 10^2 = 100$

4 Triangular sides: $\frac{1}{2}bh = \frac{1}{2}(10)(12) = 60 \times 4 = 240$

Surface area of composite figure = $1{,}280 + 100 + 240 = 1{,}620\ \text{ft}^2$

Let's try another composite figure in test problem format:

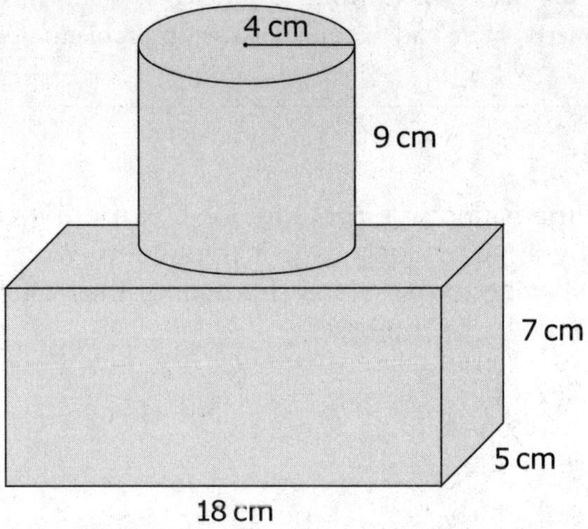

1. Which of the following represents the approximate volume, in cubic centimeters, of this figure?

   A. 22,680
   B. 1,082.16
   C. 527
   D. 780.72

Here's How to Crack It

Identify the shapes you know and get their formulas ready. Since this is volume, all you have to do is calculate the volume of the rectangular prism and the volume of the cylinder, and then add them together.

Rectangular prism: $V = lwh = (18)(5)(7) = 630$

Cylinder: $V = \pi r^2 h \approx (3.14)(4^2)(9) \approx 452.16$

Composite Figure: $630 + 452.16 \approx 1{,}082.16$ cm^3. The answer is (B).

SETUP GEOMETRY

A few GED® problems will ask you to set up a geometry problem but then not solve it. Just like the setup problems we saw in the Applied Arithmetic chapter—which tested the same arithmetic concepts as all the other arithmetic problems—setup geometry tests the same concepts as regular geometry. Here's an example of a setup problem:

1. The dimensions of a rectangular box are 3 inches wide by 4 inches long by 2 inches deep. Which of the following expressions represents the volume, in cubic inches, of the box?

   A. 3(2)(4)
   B. 3 + 2 + 4
   C. 3(2) + 4
   D. 3(4) + 2

Here's How to Crack It

Essentially, this is almost exactly the same problem you just saw before. The key words again are *volume* and *rectangular*. The only real difference is that this time the question does not ask you to find the volume, but to set up the work involved in finding the volume.

As we said in the "Applied Arithmetic" chapter, take your time with these problems. It's easy to pick an answer choice that is almost (but not quite) right. You need to multiply length by width by height. In this problem, that means $4 \times 3 \times 2$. The correct answer is (A).

GRAPHING

Graphing is a way of representing a point in two dimensions on what is known as a Cartesian grid or coordinate plane. This may sound intimidating, but it's actually pretty simple. Here's a Cartesian grid:

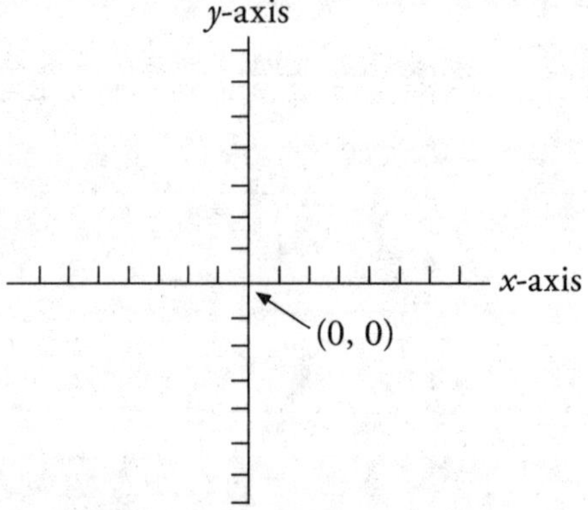

Graphing is a way of assigning points to this grid. Both the x-axis and the y-axis are number lines (as we discussed in Chapter 13) with positive and negative sides. These number lines cross at their zeros. Every point has two numbers assigned to it: an x-coordinate and a y-coordinate. Let's take the point A (3, 1). The first number is considered the x-coordinate. The second number is the y-coordinate. To plot this point on the graph, we start at (0, 0) and count over three to the right (the positive side) on the x-axis, and then count one up (the positive side of the y-axis). To find point B (5, 4), we count over five places to the right on the x-axis and then up four places.

Try plotting these two points on the graph above. Then, check your work by looking at the graph below.

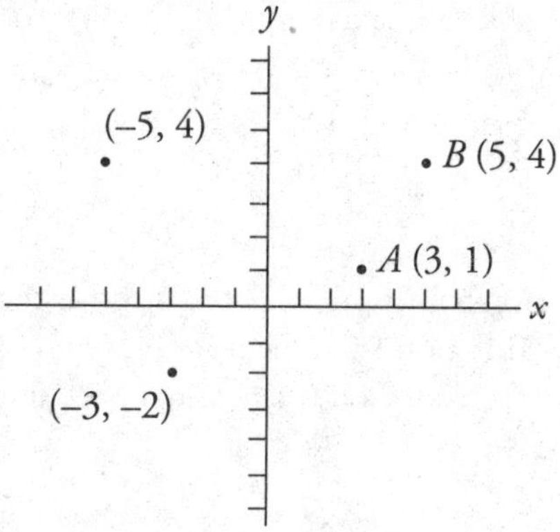

If the first number in an (x, y) point (in other words, the x-coordinate) is negative, then to graph this point, you count to the *left* along the x-axis. If the second number in an (x, y) point (in other words, the y-coordinate) is negative, then you count downward. Look at the graph above and see how points (–5, 4) and (–3, –2) were plotted.

GED® questions about graphing are fairly rare. There are three types of GED® graphing questions: questions in which you graph a point on the coordinate plane, questions about the slope of a line, and questions about the distance between two points.

Slope

The slope of a line tells you its slant—how sharply it is inclining or declining. To find the slope, you need to know two points anywhere on the line. The slope formula (which always appears on the formula page of the Mathematical Reasoning test) looks like this:

$$\textbf{Slope} = \frac{\text{change in } y}{\text{change in } x} = \frac{y_2 - y_1}{x_2 - x_1}$$

For example, to find the slope of a line that went through points (5, 6) and (3, 2), all you have to do is subtract one y-coordinate from the other (the result of this subtraction becomes your numerator—also sometimes known as the **rise**) and subtract one x-coordinate from the other (the result of this subtraction becomes your denominator—also known as the **run**):

$$\frac{6-2}{5-3}=\frac{4}{2}=2$$

Therefore, the slope of the line that goes through points (5, 6) and (3, 2) is 2.

Note that dividing $y_1 - y_2$ by $x_1 - x_2$ gives the same result as dividing $y_2 - y_1$ by $x_2 - x_1$ (try it using the above example). Just make sure to subtract the corresponding x- and y-values in the same order, and be careful not to mix up the coordinates of the first point (x_1, y_1) and the second point (x_2, y_2). Finally, make sure that you are finding the difference between ys (rise) and the difference between xs (run)!

Distance

To find the distance between two points on a Cartesian grid, there is a long formula that we think is *one* equation you shouldn't bother to memorize. It's too complicated, it comes up too rarely on the test, and besides, it's printed on the formula page of the test.

Just for practice, here it is:

$$\text{Distance between two points} = \sqrt{(x_2-x_1)^2+(y_2-y_1)^2}$$

where (x_1, y_1) and (x_2, y_2) are two points in a plane.

Let's find the distance between points (1, 2) and (5, 6). What we have to do is carefully plug these numbers into that long equation. Here's what it should look like:

$$\begin{aligned}&=\sqrt{(5-1)^2+(6-2)^2}\\&=\sqrt{4^2+4^2}\\&=\sqrt{32}\end{aligned}$$

You can see why this doesn't come up often.

When You're Given a Graph

Most of the graphing problems on the Mathematical Reasoning test concerning slope or distance will actually give you a graph to look at. This can be very helpful in Ballparking your answers. Take a look at the following question.

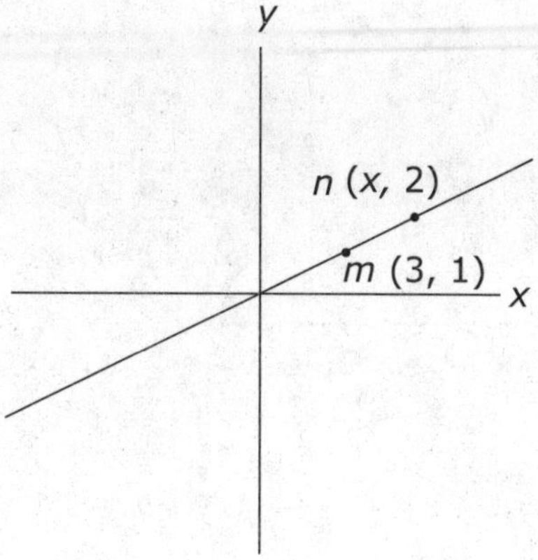

1. In the graph shown above, what is the x-coordinate of point n if the slope of the line mn is $\frac{1}{3}$?

A. 9
B. 6
C. 3
D. 2

Here's How to Crack It

First, let's get an idea of which answer choices are out of the ballpark. We are looking for the x-coordinate of point n. Well, before we start using complicated formulas, let's do a little measuring. The x-coordinate for point m is 3. This means that the horizontal distance from 0 to m is 3. Mark off this distance on your scratch paper. Now, try measuring the horizontal distance between 0 and point n. Did you get about 6? That's what we got. Because these figures are drawn only roughly to scale, we can't guarantee that the answer is going to be exactly 6, but it ought to be close to 6 anyway. So which answer choices can we get rid of? Choices (A), (C), and (D) are all out of the ballpark. The only possible answer this time is (B).

If you needed to get this one the traditional way, you would have to use the slope formula backward.

$$\text{Slope} = \frac{\text{change in } y}{\text{change in } x} \quad \frac{1}{3} = \frac{2-1}{x-3}$$

The correct answer is (B).

Graphing Drill

You can check your answers in Part IX: Answer Key to Drills.

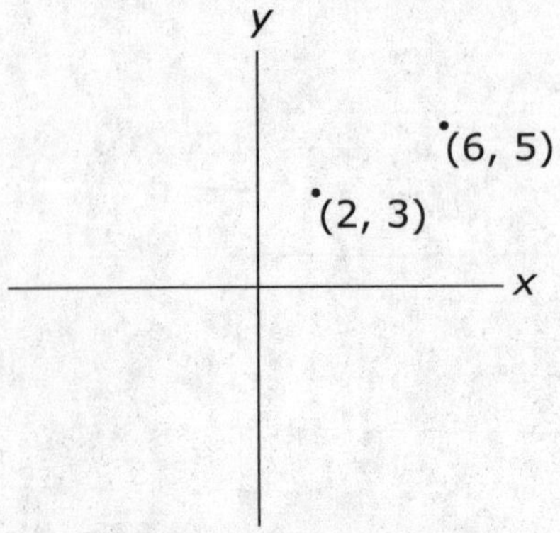

1. A line passes through the points (6, 5) and (2, 3). What is the slope of this line?

    A. $-\frac{1}{5}$

    B. $\frac{1}{4}$

    C. $\frac{1}{2}$

    D. 3

2. What is the distance between points (5, 0) and (12, 0) on the coordinate plane?

    A. 12
    B. 9
    C. 7
    D. 4

3. On the graph below, plot the following points:
Point *A* (–3, –4), Point *B* (2, 3), and Point *C* (3, 5).

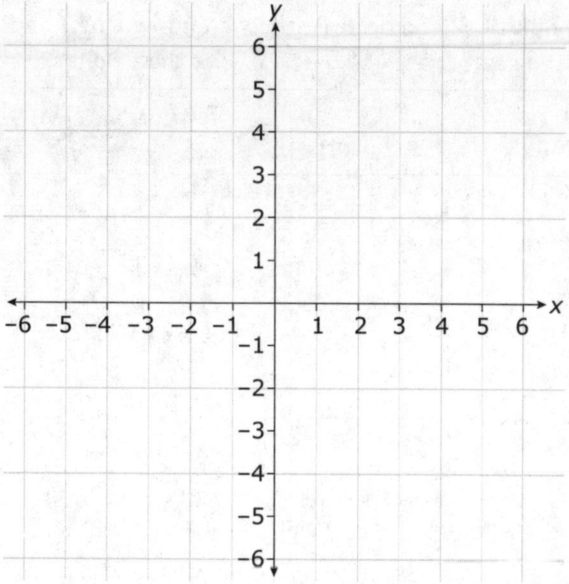

EQUATION OF A LINE

Sometimes the GED® test writers will give you an equation with two variables and ask you to graph a line representing the equation. The key is to get the equation into **slope-intercept** form

$$y = mx + b$$

in which m represents the slope and b represents the y-intercept. The y-intercept is the y-coordinate of the point on the line that crosses the y-axis and has an x-coordinate of 0. If you need to sketch a graph of the equation $y = 2x + 3$, start out with the y-intercept, 3. Since the y-intercept is 3, the graph includes the point (0, 3). Plot this on the graph as below.

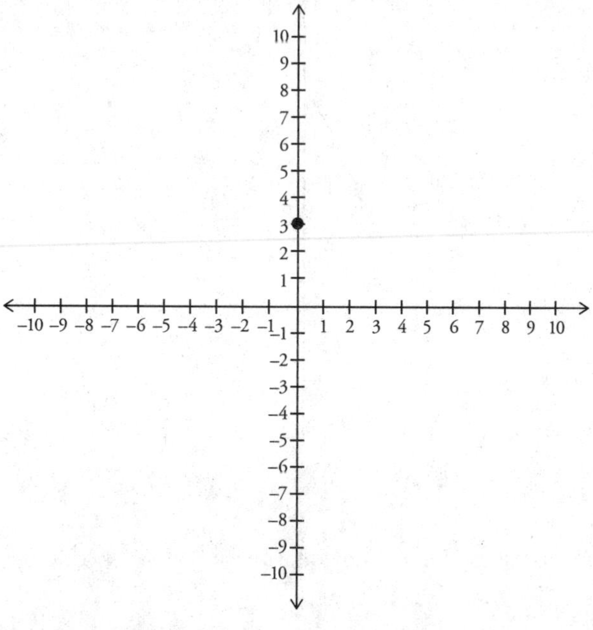

The slope is 2, so the y-coordinate increases by 2 as the x-coordinate increases by 1. Use this to plot additional points. Start with point (0, 3) and increase the x-coordinate by 1 and y-coordinate by 2 to get (1, 5). Do this again to get (2, 7) and (3, 9). Similarly, you can go backward. Go back to the point (0, 3) and decrease the x-coordinate by 1 and the y-coordinate by 2 to get (–1, 1) and again to get (–2, –1) and (–3, –3). Plot these points as well.

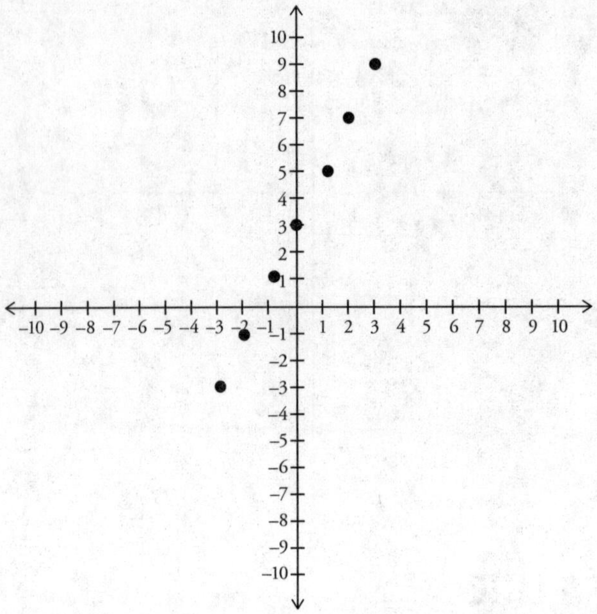

Finally, draw a line that goes through all these points as below.

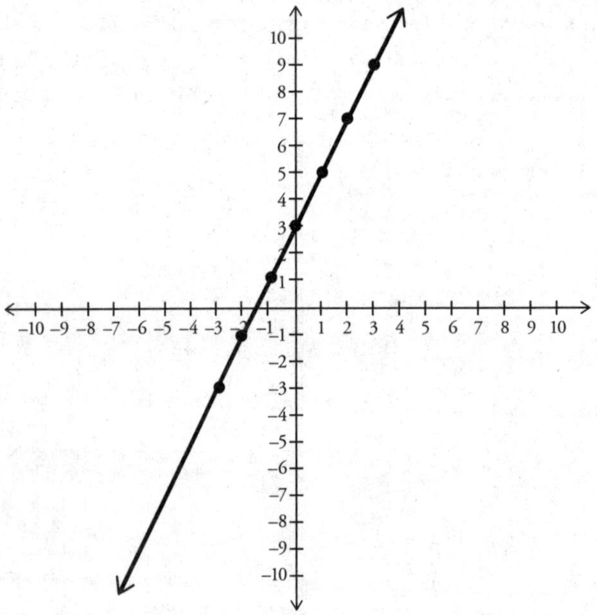

This line is a graphical representation of the equation. Try another one.

1. Which of the following represents the graph of the line $2x + 3y = 6$?

A.

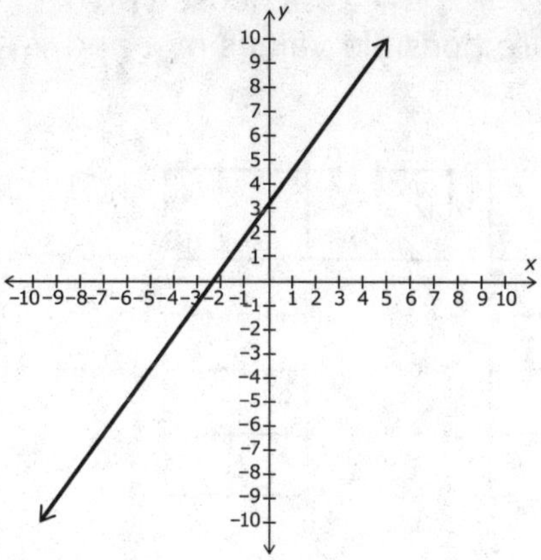

C.

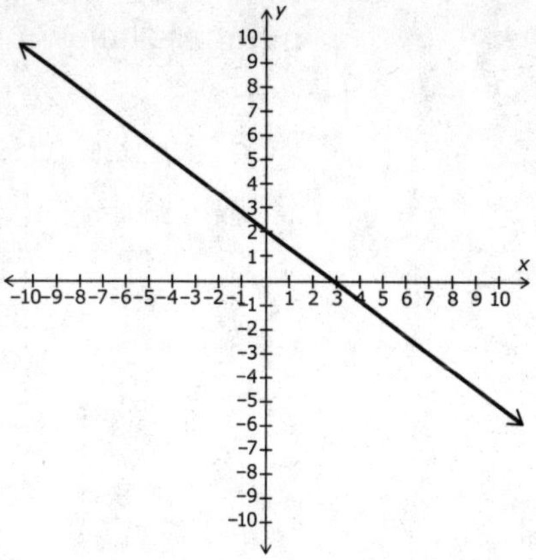

B.

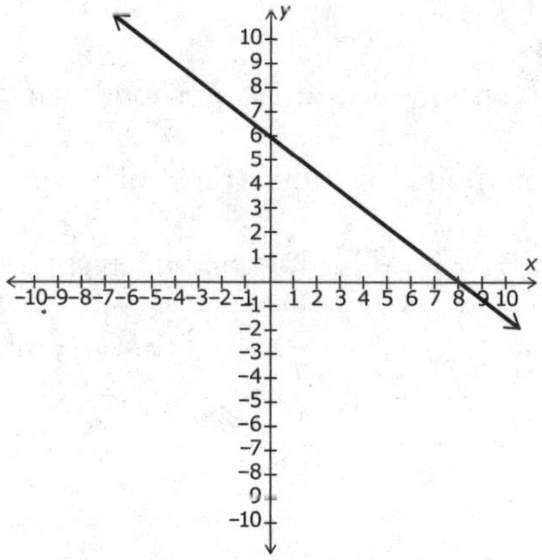

D.

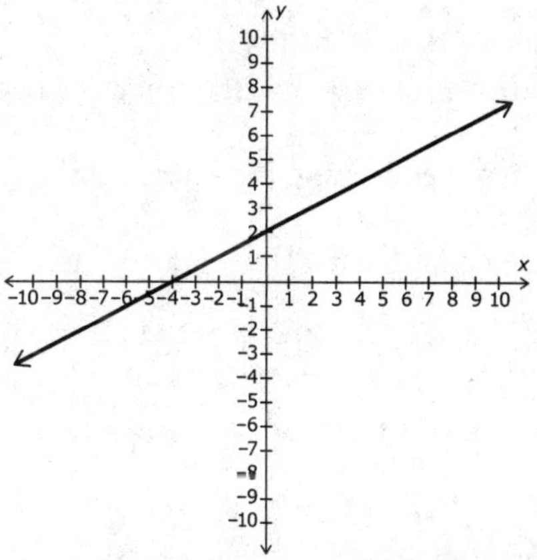

Here's How to Crack It

First, get the equation into $y = mx + b$ form. Take the given equation, $2x + 3y = 6$ and isolate y. First subtract $2x$ from both sides to get $3y = -2x + 6$. Now divide both sides by 3 to get $y = -\frac{2}{3}x + 2$. This equation has y-intercept 2, so eliminate (A) and (B). The equation also has a negative slope, $-\frac{2}{3}$, meaning that the graph has to decrease as it goes from left to right. Eliminate (D). Now, since the slope is $-\frac{2}{3}$, the y-coordinate has to decrease by 3 as the x-coordinate increases by 2. The correct answer is (C).

Now try another one.

2. If $3x + 6y = 30$ and $2x + 5y = 26$, choose two numbers below that are possible values of x and y.

$x =$			$y =$	

x options	y options
−6	−2
−2	1
6	6

Here's How to Crack It

If this problem looks familiar, it's because you solved it in the previous chapter. Last chapter, you solved it using the linear combination method. This time, you'll solve it graphically. Graph one equation at a time. Start with $3x + 6y = 30$. Get this into slope-intercept form. Subtract $3x$ from both sides; then divide both sides by 6 to get $y = -\frac{1}{2}x + 5$. This graph has a y-intercept of 5 and a slope of $-\frac{1}{2}$. Graph this as follows.

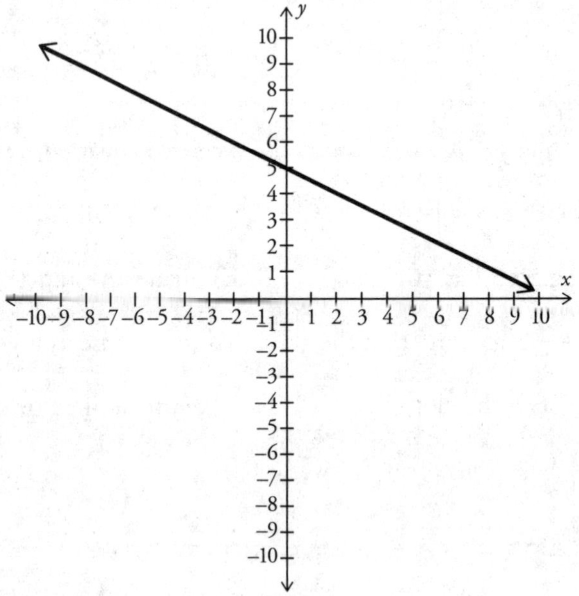

Now sketch the graph of the other line in the same axes. Take $2x + 5y = 26$, subtract $2x$ from both sides, and then divide both sides by 5 to get $y = -\frac{2}{5}x + \frac{26}{5}$. Therefore, this graph has a slope of $-\frac{2}{5}$ and a y-intercept of $\frac{26}{5} = 5.2$. Graph this to get the following:

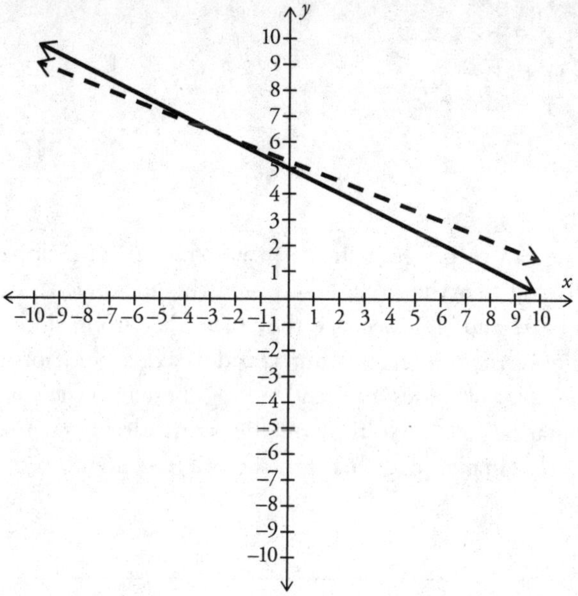

Look to see where the lines intersect. This appears to be at the point (–2, 6). Therefore, $x = -2$ and $y = 6$.

Some GED® questions will ask you to determine the equation of a line. You know the slope-intercept form of a line equation, $y = mx + b$. Therefore, if given the slope and the y-intercept, you can plug the slope in for m and the y-intercept for b and get the equation of a line. For example, suppose you were told that a line had a slope of 3 and contained the point (0, –2). You're given slope, so you can plug this value in for m and get $y = 3x + b$. But what about the y-intercept? Since the y-intercept is the point on the line for which the x-coordinate is 0, the y-intercept of this line must be –2. Therefore, the equation of this line would have to be $y = 3x - 2$. What if they gave you the slope and a point other than the y-intercept? Let's look at an example below.

3. What is the equation of a line that goes through the point (1, 3) and has a slope of −2?

A. $y = 5x - 2$
B. $y = -2x + 3$
C. $y = -2x + 5$
D. $y = 3x + 2$

Here's How to Crack It

The equation of any line can be put into the form $y = mx + b$, with slope m and y-intercept b. Since the question tells you that the slope is –2, plug this in for m to get $y = -2x + b$. Therefore, you can eliminate (A) and (D), because they have the wrong slope. But what about the y-intercept? You don't have the y-intercept, but you do have a point on the line, (1, 3). This means that you have one pair of values for x and y. Plug these into the equation to get $3 = -2(1) + b$. Now, solve this equation for b. Multiply on the right side to get $3 = -2 + b$. Now, add 2 to both sides to get $5 = b$. Finally, plug this into the original equation to get $y = -2x + 5$. The correct answer is (C).

Let's look at another one.

4. What is the equation of the line that goes through the points (−2, 5) and (8, 0)?

A. $y = -\frac{1}{2}x + 4$

B. $y = -\frac{1}{2}x + 8$

C. $y = -2x + 4$

D. $y = -2x + 8$

Here's How to Crack It

Once again, the equation of any line can be put into the form $y = mx + b$, with slope m and y-intercept b. You are not given the slope and, while it may appear that you're given the y-intercept, you're given a point in which the y-coordinate is 0, so this is actually the x-intercept. However, you can determine both the slope and the y-intercept. Remember the slope formula, $m = \frac{y_2 - y_1}{x_2 - x_1}$. Plug the points you're given into this formula to get $m = \frac{5 - 0}{-2 - 8} = \frac{5}{-10} = -\frac{1}{2}$. Plug this into the slope-intercept form of the line to get $y = -\frac{1}{2}x + b$. To get the value of b, plug in one of the points you're given. Try (8, 0). Plugging in this point gives you $0 = -\frac{1}{2}(8) + b$. Multiply on the right side to get $0 = -4 + b$. Add 4 to both sides to get $4 = b$. Plug this into the equation to get $y = -\frac{1}{2}x + 4$. The correct answer is (A).

Earlier in this chapter, we talked about parallel and perpendicular lines. In plane geometry, parallel means not intersecting, and perpendicular means intersecting at right angles. In coordinate geometry, this is also true, but parallel and perpendicular lines also have another interesting property relating to their equations. That's right; if you know the equations of the two lines, you can determine whether they're parallel and whether they're perpendicular without even needing to look at the graph. Simply use the facts that the slopes of parallel lines are equal, and the slopes of perpendicular lines are negative reciprocals. (A reciprocal is a fraction flipped upside down, so a negative reciprocal is a fraction flipped upside down and with its sign reversed. The negative reciprocal of $\frac{5}{2}$ is $-\frac{2}{5}$. The negative reciprocal of 8 is $-\frac{1}{8}$.)

Let's look at an example.

---

5. Which of the following represents the equation of a line that is parallel to the line represented by the equation $y = -3x + 1$?

   A. $y = 2x + 1$

   B. $y = -3x + 5$

   C. $y = 3x + 1$

   D. $y = \frac{1}{3}x + 5$

Here's How to Crack It

The question asks for which line is parallel to the given line. Your instinct might be to sketch the graph, but in this question there is no need. Parallel lines have equal slopes. Since the given line and the answer choices are in the form $y = mx + b$, m represents the slope. The slope of the original equation is –3. Find the equation in the answer choices with the same slope, i.e., the same value of m. This is the equation $y = -3x + 5$. The correct answer is (B).

Let's look at another.

6. The line represented by the equation $3x + 6y = 4$ is perpendicular to the line represented by which of the following equations?

   A. $-4x - 8y = -5$
   B. $3x + 2y = 4$
   C. $2x - y = -1$
   D. $-3x + 6y = -4$

Here's How to Crack It

The slopes of perpendicular lines are negative reciprocals, which are any two numbers that have a product of –1 when multiplied together. However, neither the equation of the line given in the question nor those in the answer choices are in $y = mx + b$ form. Put them in this form. Start with the equation in the question: $3x + 6y = 4$. Subtract $3x$ from both sides to get $6y = -3x + 4$. Now, divide both sides by 6 to get $y = -\frac{1}{2}x + \frac{2}{3}$. Now that this is in $y = mx + b$ form, the slope is equal to m, which is $-\frac{1}{2}$. The slope of the perpendicular line is the negative reciprocal of $-\frac{1}{2}$, which is $\frac{2}{1}$, or 2. Now, do the same to the answer choices and stop when you find a line with a slope of 2. Choice (A) is $-4x - 8y = -5$. Add $4x$ to both sides to get $-8y = 4x + 5$.

Divide both sides by –8 to get $y = -\frac{1}{2}x - \frac{5}{8}$. This is a possible trap answer since it is parallel to the line in the question. However, it is not perpendicular, so eliminate (A). Choice (B) is $3x + 2y = 4$. Subtract $3x$ from both sides to get $2y = -3x + 4$. Divide both sides by 2 to get $y = -\frac{3}{2}x + 2$. The slope is not 2, so eliminate (B). Choice (C) is $2x - y = -1$. Subtract $2x$ from both sides to get $-y = -2x - 1$. Divide both sides by –1 to get $y = 2x + 1$. Since the slope of this line is 2, the correct answer is (C).

Equation of a Line Drill

You can check your answers in Part IX: Answer Key to Drills.

1. Which of the following is the equation of a line through the point (0, –2) with a slope of 4?

   A. $y = 4x - 2$
   B. $y = 4x + 4$
   C. $y = -2x - 2$
   D. $y = -2x + 4$

2. A line goes through the points (2, 2) and (–4, –1). Show below a possible equation for the line.

   $y =$ ☐ $x +$ ☐

$-\frac{1}{2}$	–4	–2	1
2	$\frac{1}{2}$	3	4

3. Of the equations below, which best represents a line with a slope of –2 that goes through the point (–1, 3)?

A. $y = -2x + 3$
B. $y = 3x - 1$
C. $y = -2x + 1$
D. $y = 3x + 1$

4. What is true of the lines represented by the equations $2x + 8y = -5$ and $3x + 12y = 8$?

A. They are parallel.
B. They are perpendicular.
C. They have the same x-intercept.
D. They have the same y-intercept.

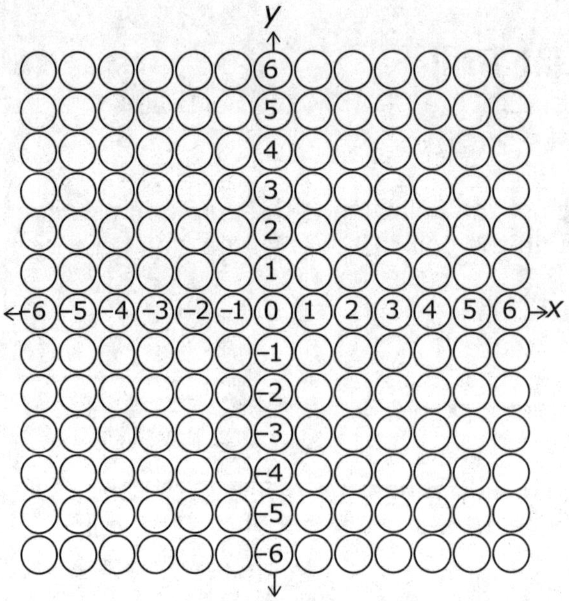

5. On the graph above, select the points on the line represented by the equation $y = -2x + 4$.

PROPORTIONS AND GRAPHS

In Chapter 14, we talked about ratios and proportions. Proportions can also be described as linear graphs through the origin. Remember that equations of lines can be expressed in the form $y = mx + b$. Since lines representing proportions go through the origin, the y-intercept, and therefore b, is 0, so these lines can be expressed by the equation $y = mx + 0$, or $y = mx$. In graphical terms, m represents the slope. In proportional terms, m represents the rate. Let's look at an example.

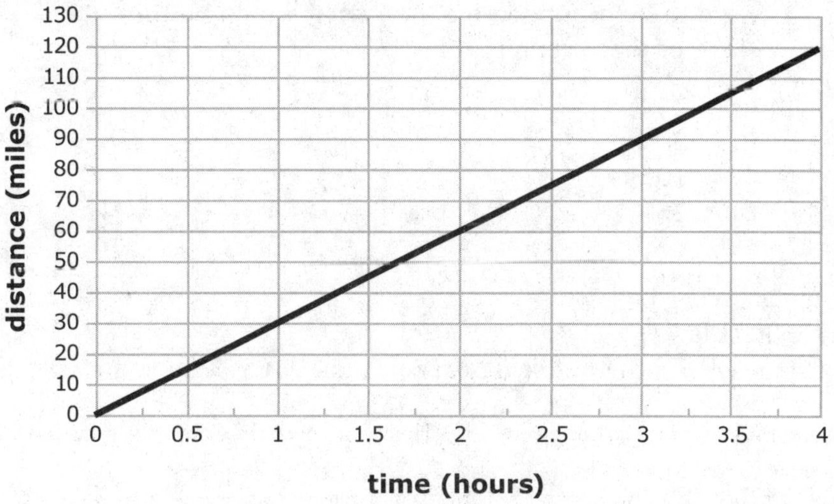

1. The graph above represents the distance traveled by a car driving at a constant speed. Which of the following is the constant speed, in miles per hour?

   A. 10
   B. 15
   C. 30
   D. 45

Here's How to Crack It

Remember that the rate, in this case speed, is always equal to the slope of the line. To determine the slope, find two points on the line. To make this as easy as possible, make one of those points the origin (0, 0). Choose another point, say (1, 30). Then, the slope, i.e., the speed, is $\frac{30-0}{1-0} = 30$. The correct answer is (C).

Let's look at another example.

2. During a certain week, a company hires a constant number of new employees each day, and no one leaves the company. On Tuesday of that week, the company has 400 employees. On Friday of that week, the company has 550 employees. If the total number of employees the company has each day were to be graphed as a line, what would be the slope of that graph?

A. 25
B. 50
C. 100
D. 150

Here's How to Crack It

The slope of the graph is the rate of increase. Look at the data given. On Tuesday, there were 400 employees, and on Friday, there were 550. Therefore, over the course of 3 days, the number of employees increased by 150. The rate of increase, therefore, is $\frac{150}{3} = 50$. The correct answer is (B).

Proportions and Graphs Drill

You can check your answers in Part IX: Answer Key to Drills.

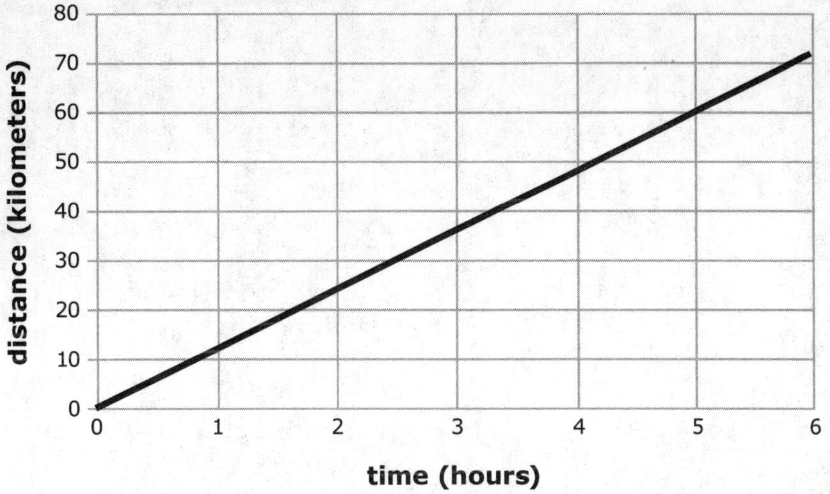

1. Elizabeth rides her bike over a period of 6 hours and records the distance she traveled in the graph above. If d represents her distance traveled in kilometers and t represents time, in hours, from the beginning of her trip, select the value that completes the equation below.

$$d = \boxed{}\, t$$

10	12	15
18	20	24

2. A certain toy store sells marbles only in boxes that each contain 2 red marbles and 5 blue marbles. Which of the following plots the possible number of red marbles and blue marbles a customer can buy?

A.

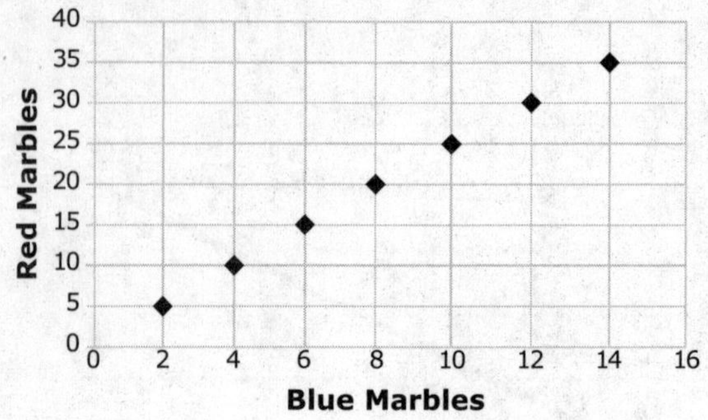

B.

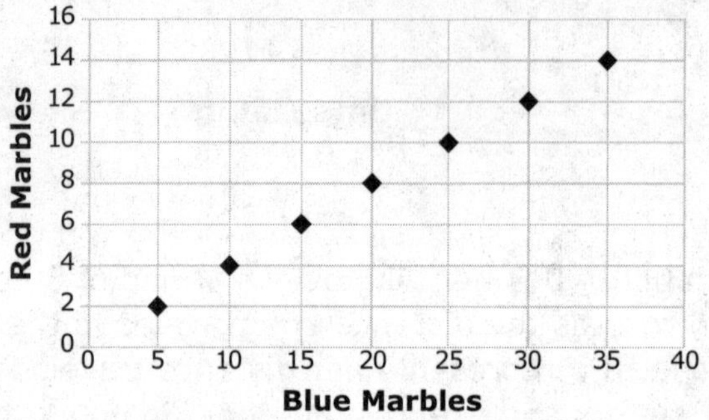

C.

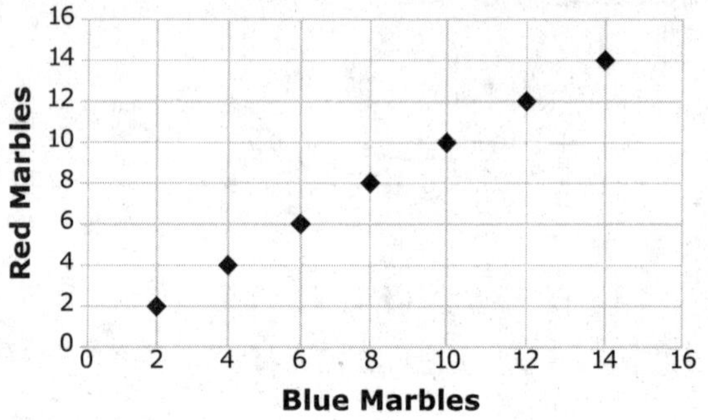

D.

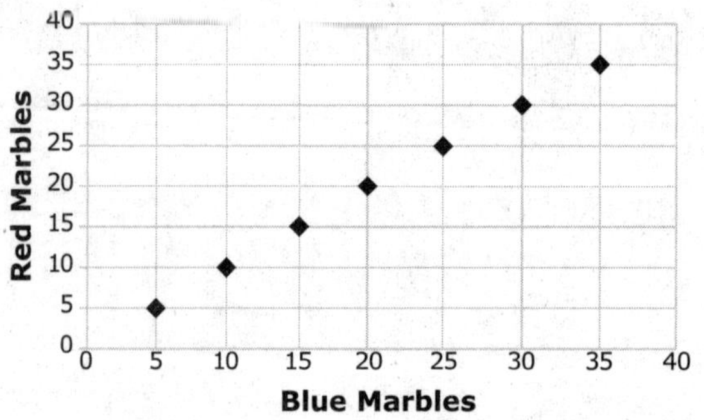

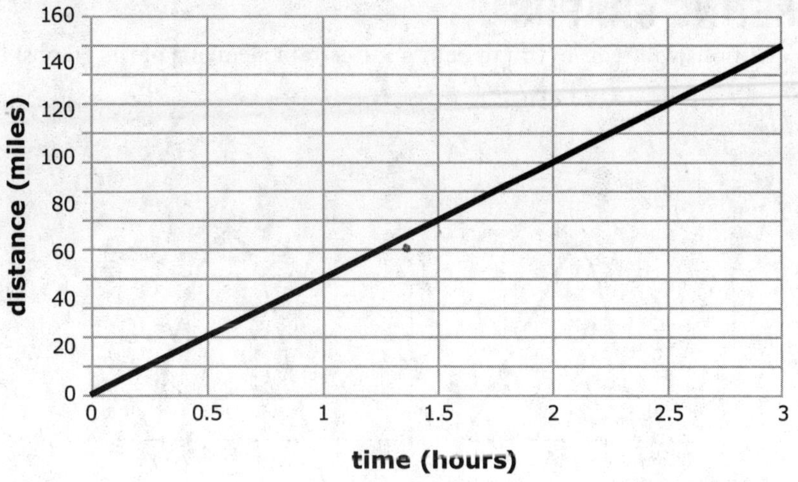

3. Naomi and Ravi are both driving on a highway at different constant speeds. Naomi's driving is expressed by the graph above. Ravi's driving is expressed by the equation $d = 40t$. Naomi's speed is

Select... ▼ Ravi's speed.

- greater than
- the same as
- less than

INTERPRETING GRAPHS

Some graph questions will require you to determine certain elements of the graphs. Look at the graph below.

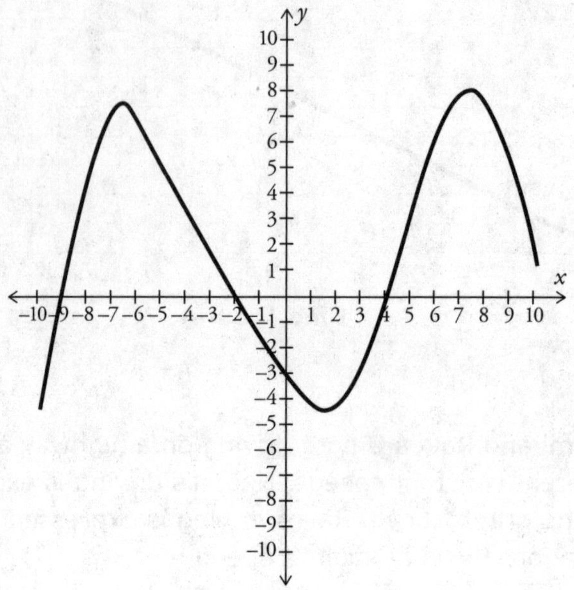

Let's identify some key elements. Start with the x- and y-intercepts, i.e., where the graph crosses the x-axis and y-axis, respectively. A graph, particularly a nonlinear graph, may have multiple x-intercepts. Where does the graph cross the x-axis? It crosses at three points: (–9, 0), (–2, 0), and (4, 0). Therefore, these are the x-intercepts. If a graph is of a function, it can have only one y-intercept (otherwise it would fail the vertical line test). Where does this graph cross the y-axis? It crosses it about halfway between the hashmarks for –3 and –4, so the y-intercept is about (0, –3.5).

Now let's determine the positive and negative ranges of the graph. The y-values of a graph are negative below the x-axis and positive above the x-axis. Use the x-intercepts to your advantage. The x-intercepts are –9, –2, and 4. To the left of the –9, the y-values of the graph are below the x-axis or negative. Between –9 and –2, the y-values of the graph are above the x-axis or positive. Between –2 and 4, the y-values of the graph are below the x-axis or negative. To the right of 4, the y-values of the graph are above the x-axis or positive. Therefore, the graph is negative at ranges $-2 < x < 4$ and $4 < x < 10$ and positive at ranges $-9 < x < -2$ and $4 < x < 10$.

Now determine relative maximums and minimums. These are points for which the y-coordinate is either greater or less than all the surrounding points. Look for peaks and valleys in the graph. The graph reaches peaks at about (–6.5, 7.5) and at about (7.5, 8). These are the relative maximums. The graph reaches a valley at (1.5, –4.5). This is the relative minimum.

Now determine where the graph is increasing and decreasing. Use the relative maximums and minimums. The graph is increasing to the left of its relative maximum at $x = -6.5$. Then, it decreases to its relative minimum at $x = 1.5$. Then, it increases to its other relative maximum at $x = 7.5$. Then, it decreases to the right of this point. Therefore, it increases from $-10 < x < -6.5$ and $1.5 < x < 7.5$ and decreases from $-6.5 < x < 1.5$ and $7.5 < x < 10$.

Some graphs have two sides that are mirror images of each other. Let's look at an example.

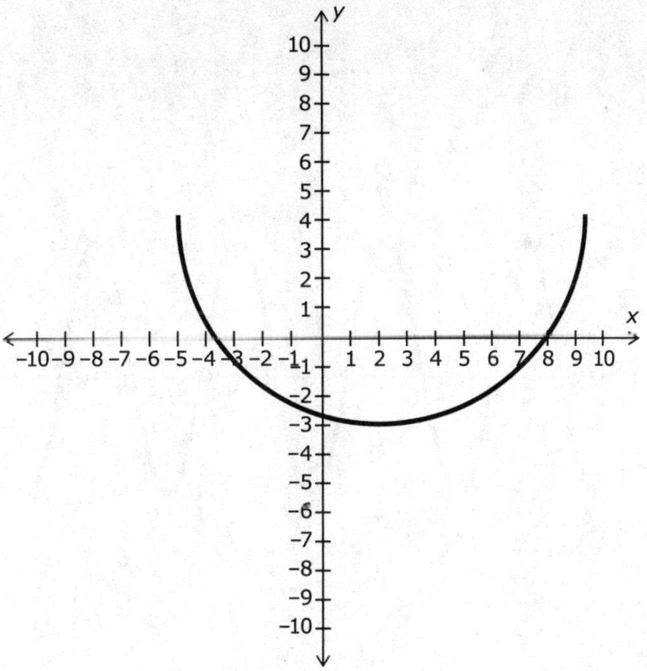

1. Which of the following represents the axis of symmetry in the graph above?

A. $x = 2$
B. $x = -3$
C. $y = 2$
D. $y = -3$

Here's How to Crack It

The axis of symmetry is the line that divides that graph into two mirror images. First, determine whether the axis of symmetry is horizontal or vertical. Since the left side of the graph is a reflection of the right side, the axis of symmetry is the vertical line separating the two sides. Since vertical lines have a constant *x*-value, they must be represented by "$x =$" and some constant. Eliminate (C) and (D). Imagine the lines represented by the two remaining choices. The line $x = 2$, the vertical line though 2 on the *x*-axis, does appear to divide the graph into mirror images. The line $x = -3$, the vertical line though –3 on the *x*-axis, clearly does not. The correct answer is (A).

Some graphs are periodic. Periodic means that the graph is made up of a repeating section. The horizontal length of this section is called the period. Let's look at an example.

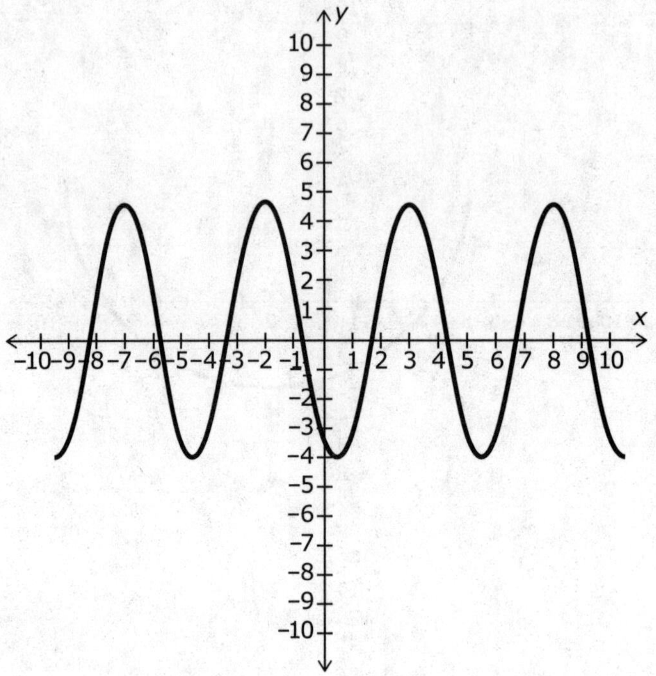

2. What is the period of the graph above?

A. 2
B. 5
C. 8
D. 10

Here's How to Crack It

This graph has a section that's repeating. To determine the length of this section, look at the relative maximums. The graph has a relative maximum at about $x = -7$, $x = -2$, $x = 3$, and $x = 8$. Since the difference between each of these relative maximums is 5, the period is 5. The correct answer is (B).

Interpreting Graphs Drill

You can check your answers in Part IX: Answer Key to Drills.

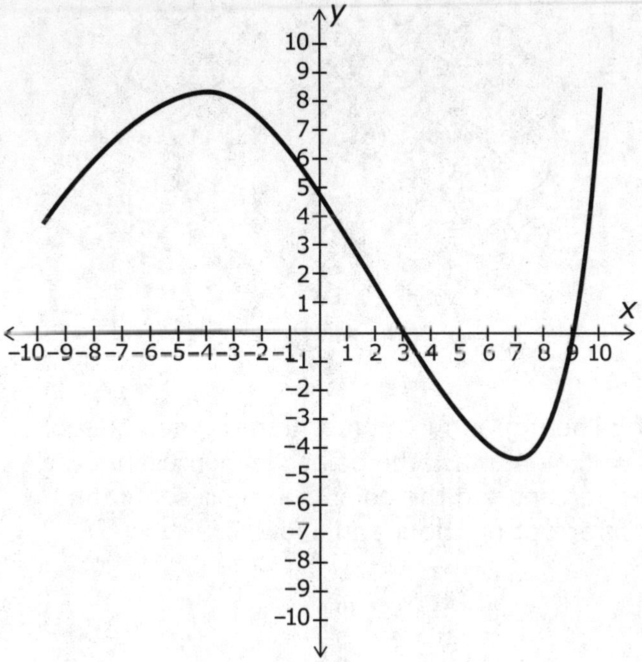

1. In the graph above, in which interval are the *y*-values of the graph negative?

   A. $-10 < x < 0$
   B. $-4 < x < 7$
   C. $3 < x < 9$
   D. $5 < x < 7$

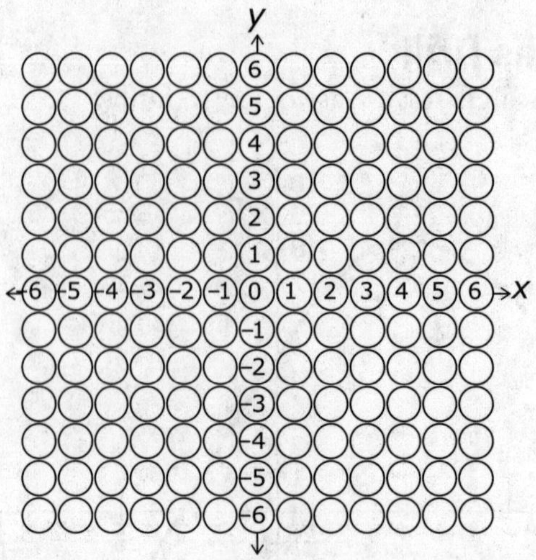

2. If a linear graph is represented by the equation $y = 2x + 4$, mark the point that represents the *x*-intercept and the point that represents the *y*-intercept on the graph above.

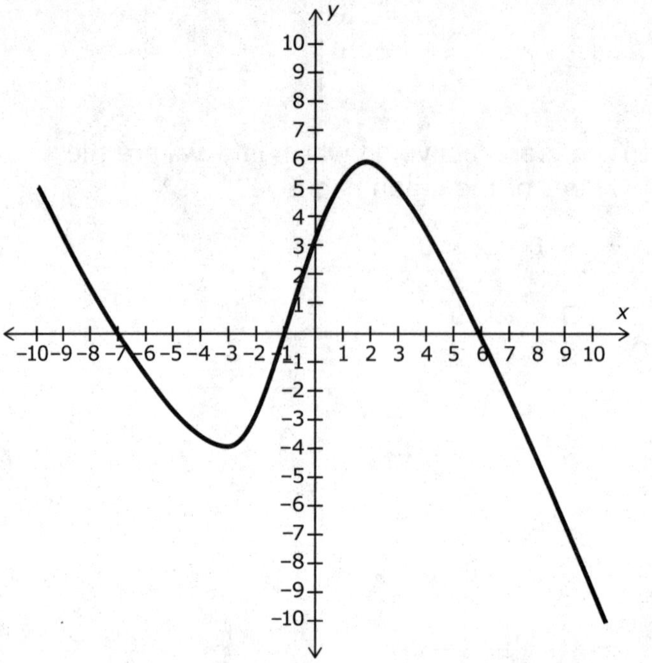

3. In the graph above, which of the following intervals represents the interval on which the graph is increasing?

A. $-7 < x < -1$ and $6 < x < 10$
B. $-3 < x < 2$
C. $-10 < x < -3$ and $2 < x < 10$
D. $-1 < x < 6$

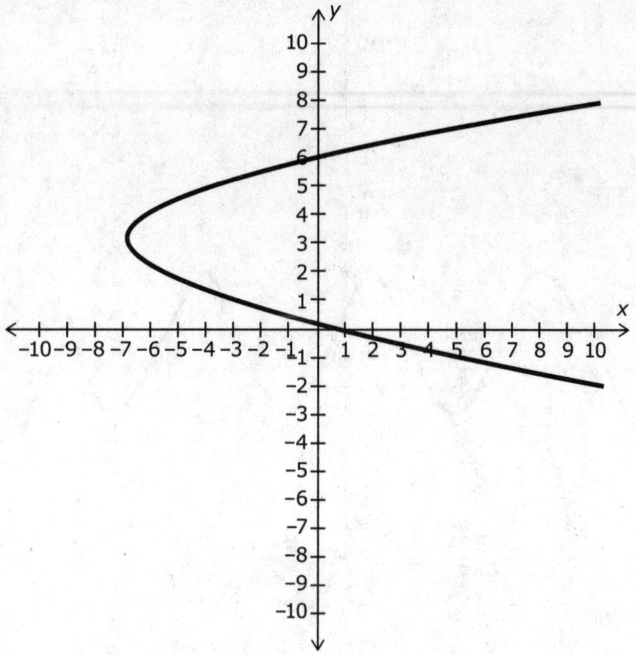

4. In the graph above, which of the following equations represents the axis of symmetry?

   A. $x = 3$
   B. $x = -7$
   C. $y = 3$
   D. $y = -7$

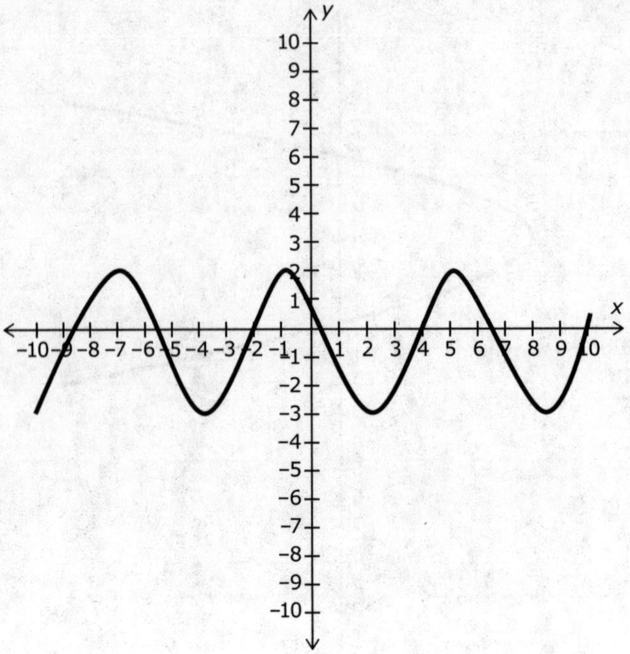

5. Which of the following is the period of the graph above?

A. 3
B. 6
C. 12
D. 24

PUTTING IT ALL TOGETHER

Now that you've seen the basics of geometry one topic at a time, we're going to give you a drill that mixes up all the different geometric concepts we've discussed in this chapter. This drill will help show you whether you're having trouble *recognizing* individual types of problems, as we've discussed in all the previous chapters. As you do this drill, make it a point to identify each question before you start calculating:

> *"This one is a triangle question."*
>
> *"That is a setup volume problem."*
>
> *"This one is a graphing question."*

Examine every diagram to see whether you can eliminate any answers that are out of the ballpark. Remember, if two answers are close together, you can't rely on the diagram to tell you which is exactly right. The figures are drawn only *roughly* to scale.

If there is no diagram provided, try to make your own. By taking something conceptual and making it concrete, you may be able to ballpark your *own* diagram.

Online Practice Drills
More math questions await you in your online Student Tools. Check out the digital Mathematical Reasoning drills as well as the Targeted Math Drills for support with the most challenging topics.

Geometry Drill

You can check your answers in Part IX: Answer Key to Drills.

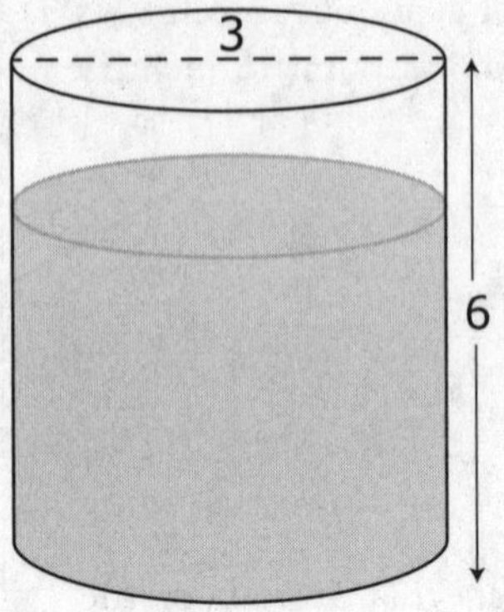

1. The cylindrical glass above is filled $\frac{3}{4}$ with water. What volume of water is in the glass, rounded to the nearest unit?

   A. 170
   B. 127
   C. 42
   D. 32

2. The radius of a circular traffic island is 7 feet. What is the approximate area of the traffic island, in square feet?

   A. 154
   B. 148
   C. 21
   D. 15

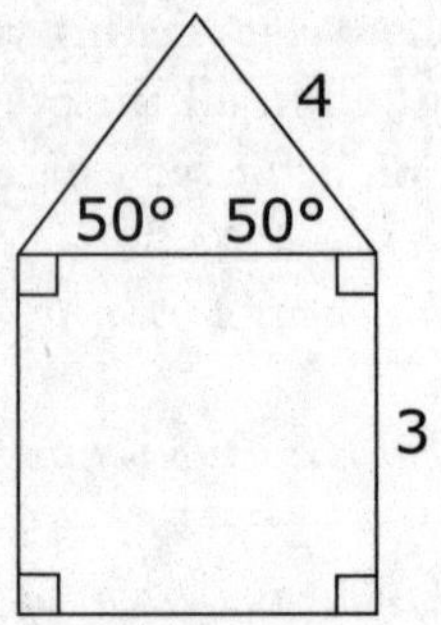

3. The figure above shows a square attached to a triangle. If the triangle is isosceles, what is the perimeter of the entire figure?

   A. 12
   B. 17
   C. 20
   D. 34

4. A three-sided figure has sides in a ratio of 2:2:1. What type of figure is this?

   A. an equilateral triangle
   B. a square
   C. an isosceles triangle
   D. Not enough information is given.

5. If a cube has a volume of 27, which of the following is the length of one side of the cube?

   A. 3
   B. 9
   C. 81
   D. 144

6. An isosceles triangle has one internal angle of 45 degrees. What is the sum of the measures of the other two interior angles, in degrees?

   A. 180
   B. 135
   C. 90
   D. 45

7. A rectangular flower garden has an area of 168 square feet. If the width of the garden is 12 feet, then what is the length, in feet, of the garden?

A. 23
B. 20
C. 15
D. 14

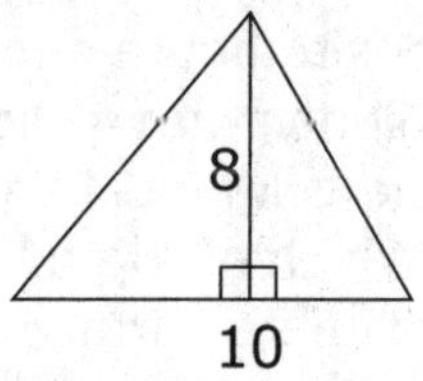

8. The triangle above has a base of 10 and a height of 8. Which of the following expressions gives the area of the triangle?

A. $\frac{1}{2}(10)(8)$
B. $2(10 + 8)$
C. $\frac{1}{2}(10 + 8)$
D. $\frac{1}{2}(10 - 8)$

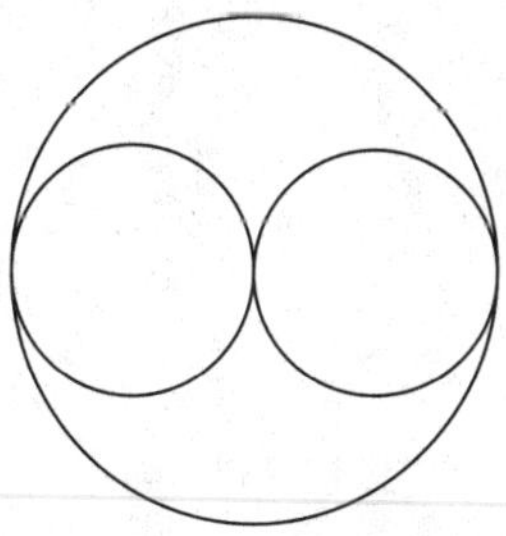

9. Two circles with identical radii are inscribed inside a third circle, as shown above. If the diameter of the large circle is 20, what is the radius of one of the small circles?

A. 40
B. 20
C. 10
D. 5

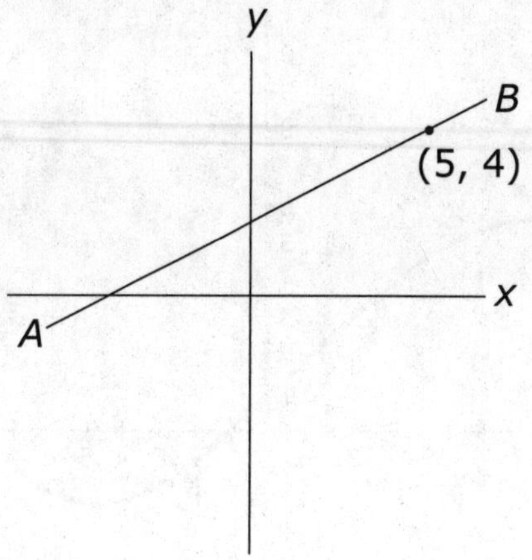

10. Point (5, 4) is on line *AB* as shown. Which of the following represents the slope of line *AB*?

A. $\frac{4}{5}$
B. $\frac{5}{4}$
C. $\frac{4 \pm 5}{5 - 4}$
D. Not enough information is given.

11. Which of the following represents the equation of a line that goes through the points (1, 2) and (−2, 8)?

A. $y = -2x - 4$
B. $y = -2x + 4$
C. $y = 2x + 4$
D. $y = 2x - 4$

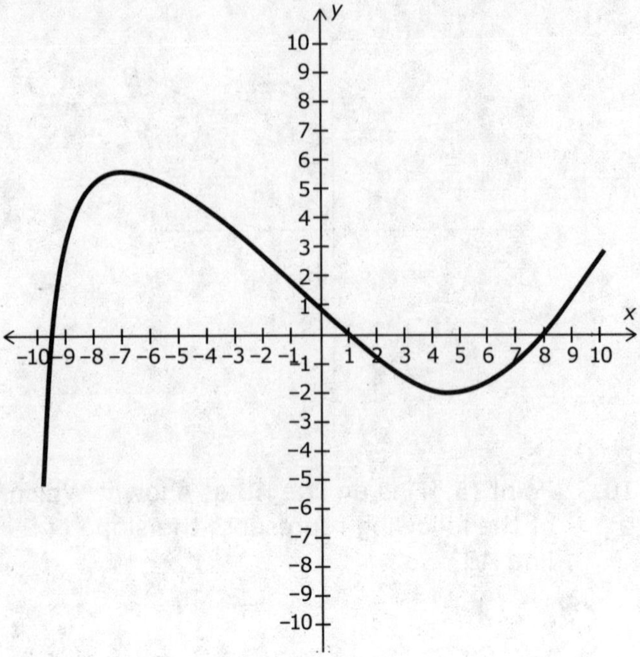

12. Which of the following intervals on the above graph is positive?

A. $-9.5 < x < 1$ and $x > 8$
B. $x < -9.5$ and $1 < x < 8$
C. $x < -6.5$ and $x > 4$
D. $-6.5 < x < 4$

13. A regular hexagon has an area of $24\sqrt{3}$.

If the area of a regular hexagon can be computed using the formula $A = \frac{3\sqrt{3}}{2}s^2$, where s is the side of the hexagon, what is the perimeter of the hexagon?

A. 2
B. 4
C. 16
D. 24

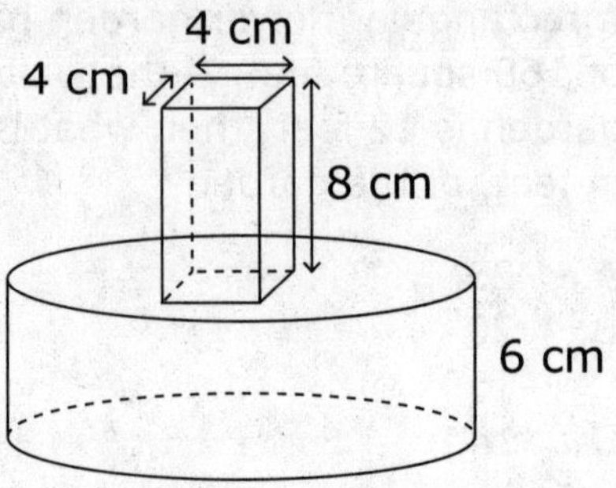

14. The composite figure above is made up of a right cylinder with a rectangular prism on top. The cylindrical base has a radius of 5 cm. Which of the following represents the approximate surface area of the composite figure, in square centimeters?

A. 160
B. 345.4
C. 473.4
D. 505.4

15. Which of the following is the volume, in cubic inches, of a right triangular prism with a base of 5 inches, a height of 9 inches, and a prism length of 12 inches?

A. 45
B. 153
C. 270
D. 540

Part VII
Social Studies

Chapter 17
Social Studies Overview

If you look in some of the other study guides for the GED® test, you may get the impression that you will have to memorize a huge number of facts for the GED® Social Studies test. In fact, the Social Studies test does not require *much* specific knowledge of history, economics, or geography (or any other social studies topics). Every question will be based on a document, chart, map, picture, or some type of graphic organizer, and the information you need to answer the question will almost always be contained in that accompanying piece of information.

The questions asked on the Social Studies test are twofold: The test writers want to make sure you have a *background* in the ideas covered in a typical social studies curriculum, and they want to assess what we will call "social studies skills" (reading passages and charts for relevant information). Thus, a strong familiarity with the major topics of social studies along with a smart approach to locating key facts will be just what you need for success on this test. In the following chapters, we will cover both of these elements.

What Do the Questions and Passages Look Like?

You will have 70 minutes to answer 35 questions. While there may be a couple of stand-alone questions, almost all questions will require you to look for information contained in one of the following: document; map; timeline; chart, graph, or table; or graphic organizer. Each of these sources will include one to three questions that can be answered with information found in the accompanying source.

Document

Documents can include newspaper editorials, speeches, letters, pieces of legislation, Supreme Court opinions, essays, and Amendments to the Constitution.

This excerpt is from a speech given by Abraham Lincoln in 1863, following the Battle of Gettysburg.

> But, in a larger sense, we cannot dedicate—we cannot consecrate—we cannot hallow—this ground. The brave men, living and dead, who struggled here, have consecrated it, far above our poor power to add or detract. The world will little note, nor long remember what we say here, but it can never forget what they did here. It is for us the living, rather, to be dedicated here to the unfinished work which they who fought here have thus far so nobly advanced. It is rather for us to be here dedicated to the great task remaining before us—that from these honored dead we take increased devotion to that cause for which they gave the last full measure of devotion—that we here highly resolve that these dead shall not have died in vain—that this nation, under God, shall have a new birth of freedom—and that government of the people, by the people, for the people, shall not perish from the earth.

Map

Timeline

Events in the Civil Rights Movement

1954	*Brown v. Board of Education* Supreme Court decision
1955	Rosa Parks's arrest in Montgomery
1959	Little Rock Nine attend Central High School
1963	Martin Luther King Jr. delivers "I Have a Dream" speech
1964	Civil Rights Act is passed by Congress and signed by President Johnson

Chart, Graph, or Table

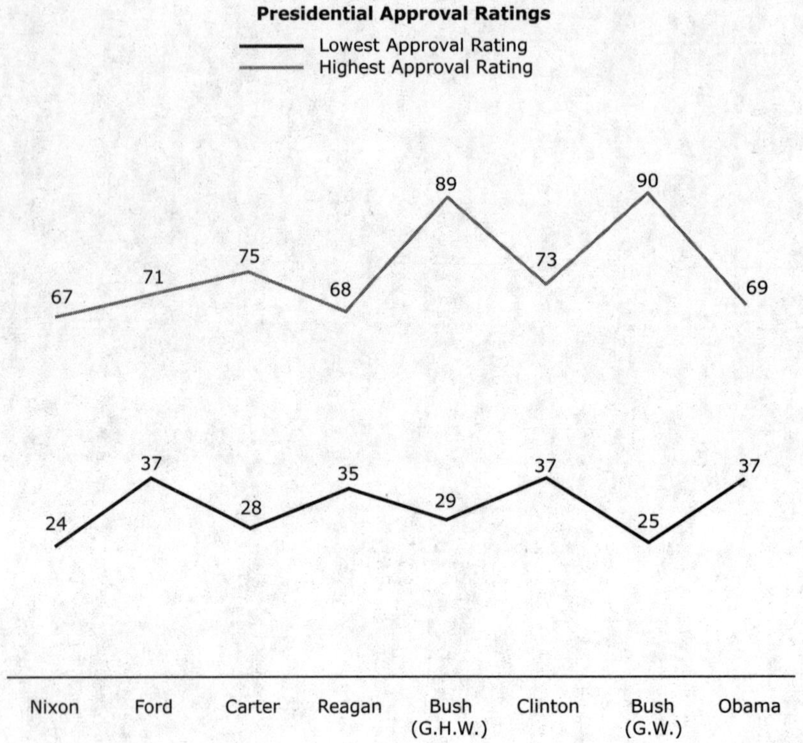

Graphic Organizer

Causes of the Great Depression			
Stock Market Crash of 1929	High tariffs against European countries	Bank failures	Widespread drought

Question Formats

Since the GED® test is to be taken on a computer, the test writers have included a few fancy kinds of question formats. You have seen these question formats earlier in this book, but here are some examples of how they will look on the Social Studies test.

Multiple Choice

The following text is taken from the Articles of Confederation (1781).

> Each state retains its sovereignty, freedom, and independence, and every power, jurisdiction, and right, which is not by this Confederation expressly delegated to the United States, in Congress assembled.

1. According to the passage above, the Articles of Confederation gave priority to

   A. the development of a strong, central government.
   B. the rights of individuals.
   C. a powerful Congress.
   D. states maintaining self-determination.

Hot Spot

2. Click on a power that the executive branch has directly over the legislative branch.

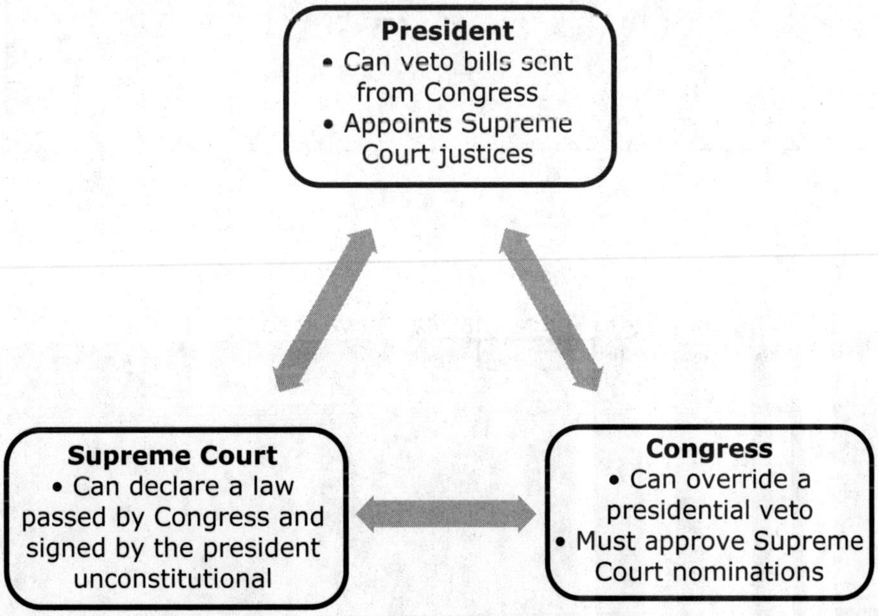

Fill in the Blank

AFRICA

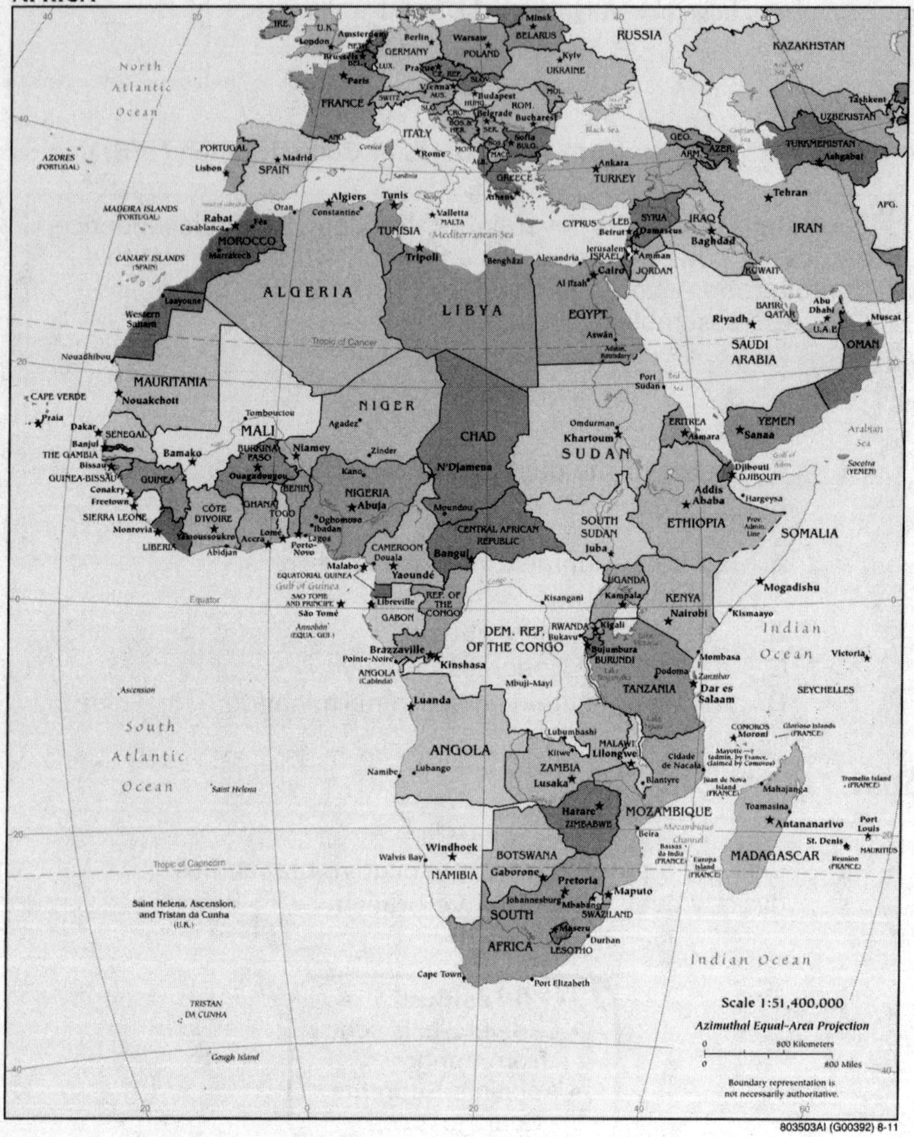

803503AI (G00392) 8-11

3. The country in Africa that can have trade ports on two oceans is ______.

Drop Down

This excerpt is from Albert J. Beveridge's "The March of the Flag" (1898).

> The Opposition tells us that we ought not to govern a people without their consent. I answer, the rule of liberty that all just government derives its authority from the consent of the governed, applies only to those who are capable of self-government. We govern the Indians without their consent, we govern our territories without their consent, we govern our children without their consent. How do they know that our government would be without their consent? Would not the people of the Philippines prefer the just, human, civilizing government of this Republic to the savage, bloody rule of pillage and extortion from which we have rescued them?
>
> And, regardless of this formula of words made only for enlightened, self-governing people, do we owe no duty to the world? Shall we turn these peoples back to the reeking hands from which we have taken them? Shall we abandon them, with Germany, England, Japan, hungering for them? Shall we save them from those nations, to give them a self-rule of tragedy? ... Then, like men and not like children, let us on to our tasks, our mission, and our destiny.

4. The perspective offered in this passage is most directly influenced by [Select... ▼].
   - isolationism
   - imperialism
   - suffrage
   - sectionalism

Drag and Drop

Natural gas reserves are plentiful throughout the planet. Most active sources for natural gas are located in central Asia and in the Americas. Iran and Russia each sit on approximately 33 trillion cubic meters of natural gas, which together account for $\frac{1}{3}$ of the earth's natural gas supply. Qatar, which is a mere 150th the size of Iran, contains $\frac{2}{3}$ of the oil reserves that Iran does. Rounding out the Asian natural gas powerhouses are Turkmenistan (18 trillion) and Saudi Arabia (8 trillion).

Despite the talk of the United States' dependence on foreign energy sources, it sits on between 9 and 10 trillion cubic meters of natural gas, making it the largest such resource holder in the Americas. Venezuela, the next most natural gas-rich country in the Americas, has the equivalent of just over half of the United States' reserves.

5. Drag and place the appropriate country under the bar graph that best describes its natural gas reserves.

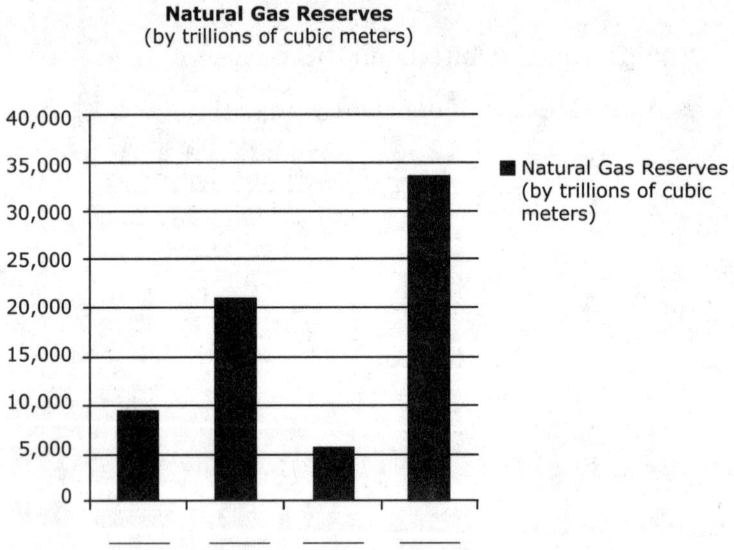

Iran | United States | Qatar

Turkmenistan | Venezuela

Question Tasks

The following are the four types of question tasks that you'll be asked to perform on the Social Studies test.

Comprehension Questions

A comprehension question asks you to find a particular piece of information and then recognize it, slightly restated, among the answer choices. Occasionally, comprehension questions will ask you to go just a bit further to identify a logical implication of that information.

The following passage is taken from the Supreme Court's majority opinion in *Brown v. Board of Education* (1954).

> We conclude that, in the field of public education, the doctrine of "separate but equal" has no place. Separate educational facilities are inherently unequal. Therefore, we hold that the plaintiffs and others similarly situated for whom the actions have been brought are, by reason of the segregation complained of, deprived of the equal protection of the laws guaranteed by the Fourteenth Amendment.

1. Which of the following inferences about the 14th Amendment is supported by the majority opinion?

   A. The plaintiffs have no standing in cases of educational discrimination.
   B. Institutions related to education may in some instances segregate.
   C. "Separate but equal" is a valid interpretation of the 14th Amendment.
   D. The 14th Amendment implies that schools may not segregate.

Comprehension Questions
These questions ask you to recognize information in a slightly altered form.

Here's How to Crack It

This is a comprehension question designed to see whether you understood what you read. The correct answer is (D) because the final sentence clearly states that segregated schools deprive students of a central guarantee of the 14th Amendment. Since all segregation in schools violates the 14th Amendment, (B) cannot work. Furthermore, the final sentence mentions that the court declared that the plaintiffs were wronged, so you can eliminate (A). Choice (C) is incorrect because the text declares that "separate but equal has no place."

Application Questions

To answer an application question, you must first understand the meaning of a concept conveyed in the document, chart, or map and then apply that concept to an entirely different situation.

2007 United States Population Distribution

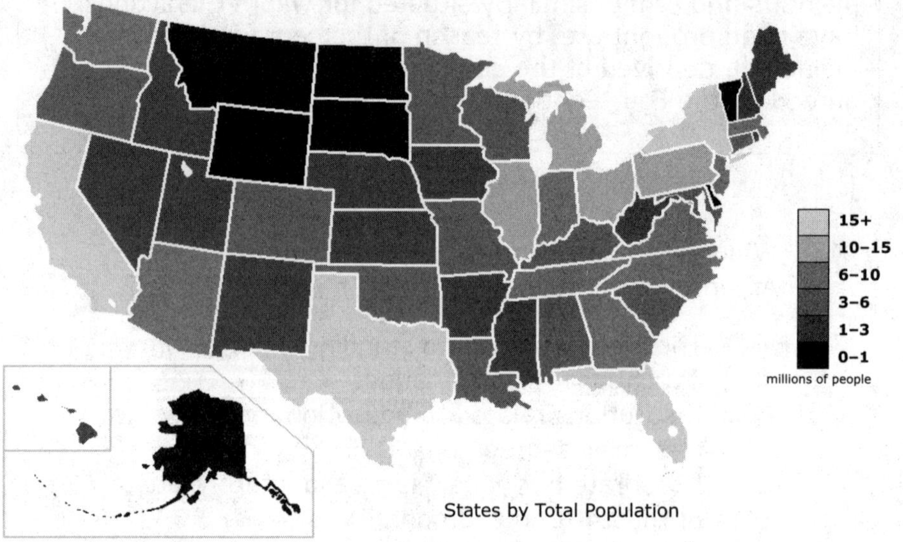

2. Population density can be defined as the number of people living in an area, relative to the size of that area. Which area of the U.S. has the lowest population density?

A. the West Coast
B. the Southeast
C. the Northern Mountain region
D. New England

Application Questions
These questions ask you to apply a concept from one situation to another situation.

Here's How to Crack It

Here we have a population map, and we're asked about population density. Since we're looking for the lowest population density, we need to find big states with small populations. The West Coast contains large states, but they have higher populations, so we can eliminate (A). The Southeast has moderate-sized states, most of which also have medium-sized populations—plus Florida, which is very populous—so eliminate (B). That leaves us with the Northern Mountain region and New England. Both have low populations, but New England's area is also quite small, whereas the Northern Mountain region spreads its small population over a very large area. So, we can eliminate (D). Choice (C) is our answer.

Analysis Questions

An analysis question asks you to break down the accompanying information into more specific categories and explore the relationship between those categories.

The following poster was created during World War I.

3. This poster was most likely created with the intention to

   A. recruit soldiers to fight in the war.
   B. give factual information about the destruction caused by the German Empire.
   C. praise the military might of Germany.
   D. raise funds for the war effort.

Analysis Questions
These questions ask you to explore the relationship of implied categories within the passage.

Here's How to Crack It

The key to an analysis question is to understand the motives of the document's creator. The image shows a menacing figure of a person called a Hun and asks its audience to purchase war bonds. War bonds were sold to help fund the war effort, so (D) is correct. It is not asking for soldiers to fight in the war, so you can eliminate (A). The Huns were a Germanic people, so this poster does not seem to be praising Germans; rather, it depicts them as menacing and inhuman. Eliminate (C) and (B).

Evaluation Questions

To answer an evaluation question, you must make a judgment or prediction about the information provided in the passage—sometimes by applying outside knowledge.

Evaluation Questions
These questions ask you to make a prediction based on the passage.

4. Gadzooks Cola has been a favorite in the Pacific Northwest since its introduction five years ago. This year, the manufacturer decided to finally raise the price it charges per bottle. This is most likely due to

A. an increase in demand.
B. a loss in profits.
C. an increase in supply.
D. deflation.

Here's How to Crack It

We are given an effect and have to imagine what cause is responsible for it. Work backward and see whether each answer choice would yield a price increase. The law of demand indicates that more quantity demanded by consumers leads to price increases. Therefore, (A) is correct. Choice (C) is incorrect because that would lead to a decrease in price. Deflation is also related to a decrease in price, so eliminate (D). Choice (B) is not necessarily true, as a loss in profits could mean low sales, which would necessitate a drop in prices.

Another type of evaluation question may ask you to distinguish fact from opinion or judgment in a primary or secondary source document.

Let's try a question.

The following text is adapted from President Richard Nixon's speech, "The Great Silent Majority" (November 3, 1969):

> Tonight I want to talk to you on a subject of deep concern to all Americans and to many people in all parts of the world, the war in Vietnam.
>
> I believe that one of the reasons for the deep division about Vietnam is that many Americans have lost confidence in what their Government has told them about our policy. The American people cannot and should not be asked to support a policy which involves the overriding issues of war and peace unless they know the truth about that policy.
>
> Now let me begin by describing the situation I found when I was inaugurated on January 20: The war had been going on for four years. Thirty-one thousand Americans had been killed in action. The training program for the South Vietnamese was beyond [behind] schedule. Five hundred and forty-thousand Americans were in Vietnam with no plans to reduce the number. No progress had been made at the negotiations in Paris and the United States had not put forth a comprehensive peace proposal.
>
> Tonight, I do not tell you that the war in Vietnam is the war to end wars, but I do say this: I have initiated a plan which will end this war in a way that will bring us closer to that great goal to which—to which Woodrow Wilson and every American President in our history has been dedicated—the goal of a just and lasting peace.

5. Click the selection of text in President Nixon's speech above that best represents an opinion, rather than a fact.

Here's How to Crack It

Facts are statements that can be proven true or false, whereas opinions are statements that can neither be proven nor disproven. In this question, the first highlighted quote (starting with "I believe") is the opinion, whereas the other two highlighted sentences are facts. There is no way to prove or disprove Nixon's statement that societal division about Vietnam was caused by Americans' lack of confidence in the government, but the other two statements are numerical and can thus be proven.

Yet another type of evaluation question, similar to the one above, may ask you to judge whether or not a particular author or source is credible and relevant to historical or modern political conversations.

Let's try a question.

The following text is adapted from President Barack Obama's speech on climate change delivered at Georgetown University (September 25, 2013):

> Now, we know that no single weather event is caused solely by climate change. Droughts and fires and floods, they go back to ancient times. But we also know that in a world that's warmer than it used to be, all weather events are affected by a warming planet. The fact that sea levels in New York, in New York Harbor, are now a foot higher than a century ago—that didn't cause Hurricane Sandy, but it certainly contributed to the destruction that left large parts of our mightiest city dark and under water.

6. An analysis of which of the following sources would be most relevant to a thoughtful and unbiased discussion of the issue described above?

   A. an advertising campaign funded by a major coal mining company
   B. a political speech hosted by an environmentalist group
   C. a peer-reviewed academic paper published by a leading scientist
   D. a disaster film produced by one of Hollywood's most respected filmmakers

Here's How to Crack It

In order to determine whether a particular source or author is credible and relevant to a particular topic, one must consider the source's bias, credentials, level of expertise, etc. Since the issue above deals with climate change, any sort of advertising campaign would have inherent bias—especially an advertising campaign funded by a coal company; eliminate (A). Political speeches are rarely neutral, and those hosted by particular interest groups are less likely to be so; eliminate (B). A Hollywood film may provide the viewer with interesting things to think about, but a filmmaker is certainly not a credentialed expert on scientific matters; eliminate (D). The best answer is thus (C); among these four choices, a published and respected scientist is most likely to be unbiased and knowledgeable about the subject in question.

Graphic Material Questions

The Social Studies test will also include comprehension, application, analysis, and evaluation questions based on graphic materials. If you've already read the downloadable supplement, "Understanding Graphics," you're well on your way toward acing these questions. But there are three types of graphics that appear on the Social Studies test that the supplement doesn't cover: cartoons, photos, and famous pieces of art.

The GED® Test Cartoon

The test writers want to see whether you can figure out the point behind these mostly political cartoons. Sometimes the cartoons will be fairly recent; other times they may be more than 200 years old. Here's an example from somewhere in between:

THE CROWNING ACHIEVEMENT

THIS LATEST SUBMARINE VICTIM MAY BE THE LAST

1. This American World War I cartoon was published in 1916, before the United States entered the war. The U.S. ship has just been torpedoed by a German submarine. What is the sinking ship in the cartoon meant to imply?

   A. The United States' patience with Germany was about to run out.
   B. The ship was carrying illegal war supplies and was a legitimate war target.
   C. The United States should be more patient.
   D. In wartime, even innocent people can get hurt by mistakes.

Graphic Material Questions
These questions may ask you to evaluate cartoons or photos.

Here's How to Crack It

Read this comprehension question carefully, and then study all information in the cartoon itself, including any words contained as a caption or inside the drawing itself. We know from the question that a U.S. ship has been torpedoed by a German submarine in the early days of World War I, before the United States entered the war. Even if you don't know much about World War I, you can imagine how the people of the United States probably felt about one of their ships being torpedoed: pretty mad.

The cartoonist has labeled the ship the *U.S. Patience*, and it's about to sink. What is the cartoonist implying by this? If you picked (A), you are doing just fine. The cartoonist was implying that the patience of the United States was about to run out in the face of Germany's sinking one of its ships—and, in fact, less than a year later, the United States did enter the war and helped to defeat Germany.

Choices (B) and (C) made new assumptions without any basis in information supplied in the cartoon or the question. Choice (D) certainly could have been true, but made no use of the important information contained in the drawing itself: the labeling of the ship as the *U.S. Patience.*

The GED® Test Photo

As with cartoon questions, the key to photo questions is to understand the point behind the photos and the relationship of a photo to any text that goes with it. Here's an example.

2. The men in this photograph are demonstrating against

   A. nationalism.
   B. segregation.
   C. fascism.
   D. suffrage.

Here's How to Crack It

Read this evaluation question carefully, and then study all information in the photo itself. Jim Crow is a symbol of the era of racial segregation, so (B) is correct. Nationalism, or pride in one's nation, is not depicted in this protest against segregation, so eliminate (A). Fascism was present in *Europe* during the 1930s and 1940s, not in the United States, the country indicated by the presence of the Jim Crow banner. Eliminate (C). Suffrage, the right to vote, was a cause for many Americans, but Jim Crow laws existed even after African Americans had the right to vote, so (D) is incorrect.

The GED® Test Famous Work of Art

When the GED® test gives a famous work of art as your information source, it will be of some historical significance. Fear not—there will be a historic document that will help you understand its context. Here is an example of how the test will present a famous work of art.

The painting below depicts the signing of the Declaration of Independence:

The following text is taken from the Declaration of Independence:

> When in the Course of human events, it becomes necessary for one people to dissolve the political bands which have connected them with another, and to assume among the powers of the earth, the separate and equal station to which the Laws of Nature and of Nature's God entitle them, a decent respect to the opinions of mankind requires that they should declare the causes which impel them to the separation.

3. What event was ongoing when the meeting in the painting occurred?

A. the Civil War
B. the War of 1812
C. the Revolutionary War
D. World War I

Here's How to Crack It

Use the historic context surrounding the painting to determine its central issue. The Declaration of Independence was created to assert the United States' freedom from England. This is exactly why the Revolutionary War was fought, so (C) is correct. The United States had already gained its independence by the time the events in the other three answer choices occurred.

What Topics Are Covered on the Social Studies Test?

Here are the topics as they are described by the people who write the test:

Civics and Government	50%
United States History	20%
Economics	15%
Geography and the World	15%

This is a pretty vague list. Just trying to acquaint yourself with all the topics covered in high school economics classes alone would take a long time. Fortunately, we will be able to give you much more exact information in the three chapters that follow.

Our Approach

While no particular knowledge of the facts of history, economics, or political science is necessary to do well on this test (you can virtually always find the correct answers contained in the passages), some *general* knowledge of these subjects and the specialized **vocabulary** that comes with them can be extremely helpful, if only because it will give you confidence. It's no fun answering questions about a topic you haven't heard about before.

We're going to discuss the topics that come up most often on the GED® Social Studies test. Don't try to memorize them. The idea is simply to become familiar with the subject matter and to practice answering social studies questions.

Chapter 18
United States History

In this chapter, we'll go over the topics of United States history that you may see on the GED® test.

While it is impossible to predict *exactly* what is going to be on the GED® Social Studies test that you take, we can be pretty sure that it will include certain topics that come up on the test all the time. And while it isn't necessary to take any specific outside social studies knowledge to the test, some general understanding of the processes of social studies can be very useful.

In this chapter, we'll present a summary of each era of United States history. After each review, we'll give you some helpful vocabulary words to think about, and we'll ask some GED®-type questions based on that particular area.

Learning how to think about the social studies questions is probably more important than learning facts, so at the end of each review, there will also be a short drill for you to try on your own.

Here are the topics we'll cover in this chapter:

- Colonial America
- American Revolution
- Westward Expansion
- Civil War
- Reconstruction
- Progressive Era
- WWI
- Great Depression
- WWII
- Cold War
- Civil Rights Movement
- Vietnam War
- Globalization and the Information Age
- War on Terror and post-9/11

COLONIAL AMERICA

Beginning in the early 1600s, the traditional story of colonial America traces the founding of the United States to 13 original **colonies**, which were settled along the eastern coast primarily by groups of people from England. Although other countries from across the Atlantic Ocean (namely France, Spain, and the Netherlands) had established claims on the continent at this time, it is the story of those settlers from England—their fight for independence from their home country—that develops into the story of a new nation.

Colonies are basically business ventures, a way for wealthy countries to compete with one another through trade. By exploiting the colony for **exports**, goods produced to be sold to other countries, the home country would maximize profits for itself in a practice called **mercantilism.** In this system, the primary purpose of the English colonists was to make money for sponsors back in England (also called Britain). Many settlers came as **indentured servants**, paying for their costly passage by signing a contract to work off the debt for a number of years. Britain also populated the labor force of the English colonies in North America through the **transatlantic slave trade**.

The original 13 colonies can be divided into three regions with characteristics or common ways of life based on their geography:

- In the Northeast, the **New England colonies**—Massachusetts, Connecticut, Rhode Island, and New Hampshire—were founded by groups of settlers who wanted to practice religion in their chosen way. They struggled to grow food in a cold climate and rocky soil, and had to rely on fishing, whaling, and ship building. The **port city** of Boston emerged as an economic center in this New England region.
- The **Middle colonies** of New York, New Jersey, Pennsylvania, and Delaware could benefit from a milder climate by growing plenty of wheat and other grains. Cities in this region also supplied materials through paper, textile, and iron factories. With Dutch, German, French, and Irish settlers, the Middle colonies were originally the most diverse.
- Further south, Virginia, Maryland, North and South Carolina, and Georgia established **plantation**-based economies; the rich soil in the **Southern colonies** allowed them to grow **cash crops** (like cotton, rice, and tobacco) in large fields, using slave labor to increase profits.

By the mid-1700s, the 13 colonies had developed different ways of defining and sustaining themselves, but they still had in common a life under British rule.

How might colonial America appear on the GED® test? Try this question.

1. Drag and drop the Colonial regions that match the economic activities below.

Cash crops	**Ocean-based**	**Staples**
Tobacco Rice Cotton	Shipbuilding Trade Fishing	Wheat Barley Rye

Colonial Regions
New England
Middle
Southern

Here's How to Crack It

Use the details given in the question and what you already know: the colonial region names (New England, Middle, and Southern) tell you their geographic locations from north to south along the Atlantic coast. Since you know that the climate in the North would not support farming, you can reason that the Northern colonies would rely on ocean-based activities (shipbuilding, trade, and fishing). Next, you might recognize tobacco, rice, or cotton as Southern crops, or recall what you know about the Southern colonies, where the production of cash crops was organized on plantations to maximize profits using slave labor for the heavy fieldwork. This reasoning leaves the staple crops (wheat, barley, and rye) for the Middle colonies.

Vocabulary

colony—an area or country occupied by settlers from another, often distant country and ruled or controlled by that home country

exports—goods produced within a country to be sold to other countries

mercantilism—trading for profit by producing and shipping more exports to increase a country's wealth

indentured servants—workers who signed a contract to work for a number of years to pay off a debt, often their passage to the colonies

transatlantic slave trade—system of trade taking millions of enslaved Africans across the Atlantic Ocean to the American colonies

port city—a city where ships dock to load or unload goods for transport

plantation—an estate designed for large-scale farming using resident slave labor

cash crops—products grown for commercial profit, not for use or consumption by the producer

Colonial America Drill

You can check your answers in Part IX: Answer Key to Drills.

<u>Questions 1 and 2</u> refer to this title page of a pamphlet.

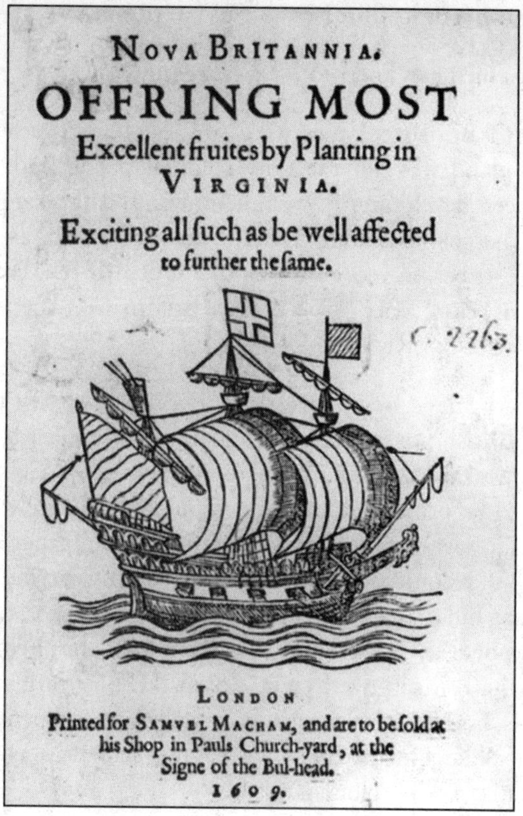
NOVA BRITANNIA.
OFFRING MOST
Excellent fruites by Planting in
VIRGINIA.
Exciting all ſuch as be well affected
to further the ſame.

C. 2263.

LONDON
Printed for SAMVEL MACHAM, and are to be ſold at
his Shop in Pauls Church-yard, at the
Signe of the Bul-head.
1609.

Title page, *Nova Britannia. Offring most excellent fruites by planting in Virginia. Exciting all such as be well affected to further the same* (London, 1609).

1. This document was most likely created with the intention to

   A. sell fruit.
   B. recruit colonists.
   C. praise the bravery of seafarers.
   D. raise funds for shipbuilding.

2. This document was meant to be read by people in

   Select... ▼ .
   - London, England
   - a New England colony
   - Jamestown, Virginia
   - a shipbuilding yard

AMERICAN REVOLUTION

During the American Revolution, the colonies united in their fight for independence from the British empire. The heart of their revolt pushed for **"no taxation without representation"**: the colonists had to pay taxes and follow laws enforced by England, but they had no voice, no say, and no influence in this distant government ruling over them. They began to **protest** the British government's **tyranny**, or its unreasonable use of power.

What led up to these extreme taxes and protests?

By the mid-1700s, the 13 British colonies were well-established along the eastern coast of North America. But England was not the only colonial power with claims to land on the continent; France had been developing its own colonies, and the English and French started fighting over territory. The colonists were drawn into the conflict as **subjects** of the British empire, and most native tribes served as **allies** of France in the **French and Indian War**, also known as the **Seven Years' War** (1754–1763). Britain won the war and control of land extending west to the Mississippi River.

Even though England had gained new territory, it had spent a lot of money, and to help pay for this costly war, the British government (or **Parliament**) forced the colonists to pay new taxes. For example, the **Stamp Act** of 1765 required payment for a stamp on all important documents, which had to be printed in England. The colonists grew angry at having to pay undue taxes to the British government for everyday items like paper and tea. They began to protest. In 1773, a group of colonists in Boston boarded ships carrying goods made in another British colony by the East India Tea Company, and dumped all the tea into the harbor. This act of protest became known as the **Boston Tea Party** and resulted in several measures to discipline the colonies: the British government closed the Boston Harbor until the colonists paid for the ruined goods, limited town meetings for colonists and penalties for British officials, and even placed British soldiers in the homes of colonists; these acts, called the **Coercive** or **Intolerable Acts**, only angered the colonists more.

After the first armed clashes with British troops in 1775, the Revolutionary War began. Representatives of all 13 colonies met as an organization called the **Continental Congress**, and on July 4, 1776, they issued the **Declaration of Independence**, officially rejecting British rule. Although Thomas Jefferson is considered the primary author of this document, other Founders, namely Benjamin Franklin and John Adams, helped to write it. The colonists would still have to fight many bloody battles for their independence, but with the help of the French, they forced the British to surrender in 1781 and signed a peace treaty in 1783.

After England was defeated, representatives of the new states had to define how their government would operate. It took several years to draft the **U.S. Constitution**, a document laying out the structure and principles of the new government. After the Constitution was **ratified,** or signed for approval, by the states between 1787 and 1789, George Washington was elected the nation's first president. By 1791, many additions or **amendments** had already been made to the Constitution; these first 10 amendments, known as the **Bill of Rights**, include important protections like freedom of speech and the right to a fair trial.

How might the American Revolution appear on the GED® test? Try this question.

1765 Stamp Act taxed printed products	1765 Boycott of British goods	1766 Stamp Act repealed	1767 Townshend Act taxed paper, paint, lead, and tea	1773 Monopoly on tea from British company	1773 Boston Tea Party protest	1774 Coercive or Intolerable Acts punished colonists

1. Which of the following inferences can be made based on the timeline above?

   A. The colonists' boycott of British goods had a significant impact.
   B. The Boston Tea Party resulted in a monopoly on tea.
   C. The Coercive (or Intolerable) Acts punished the colonists harshly.
   D. Stamps were an expensive product.

Here's How to Crack It

Eliminate any answer options that you could not argue using the information given in the timeline: You can point to the fact that the Stamp Act was repealed or taken back *after* the boycott of British goods; this suggests that the colonists' reaction had a significant enough impact for the British to reverse a previous action, supporting (A). Further, you can rule out (B) because the Boston Tea Party comes *after* the British monopoly on tea. There is no information given about the content of the Coercive (or Intolerable) Acts, only that they were intended as punishment; you don't know how harsh these acts were, so you could not argue for (C) using the timeline. Lastly, the Stamp Act has nothing to do with the price of stamps, so you cannot speculate about their cost; dismiss the remaining choice, (D).

Vocabulary

"No taxation without representation"—the basic idea of the American Revolution, a phrase rejecting government control without the participation of the people
protest—expressing a strong objection to something or someone
tyranny—unreasonable use of power
subject—a citizen or member of a state or ruling system
ally—one party cooperating with another for military or other purposes
French and Indian War—the expensive, 7-year war that Britain fought and won against the French and their Indigenous allies (also called the **Seven Years' War**)
Parliament—the law-making body of the British government
Stamp Act—law requiring North American colonists to pay a tax on all printed documents from England
Boston Tea Party—anti-Britain protest involving colonists throwing tea into the Boston Harbor

Coercive Acts—several British laws that further restricted the colonists in response to the Boston Tea Party (also called the **Intolerable Acts**)
Continental Congress—organization that represented the colonies and issued the Declaration of Independence in 1776
Declaration of Independence—document that detailed England's abuse of power and rejected British rule over the colonies
U.S. Constitution—document establishing the structure and principles of the U.S. government
ratify—to sign approval or consent, making an agreement or contract valid
Bill of Rights—first 10 **amendments,** or additions, to the U.S. Constitution, including individual rights, liberties, and protections

American Revolution Drill

You can check your answers in Part IX: Answer Key to Drills.

Questions 1 and 2 refer to the following text, the "Preamble" of the U.S. Constitution.

> We the People of the United States, in Order to form a more perfect Union, establish Justice, insure domestic Tranquility, provide for the common defence, promote the general Welfare, and secure the Blessings of Liberty to ourselves and our Posterity, do ordain and establish this Constitution for the United States of America.

1. Click to highlight the selection of text where you find the action of adopting the Constitution. (For this drill, underline the text.)

2. According to the "Preamble" text, which of the following is a goal of the U.S. Constitution?

   A. to declare independence from England
   B. to free enslaved people in the American colonies
   C. to define the idea of nationhood
   D. to appoint people to jobs in the new government

WESTWARD EXPANSION

During the 1800s, the United States began to stretch its geography westward. In 1803, President Thomas Jefferson bought the **Louisiana Purchase** from France, doubling the size of the young country. The **War of 1812**, a second war for independence from the British empire, secured the boundaries of the nation and defeated native tribes, paving the way for settlement of the western territories. The West held the promise of freedom for all in enough land for U.S. citizens to own property and gain independence.

Westward Expansion was the driving force of growth in 19th-century America. For individuals and families, the expanse of empty land stretching to the West represented opportunity and the dream of creating wealth. It was also considered the divine duty of the nation, or America's **"manifest destiny,"** to spread the special freedom of democracy to the edge of the continent. But the western territories were not empty; native populations had established ways of life on their lands, and they did not simply bow down to Christian American civilizers. Millions of natives were forced out of territories to make room for others to pursue their destiny.

The movement west involved a few major routes across the country. Sent by President Jefferson, **Lewis and Clark** led an expedition to explore the Louisiana Purchase and Pacific Northwest; with their guide Sacagawea, they traveled from St. Louis, Missouri, to the mouth of the Columbia River from 1803 to 1806. The **Oregon Trail**, more than 2,000 miles of wagon trail running from Independence, Missouri, to Oregon City, Oregon, was braved by hundreds of thousands of American pioneers in the mid-1800s. Another short-lived trail between Missouri and California was used by the **Pony Express** to carry mail on horseback across the country. By land and by sea, around 300,000 people migrated to California in hopes of striking it rich during the **California Gold Rush** (1848–1855).

While Westward Expansion moved toward the vision of a nation of one people under one government, the settlement of the West also splintered the union of the states. Each time a territory was about to become a state, the question of slavery would have to be addressed: would the new state enter the union as a free or slave state? And each time it was decided, this question would shake the delicate balance on which the union stood.

Meanwhile, movement to and through the country accelerated. The technologies of the **Industrial Revolution** boosted American manufacturing and gave birth to new industries, creating new jobs and new modes of transportation. Workers built a network of canals and railroads, including the **Transcontinental Railroad** connecting the major cities of New York and San Francisco. By 1860, 31 million people were living in a total of 33 states.

How might Westward Expansion appear on the GED® test? Try this question.

Question 1 refers to the following map.

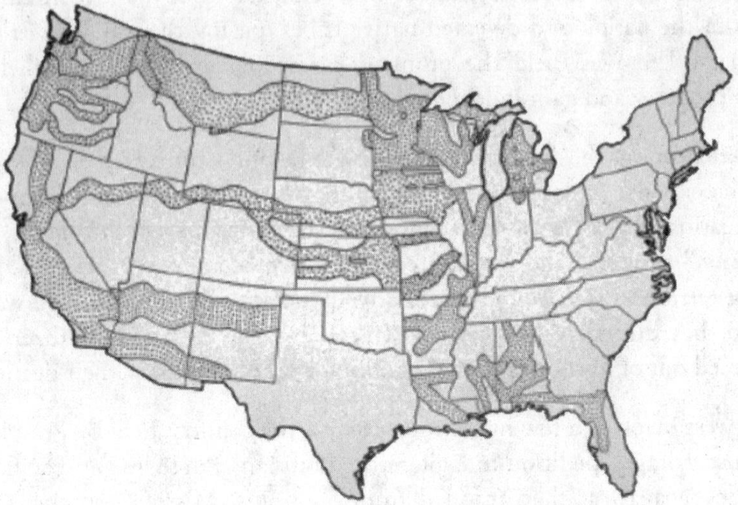

1. The shaded areas of this map from the late 1800s most likely indicate

A. pathways of the Underground Railroad.
B. land grants provided to railway companies.
C. major rivers used for transporting manufactured goods.
D. the Lewis and Clark trail.

Here's How to Crack It

The shaded areas mostly run from east to west, with little shading in the Northeastern region of the United States. The Underground Railroad was a network helping enslaved people to escape from the South to Canada north of the United States, so this option, (A), does not match the pattern on the map. Major rivers used for transporting manufactured goods would include part of the Mississippi River, which is not indicated on the map, and would also involve routes carrying manufactured goods from the production centers in major cities of the Northeast, so you can rule out (C). Lewis and Clark led a small expedition to explore the land along one trail across the West, not a complex network of pathways you see on the map; eliminate (D). This reasoning leaves (B): the shaded regions represent the major railroads running east to west, including the Transcontinental Railroad, Northern Pacific, and Southern Pacific.

Vocabulary

Louisiana Purchase—bought from France in 1803, this land stretched from the Mississippi River to the Rocky Mountains

War of 1812—second war fought against England for complete independence of the United States from the British empire

Westward Expansion—growth of the United States during the 19th century as settlers moved to the West
"manifest destiny"—belief that "civilizing" (conquering and controlling) the Western United States was fulfilling God's plan
Lewis and Clark—two explorers sent by Thomas Jefferson to survey Northwestern lands
Oregon Trail—more than 2,000 miles of wagon trail traveled by American pioneers bound for the West in the mid-1800s
Pony Express—temporary horseback mail service between Missouri and California
California Gold Rush—mass migration to California after gold was found there in 1848
Industrial Revolution—changes in manufacturing and transportation that led to large-scale factory production
Transcontinental Railroad—continuous railroad line connecting the eastern and western U.S. cities

Westward Expansion Drill

You can check your answers in Part IX: Answer Key to Drills.

Questions 1 and 2 refer to the following excerpt, taken from John O'Sullivan's treatise "Manifest Destiny" (1839).

> The American people having derived their origin from many other nations, and the Declaration of National Independence being entirely based on the great principle of human equality, these facts demonstrate at once our disconnected position as regards any other nation; that we have, in reality, but little connection with the past history of any of them, and still less with all antiquity, its glories, or its crimes. On the contrary, our national birth was the beginning of a new history, the formation and progress of an untried political system, which separates us from the past and connects us with the future only; and so far as regards the entire development of the natural rights of man, in moral, political, and national life, we may confidently assume that our country is destined to be the great nation of futurity...

1. Click on the description that does NOT correspond with O'Sullivan's views of the American nation presented in the passage above. (For this drill, circle the description.)

American democracy is oriented toward the future.	The American people are a nation of immigrants.	The greatness of the U.S. is its connection to the past.	Equality is a founding principle of the country.

2. According to the passage, which of the following describes the destiny of the United States?

   A. The United States will follow the same path of development as other nations.
   B. The United States will establish a superior economic system.
   C. The United States will grow into a vast empire.
   D. The United States will develop a new history of democracy.

CIVIL WAR

By the mid-1800s, the country was deeply divided, with Southerners fearing the end of slavery, and Northerners concerned over its expansion west. The growth of the country also gave rise to doubts about whether one government could represent such a vast land.

Several events added fuel to the fire. In 1852, Harriet Beecher Stowe published the book ***Uncle Tom's Cabin***, exposing the brutality of slavery to people worldwide. When residents of Kansas and Nebraska were allowed to decide for themselves whether they would be free or slave states, violence erupted between pro-slavery activists and **abolitionists**. The fighting would go on for years in **"Bleeding Kansas"** (1854–1861). In the **Supreme Court**, **Dred Scott** appealed for his freedom from slavery, having lived previously in a free territory; the Court ruled that a Black man did not have the rights of a citizen. Finally, after the **Presidential Election of 1860**, when antislavery candidate Abraham Lincoln was elected, Southern states left the Union to secure their economic system and rights to property. The **secession,** or separation, of the **Confederate States** ignited the Civil War. The first shots were fired when Confederates attacked **Fort Sumter**.

The North had many advantages over the South during the Civil War: the North had 22 million people, significantly more than the 9 million in the South; industries in the North produced nearly all of the firearms in the United States; there was generally more support for the Union cause; the Union army's strategy of cutting off supply lines in the South was very effective; and the North had the additional power of **freedmen**. In 1863, in the middle of the Civil War, Lincoln issued the **Emancipation Proclamation** as a military order to free enslaved people in rebel states; these freedmen joined the Union forces in large numbers, helping the North to defeat the South.

The Civil War was fought in places all over the country, although Virginia and Tennessee were the major battleground states. One in fifty Americans died during the war. Homes, fields, and entire towns were destroyed. How should the country be rebuilt? Leaders would continue fighting over this question in the years that followed the end of the war.

How might the Civil War appear on the GED® test? Try this question.

1. Drag and drop the contrasting features of the North and South into the appropriate boxes.

North	South

Agricultural	Immigrant labor	Slave labor
Population 9 million	Industrial	Population 22 million

Here's How to Crack It

Sort the pairs of contrasts: since the South fought to keep slave labor, immigrant labor must belong to the North. The reason for the South's reliance on slave labor was its agricultural economy; that means the North must have been more industrial. And given that an industrial economy would attract larger populations to cities, you can reason that the population of 22 million goes with the North, leaving the population of 9 million for the South.

Vocabulary

Uncle Tom's Cabin—novel depicting the cruel treatment of enslaved people, gaining support for abolition, or the end of slavery

abolitionist—antislavery stance or an activist fighting to end slavery

"Bleeding Kansas"—years of bloodshed in Kansas over the people's decision about whether to be a free or slave state when joining the Union

Supreme Court—the highest federal court consisting of nine justices who rule on whether existing laws or acts align with the U.S. Constitution

Dred Scott—man who appealed to the Supreme Court for freedom from slavery only to be denied the rights of a U.S. citizen in the Court's ruling

Presidential Election of 1860—election of Abraham Lincoln, prompting the secession of 11 southern states

secession—act of withdrawing from a political body

Confederate States—the Southern states who left the Union at the start of the Civil War

Fort Sumter—federal base that was the site of the first gunfire in the Civil War

freedmen—those who had been recently freed from slavery

Emancipation Proclamation—military order issued by Abraham Lincoln in 1863, calling for all enslaved people in rebel/Confederate states to be set free

Civil War Drill

You can check your answers in Part IX: Answer Key to Drills.

Questions 1 and 2 refer to the excerpt below, which is taken from the "Emancipation Proclamation" (1863).

> That on the first day of January, in the year of our Lord one thousand eight hundred and sixty-three, all persons held as slaves within any State or designated part of a State, the people whereof shall then be in rebellion against the United States, shall be then, thenceforward, and forever free; and the Executive Government of the United States, including the military and naval authority thereof, will recognize and maintain the freedom of such persons, and will do no act or acts to repress such persons, or any of them, in any efforts they may make for their actual freedom.

1. The purpose of the Emancipation Proclamation was to

   A. release the rebel states from the Union.
   B. declare the end of the Civil War.
   C. free enslaved people in certain states to weaken the South.
   D. grant temporary freedom to all enslaved people.

2. Click to highlight the selection of text where Lincoln invokes the authority to enforce his Emancipation Proclamation order. (For this drill, underline the text.)

RECONSTRUCTION

The Union may have declared victory in the Civil War in April 1865, but reunifying the country would be a continuing battle during the period of **Reconstruction** (1865–1877).

Lincoln's **10% Plan** required 10 percent of the voters in a Southern state to swear an **oath of allegiance** before it could rejoin the Union. He also offered to pardon all Confederates and promised to protect private property. In these forgiving plans, Lincoln pushed to reunify the nation quickly. But it is impossible to know what he would have done further, as Lincoln's **assassination** cut short his plans for Reconstruction.

Lincoln's successor, Andrew Johnson, took over the process of Reconstruction. Putting states' rights first, Johnson wanted to let Southern landowners and state governments rebuild themselves. For example, he returned all land that had been seized during the war to its original owners, even property that had already been redistributed through the **Freedmen's Bureau**, a temporary relief organization for assisting formerly enslaved and other poor or displaced people after the Civil War.

Under Johnson's administration, many Southern states passed laws to restrict the rights of formerly enslaved people. Some of these **"black codes"** prohibited Black people from owning property, owning firearms, testifying in court, or simply occupying certain places. One such law justified the arrest of Black people for **vagrancy**—loitering, wandering, or homelessness. Once arrested, they could be forced to work for punishment in prison or back on plantations; this exception to the **13th Amendment**, which ended slavery except as penalty for a crime, enabled slavery to continue through the **penal labor** system. Formerly enslaved people also sought work through **sharecropping**, a system in which families rented land from owners who took a share of their crops in exchange.

Northern members of Congress rejected Johnson's policies and used their majority to pass laws despite the President's **veto**; these include the Civil Rights Act of 1866, affirming that all citizens have equal protection under the law, and the Reconstruction Act of 1867, which divided the South into five districts under military control and prepared the way for freedmen to vote. To rejoin the Union, Southern states were required to ratify the **14th Amendment** to the Constitution, granting the rights of citizenship and equal protection under the law to formerly enslaved people. By 1870, the right to vote regardless of race would be protected by the **15th Amendment.**

How might Reconstruction appear on the GED® test? Try this question.

1. Below are transcripts of the 13th, 14th, and 15th Amendments to the U.S. Constitution.

AMENDMENT XIII	**AMENDMENT XIV**	**AMENDMENT XV**
Neither slavery nor involuntary servitude, except as a punishment for crime whereof the party shall have been duly convicted, shall exist within the United States, or any place subject to their jurisdiction.	All persons born or naturalized in the United States, and subject to the jurisdiction thereof, are citizens of the United States and of the State wherein they reside. No State shall make or enforce any law which shall abridge the privileges or immunities of citizens of the United States; nor shall any State deprive any person of life, liberty, or property, without due process of law; nor deny to any person within its jurisdiction the equal protection of the laws.	The right of citizens of the United States to vote shall not be denied or abridged by the United States or by any State on account of race, color, or previous condition of servitude.

Click on the amendment that expanded citizenship to formerly enslaved people.

Here's How to Crack It

All three amendments mention enslaved people or slavery, so the keyword here is citizenship (or citizens), which you can find only in the 14th Amendment. To sort through the very dense language of these amendments, try tracking the subject of a sentence to its verb to get to the point. The 13th Amendment declares only that slavery no longer exists; the 15th Amendment concerns only the right to vote.

Vocabulary

Reconstruction—period after the Civil War when Southern states and freedmen were being reintegrated into the United States
10% plan—Lincoln's plan requiring 10 percent of voters in a Southern state to swear allegiance to the Union before it could be readmitted
oath of allegiance—pledge acknowledging one's duty and swearing loyalty
assassination—politically motivated killing
Freedmen's Bureau—temporary organization for assisting formerly enslaved people and other poor or displaced people after the Civil War
black codes—laws passed in many Southern states to restrict formerly enslaved people and continue the labor practices of slavery
vagrancy—loitering, wandering, or homelessness that is recognized as a criminal act
penal labor—forcing people to work in prison or as punishment
sharecropping—system in which families rent land and pay the owner a share of their crops
veto—rejection of a proposed law or decision
13th Amendment—amendment that abolished slavery (except as punishment)
14th Amendment—amendment that extended citizenship to formerly enslaved people born in the Unites States and granted "equal protection" under the law
15th Amendment—amendment that granted the right to vote to Black men

Reconstruction Drill

You can check your answers in Part IX: Answer Key to Drills.

Questions 1 and 2 refer to this political cartoon.

Harding, Nelson. "Get to Work." *The Independent* (January 24, 1920).

1. This political cartoon belongs to which of the following eras of U.S. History?

   A. Civil War
   B. Reconstruction
   C. World War I
   D. American Revolution

2. Which of the following describes the cartoonist's attitude toward the action depicted?

   Select... ▼
   - admiring, praising
   - skeptical, doubting
   - neutral, indifferent
   - confident, optimistic

THE PROGRESSIVE ERA

From the 1890s to the 1920s, social activism and political reform defined the **Progressive Era** in the United States. The main goal of the Progressive Era was to improve the conditions for a democratic society, either by creating solutions or getting rid of corruption. These efforts took many different targets and forms of effort.

Progressive Era activists responded to the living and working conditions of **urbanization**. As American workers and immigrant laborers moved into cities for jobs in factories, they often ended up living in overcrowded **tenement houses**. Jane Addams's **Hull House** in Chicago is the most famous example of an urban housing solution from this time. Activists also took on unsafe and unfair practices in factories. **Labor unions** formed to push for changes by organizing individual workers. Union-organized **strikes** were one tactic used to bargain with industry leaders; by refusing to work, employees showed the value of their labor to employers and, in many cases, won better pay and safer working environments. Other activists called **muckrakers** used journalism to expose corruption. Upton Sinclair's account from inside the meat-packing industry in ***The Jungle*** led to investigation and reform. In general, industries were improved and standardized during the Progressive Era.

Women played a large role in Progressive Era activism as they gained more political influence. The **Temperance movement**, led by a majority of women, resulted in the **Prohibition**, the time period when alcohol was illegal in the United States under the **18th Amendment**. In 1920, the **19th Amendment** finally granted women **suffrage,** or the right to vote.

Other major changes to the political system cleaned up corruption and strengthened American democracy. The first **"trust-busting"** law, the **Sherman Antitrust Act**, banned **monopolies,** or companies so large that they exclude any competition. Congress also promoted a fair market through the **Federal Trade Commission Act**, which outlawed other anticompetitive practices. With the regulation of corporate bosses came other changes to support more direct democracy: the **16th Amendment** created the **income tax** based on a percentage of one's earnings to fund the government, and the **17th Amendment** established the **direct election of senators**.

How might the Progressive Era appear on the GED® test? Try this question.

Progressive Era Reforms				
1890	**1906**	**1913**	**1919**	**1920**
Sherman Antitrust Act outlawed monopolies	Meat Inspection Act protected consumers	Department of Labor formed	18th Amendment made alcohol illegal	19th Amendment gave women the right to vote

1. Click on the Progressive Era reform that most directly relates to the impact of union-organized strikes.

Here's How to Crack It

Monopolies have to do with the market and competition between businesses, not individual workers who organized in unions to negotiate better working conditions and pay, so you can rule out the Sherman Antitrust Act. Meat inspection came about as a result of muckraking that exposed unsafe practices to consumers. The activism led by women resulted in the 18th and 19th Amendments. The formation of the Department of Labor would respond most directly to the concerns of workers, so this reform makes the most sense.

Vocabulary

Progressive Era—period of widespread social activism and political reform addressing problems of urbanization and political corruption in the United States from the 1890s to the 1920s

urbanization—process of concentrating the population of cities

tenement house—a house divided into separate rented rooms, usually in poor condition and overcrowded

Hull House—one of the first settlement houses in the United States (Chicago, 1889); founded to provide needed social programs

labor union—organization of workers in a trade or profession that can stand up for their rights and interests

strike—protest when employees refuse to work and demand a change from their employer

muckraker—journalist exposing corruption of industries, systems, and/or individual leaders during the Progressive Era

The Jungle—work written by Upton Sinclair that resulted in regulation of the meat-packing industry

Temperance movement—organized effort to outlaw alcohol in the United States

18th Amendment—amendment that made alcohol illegal in the United States

Prohibition—period when alcohol was illegal in the United States (1920–1933)

19th Amendment—amendment granting women the right to vote

suffrage—right to vote

"trust-busting"—efforts to promote competition by limiting or eliminating corporate trusts or monopolies

Sherman Antitrust Act—first "trust-busting" law passed by the U.S. Congress (in 1890): outlawed trusts or monopolies

monopoly—a company that dominates an entire industry or sector of the market, excluding any competition

Federal Trade Commission Act—law of 1914 that banned certain commercial practices to protect the competitive market

16th Amendment—amendment that established **income tax**, a percent amount of pay owed to fund the government

17th Amendment—amendment that established **direct election of senators**, which enabled the people to vote for their representatives

Progressive Era Drill

You can check your answers in Part IX: Answer Key to Drills.

<u>Questions 1 and 2</u> refer to this political cartoon from the Progressive Era.

Chapin, Archibald. "The Last Few Buttons Are Always the Hardest." *St. Louis Star* (1919)

1. The label "national suffrage" in the political cartoon refers to [Select... ▼].
   - women's struggle to fit new social roles
   - low wages
   - the right to vote
   - high prices

2. The numbers above the label "ratification" represent

   A. numbers of states.
   B. measurements.
   C. numbers of women.
   D. years.

WORLD WAR I

World War I (WWI), or "The Great War" as it was called at the time, began in 1914 and lasted until 1918. The root causes of WWI had been building up in Europe for years before the war was triggered.

First, countries had formed a network of **alliances**: Russia and Serbia; Germany and Austria-Hungary; France and Russia; Britain and France and Belgium; and Japan and Britain. If any one of these countries were to be attacked, its allies would be pulled into the conflict because they were bound to defend them. These alliances laid the groundwork for war involving many countries.

Another trend paving the way for conflict was **imperialism**, or the growth of empires by taking over new lands and their resources. Several European countries were fighting over claims in Africa and Asia before WWI. This tension pushed the competing countries toward confrontation.

Along with these imperialist tendencies, countries had begun competing to develop their military power, beefing up their armies and battleships, developing new weapons and defense methods, as if preparing for war. Through this military buildup or **militarism**, powerful nations set course for WWI.

The desire to increase the power of one's nation through military might and expansion is an expression of **nationalism**. WWI became an opportunity for nations to try proving their greatness.

Nationalism also motivated the event that sparked off the war: the **assassination of Archduke Franz Ferdinand** of Austria-Hungary, which was committed by a Serbian Nationalist group protesting the control of Austria-Hungary. This assassination led to Austria-Hungary declaring war on Serbia, drawing Russia into the conflict, and thus Germany, and so on, according to the lines drawn by alliances.

World War I began in 1914, but the United States would not enter the conflict until 1917. As a nation of immigrants, the United States was a refuge for many Europeans who had fled increasing tensions. Americans were also not interested in getting involved in foreign interests. President Woodrow Wilson had just won re-election in 1916 with the campaign slogan "He Kept Us Out of War." The United States sought to maintain **neutrality** until hit directly by Germany's actions: first, Germany resumed **unrestricted submarine warfare** and sank a British ship, the *Lusitania*, carrying more than a hundred Americans; secondly, in the **Zimmermann Telegram** discovered by British allies, Germany had asked Mexico to join the war in exchange for the lands it had lost to the United States. The United States declared war on Germany on April 6, 1917.

In addition to more than a million Americans who joined the armed forces, citizens participated in the war effort by producing war materials, rationing supplies, and purchasing bonds to fund the war. U.S. government **propaganda** appealed to citizens' patriotism and sense of duty, linking domestic efforts to the defense of democracy.

How might World War I appear on the GED® test? Try this question.

This propaganda poster was circulated during World War I.

Britton, L.N. "Eat more corn, oats and rye products..." (1917)

1. The purpose of this poster was to encourage people in the U.S. to

Select... ▼
ration a limited supply
buy more U.S. produce
get fit to join the U.S. army
save money

.

Here's How to Crack It

The text on the poster tells you about the connection between action and effect: the poster is calling people to "eat more" of certain foods and "eat less" of others "to save for the army and our allies." Restricting how much you consume of a limited supply, as during war time, is called rationing. Even if the term *rationing* is not familiar, "limited supply" can be your clue that this is the correct answer. The poster is talking only about food choices, not about the U.S. market, fitness, or money. Including "our allies" also suggests that consumers are being asked to help the war effort more generally by helping to manage the food supply for others.

Vocabulary

World War I (WWI)—international conflict fought mostly in Europe from 1914 to 1918
alliance—an association between two or more countries in which they agree to come to one another's defense
imperialism—increasing a nation's influence and power by taking over other territories
militarism—building up armed forces as if in preparation for war
nationalism—pride in the dominance of one's nation
assassination of Archduke Franz Ferdinand—political assassination that started WWI; a protest against Austria-Hungary's control of regions that wanted to be part of Serbia
neutrality—status of not helping either side in a conflict
unrestricted submarine warfare—wartime practice of sinking ships without warning
Zimmermann Telegram—communication in which the United States learned that Germany asked Mexico for help in WWI in exchange for returned lands
propaganda—information designed to manipulate public opinion to promote a point of view or cause

World War I Drill

You can check your answers in Part IX: Answer Key to Drills.

Causes of World War I			
Militarism	Nationalism	Alliances	Imperialism

Click on the cause of WWI that is described in each of the events below (for this drill, circle the cause):

1. The rivalry between Britain and Germany intensified when they competed for claims to land in Northern Africa.

2. Russia entered WWI in defense of Serbia after Austria-Hungary declared war.

GREAT DEPRESSION

During the period known as the **Great Depression** (1929–1939), Americans suffered the consequences of the economic boom that they had enjoyed in the 1920s. In the years after WWI ended, there were plenty of opportunities to make and spend money. Businesses were adding jobs and investors. Even ordinary people started putting their money into the **stock market** or **speculating**, betting on the future profits of businesses by buying **shares** in companies. They were even speculating on **credit**, borrowing money from banks to invest in the rising stock market.

In the summer of 1929, business started to slow down; prices dropped, profits declined, and investors started selling their shares, further tanking the value of stocks that people had purchased. On October 29, 1929, the date known as **Black Tuesday**, millions of shares were traded, causing the stock market to bottom out. Panic spread, and crowds gathered in **bank runs** to demand the money in their accounts. But the banks had most cash tied up in loans that were not being paid back. Many people also suffered **foreclosures**, losing their homes when they could not make loan payments, and jobs were lost as businesses downsized, sending families into poverty.

To make matters worse, in 1933, a drought in the Midwest caused food shortages. Because of the damage wrought by dust storms, this prairie region came to be known as the **Dust Bowl**.

The Great Depression worsened before any relief came. President Hoover did not believe that the government should step in to solve the problems that Americans were facing. He was harshly criticized for this lack of action. For example, people who lost their homes built **shantytowns** out of whatever materials were available; these unsafe, makeshift residences were called **Hoovervilles**.

When Hoover lost the Presidential election of 1932, Franklin Delano Roosevelt (FDR) steered the government toward recovery. One of his first executive actions was to try stabilizing the banking system with the **Emergency Banking Act**. In 1933, FDR launched a set of programs called the **New Deal** to create jobs and provide security. Helping to bring down the **unemployment** rate, which peaked at 25%, the **Works Progress Administration (WPA)** employed millions to build infrastructure throughout the United States. Another New Deal measure, the **Social Security Act** of 1935, guaranteed unemployment pay, and pensions for retired elderly citizens.

While FDR's New Deal provided some relief during the Great Depression, it was the start of WWII that pulled the U.S. economy out of crisis. All factories turned their production to the war effort. Americans were participating in this **"arsenal of democracy"** years before the country entered the armed conflict. Seventeen million new jobs were created during WWII, allowing workers to pay off debts and even begin saving.

How might the Great Depression appear on the GED® test? Try this question.

The following chart lists many of the programs implemented under President Franklin D. Roosevelt's "New Deal":

1933	
Emergency Banking Act	Closed down all banks, examined their books, and reopened those that were solvent
Farm Credit Administration	Made low-interest, long-term loans to farmers for mortgages, equipment, and taxes
Economy Act	Proposed balancing the federal budget
Civilian Conservation Corps	Paid $30 a month to boys and young men to work in national parks and plant trees throughout the West
Federal Emergency Relief Administration	• Distributed $500 million to states for direct aid to families • Matched every $3 that cities and towns spent on relief projects with $1 in federal aid
Agricultural Adjustment Administration	Paid farmers to grow fewer crops, thus bringing prices up (later declared unconstitutional)
Tennessee Valley Authority	Built dams, provided electricity, and otherwise greatly improved conditions in the Tennessee Valley, one of the nation's poorest regions
Home Owners' Loan Corporation	• Made low-interest, long-term mortgage loans • Protected people from losing their houses
Banking Act of 1933	• Created the FDIC (see next row) • Authorized branch banking
Federal Deposit Insurance Corporation	Insured individual bank deposits of up to $5,000
National Recovery Administration	Regulated businesses by establishing minimum wages and other standards to protect workers
Public Works Administration	Contracted private firms to hire millions of people to build bridges, post offices, highways, and other structures
Civil Works Administration	Created millions of low-skill jobs such as cleaning city streets
1934	
Securities and Exchange Commission	Regulated companies that sold stocks and bonds
Federal Housing Administration	Insured all bank loans made for the construction and repair of houses

1. Which of the boxed New Deal programs below directly provided jobs to the unemployed?

Click on the programs you want to select and drag them into the box below.

Job Programs Under the New Deal

(a) Emergency Banking Act
(b) Civil Works Administration (CWA)
(c) Public Works Administration (PWA)
(d) Federal Housing Administration (FHA)
(e) Civilian Conservation Corps (CCC)
(f) Economy Act

Here's How to Crack It

Look for the words related to employment: jobs, hire, paid. According to the descriptions in the chart, only the (b) Civil Works Administration, (c) Public Works Administration, and (e) Civilian Conservation Corps involved putting people to work. Be careful: Federal Housing Administration relates to the construction and repair of houses, but only in terms of financing through bank loans, not hiring people to do the work.

Vocabulary

Great Depression—poor economic times that began after the stock market crash of 1929 and continued for a decade in the United States
stock market—where shares of a company are bought and sold
speculation—investing in future profits of businesses
share—an equal part of a company's value owned by an investor who will receive a proportional amount of its profits
credit—money lent or advanced, often to be paid back with interest
Black Tuesday—October 29, 1929, date when share prices on the stock market fell dramatically, marking the start of the Great Depression
bank run—event when customers demand more money than a bank has available
foreclosure—forced sale of a home or other asset when a loan is not being repaid

Dust Bowl—name for plains region of the United States that suffered severe dust storms and drought during the 1930s
shantytowns—crudely made dwellings
Hoovervilles—grouped shelters built by people who were homeless during the Great Depression
Emergency Banking Act—legislation passed by FDR in an attempt to stabilize the banking system
New Deal— FDR's plan for relief and recovery from the Great Depression
unemployment rate—percentage of labor force that is not working
Works Progress Administration (WPA)—government program that employed millions of workers in construction and other projects during the Great Depression
Social Security Act—law establishing benefits for retired workers, the unemployed, and people with workplace injuries and disabilities
"arsenal of democracy"—phrase used by FDR calling for workers to ramp up production for WWII

Great Depression Drill

You can check your answers in Part IX: Answer Key to Drills.

Questions 1 and 2 refer to the graph below.

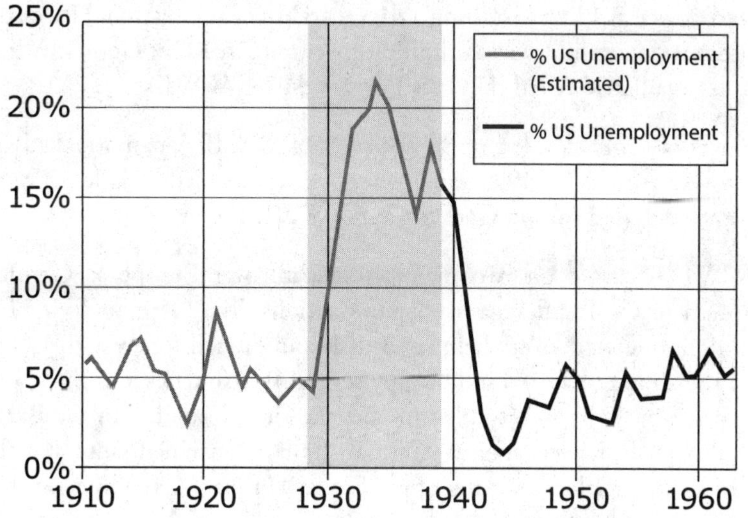

U.S. Unemployment 1910–1960

1. Click on the year in which the highest number of Americans were unemployed. (For this drill, circle the year.)

1929	1933	1939	1943

2. During which of the following years did unemployment decline at the fastest rate?

A. 1914–1918
B. 1929–1933
C. 1940–1942
D. 1949–1953

WORLD WAR II

World War I may have ended in 1918, but this conflict led directly to **World War II**. Large-scale war had traumatized an entire generation of people, who looked to leaders offering radical solutions to political and economic instability.

In Germany, the harsh terms of the peace treaty ending WWI, the **Treaty of Versailles**, set the stage for the rise of **Adolf Hitler**. Hitler stoked the anger of the German people and blamed all their problems on the Jewish population. Once he became the Führer, or absolute leader, he led a campaign to remove Jewish people, rounding up families to live in ghettos, work to death in **concentration camps**, or to be killed outright. Millions of people, not only Jews but also other targeted minorities, died in the **Holocaust**.

Hitler may be most remembered for the scale of invasion and mass murder that he led, but there were other **fascist** leaders who took control of nations by force at this time. In Italy, Mussolini seized power in 1922, installing a **dictatorship** of the National Fascist Party. And in Japan, Hirohito started a military expansion of his empire in 1926. Germany, Italy, and Japan would operate as an alliance called the **Axis Powers** during WWII.

Several major acts of aggression led up to the start of WWII: Japan attacked China in 1937, Germany took over Austria in 1938, and when Hitler invaded Poland in September 1939, Britain and France declared war on Germany, and WWII began.

Fighting in WWII occurred on two major fronts: all over Europe as Germany expanded its occupation and in the Pacific against Japan's actions. The German style of assault called **blitzkrieg** or "lightning war" overwhelmed British and French forces with its speed of attack on land and in the air. Germany would occupy several British cities and the seat of the French government in Paris by 1940, but it failed to take the city of London in the **Battle of Britain**. British forces also pushed back against German-Italian movement into North Africa, and Russia defended against Hitler's invasion of the **Soviet Union**. Meanwhile, on the Pacific front, Japan continued its assault on China.

On December 7, 1941, Japan attacked **Pearl Harbor**, an American base in Hawaii, and the United States declared war on Japan. Days later, Germany and Italy declared war on the United States, and American forces were fully engaged in WWII combat as part of the alliance of **Allies**: Britain, France, and eventually the **USSR,** or Soviet Union.

Major turning points in WWII include the **Battle of Midway** (June 1942), when the United States destroyed Japan's naval fleet to establish its dominance early on in the Pacific, and **D-Day** (June 1944), when the Allies bombarded German forces on the shores of Normandy, France.

WWII was also fought on the U.S. homefront in different ways. Americans participated in the war effort by rationing, recycling, buying government bonds, and planting **Victory Gardens** to increase the supply of fresh foods. From 1942 to 1946, the U.S. government imprisoned Japanese Americans, which included separating families with children, in **internment camps** or military housing.

WWII came to an end in 1945. (Italy had already surrendered in 1943.) In April 1945, Germany surrendered after the death of Hitler. Months later, in August 1945, the United States dropped **atomic bombs** on the cities of Hiroshima and Nagasaki to force Japan's surrender. The Allies divided up Germany into districts that they would control. To help rebuild the rest of Europe, the United States passed the **Marshall Plan** to provide economic assistance. In the hope of preventing yet another World War, the **United Nations** was formed with a commitment to maintaining international peace.

American soldiers returning home from the war could take advantage of housing and educational opportunities offered through the **GI Bill**, which strengthened the U.S. economy and its middle class after WWII.

How might World War II appear on the GED® test? Try this question.

Causes of World War II			
Political tensions and economic insecurity across Europe	Rise of dictators using nationalism to control populations	Acts of aggression by other countries	Failure of the League of Nations

1. Click on the cause of WWII that led most directly to the United States entering the war.

Here's How to Crack It

Remember that the United States stayed out of WWII until it was attacked by Japanese forces at Pearl Harbor. What was happening in Europe and in Southeast Asia did not prompt the United States to get involved. The failure of the League of Nations (which the United States did not join) had more to do with the rise of the Axis Powers, but this threat is not the reason for U.S. entry into WWII. The correct selection is acts of aggression by other countries—in this case, Japanese aggression against the United States.

Vocabulary

World War II—war involving the world's great national powers in two opposing alliances: the Allies and the Axis Powers (1939–1945)

Treaty of Versailles—treaty that punished Germany at the end of World War I

Adolf Hitler—leader of Nazi Germany who provoked World War II in Europe and directed the imprisonment and execution of the Jewish population

concentration camp—facility where masses of people are detained in poor conditions, and often forced to work or be put to death

Holocaust—systematic killing of millions of Jewish people and others by the German state during World War II

fascism—movement or government characterized by absolute control of social and economic systems and populations, extreme nationalism, and brutal suppression of opposition

dictatorship—type of government in which one person (a dictator) exercises unrestricted power

Axis Powers—the alliance between Germany, Italy, and Japan in World War II

blitzkrieg—German word meaning "lightning war," military strategy that overwhelmed enemy forces with firepower and shocking speed

Battle of Britain—successful defense of Great Britain against German air raids from July through September 1940

USSR (Soviet Union)—former country called the Union of Soviet Socialist Republics that included Russia and several other present-day countries (1922–1991)

Pearl Harbor—Hawaiian coastal site of a U.S. naval base that was attacked by Japanese air bombers on Sunday, December 7, 1941

Allies—the WWII alliance between Great Britain, France, the United States, and eventually the Soviet Union

Battle of Midway—defeat of Japanese by American forces in June 1942

D-Day—invasion of northern France by Allied forces on June 6, 1944

Victory Gardens—gardens planted to increase food production during a war

internment camp—military housing used to confine members of national or minority groups for reasons of state security

atomic bomb—weapon using nuclear energy to cause widespread damage

Marshall Plan—American aid plan to help Western Europe rebuild after WWII

United Nations—international organization formed after WWII with the goal of maintaining peace and security among nations

GI Bill—benefits for WWII veterans returning to the United States that increased access to college education and home ownership

World War II Drill

You can check your answers in Part IX: Answer Key to Drills.

Questions 1 and 2 refer to the following text, taken from a speech by President Franklin Delano Roosevelt.

> As Commander in Chief of the Army and Navy, I have directed that all measures be taken for our defense. But always will our whole nation remember the character of the onslaught against us.
>
> No matter how long it may take us to overcome this premeditated invasion, the American people in their righteous might will win through to absolute victory.
>
> I believe that I interpret the will of the Congress and of the people when I assert that we will not only defend ourselves to the uttermost, but will make it very certain that this form of treachery shall never again endanger us.
>
> Hostilities exist. There is no blinking at the fact that our people, our territory, and our interests are in grave danger.
>
> With confidence in our armed forces, with the unbounding determination of our people, we will gain the inevitable triumph—so help us God.
>
> I ask that the Congress declare that since the unprovoked and dastardly attack by Japan on Sunday, December 7th, 1941, a state of war has existed between the United States and the Japanese empire.

1. Based on the excerpt, what event was Roosevelt addressing when he made this speech?

   A. the Battle of Midway
   B. the attack on Pearl Harbor
   C. the invasion of Allied territory
   D. the fall of Singapore

2. Click to highlight the selections of text where President Roosevelt presents the U.S. response to Japan as defensive. (For this drill, underline the text.)

COLD WAR

At the end of WWII, the United States and the Soviet Union emerged as rival superpowers, and the **Cold War** began. Lasting decades from 1947 to 1991, the Cold War was not a direct, combat-based war; it was a long period of tension between Western democracies and the sphere of communist influence with the Soviet Union at its center. The United States and the Soviet Union fought each other indirectly by fueling **proxy wars** and competing in the **arms race** and the **space race**.

As the Allies worked to reset international relations in the wake of WWII, the Americans and the British worried that democracies within the reach of the Soviet Union would fall to **communism**, a social system based on the idea of economic equality established through government control of property and production. The Soviets were interested in widening the influence of communism while also trying to maintain a buffer against potential threats.

The United States began to get involved in the affairs of Europe after an important speech in 1946 by **Winston Churchill**, the prime minister of Britain who had been a United States ally in WWII. Churchill came to address Congress about the growing communist threat in Europe. He described an **Iron Curtain** dividing the democratic nations of the West and the **Eastern Bloc** under communist influence—not a physical wall, but a very real division. The United States decided to respond by providing foreign aid to support democracy against the threat of communism. This policy of intervention was called the **Truman Doctrine** after President Harry S. Truman. The United States also adopted the **policy of containment** by acting to stop the spread of communist influence and the **domino effect** of one country falling to communism, causing another to fall. In 1949, the United States and several European allies formed the **North Atlantic Treaty Organization (NATO)** to protect democracy against Soviet influence.

Sometimes the Cold War turned hot or erupted into armed conflict. When the Soviet-supported communist government of North Korea invaded U.S.-supported South Korea in 1950, the **Korean War** began and lasted until 1953. In other examples of proxy wars, Soviet troops occupied countries to prop up communist governments in East Germany (1953), Hungary (1956), Czechoslovakia (1968), and Afghanistan (1979), while the United States tried to undermine communist rule in Guatemala (1954), Cuba (1961), the Dominican Republic (1965), and Vietnam (1964–1975).

The United States and the Soviet Union committed their countries' resources to developing weapons and achieving space exploration. They avoided war while stockpiling nuclear arms because these weapons amounted to **"mutually assured destruction"**; if one country used a nuclear weapon on another with the same power, both would be annihilated. The **Cuban Missile Crisis**, a standoff between the United States and the Soviet Union over nuclear missiles in Cuba, was a dangerous game of chicken based on this idea. Being the first to reach milestones in space exploration also allowed Americans and Soviets to compete with one another. In this space race, the Soviet Union launched the first satellite, named **Sputnik**, in 1957, and the United States followed with the **Moon landing** of Apollo 11 in 1969.

The Cold War also had a significant impact on American society. U.S. citizens, among them many celebrities, were accused of being communists during the era of **McCarthyism**. Americans were even made suspicious of their own neighbors during this **Red Scare**.

The year 1991 marked the end of the Cold War when the Soviet Union collapsed and tensions lifted. Already in 1989, the fall of the **Berlin Wall**, the physical barrier separating communist East Berlin and capitalist West Berlin, announced to the world that democracy was winning.

How might the Cold War appear on the GED® test? Try this question.

This excerpt is from a speech by President Harry Truman:

> Members of the Congress of the United States:
>
> The very existence of the Greek state is today threatened by the terrorist activities of several thousand armed men, led by Communists, who defy the government's authority at a number of points, particularly along the northern boundaries.... Meanwhile, the Greek Government is unable to cope with the situation. The Greek army is small and poorly equipped. It needs supplies and equipment if it is to restore the authority of the government throughout Greek territory. Greece must have assistance if it is to become a self-supporting and self-respecting democracy...The United States must supply that assistance.

1. Based on the excerpt, what event was Truman addressing when he made this speech?

   A. the desegregation of the military
   B. the final stages of World War II
   C. his reelection campaign
   D. the early stages of the Cold War

Here's How to Crack It

There is a key phrase in this document that states rebellion in Europe is "led by Communists." Communism characterized the Soviet Union during the Cold War and the Soviets attempted to gain influence in Europe by infiltrating European governments. The U.S. response was containment policy, which aimed to disallow the spread of communism beyond Soviet borders. This is called the Truman Doctrine, which set the stage for the Cold War. Choice (D) is correct. While Truman is responsible for the desegregation of the military, there is no evidence in the text of this action, so (A) is incorrect. Truman oversaw the final stages of World War II as president, but did not declare the Truman Doctrine until after the war was over, so (B) is incorrect. There is no evidence of a political campaign, so eliminate (C).

Vocabulary

Cold War—decades-long period of hostile relations between the United States and the Soviet Union over the influence of communism

proxy war—conflict incited by or fought on behalf of actors that are not fighting directly, but through the war between other parties

arms race—competition between nations to develop weapons as a show of dominance

space race—competition between Soviet and American rivals to achieve firsts in space exploration during the Cold War

communism—a social system based on state control of the economy and means of production

Winston Churchill—prime minister of Great Britain who led the country through World War II and the start of the Cold War

Iron Curtain—dividing line between Western democracies and the Eastern Bloc of Soviet-influenced communist states, a term used by Winston Churchill to define the communist threat to the West

Eastern Bloc—communist nations under Soviet influence during the Cold War

Truman Doctrine—U.S. policy of supporting nations under communist threat; originated with President Truman's speech to Congress concerning aid to Greece and Turkey in 1947

policy of containment—U.S. policy of intervening in foreign nations to stop the influence of communism from spreading

domino effect—chain reaction when one event leads to a cascade of events, much like falling dominoes; used to describe the spread of communism

North Atlantic Treaty Organization (NATO)—organization formed by the United States, Canada, Britain, and other European countries to defend one another for the sake of democracy, which at the time was threatened by Soviet influence

Korean War—proxy war fought in the early 1950s between U.S.-supported forces and communist North Korea, who had invaded South Korea

"mutually assured destruction"—state of war when nuclear weapons would cause the destruction of both sides

Cuban Missile Crisis—13-day confrontation between the United States and the Soviet Union over Soviet nuclear missiles in Cuba

Sputnik—Soviet satellite that was the first to be launched into Earth's orbit (October 4, 1957)

Moon landing—U.S. landing of the Apollo 11, which was the first astronaut-navigated mission on the Moon (July 20, 1969)

McCarthyism—campaign led by Senator Joseph McCarthy accusing many Americans of being communists in the 1950s

Red Scare—period when the fear of communism was elevated

Berlin Wall—physical barrier separating communist East Berlin and capitalist West Berlin from 1961 to 1989

Cold War Drill

You can check your answers in Part IX: Answer Key to Drills.

Questions 1 and 2 refer to this timeline of the Cold War.

1946	British Prime Minister Winston Churchill addresses U.S. Congress about "the Iron Curtain" across Europe
1947	U.S. President Truman appeals to Congress for aid to the democracies of Western Europe under Communist threat
1950	The Korean War begins between Communist North Korea supported by the Soviets and South Korea supported by the United States
1957	Soviets launched the Sputnik satellite into Earth's orbit
1962	U.S. President Kennedy avoids war with Soviet Union over nuclear-armed missiles in the Cuban Missile Crisis

1. The timeline above includes examples that illustrate the terms below. Drag and drop one event into each box (for this quiz, you may simply write the year of the event in the appropriate box).

proxy war	space race	mutually assured destruction

2. What was "the Iron Curtain" that Churchill described in his address to U.S. Congress?

   A. a physical wall dividing Germany into East and West
   B. a trade barrier between the United States and England
   C. the boundary between warm and cold countries
   D. the dividing line between democratic and communist influence in Europe

CIVIL RIGHTS MOVEMENT

Even though Black Americans were granted the rights of U.S. citizens, including the right to vote, and "equal protection of the laws" during Reconstruction, the legacy of racism persisted in the social and legal institutions of the South. Southern states passed **"Jim Crow" laws** based on the **"separate but equal"** status of Black Americans established in ***Plessy v. Ferguson*** (1896). This Supreme Court ruling concerned a New Orleans man of mixed racial heritage who tried to ride the whites-only streetcar and was arrested when he refused to leave. But the ruling gave broad legal license to **racial segregation**, which organized life in the South; places where people lived, worked, ate, shopped, gathered, and used services of all sorts were separated by race. Jim Crow restricted Black people to inferior treatment and facilities, like schools, hospitals, restaurants, water fountains, bathrooms, and public transportation.

In 1954, the Supreme Court reversed the "separate but equal" doctrine in ***Brown v. Board of Education***, which concerned the segregation of schools. The Court ruled that "separate educational facilities are inherently unequal"—the very act of separating people by race creates conditions that are not equal. The Court's decision, stripping racial segregation of its legal status, was not honored in the South. As schools were forced to desegregate, Black students had to be escorted to schools by United States marshals and were met with violent backlash.

The fight against continued racial segregation took the form of **civil disobedience**, bringing attention to the injustice of laws by breaking them. In Montgomery, Alabama, Black people were allowed to sit only in seats remaining in the backs of buses. When **Rosa Parks** refused to give up her seat to a white man, she was arrested, and her case stirred up the energy of resistance. The **Montgomery Bus Boycott**, organized in response to Parks's arrest, was one of the largest mass protests against racial segregation, and it set **Martin Luther King Jr.** (MLK) on his way to becoming a leader of the Civil Rights Movement. Other tactics of civil disobedience included **sit-ins**, or sitting at whites-only counters to provoke a response, and **freedom rides**, multi-racial groups who rode buses together across states, peacefully, but often triggering an extreme response. The **Congress of Racial Equality (CORE)** organized most of these freedom rides, but some were organized by the **Student Nonviolent Coordinating Committee (SNCC)**, which was formed to give young people more of a voice in the Civil Rights Movement. On August 28, 1963, an estimated 250,000 people gathered for the **March on Washington**, a mass demonstration for racial equality. It was here, in front of the Lincoln Memorial, that MLK gave his famous **"I Have a Dream Speech."** President John F. Kennedy began to push for legislation that would respond to the concerns of the Civil Rights Movement. Kennedy was assassinated in 1963, so it was his successor, Lyndon B. Johnson, who signed the **Civil Rights Act of 1964**.

Demonstrations during the Civil Rights Movement also focused on voting rights. After protesters were violently stopped on their march from Selma to Montgomery, Alabama, President Johnson ordered federal protection for a second organized march; the **Selma to Montgomery March** led directly to the **Voting Rights Act of 1965**, which outlawed practices like **literacy tests** that were used to keep Black Americans from voting.

The activism of the Civil Rights Movement brought the country closer to the promise of equal rights and opportunities.

How might the Civil Rights Movement appear on the GED® test? Try this question.

The following passage comes from the majority opinion of *Plessy v. Ferguson* (1896):

> The argument...assumes that social prejudice may be overcome by legislation, and that equal rights cannot be secured except by an enforced commingling of the two races.... If the civil and political rights of both races be equal, one cannot be inferior to the other civilly or politically. If one race be inferior to the other socially, the Constitution of the United States cannot put them upon the same plane.

The following passage comes from the majority opinion of *Brown v. Board of Education* (1954):

> A sense of inferiority affects the motivation of a child to learn. Segregation with the sanction of law, therefore, has a tendency to [retard] the educational and mental development of Negro children and to deprive them of some of the benefits they would receive in a racially integrated school system.... We conclude that, in the field of public education, the doctrine of 'separate but equal' has no place. Separate educational facilities are inherently unequal.

1. Drag the consequences of each Supreme Court decision into the proper box:

Legacy of *Plessy v. Ferguson*	**Legacy of *Brown v. Board of Education***

- desegregation of schools
- increase of Jim Crow laws
- further division between Black and white people
- some Southerners resisting forced integration
- the rapid acceleration of the civil rights movement
- the creation of "separate but equal" facilities

Here's How to Crack It

Plessy v. Ferguson sets up the "separate but equal" doctrine. Therefore, any answer choice that deals with promoting segregation based on race will go in the box on the left. These are as follows: increase of Jim Crow laws, further division between Black and white people, and the creation of "separate but equal" facilities. *Brown v. Board of Education* ended segregation in schools, effectively shooting down the "separate but equal" doctrine and jump-starting the civil rights movement of the 1950s and 1960s. Any choice that shows the promotion of racial integration or the start of the civil rights movement should go on the right. These are as follows: desegregation of schools, some Southerners resisting forced integration, and the rapid acceleration of the civil rights movement.

Vocabulary

"Jim Crow" laws—state and local laws ordering racial segregation, named after an insulting slang term

"separate but equal"—doctrine that justified the legal status of racial segregation because it did not violate the right to "equal protection of the laws"

Plessy v. Ferguson—U.S. Supreme Court ruling from 1896 that gave legal status to laws ordering racial segregation

racial segregation—systemic separation of people by race

Brown v. Board of Education—U.S. Supreme Court ruling from 1954 that declared segregation in public schools to be unconstitutional

civil disobedience—refusing to obey rules as a form of nonviolent protest

Rosa Parks—African American woman who was arrested for refusing to give up her seat on a Montgomery city bus

Montgomery Bus Boycott—mass protest against segregated seating on Montgomery city buses from December 5, 1955 to December 20, 1956

Martin Luther King Jr.—organizer and Baptist minister who was a prominent leader of the civil rights movement until his assassination in 1968

sit-in—the practice of occupying a place and refusing to leave as a form of nonviolent protest

freedom ride—interracial group of bus riders who challenged racial segregation on interstate buses

Congress of Racial Equality (CORE)—group founded in 1942 that organized nonviolent protests during the Civil Rights Movement

Student Nonviolent Coordinating Committee (SNCC)—group formed in 1960 to give younger Black people more of a voice

March on Washington—mass demonstration that occurred in August 1963, when an estimated 250,000 people gathered in Washington, D.C. for racial equality

"I Have a Dream" Speech—memorable speech given by MLK on the steps of the Lincoln Memorial at the March on Washington

Civil Rights Act of 1964—law that ended discrimination on the basis of race, color, religion, sex, or national origin

Selma to Montgomery March—mass protest for voting rights that was met with violence and then reattempted with federal protection

Voting Rights Act of 1965—law that outlawed practices that prevented Black Americans from voting

literacy test—test determining one's ability to read and write, required for voting

Civil Rights Movement Drill

You can check your answers in Part IX: Answer Key to Drills.

Questions 1 and 2 refer to the following information.

The Montgomery Bus Boycott was among the first mass protests against segregation laws.
If the Voting Rights Act had been passed before 1965, the Civil Rights Movement would have ended earlier.
Many civil rights activists used nonviolent civil disobedience to protest racial inequality.
The struggle for equal rights moved President John F. Kennedy to push for civil rights legislation.

1. Three of the above statements about the Civil Rights Movement are based on facts and evidence. Click to select the one based on speculation or opinion. (For this drill, circle the statement.)

2. Which of the following would NOT be an example of "nonviolent civil disobedience"?

   A. refusing to move from certain lunch counters
   B. refusing to move from a bus seat
   C. participating in a bus boycott
   D. riding on a bus across states lines as an interracial group

VIETNAM WAR

The **Vietnam War** was a long, unpopular war in which the United States stepped into another country's conflict to stop the spread of communism.

When Vietnam won its independence from France in 1954, the country was divided into North and South Vietnam. North Vietnam was communist, while South Vietnam was anti-communist. When it became apparent that the South would resist unifying as one country, communists in South Vietnam, **guerrilla fighters** known as the **Vietcong**, began trying to overthrow the government. The communist North aided in this effort, training fighters and providing supplies that were transported North to South via the **Ho Chi Minh Trail**.

To support South Vietnam in resisting communist takeover, the United States sent thousands of military advisors. The situation worsened, and in 1965, President Lyndon B. Johnson ordered airstrikes and deployed American troops on the ground in South Vietnam, which by this time was mostly under the control of the Vietcong. While U.S. forces had more advanced weapons, including jet bombers and helicopters, the Vietcong knew the jungle terrain and engaged in brutal surprise tactics.

By 1968, more than 500,000 American soldiers were fighting the Vietcong in South Vietnam. The United States was spending billions of dollars on the war, and Americans were watching soldiers and civilians die on television. When the Vietcong and North Vietnamese carried out the **Tet Offensive**, a coordinated series of surprise attacks on villages and cities all over South Vietnam, Americans began to doubt the U.S. government's claims that the war was all but won. Public opinion turned against the Vietnam War as Americans began to ask whether it was worth the cost, even whether the United States should be fighting communism in other countries at all.

People began to protest the Vietnam War, especially the **draft**, which randomly selected young men to go fight in the jungles of Vietnam. As a result of these antiwar demonstrations, support grew for lowering the voting age from 21 to 18, since young men were being called to give their lives for their country when they could not even vote. The **26th Amendment** was passed in March 1971, extending voting rights to American citizens at age 18.

When Richard Nixon was elected president in 1969, the United States moved toward **Vietnamization**, the process of withdrawing American troops and letting South Vietnam take more responsibility for fighting the war. U.S. soldiers started coming home, but the bombing of North Vietnam and neighboring Cambodia increased, targeting the flow of supplies and soldiers into South Vietnam. Through efforts to end the war with diplomacy, a **cease-fire** agreement was reached in the **Paris Peace Accords** of 1973. In 1975, South Vietnam surrendered and the country was reunified under Communist rule.

The Vietnam War cost more than a million lives, a large number of these Vietnamese civilians, and billions of U.S. dollars. As a result of American involvement in Vietnam, the U.S. Congress passed the **War Powers Act** in 1973, requiring the president to seek approval from Congress before sending U.S. troops to war.

How might the Vietnam War appear on the GED® test? Try this question.

1954 Vietnam gained independence, divided into North and South	1960 Northern guerrilla fighters, the Vietcong, or Vietnamese communists, attack South Vietnam	1965 United States bombs North Vietnam and sends combat troops to South Vietnam	1968 Tet Offensive attacks shock the United States, which begins gradual withdrawal of troops

1. The United States fought against the Vietcong in the Vietnam War to stop the spread of ______________.

Here's How to Crack It

This fill-in-the-blank question doesn't *necessarily* require that you know the cause of U.S. involvement in the Vietnam War (although that would make it easier!). You can use the information given in the timeline to connect the Vietcong (Vietnamese communists) to communism, the correct answer, as a threat to be contained. The only word that would fit in the blank is something that could spread, like influence or ideas, not a small group of fighters in a faraway country.

Vocabulary

Vietnam War—military conflict (1954–1975) in which the United States supported South Vietnam against communist North Vietnamese fighters

guerrilla fighter—one who engages in warfare usually in less organized groups using surprise tactics

Vietcong—communist guerrilla fighters of North Vietnam who fought South Vietnam and United States forces in the Vietnam War

Ho Chi Minh Trail—military supply route that sent men, weapons, and other supplies from North Vietnam to South Vietnam during the Vietnam War

Tet Offensive—coordinated series of attacks on South Vietnamese cities and towns that shocked the United States with its swift brutality

draft—selection for mandatory military service by a lottery system

26th Amendment—amendment that lowered the voting age from 21 to 18

Vietnamization—U.S. policy of withdrawing troops and making South Vietnam more responsible for the Vietnam War

cease-fire—a pause in fighting, usually for negotiations to take place

Paris Peace Accords—agreement between North Vietnam, South Vietnam, and the United States to end the Vietnam War

War Powers Act—law passed after the Vietnam War to limit the president's power to declare war, requiring a Congressional vote

Vietnam War Drill

You can check your answers in Part IX: Answer Key to Drills.

Questions 1 and 2 refer to this image, capturing an antiwar protest in New York City in 1967.

Footage of Draft Card Burning in New York City, 1967

1. This group of demonstrators was burning draft cards to protest

   A. the U.S. military strategy of burning lands in Vietnam.
   B. the lottery system selecting men for mandatory service during the Vietnam War.
   C. age restrictions on military service.
   D. their university's support for the Vietnam War.

2. Youth protests during this time used the slogan "Old enough to fight, old enough to vote" to push for which of the following?

   A. Voting Rights Act
   B. universal suffrage
   C. abolishing poll taxes
   D. lowering the voting age to 18

GLOBALIZATION AND THE INFORMATION AGE

Ending the Cold War politics of division allowed for a global marketplace to emerge in the 1990s. International trade and investment, immigration, and cultural exchange increased as barriers were lifted, and new technologies, including the Internet and mobile devices, connected people instantly. This trend of linking nations in a network of economic and cultural commerce is known as **globalization**. Globalization can create opportunities in less developed countries, while eliminating jobs in more developed countries as production moves to cheaper labor markets.

Cooperation between nations coming out of the Cold War era changed how business would be done based on new agreements. **Free trade agreements** removed barriers to the flow of people, goods, and services across national borders. These agreements had both positive and negative effects. For example, the **North American Free Trade Agreement (NAFTA)** signed by the United States, Canada, and Mexico in 1992 increased trade and economic growth, but also led to the loss of certain jobs, such as U.S. manufacturing jobs that moved to Mexico. Trade rules between nations fell under the direction of the **World Trade Organization**. The ability to operate in multiple countries gave rise to **multinational corporations.**

The end of the Cold War also strengthened international organizations focused on global issues. In addition to the United Nations, the annual meetings of the **G20** address crises facing the world. Nations also unite under commitments like the **Universal Declaration of Human Rights** and the **Paris Climate Agreement.**

The development of public information technologies played a vital role in globalization. The network of information accessible through the **World Wide Web** enables the international exchange of goods, services, and ideas. The **Internet** and the growth of the mobile technologies makes this marketplace increasingly accessible anytime and anywhere.

How might Globalization and the Information Age appear on the GED® test? Try this question.

1. Drag and drop the items below into the appropriate box to organize the causes and effects of globalization.

Causes	**Effects**

Decreased cultural diversity
Networked computers and information
Free trade agreements
Increased movement of jobs

Here's How to Crack It

Globalization is the process of people across the globe becoming more connected. This would happen through the easier flow of goods (free trade agreements) and information (networked computers and information) across national borders and geographical distances. Trade agreements also increase the movement of jobs to other countries where labor and production costs are cheaper. And the interconnections made possible by multinational corporations and the Internet promote one global culture over local differences. The items that indicate changes (decreased diversity, increased movement) would belong to the effects of globalization.

Vocabulary

globalization—spread of products, technology, information, and jobs across national borders and cultures. In economic terms, it describes an interdependence of nations around the globe fostered through free trade.

free trade agreement—a pact between two or more nations to reduce barriers to imports and exports between or among them. Under a free trade policy, goods and services can be bought and sold across international borders with little or no government tariffs, quotas, subsidies, or prohibitions to inhibit their exchange.

North American Free Trade Agreement (NAFTA)—an agreement among the United States, Canada, and Mexico designed to remove tariff barriers between the three countries, signed in 1992

World Trade Organization—international institution that oversees the global trade rules among nations

multinational corporation—company that owns or controls production of goods or services in at least one country other than its home country

G20 (or Group of Twenty)—an international forum for the governments and central bank governors from 19 countries and the European Union (EU), which meets annually to address the world's crises

Universal Declaration of Human Rights—a milestone document in the history of human rights. It sets out, for the first time, fundamental human rights to be universally protected and it has been translated into more than 500 languages.

Paris Climate Agreement—global agreement within the United Nations Framework Convention on Climate Change aimed at reducing greenhouse gas emission

World Wide Web—system of networked information, including web pages linked to other related pages, files, source documents, definitions, and other web-based resources

Internet—global-wide area network that connects computer systems across the world

Globalization and Information Age Drill

You can check your answers in Part IX: Answer Key to Drills.

Questions 1 and 2 refer to the following text, an excerpt from a speech given by President Bill Clinton concerning Internet commerce on July 1, 1997.

> Because the Internet has such explosive potential for prosperity, it should be a global free trade zone. It should be a place where government makes every effort, first...not to stand in the way, to do no harm. We want to encourage the private sector to regulate itself as much as possible. We want to encourage all nations to refrain from imposing discriminatory taxes, tariffs, unnecessary regulations, cumbersome bureaucracies on electronic commerce.

1. According to Clinton's speech, what is the role of government in Internet commerce?

   A. to provide a regulatory structure
   B. to support a global free market
   C. to promote American business through tariffs
   D. to negotiate new laws with other nations

2. Clinton expresses a commitment to

   Select... ▼.
   - isolationism
   - nationalism
   - bureaucratization
   - globalization

WAR ON TERROR AND POST-9/11

Along with advances in transportation and information exchange, globalization also enabled the organization and movement of international **terrorists**.

This rising threat shook the world one morning: on September 11, 2001, terrorists hijacked four planes, crashing two into the **World Trade Center** in New York City, one into the **Pentagon** in Washington, D.C., and another into a field in Pennsylvania, missing its target. Nearly 3,000 people died in this attack, the deadliest in U.S. history.

The 9/11 attackers had been trained and organized through **al Qaeda**, a radical **Islamist** network devoted to fighting Western influence and linked to leader **Osama bin Laden**. President George W. Bush named this enemy in his speech declaring a **"War on Terror,"** which he called on world leaders to join.

Under the official name of **Operation Enduring Freedom**, U.S. forces led airstrikes in Afghanistan, where bin Laden and al Qaeda members were harbored by the militant Islamist regime, the **Taliban**. The Taliban government was quickly removed from power in late 2001, but Taliban leaders and fighters regrouped in Pakistan and continued an insurgency. As other countries joined the war effort, Taliban control weakened in some areas but later recovered in others, contributing to a **War in Afghanistan** that lasted until the U.S. withdrawal in 2021.

The War on Terror entered a second phase when in 2003, U.S.-led forces invaded Iraq in response to intelligence that the country's dictator, **Saddam Hussein**, had **"weapons of mass destruction."** Months later, President Bush declared "Mission Accomplished" in Iraq as a victory in the War on Terror. Saddam Hussein was captured by U.S. soldiers and later executed for crimes against humanity.

Meanwhile, terrorists continued to carry out significant attacks, killing and injuring dozens to several hundred people in a single strike. The War on Terror was not like any war that had been won.

The War in Afghanistan, which had involved U.S. troops since 2001, took a turn in 2011 when bin Laden was killed in a raid in Pakistan. President Barack Obama soon announced the withdrawal of U.S. forces from Afghanistan with the intention of handing over responsibility to Afghans. The U.S. did not withdraw completely until 2021, making the War in Afghanistan the longest war in U.S. history.

Congress also passed the **USA PATRIOT Act** in 2001 and created the **Department of Homeland Security** in 2002 as part of the domestic response to 9/11.

The hostility and suspicion stirred up by the War on Terror persists in anti-Muslim sentiment in the United States and European populations and in radicalized recruitment techniques of terrorist organizations.

How might the War on Terror and post-9/11 appear on the GED® test? Try this question.

1. Drag and drop the items below into the appropriate box to organize the causes and effects of the 9/11 attacks.

Causes	Effects

Formation of terrorist group al Qaeda

Increased security and surveillance in the United States

Globalization of Western influence in Islamic nations

Invasion of Afghanistan by U.S.-led forces

Here's How to Crack It

Al Qaeda was responsible for carrying out the 9/11 attacks, so the formation of this group would be a cause of the event. The United States increased security and surveillance in response to the threat of terrorism, with the aim of preventing other such attacks, so this would be among the effects of 9/11. Radical Islamic terrorist organizations are dedicated to fighting Western influence that reached Islamic cultures through globalization, so this would be a cause. And the United States invaded Afghanistan in response to the 9/11 attacks, launching the War on Terror, so this would be an effect, not a cause.

Vocabulary

terrorist—a person or group who uses violence to incite fear for political or ideological purposes

World Trade Center—skyscrapers, also known as the Twin Towers in New York City, that housed offices of international commerce; were destroyed in the September 11 terrorist attacks

Pentagon—building in Arlington, Virginia, that contains offices of the U.S Department of Defense; partly destroyed in the September 11 terrorist attacks

al Qaeda—a radical Islamist network devoted to fighting Western influence

Islamist—a person or group who supports or participates in militant advocacy of Islam

Osama bin Laden—leader of al Qaeda who organized the 9/11 attacks; was killed by U.S. forces

"War on Terror"—international campaign to fight terrorism launched by U.S. President George W. Bush in response to the 9/11 attacks

Operation Enduring Freedom—official name of U.S.-led operations in Afghanistan as part of the War on Terror

Taliban—militant Islamist regime controlling Afghanistan at the time of U.S.-led attacks on al Qaeda terrorists

War in Afghanistan—longest war in U.S. history; it began with airstrikes against al Qaeda terrorists and continued in efforts to topple the Taliban regime

Saddam Hussein—dictator of Iraq who was captured by U.S.-led forces and executed for crimes against humanity

"weapons of mass destruction"—class of weapon with the capacity for inflicting death on a massive scale; cited as reason for U.S. invasion of Iraq as part of the War on Terror

War on Terror and Post-9/11 Drill

You can check your answers in Part IX: Answer Key to Drills.

Questions 1 and 2 refer to the following text, an excerpt from President George W. Bush's televised address to Congress in September 2001.

> Our response involves far more than instant retaliation and isolated strikes. Americans should not expect one battle, but a lengthy campaign, unlike any other we have ever seen. It may include dramatic strikes, visible on TV, and covert operations, secret even in success. We will starve terrorists of funding, turn them one against another, drive them from place to place, until there is no refuge or no rest. And we will pursue nations that provide aid or safe haven to terrorism. Every nation, in every region, now has a decision to make. Either you are with us, or you are with the terrorists. From this day forward, any nation that continues to harbor or support terrorism will be regarded by the United States as a hostile regime.

1. What event is President Bush responding to in this speech?

   A. surprise bombing of a U.S. military base
   B. terrorist attack on United Nations headquarters
   C. crashing of hijacked planes into American targets
   D. development of weapons of mass destruction in Iraq

2. Which of the following describes the scope of the response to terrorism?

   A. It will take action against any state that enables terrorism.
   B. It will focus only on known locations of terrorists.
   C. It will include only targeted airstrikes.
   D. It will be limited to one well-executed attack.

THE GED® TEST'S VERSION OF U.S. HISTORY

The following is a quick reference to the United States history you need to know for the GED® test.

- **1607–1732—Colonial America**
  Settlers from England and other European countries brave the journey across the Atlantic to seek opportunities on the North American continent. The 13 colonies along the Eastern seaboard remain subject to British rule as they begin to establish their own way of life.

- **1776–1789—American Revolution**
  The American colonies proclaim their independence from England. The big movers and shakers are Benjamin Franklin, Thomas Jefferson, John Adams, and George Washington. After the Revolutionary War is won in 1781, the 13 colonies attempt to create a national government by drafting a constitution called the Articles of Confederation that fails because of its over-reliance on state sovereignty. The dissolution of the Articles of Confederation is followed up by discussions that will lead to the U.S. Constitution, which is ratified in 1789.

- **1789–1865—Westward Expansion**
  The United States fights one more war with Great Britain (War of 1812) and goes on to expand its geography. Following Manifest Destiny, a belief that Americans are destined to settle the entire continent, the United States adds to its territories, buying some lands and gaining others through annexation and war. The Native Americans are gradually pushed off their lands onto reservations. City populations explode as the Industrial Revolution gains force.

- **1860–1865—Civil War**
  The election of Abraham Lincoln on an antislavery ticket causes Southern states to secede from the Union. This begins the Civil War. During the war, Lincoln issues the Emancipation Proclamation, freeing the enslaved people in the seceding states.

- **1867–1877—Reconstruction**
  In the Reconstruction period, the Northern states ratify the 13th, 14th, and 15th Amendments, extending civil rights and voting privileges to African Americans.

- **1877–1920—Progressive Era**
  The Industrial Revolution continues. Large industrial empires are born in the United States, including railroad and shipbuilding companies. These companies are major employers for the "new immigrants," groups of people from Southern and Eastern Europe who have arrived in major cities, such as New York, Philadelphia, and Chicago, to find new economic opportunities. Progressive activists address the issues of industrialization, including poor living and working conditions and corruption within business and politics. The Women's Suffrage movement culminates in the 19th Amendment, which prohibits citizens from being denied the right to vote on the basis of sex.

- **1914–1918—World War I**
World War I begins in Europe because of extreme nationalism and an alliance system among the countries. The United States enters the war in 1917 on the side of the Allies after Germany's attack on U.S. civilian boats. Russia, a strong member of the Allies, drops out because of its own communist revolution, but Germany still loses the war. The Allies develop the Treaty of Versailles (which the United States never actually ratifies) to punish Germany after the war. President Woodrow Wilson attempts to create a League of Nations with his Fourteen Point plan that will prevent such wars from happening in the future, but he is met with resistance from the Senate.

- **1929–1939—The Great Depression**
The stock market crash of 1929 sends the country spiraling into an economic crisis. War-weary Americans wish to practice isolationism following World War I. Franklin Delano Roosevelt is elected president and promises to try to bring the country back to prosperity. His New Deal policies bring more regulation to the business world, and his social programs employ hundreds of thousands.

- **1939–1945—World War II**
Germany, falling under control of the totalitarian Nazi party, is persuaded by a new leader, Adolf Hitler, to expand by invading other countries. Hitler begins to systematically persecute and kill Jews and political enemies as the Holocaust escalates. This begins World War II. The United States passes the Neutrality Acts to avoid entry but is forced to participate after Japan (an ally of Germany) bombs Pearl Harbor in 1941. The United States joins the Allies (Great Britain, the Soviet Union, and others) to oppose the Axis Powers (Germany, Japan, Italy). During the war, the United States imprisons Japanese Americans out of fear that they may be spies. The war ends with an Allied victory and leads to a period of decolonization in which colonies in Africa and Asia gain independence. Soldiers return home to the United States greeted by the G.I. Bill, which allows veterans to go to college and secure home loans.

- **1945–1953—Cold War**
The United States enjoys a period of economic prosperity, although political tensions between the capitalist United States and communist Russia increase. The period begins what is known as the "Cold War," during which both sides start a nuclear arms race. The Truman Doctrine, articulated by President Truman, emphasizes the need to contain communism so that it will not follow the same path as the unchecked Nazism did. The United States forms NATO, which consists of allegiances with Western European countries that wish to stop the expansion of communism. The Soviets and Eastern European countries respond with the Warsaw Pact. Caught in the middle of this conflict is Germany, which is divided into East Germany and West Germany. Tensions grow early on as the Soviets block the United States from entering West Berlin, Germany, and the United States utilizes an airlift to take supplies to the region. From 1950 to 1953, the United States takes part in the Korean War in an attempt to prevent Korea from becoming a communist state.

- **1954–1963—Civil Rights Movement**
  The civil rights movement begins. The Supreme Court rules school segregation unconstitutional. Martin Luther King Jr. becomes a national figure and delivers his "I Have a Dream" speech.

- **1963–1973—Vietnam War**
  The United States gradually becomes entangled in the Vietnam War. The civil rights movement continues to gain ground, bolstered by a Supreme Court led by Earl Warren that is notable for its expansion of civil liberties and civil rights. President Johnson's Great Society plan champions equality and a war on poverty. The Watergate scandal forces President Nixon to resign and brings American confidence in its political system to a low point.

- **1973–1990s—Globalization and the Information Age**
  Nuclear armaments around the world begin to dismantle as the Cold War wanes. The USSR is disbanded, and many of the Eastern Bloc (formerly communist) countries begin to move toward capitalism. A new awareness of the environment leads to the ecology movement, and new technologies begin what will be called the Information Age.

- **2000–2010—War on Terror and Post-9/11**
  The September 11 attack on New York's World Trade Center in 2001 leads the United States to declare a "war on terror" resulting in the invasion of Afghanistan and Iraq. Several large natural disasters (including Hurricane Katrina) help propel global warming to the forefront of public debate. Both China and India come into their own as economic forces to be reckoned with, just as a credit and housing crisis in the United States leads to the bankruptcy of major banks and other financial institutions, resulting in a global recession.

Chapter 19
Civics and Government

In this chapter, we'll go over some of the topics in Civics and Government, including types of governments, the structure of U.S. government, founding documents, the Supreme Court, amendments, civil rights, and voting and elections.

In this chapter, we'll cover some of the topics in Civics and Government that may come up on the GED® test. After each review, we'll give you some helpful vocabulary words to think about, and we'll ask some GED®-type questions based on that particular area. At the end of each review, there will also be a short drill for you to try on your own.

Here are the topics we'll cover in this chapter:

- Types of government
- Foundation and structure of the U.S. government
- Amendments and civil rights
- Voting and elections

TYPES OF GOVERNMENT

A **government** is the set of legal institutions, practices, and processes that determine how a state functions. The structure of government is often bound up with the social interactions that make up its economic system. Types of government found throughout world history include authoritarian or totalitarian, socialism or communism, monarchy, oligarchy, and democracy.

Authoritarian government imposes the state's authority upon many aspects of its citizens' lives. Power is concentrated in the hands of one leader or small elite. Examples include the military dictatorships of 20th-century Latin America. **Totalitarian** government extends absolute control over individuals' attitudes and beliefs, often mobilizing its population toward one party's national aim. Examples include Nazi Germany and Italy under Mussolini's National Fascist Party.

Socialism is based on public ownership of economic resources and property to ensure wealth equality. In theory, the economic system is managed by the community. **Communism** is also based on common ownership of the means of production in a classless society, but a central, controlling government provides citizens with basic necessities. Examples of communist government include Soviet Russia, Cuba, and North Korea.

A **monarchy** is ruled by one person called a monarch, who usually holds their lifetime position by **divine right** or **hereditary succession**. Monarchies range from **absolute monarchies**, such as the royal line of kings in pre-Revolution France, to **constitutional monarchies**, like present-day Great Britain, where the monarch holds the power of tradition as a figurehead or symbol, but the government is actually administered through elected officials.

In an **oligarchy**, the power resides in a few people at the top; this ruling elite is interested in holding onto or increasing its power. Twentieth-century South Africa is considered an oligarchy based on race, in that a small number of white people dominated the majority Black population.

A **democracy**, in theory, is government by the people. People elect representatives in democratic governments, but democracy can take different forms based on the structures of power.

Types of Democracies

The American **constitutional democracy**—a system in which the people consent to the structure and limits of a government as outlined in a constitution—developed through its rejection of a **monarchy**, rule by a king or queen. Other kinds of democracies have both influenced and been influenced by the American system.

- **Parliamentary democracy**—system in which the elected legislators (lawmakers) appoint a person to be chief of government (e.g., United Kingdom)
- **Presidential democracy**—system in which the people elect a president to be the chief of government *and* head of state (e.g., United States)
- **Direct democracy**—a system in which the people decide on laws and decisions, as opposed to electing representatives to decide for them (e.g., ancient Athens)
- **Representative democracy**—a system in which people elect representatives to make decisions and create policies (e.g., United Kingdom and United States)

Let's try an example of a question dealing with types of democracies.

The following text comes from James Madison's *Federalist Paper* #10.

> ...a pure Democracy, by which I mean a Society consisting of a small number of citizens, who assemble and administer the Government in person, can admit of no cure for the mischiefs of faction. A common passion or interest will, in almost every case, be felt by a majority of the whole; a communication and concert result from the form of Government itself; and there is nothing to check the inducements to sacrifice the weaker party, or an obnoxious individual. Hence it is, that such Democracies have ever been spectacles of turbulence and contention.

1. In this text, James Madison most directly warns against

   A. presidential democracy.
   B. parliamentary democracy.
   C. representative democracy.
   D. direct democracy.

Here's How to Crack It

The text considers the "pure Democracy" to be "spectacles of turbulence and contention." This is a critical view of direct democracies, in which the people vote directly on decisions. Choice (D) is correct. No mention is made of a president, so (A) is incorrect. There is also no discussion of elected representatives, so eliminate (B) and (C).

Vocabulary

government—set of legal institutions, practices, and processes that determine how a state functions
authoritarian—system of government that imposes the state's authority upon many aspects of its citizens' lives
totalitarian—system of government with absolute control over individuals' attitudes and beliefs, often mobilizing its population toward one party's national aim
socialism—theory of social organization based on community ownership of economic resources
communism—system of government in which economic resources are publicly owned and controlled by the state, which provides basic necessities to citizens
monarchy—system of government ruled by one person
divine right—belief that a ruler has been selected by God
hereditary succession—inheritance of a title along family blood lines
absolute monarchy—monarchy in which the ruler has absolute authority, unrestricted by laws or other forms of government
constitutional monarchy—monarchy in which a nonelected authority functions within the limits of a constitution or founding legal document of a government
oligarchy—system of government ruled by a few, self-interested elite
democracy—system of government by the people, who elect representatives

Types of Government Drill

You can check your answers in Part IX: Answer Key to Drills.

No public property and community management of economic system	No individual freedom and absolute control by one leader or party with nationalist vision	One head of state who holds power by divine right or family inheritance	No government and lawlessness create a state of total disorder

1. Click on the description of totalitarian government above. (For this drill, circle the description.)

2. Great Britain is an example of a country that has different types of government. It has a monarch, a king or queen from a royal family who symbolizes traditional power, but elected representatives make its laws and policies. This system is an example of

Select... ▼
representative democracy
communism
direct democracy
authoritarian government

.

FOUNDATION AND STRUCTURE OF U.S. GOVERNMENT

The Documents That Started It All

For nearly a millennium, societies have attempted to put forth the ideals later captured by the American system. Notably, in 1215, nobles from England wrote the **Magna Carta**, which sought to limit the power of the king and protect the rights of individuals. Centuries later, some of the first Europeans to arrive in North America, the English Pilgrims, created the **Mayflower Compact** in 1620. All who signed this document consented to laws voted upon by the majority in exchange for protection and survival. Such constitutions became increasingly common in the New World and within a century and a half, the colonists were ready to cut ties with England.

Angered at Britain's refusal to grant them the rights of British citizens, the people of the 13 colonies decided to revolt. The **Declaration of Independence** was written by Thomas Jefferson in 1776. It said, in part,

We hold these truths to be self-evident, that all men are created equal, that they are endowed by their Creator with certain inalienable Rights, that among these are Life, Liberty, and the Pursuit of Happiness....

It went on to list the colonists' grievances against the king of England. The declaration was adopted on July 4, 1776.

During the war with England that followed (called the **Revolutionary War**), the colonists ruled themselves through an organization called the **Continental Congress**. However, after England was defeated, the former colonists wrote the **U.S. Constitution** in 1787, which created principles of government that are still in use today. The Constitution was designed to compromise between the need for autonomy of the individual states and the need for a strong central government. It began

We, the people of the United States...

The U.S. Constitution listed the powers of the states and the powers of the federal government and set up the system of government that we have described above. Worried that the rights of individuals were not sufficiently protected, the Founders wrote the first 10 amendments to the Constitution in 1791. These have come to be known as the **Bill of Rights**. These rights include freedom of speech, the right to bear arms, the right to a trial by jury, protection against illegal search and seizure, and protection against cruel and unusual punishment.

Let's try the following question.

The following text is taken from the Mayflower Compact:

> Having undertaken, for the Glory of God, and advancements of the Christian faith and honor of our King and Country, a voyage to plant the first colony in the Northern parts of Virginia, do by these presents, solemnly and mutually, in the presence of God, and one another, covenant and combine ourselves together into a civil body politic; for our better ordering, and preservation and furtherance of the ends aforesaid; and by virtue hereof to enact, constitute, and frame, such just and equal laws, ordinances, acts, constitutions, and offices, from time to time, as shall be thought most meet and convenient for the general good of the colony; unto which we promise all due submission and obedience.

1. Click the section of the text that best shows the authors' concern for all decisions being made with the common welfare of the Mayflower community in mind.

Here's How to Crack It

When reading the passage, look for clues related to "welfare" and "community." The "general good" is synonymous with welfare. Therefore, "**the general good of the colony**" is most accurate.

Vocabulary

Magna Carta—document signed by King John of England in 1215 establishing that the king was subject to the same laws as citizens

Mayflower Compact—document written by male passengers of the *Mayflower* setting up how their settlement would govern itself

Declaration of Independence—document outlining England's abuses of power and declaring the American colonies' independence from the British Empire

Revolutionary War—war fought by American colonists for independence from Britain, 1775–1783

Continental Congress—organization of representatives from the 13 American colonies that issued the Declaration of Independence in 1776

U.S. Constitution—founding document of the U.S. government

Bill of Rights—first 10 amendments or additions to the U.S. Constitution

Constitutional Powers

The formation of the United States government was highly influenced by the philosophers of the 1600s and 1700s. These philosophers emphasized the importance of **individual rights**, **popular sovereignty** (consent of the governed), and the rule of law over the arbitrary rule of monarchs.

With these **federalist** concerns in mind, the writers of the U.S. Constitution designed the structure of the federal government. This document establishes three branches of government: **executive**, **legislative**, and **judicial**. These three branches are **coequal**, meaning that the power within each one is equal to the others. This **separation of powers** ensures that authority is never concentrated in the hands of one person or body. Let's explore each branch more thoroughly and then see how they interact.

The executive branch of the U.S. government includes the **president**, elected by the people to serve as head of state and commander-in-chief of the armed forces, the **vice president**, and the **cabinet**, which consists of the department heads appointed by the president. The powers of the executive branch include signing bills into law, vetoing bills, nominating federal judges and Supreme Court justices, issuing pardons, and making treaties.

The legislative branch is charged with making laws. It is a **bicameral** branch of government, meaning that there are two chambers of the legislature, or **Congress**: the **Senate** and the **House of Representatives**. While both the Senate and the House propose, debate, and vote on bills that may or may not become laws, there are some key differences between them: The Senate has 100 members, 2 from each state, elected in statewide elections to serve 6-year terms. The House of Representatives totals 435 members, elected by **constituents** or voters in their home districts, meaning the number of representatives per state varies by population. Representatives serve 2-year terms.

The process of making a law is long and complicated: an idea may originate in either chamber of Congress (the Senate or the House); it then goes to a **committee** to be developed; if it makes it through the committee, the Senate or the House will discuss and vote on it; if it passes one chamber, it must go on to the other one for the same process; if it passes both chambers, the bill arrives at the president's desk for a signature, but the executive may decide to **veto**, and then it would take a two-thirds majority of Congress to vote the bill into law.

In addition to introducing laws and overriding a presidential veto, the legislative branch has the power to coin and borrow money, declare war, and **impeach** or remove a president.

The judicial branch is charged with interpreting laws. It consists of U.S. district courts and the **Supreme Court**, the highest court in the nation. These courts decide whether or not a law or action goes against the principles written in the Constitution; if a law or action is declared **unconstitutional**, then it will be struck down. Decisions in the lower federal courts can be appealed all the way up to the Supreme Court, which will first decide whether they will hear the case or not. Supreme Court rulings are the final word on laws or actions that they review. There are 9 Supreme Court justices, nominated by the president, confirmed by the Senate, appointed to serve for life. The uneven number ensures that there cannot be a split decision; there will always be a **majority opinion** held by at least one more justice than the **dissenting opinion** in a case.

The powers of the judicial branch—interpreting the meaning of laws and declaring them unconstitutional—are critical in the system of **checks and balances** within the separation of powers in the U.S. government. The legislative branch can make a law and the president can take an executive action, but the Supreme Court can decide whether a law or action can stand or whether it is unconstitutional. The president may reject a bill passed by the legislature, but Congress may still vote to override a presidential veto. The executive branch can nominate justices to the Court, but they must be approved by the legislative branch. Congress can also impeach a president, who can be removed from office by a vote in the Senate. These checks and balances prevent the concentration and abuse of power through interactions between the three branches.

Try the following question.

The following image is a political cartoon from 1833 featuring President Andrew Jackson.

1. The cartoonist most likely wishes to convey the idea that
   - A. Andrew Jackson comes from royal lineage.
   - B. the executive branch can disrupt the system of checks and balances by overusing the veto.
   - C. President Jackson should be praised for his decisive leadership.
   - D. the president opposes Congress's use of the veto.

Here's How to Crack It

Andrew Jackson is declared a king who is stomping on the Constitution, all the while holding a scroll that says "veto." This shows that the cartoonist sees Jackson as ignoring the Constitution and using the veto to overreach executive power. Therefore, (B) is correct. Choice (A) is wrong because it takes the symbolism of this political cartoon too literally. The cartoon is quite critical toward Jackson's approach, so (C) would not make sense. Choice (D) is incorrect because Congress does not have the power to use a veto.

Vocabulary

individual rights—protections that make sure individuals do not suffer from the interference of the government or other people
popular sovereignty—principle that the authority of government comes from the people agreeing to be governed
federalism—sharing power between national (federal) government and states
executive—branch of government with the power to execute laws
legislative—branch of government with the power to make laws
judicial—branch of government with the power to interpret laws
coequal—equal with one another in importance, describes the three branches of U.S. government
separation of powers—division of executive, legislative, and judicial powers into different bodies of government
president—elected head of state
vice president—executive ranking below the president
cabinet—appointed heads of departments who advise the executive
bicameral—two chambers, describes U.S. Congress
Congress—the legislative or law-making body of United States government
Senate—100-member body of lawmakers elected by people in their states
House of Representatives—435-member body of lawmakers elected by people in their home districts
constituent—a voter, part of the voting population represented by an elected official
committee—a group charged with a specific duty
veto—rejection of a decision or proposal
impeachment—the process of charging a government official with wrongdoing
Supreme Court—the highest federal court in the United States whose decisions become the standard
unconstitutional—contrary to the principles of the Constitution and thus not allowed
majority opinion—the opinion that most justices agree to and thus the Supreme Court's decision
dissenting opinion—the opinion that disagrees with the majority in a Supreme Court ruling
checks and balances—system that allows the interactions between branches of U.S. government to prevent too much power in any one branch

Foundation and Structure of U.S. Government Drill

You can check your answers in Part IX: Answer Key to Drills.

1. Click on (or circle) the power below that the U.S. Constitution grants to the executive branch of government.

Declare war	Declare a law unconstitutional	Sign a bill into law	Introduce a law

2. Which of the following is a difference between the Senate and the House of Representatives?

   A. The number of representatives in the House varies with population, while the Senate remains constant.
   B. Members of the Senate are older than members of the House.
   C. The House of Representatives deals with local issues, not federal laws.
   D. The Senate can make laws without a signature from the president.

Question 3 refers to Article I, Section 7, of the U.S. Constitution.

> ...Every Bill which shall have passed the House of Representatives and the Senate, shall, before it become a Law, be presented to the President of the United States; If he approve he shall sign it, but if not he shall return it, with his Objections to that House in which it shall have originated, who shall enter the Objections at large on their Journal, and proceed to reconsider it. If after such Reconsideration two thirds of that House shall agree to pass the Bill, it shall be sent, together with the Objections, to the other House, by which it shall likewise be reconsidered, and if approved by two thirds of that House, it shall become a Law.

3. The process outlined in this section of the Constitution is

   A. how a president is removed from office.
   B. how a law that is unconstitutional can be changed.
   C. how a law is introduced in Congress.
   D. how a bill is made a law.

POLITICS IN ACTION AND ACTIVISM

Amendments

In addition to making laws, Congress can propose **amendments**, changes or additions to the Constitution. Amendments are rare—there are currently only 27—in part because they are difficult to make happen: first, two-thirds of Congress (both the Senate and House) have to vote for one; then three-fourths of state legislatures (or special conventions) must sign off on it.

The first 10 amendments, also called the **Bill of Rights** because they protect many individual liberties, came about during the process of ratifying the Constitution itself. These amendments include freedoms of speech, religion, the press, and assembly; the right to bear arms; protections for suspected, accused, and convicted persons throughout the legal process; and unlisted rights kept by the people and the states.

Amendments were used to extend the rights of citizens to those recently freed during the Reconstruction period after the Civil War: the 13th Amendment abolished slavery, the 14th Amendment made citizenship a native-born right and granted all U.S. citizens equal protection under the law, and the 15th Amendment outlawed racial discrimination in voting, so that Black men could have the right to vote.

Women won the right to vote by pushing for the 19th Amendment, ratified in 1920. And the protests of young activists during the Vietnam War led to a lowered voting age of 18 (26th Amendment).

Supreme Court

Amendments are considered equal parts of the Constitution, which is the document that the Supreme Court uses to make decisions. Justices interpret the meaning of what is written in the context of the cases that they hear, but also consider the broader implications of the principles that are at stake.

For example, in the case of *Gideon v. Wainwright* (1963), the Court ruled that when a defendant cannot afford a lawyer, the court must provide one, since representation is key to a fair trial, which is a right secured by the 6th Amendment. The Court's ruling in *Texas v. Johnson* (1989) involved interpreting the 1st Amendment to conclude that even offensive speech (in this case, burning an American flag) is protected speech.

The Supreme Court played a large role in the history of civil rights. In ***Plessy v. Ferguson*** (1896), the Court ruled that a law requiring separate streetcars for white and Black people did not violate a person's constitutional right to equal protection of the law (14th Amendment) as long as the cars were **"separate but equal."** This phrase established the legal status of segregation across public facilities and services. In 1954, the ruling in ***Brown v. Board of Education*** reversed this decision; when considering racial segregation in public schools, all justices agreed that separate is inherently unequal, making racial segregation laws unconstitutional. When Southern institutions refused to integrate, another Supreme Court decision (*Cooper v. Aaron*, 1958) stated that states must follow the rulings of federal courts.

Voting Rights and Elections

The first voters in the United States were white, property-owning men. As the country was expanding westward in the 1830s, the right to vote was extended to include those farmers who did not own their own land. Black men were still excluded until after the Civil War, when the 15th Amendment was passed. Still, women could not vote until the 19th Amendment in 1920.

These amendments changed the Constitution, but they did not change certain practices that continued to deny the right to vote to Southern Black and poor people. **Poll taxes**, which charged a person to vote, were not abolished until the 24th Amendment in 1962. Violence and intimidation, irregularities at **polling places**, and **literacy tests** continued to discourage Black voters from exercising their right until the protections of the Voting Rights Act of 1964.

Today, all U.S. citizens over the age of 18 who have proper state requirements (identification, registration, and no felony restrictions) can vote.

Elections at the local and state levels are decided by **popular vote**, the total number of individual votes within a **constituency**. (Senators have been elected directly by popular election since the 17th Amendment in 1913.)

Presidential elections run differently: presidents (and vice presidents) are not elected directly by citizens, but by **electors** through a process called the **Electoral College**.

The Electoral College, which was created in the Constitution, is like a compromise between a popular vote by the people and a vote in Congress: states are assigned numbers of electors in proportion to their populations, and when a candidate wins the majority of individual votes in a state, they win the **electoral votes** for that state. There is a total of 538 electoral votes available, which is equal to the representation in Congress of 100 Senators and 435 Representatives, plus 3 votes for the District of Columbia (D.C.). A candidate who wins the majority of electoral votes (more than half, or 270) wins the election, regardless of the popular vote. In recent elections, those in 2000 and 2016, the candidate who won the popular vote did not win the presidency.

Other Actors

Elected officials may pass laws, but those laws are enforced by the executive branch through **federal agencies**. Federal agencies belong to **executive departments**, the primary units of the executive branch. The president appoints secretaries to head each department (the Department of State, the Department of Justice, and so on) and thereby oversees the execution of all federal laws and policies.

The GED® test may also ask questions that involve the political process from other angles. For instance, you should be familiar with the function of **political parties**, which are organizations composed of people with similar ideologies that seek to get like-minded candidates elected and pass laws consistent with their ideologies. Another influential political actor is an **interest group**. Interest groups represent a cause, a group of people, or even an industry. They attempt to get officials elected or laws passed that support their respective causes, groups, or industries.

Let's try a question.

The following chart describes the United States constitutional amendment process:

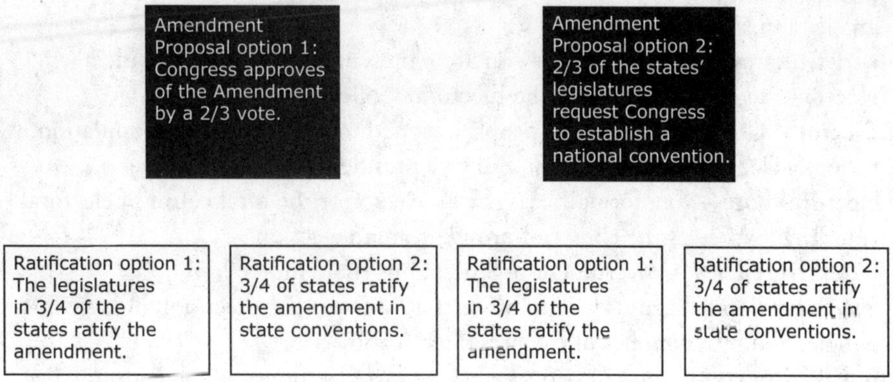

1. It is NOT possible for an amendment to be passed without the input of [Select... ▼].
   - the president
   - the state legislatures
   - Congress
   - state conventions

Here's How to Crack It

Since both methods of proposal involve Congress in some respect, it is not possible for an amendment to be passed without its input. Therefore, **Congress** is the correct answer. The president is not officially involved at all in the process. State legislatures can be avoided with proposal option 1 and ratification option 2. "State conventions" is incorrect because they are involved only in ratification option 2.

Vocabulary

amendment—change or addition to the Constitution, made by two-thirds majority vote in Congress and three-quarters of states
Bill of Rights—first 10 amendments of the Constitution, protecting many individual rights
appeal—to ask a higher court to hear a case that has been decided
judicial review—procedure in the Supreme Court of considering whether a pre-existing law is constitutional or not
Plessy v. Ferguson—Supreme Court case establishing the legal status of segregation
"separate but equal"—doctrine justifying racial segregation
Brown v. Board of Education—Supreme Court case making segregation illegal

poll tax—a voting fee used to limit the right to vote until it was eliminated in 1962
polling place—location assigned to a person for casting their vote
literacy test—assessment of a person's ability to read and write, used to discriminate against voters until it was outlawed in 1964
popular vote—total count of individual votes that expresses the people's choice in an election
constituency—body of people who are represented by an elected official
elector—a voting member of the Electoral College
Electoral College—a body of people assigned to states based on population, who formally elect the U.S. president and vice president
electoral vote—vote formally cast by an elector or the total count of electoral votes that expresses the choice of president in an election
federal agencies—government organizations that enforce laws
executive department—federal office that oversees the execution of laws and policies, led by a member of the president's cabinet
political party—group of people who organize to support an agenda and candidates for election
interest group—group of people who organize around a common interest and aim to influence public policy

Politics in Action and Activism Drill

You can check your answers in Part IX: Answer Key to Drills.

Question 1 refers to the following information.

Timeline of Voting Rights			
1870 15th Amendment ends racial discrimination	**1920** 19th Amendment grants women's suffrage	**1962** 24th Amendment abolishes poll taxes	**1971** 26th Amendment lowers voting age to 18

1 Which of the following could prevent a U.S. citizen from voting in 1950?

A. identity as a woman
B. unable to afford to vote
C. age of 21 years
D. slave ancestry

Question 2 refers to the text of the 1st Amendment.

> Congress shall make no law respecting an establishment of religion or prohibiting the free exercise thereof, or abridging the freedom of speech or of the press, or the right of the people peaceably to assemble and to petition the government for a redress of grievances.

2. Which of the following is NOT protected by the 1st Amendment?

   A. an individual's religious identity
   B. an individual's right to bear arms
   C. a newspaper's right to quote a source
   D. a peaceful protest

3. "Laws permitting, and even requiring, their separation in places where they are liable to be brought into contact do not necessarily imply the inferiority of either race to the other, and have been generally, if not universally, recognized as within the competency of State Legislatures in the exercise of their police power. The most common instance of this is connected with the establishment of separate schools for white and colored children, which has been held to be a valid exercise of legislative power."

   —*Plessy v. Ferguson* (1896)

   The above quote best exemplifies which of the following ideas?

   A. civil rights and racial equality
   B. separation of powers
   C. racism
   D. separate but equal

Chapter 20
Economics and Geography

In this chapter, we'll cover economics, statistics, geography, the environment, and human geography.

ECONOMICS

Economics is not just the study of money—it's the study of how a society meets its needs through the production and distribution of goods and services.

How successful a country is in meeting its needs is a function of many interconnected things such as the following:

Natural resources: Every country has some natural resources. Some have oil or valuable metal deposits in their lands, others have rich farmland, and others have miles of coastline that can be used for fishing or shipbuilding.

The labor pool: Are the country's workers highly skilled or uneducated? Are there enough workers to meet the needs of production, or are there too many, leaving some unemployed?

The industrial base: Does a country have the technical know-how, the factories, and the ability to raise money to acquire new knowledge and new factories?

Types of Economies

Capitalism is a system in which the means of production and development are privately owned and traded. The concept of pure capitalism was first described in 1776 by a Scottish economist named Adam Smith, in a book called *The Wealth of Nations*. Smith advocated a **laissez-faire** (from the French "to let alone") economic system in which the government does not interfere with the free market at all, allowing the interplay of supply and demand to determine prices. In later years, other economists, such as John Maynard Keynes, argued that in the real world, governments must use a combination of tax and spending programs to stabilize a capitalist-based economy.

Some countries have installed economies based on **central planning**—in other words, government ownership of a country's resources and government control of its economic activities. **Communism**, as it was practiced in the former Soviet Union, is an example of such an economy. All the means of production in the Soviet Union were owned by the state, which decided what would be produced and when. **Socialism** is also an example of an economy based at least in part on central planning. In a socialist country, many of the largest industries (such as the transportation industry or the steel industry) are owned and operated by the government, as is a comprehensive system of public welfare.

The United States, like most countries today, practices a modified version of capitalism, sometimes called a **mixed economy**. The government regulates some aspects of business (for example, the Food and Drug Administration makes sure that products sold in our stores will not poison us) and offers some social welfare systems, but the majority of economic decisions are made by private individuals and companies. Such a system encourages **entrepreneurialism**, the practice of taking on the risk of starting a business with the hope of it paying off in substantial profits.

Microeconomics

In a capitalist economy, prices are determined by supply and demand. **Supply** is the amount of goods and services available at a particular time. **Demand** is the consumers' need for those goods and services. For example, a sneaker company might produce 200,000 pairs of sneakers. This is its supply. The public might end up buying 150,000 pairs. This is the demand for this particular product. If supply and demand are equal, then the price will remain the same. However, if there is more supply than demand, then prices fall. For example, because there was a surplus of 50,000 pairs of sneakers that were not sold, the company is going to have to reduce its price to make the public want to buy them.

However, if there is more demand than supply, then prices rise. For example, if these sneakers become very popular, then there will be a shortage, and the sneaker company may charge more for the sneakers because they are scarce.

Simple Economics
If supply is greater than demand, prices fall. If demand is greater than supply, prices rise.

These forces work on a global scale, which is why the prices of oil, gold, and shares of stock in different companies go up and down every day in reaction to the supply and demand of the market.

If an economy is functioning properly, there is an ever-increasing demand for goods and services that is met by an ever-increasing supply. However, if there is too much demand and not enough supply, then **inflation** can result. Inflation is a general rise in prices. A little inflation is to be expected, but too much can start a spiraling effect in which prices rise so rapidly that a country's currency loses its value. During the 1930s in Germany, it was not uncommon to see people taking wheelbarrows full of money to the store to pay for their groceries.

When there is too little demand and too much supply, then **deflation** can result. Most of the countries of the world experienced deflation during the Great Depression.

Let's try a problem.

A company produces and sells widgets. A demand curve for that product is shown below:

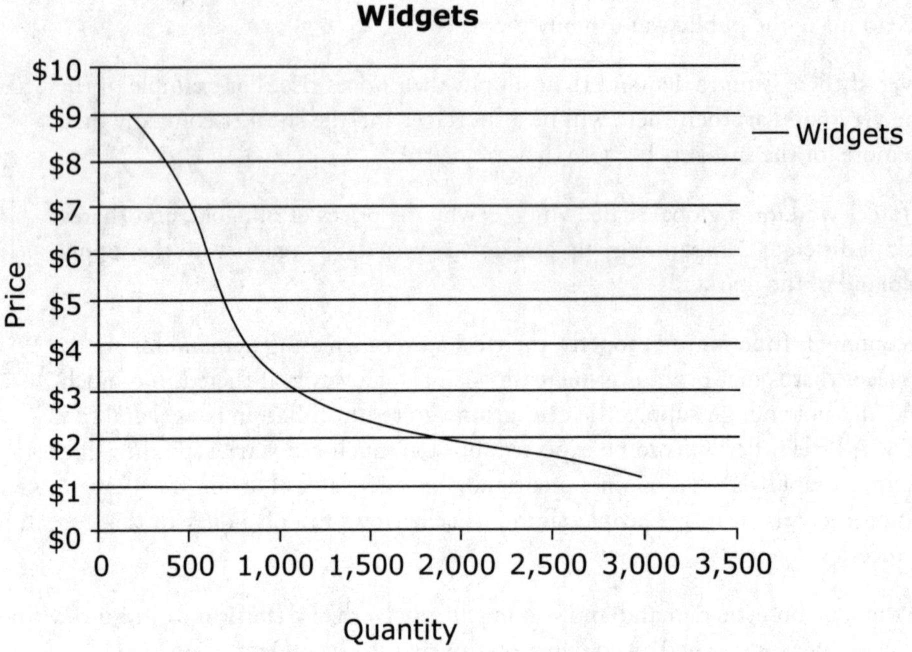

1. If the price for a widget drops to $3, the company can expect to sell an amount of ______ widgets.

Here's How to Crack It

The demand curve shows how much quantity a firm can expect to sell when it marks the product at a certain price. Look at the prices on the *y*-axis (vertical) and locate $3. Scan right until you find the line representing widgets. When you find the line, move straight down (to the *x*-axis) to see that the expected quantity sold is **1,000**.

Production

Capital is the primary catalyst for industrial production. Both material wealth and the ability to produce wealth are known as capital (hence the term *capitalism*). In many industries, the most important form of capital is human **labor**—the people who produce a given product.

Another factor in production is the concept of **incentives**. Incentives are anything that motivates or encourages economic behavior. For example, if a company receives tax breaks for hiring more employees, then it has an incentive to increase its labor force, thus increasing production. Other incentives occur at the consumer level. If a company wants to encourage people to purchase its product, it may create an incentive by lowering the price.

A further factor of production is **opportunity cost**. Opportunity cost is the option not chosen when a more advantageous option is chosen. For instance, a person may choose to purchase Brand X or Brand Y. If she chooses Brand X, then Brand Y is the opportunity cost. In matters of production, opportunity costs can come in the form of materials used, the decision to hire more or fewer workers, the price set for a product, and other decisions related to economic behavior. The ability of a company in a particular country to produce its product at a lower opportunity cost than a company in another country is referred to as a **comparative advantage**.

Let's try a problem.

Ben creates a company that sells and repairs musical instruments. When the economy experiences a recession and Ben's business slows down, he realizes that he cannot continue selling musical instruments. He decides to move into a smaller building with cheaper rent and continue his business by doing only musical instrument repairs.

1. Click on the phrase that represents Ben's opportunity cost after the recession occurs.

Here's How to Crack It

Since opportunity cost refers to the option not taken, you want to look for something that Ben gave up. In this case, he stopped *selling musical instruments,* making that his opportunity cost. Since he is not forgoing a smaller building, cheaper rent, or instrument repairs (instead, he is choosing those options), these are not opportunity costs.

Balance of Payments Quiz

Q: The United States buys more goods from Japan than it sells to Japan. Does it have a balance of payments deficit or a surplus?

Turn the page for the answer.

Markets

A market is a system in which goods, services, and capital are exchanged. If one company controls an entire industry or becomes the only company to make a certain product, that company is said to have a **monopoly**. In the United States, this is illegal. If the government believes that one company is gaining control of an industry, it will institute an **antitrust** court action to force that company to let other companies into the field. An example of this was the antitrust action that forced AT&T to break up into smaller independent telephone companies. The case against Microsoft was another antitrust action.

Because all countries lack some natural resources, each country trades certain goods and services in exchange for other goods and services that it needs. This is known as **international trade.** If a country buys more goods from foreign countries than it sells, it has a **balance of payments deficit.** If it sells more than it buys, it has a **balance of payments surplus.**

Let's try a problem.

The graph below summarizes Country X's international trade:

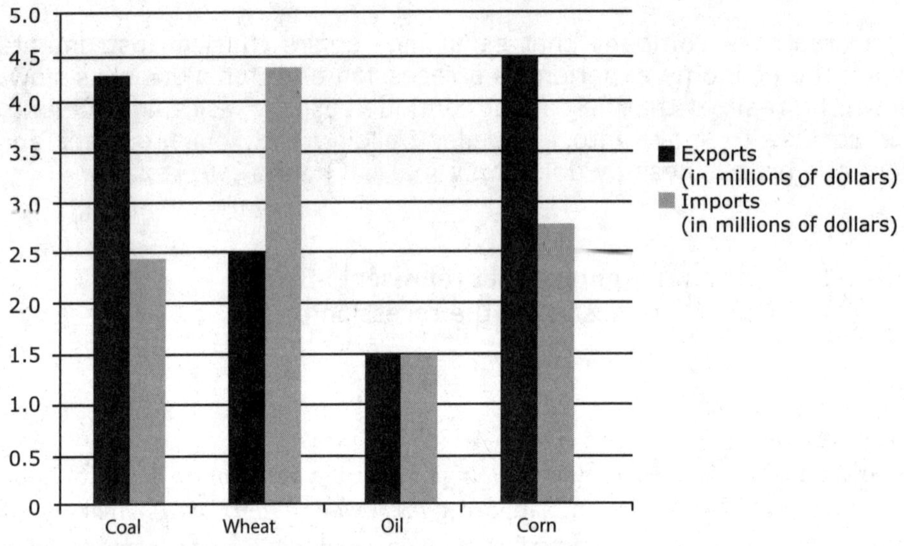

1. For which product does Country X have a balance of payment deficit?

   A. coal
   B. wheat
   C. oil
   D. corn

Here's How to Crack It

The balance of payment deficit occurs when spending on imports exceeds revenue from exports. Therefore, you should look for the product with an import amount higher than its export amount. Wheat is the only product that has a higher bar for imports than exports. Both corn and coal have a balance of payment surplus, while oil is revenue neutral.

Macroeconomics

Instead of viewing individual markets, as the field of microeconomics does, **macroeconomics** looks at the entire economy. This is useful when it comes to government policies that attempt to strengthen the economy. There are two types of economic policies: **fiscal policy** and **monetary policy**.

Fiscal policy consists of the processes of taxation and government spending as they relate to the health of the overall economy. If there is widespread **unemployment**, the government may increase its spending to create programs that help people get back to work. In order to do this, the government must also increase its revenue by raising taxes. For obvious reasons, this may also have short-term drawbacks.

Monetary policy deals with the amount of money put into or taken out of the market. The intention of monetary policy is to adjust the value of currency in order to reverse inflation or deflation. For example, the rules of supply and demand tell us that the presence of too much money in a market lowers the value of an individual dollar. When the value of the dollar is low, people cannot easily afford the products they used to be able to purchase. This is called **inflation**. By removing some of the currency from the market, prices should drop back to normal levels.

Let's try a problem.

The following text is from a radio address given by President Franklin Roosevelt in 1933:

> Two months ago we were facing serious problems. The country was dying by inches. It was dying because trade and commerce had declined to dangerously low levels; prices for basic commodities were such as to destroy the value of the assets of national institutions such as banks, savings banks, insurance companies, and others.... The legislation which has been passed or is in the process of enactment can properly be considered as part of a well-grounded plan.
>
> First, we are giving opportunity of employment to one-quarter of a million of the unemployed, especially the young men who have dependents, to go into the forestry and flood prevention work. This is a big task because it means feeding, clothing, and caring for nearly twice as many men as we have in the regular army itself. In creating this civilian conservation corps we are killing two birds with one stone. We are clearly enhancing the value of our natural resources and second, we are relieving an appreciable amount of actual distress.

1. According to the speech, Franklin Roosevelt combated the economic crisis by

   A. cutting taxes to save federal money.
   B. saving banks to protect America's credit.
   C. selling natural resources to stabilize funds.
   D. allowing the government to spend money in order to invest in workers.

Balance of Payments Quiz

A: The United States has a balance of payments deficit with Japan.

Here's How to Crack It

The text mentions that the government is "giving opportunity of employment to one-quarter of a million of the unemployed." This is closest to (D). Roosevelt's plan would actually raise taxes to pay for these programs. Therefore, (A) is incorrect. The phrase "savings banks" is located in the passage, but there is no evidence that Roosevelt sought to save banks. Choice (B) was meant to trick test takers who did not read for content. Natural resources are mentioned in the final sentence, but there is no evidence of selling them. Eliminate (C).

Vocabulary

Economics and Types of Economies

natural resources—resources drawn from nature, such as water, land, minerals, and agricultural products

labor—workers considered as a group

industrial base—the entire system of manufacturing in an economy

capitalism—an economic system in which the means of production and distribution are privately or corporately owned

laissez-faire—an economic doctrine that opposes governmental regulation of commerce beyond the minimum necessary for a free-enterprise system to operate according to its own economic laws

central planning—a system in which the government can use land, labor, and capital to serve the economic needs of the country

communism—an economic system characterized by the collective ownership of property and by the organization of labor for the common advantage of all members

socialism—an economic system in which the means of producing and distributing goods is at least partially controlled by a centralized government

mixed economy—an economic system blending elements of the free market with a planned economy

entrepreneur—a person who organizes, operates, and assumes the risk for a business venture

Microeconomics

microeconomics—the study of how businesses, households, and individuals within an economy allocate limited resources

supply and demand—the determination of prices for a good or service as a balance between the amount of available goods (supply) and the corresponding need or desire for those goods (demand)

inflation—a persistent increase in the level of consumer prices or a persistent decline in the purchasing power of money

deflation—a persistent decrease in the level of consumer prices or a persistent increase in the purchasing power of money

recession—a significant period of economic decline, characterized by decreased production and rising unemployment

depression—a period of drastic economic decline, falling prices, and rising unemployment

import—to bring in goods or materials from a foreign country for trade or sale

export—to send merchandise over country boundaries in order to sell it

Production and Markets

capital—wealth, especially in the form of financial or physical assets, used in the production or accumulation of more wealth

incentives—things that cause economic actions or motivate economic effort

opportunity cost—the net value of the most desirable alternative to a course of action

comparative advantage—a situation in which people or businesses can produce a good or service at a lower cost relative to others

monopoly—exclusive control by one group of the means of producing or selling a product or service

antitrust legislation—laws intended to prevent business monopolies

international trade—the exchange of capital, goods, or services across international borders

balance of payments—a record of a nation's total payments to foreign countries, including the price of imports, along with the total receipts from abroad, including the price of exports

gross national product (GNP)—the total market value of all the goods and services produced by a nation during a specified period

Macroeconomics

macroeconomics—the study of the overall aspects and workings of a national economy
fiscal policy—the use of taxes or spending to influence the economy
monetary policy—measures taken by a government to control banking, interest rates, and the supply of money

Economics Drill

You can check your answers in Part IX: Answer Key to Drills.

Questions 1 and 2 refer to the graph below.

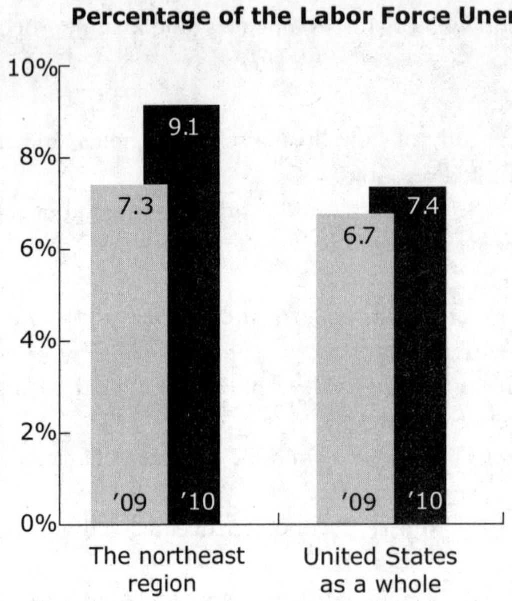

1. According to the graph, the difference in the employment rate in the northeast region from 2009 to 2010 represented a change of what percent?

   A. 16.4%
   B. 10.9%
   C. 3.1%
   D. 1.8%

2. An evaluation of the graph above would show that the overall economy of the United States in 2010 probably performed

   A. worse than it did in 2009.
   B. worse than it did in the northeast region.
   C. better than the economies of other nations.
   D. better than it did in 2009.

Paid Civilian Employment of the Federal Government, 1911–1970

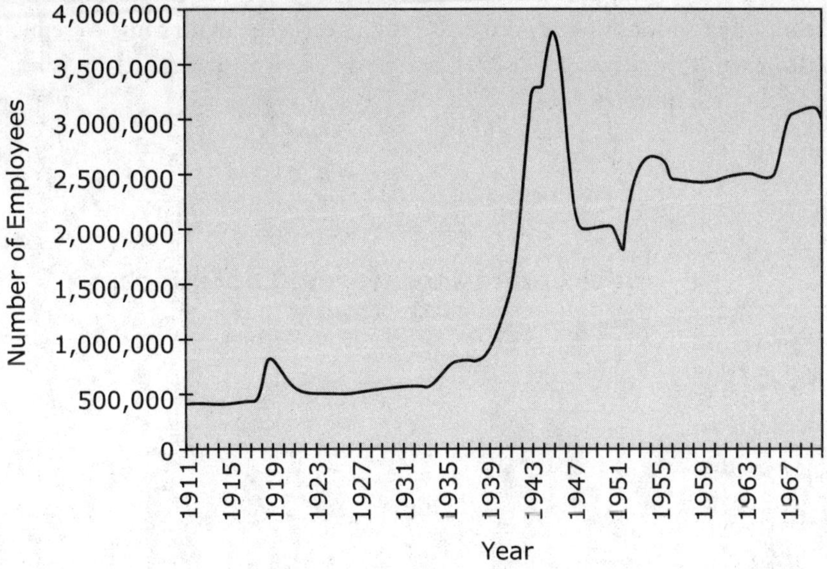

3. Which of the following is most supported by the graph above?

   A. The government grows most rapidly in wartime.
   B. The population of the country grew most rapidly during the 1940s.
   C. Civilian employment increased most rapidly during the Great Depression.
   D. Civilian employment was at its lowest levels in the years after World War I.

4. Select the answer that best describes the difference between a capitalist and communist economic system.

   A. Capitalism strives to eliminate differences in wealth among people of different classes; communism strives to maximize profits for individual entrepreneurs and private corporations.
   B. Capitalism strives to maximize profits for individual entrepreneurs and private corporations; communism strives to protect the private ownership of land and capital.
   C. Capitalism strives to maintain competition among entrepreneurs and private investors; communism strives to maximize profits for individual entrepreneurs and private corporations.
   D. Capitalism strives to maximize profits for individual entrepreneurs and private corporations; communism strives to redistribute wealth among all members of a society.

STATISTICS

While you don't need to know much about statistics for the GED® test, one topic that occasionally shows up involves interpreting data in social studies contexts. You may, for example, be asked to distinguish between **correlation** (a mutual relationship or connection) and **causation** (the relationship between cause and effect). The main thing to remember in this context is that even if there is a close correlation between two variables, there is not necessarily a cause-and-effect relationship.

Let's try a question.

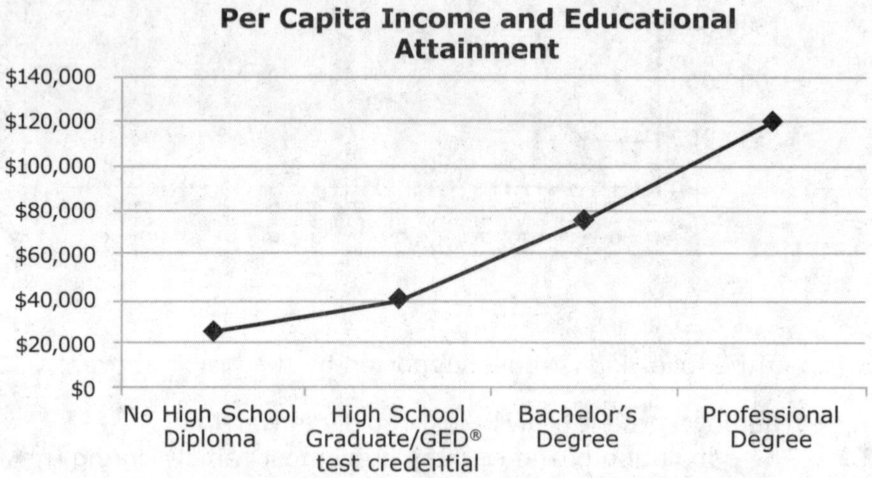

1. The graph above shows the relationship between average per capita income and educational attainment in the United States. Which of the following statements is best supported by the data?

   A. There is a causal relationship between educational attainment and per capita income.
   B. There is no causal relationship between educational attainment and per capita income.
   C. There is a correlation between educational attainment and per capita income.
   D. There is no correlation between educational attainment and per capita income.

Here's How to Crack It

According to the graph, average per capita income increases as educational attainment increases. Be careful, however—this is a correlation, and not necessarily a cause-and-effect relationship. Simply based on a correlation between two variables, it is impossible to state with certainty that one of those variables caused (or didn't cause) the other; eliminate (A) and (B). Since there is definitely a correlation between the two variables in question, eliminate (D) and choose (C).

A final area of statistics that is occasionally tested on the GED® test requires you to understand the difference between **average, median, mode,** and **range.** While this may seem like something that would fit better in the math chapter, the GED® test may ask you to apply these math concepts in a social studies context.

These topics are covered in Chapter 14, beginning on page 343.

Let's try another question.

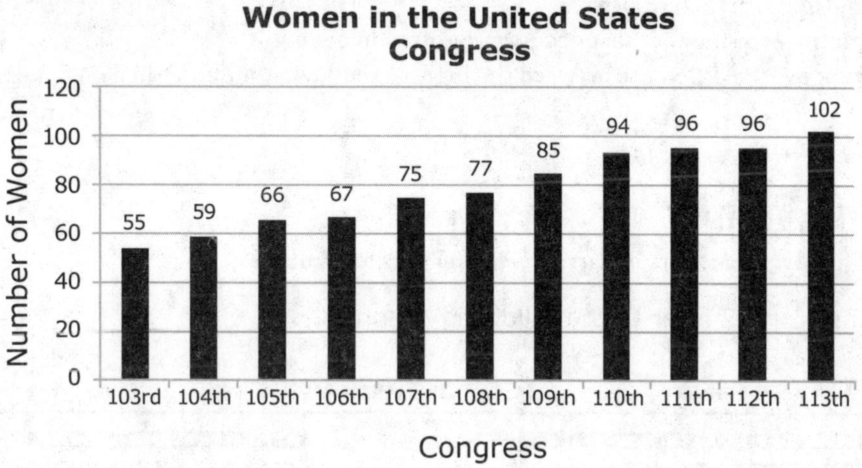

1. The graph above shows the number of women serving in the United States Congress (both House and Senate) from the 103rd to the 113th Congress (1993–2015). Drag the average, median, mode, and range of the number of women serving in Congress during this period into the appropriate boxes below.

Average	Median	Mode	Range

47	$79.\overline{27}$
77	96

Here's How to Crack It

To find the average, you need to add up all the numbers in the chart and divide by the number of items: (55 + 59 + 66 + 67 + 75 + 77 + 85 + 94 + 96 + 96 + 102) ÷ 11 = 79.27 To find the median, list the numbers in increasing order and find the one in the middle: 77. To find the mode, look for the number that occurs most often: 96. To find the range, subtract the smallest number from the largest number: 102 – 55 = 47. Since finding the average is the most work-intensive of these four operations, you could also find the median, mode, and range first and then whatever answer choice is left over must be the average.

Vocabulary

causation—a relationship in which one thing causes another thing to occur
correlation—a relationship between two things that occur at the same time, whether or not one is the cause of the other
average (arithmetic mean)—the sum of a set of numbers divided by the number of items in that set
median—the middle number in a set (when those numbers are arranged in increasing order); if there is an even number of items, the median is the average of the middle two numbers
mode—the number that occurs most often in a set
range—the difference between the highest and lowest numbers in a set

Statistics Drill

You can check your answers in Part IX: Answer Key to Drills.

Questions 1 and 2 refer to the following graph.

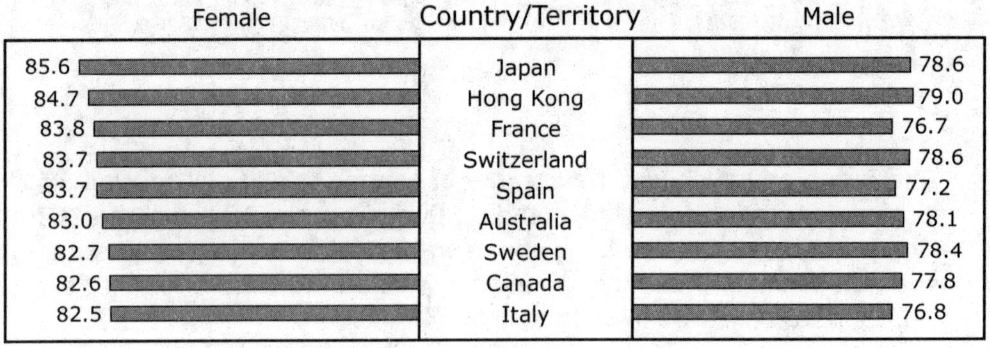

Average life expectancy in years

1. What is the mode of years of life expectancy for females in the countries listed?

   A. 3.4
   B. 78.6
   C. 83.6
   D. 83.7

2. How much greater is the median of the years of life expectancy for females than the median of the years of life expectancy for males in the countries listed?

   A. 5.1
   B. 5.6
   C. 6.5
   D. 7

GEOGRAPHY

Geography is the study of the physical features of the Earth and the ways in which these features affect the people who live on the Earth. When most people think about geography, they think only of surface terrain, but the study of geography also includes the natural resources underneath the surface of the Earth and the climates of, and atmosphere above, the various regions of the world.

Globes

A globe is a three-dimensional representation of the Earth. On the GED® test, you may see two-dimensional drawings of a globe such as the one below:

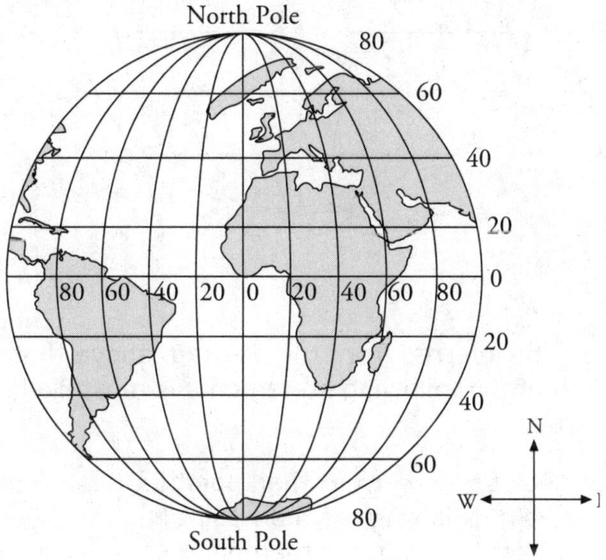

In this figure, you can see about half of the Earth's surface. You are looking at Africa in the middle of the globe. Above Africa, you can see most of Europe. At the bottom left of the globe, you can see most of South America. The line running horizontally across the center of the globe is called the **equator**. This line, like all the lines on this map, is imaginary. If you go to the equator, you will not, of course, find a line drawn all the way around the globe. The part of the Earth above the equator is called the **Northern Hemisphere.** The part below is called the **Southern Hemisphere.** The horizontal lines above and below the equator are called lines of **latitude.** Any point on the equator has a latitude of 0 degrees. A point 20 degrees above the equator would be called 20 degrees north; a point 20 degrees below the equator would be called 20 degrees south. The vertical lines running along the globe are called lines of **longitude.** A longitude of 0 degrees describes an imaginary line called the **Prime Meridian** that runs right through Greenwich, England, dividing the globe into the **Eastern** and **Western Hemispheres.** A point 60 degrees to the left of the Prime Meridian would be called 60 degrees west; a point 60 degrees to the right of the Prime Meridian would be called 60 degrees east. Using a combination of latitude and longitude, you can locate the position of any point on the Earth.

Let's try a question.

Map Lines
horizontal lines = latitude
vertical lines = longitude

Question 1 refers to the following diagram of the globe.

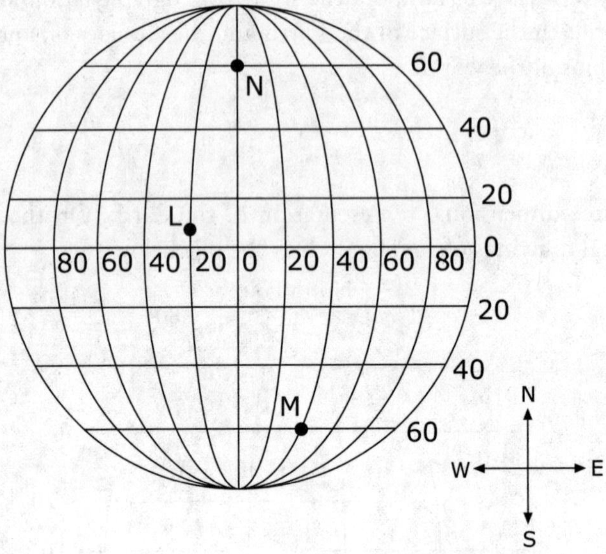

1. It can be inferred from the diagram above that which of the following statements is most likely to be true?

   A. Point M is warmer than point L.
   B. Point N is warmer than point M.
   C. Point N is warmer than point L.
   D. Point L is warmer than point N.

Here's How to Crack It

The nearer the equator, the warmer the average temperature. Which point is nearest the equator? If you said point L, you are absolutely right. The correct answer to this analysis question is (D).

Maps

A map is a drawing of a smaller part of the globe. Below, you can see one of the GED® test's favorites: a map of the United States.

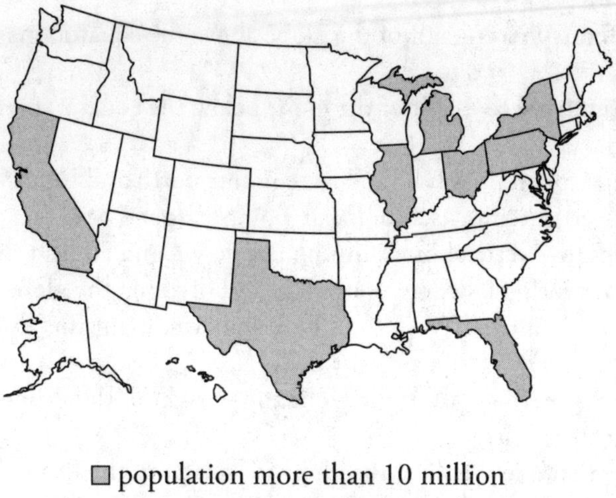

(Source: U.S. Bureau of Census)

This map shows the different states of the United States. There's a similar one in the "Understanding Graphics" supplement. However, note that on this map, you are also given some additional information. States with a population of more than 10 million are shaded. Almost certainly, this information will be necessary to answer the question that comes with this map. As we said in the "Understanding Graphics" supplement, the information you need to answer map questions is almost always located on the map itself, in the title and the **key**. You will find that some maps include **demographic** information on the population living in the area, others will show **climate** patterns, and others will give **topographical** information, such as how far the land is above **sea level**.

As with almost all maps, north is at the top of the page, which means that south is at the bottom, west is toward the left, and east is toward the right. Let's look at the question that went with this map:

1. According to the map above, the biggest concentration of states with large populations can be found in which region of the United States?

   A. the central region
   B. the southwestern region
   C. the northwestern region
   D. the northeastern region

Here's How to Crack It

Where are most of the high-population states? That's right, the top right-hand corner of the United States. Which region is that? If you're stuck, consult the paragraph right above the question. The correct answer to this comprehension question is (D).

Vocabulary

equator—horizontal line running around the center of the globe representing 0 degrees latitude and dividing the globe into two hemispheres (Northern and Southern)

Northern Hemisphere—half of the globe above the equator, marked in degrees north

Southern Hemisphere—half of the globe below the equator, marked in degrees south

latitude—horizontal lines used to locate points north and south

longitude—vertical lines used to locate points east and west

Prime Meridian—vertical line running up, down, and around the middle of the globe representing 0 degrees longitude and dividing the globe into two hemispheres (Eastern and Western). The Prime Meridian runs through Greenwich, England.

Eastern Hemisphere—half of the globe to the right of the Prime Meridian, marked in degrees east

Western Hemisphere—half of the globe to the left of the Prime Meridian, marked in degrees west

key—part of a map that explains what its markings or symbols represent; also called a legend

demographic—of or relating to information about population

climate—the usual or average weather conditions in an area over a long time period

topographic—of or relating to detailed information about the natural or human-made features of the land in an area

sea level—base level corresponding to the surface of the sea, used to describe elevation as above or below

Online Practice Drills

We've got more questions for you online. Check out the two digital Social Studies drills in your Student Tools. Register here for access if you haven't done so already:

Geography (Globe and Maps) Drill

You can check your answers in Part IX: Answer Key to Drills.

Questions 1 and 2 refer to the globe below.

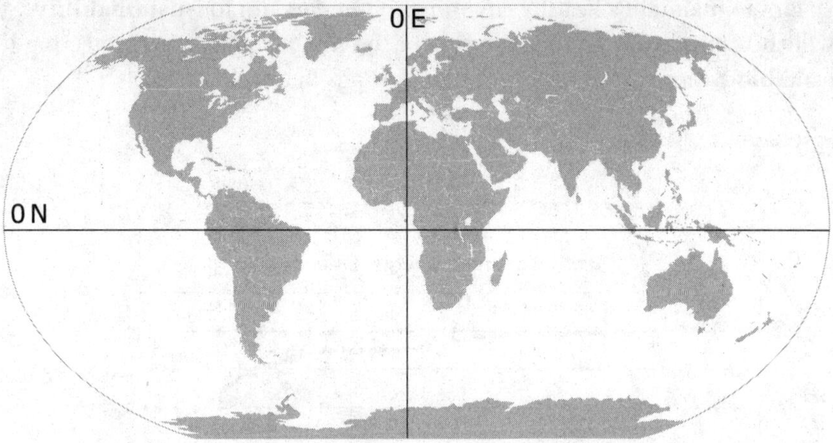

1. 0 degrees latitude and 0 degrees longitude intersect in which ocean?

   A. Pacific Ocean
   B. Atlantic Ocean
   C. Arctic Ocean
   D. Indian Ocean

2. The continent that is found entirely within the Southern and Eastern Hemispheres is ______________.

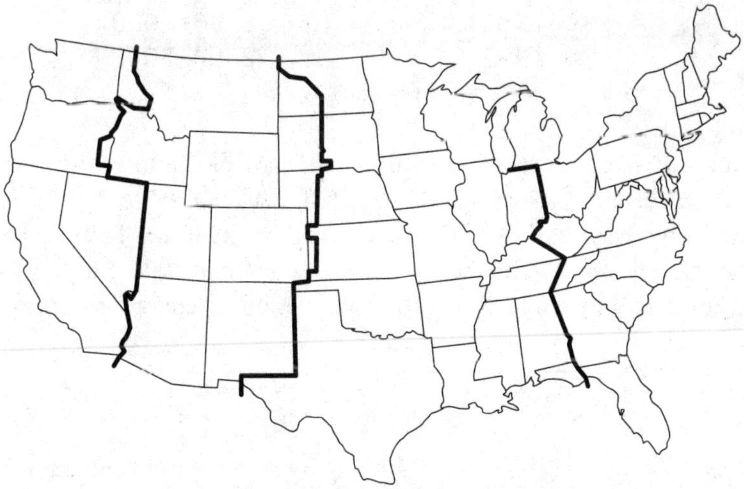

3. The bold lines on the U.S. map above represent

   A. mountain ranges.
   B. major rivers.
   C. time zones.
   D. climate zones.

ENVIRONMENT

Humans have left an impact on the environment through their interaction with the world around them. Some of these interactions can have harmful effects on the environment, such as pollution, while others can have positive effects, such as the protection of endangered species.

Policies that aim to maintain a healthy environment tend to aim for **sustainability**. Sustainable practices will theoretically allow an environment to remain stable, thus protecting its **natural resources** and **biodiversity** (the variety of living things in a region).

Let's try a problem.

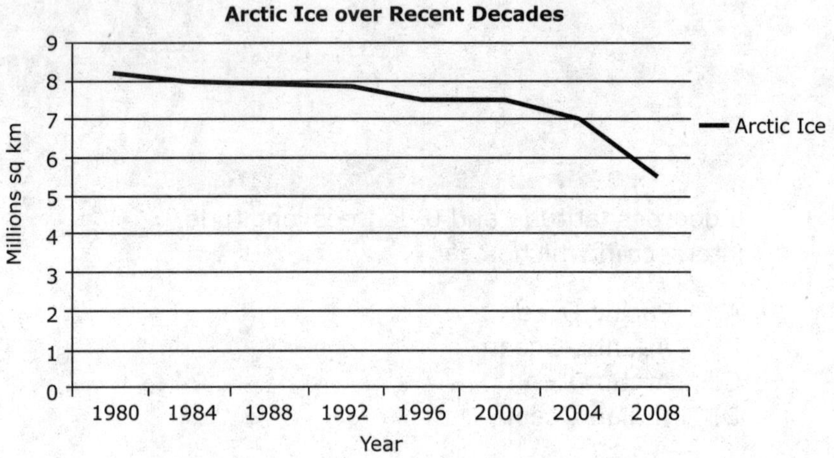

1. In which set of years was the most significant change in arctic ice recorded?

A. 1980–1984
B. 1988–1992
C. 1996–2000
D. 2004–2008

Here's How to Crack It

The most significant change in arctic ice will be the part of the line with the steepest slope. The steepest part of this line is closest to 2004–2008, when arctic ice drops from around 7 to 5.5 million square kilometers. Choice (D) is correct. From 1980 until 1992, the line is mostly flat, so eliminate (A) and (B). While the amount of arctic ice in 1996–2000 is less than that of previous years, it is relatively stable during this time period. Therefore, eliminate (C).

Vocabulary

biodiversity—the variability among living organisms on the Earth, including the number and variety of species found within specific geographic areas

natural resources—resources drawn from nature, such as water, land, minerals, and agricultural products

sustainability—activities that are capable of being continued with minimal long-term effect on the environment

Environment Drill

You can check your answers in Part IX: Answer Key to Drills.

<u>Questions 1 and 2</u> refer to the following graphic.

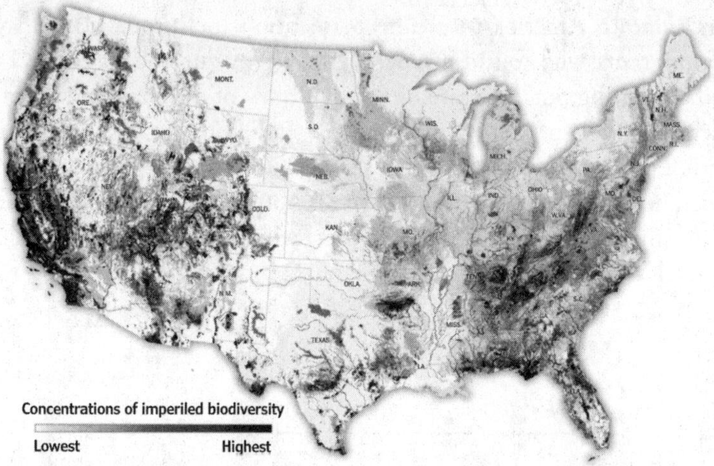

1. The map shows the contiguous United States with regional concentrations of imperiled (endangered) biodiversity from lowest to highest. Which conclusion can best be reached from the information on the map?

   A. The patterns of biodiversity across the United States are random in nature, unrelated to climate or population.

   B. Imperiled biodiversity is found only on the East and West coasts of the United States.

   C. The Southwestern region of the United States has the most imperiled biodiversity of any region in the United States.

   D. Biodiversity is distributed equally across all regions of the United States.

2. Based on the graphic above, determine whether the following statement is true or false. Drag and drop the statement into the appropriate box. (For this drill, write the statement letter in the box.)

True	False

(a) The Southern United States is a hotspot for species at risk of vanishing.

HUMAN GEOGRAPHY

Throughout history, humankind has migrated from one area to another in search of trade, food, adventure, and freedom. This dispersal of a population into new areas around the world is known as a **diaspora**.

The early settlers came to America to escape persecution in Europe. These were the first of a long line of immigrants who found a new beginning in our country. The United States is sometimes called a "melting pot" because of the rich brew of different cultures that has helped form the American culture. In melting pots such as the United States, **cultural diversity** can lead to the spread of practices beyond the original culture. This phenomenon is called **cultural diffusion**. For instance, Mexican food's popularity is not unique to Mexican Americans. Rather, it has diffused into mainstream American cultures, while undergoing some changes. Groups also practice **assimilation** as they sacrifice some of their cultural identity in order to fit into a new culture.

Let's try a question.

The following is from an 1818 letter that an Irish immigrant to the United States wrote back to his family in Ireland six months after settling in America:

> One thing I think is certain that if the emigrants knew before hand what they have to suffer for about the first six months after leaving home in every respect they would never come here. However, an enterprising man, desirous of advancing himself in the world will despise everything for coming to this free country, where a man is allowed to...act and speak as he likes, abuse public men in their office to their faces, wear your hat in court and smoke a cigar while speaking to the judge as familiarly as if he was a common mechanic, hundreds go unpunished for crimes for which they would be surely hung in Ireland; in fact, they are so tender of life in this country that a person should have a very great interest to get himself hanged for anything!

1. What does the author of this letter indicate was a primary reason for his emigration?

   A. freedom of religion
   B. freedom of speech
   C. freedom of privacy
   D. freedom to work

Here's How to Crack It

The author says that one can "act and speak as he likes" and goes on to give examples of how this is possible in the United States. He most values his freedom of speech, which makes (B) the correct answer. There is no evidence that the author values religious freedom, privacy, or the right to work. Eliminate (A), (C), and (D).

Vocabulary

refugee—someone fleeing from one country to another out of fear or necessity
immigrate—to enter a new country
emigrate—to leave your own country
diaspora—a dispersion of a people from their original homeland
cultural diversity—different cultures within a specific country or region
cultural diffusion—the spread of cultural ideas, such as religion, language, or customs, among groups of people
assimilation—the process by which a minority group gradually adopts the customs and attitudes of the prevailing culture

Human Geography Drill

You can check your answers in Part IX: Answer Key to Drills.

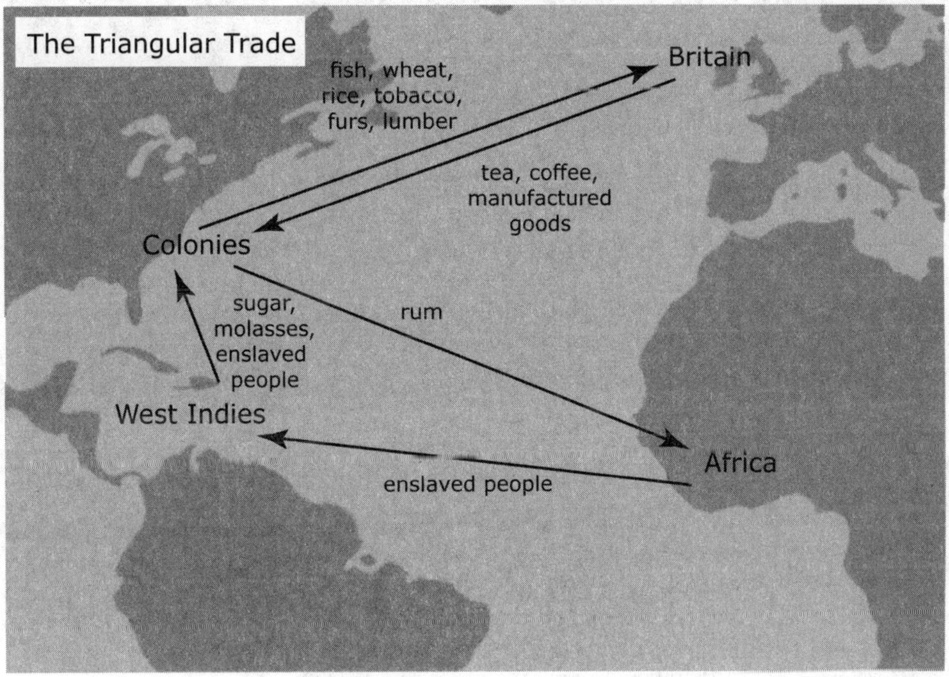

1. According to the map above, one of the colonies' major exports was

    A. tobacco.
    B. manufactured goods.
    C. enslaved people.
    D. sugar.

2. The following represents patterns of immigration to the United States from 1880 to 1930:

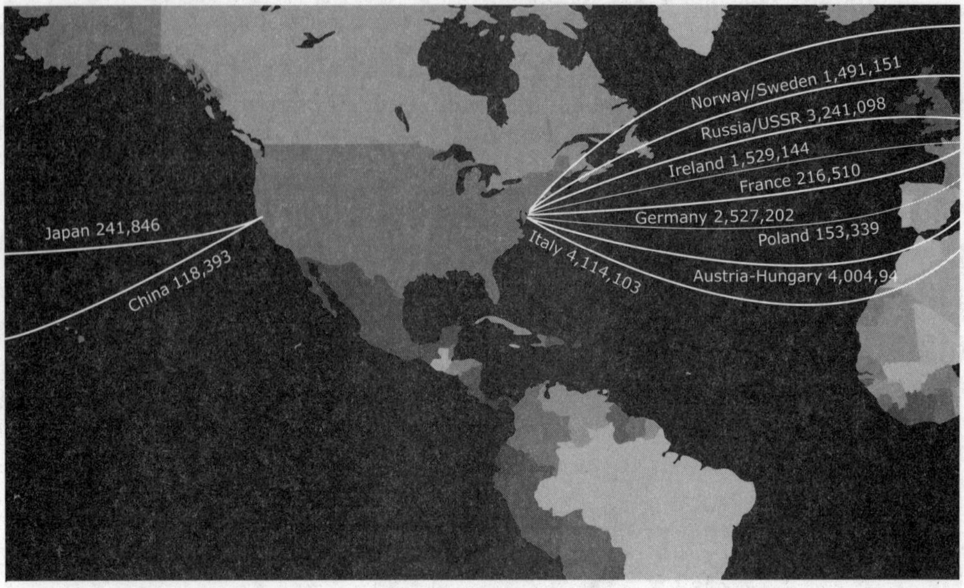

According to the map above, determine whether the following statements would be "True" or "False." Drag and drop the statements into the appropriate boxes. (For this drill, write the statement letters in the boxes.)

True	**False**

(a) European immigrants were more likely to arrive in the Eastern United States than in the West.

(b) Italian immigrants outnumbered Irish immigrants by at least 2 to 1.

(c) For a time, there were more Japanese than French immigrating to the United States.

(d) Chinese and Japanese immigrants did not settle in the East from 1880 to 1930.

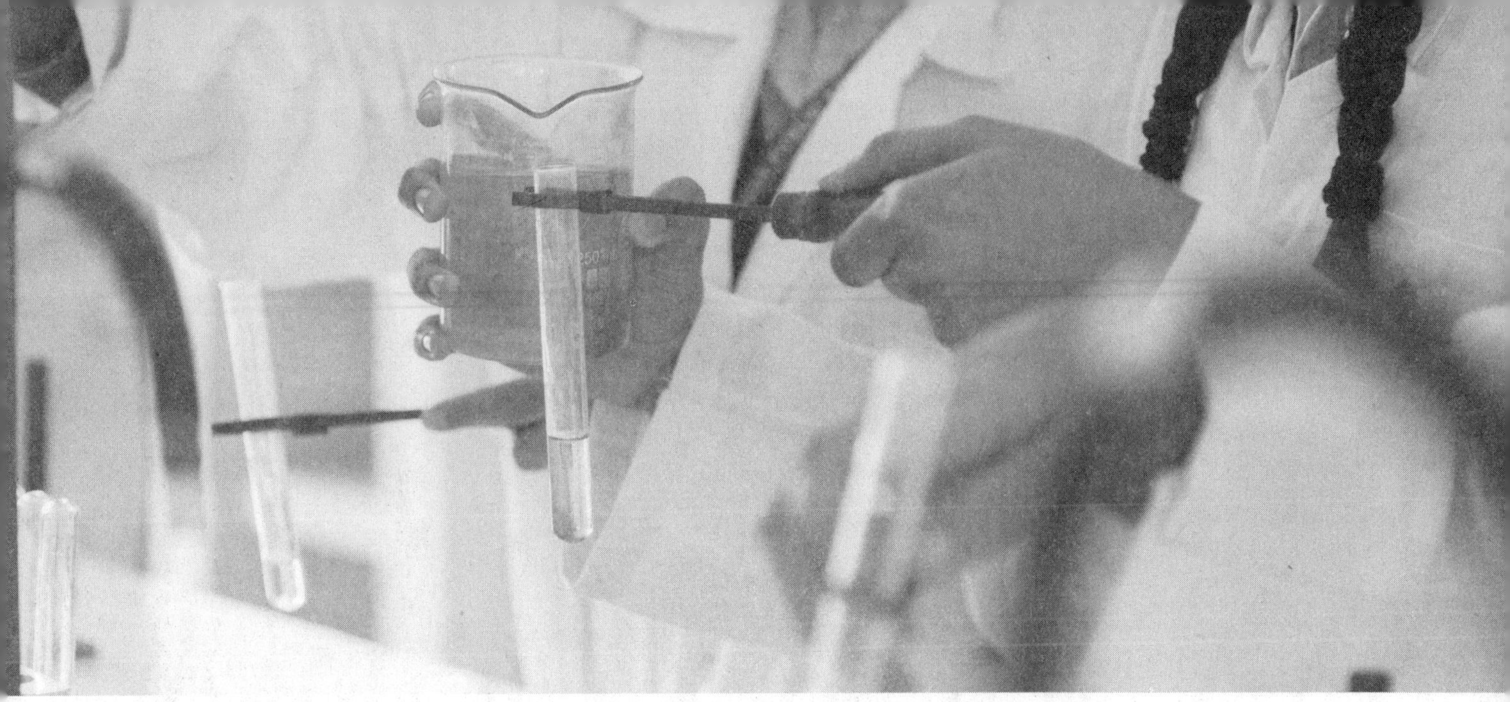

Part VIII
Science

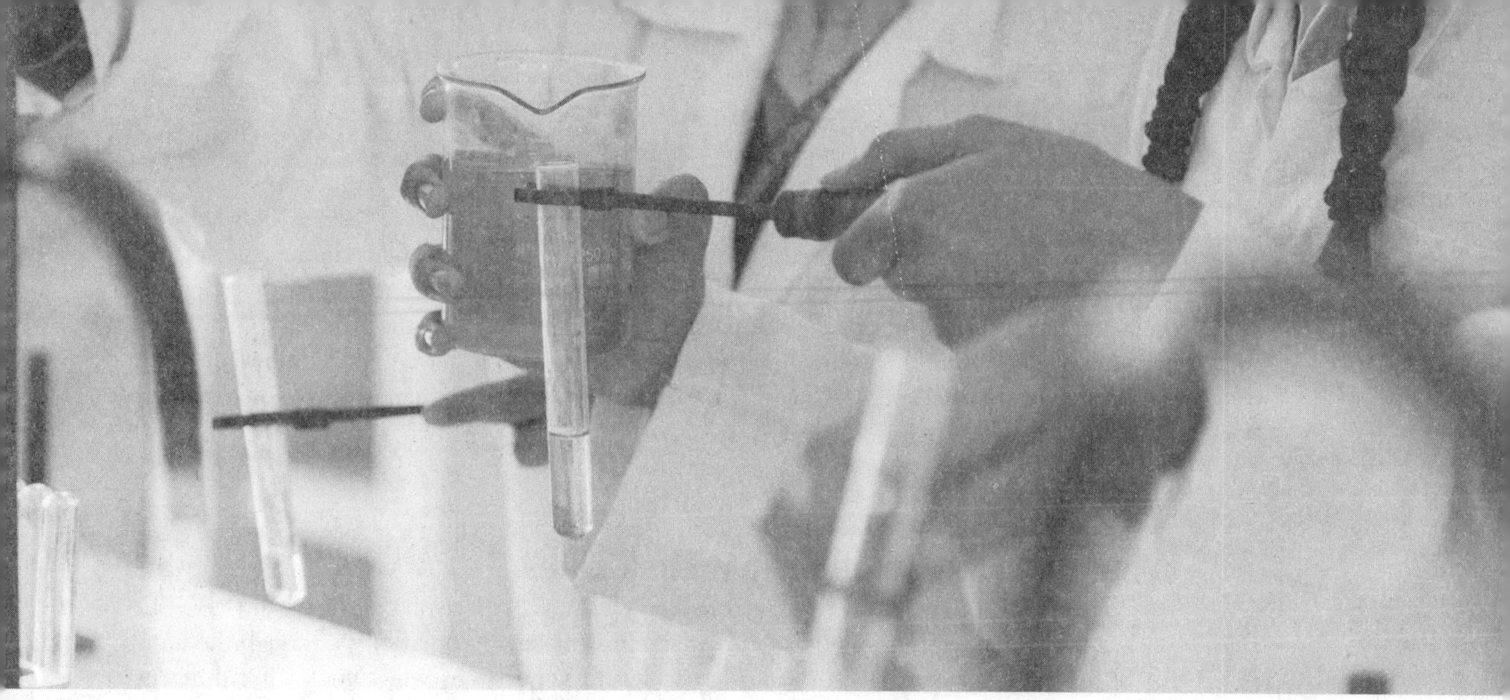

Chapter 21
Science Overview

If you find that the idea of spending an hour and a half answering science questions sends you into a cold sweat, have no fear! While you will need to have some basic science knowledge in order to work the questions successfully, you won't need to memorize the periodic table or learn how to do quantum physics. In fact, you'll find that you can answer many of the questions in the Science test simply by reading the passages, charts, and graphs that the test provides, or by using scientific thinking. Some questions will require you to have outside knowledge, but in the chapters that follow we'll address the topics that the test covers, so that you'll be well prepared by the time that test day arrives.

What Does the Science Test Look Like?

To score well on the test, you first need to know what to expect on test day. On the GED® Science test, you'll have 90 minutes to answer approximately 34 questions, although the number of questions can vary slightly from test to test. The questions will come in five different formats.

Question Formats

Multiple-choice questions give you a question with four possible answers, and your job will be to choose the best answer. For example, you may see a passage-based multiple-choice question, such as the one that follows.

1 Biologists have long known that some types of electromagnetic radiation, such as X-rays and gamma rays, can be dangerous to human beings.

2 However, until now, no one has ever suggested that microwave radiation might also be harmful. In preliminary test-tube laboratory results, a scientist has found elevated growth rates in cancer cells exposed to low doses of microwaves.

3 These results are only preliminary because, first, there has been no controlled study of the effects of microwaves on human beings. Second, this study was of short duration, raising the possibility that the dangers of long-term exposure have not yet been assessed.

4 Although federal guidelines for how much electromagnetic energy can be allowed to enter the work and home environment have been made more stringent since they were first implemented in 1982, the recent study poses troubling questions about the safety of microwaves.

1. According to the information presented, the cancer cells' increasing growth rates in the laboratory experiment were most likely due to

   A. the cancer cells' natural reproductive cycle.
   B. a short-term growth spurt that may not indicate a general trend.
   C. exposure to microwave radiation.
   D. accidental contamination of cell samples during laboratory procedures.

Fill-in-the-blank questions won't provide you with any answer choices; you'll just need to fill a word or number into a blank space in order to answer the question. Note that if the question requires you to do any calculations, you will generally receive access to an online calculator. After all, the Science test is about understanding science concepts and scientific thinking, not your ability to do math! Here's an example of a fill-in-the-blank question.

2. Each day for one week, doctors measured the flow rate—the amount of fluid passing through a given area of a pipe per second—of blood flowing through a patient's aorta. The day of the week, the velocity of the blood, and the flow rate are shown in the chart below.

Day	Blood Velocity	Flow Rate
Monday	40 cm/s	120 cm/s^3
Tuesday	38 cm/s	114 cm/s^3
Wednesday	39 cm/s	117 cm/s^3
Thursday	42 cm/s	126 cm/s^3
Friday	41 cm/s	123 cm/s^3
Saturday	39 cm/s	117 cm/s^3
Sunday	43 cm/s	129 cm/s^3

What is the mean of the flow rates shown in the chart above, to the nearest hundredth?

You may use the calculator.

Drop-down menu questions are similar to multiple-choice questions, but you'll need to choose your answers from a drop-down menu. Additionally, you may find that a single question will involve more than one drop-down menu. For example, you may see a question such as the following.

3. Scientists calculate the buoyant force, the upward force that a liquid exerts on an object submerged or floating in that liquid, by using the formula $F_B = \rho_f Vg$, where F_B is the buoyant force, ρ_f is the density of the fluid, V is the volume of the displaced fluid, and g is a constant and is the acceleration due to gravity.

Based on the information above, an object would

experience a Select... ▼
greater buoyant force
lesser acceleration due to gravity

in a fluid that had Select... ▼.
greater density
lesser volume

Hot-spot questions will typically provide you with a chart or a graph, and ask you to identify a point on the chart or graph that answers a particular question. You'll be able to select that point using your computer cursor. A typical hot-spot question might look like the following.

4. The term *solubility* refers to the amount of a substance (solute) that will dissolve in a given amount of a liquid substance (solvent). The solubility of solids in water varies with temperature. The graph below displays the water solubility curves for six crystalline solids.

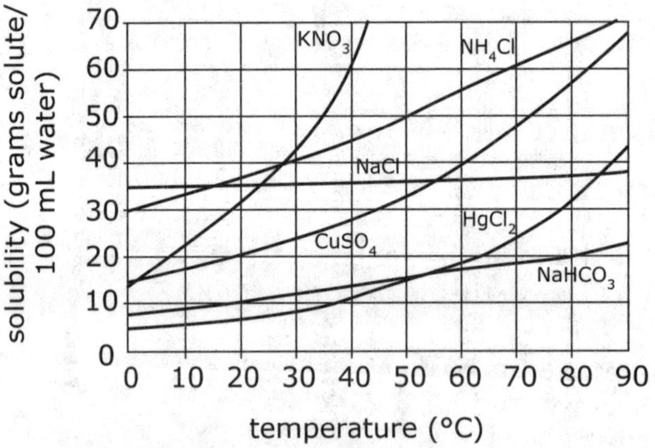

Click the point on the graph at which the solubility of NaCl is equal to the solubility of $CuSO_4$.

Drag-and-drop questions will provide you with multiple options, and you'll be asked to select one or more of those options in order to complete the question. A typical drag-and-drop question may appear as follows.

5. The term *solubility* refers to the amount of a substance (solute) that will dissolve in a given amount of a liquid substance (solvent). The solubility of solids in water varies with temperature. The graph below displays the water solubility curves for six crystalline solids.

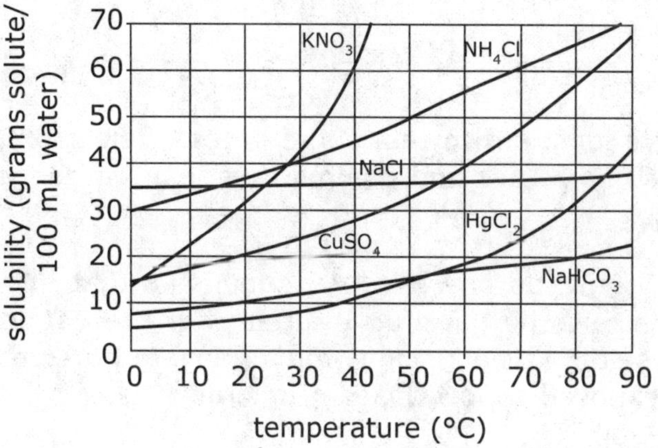

Identify the substances with the least change in solubility and the greatest change in solubility. Drag and drop your choices into the appropriate boxes.

Least Change in Solubility	**Greatest Change in Solubility**

NaCl

$CuSO_4$

$NaHCO_3$

$HgCl_2$

What Skills Will Be Tested?

In addition to knowing the format in which the questions will appear, you should also know which skills those questions will test. Fortunately, GED® Science questions really test only a few skills. Once you master those skills, then you'll find it much easier to ace the Science test!

Comprehension Questions

Comprehension questions ask you to find a particular piece of information from a passage, chart, or graph, and then recognize that information, slightly restated, in an answer choice. Comprehension questions may also ask you to go just a bit further and identify a logical implication of that information. The question that follows is a comprehension question related to a passage you've already seen.

1 Biologists have long known that some types of electromagnetic radiation, such as X-rays and gamma rays, can be dangerous to human beings.

2 However, until now, no one has ever suggested that microwave radiation might also be harmful. In preliminary test-tube laboratory results, a scientist has found elevated growth rates in cancer cells exposed to low doses of microwaves.

3 These results are only preliminary because, first, there has been no controlled study of the effects of microwaves on human beings. Second, this study was of short duration, raising the possibility that the dangers of long-term exposure have not yet been assessed.

4 Although federal guidelines for how much electromagnetic energy can be allowed to enter the work and home environment have been made more stringent since they were first implemented in 1982, the recent study poses troubling questions about the safety of microwaves.

1. According to the information presented, the cancer cells' increasing growth rates in the laboratory experiment were most likely due to

   A. the cancer cells' natural reproductive cycle.
   B. a short-term growth spurt that may not indicate a general trend.
   C. exposure to microwave radiation.
   D. accidental contamination of cell samples during laboratory procedures.

Here's How to Crack It

Before you begin the questions from any passage, you should always make sure that you understand the *structure* of the passage. For example, someone in a hurry might have read the first paragraph of *this* passage and gotten the impression that it was going to be about the danger of gamma rays and X-rays. However, if you looked past the first paragraph, you would realize that the introduction provides background historical context for the subject of the passage. It began by talking about the kind of rays scientists have "long known" to be dangerous and then segued in the second paragraph to another type of ray that may, it turns out *now,* be dangerous as well. The passage describes a laboratory study, gives two reasons that the results are only preliminary, and then summarizes. This question asks about a "laboratory experiment." Where does the passage discuss a laboratory experiment? Check out the second paragraph. Briefly reread the paragraph, and then use Process of Elimination to remove answers that don't agree with the information in the passage. The passage states that cancer cells exposed to microwave radiation experienced "elevated growth rates," so the increasing growth rates are due to microwave radiation, and are not natural. Eliminate (A). While the passage does state that the effects of microwave radiation are unknown, it doesn't provide any evidence that the growth spurt does not indicate a general trend, so (B) is incorrect. Choice (C) agrees with the passage, which states that "a scientist has found elevated growth rates in cancer cells exposed to low doses of microwaves." Thus, (C) is the correct answer. The passage doesn't mention accidental contamination, so (D) is not the correct answer.

Here's another example of a comprehension question. It's based on the same passage as the question on the previous page.

Scientists hypothesize that meteorologists who use remote sensing microwave radiometers to measure the temperature of objects and terrain may suffer adverse health effects because of frequent exposure to microwave radiation.

2. Which excerpt from the passage supports this hypothesis?

   A. "These results are only preliminary, because, first, there has been no controlled study of the effects of microwaves on human beings."
   B. "Biologists have long known that some types of electromagnetic radiation, such as X-rays and gamma rays, can be dangerous to human beings."
   C. "A scientist has found elevated growth rates in cancer cells exposed to low doses of microwaves."
   D. "Federal guidelines for how much electromagnetic energy can be allowed to enter the home and work environment have been made more stringent since they were first implemented in 1982."

Here's How to Crack It

In this question, you're asked about "adverse health effects due to frequent exposure to microwave radiation." Where can you find information about possible adverse health effects caused by microwave radiation? Check out paragraph 2, and then use Process of Elimination to remove answer choices that don't discuss adverse health effects and microwave radiation.

Choice (A) discusses the fact that there has been no controlled study of the effects of microwave radiation on humans. While this might suggest that the effects of microwave radiation on humans are unknown, it doesn't show that meteorologists have cause for concern regarding their health; it merely shows that they don't know whether they should be concerned. Thus, you can eliminate (A). Choice (B) does discuss the dangers of some types of electromagnetic radiation, but it discusses X-rays and gamma rays, rather than microwaves, so (B) is incorrect. Choice (C) mentions that microwaves may be associated with increased cancer cell growth rates, which is a potential health hazard associated with microwaves, and is the correct answer. Choice (D) discusses the fact that there are laws in place that regulate the amount of electromagnetic radiation allowed to enter homes and workplaces, but it does not deal specifically with microwave radiation, and does not state that the reason for such regulations is that such radiation poses a health hazard. Thus, (D) is also incorrect. The correct answer is (C).

Application Questions

To answer an application question, you must understand the meaning of a concept described in the passage and then apply that concept in a different context.

The following is an example of an application question.

1. Each day for one week, doctors measured the flow rate—the amount of fluid passing through a given area of a pipe per second—of blood flowing through a patient's aorta. The day of the week, the velocity of the blood, and the flow rate are shown in the chart below.

Day	Blood Velocity	Flow Rate
Monday	40 cm/s	120 cm/s^3
Tuesday	38 cm/s	114 cm/s^3
Wednesday	39 cm/s	117 cm/s^3
Thursday	42 cm/s	126 cm/s^3
Friday	41 cm/s	123 cm/s^3
Saturday	39 cm/s	117 cm/s^3
Sunday	43 cm/s	129 cm/s^3

What is the mean of the flow rates shown in the chart above, to the nearest hundredth?

You may use the calculator.

[ ]

Here's How to Crack It

To find a mean, or average, you must add up all of the numbers given, and then divide your total by the number of items you added up. Be careful to make sure you're solving for the correct thing; in this case, you want to find the mean of the flow rates, not the blood velocity, so be sure to use the numbers given for flow rate. In this case, adding up all of the numbers given for flow rate gives you 120 + 114 + 117 + 126 + 123 + 117 + 129 = 846. Divide 846 by 7 to get 120.86.

Here's another application question.

---

2. Scientists calculate the buoyant force, the upward force that a liquid exerts on an object submerged or floating in that liquid, by using the formula $F_B = \rho_f Vg$, where F_B is the buoyant force, ρ_f is the density of the fluid, V is the volume of the displaced fluid, and g is a constant and is the acceleration due to gravity.

   Based on the information above, an object would

   experience a [Select... ▼]
   - greater buoyant force
   - lesser acceleration due to gravity

   in a fluid that had [Select... ▼].
   - greater density
   - lesser volume

Here's How to Crack It

The passage states that g, the acceleration due to gravity, is a constant. Thus, you can eliminate "lesser acceleration due to gravity" from the answer choices in the first drop-down menu, since acceleration due to gravity does not change. Thus, the correct answer in the first drop-down menu must be "greater buoyant force." Now check out the formula $F_B = \rho_f Vg$. If density, or ρ_f, increases, then F_B, or the buoyant force, must also increase. On the other hand, if volume, or V, decreases, then F_B must actually decrease. Thus, the correct answer in the second drop-down menu is "greater density."

Analysis Questions

An analysis question asks you to break down information from a passage, chart, or graph into more specific categories, and then explore the relationships between those categories. An analysis question might be similar to this one.

1. The term *solubility* refers to the amount of a substance (solute) that will dissolve in a given amount of a liquid substance (solvent). The solubility of solids in water varies with temperature. The graph below displays the water solubility curves for six crystalline solids.

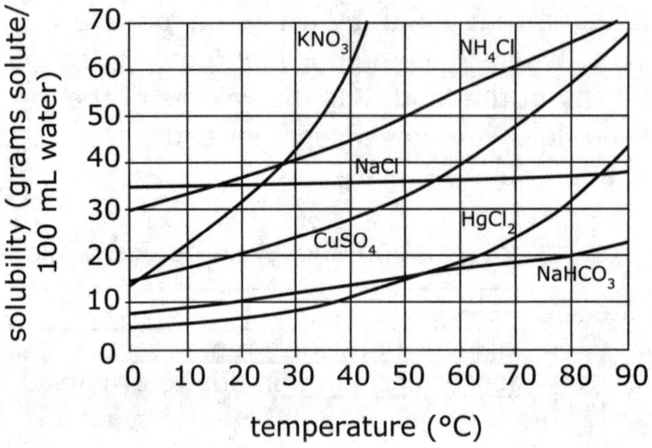

Identify the substances with the least change in solubility and the greatest change in solubility. Drag and drop your choices into the appropriate boxes.

Least Change in Solubility	**Greatest Change in Solubility**

NaCl
$CuSO_4$
$NaHCO_3$
$HgCl_2$

Here's How to Crack It

To find the substance with the least change in solubility, look at the slope of the graph of each of the substances. Note that NaCl has the flattest graph, which therefore means that it has the least change in solubility. The initial solubility of the substance is approximately 35 grams solute per 100 mL of water, and the final value is only approximately 38 grams solute per 100 mL of water. Thus, its change in solubility is very small. $CuSO_4$ has an initial solubility of approximately 15 grams solute per 100 mL of water, and a final solubility of approximately 68 grams solute per 100 mL of water, and does not have the flattest graph, so it does not have the least change in solubility. $NaHCO_3$ has an initial solubility of approximately 8 grams solute per 100 mL of water, and a final solubility of approximately 23 grams solute per 100 mL of water, and does not have the flattest graph, so it does not have the least change in solubility. Finally, $HgCl_2$ has an initial solubility of approximately 5 grams solute per 100 mL of water, and a final solubility of approximately 43 grams solute per 100 mL of water, and does not have the flattest graph, so it does not have the least change in solubility. Note that of the substances, $CuSO_4$ has the greatest difference between its initial solubility and its final solubility, and its graph has the steepest curve, so it is the substance with the greatest change in solubility.

Evaluation Questions

To answer an evaluation question, you must make a judgment or prediction about the information provided in a passage, chart, or graph—sometimes by applying outside knowledge or information that you bring with you to the test.

1 Biologists have long known that some types of electromagnetic radiation, such as X-rays and gamma rays, can be dangerous to human beings.

2 However, until now, no one has ever suggested that microwave radiation might also be harmful. In preliminary test-tube laboratory results, a scientist has found elevated growth rates in cancer cells exposed to low doses of microwaves.

3 These results are only preliminary because, first, there has been no controlled study of the effects of microwaves on human beings. Second, this study was of short duration, raising the possibility that the dangers of long-term exposure have not yet been assessed.

4 Although federal guidelines for how much electromagnetic energy can be allowed to enter the work and home environment have been made more stringent since they were first implemented in 1982, the recent study poses troubling questions about the safety of microwaves.

2. Which of the following, if true, would lend weight to the scientists' initial findings regarding microwaves?

   I. Individuals who extensively use point-to-point telecommunications, which heavily utilize microwaves, have higher-than-average incidences of cancer.
   II. A long-term study of cancer cells exposed to microwaves in the laboratory shows the same pattern of growth found in the short-term study.
   III. A study of dental associates who regularly work with X-rays shows that such individuals have higher-than-normal incidences of cancer.

   A. I only
   B. II only
   C. I and II
   D. I and III

Here's How to Crack It

One of the most useful things you can know for the GED® Science test is the **scientific method.** We will cover it in the review that begins in the next chapter, but for now, you should know that evaluation questions often ask you to bring some knowledge of the scientific method to bear on the question—and that is certainly the case here.

Given what the passage said about the preliminary nature of the study and what needs to be done next, which of the answer choices would help to prove the initial findings? The passage gave two reasons that the findings were only preliminary. First, the study was only at the test-tube stage. No studies involving people have been done yet. Second, it was only a short-term study. To know for sure whether microwaves cause increased growth in cancer cells, a long-term study is needed.

Now check out the possibilities. Statement I addresses the first reason presented in the passage—as yet there has been no study on human beings—and provides you with a study that supports the initial findings with new findings on human subjects. Statement II addresses the second reason presented in the passage—there has been no long-term study as of yet—by providing information from a long-term study of cancer cells exposed to microwaves. Statement III, however, focuses on people who have been exposed to X-rays, rather than microwaves. Since this study does not relate to microwaves, the results would not lend any weight to the initial results described in the passage. Thus, I and II, but not III, support the initial results, and the correct answer is (C).

What Topics Are Covered on the Science Test?

Here are the topics as they are described by the people who write the test:

Life Science	40%
Physics and Chemistry	40%
Earth and Space Sciences	20%

If this list seems slightly vague, have no fear. While trying to acquaint yourself with all of the topics covered in a high school biology class might take a long time, you don't need an in-depth knowledge of all of those topics in order to ace the Science test. In the chapters that follow, you'll discover just exactly what information you will need.

Our Approach

While some questions won't require you to have any particular knowledge of biology, earth science, physics, or chemistry, others will require you to have some general knowledge of these topics, including a knowledge of their specialized vocabularies. As you read, you'll discover just exactly what basic knowledge of these subjects you'll need. You may even find that science is more fascinating than you imagined, and want to learn more about these topics!

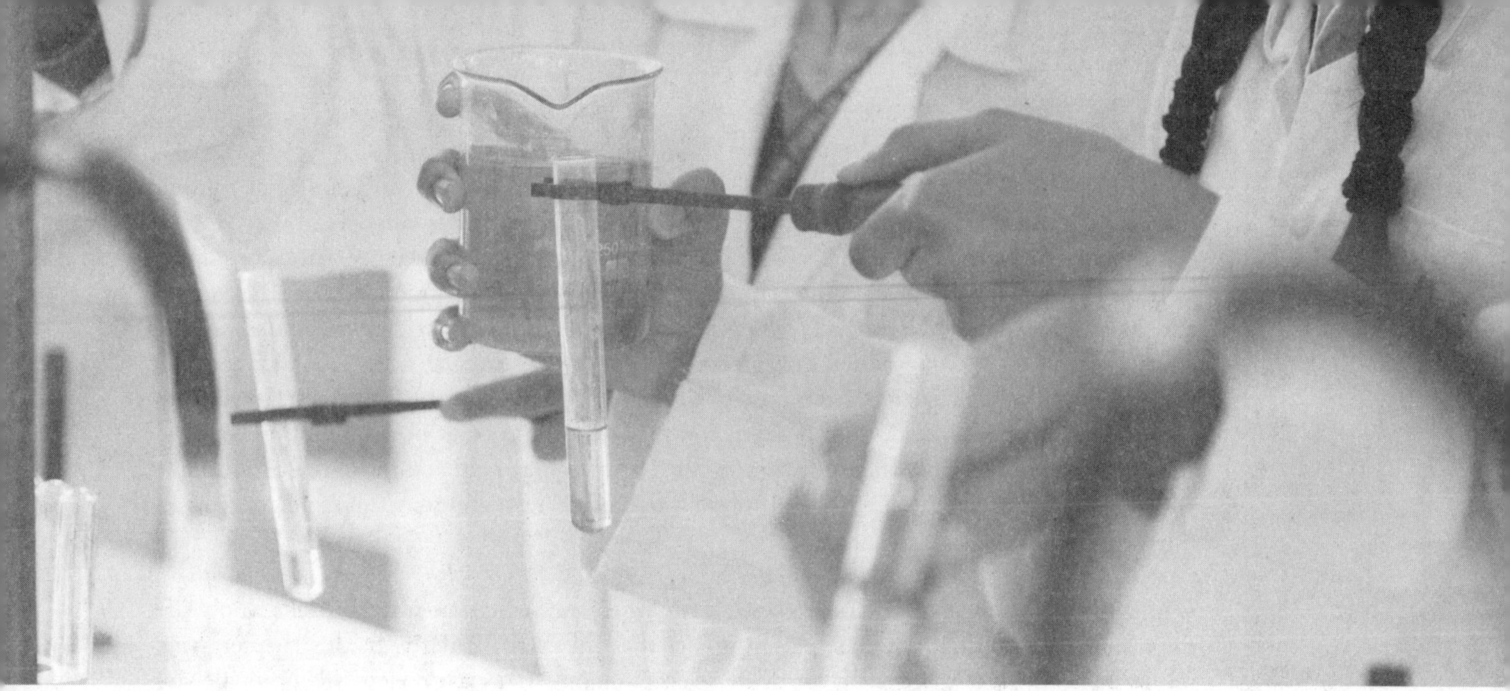

Chapter 22
Life Science

In this chapter, we'll go over some of the topics covered on the Science test—including the scientific method, cell theory and the origins of life, genetics, evolution and natural selection, plants, ecosystems and food chains, and the human body and human health.

Sometimes teachers can be knowledgeable about a subject but not especially skilled at communicating that knowledge in ways that inspire. If you had one of these teachers in your science class, you might be convinced that science is dull and tedious. In fact, science can be fun if you learn to look in the right places. The GED® test writers say that they frequently get their topics and ideas from *Discover, Science News, National Geographic, Popular Science,* and *American Health.* If you want some added confidence for the GED® Science test, you may consider reading one of these magazines from time to time as you prepare for the GED® test. It will help you get into a "science head," and besides, you may be astonished at how interesting you find these magazines. Not only that, but reading such articles may help you feel more comfortable with the topics tested on the science portion on the GED® test, and may therefore give you an important psychological advantage.

While it is impossible to predict *exactly* what you'll see on the Science test, the folks who write the test do indicate that there are certain topics that they test regularly. In this chapter, we'll review some of the test writers' favorite life science topics. After each review, we'll provide you with GED®-style practice questions based on those particular topics.

Here are the specific subjects we'll cover in this chapter:

- Scientific method
- Cell theory and the origins of life
- Genetics
- Evolution and natural selection
- Plants
- Ecosystems and food chains
- The human body and human health

Science Can Be Fun!
Articles from *Discover,* in addition to appearing in GED® test passages, cover interesting topics such as:

- how scientists analyze dinosaur excrement
- how to catch a flying gopher
- how to beat a champion chess-playing computer

THE SCIENTIFIC METHOD

How did scientists learn anything about biology, the solar system, or the movement of continents in the first place? In each case, a scientist first came up with a hypothesis to explain an event that was not yet understood. A **hypothesis** is simply a possible explanation of an event or a phenomenon. Once she has her hypothesis, the scientist performs experiments to see whether the hypothesis is correct. These experiments must be carefully designed to make sure that the information they provide is accurate and that each experiment tests only one phenomenon at a time. For example, if you were testing whether aspirin alleviates headaches, you would have to make sure that the test subjects took only aspirin—nothing else. A good scientist would properly wonder whether it might be the water the subjects took to swallow the aspirin that actually alleviated the headache. As you refine your hypothesis, you are attempting to remove any confounding external forces or internal sources of error. By controlling for both internal and external factors, you are establishing a controlled sample that reduces the potential of encountering issues with validity and reliability.

Often, an experiment will be repeated many times to make sure that the same results occur. Sometimes the scientist will use what is called a **control group**—a group of test subjects that are not subjected to the phenomenon being tested. For example, a scientist who is studying the effect of microwaves on cancer cells (like the man in the passage you just read in the last chapter) may also study a second group of cancer cells that are *not* exposed to microwaves. This is called the control group. The scientist will watch both groups closely. After all, how will he know if the cells exposed to microwaves behave abnormally if he doesn't know what normal is?

Only after other scientists have conducted the same experiments and obtained the same results is a hypothesis accepted as fact. And even then, scientists continue to reexamine their own thinking and the thinking of their predecessors. Sometimes accepted facts turn out to be wrong.

On the GED® Science test, you will occasionally be asked to evaluate the accuracy of information or the relevance of a method. These can be the most complicated questions on the test—and they almost always involve your thinking through the question based on the scientific method. Let's look at an example.

Scientists conducted a study to determine whether drinking a small amount of alcohol each day reduces one's chances of suffering from a heart attack. They tested 400 first-heart-attack survivors who maintained daily fitness routines and healthy diets by giving these individuals one alcoholic drink per day for 20 years. The results of the study are shown in the chart below, along with the incidence of second heart attacks among first-heart-attack survivors nationwide.

The Scientific Method Quiz

Q: If you were testing the effectiveness of a cream that's supposed to grow hair on bald men's heads, which of the following would be a good control group?

(1) a group of bald women
(2) a group of men with full heads of hair who are also given the cream
(3) a group of bald men who are given a harmless cream that has no effect

Turn the page for the answer.

Incidence of Second Heart Attacks Among Study Participants

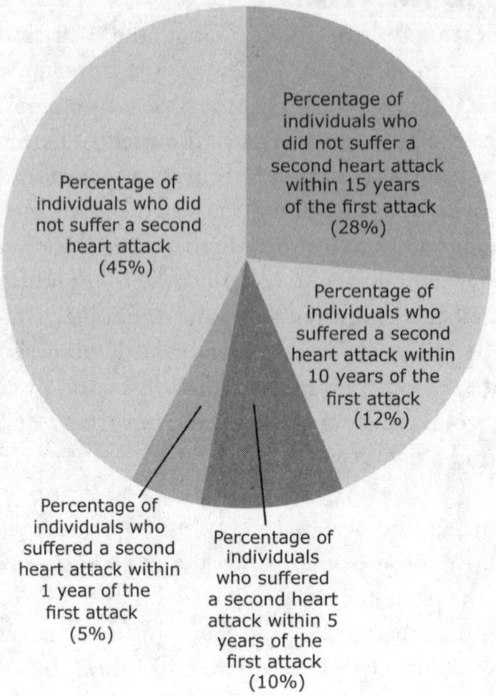

Incidence of Second Heart Attacks Among Average First-Heart-Attack Survivors Nationwide

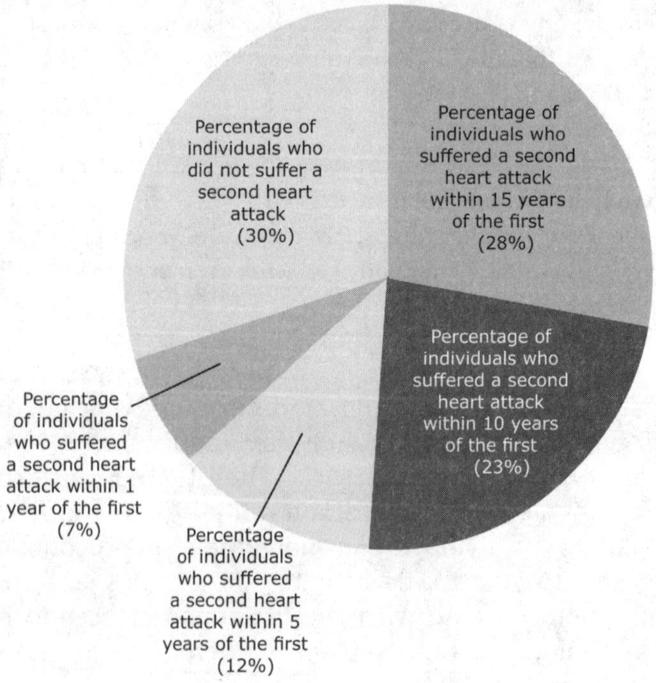

The Scientific Method Quiz

A: A control group should be a group that's representative of the group that you're testing but does not receive any medication or treatment. Since this study aims to test the effectiveness of the treatment on men, the control group should be men, rather than women. Thus, the first choice is incorrect. Additionally, since the study is testing the effects of the cream specifically on bald men, a control group of men with full heads of hair would not be appropriate. However, a control group of bald men who receive only a cream that has no effect would help scientists see bald men under normal conditions, so that they could see the difference between those who receive the cream and those who do not.

1. Based on the results of the study, scientists concluded that drinking alcohol in small amounts lowers the risk of heart attack.

   Which of the following represents a flaw in the study above?

   A. The sample size of the study was too small to be effective.
   B. The study was not performed over a long enough period of time to provide reliable data.
   C. The exercise and diet routines of the subjects may have affected their incidence of heart attack.
   D. The scientists did not perform the study on animals before attempting to study humans.

Here's How to Crack It

As soon as you see the word "study," you can be pretty sure that this passage will concern the scientific method. Not every evaluation question is about a study or experiment, of course, but clearly this one is. You're asked to find a flaw in the study, so start by using Process of Elimination to get rid of some of the more clearly wrong answers. Choice (A) would be a good answer if the number of study participants was small, but a **sample size** of 400 individuals seems large enough to be meaningful. Thus, (A) is incorrect. Similarly, the study was conducted over a period of 20 years, so the length of the study appears to be long enough to provide reliable data. Therefore, (B) is incorrect. Choice (D) seems unrealistic; even if testing animals before testing humans is preferable, you can't recommend a new form of treatment for mass human consumption without first testing it on at least a few human subjects. Choice (C), however, describes a serious flaw in the study. This choice points out that the study observed the effects not just of a single variable—alcohol consumption—but of other variables—exercise and diet routines. In this case, the lower incidence of second heart attacks among study subjects might be due, not to alcohol consumption, but to better-than-average exercise and diet routines. As noted above, it's much better to measure a single variable at a time than to attempt to measure multiple variables; other wise, you don't know which of the variables is really responsible for the results.

In a scientific experiment, the **independent variable** is the variable that is deliberately changed.
The **dependent variable** changes as a result of changes in the independent variable.

If you found this question challenging, it might help to remember that when the GED® test writers select a passage about an experiment, they like to see how much you know about the scientific method. Typical flaws in experiments include relying on a sample size that is too small, failing to include a control group, and allowing a sample to be tainted by other possible causes of the phenomenon in question (as was the case in this question).

When scientists draw conclusions about a certain population (as in the heart attack study we just discussed), they rely on the observations that they can make with a much smaller group. This technique is called **sampling**, and it is most reliable for drawing general conclusions about a population when the sample is random and representative. In a simple **random sample**, every member of the population has an equal chance of being selected. To make a sample more representative, **stratified random sampling** divides the population into particular groups (based on differences) and then randomly selects subjects within those groups. In experiments, **random assignment** is used to set up the experimental and control (untreated) groups. For example, scientists studying the effects of a particular drug would not choose their sample from among their colleagues, families, or neighbors; this would not be a representative sample. Choosing randomly from within varied collections of people (age, gender, race, family medical history, etc.) would be more representative of the population as a whole, with all its variation. Then, randomly assigning subjects to the two groups in their study—the group receiving the treatment and the untreated control group—would prevent further biases or uncontrolled variables from affecting their results.

Let's apply these terms in a test question about sampling nonhuman populations.

2. Researchers investigating an invasive bug species used samples of marshland habitat to make general observations about population trends. Throughout the entire ecological area of interest, they marked out 10-yard squares and labeled each with coordinates. Then, they used randomly generated numbers to select which plots of marshland they would analyze.

   Based on the information above, the scientists set up their ecological study using

   Select... ▼.
   - random sampling
   - stratified random sampling

Here's How to Crack It

Researchers are divvying up the "entire area" where they are studying the population of interest, and they are selecting using "random numbers," so any quadrant of marshland is equally likely to get picked. This is random sampling. If this study had used stratified random sampling, the marshland would have been divided into different zones based on variations like soil composition, type or density of vegetation, etc. (whatever differences researchers define as significant), and then randomly sampled *within* those zones, rather than from the whole area.

Vocabulary

hypothesis—a possible explanation of an event or phenomenon
control group—the group of subjects not being subjected to a phenomenon in a study
independent variable—the variable in a scientific experiment that is deliberately changed
dependent variable—the variable in a scientific experiment that changes as a result of changes in the independent variable
sample size—the number of subjects in a study
variable—an element that changes in a study
random sampling—creating a sample in which every member of the population has an equal chance of being selected
stratified random sampling—dividing the population into particular groups (based on categorical differences) and then randomly selecting *within* those groups
random assignment—the process of blindly sorting subjects into the experimental and control (untreated) groups of a study

Scientific Method Drill

You can check your answers in Part IX: Answer Key to Drills.

Questions 1 and 2 refer to the following passage.

1 In the year 79 A.D., Mount Vesuvius erupted and covered the town of Pompeii in about 5 m of ash, killing most of the inhabitants. However, much of the town was preserved under the volcanic debris, which allowed researchers to learn a lot about the way of life in Pompeii when it was discovered 1,500 years later. Over the next two hundred years, it was determined that Pompeii must have had an intricate system for transporting water as well as an amphitheater that was used for entertainment and even a gymnasium for exercise.

2 Scientists found remains that also included many fossilized animals, which have been used to better understand the wildlife that was present during that time period. Among the fossils was a bird that scientists believe to be part of a species that is now extinct. The bird had a slightly longer wing-to-body ratio than any known species that is alive today. It also has a stout and strangely pointed beak that may have given it a foraging advantage over competitors.

1. Based on the information in the passage, which of the following scientific conclusions is the most reasonable?

   A. The volcanic eruption at Pompeii was responsible for the extinction of this species.
   B. The bird did not live in Pompeii, but was on its way south for the winter.
   C. No one survived the volcanic eruption at Pompeii.
   D. The bird lived at the same time as the eruption.

2. Determine whether each of the following statements is a scientific observation or conclusion. For this drill, write the letters of the statements in the appropriate boxes.

Observations	**Conclusions**

(a) Mount Vesuvius erupted in 79 A.D.

(b) The bird would have been able to eat more than its competitors.

(c) The bird found at Pompeii is the only living version of that species that is alive today.

(d) The bird's wings are abnormally long.

CELL THEORY AND THE ORIGINS OF LIFE

All living organisms are made up of cells. Some organisms, such as amoebas, consist of single cells, while other organisms, such as humans, are composed of trillions of different cells. For instance, long tubular muscle cells, also known as myocytes, make up your muscle tissue, while your skin is comprised of skin cells. While the cells in your body may look different and have different functions, they are genetically identical.

There are two main types of cells: **prokaryotic cells**, which lack a nucleus and membrane-bound organelles, and are generally found in single-celled organisms such as bacteria and archaea, and **eukaryotic cells**, which have a nucleus and membrane-bound organelles. Eukaryotic cells are found in more complex, multicellular organisms such as animals, plants, and fungi, though some unicellular eukaryotes, like amoebas, also exist.

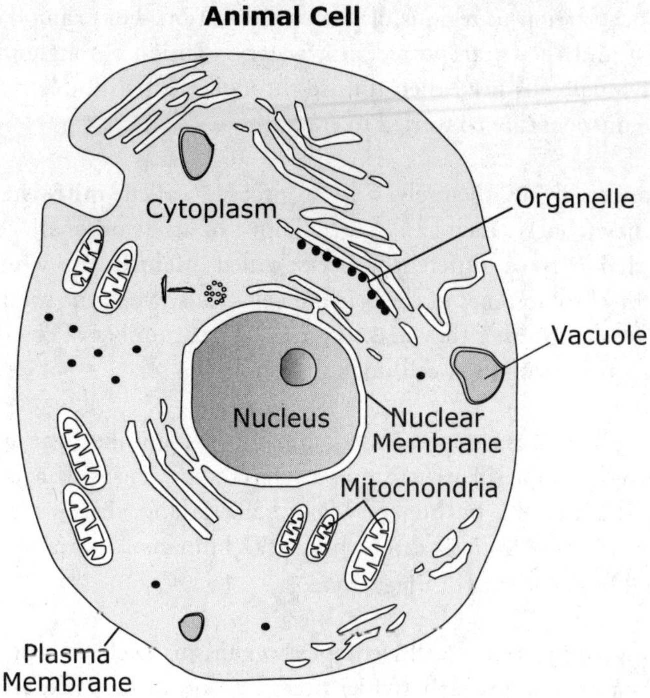

The **cell membrane,** also known as the plasma membrane, serves as a protective barrier that surrounds the cell, separating its internal environment from the external environment. It controls the movement of substances in and out of the cell, allowing nutrients to enter and waste products to exit. The **cytoplasm** is a gel-like substance that fills the interior of the cell. It contains various organelles suspended within it and serves as a medium for the transport of materials within the cell. Most types of cells have a **nucleus** containing the essential genetic information of the organism of which they form a part. This information is made up of DNA and is contained in structures called **chromosomes.** The nucleus regulates gene expression and directs the synthesis of proteins necessary for cell function. **Mitochondria** are often called the powerhouse of the cell because they generate energy in the form of adenosine triphosphate (ATP) through a process called cellular respiration. They have their own DNA and are believed to have originated from ancient symbiotic bacteria. The **endoplasmic reticulum (ER)** is a network of membranes that extends throughout the cytoplasm. It is involved in the synthesis, folding, and transport of proteins and lipids within the cell. **Ribosomes** are small, spherical organelles responsible for protein synthesis. They can be found free-floating in the cytoplasm or attached to the surface of the endoplasmic reticulum. The **Golgi apparatus** is responsible for modifying, sorting, and packaging proteins and lipids for transport to their final destination within or outside the cell. It consists of a series of flattened membrane sacs called cisternae.

Cell Division Quiz

Q: If a cell divides into two cells, which process would ensure that each of the new cells had the same number of chromosomes as the original?

(1) mitosis
(2) meiosis

Turn the page for the answer.

Understanding these basic components of a cell is crucial for comprehending more complex biological processes and phenomena. These components work together in a coordinated manner to maintain the cell's structure and function, allowing it to carry out its various activities essential for life.

Cells receive nourishment through **diffusion,** the process by which molecules spread from regions of high concentration to regions of low concentration. For example, the food that we eat is broken down and then transported in a watery solution throughout our bodies. The nutrients that individual cells need then diffuse through the permeable outer membranes of the cells, where the nutrients are converted to energy.

Most cells reproduce all by themselves in a process called **mitosis,** in which a cell splits into two new ones, each an exact copy of the original cell. Reproductive cells in animals divide by a different process called **meiosis,** in which the new cells contain only half the chromosomes of the original cell. Thus, when the sperm of a male unites with the egg of a female, together they make up the correct number of chromosomes, because the two "halves" (sperm cell and egg cell) make a "whole."

Single-cell organisms can be as complex in structure as the plantlike algae and the animal-like amoeba or as relatively simple in structure as bacteria and viruses. If a microbial organism can cause disease, it is called a **pathogen.** Many bacteria and viruses are considered pathogens, although some kinds of bacteria can be helpful to humans. For example, certain kinds of bacteria in the small intestine help us digest food.

In addition to being composed of cells, complex organisms such as humans require organ systems to assist them in completing activities necessary for life. These **essential functions of life** include the following:

- **Circulation.** This involves the movement of substances within an organism or its cells.
- **Excretion**. This process involves removal of waste, whether that waste be in the form of carbon dioxide, urine, or sweat.
- **Growth**. This is the process by which organisms increase in size—that is, increase the number of cells of which they are composed.
- **Reproduction**. A single organism may not need to reproduce in order to maintain its own health, but each species as a whole cannot survive unless its organisms reproduce. There are two types of reproduction: asexual reproduction, which involves only one parent, and which produces offspring identical to that parent, and sexual reproduction, which requires two parents, and which produces offspring that possess features that are a combination of both parents.
- **Movement**. This simply involves a change in position of a living thing, and allows shifts in circulation, muscles, and other systems.
- **Nutrition.** This is the process in which living things take in substances that allow them to grow and repair themselves. There are two types of nutrition: autotrophic nutrition, in which living organisms make their own food, and heterotrophic nutrition, in which organisms acquire food from their environments.
- **Synthesis.** This is the process by which organisms take small, simple substances, and combine them to form larger, more complex substances.

Now that you know a few basics of cell theory, check out the question on the next page to discover how the GED® test writers might construct a question based on cell theory.

When a cell undergoes mitosis, it duplicates into two genetically exact replicas of itself, so that the new cells have exactly the same number of chromosomes as did the original cell. When a cell undergoes meiosis, it creates four cells, each with half the number of original chromosomes. Meiosis, unlike mitosis, takes place in two rounds.

Scientists conduct an experiment on three different cells, and track the number of resulting cells and chromosomes after each cell undergoes either meiosis or mitosis, according to the cell type. The results are shown below.

Trial	Number of Initial Chromosomes	Number of Final Chromosomes in Each Resulting Cell	Number of Final Cells
1	6	6	2
2	4	2	4
3	46	x	4

Cell Division Quiz
A: In mitosis, a cell divides into two identical cells, each with the same number of chromosomes as the original cell.

1. In trial 3, the cell undergoes

   Select... ▼ and each resulting
   - meiosis
   - mitosis

   cell has Select... ▼ chromosomes.
   - 23
   - 46

Here's How to Crack It

Note that the final number of cells, after the cell in trial 3 divides, is 4. Thus, according to the information in the passage, the cell must have undergone meiosis, rather than mitosis. In meiosis, each resulting cell has half of the number of chromosomes of the original cell, so each resulting cell will have half of 46, or 23 chromosomes.

Vocabulary

organelles—specialized structures within a living cell
cytoplasm—area between the membrane and nucleus that contains organelles
mitochondria—the powerhouses of the cell that supply energy and break down food and sugar into water
vacuole—large water-filled sac that stores food, water, and waste
plasma membrane—boundary between the cell and environment that regulates the products that enter and exit the cell

nuclear membrane—boundary between the nucleus and the rest of the cell that is permeable to molecules like DNA, RNA, and ATP
permeable membrane—a barrier that lets certain molecules through it
prokaryotic cells—cells that lack structure
eukaryotic cells—cells that are structured and work together
nucleus—part of a cell containing its essential genetic information
chromosomes—structures of DNA
diffusion—the process by which molecules spread from regions of high concentration to regions of low concentration
mitosis—the process in which cells divide into new ones, each of which is an exact copy of the original
meiosis—the process by which cells split into new ones, each of which contains only half as many chromosomes as the original cell
pathogens—microbial organisms that can cause disease
essential functions of life—processes that include circulation, excretion, growth, reproduction, movement, nutrition, and synthesis
mitochondria—cell's energy powerhouse, producing ATP through cellular respiration; contains its own DNA
endoplasmic reticulum (ER)—membrane network for protein and lipid synthesis and transport
ribosomes—sites of protein synthesis in cells, translating genetic information into amino acids
Golgi apparatus—modifies, sorts, packages proteins and lipids for cell transport; near nucleus

Cell Theory and the Origins of Life Drill

You can check your answers in Part IX: Answer Key to Drills.

Questions 1 through 3 refer to the following information.

1 Tuberculosis is caused by the mycobacterium, *Mycobacterium tuberculosis,* which kills approximately half of all infected patients. For many years, *M. tuberculosis* was susceptible to drug therapy; however, like many other disease-causing organisms, new drug-resistant strains of tuberculosis have emerged. Many theories have been postulated to explain the emergence of these resistant strains (also known as "superbugs") but most health-care professionals blame the over-prescription of antibiotics as well as their misuse by patients.

2 Today, before a tuberculosis patient can be treated, it is first necessary to find out which strain of bacterium is causing the disease and then to find a drug that will kill that particular strain. Fortunately, a new technique has been discovered that aids this process. Scientists can now insert *luciferase*, the enzyme that makes fireflies glow in the dark, into tuberculosis cells taken from the patient, which makes the tuberculosis cells glow in the dark (see Figure).

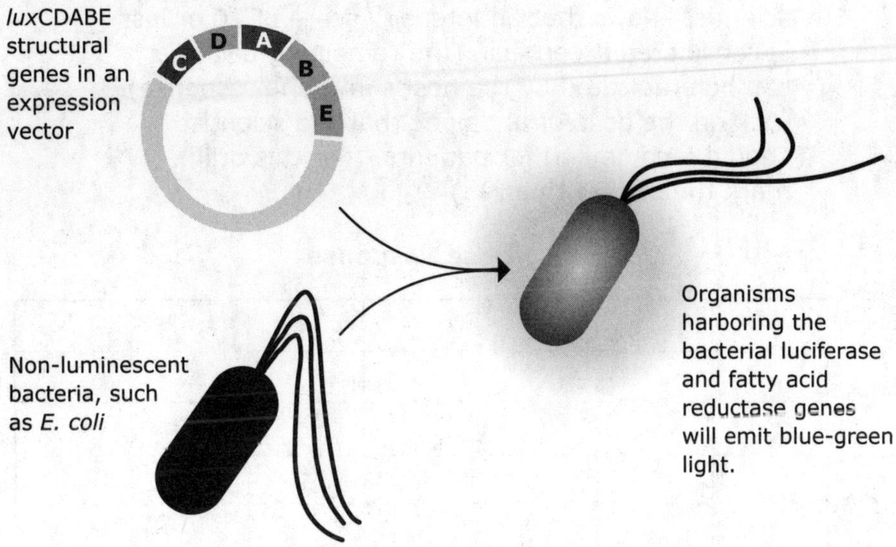

3 With their new glow-in-the-dark organisms, scientists can then test different drugs to see whether they kill the bacteria (which stop glowing). This new test can be done in days, which is faster than previous tuberculosis tests which required up to five weeks.

1. If a tuberculosis cell with luciferase is treated with a drug but keeps on glowing, which of the following is most likely the case?

   A. A higher dosage of the drug is needed.
   B. The tuberculosis cell has been destroyed.
   C. The cell is resistant to that particular drug.
   D. Both A and C are correct.

2. What is likely to be the most important reason to save time on a tuberculosis test?

   A. The patient can begin effective drug therapy that much sooner.
   B. The scientists can perform twice as many tests and thus have more time for other experiments.
   C. The enzyme luciferase lasts almost indefinitely.
   D. Other types of bacteria have shown themselves less able to mutate.

3. The following chart depicts the dose response curve of *M. tuberculosis* to an antibiotic drug. If a scientist knows that an intensity score of 20 or less is considered acceptable (the remaining bacteria can be eradicated by the host's immune response), click on the dose of antibiotic that the scientist should recommend for patients. (For this drill, mark the dose with an X.)

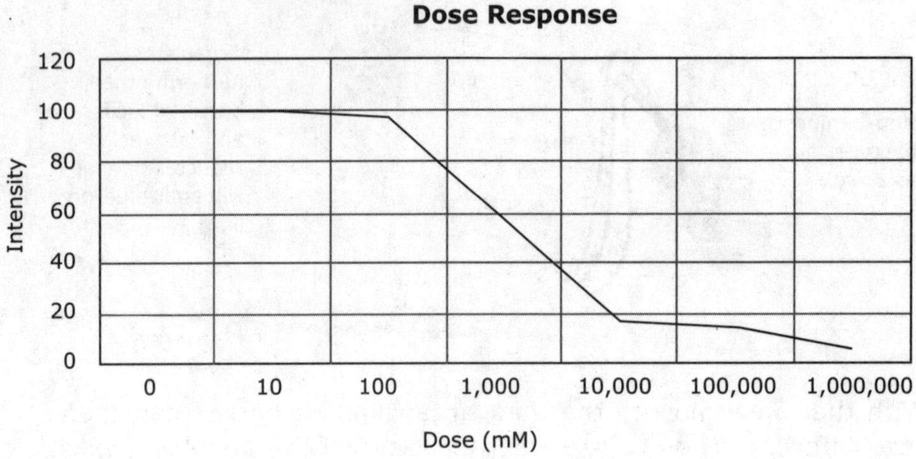

GENETICS

Genetics is the science of genes, and it involves the study of how parents pass on traits to their offspring. In order to begin learning the vocabulary of basic genetics, the first two genetics terms that you need to know are **genotype** and **phenotype.** A person's genotype is the genetic code that person carries, and it provides information about particular traits. Phenotypes are the expressions of those traits. For example, your hair color, which is an expression of instructions carried in your genetic code, is a phenotype. Phenotypes often depend upon genotype, but they can also result from environmental factors.

You have inherited many of your traits from your parents; perhaps people tell you that you have your mother's smile or your father's eyes. Your parents passed along these traits through chromosomes, which were introduced in the previous section, and which are made up of wound-up DNA. Each human chromosome pair consists of one chromosome from the father and another from the mother, which is why you resemble, at least to some extent, both your father and your mother. You could think of the **genes**, or sections of DNA, as sets of instructions for proteins, or traits. Of course, children inherit multiple traits from their parents, so it's not surprising that human cells have not only more than one gene, but also more than one chromosome. In fact, human cells have 23 pairs of chromosomes, or 46 chromosomes each. Of those 23 pairs, one pair is made up of sex chromosomes. Male chromosomes are known as XY chromosomes, while female chromosomes are known as XX chromosomes. The remaining 22 pairs of chromosomes are called **autosomes**, and each autosome pair is a **homologous pair**, or a pair of chromosomes, one from the father and one from the mother, with the same structure.

If genes are instructions for traits, **alleles** are versions of the instructions for traits. For example, you might have an allele for attached earlobes, or you might have an allele for detached earlobes. Each allele is a different form of the same gene.

So how might GED® test writers test genetics concepts? Check out the following question.

1 Chromosomes come in pairs and contain genes, which code for inherited traits. If a gene is always expressed when present, it is called dominant and is represented by a capital letter. A dominant gene will be expressed whether an individual is pure and has two copies of the dominant gene or is hybrid and contains one dominant copy and one copy of another gene. In the case of hybrids, the dominant gene hides the expression of the recessive gene. A recessive gene is expressed only when it is pure, and it is represented by a lowercase letter.

2 In pea plants, the gene for round pea shape is dominant and the gene for wrinkled pea shape is recessive. A plant that produces wrinkled peas must be pure for the wrinkled gene, meaning it must contain two copies of the wrinkled gene. A plant that produces round peas can either be pure for the round gene or be hybrid and have one gene for round shape and one gene for wrinkled shape.

3 Punnett Squares are charts used to predict the odds of specific gene combinations in offspring. Below is a Punnett Square of a cross between a pea plant purebred for wrinkled peas and a pea plant that produces round peas.

Punnett Square—Shape in Pea Plants

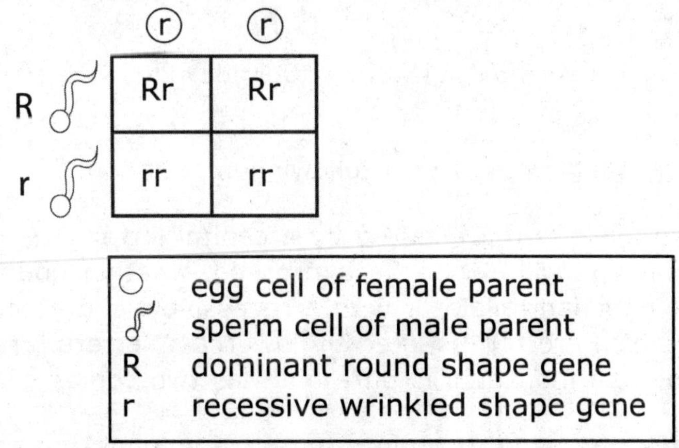

1. Which of the following describes the offspring of this cross?

    A. Half produce round peas and half produce wrinkled peas.
    B. All produce wrinkled peas.
    C. All produce round peas.
    D. Half produce wrinkled peas and half produce both round and wrinkled peas.

Here's How to Crack It

Half of the offspring (rr) possess only the genes for wrinkled peas, and will therefore produce wrinkled peas. The offspring in the other half of the square (Rr) possess one gene for wrinkled peas and one for round peas. Since the round gene is dominant over the wrinkled gene, these offspring will produce round peas. Thus, (A) is correct.

Vocabulary

genotype—genetic code that a person carries and that provides information about particular traits
phenotype—expression of genetic traits and traits that result from interactions of the genotype with the environment
genes—sections of DNA
autosomes—pairs of chromosomes other than the sex chromosomes
homologous pair—a pair of chromosomes, one from the father and one from the mother, with the same structure
alleles—versions of the instructions for genetic traits
hybrid—having one gene for one trait and another gene for a different trait

Genetics Drill

You can check your answers in Part IX: Answer Key to Drills.

Questions 1 through 3 refer to the following information.

1 When an allele is represented by a capital letter, it is said to be dominant, and will always be expressed, whether coupled with another dominant allele or with a recessive allele. Recessive genes, which are represented by lowercase letters, are expressed only when an individual is pure and has two copies of the allele.

2 In kittens, the gene for pointy ears is dominant and the gene for floppy ears is recessive. A kitten will express the pointy ear trait if the kitten is pure or has a hybrid of alleles. In order for floppy ears to be expressed on a kitten, the kitten must be pure for the recessive gene.

3 Punnett Squares are charts used to predict the odds of specific gene combinations in offspring. Below is a Punnett Square of a cross between two heterozygous parents.

	P	p
P	?	Pp
p	Pp	pp

P	dominant pointy ear allele
p	recessive floppy ear allele
?	unknown allele

1. What is the probability that an offspring will have pointy ears?

   [ ] %

2. According to the information presented, what genotype should replace the "?" in the Punnett Square?

   A. PP
   B. Pp
   C. pP
   D. pp

3. The genotypic ratio of this Punnett Square is best expressed as [Select... ▼].

   3:1
   1:3
   1:2:1
   2:1:2

EVOLUTION AND NATURAL SELECTION

Survival of the Fittest Quiz

Q: Which of the following is an example of natural selection?

(1) A frog survives by hiding under a rock.

(2) Over thousands of years, a frog species gradually changes color to mimic the color of the rocks it likes to sit on.

Turn the page for the answer.

It was Charles Darwin who first published the **theory of evolution.** This theory holds that species change slowly in response to factors in their environment. For example, if the Earth's climate started to get colder, dogs that happened to have thicker, warmer fur would tend to survive better than members of their species with thinner fur, thus allowing the **survival of the fittest**. The surviving dogs would pass on the thicker fur gene to their puppies, and so this trait would gradually become a prevailing characteristic of their species. This process in which traits that help an organism survive gradually triumph over traits that don't is called **natural selection.**

The other way evolution operates is **genetic drift**. Genetic drift is the accumulation of changes in the frequency of alleles (versions of a gene) over time due to sampling errors—changes that occur as a result of random chance. For example, in a population of owls there may be an equal chance of a newly born owlet having long talons or short talons, but due to random breeding variances a slightly larger number of long-taloned owlets are born. Over many generations, this slight variance can develop into a larger trend, until the majority of owls in that population have long talons. These breeding variances could be a result of a chance event—such as an earthquake that drastically reduces the size of the nesting population one year. Small populations are more sensitive to the effects of genetic drift than large, diverse populations.

Just as new species are formed by natural selection and genetic drift, other species may become extinct. Extinction occurs when a species cannot adapt quickly enough to environmental change and all members of the species die.

Darwin theorized that all species on Earth descended from one or two very simple organisms that gradually evolved into different kinds of more complex organisms. Thus, according to Darwin, human beings are thought to have evolved from simple sea creatures that gradually changed over millions of years into a common ape-like ancestor that in turn gradually evolved into *Homo sapiens*.

Today, animals are divided into two categories: invertebrates and vertebrates. **Invertebrates** do not have backbones—they include worms, jellyfish, and insects. **Vertebrates** *do* have backbones and include most of the animals you know, including fish, birds, and mammals. **Mammals** are animals that nurse their young. The whale is the largest mammal. *Homo sapiens* (otherwise known as human beings) are also mammals.

Ready to try a question on evolution and natural selection? Work the problem below.

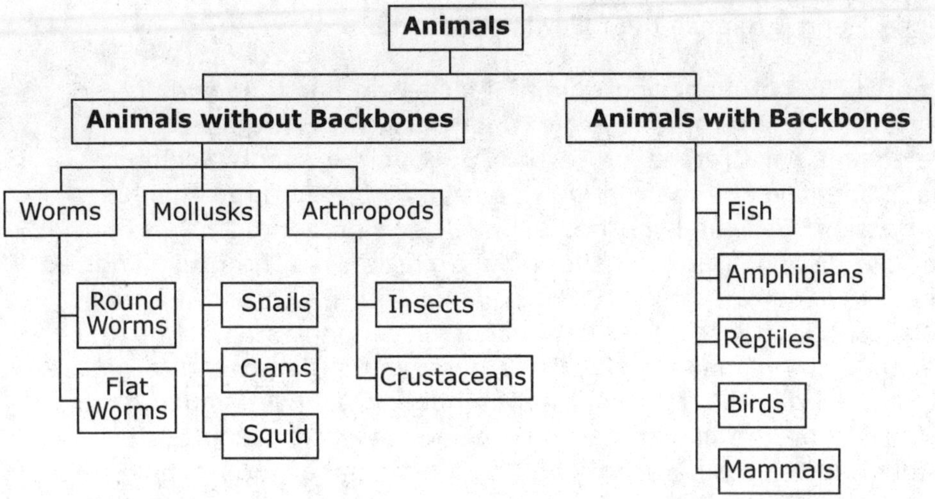

1. Based on the information in the chart above, which of the following animals are vertebrates?

   A. crustaceans
   B. amphibians
   C. insects
   D. round worms

Here's How to Crack It

Vertebrates are animals with backbones, so look for an animal that appears on the right-hand side of the chart. Crustaceans, insects, and round worms are all animals that appear on the left-hand side of the chart, under "Animals without Backbones," so (A), (C), and (D) are incorrect. Amphibians appear under the right-hand side of the chart, under "Animals with Backbones," so (B) is the correct answer.

Vocabulary

theory of evolution—scientific explanation that species change over time through genetic variation and natural selection
survival of the fittest—another name for natural selection
adaptation—short-term changes in a species
natural selection—mechanism of evolution in which organisms better adapted to their environment tend to survive and reproduce
genetic drift—the accumulation of changes in the frequency of versions of a gene over time due to changes that occur as a result of random chance
invertebrates—animals without backbones
vertebrates—animals with backbones
mammals—animals that nurse their young

Evolution and Natural Selection Drill

You can check your answers in Part IX: Answer Key to Drills.

Questions 1 and 2 refer to the following passage.

1 Nearly 75% of plant and animal species on Earth, including all non-bird dinosaurs, went extinct during the Cretaceous-Paleogene (or Cretaceous-Tertiary) extinction event. Scientists have spent years speculating about what precipitated this extinction. Various hypotheses have been presented to account for the disappearance of these huge creatures. The prevailing theory is that a large asteroid collided with Earth and its impact raised a cloud of dust that reduced the amount of sunlight that reached the planet's surface for many years. Temperatures fell rapidly, and without the normal amount of sunlight, much of the plant life on the planet's surface disappeared. Unadapted for sudden lower temperatures and a much smaller food supply, the dinosaurs, as well as many other species, became extinct.

2 In support of this theory, scientists have found a thin layer of sediment in marine and terrestrial rocks that contains metals that are rare on Earth but abundant in asteroids. Additionally, a large crater was found in the Gulf of Mexico that must have been formed when an asteroid hit Earth at roughly the same time as the extinctions took place.

3 Amid the destruction was opportunity for evolution. There were countless vacated ecological niches and the surviving organisms rapidly adapted and developed in order to occupy these niches. It is believed that several of the mammals, including the ancestors of primates, that are alive today developed during this time.

Survival of the Fittest Quiz

A: A frog species that gradually changes color to adapt to its environment is a good example of natural selection.

1. If the preceding information is true, which of the following is the most likely explanation for the fact that there is still life on Earth today?

   A. Some forms of life were able to survive in spite of the decrease in available sunlight.
   B. The dinosaurs went into hibernation.
   C. Sunlight is unnecessary for the survival of plant forms.
   D. There was no food at all on the planet's surface during these years.

2. If Charles Darwin read this passage, would he agree with the statements made in the last paragraph?

   A. No. According to Darwin's theory of natural selection, organisms were destined to fulfill specific niches only when it was best for their evolutionary fitness.
   B. No. Darwin would not have considered a tragedy to be an opportunity.
   C. Yes. Darwin believed that slight differences between organisms can be selected for through natural selection and that this would be exacerbated in a time when there were many potential ecological niches.
   D. Yes. Darwin believed that individual organisms were capable of evolution.

PLANTS

Most plants are made up of many cells. Plants make their own food through a fascinating process called **photosynthesis.** Plant cells contain a chemical called **chlorophyll,** which gives plants their green color. When a plant's leaves absorb sunlight, the chlorophyll in the leaves converts the sunlight into energy. Meanwhile, the roots of the plant have been drawing water from the ground all the way up into the leaves. The plant uses the energy it has just converted to split the water (H_2O) into its two components—hydrogen and oxygen. The hydrogen is used by the plant, along with carbon dioxide from the air, to create sugar and starches for its own nutrition. The oxygen is released into the atmosphere—incidentally making it possible for humans to go on breathing.

The growth process of plants is dependent on the seasons. Some plants last only one growing season and die during the winter. To carry on the species, these plants produce **seeds,** which lie dormant during the winter months and then **germinate** in the spring. Other plants, called **perennials,** live for many years. The upper shoots of a perennial wither and die during the winter, but the roots live through the winter and produce new shoots in the spring.

Trees are also a kind of plant whose stalks have become woody. Trees survive the winter because their trunks protect them from the cold. If you were to cut down a tree and look at a horizontal cross section inside, you would find many circular rings. This is because in the spring and summer, the tree grows more rapidly, producing wider pores. During the winter, the growth is slower, producing denser wood. By counting the rings of a tree, you can tell how old it is.

Check out the passage on plants below, and answer the question that follows.

When plants respond to an environmental stimulus by growing in a particular way, that response is called a tropism. There are five kinds of tropism:

phototropism—a response in which plants turn toward the light

geotropism—a response in which roots grow toward the earth and the shoots and flowers grow toward the sky

thigmotropism—a response in which plants curl around any object they touch

hydrotropism—a response in which plants' roots grow toward a source of water

chemotropism—a positive attraction of roots toward the presence of certain chemicals

A student decides to study the way in which a particular plant responds to sunlight over a six-month period. At the beginning of the study, the student moves the plant, which originally bent toward a nearby window, so that the plant bends directly away from the window, and the angle between the direction in which the plant bends and the window is 180°. The graph below shows the changes in the way that the plant bends as the year progresses.

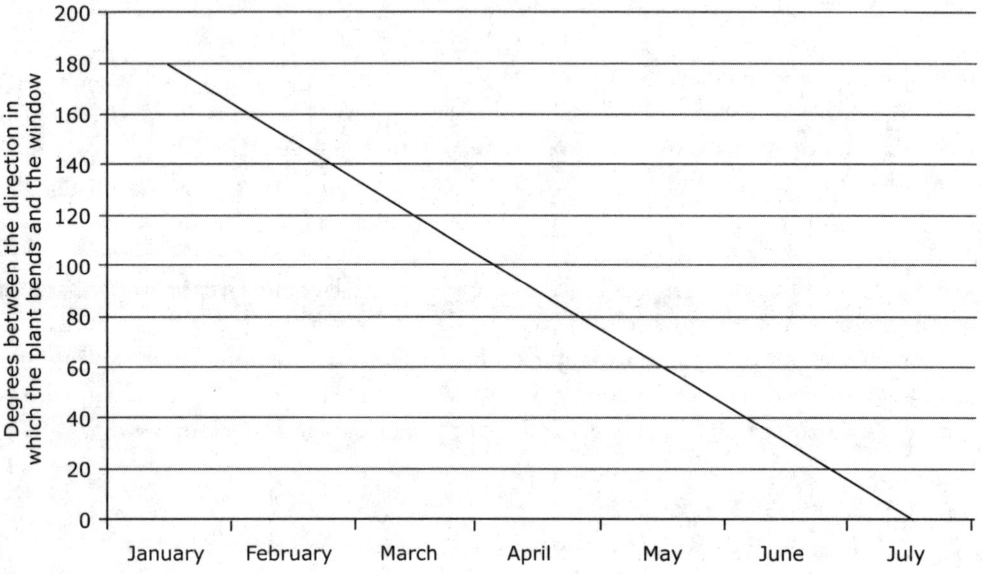

1. The plant's movements toward the window are an expression of which of the following?

   A. phototropism
   B. geotropism
   C. thigmotropism
   D. chemotropism

Here's How to Crack It

This question is not about the roots but about the visible part of the plant above the soil. Based on that information, only two choices are possible: phototropism and thigmotropism. Because the question does not mention curling, and according to the graph, the plant bends toward the window at the end of the study, the correct answer to this question must be (A).

Vocabulary

stomates—the microscopic openings through which gases diffuse into and out of leaves during photosynthesis
pistil—female reproductive organ of a flower
stamen—male reproductive organ of a flower
photosynthesis—the process through which plants make their own food
chlorophyll—the chemical that provides plants with their green color
seeds—reproductive structures of plants containing an embryo, stored nutrients, and a protective outer covering
germinate—begin to grow or put out shoots
perennials—plants that live for many years

Plants Drill

You can check your answers in Part IX: Answer Key to Drills.

Questions 1 through 3 refer to the following passage.

1 If you cut a horizontal cross section through the trunk of a tree, you can see the tree's growth rings (also known as tree rings). Each ring inside the trunk of a tree represents the annual growth of the tree. There are two parts of a growth ring. The inner part is formed during the early growth season (spring and early summer in North America) and is relatively less dense. The outer part of each ring is denser and is formed during the late summer and autumn.

2 The growing conditions of a particular year will affect the size of a ring. In ideal growing conditions (such as adequate moisture and a relatively long growing season), a ring may be larger because the tree was able to grow more during that time. However, a cold summer or a drought can cause the ring size to be smaller than normal.

3 Researchers can use tree rings to learn about the growing conditions that were present during a particular time period. The tree depicted below was cut down at the end of the growing year in 2000.

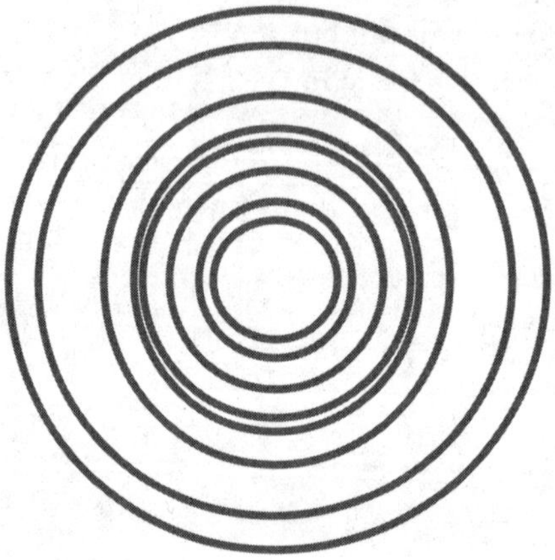

1. Based on the figure, which of the following years was the best growing season?

    A. 2000
    B. 1999
    C. 1998
    D. 1997

2. How old, in years, is the tree represented in the figure?

   A. 6
   B. 7
   C. 8
   D. 9

3. The following graph compares tree ring size to the average amount of monthly rainfall.

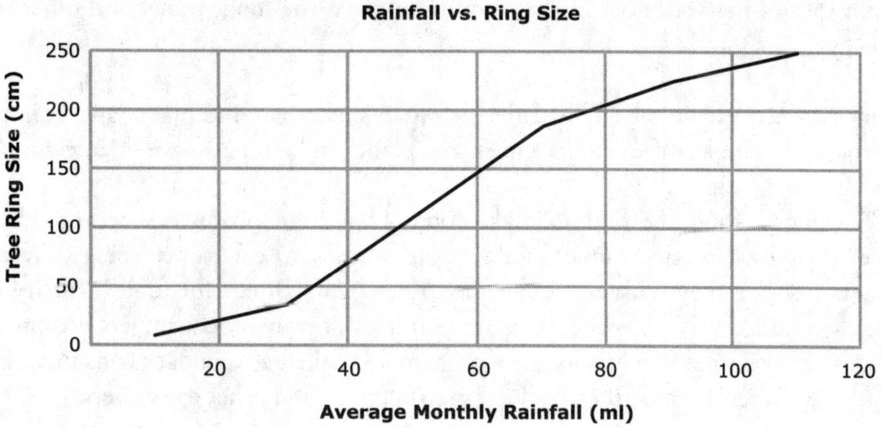

In the graph above, average monthly rainfall is the

Select... ▼ variable, while tree ring size is
independent
dependent

the Select... ▼ variable.
independent
dependent

ECOSYSTEMS AND FOOD CHAINS

An **ecosystem** is a place where many organisms live and depend on other organisms for survival. For example, grass uses the energy of the Sun to grow; a rabbit eats the grass; a hawk eats the rabbit. Every organism is eating something else to get energy, except for the grass, which gets its energy from sunlight through photosynthesis.

In any given ecosystem, the total number of resources is limited. A given region, for example, can support only so many rabbits before the rabbits begin to run out of grass to eat and their population begins to dwindle. When this happens, the hawk population will also begin to dwindle. The **carrying capacity** of a particular ecosystem is the maximum population size of a given species that can exist in that ecosystem given the food, water, and other resources available in the region.

To balance an ecosystem, all of the different organisms, including plants and animals, have certain roles. Let's look at the different roles that plants and animals have in an ecosystem.

Plants get energy from the Sun to make food. Plants are **producers** because they make (produce) their own food. Animals, unlike plants, need to eat to get energy. Animals are **consumers** because they must eat (consume) other living things for food. Primary consumers eat only producers. Rabbits and cows are examples of primary consumers because they eat only plants. A consumer that eats another consumer is called a secondary consumer. Frogs are secondary consumers because they eat flies, grasshoppers, and other consumers.

All primary consumers eat plants, and the scientific term for these consumers is **herbivores**. Secondary consumers that eat only animals and not any plants are called **carnivores**. Many consumers eat both plants and animals, depending on what is available. These consumers are called **omnivores**.

There are other organisms in an ecosystem besides producers and consumers. These organisms, like earthworms, bacteria, and fungi, eat dead organisms and return nutrients back to the soil for plants to use. These organisms are called **decomposers** because they break down other organisms to get energy.

The **food chain** is the process by which organisms pass energy from one to another. The first step in a food chain occurs when a green plant absorbs energy from the Sun and converts it to chemical energy through photosynthesis. The second step occurs when an animal eats the plant, converting the energy contained in the plant into energy that the animal can store in its cells. Following this, a larger animal then eats the first animal, and stores the energy from that animal in its own cells. This process may continue through several steps. Eventually, a fungus or bacterium breaks down decaying organic matter. The figure on the next page shows an example of a food chain.

Food Chain

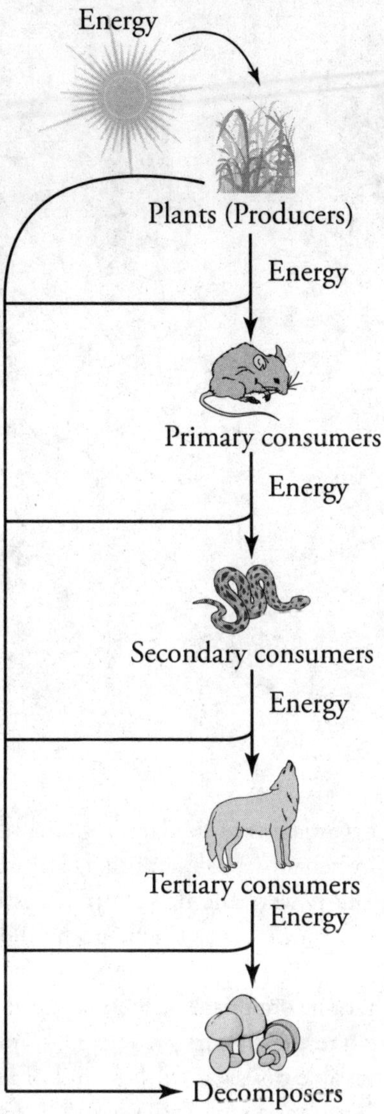

Arrows represent the direction in which energy and nutrients flow, pointing from the organism that is consumed to the organism that consumes.

An alternative way to show how animals transfer energy to one another is by using a **food web**. This is a slightly more complicated chart that takes into account the fact that there is often more than one animal vying for a particular kind of food.

Food Web

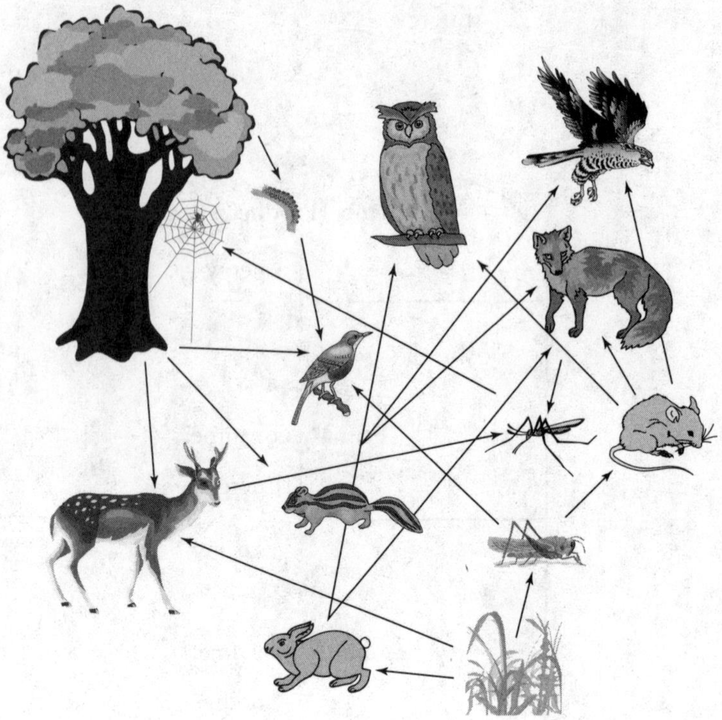

Not all relationships between organisms are predatory. Some are **mutualistic**, meaning that both organisms in a relationship benefit from each other. For example, insects that eat nectar from a flower are also helping the flower. The flower's pollen sticks to the insects as they eat, and then some of the pollen rubs off when they reach another flower, pollinating it.

Some are **parasitic**, meaning that one organism benefits while another organism suffers. Think about fleas on a dog. The fleas bite the dog to get energy from its blood and in return, the poor dog gets itchy welts and possible diseases. In this kind of relationship, the flea is called a parasite and the dog is called a host. Tapeworms, ticks, and lice are other examples of parasites.

Some exhibit **commensalism**, meaning that one organism is helped while the other organism is neither helped nor harmed. A great example of commensalism is the relationship between a remora and a whale. The remora has a sucker on the top of its head that attaches to the whale's top, mouth, or underside. Through this attachment, the remora can travel around more easily and eat any debris that falls from the whale. The whale is left unharmed.

1. A food web in an ecosystem is shown below:

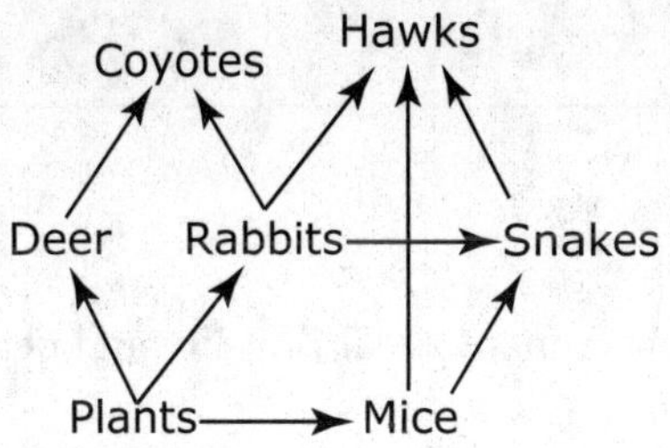

Select the producer from the list below, and drag it into the box.

[ ]

Select the herbivores from the list below, and drag them into the box.

[ ]

Select the carnivores from the list below, and drag them into the box.

[ ]

Coyotes | Rabbits | Snakes | Deer

Plants | Mice | Hawks

Here's How to Crack It

Plants make their own food, and are therefore producers. Thus, you should select plants as the producers. Herbivores eat plants, and based on the food web, deer, rabbits, and mice eat plants, so you should select these as the herbivores. Carnivores are animals that eat other animals. Coyotes eat deer and rabbits; hawks eat rabbits, mice, and snakes; and snakes eat mice and rabbits. Therefore, coyotes, hawks, and snakes are carnivores.

Vocabulary

ecosystem—a place where many organisms live and depend upon other organisms for survival

carrying capacity—the maximum population size of a given species that a certain ecosystem can support

producers—green plants and algae that take the Sun's energy and convert it into chemical energy

consumers—animals that eat the producers and/or sometimes each other

herbivores—primary consumers, or living things that eat plants

carnivores—secondary consumers, or animals that eat only animals

omnivores—animals that eat both plants and animals

decomposers—organisms such as bacteria that live on dead or decaying organic matter, breaking it down into its basic ingredients and beginning the life process all over

food chain—the process by which organisms pass energy from one to another

food web—a chart that shows the way that organisms pass energy from one to another, and that takes into account the fact that there is often more than one animal vying for a particular kind of food

mutualistic relationships—relationships in which organisms benefit from helping each other

parasitic relationships—relationships in which one organism benefits while another suffers

commensalism—a class of relationships in which one organism benefits while another is neither helped nor harmed

Ecosystems and Food Chain Drill

You can check your answers in Part IX: Answer Key to Drills.

Questions 1 through 3 refer to the food web below.

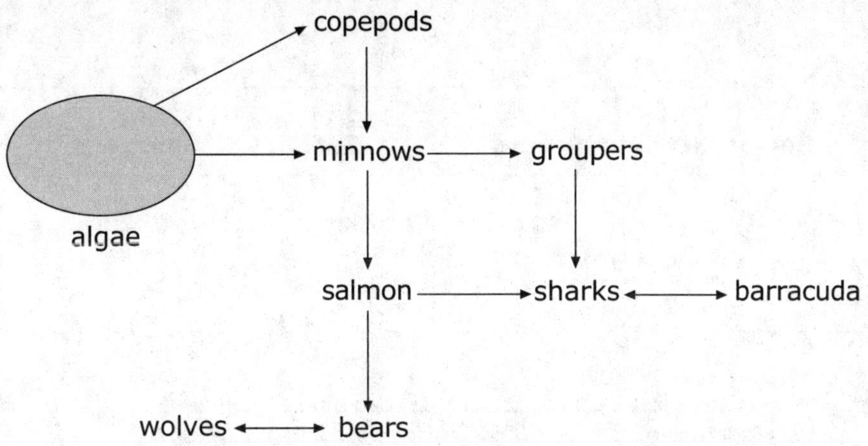

1. Which of the following organisms in the food web above are eaten by both land and sea creatures?

   A. minnows
   B. wolves
   C. salmon
   D. groupers

2. The absence of which organism in the food web above would most devastate the rest of the web?

   A. minnows
   B. wolves
   C. salmon
   D. algae

3. Drag and drop the organisms from the list below into the following categories. (For this drill, write the letter next to each organism into the appropriate category).

Primary Producers	Primary Consumers

Secondary Consumers	Tertiary Consumers

(a) Algae	(d) Groupers	(g) Bears
(b) Copepods	(e) Salmon	(h) Barracuda
(c) Minnows	(f) Sharks	(i) Wolves

THE HUMAN BODY AND HUMAN HEALTH

The human body is truly remarkable. Eleven different systems work together to keep your heart pumping, air in your lungs, and the rest of your body functioning. You'll need to know something about these systems in order to successfully tackle the GED® Science test, so you may find it helpful to familiarize yourself with them.

First, the **circulatory system** allows blood to circulate through your body and deliver oxygen, nutrients, and hormones to your cells, and carry away wastes such as carbon dioxide. It helps you to stay nourished, maintain a constant body temperature, and fight disease. Your **lymphatic system** is actually part of your circulatory system, and is composed of lymphatic vessels that carry lymph, a clear fluid, toward your heart. Each day, approximately 17 of your 20 liters of body's plasma are reabsorbed into your blood vessels, but 3 liters get left behind. The lymphatic system creates an alternative way for this plasma to return to your blood.

Next, the **integumentary system** is composed of your skin, hair, and nails, and helps to protect your body from damage from its environment. The **urinary system**, otherwise known as the renal system, includes your bladder, kidneys, ureters, and urethra. This system is responsible for eliminating waste from your body, regulating blood pH, controlling your electrolyte and metabolite levels, and regulating your blood pressure and volume. Your lungs make up your **respiratory system,** which moderates your intake of oxygen and expulsion of carbon dioxide. Your **muscular system** consists of your skeletal, cardiac, and smooth muscles, and allows you to move, remain upright, and circulate blood through your body. It works closely with your **nervous system**, which controls your muscular system and regulates both voluntary and involuntary motions by transmitting signals to various parts of your body. Your bones—all 270 of them at birth—make up your **skeletal system**, which supports your body and allows it to move, produces blood cells, regulates endocrine, and stores ions. Your **digestive system** includes your mouth, esophagus, stomach, intestines, anus, and rectum. It helps you break down food so that it can be absorbed into your body, and it eliminates waste. The **reproductive system,** which is made up of the sex organs, as well as fluids, pheromones, and hormones, allows humans to have offspring. Your **endocrine system,** which consists of glands that secrete hormones into your circulatory system, regulates functions throughout the body.

Why do you need so many systems? One reason is that your body needs to maintain **homeostasis**, or stable internal conditions. For example, you need to maintain a constant internal temperature, a constant pH, and constant blood glucose levels. Your body's systems work together to maintain homeostasis.

Of course, nutrition and environment also strongly contribute to your health. Poor nutrition may cause diseases such as diabetes, scurvy (a disease that results from a lack of vitamin C), and cardiovascular disease, among others.

Try out the following human health and human body question.

The human body maintains itself through several systems. For example, the integumentary system, which is composed of skin, hair, and nails, helps to protect the body from harm. The endocrine system consists of glands that secrete hormones into your circulatory system, such as the pituitary glands, thyroid, pancreas, and adrenal glands. Lungs make up the respiratory system, and moderate intake of oxygen and expulsion of carbon dioxide. The muscular system consists of skeletal, cardiac, and smooth muscles, and allows humans to move and remain upright, and circulates blood through the body. These, along with seven other systems, maintain homeostasis, or stable internal conditions. When the body is no longer in homeostasis, these systems act to bring the body back to equilibrium.

1. After a large meal, glucose enters the bloodstream as carbohydrates are broken down. The rise in blood sugar levels signals the pancreas to release insulin.

   This is an example of the [Select... ▼]
   - muscular
   - integumentary
   - endocrine

   system glands being activated to

   [Select... ▼].
   - return the body to homeostasis
   - circulate blood through the body
   - expel carbon dioxide

Here's How to Crack It

According to the passage, "the endocrine system consists of glands that secrete hormones into your circulatory system, such as the pituitary glands, thyroid, pancreas, and adrenal glands." Thus, the pancreas is part of the endocrine system, so the answer to the first question is "endocrine." The passage also states that the bodily systems listed, "along with seven other systems, maintain homeostasis, or stable internal conditions. When the body is no longer in homeostasis, these systems act to bring the body back to equilibrium." When blood sugar rises, the body's systems act to store glucose as energy and restore balance to levels in the blood. Thus, the correct answer to the second question is "return the body to homeostasis."

Vocabulary

systems of the human body—the circulatory system, the lymphatic system, the integumentary system, the urinary system, the respiratory system, the muscular system, the nervous system, the skeletal system, the digestive system, the reproductive system, and the endocrine system

homeostasis—stable internal conditions

The Human Body and Human Health Drill

You can check your answers in Part IX: Answer Key to Drills.

Questions 1 through 3 refer to the following information.

The human body maintains equilibrium through the use of multiple bodily systems. For example, the muscular system, which circulates blood through your body and allows you to move, is comprised of skeletal, cardiac, and smooth muscles. Working closely with the muscular system, the nervous system controls your muscular system and regulates both voluntary and involuntary motions by sending signals to parts of the body. Likewise, the skeletal system works in harmony with the muscular system, providing internal organs with protection and working with muscles to enable movement. Along with the other bodily systems, the muscular, nervous, and skeletal systems work together to keep the body in equilibrium.

1. Which of the following bodily systems from the list below play a role in movement? Choose all that apply. (For this drill, write the option letters in the box below.)

Bodily Systems that Play a Role in Movement

(a) Endocrine

(b) Muscular

(c) Skeletal

(d) Digestive

(e) Nervous

2. Susan suffered from a heart attack in February,

which primarily impacted the [Select... ▼ | skeletal | cardiac | smooth]

muscles within her [Select... ▼ | muscular | skeletal | nervous] system.

3. Franklin is walking through the desert when he comes upon a poisonous scorpion. Franklin's "flight or fight" response is initiated by his endocrine system and he then reacts by running in the opposite direction of the scorpion. Which system is responsible for triggering Franklin's movement?

A. skeletal
B. endocrine
C. muscular
D. nervous

BACTERIA AND VIRUSES

When we think of a **disease,** we often think of an illness (which can have a variety of symptoms and effects) that negatively impacts humans, animals, and plants. While you won't need to know the scientific names of every disease on the GED® test, you should have a general idea about the way in which disease spreads, the impact of disease on a population, and how to combat disease.

Bacteria are single-celled, living organisms. Despite their small size, bacteria have ribosomes and a single loop of DNA, which contains approximately 5,000 genes. Bacteria are also capable of reproduction through a process called **binary fission,** which occurs when the DNA replicates and the bacterial cell splits into identical daughter cells. So, how can you catch a bacterial infection? A bacterial infection can be transmitted through the air, tainted food or water, an insect bite, or direct contact with open sores on the body. Consider the bubonic plague, which is usually transmitted via flea bites, and dysentery, which is contracted when an individual consumes contaminated food or water. Thankfully, most harmful bacteria can be killed with chemicals or boiling water, and many bacterial infections can be treated with antibiotics, which are substances that can destroy or inhibit the growth of infectious bacteria by interfering with their cellular processes. It should be noted that not all bacteria are harmful. There are a number of "friendly" bacteria, such as *L. acidophilus,* that aid in the digestive process.

A **virus** is a piece of DNA or RNA encapsulated by a protein coat, or **capsid**. While a complex virus can have a hundred genes, all viruses are extremely small, and no virus is alive. Viruses can't reproduce independently, don't perform any biological functions, and rely on living cells for replication through a process called lysis, or the lytic cycle. In the **lytic cycle**, a virus attaches to a host cell, injects its DNA or RNA into the host cell, and makes hundreds of copies of itself. Eventually, the host cell bursts, releasing the viral copies into the organism. Once replicated, viruses can be transmitted through either air or direct contact. For example, a child could contract the chicken pox through inhalation, but could contract AIDS only through direct contact with infected bodily fluids. Unlike bacterial infections, however, viral infections cannot be treated with antibiotics. Instead, the most effective preventative treatment against contracting a viral infection is **immunization** or **vaccination**, the process of stimulating the immune system to produce defenses against harmful viruses by introducing harmless, yet similar, viruses or viral components. Unfortunately, vaccines must be continually adapted, as many viruses (such as the common cold) are capable of rapid mutation.

Viral and bacterial **pathogens**, or disease-causing agents, can have devastating consequences on human, animal, and plant populations. During the Middle Ages, the bubonic plague spread throughout Europe, killing more than one-third of the continent's population. Referred to as the Black Death, victims of the plague suffered from diarrhea, vomiting, chills, and blood-filled boils. Due to the lack of antibiotics and unsanitary living conditions during this time period, tens of millions had died by the time the plague ran its course. If a disease is particularly brutal, it can have a severe impact on the population demographics. In animal populations, for example, a virulent pathogen could cause the species to become extinct. While such fatal bacterial infections, such as the bubonic plague, sometimes occur today in pre-industrialized countries, modern medicine and sanitation practices have greatly reduced mortality rates by mitigating the spread of bacterial infections. Conversely, modern sanitation and medicine have not been able to mitigate the consequences of many viral infections.

Acquired immunodeficiency syndrome (**AIDS**), caused by the human immunodeficiency virus (**HIV**) and spread via bodily fluids, is one of the most notorious viral diseases today. While cells in the immune system fight pathogens in a healthy individual, cells in the immune system are infected and attacked by HIV in an individual with AIDS. In turn, the individual's immune system is compromised, and the person becomes more susceptible to illness. New treatments have considerably extended the life expectancy of those with HIV, but the virus still takes a large toll on public health.

Try out the following question.

1 The genetic material within virus particles, and the method by which the material is replicated, varies considerably between different types of viruses.

DNA viruses

2 The genome replication of most DNA viruses takes place in the cell's nucleus. If the cell has the appropriate receptor on its surface, these viruses enter the cell either by direct fusion with the cell membrane (e.g., herpesviruses) or—more usually—by receptor-mediated endocytosis. Most DNA viruses are entirely dependent on the host cell's DNA and RNA synthesizing machinery and RNA processing machinery. Viruses with larger genomes may encode much of this machinery themselves. In eukaryotes, the viral genome must cross the cell's nuclear membrane to access this machinery, while in bacteria it need only enter the cell.

RNA viruses

3 Replication of RNA viruses usually takes place in the cytoplasm. RNA viruses can be placed into four different groups depending on their modes of replication. The polarity (whether or not it can be used directly by ribosomes to make proteins) of single-stranded RNA viruses largely determines the replicative mechanism; the other major criterion is whether the genetic material is single-stranded or double-stranded. All RNA viruses use their own RNA replicate enzymes to create copies of their genomes.

1. Which of the following statements is true regarding the replication of DNA viruses?

   A. Replication primarily occurs in the cell's cytoplasm.
   B. Viruses with larger genomes encode their own RNA replicase enzymes.
   C. Entry into the cell typically involves receptor-mediated endocytosis.
   D. Host cell machinery is not utilized in the replication process.

Here's How to Crack It

Choice (C) is a true statement because the text explicitly states that DNA viruses, such as herpesviruses, enter the cell primarily through receptor-mediated endocytosis. Now, let's evaluate why the other options are incorrect. Choice (A) is incorrect because the text clearly states that replication of DNA viruses takes place in the cell's nucleus, not the cytoplasm. Choice (B) is incorrect because the text mentions that most DNA viruses are entirely dependent on the host cell's DNA and RNA synthesizing machinery. And (D) is incorrect because the text explicitly mentions that most DNA viruses are entirely dependent on the host cell's DNA and RNA synthesizing machinery for replication. This machinery includes enzymes and other components necessary for the replication of viral genetic material and the production of viral proteins. Therefore, host cell machinery is indeed utilized in the replication process of DNA viruses.

Vocabulary

disease—an atypical condition that compromises the normal bodily functions of an organism, typically associated with negative symptoms and feelings of pain and weakness

bacteria—typically single-celled, prokaryotic organisms that exist in large groups. Bacteria can be either beneficial, such as bacteria that decompose organic matter, or harmful, such as bacteria that cause infections.

binary fission—a type of asexual reproduction most common in prokaryotes. Bacterial binary fission is the process utilized by bacteria to carry out cell division, reproduce, and increase the bacterial population.

infection—a condition in which a pathogen invades and multiplies within the tissues and organs of a living organism. An infection can cause the immune system to be activated, at which point symptoms and disease will present themselves.

virus—a small, nonliving, infectious agent that is composed of both nucleic acid and a protein coat. While a virus cannot reproduce on its own, a virus can invade an organism's cell, reproduce within the cell, and then destroy the cell.

capsid—a protein sheath that surrounds the genetic material of a virus

lytic cycle—a portion of the viral reproduction cycle during which the virus replicates itself, leading to the destruction of both the infected cell and its membrane

immunization—the process by which an organism is made immune or resistant to an infectious disease. Generally, immunization occurs via the administration of a vaccine.

vaccination—a process that allows an organism to achieve a state of immunity to a particular pathogen through artificial means. In active immunization, a weakened or inactive form of a pathogen is introduced to an organism that causes the immune system to respond and create immunological memory, or the ability to remember pathogens for future infections. Passive immunization involves the administration of specific antibodies that provide immediate, temporary protection against a pathogen.

pathogen—a bacterium, virus, fungus, or other microorganism that can cause disease

AIDS—acquired immune deficiency syndrome (AIDS) is a disease caused by HIV that is characterized by a greatly increased susceptibility to infection due to compromised cellular immunity. An individual with AIDS can develop a number of health conditions including pneumonia, tuberculosis, toxoplasmosis, and fungal infections. There is currently no cure for AIDS.

HIV—human immunodeficiency virus (HIV) is a virus that attacks the immune system by destroying T-helper white blood cells, leaving an individual with a damaged immune system. HIV can be transmitted through the exchange of bodily fluids such as blood and semen. There is currently no cure for HIV and without antiretroviral treatment, HIV can progress to AIDS.

You should now have a firm grasp of concepts related to disease transfer that will be tested on the GED® test. Let's try some sample questions.

Bacteria and Viruses Drill

You can check your answers in Part IX: Answer Key to Drills.

Questions 1 through 3 refer to the following information.

1 Maria is a doctor at the World Health Organization who analyzes bacterial infections, which can be cured with antibiotics that disrupt the living cellular structures of the diseased cells, and viral infections, for which vaccines can be developed. Maria also analyzes the way in which disease is transferred among individuals, determining whether an infection is spread through the air, contaminated water, animal bites, or direct contact.

2 Maria has been sent to Ezralia, a small, pre-industrialized state, where most homes lack indoor plumbing and other innovations related to modern sanitation. Over the past six weeks, the people of Ezralia have been suffering from an unidentified disease, known as Mooshika, that is decimating the population. Maria interviews a number of individuals suffering from Mooshika and finds that the majority of the individuals who have suffered from Mooshika drink water from the well on the north side of town, and over 85% of the victims support themselves by raising goats and selling them at the local market.

1. After analyzing the disease, Maria determines that the infection is alive. Therefore, the disease is

Select... ▼
viral
bacterial

and can be addressed with

Select... ▼
antibiotics
vaccinations

.

2. Based on Maria's findings, how could Mooshika be transferred? Choose all that apply. (For this drill, write the option letters in the box below.)

Potential Methods of Transfer

(a) Contaminated food or water

(b) Air

(c) Blood

(d) Bite of infected animal

(e) Human saliva

3. All of the following are potential ways to treat and prevent viral infections EXCEPT

A. vaccination.
B. quarantining infected animals.
C. antibiotics.
D. avoiding contact with infected persons.

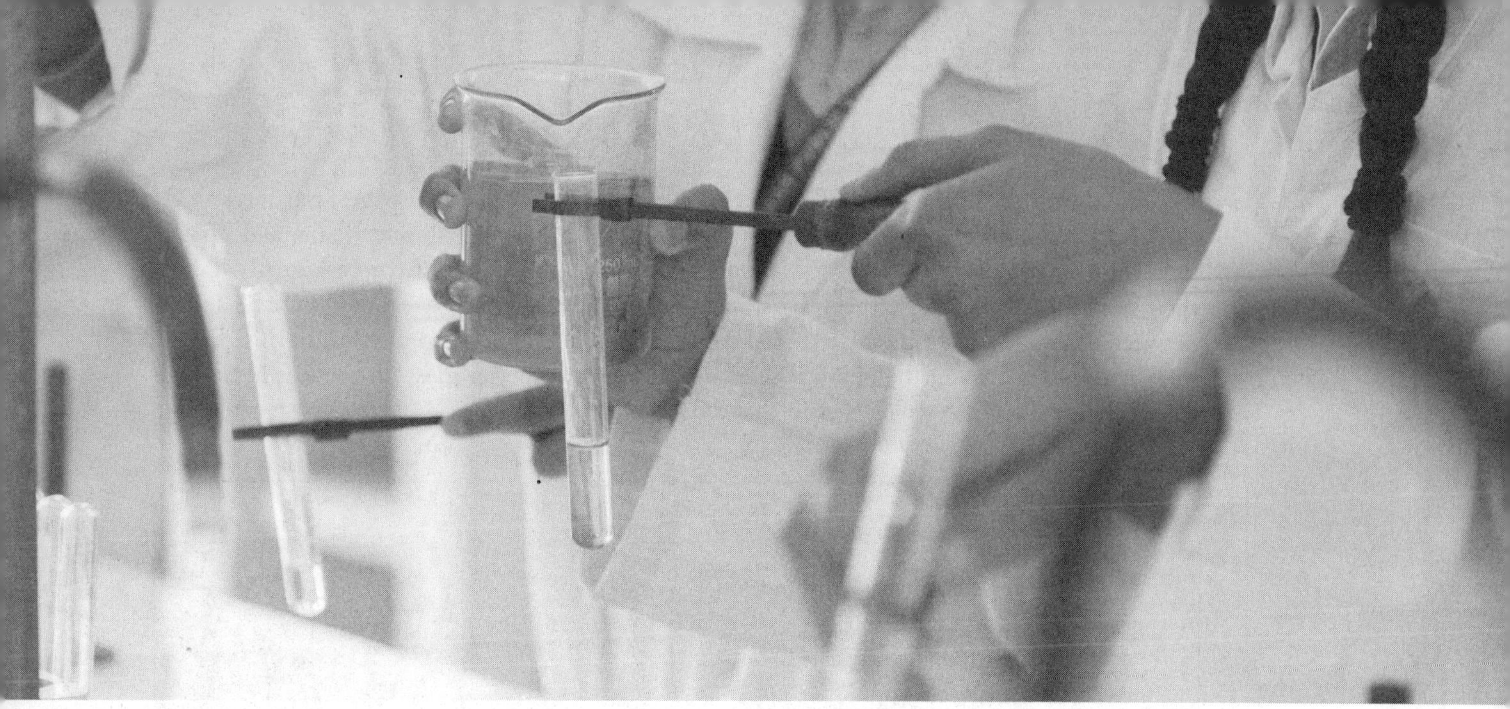

Chapter 23
Physical and Earth Sciences

In this chapter, we'll cover physical laws; solids, liquids, and gases; chemical reactions; the changing earth; glaciers, erosion, and the ice ages; fossils; and astronomy.

A study of any *one* of the physical sciences could take several hundred pages, but fortunately the GED® test writers don't delve very deeply into any of the subjects that make up the physical sciences—for the very good reason that they've already decided to ask nearly half of their questions about life sciences. This means that the remaining questions must be spread between three different topics: Earth and space science, chemistry, and physics. In this chapter, we're going to show you the physical science topics that come up most on the GED® Science test. Here are the topics we'll cover in this chapter:

- Energy and heat
- Physical laws, work, and motion
- Waves and radiation
- Solids, liquids, and gases
- Chemical reactions
- The changing Earth
- Glaciers, erosion, and the ice ages
- Natural resources
- Fossils
- Astronomy

ENERGY AND HEAT

No doubt you've been studying for the GED® test and at some point thought to yourself, "I just don't have the energy to study anymore right now." According to physics, you might be right. An object possesses **energy** if it has the ability to do work. So, if you don't have the energy to study, you don't have the ability to do work. Makes sense, right? All energy is either potential or kinetic. While **potential energy** cannot be observed, it is the amount of energy an object has due to its position or shape, which can be measured in terms of the amount of work an object *could* perform. Conversely, **kinetic energy** is directly related to motion, and can be thought of as the energy an object possesses because of its motion. Potential energy can be classified even further. **Gravitational potential energy** is energy that an object has due to its vertical or horizontal position in a gravitational field. The amount of gravitational potential energy an object has is dependent upon the mass of an object and its height in the environment. For example, if you were to hold a bowling ball a few inches from the ground, it would have less gravitational potential energy than would a bowling ball held a few feet from the ground.

The second type of potential energy is **elastic potential energy**, which is the energy stored in elastic objects resulting from stretching and compressing. Elastic potential energy is based on both the mass and speed of an object. Consider the following. Imagine that you put a rock in a slingshot and pull back, increasing the tension of the slingshot. The further back you pull the slingshot, the more elastic potential energy the object acquires. When you release the slingshot, the elastic potential energy is converted into kinetic energy. An object's **mechanical energy** is the sum total of the object's gravitational potential energy, elastic potential energy, and kinetic energy. It is important to remember that energy can be transformed from one type to another.

In fact, an important physics principle is the **law of conservation of energy**, which states that energy cannot be created or destroyed.

While an object can have mechanical energy, there are many other types of energy. Indeed, energy can come in many forms, such as light, sound, and electricity, but one important form of energy is heat. **Heat** is the energy transfer from the particles of one object to another because of the objects' different temperatures. It is important to note that energy will always move from a hotter object to a cooler object. An **exothermic reaction** occurs when heat is generated in a system and released to its surroundings, while an **endothermic reaction** is one that absorbs heat from its surroundings. Think about the last time you burned your tongue on a hot drink. You felt the burn as the energy transferred from the hotter liquid to your cooler mouth; this was an endothermic reaction, as your mouth absorbed the energy by getting burned.

The scale for measuring heat is **temperature**, or the kinetic energy of the molecules in an object, and is measured using either the **Celsius** or **Fahrenheit** scale. You should know that water freezes at 0° Celsius (32° Fahrenheit) and boils at 100° Celsius (212° Fahrenheit). Interestingly, the particles can stop moving altogether if the temperature is low enough—this point is referred to as **absolute zero** and is the basis of a third scale of measurement for temperature, the **Kelvin** scale. The amount of energy required to raise the temperature of 1 kg of a substance by 1°C is referred to as **specific heat**. Heat can also move through an object via either convection or conduction. **Convection** is a process that occurs in liquids and gasses when heated molecules carrying energy rise before eventually cooling and sinking, thus producing a continuous cycle of heat transfer; this cyclic process is known as a **convection current**. Heat can also be transferred through **conduction**. Conduction is a process of heat energy transfer that occurs when particles are in direct contact and have different temperatures.

> The **kilogram (kg)** is the base unit of mass in the International System of Units (the Metric System).

Try out the following question.

1. Which of the following best describes the transfer of heat energy?

   A. Convection currents in a liquid medium
   B. Electrical energy through a conductor
   C. Sound energy propagating through a solid
   D. Mechanical energy in the form of motion

Here's How to Crack It

Convection is the transfer of heat energy through the movement of a fluid (liquid or gas). In the case of a liquid medium, such as water or air, convection currents occur as warmer, less dense fluid rises while cooler, denser fluid sinks, creating a continuous circulation of heat energy. This process is a common mechanism for transferring heat within fluids, such as in heating systems or ocean currents. Therefore, (A) best describes the transfer of heat energy and is the correct answer. Choices (B), (C), and (D) describe other forms of energy transfer but are not specifically related to the transfer of heat energy.

Vocabulary

energy—the capacity to do work

potential energy—the energy of an object due to the position, shape, or condition of the object

kinetic energy—the energy of an object due to the motion of the object

gravitational potential energy—the energy held in an object due to the object's gravitational attraction to another object

elastic potential energy—potential energy that is stored due to the application of force that deforms an elastic object. When the force is removed from the object, the energy is released, and the object returns to its original shape.

mechanical energy—the amount of work an object is capable of due to the object's potential and kinetic energies

law of conservation of energy—a law of science that states that energy cannot be created or destroyed, but that energy can be changed from one form to another

heat—either the transfer of kinetic energy from an energy source to a medium or object or the transfer of kinetic energy from one medium or object to another. Heat transfer can occur as conduction, convection, or radiation.

exothermic reaction—a chemical reaction during which heat is released

endothermic reaction—a chemical reaction during which heat is absorbed

temperature—a measure of the heat present in either a substance or an object that is defined according to a given scale. The three main temperature scales are Celsius, Fahrenheit, and Kelvin.

Celsius—in the Celsius scale of temperature, water will freeze at 0° and water will boil at 100° under normal conditions.

Fahrenheit—in the Fahrenheit scale of temperature, water will freeze at 32° and water will boil at 212° under normal conditions.

absolute zero—defined as 0° Kelvin, or –459.67° F, and is the lower limit of the thermodynamic temperature scale. At absolute zero, atoms would stop moving altogether and, therefore, it is considered a physically impossible temperature to reach.

Kelvin—in the Kelvin scale of temperature, water will freeze at 273.15 kelvins and water will boil at 373.15 kelvins under normal conditions.

specific heat—a quantity that dictates the amount of heat energy required to raise the temperature of a single unit of an object's mass 1° Celsius relative to the amount of heat energy required to raise the temperature of a single unit of water's mass 1° Celsius, given constant volume and pressure

convection—the flow of heat energy that occurs when warmer areas of liquid or gas rise to cooler areas within the liquid or gas. As the cooler substance takes the place of the warmer substances, a continuous circulation pattern, or convection current, results with thermal energy moving from hot areas to cooler areas.

convection current—convection currents move gas or fluids when differences exist in density or temperatures within a substance.

conduction—the flow of heat energy between substances that are in direct contact with one another. In conduction, heat energy flows from a higher temperature region to a lower temperature region.

photovoltaic cells—photovoltaic cells, which are generally composed of treated silicon, are used to convert solar energy to electrical energy.

radiation—a form of heat transfer that does not rely upon any contact between the heat source and the heated object. Instead, heat is transmitted through empty space by thermal radiation.

Energy and Heat Drill

You can check your answers in Part IX: Answer Key to Drills.

Questions 1 through 3 refer to the following information.

1 The transfer of heat occurs when particles move from an object with a high temperature to an object with a low temperature. An exothermic reaction occurs when heat is released in an energy transfer, while an endothermic reaction occurs when heat is absorbed in the energy transfer. Heat transfer can occur via either conduction, which occurs when objects are in direct contact with one another, or convection currents, which involve the cyclic movement of fluid or gas, away from a heat source. Consider the following situation:

2 When setting up their campsite, Kristy and Eliz decided to build a campfire. After starting the fire, both girls felt much warmer than they did before the fire was made.

1. When Kristy and Eliz lit the campfire, an

   Select... ▼ reaction took place
   - endothermic
   - exothermic

   because heat was Select... ▼.
   - absorbed
   - released

2. Based on the information provided, which of the following is true?

   A. Via conduction, the girls absorbed heat from the campfire.
   B. Via convection, the girls absorbed heat from the campfire.
   C. Via conduction, the campfire absorbed heat from the girls.
   D. Via convection, the campfire absorbed heat from the girls.

3. Suppose that Kristy takes a metal pole, places it in the fire, and then burns her hand by touching the pole. Which of the following applies to the reaction that takes place when Kristy touched the pole? Choose all that apply. (For this drill, write the option letters in the box below.)

The Chemical Reaction Is/Involves:

(a) Conduction

(b) Convection

(c) Endothermic

(d) Exothermic

(e) Heat Transfer

PHYSICAL LAWS, WORK, AND MOTION

Physics studies the *behavior* of matter. Have you ever been in a car, and the car next to you began to go forward, but you felt as if you were moving *backward*? Interestingly, in relation to the car next to you, you were moving backward. This is because **motion** is a change in an object's position relative to time and a distinct reference point. Motion is a part of all matter in the universe and is affected by **forces**, which are push or pull factors that change an object's speed or direction.

Speed refers to how fast an object moves. When an object travels equal distances in equal amounts of time, the object is traveling at a **constant speed**. In order to calculate the speed of an object, you will use the equation $speed = \frac{distance}{time}$. Related to speed is the concept of **momentum**, which can be thought of as the amount of motion an object has or the power behind an object. Heavier objects (objects with greater mass) have more momentum than lighter objects. Consider a car and a truck that are traveling at the same speed and in the same direction. If the vehicles were asked to stop moving, it would be harder to stop the truck because it has greater momentum than the car. An object's momentum is dependent upon its mass and its **velocity**, which refers to both the direction and speed of an object. Momentum can be calculated with the following equation: *momentum* = *mass* × *velocity*. If I say the word "accelerate," you may think of pushing the gas pedal down in a car to increase the speed. In physics, the meaning of **acceleration** is any change in velocity—i.e., either an increase or decrease in speed or a change in direction.

One of the basic physical laws that affects all matter is the law of **gravity**. Gravity is the force that attracts any two objects toward each other. The strength of the gravitational pull depends on the masses of the two objects and the distance between them. Earth's gravitational force keeps the Moon orbiting around it, just as the Sun's gravitational pull keeps Earth and the other planets orbiting around it. Earth's gravitational force also keeps your feet anchored firmly to the ground.

Sir Isaac Newton, a scientist working in the early 1700s, came up with three laws of motion.

- **The First Law** states that an object will remain at rest, or continue moving at the same speed and in the same direction, unless an unbalanced force acts on the object. This is called the law of **inertia**. Imagine an air hockey table: a puck moves at a constant speed in a straight line, until it hits the table bumper, or is struck by a player's striker.
- **The Second Law** states that if an object experiences an unbalanced force, it will accelerate. The acceleration depends on the magnitude of the force (imagine kicking a soccer ball hard rather than softly) and the mass of the object (imagine kicking a bowling ball instead).
- **The Third Law** states that if Object A exerts a force on Object B, then B will exert an equal force on A, but in the opposite direction. Gun recoil is a good example of this. While the forces are ALWAYS equal, different masses cause different accelerations (see above). A force propels the (small) bullet forward, and an equal force makes the (much larger) gun "kick" back.

When we think of work, we think of something we have to do and, usually, it requires us to expend some effort. If you have to mow the lawn, you use force to push the lawnmower forward across the grass—you are doing work. **Work**, when physicists use the term, occurs when a force moves an object in the direction of the force. Work is calculated with the following equation: *work* = *force* × *distance*. As you are probably aware, not all work is equal. After all, it would take a team of five people less time to mow a lawn than it would take you to mow the same lawn by yourself. **Power** is the rate at which a certain amount of work is accomplished, and is calculated with the following equation: $power = \frac{work}{time}$. Power is measured in watts. One watt is the amount of power it takes to complete one joule of work in one second.

With all this work, wouldn't it be nice to catch a break? Thankfully, with the advent of machines, work is much easier than it was in the past. **Machines** are implements that make work easier by redirecting or multiplying forces. Just like work, not all machines are created equal. Machines that can complete work faster are said to have a **mechanical advantage**. The mechanical advantage of a simple machine is a ratio between the force put into the machine and the force put out by the machine.

There are *six* **simple machines** (machines that change the direction or magnitude of a force) that you should know for the GED® test. The **inclined plane** category of simple machines includes tools that both magnify and redirect force. An inclined plane can be thought of as a ramp, which requires less force to move an object than would be necessary with direct vertical movement. Historians often discuss the use of inclined planes in relation to the ancient pyramids in Egypt. Many researchers hypothesize that the Egyptians used a series of inclined planes to transport the giant stones that make up each pyramid. **Wedges** are inclined planes that redirect downward force into two forces pointing outward. **Screws** are spiral inclined planes that redirect a linear force into a rotational one, thus requiring less work. Levers and pulleys, which comprise the second category of simple machines, are tools in which the object and the force move in opposite directions. A **lever** consists of a long object, often a bar, and a **fulcrum**, or pivot point. When force is applied to one end of the bar, it pivots at the fulcrum, multiplying the force at the opposite end of the bar. There are three types of levers: first-class levers, such as a seesaw; second-class levers, such as a wheelbarrow; and third-class levers, exemplified by the act of hammering in a nail. Closely related to the lever is the **pulley**, which can be created by looping rope around two or more wheels to alter the direction of force, thus providing a mechanical advantage. The last simple machine is the **wheel and axle**, which consists of a wheel or lever connected to a shaft. When a small input of force is applied to the wheel, and the wheel is turned, the shaft turns as well, but with a larger resulting output of force. Consider the steering wheel of a car; minor adjustments to the steering wheel result in much larger changes to the overall movement of the car.

Try the forces problem below.

Newton's Law of Gravity states that the gravitational force that two objects exert on each other is equal to the following:

$$F = \frac{G \times M \times m}{r^2}$$

In the equation,

F is the force of gravity;

G is a constant;

M is the mass of one of the objects;

m is the mass of the second object;

r is the distance between the centers of the objects.

1. If the distance between two objects doubles but the masses of the objects remain constant, then the force between the two objects will [Select... ▼].

Select... ▼
decrease by a factor of 4
decrease by a factor of 2
increase by a factor of 2
increase by a factor of 4

Here's How to Crack It

In the equation, the distance between the two objects is represented by the r in the r^2 term in the denominator of the fraction. If the distance between the two objects doubles, then the denominator of the fraction becomes bigger. Making the denominator of a fraction larger makes the fraction as a whole smaller, so you can eliminate (C) and (D). Since the r in the equation is squared, then doubling the distance will give you a term of $(2r)^2$, or $4r^2$ in the denominator. Thus, the denominator increases by a factor of 4, making the fraction as a whole smaller by a factor of 4. Thus, the correct answer is that the force between the two objects will decrease by a factor of 4.

Vocabulary

motion—a change in an object's position relative to time and a distinct reference point
forces—push or pull factors that change an object's speed or direction
speed—how fast an object moves
constant speed—when an object travels equal distances in equal amounts of time
momentum—the amount of motion an object has or the power behind an object
acceleration—any change in velocity
gravity—the force that causes all physical objects to attract each other
inertia—another term for Newton's First Law, which states that objects at rest tend to remain at rest unless acted upon by an outside force, and that objects in motion tend to remain in motion at constant velocity unless acted upon by an outside force
work—occurs when a force moves an object in the direction of the force
power—the rate at which a certain amount of work is accomplished
machines—implements that make work easier by redirecting or multiplying forces
simple machines—inclined plane, wedge, screw, lever, pulley, axle and wheel
velocity—speed of an object in a specific direction, usually measured in meters per second (m/s)
mechanical advantage—ratio of output force to input force in a machine, indicating its effectiveness
fulcrum—point around which a lever pivots or rotates, facilitating mechanical work or force multiplication

Physical Laws, Work, and Motion Drill

You can check your answers in Part IX: Answer Key to Drills.

Questions 1 and 2 refer to the following information.

1 Bob pushes against a rock of mass 50 kg for 20 minutes, exerting an average force of 100 N, but the rock never budges. He really wants to move the rock, so he asks his wife Barbara to come out and help. She pushes on the rock with another 100 N and eventually the rock starts to move. As the couple keeps pushing, it becomes easier and easier to move.

2 At the end of the driveway is a ledge, and the couple push the rock off the ledge. The rock falls for 3 seconds and eventually crashes into the riverbed below.

1. Drag the correct force into the box that describes it. You might need to use a force more than once. (For this drill, write the force letters in the boxes.)

Original scenario before Bob asks for help

When Barbara is helping

When the rock falls over the ledge

(a) Gravity
(b) Bob on the rock
(c) Barbara on the rock
(d) Friction
(e) Air resistance

2. According to a physicist, *work* is defined as the force applied to an object multiplied by the distance the object moves during the time the force is applied. Using this definition, how much work did Bob do before Barbara helped him?

   A. none
   B. more than was necessary
   C. enough work to get the job done
   D. 20 minutes' worth

WAVES AND RADIATION

Generally, when we hear the word *wave*, we think either of the ocean's waves on the beach or of moving our hand. You don't have to go to the beach to be surrounded by waves—they surround us all the time. We use microwaves to cook our food, light waves help us see, and sound waves cause vibrations in our eardrums that allow us to hear. In physics, and for the science portion of the GED® test, you should know that a **wave** is a disturbance that carries energy from one point to another through a **medium** or space. A medium is the matter that carries a wave between locations. As noted in its definition, a wave is a disturbance. Usually, the disturbance is some sort of vibration that provides energy for the wave; for example, a plucked guitar string vibrates to cause sound waves, and friction between tectonic plates can cause shock waves. It is important to remember that waves transfer energy, *not* matter.

For the GED® test, you should know that all waves can be categorized as either **electromagnetic** or **mechanical**. Electromagnetic waves, such as light, radio, and microwaves, can travel through empty space and do not require a medium to transfer energy. On the other hand, mechanical waves, such as sound and water waves, require a medium to transfer their energy.

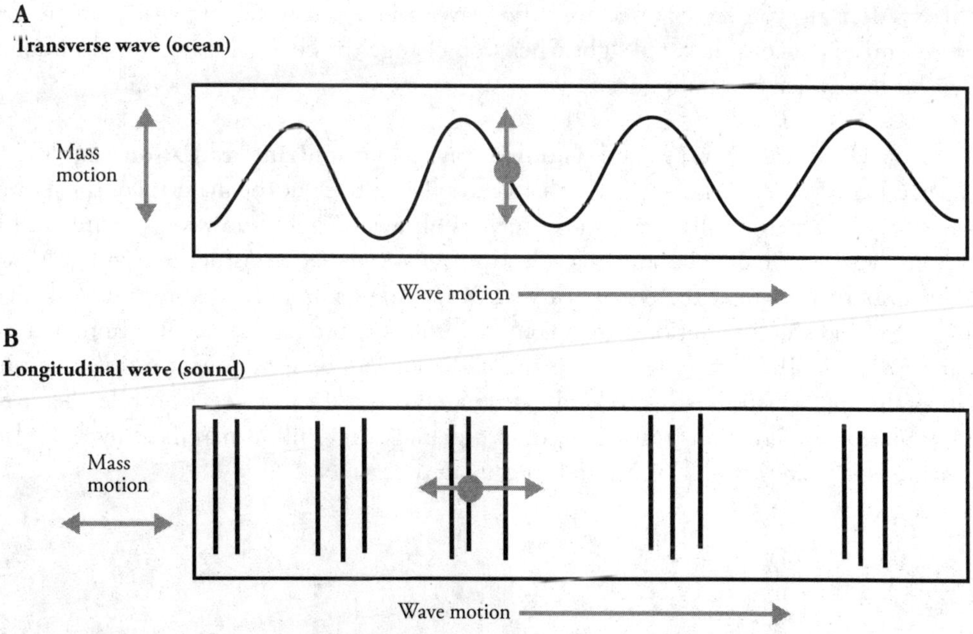

Transverse and Longitudinal Waves

Mechanical waves can be further categorized based on the direction of the medium's particle motion in relation to the direction of the wave's motion. A **transverse wave** is one in which particle motion is perpendicular to the wave motion. As shown in the figure above, the direction of energy travel is at a right angle to the direction of the disturbance, or wave. Conversely, a **longitudinal wave** is a mechanical wave in which particle motion moves in the same direction as the wave motion. In a longitudinal wave, particles alternate between **compressions**, when particles are pushed together, and **rarefactions**, when particles are pulled apart.

In a wave, the highest point is known as the **crest** and the lowest point is called the **trough** (pronounced "troff"). The height of a wave, which is referred to as **amplitude**, is found by dividing in half the vertical distance between the crest and the trough. As you notice in Figure A, a wave cycles, with each crest followed by a trough, when traveling from the origin to the final destination. A single **wavelength** is equal to the distance between two consecutive crests or troughs. The number of times a wave cycles in one second is referred to as **frequency**. Frequency is measured in **hertz**, or cycles per second. Related to frequency is the **period** of the wave, which is the time it takes for a single wave cycle, or the time between two consecutive crests of the wave. Waves that have a short period will have a high frequency, while waves that have a longer period will have a lower frequency.

Recall that, unlike mechanical waves, electromagnetic waves do not require a medium and can travel through space. Electromagnetic waves are induced by disturbances, such as changes in magnetic and electric fields. Like transverse waves, charged particles move in a perpendicular direction to the direction of the wave's movement. The energy transferred through electromagnetic waves is referred to as **radiant energy**, or **radiation**.

The following electromagnetic waves are ordered from lowest to highest frequency: radio waves, microwaves, infrared waves, visible light, ultraviolet (UV) light, X-rays, and Gamma rays. Radio waves, microwaves, infrared rays, and visible light emit **non-ionizing radiation**, due to their inability to ionize atoms and break chemical bonds, and are considered relatively harmless. After all, you are exposed to radio waves when you watch television, microwaves when you make popcorn, infrared light when you change the channel using a remote control, and visible light when you walk outside.

Conversely, **UV light**, **X-rays**, and **Gamma rays** emit **ionizing radiation** and can be considered harmful. Thankfully, the Earth's atmosphere filters out the majority of the harmful rays associated with electromagnetic waves such as ultraviolet light. However, we are not fully protected—you can thank the ionizing, electromagnetic radiation associated with UV light for that sunburn you got at the beach last year. X-rays are commonly used for medical exams, during which special precautions are taken to protect reproductive organs from harmful ionizing radiation. The true danger of ionizing radiation can be seen in cancer treatments like radiation therapy, which uses X-rays and Gamma rays to kill cancer cells. While effective at killing cancer cells, radiation treatment can also damage and kill normal, healthy cells. Thus, treatment sessions are generally short and spread out over time.

Try out the following question.

1 James Clerk Maxwell was a 19th-century Scottish physicist with broad interests. He was responsible for the classical theory of electromagnetic radiation, which was the first theory to describe electricity, magnetism, and light as different manifestations of the same phenomenon. Maxwell's equations for electromagnetism have been called the "second great unification in physics" where the first one had been realized by Isaac Newton.

2 With the publication of "A Dynamical Theory of the Electromagnetic Field" in 1865, Maxwell demonstrated that electric and magnetic fields travel through space as waves moving at the speed of light. He proposed that light is an undulation in the same medium that is the cause of electric and magnetic phenomena. The unification of light and electrical phenomena led to his prediction of the existence of radio waves. Maxwell is also regarded as a founder of the modern field of electrical engineering.

1. Which statement from the passage best supports Maxwell's contribution to the unification of different natural phenomena?

   A. Maxwell's equations describe electricity, magnetism, and light as different manifestations of the same phenomenon.
   B. Maxwell's work laid the foundation for the study of radio waves and modern electrical engineering.
   C. Maxwell's theory proposed that electric and magnetic fields travel through space as waves at the speed of light.
   D. Maxwell's publication in 1865 demonstrated the dynamic nature of the electromagnetic field.

Here's How to Crack It

The correct answer is (A), as this statement directly reflects Maxwell's contribution to the unification of different natural phenomena. His classical theory of electromagnetic radiation described electricity, magnetism, and light as interconnected aspects of the electromagnetic field, thus unifying them under a single theoretical framework. Choices (B), (C), and (D) highlight specific aspects of Maxwell's work but do not explicitly emphasize the unification of different natural phenomena as (A) does.

Vocabulary

wave—a disturbance that carries energy between locations through a medium or space
medium—matter that carries mechanical waves between locations
electromagnetic wave—a wave that does not require a medium to transfer energy and can travel through empty space. Examples of mechanical waves include light waves, radio waves, and microwaves.
mechanical wave—a wave that requires a medium to transfer energy. Examples of mechanical waves include both sound and water waves.
transverse wave—a wave in which the particle motion of the medium is perpendicular to the motion of the wave
longitudinal wave—a mechanical wave in which the particle motion of the medium moves in the same direction as the motion of the wave
compressions—regions in a longitudinal wave where the particles are crowded together, resulting in increased density and pressure
rarefactions—regions in a longitudinal wave where the particles are spread out, resulting in decreased density and pressure compared to the surrounding medium
crest—the highest point on a transverse wave, where the displacement of the medium is at a maximum
trough—the lowest point on a transverse wave, where the displacement of the medium is at a minimum
amplitude—the maximum displacement of points on a wave, or the height of a wave. The amplitude of a wave is equal to the vertical distance between the equilibrium point, or rest position, of the wave and the highest point, or crest, of the wave.
wavelength—the distance between two consecutive crests or two consecutive troughs of a wave. A single wavelength is referred to as a cycle.
frequency—the number of wavelengths per second. The frequency of a wave is inversely related to the period of a wave; i.e., a wave with a high frequency will have a small period and vice-versa.
hertz (Hz)—the unit used to measure the frequency of a wavelength, or the number of wavelengths per second
period—the amount of time it takes a wave to complete a single cycle. The period of a wave is inversely related to the frequency of a wave; i.e., a wave with a large period will have a low frequency and vice-versa.
radiation (radiant energy)—energy that travels by either waves or particles, such as heat or light
non-ionizing radiation—any type of electromagnetic radiation that does not have enough energy to remove an electron from an atom. Accordingly, non-ionizing radiation, such as radio waves, microwaves, and UV light, is not harmful to humans.
ultraviolet (UV) light—a type of high-frequency electromagnetic radiation produced by the Sun, but invisible to the naked eye. In excess, UV light can be harmful to the human body.
X-rays—a type of mid- to high-frequency electromagnetic radiation produced by accelerating electrons. X-rays are used in the medical field to create images, also known as X-rays, which penetrate soft tissues, but not bone. Prolonged exposure to X-rays can lead to negative health effects, as X-rays kill healthy cells.
gamma rays—a type of high-frequency electromagnetic radiation that is used in both the medical and astronomical fields. Gamma rays are used to treat cancerous tumor cells.

ionizing radiation—any type of electromagnetic radiation that carries enough energy to remove electrons from an atom. While ionizing radiation, such as X-rays and Gamma rays, is used in many fields of research, prolonged exposure is harmful to humans and can cause illness, mutations, cancer, and death.

Phew! You should now have a solid grasp of the wave and radiation concepts that will be asked on the GED® test. Now, let's try out some sample questions.

Waves and Radiation Drill

You can check your answers in Part IX: Answer Key to Drills.

Questions 1 through 3 refer to the following information.

Employees at GetWell research labs are analyzing mechanical waves, which require a medium to pass through, and electromagnetic waves, which travel through space. José Gonzalez IV is studying electromagnetic waves and their potential, real-world health and medical applications. He records the wavelengths of the various waves, noting that radio waves are the longest, while Gamma rays are the shortest. When calculating the frequency of the wave, or the number of wavelengths that occur in a distinct amount of time, José notes that there is an inverse relationship between the frequency of a wave and its period, which is the time it takes for a single wave to occur.

Wave Type	Wavelength	Application
Radio Waves	Greater than 30 cm	Aircraft Navigation, TV, AM/FM Radio
Microwaves	30 cm–1 mm	Microwave Ovens, Mobile Phones
Infrared Waves	1 mm–700 nm	Remote Controls, Toasters, Night Vision
Visible Light	700 nm–400 nm	Physical Therapy, Light Bulbs, Photography
Ultraviolet Light	400 nm–60 nm	Sanitation, Air Purification, Forgery Detection
X-Rays	60 nm–1 x 10^{-4} nm	Medical Examination, Cancer Treatment
Gamma Rays	0.1 nm–1 x 10^{-5} nm	Cancer Treatment, Food Irradiation

1. Based on the information provided, only

   [Select... ▼] waves can pass through
   - electromagnetic
   - mechanical

   empty space. The relationship between waves of longer and shorter wavelengths is such that as

   the [Select... ▼] of a wave increases, the
   - period
   - frequency
   - amplitude

   period [Select... ▼].
   - increases
   - decreases
   - stays the same

2. Based on the information provided, which types of waves have potential medical applications? Choose all that apply. (For this drill, write the option letters in the box below.)

Waves with Potential Medical Applications

(a) Microwaves

(b) Radio Waves

(c) X-rays

(d) Ultraviolet Light

(e) Visible Light

(f) Gamma Rays

(g) Infrared waves

3. José identifies a new medical technology that utilizes a wave with a wavelength of 1 nm. Which type of electromagnetic wave is used in this technology? (Write the name of the wave in the provided box—e.g., Microwaves, Infrared Waves, or Gamma Rays.)

SOLIDS, LIQUIDS, AND GASES

Chemistry is the study of matter. All matter is made up of **molecules,** tiny invisible pieces of matter. However, even molecules are not the smallest particles in the world. Molecules are made up of **atoms,** which are in turn composed of **protons** and **neutrons** (at the atom's center, which is known as the **nucleus**) and **electrons** that circle the nucleus.

Certain types of atoms break down slowly over time. The nuclei of these atoms gradually decay over thousands of years and give off charged particles of energy. The particles that are discharged are called radioactive, and because they are coming from the nucleus of an atom, the process is called **nuclear radiation.** Some radioactive elements are highly dangerous—uranium comes to mind—but other elements are essentially harmless.

Matter exists in one of three states. When its temperature is low, matter exists in a **solid** state, with its molecules closely joined, barely moving. As the temperature increases, the molecules begin to move more freely, and the matter changes into a **liquid.** If the matter is heated even further, the molecules will break away from one another to form a **gas.** The point at which a solid turns into a liquid is called its **melting point.** The temperature at which a liquid turns into a solid is called its **freezing point.** Each element in nature changes from a solid into a liquid and from a liquid into a gas at different temperatures. Ice turns to a liquid (water) when the temperature is above 32 degrees Fahrenheit. Iron, however, does not turn into a liquid unless the temperature is much hotter.

Matter Quiz

Q: What happens if you freeze a pipe full of water?

Turn the page for the answer.

Solids keep their own shape. Liquids will flow into any container but still have chemical bonds that hold the liquid together. Gases have no shape and will disperse unless they are contained. By increasing the temperature, in most cases you increase the volume of a substance. One exception is water, which actually increases slightly in volume *when frozen.*

An **element** is a pure substance consisting of only one type of atom. For example, hydrogen and oxygen are elements. When two elements are mixed together, the result is called a **mixture.** However, if you mix the two elements and they bond together through a chemical interaction, then the new product formed is called a **compound.** For example, water (H_2O) is a compound. Many compounds can be classified either as **acids** or **bases**. Acids, such as lemon juice, taste sour. Bases neutralize acids. An example of a base is baking soda.

When a substance such as salt is **dissolved** in water or another liquid, the result is called a **solution.** You can keep adding more of the substance until the solution reaches its **saturation point,** the point at which the solution can no longer dissolve more of the substance. A higher temperature will often increase the saturation point.

Try your skills at the solids, liquids, and gases problem below.

Ethylene glycol (EG) is the main ingredient in antifreeze and has the chemical structure shown below:

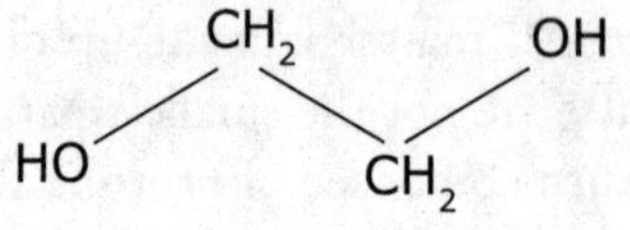

The figure below shows how the melting point (the temperature at which solid antifreeze would begin melting) of antifreeze varies with % EG.

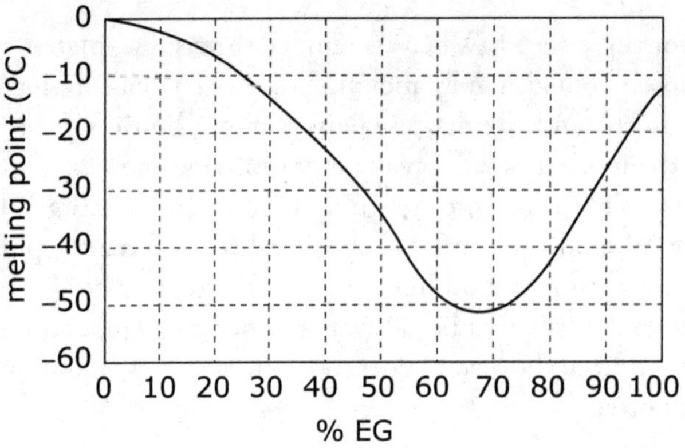

1. A company that creates antifreeze wants to create an antifreeze solution that is effective at the coldest possible temperatures. Select the point on the graph that represents the ideal % EG that the company should use in its solution and the temperature that such an antifreeze solution could withstand before freezing. Mark the point with an X.

Here's How to Crack It

According to the graph, antifreeze is most effective when it is composed of approximately 67% EG. At that point, antifreeze melts at temperatures as low as approximately –52°C. Thus, the correct point on the graph is the point at (67%, –52°C).

Matter Quiz

A: The pipe might break because when water freezes, it increases slightly in size.

Vocabulary

pH value—a scale to measure the basicity or acidity of a compound
evaporation—the process by which a liquid becomes a gas
half-life—the amount of time it takes half of a sample of a radioactive element to decay
molecules—tiny particles of matter
atoms—tiny particles that make up molecules
protons—tiny, positively charged particles that make up an atom's nucleus
neutrons—tiny particles that make up an atom's nucleus that do not have charge
nucleus—the center of an atom
electrons—tiny, negatively charged particles that circle the nucleus of an atom
nuclear radiation—the process in which the nuclei of certain atoms break down over time, releasing charged particles of energy
solid—a state of matter that occurs at low temperatures and in which the matter's molecules are closely joined and barely move
liquid—a state of matter that occurs at higher temperatures than does the solid state, and in which the matter's molecules move more freely than they do in the solid state
gas—a state of matter that occurs at higher temperatures than does the liquid state, and in which molecules break away from one another
melting point—the temperature at which a solid turns into a liquid
freezing point—the temperature at which a liquid turns into a solid
element—a pure substance consisting of only one type of atom
compound—a substance that results when two elements bond together through chemical interaction
saturation point—the point at which a solution contains enough of a particular substance that it can no longer dissolve more of that substance
mixture—combination of two or more substances physically intermingled but not chemically bonded
dissolved—process of a substance dispersing uniformly in a solvent, forming a solution
solution—homogeneous mixture of two or more substances in which one substance is dissolved in another
acids—chemical compounds that release hydrogen ions when dissolved in water, having a sour taste
bases—chemical compounds that accept hydrogen ions in solution, having a bitter taste and slippery feel

Solids, Liquids, and Gases Drill

You can check your answers in Part IX: Answer Key to Drills.

Questions 1 through 3 refer to the following passage.

1 All matter exists in one of three phases: as a solid, liquid, or gas. Solids are rigid in shape and usually the densest form of matter. Both liquids and gases are generally less dense and able to deform to take on the shape of a container, with gas molecules being the least constrained. The most notable exception to the density rule is water. Liquid water is actually denser than solid water (ice). You know that this is true because you have probably noticed that lakes and waterways freeze from the top down as opposed to the bottom up. For the same reason, ice cubes float in a glass of water.

2 Pressure and temperature affect the phase in which matter is found. For example, at high pressure and low temperature, matter is more likely to be solid. Conversely, at low pressure and high temperature, matter is often found in gaseous state. By changing pressure and temperature, researchers can change the phase of a substance. The following diagram depicts the phase that carbon dioxide will be found in based on the temperature and pressure.

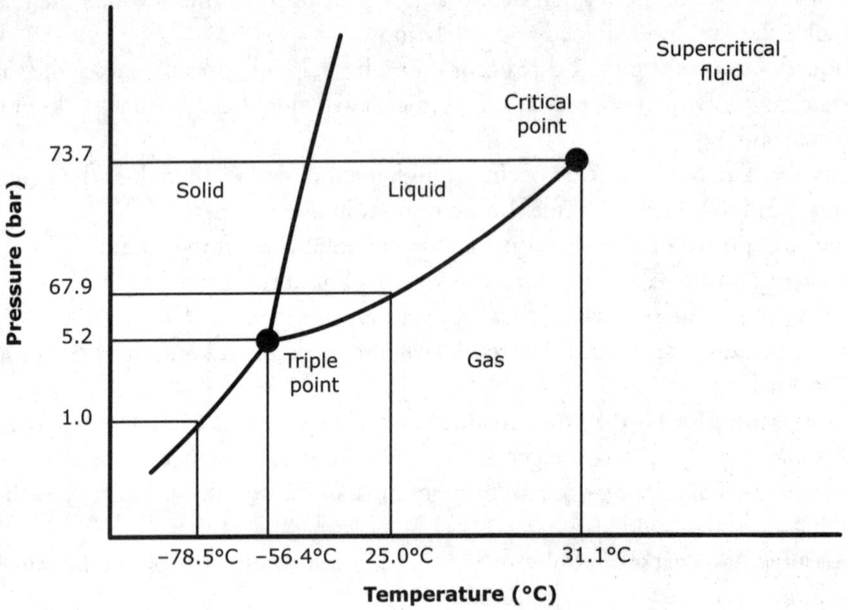

The dark black lines represent phase equilibria where there is more than one phase present at a given temperature and pressure.

1. What can you do to increase the amount of gas that you can store in a fixed container?

Select... ▼	the pressure and
Increase	
Decrease	

Select... ▼	the temperature.
increase	
decrease	

2. Adding salt to a pot of boiling water temporarily stops the water from boiling. Which of the following is the best explanation for this occurrence?

   A. The salt raises the boiling point of the water.
   B. Salt prevents water from ever boiling.
   C. Salt neutralizes the water.
   D. Salt water is easier to float in than freshwater.

3. Using the figure above, determine what phase change would occur if carbon dioxide at −70°C and 70 bar was heated to 25°C and held at the same pressure.

   A. melting
   B. freezing
   C. boiling
   D. condensing

CHEMICAL REACTIONS

While you won't need to memorize the periodic table or know how to do complex organic chemistry in order to succeed on the GED® test, you will find it helpful to be able to understand basic formulas for **chemical reactions.** A chemical reaction occurs when molecules interact to create a new substance. In order to show what happens in a chemical reaction, scientists use chemical equations. A typical example of a chemical reaction might be when hydrochloric acid combines with sodium hydroxide. In the equation that demonstrates this reaction, hydrochloric acid is denoted by HCl. This tells you that a molecule of hydrochloric acid is made up of one hydrogen atom (the H in HCl is for hydrogen) and one chlorine atom (the Cl in HCl is for chlorine). Sodium hydroxide is denoted by NaOH, which means that a molecule of sodium hydroxide is made up of one atom of sodium (Na), one atom of oxygen (O), and one atom of hydrogen (H). When these two substances interact, a chemical reaction occurs. The formula for the interaction is below.

$$NaOH + HCl \rightarrow NaCl + H_2O$$

This tells you that when sodium hydroxide and hydrochloric acid interact, they create one molecule of NaCl, or sodium chloride, and one molecule of water, or H_2O. NaCl is a salt that is an ionic compound and is made up of Na^+ and Cl^- ions. H_2O is a molecule that contains two hydrogen atoms (H_2) and one oxygen atom (O). The little 2 next to the H indicates that you have two, rather than one, hydrogen atoms.

Sometimes you'll see equations that have a larger number out in front of one of the molecules in the equation. For instance, you might see $2H_2O$ in an equation. This would tell you that you had two water, or H_2O, molecules. Since each of those water molecules would have two hydrogen atoms, you would have four hydrogen atoms in total. However, each of those molecules would have only one oxygen atom, so you would have only two oxygen atoms in total.

Don't worry that you won't know the symbols for each of the elements. While the GED® test is tricky, it won't expect you to have an in-depth knowledge of chemistry! Generally, if you need to know what element a particular symbol refers to, the GED® test will give you that information. There are just three chemical symbols you may want to memorize: Hydrogen is denoted with an H, carbon is denoted with a C, and oxygen is denoted with an O. You should also know that water is H_2O.

How might you see chemical equations tested on the GED® test? Try out the following problem.

1. When propane interacts with oxygen, a chemical reaction occurs, creating carbon dioxide and water. The balanced chemical equation for this reaction is shown below.

$$C_3H_8 + 5O_2 \rightarrow 3CO_2 + 4H_2O$$

Based on the information above, which of the following is true?

A. When one molecule of propane combines with five molecules of oxygen, one molecule of water results.
B. When eleven molecules of propane combine with ten molecules of oxygen, three molecules of carbon dioxide result.
C. When one molecule of propane combines with five molecules of oxygen, four molecules of water result.
D. When one molecule of propane combines with five molecules of oxygen, one molecule of carbon results.

Here's How to Crack It

If you know that the $5O_2$ on the left-hand side of the equation represents oxygen, then you know that the C_3H_8 must represent the propane. Since there is no large number in front of the C_3H_8, you know that there is only one molecule of propane. Eliminate (B), since you do not have eleven units of propane. The right-hand side of the equation shows that the equation results in $4H_2O$, or four water molecules. Thus, you can eliminate (A), which says that one molecule of water results. Finally, the right-hand side of the equation also indicates that the reaction creates $3CO_2$. Since the $4H_2O$ represents the water molecules, the $3CO_2$ must represent the carbon dioxide molecules. Note that the number 3 appears in front, which means that you must have three carbon dioxide molecules. Eliminate (D), which states that the reaction creates one molecule of carbon dioxide. Only (C) remains, so it is the correct answer.

Vocabulary

chemical reaction—a process that occurs when molecules interact to form a new substance

Chemical Reactions Drill

You can check your answers in Part IX: Answer Key to Drills.

Questions 1 and 2 refer to the following information.

There are four basic types of chemical reactions, as shown in the table below.

Reaction Types	General Example
Combination	A + B → C
Decomposition	C → A + B
Single Displacement	A + BC → B + AC
Double Displacement	AB + CD → AC + BD

The balanced chemical equation describing the reaction between silver and hydrogen sulfide is shown below.

$$2Ag + H_2S \rightarrow Ag_2S + H_2$$

1. Which of the four basic types of chemical reactions is this?

    A. combination
    B. decomposition
    C. single displacement
    D. double displacement

2. Based on the information above, which of the following is true?

   A. When two atoms of silver combine with one molecule of hydrogen sulfide, the result is one molecule of silver sulfide and one molecule of hydrogen.
   B. When an atom of silver combines with one molecule of hydrogen, the result is one molecule of silver sulfide and two molecules of hydrogen.
   C. When two molecules of silver sulfide combine with two molecules of hydrogen, the result is two atoms of silver and one molecule of silver sulfide.
   D. When one molecule of hydrogen sulfide combines with one molecule of silver sulfide, the result is one molecule of hydrogen and one molecule of silver sulfide.

3. In a balanced chemical equation, the number of atoms associated with a given element is the same both before and after a chemical reaction. The balanced equation for photosynthesis is

   Select... ▼ $CO_2 + 6H_2O \rightarrow$

Select... ▼
2
6
12

   $C_6H_{12}O_6 + 6$ Select... ▼ $_2$.

Select... ▼
C
H
O

THE CHANGING EARTH

Although it generally feels pretty solid underfoot, the Earth is undergoing constant change. We have discovered that the continents—that's right, entire *continents*—are actually moving slowly on the face of the Earth. This is called **continental drift.** Looking at the map pictured here, you will notice that if you pushed the continent of Africa up against the continent of South America, you would have an almost perfect fit.

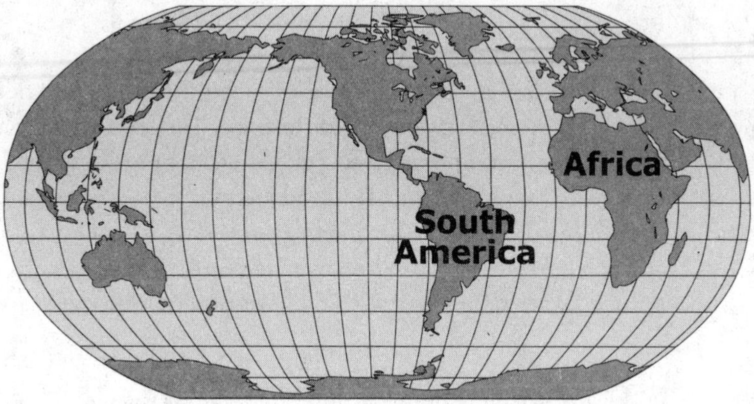

Scientists theorize that at one time, the two continents may have been joined together. Today, it is believed that the Earth's crust is composed of several large pieces—called **tectonic plates**—that move slowly over the mantle of the Earth. When these plates rub against one another, the friction between them causes **earthquakes.** The places where the plates rub together are called **fault lines.**

The Earth's Plates

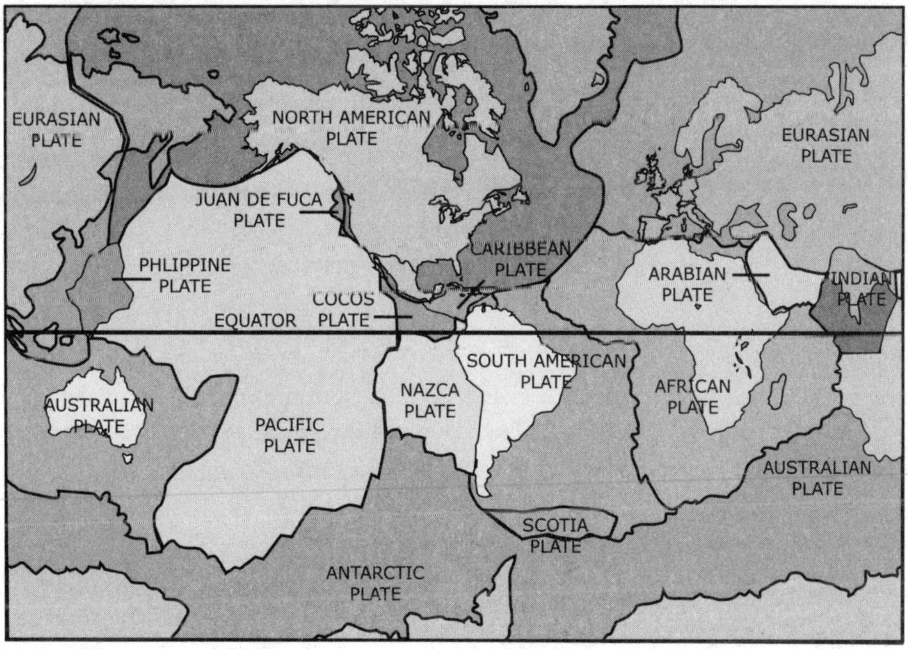

The inner portions of the Earth are under enormous pressure and are very hot. Sometimes, when the pressure becomes too great, it forces hot molten rock to the surface of the Earth. This is called a **volcanic eruption.**

So far, scientists have had little luck predicting earthquakes and volcanic eruptions, although one interesting avenue for exploration may be the fact that animals often seem to know when an earthquake is coming.

The Earth is composed of several layers. The outer layer is called the **crust.** The next layer down is called the **mantle.** The center of the Earth is called the **core.** The crust of the Earth (the only part we generally ever get to see) is composed of several different kinds of rock. **Igneous rock** is formed from cooled **magma;** magma is rock from the mantle that is so hot it has turned to liquid. **Sedimentary rock** is made up of sediment from the Earth—such as sand—that has been hardened by compression. **Metamorphic rock** is made up of either of the other two types of rock, but it has been subjected to either a great deal of pressure or heat way below the surface of the Earth.

Let's look at how the GED® test writers might ask a question about the changing Earth.

The rock cycle is a process by which old rocks are recycled into new rocks. In the rock cycle, time, pressure, and the Earth's heat interact to create three types of rocks. Sedimentary rock is formed as sediment (eroded rocks and the remains of plants and animals) builds up and is compressed. Metamorphic rock is formed as a great deal of pressure and heat is applied to rock. Igneous rock results when rock is melted by pressure below the Earth's crust into a liquid and then resolidifies.

1. Based on the passage above, which of the following would contain the greatest number of fossils?

   A. igneous rocks only
   B. sedimentary rocks only
   C. metamorphic rocks only
   D. igneous and metamorphic rocks

Here's How to Crack It

According to the passage, sedimentary rocks are formed from the eroded remains of plants and animals. Thus, sedimentary rocks would likely contain the greatest number of fossils, and the correct answer is (B).

Vocabulary

Richter scale—a scale used to measure the magnitude of earthquakes
epicenter—the place where an earthquake originates
dormant volcano—a volcano that is inactive at the moment
strata—layers of rock
continental drift—the process in which continents move slowly across the face of the Earth

tectonic plates—large pieces of earth that compose the Earth's crust
earthquakes—events that occur when tectonic plates rub together and produce friction
fault lines—places where tectonic plates rub together
volcanic eruption—event that occurs when inner portions of the Earth experience extreme heat and pressure, and pressure forces hot molten rock to the surface of the Earth
crust—outer layer of the Earth
mantle—layer of the Earth below the crust
core—center of the Earth
igneous rock—rock composed of cooled magma
magma—rock from the Earth's mantle that has become so hot that it has turned to liquid
sedimentary rock—rock made up of sediment that has been hardened by compression
metamorphic rock—rock that is made up of either of the other two types of rock, but that has been subjected to extreme heat or pressure

The Changing Earth Drill

You can check your answers in Part IX: Answer Key to Drills.

Questions 1 through 3 refer to the passage below.

1 Scientists believe that earthquake activity is the result of friction between tectonic plates of the Earth that causes the sudden release of energy, creating seismic waves. These waves can be measured, using seismometers, to describe the magnitude of an earthquake. The Richter scale provides a local measurement of the strength of an earthquake. Anything measuring below 3 on the Richter scale is nearly imperceptible; however, a quake that exceeds 7 can cause major damage. The largest earthquakes recorded have measured over 9 on the Richter scale and caused enormous amounts of damage.

2 Earthquakes can occur at different depths, and this has a significant effect on the amount of damage an earthquake causes. Shallow earthquakes, those that occur near to the Earth's surface, cause the most damage. Earthquakes that occur on land have been known to cause volcanoes to erupt and landslides while earthquakes occurring offshore can initiate tsunamis.

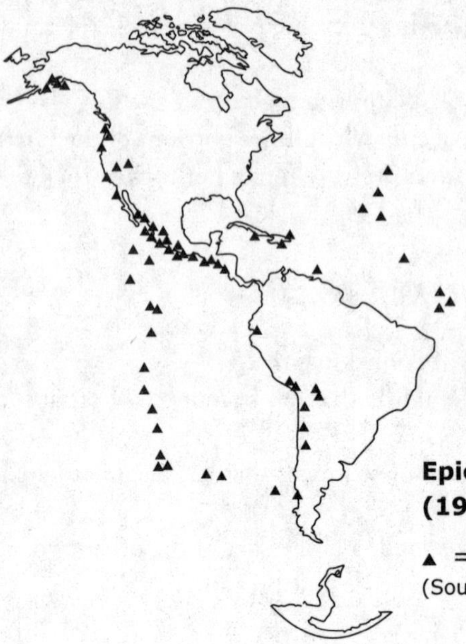

Epicenters of earthquakes (1961–1967)

▲ = earthquake epicenter

(Source: *Earth*, third edition)

3 Some locations on Earth are more prone to earthquakes than others. There has been a great deal of earthquake activity along the western coast of North and South America, as shown on the map above. Each point represents the epicenter of an earthquake: the point at ground level directly above the point where the initial rupture of the earthquake took place, referred to as the hypocenter or focus.

1. From the information presented above, which of the following statements can be concluded?

   A. The places marked on the map are the only places on Earth where earthquakes occur.

   B. Two tectonic plates are rubbing together along the west coast of the Americas.

   C. Two tectonic plates are rubbing together along the east coast of the Americas.

   D. Canada reports more earthquakes than the United States does.

2. Which of the following options from the list below can result due to an earthquake with magnitude 5 or greater? Choose all that apply. (For this drill, write the option letters in the box below.)

Outcomes of an Earthquake

(a) Tsunamis	(c) Tremors	(e) Volcanic activity
(b) Hurricanes	(d) Damage to buildings	(f) Tornadoes

3. You turn on the news to find out, for the first time, that an earthquake has taken place only a few miles from your home. You didn't feel anything, and there is no obvious sign of damage. The earthquake probably measured Select... ▼
   - 3
   - 5
   - 7

   on the Richter scale and was probably

   Select... ▼
   - deep
   - shallow

   with respect to the Earth's surface.

GLACIERS, EROSION, AND THE ICE AGES

Glaciers are large masses of ice that form over land due to the accumulation and compaction of snow over long periods. They are a critical component of Earth's climate system, influencing weather patterns, shaping landscapes, and playing a crucial role in the global water cycle. **Continental glaciers,** also known as ice sheets or ice caps, are vast ice masses that cover large land areas, often entire continents. The Antarctic and Greenland ice sheets are prime examples of continental glaciers. **Valley glaciers** are long, narrow glaciers that form in mountain valleys and flow downhill due to gravity. They are commonly found in mountainous regions worldwide, such as the Alps, Himalayas, and Andes.

Glaciers are powerful agents of **erosion** (the wearing away or removal of soil, rock, or other materials by natural forces) and **deposition** (the depositing or laying down sediments, soil, or rock fragments), reshaping landscapes over thousands of years. The movement of glaciers results in several erosional features, including the following:

- **U-shaped valleys.** Glaciers carve deep, steep-sided valleys with a characteristic U-shaped cross-section as they flow downhill.
- **Cirques** are bowl-shaped depressions at the head of valleys where glaciers originate.
- **Moraines** are deposits of sediment and rock debris carried and pushed by glaciers. Terminal moraines mark the furthest advance of a glacier, while lateral and medial moraines form along the sides and center of glaciers, respectively.
- **Erratics** are large boulders transported by glaciers and deposited far from their source.

Ice ages are periods in Earth's history when large portions of the planet's surface are covered by ice sheets and glaciers. These periods alternate with warmer interglacial periods. The most recent ice age, known as the Pleistocene Epoch, occurred from about 2.6 million to 11,700 years ago. Several factors contribute to the onset and duration of ice ages, including the following:

- **Milankovitch cycles.** Variations in Earth's orbit, axial tilt, and precession influence the distribution of solar radiation received by the planet, affecting climate patterns.
- **Plate tectonics.** Changes in the arrangement of continents and ocean currents can impact global climate by altering atmospheric circulation patterns.
- **Atmospheric composition.** Changes in greenhouse gas concentrations, such as carbon dioxide and methane, can influence global temperatures and climate.

Glaciers, erosion, and the ice ages are integral components of Earth's geological history and climate system. Understanding their formation, behavior, and impacts on landscapes and climate is essential for comprehending Earth's past and present environments and predicting future changes.

Let's try a question based on this material.

The Cape Hatteras lighthouse is located on the Outer Banks, a chain of islands off the coast of North Carolina, and was built in 1870. After the lighthouse was built, citizens of the Outer Banks noted that the ocean was eroding the beach, bringing the shoreline progressively closer to the lighthouse. The chart below shows how the distance in meters between the shoreline and the lighthouse changed between 1870 and 1990.

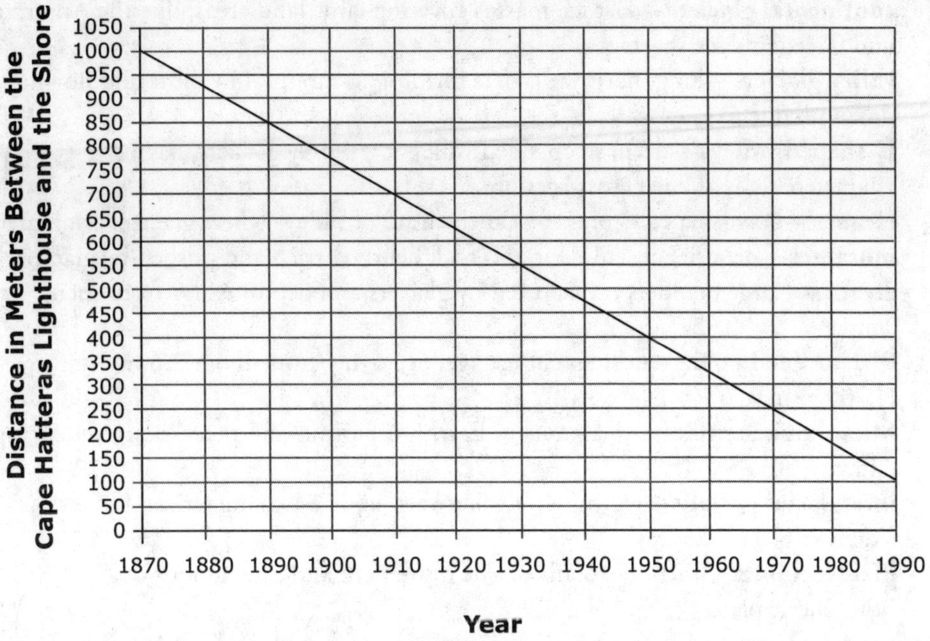

1. In 1990, scientists studied the Cape Hatteras lighthouse to determine when local residents would need to move the lighthouse before it suffered damage. According to the information above, scientists could project that in the year 2000 the distance between the shore and the lighthouse would most likely be closest to

   A. 0 meters.
   B. 25 meters.
   C. 75 meters.
   D. 100 meters.

Glaciers Quiz

Q: If the glaciers suddenly melted, what would happen to the sea levels?

Turn the page for the answer.

Here's How to Crack It

According to the chart, the distance between the shoreline and the lighthouse decreases by 75 meters every 10 years. In 1990, the distance between the shore and the lighthouse is 100 meters, so by 2000 the distance between the lighthouse and the shore should be 100 meters – 75 meters = 25 meters. Thus, the correct answer is (B).

Vocabulary

glaciers—large masses of ice that form over land due to the accumulation and compaction of snow

erosion—wearing away of soil, rock, or other materials by natural forces like water, wind, and ice

deposition—process of depositing sediments, soil, or rock fragments by natural agents such as water and ice

ice ages—periods in Earth's history when large portions of the surface are covered by ice

continental glaciers—vast ice masses covering large land areas, like the Antarctic and Greenland ice sheets
valley glaciers—long, narrow glaciers forming in mountain valleys and flowing downhill due to gravity
U-shaped valleys—deep, steep-sided valleys carved by glaciers, having a characteristic U-shaped cross-section
cirques—bowl-shaped depressions at the head of valleys where glaciers originate
moraines—deposits of sediment and rock debris carried and pushed by glaciers
erratics—large boulders transported by glaciers and deposited far from their source
Pleistocene Epoch—most recent ice age, occurring from about 2.6 million to 11,700 years ago
Milankovitch cycles—variations in Earth's orbit, tilt, and precession influencing climate patterns
interglacial periods—warm periods between ice ages, characterized by less extensive glacial coverage
plate tectonics—theory explaining the movement and interactions of Earth's lithospheric plates
greenhouse gases—atmospheric gases, such as carbon dioxide and methane, contributing to the greenhouse effect

Glaciers, Erosion, and the Ice Ages Drill

You can check your answers in Part IX: Answer Key to Drills.

Questions 1 through 3 refer to the passage below.

1 Scientists posit that ice ages, times when the temperature of the Earth fell dramatically for reasons not well understood, took place as recently as 2.5 million years ago. There have been several ice ages during which glaciers covered much of the surface of the Earth. In between ice ages and following the last one, the Earth's temperature warmed up again for reasons not fully understood.

2 Evidence for the ice ages comes in three varieties: paleontological, chemical, and geological. Fossils have provided evidence of ice ages due to their distribution. Certain organisms that would have required warm conditions went extinct during these times, while those that were better adapted to cooler climates survived and spread into warmer areas. Chemical variations in the isotopes found in fossils and sedimentary rock offer further evidence of ice ages. Finally, the valley-cutting and scratching of rocks provide geological evidence of glacial movement.

Glaciers Quiz
A: Sea levels would rise.

1. Based on the information above, which of the following is most likely true?

   A. Glaciers begin melting when their temperature rises above freezing.
   B. Glaciers are found only near the equator.
   C. When glaciers melt, the level of water in the oceans goes down.
   D. Glaciers are affected by the gravitational pull of the Moon.

2. Glaciers are formed over time as snow gradually turns to ice. Which of the following can be concluded about glaciers?

   A. When they move, glaciers move rapidly.
   B. Glaciers are composed of fresh water.
   C. Glaciers occur only in valleys.
   D. Glaciers will never again cover the Earth.

3. Click on all of the points on the following graph that represent the ice ages. (For this drill, mark the points with an X.)

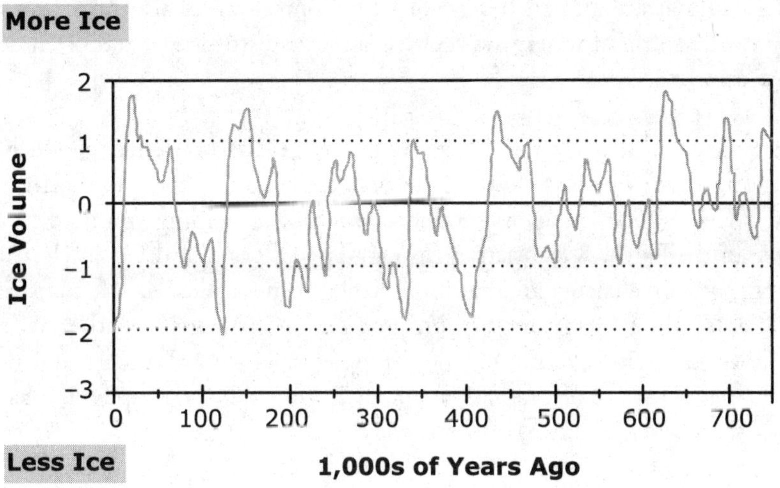

NATURAL RESOURCES

Remember when we discussed energy? Well, we are going to revisit the sources of our energy. On a daily basis, you perform a multitude of tasks that require power; e.g., you may brush your teeth, make toast, drive your car, use electricity, or a host of other power-sucking tasks. So, where does all that power come from? And, more importantly, what happens if the sources of power run dry? A large amount of energy is required to produce the power supplied throughout the world. In order to produce this energy, it is necessary to utilize a combination of human ingenuity and the Earth's resources. There are two types of **natural resources:** renewable and nonrenewable.

Renewable resources are those that can be replenished or regenerated over the course of time by natural processes and can be replaced at a sustainable rate; i.e., the supply of the energy is able to meet the demand for energy. In the United States, eight percent of electricity is produced with five main renewable resources: biomass, hydroelectric power, geothermal energy, wind, and solar power. **Biomass**, or biofuels, is organic matter such as plants, animals, or waste products from organic sources that is burned in a biomass boiler to produce energy. Using biomass as an energy source is beneficial because it is low-cost, readily available and renewable, and better for the environment than fossil fuels. Biomass can also help reduce the amount of waste in landfills, as it relies on the burning of organic matter. The major downsides of biomass include the initial cost and large land mass required for installation of a biomass boiler. **Hydroelectric power** works via the systematic placement of river dams that spin turbines to produce electricity. Despite the fact that hydroelectric power does not generate any pollution and can be cost-effective, the usefulness of this resource is limited by geography. Hydroelectric power is practical only in areas that receive significant rainfall and are located near rivers. Environmentalists also note that hydroelectric dams require the diversion of waterways that leads to the disturbance, and often destruction, of habitats and ecosystems.

An increasingly researched renewable energy source is **geothermal energy**, which is produced by harnessing the Earth's internal heat. (Fun fact: *Geo* means "from the Earth," and *thermal* means "heat.") Geothermal energy is produced when heat, coming from steam or hot water reservoirs deep in the Earth, is transferred through large pipes that drive an electrical generator. The benefits of geothermal energy are that it is reliable when installed, is safe to use, and does not produce pollutants in the energy production process. Unfortunately, geothermal energy hasn't gained popularity, is expensive to install, and can potentially release toxic gas during the drilling process. Furthermore, the use of geothermal energy is limited by geography; if a location lacks a geothermal source, energy production cannot take place.

With recent advents in technology, both **solar** and **wind power** have become increasingly accessible, affordable, and reliable. Perhaps one of the greatest benefits of both resources is that they are indefinitely renewable. Wind power produces electricity through large windmills that harness wind that spins turbines. While wind power can provide energy for a reasonable cost, it has seen a slow adoption rate. Indeed, wind power is not always practical in a given environment, as large, unobstructed areas of land are needed for windmill placement. For wind power to work effectively, large windmills with turbines must be installed, which have been met with criticism for various reasons. One criticism is regarding the aesthetic nature of a windmill farm, which can stretch over vast swaths of land. Others note the deadliness of the wind turbines, which have been known to suck in and kill migrating birds.

Solar power, however, has seen a rapid adoption rate, as individuals and corporations alike install **photovoltaic cells**, which transform the Sun's light into usable energy. Two benefits of solar energy are that passive solar energy production produces no air pollutants and that users can save significant amounts of money by receiving energy "off the grid." Unfortunately, the production of photovoltaic cells requires the use of fossil fuels, which have a detrimental impact on the environment, and the initial installation cost of a passive solar collection system is quite significant. Furthermore, areas that receive limited amounts of sunlight are not practical for solar energy systems.

In summation, it should be noted that there is a huge benefit associated with the use of renewable resources: Compared to nonrenewable energy, renewable energy is significantly less harmful to the environment and is considered **green technology**. Worldwide, renewable resources provide approximately 10 percent of the world's energy consumption. As technology continues to improve, and the world becomes increasingly aware of the environmental hazards associated with fossil fuels, researchers project that renewable resources will provide 15 percent of the world's energy by 2040.

Nonrenewable resources are those that exist in a limited supply and cannot be naturally replaced on a level to meet their consumption; i.e., the demand exceeds the supply. While **fossil fuels** are nonrenewable and the cause of many environmental problems, such as pollution, acid rain, and ozone destruction, they remain the top energy choice for many countries. Fossil fuels, such as coal, oil, and natural gas, are the world's primary sources of energy, comprising approximately 80 percent of the world's energy. Formed from fossilized remains of organic matter, fossil fuels are found deep within the earth. Oil is the most used fossil fuel. In order to locate oil, geologists dig **exploratory wells** to take samples from the earth and determine whether or not an area is a **proven reserve**, or a location known to house fossil fuel deposits. Once a proven reserve has been tapped, oil is pumped from the reserve up to the surface. This form of oil is **crude oil**, which can vary greatly in viscosity, sulfur output, and color. There are four main modes of oil extraction: primary extraction, during which oil is easily pumped to the surface; pressure extraction, during which water and CO_2 push oil out of the reserve; steam and gas extraction; and the newest mode, **fracking**, the process of injecting liquid at high pressure into the earth so existing fissures can be opened and oil can be extracted.

Another major fossil fuel is **coal**, a combustible black rock composed of fossilized organic plant matter. Coal is extracted from the earth via **underground mining**, during which coal miners enter and manually retrieve coal from a series of underground tunnels. One major issue associated with coal mining is subsidence, which is the caving in of mine shafts. Many times throughout history, cave-ins have trapped miners underground, in what would become their final resting place. Like other fossil fuels, coal releases harmful pollutants into the environment that destroy the ozone layer, pollute the air with smog and smoke, and produce **acid mine drainage**, or highly acidic water that can damage the areas surrounding the mine.

Comprised mainly of methane and pentane, **natural gas** can be found deep in the earth where it is stored in the space between rocks. Like oil extraction, natural gas extraction occurs when gas is carried to the surface and harnessed to produce power. Unlike the other types of fossil fuels, natural gas does not produce harmful pollutants. However, natural gas is quite unstable and, if not properly controlled, intense explosions can occur.

Another form of nonrenewable energy is **nuclear power**, which uses uranium in a process called **nuclear fission**, which occurs when an isotope of uranium-235 is split. Despite the low cost associated with nuclear energy, there are many concerns with widespread use. Primarily, concerns regarding the radioactive waste produced by the fission process, coupled with the potential for tragic nuclear meltdowns as seen in Chernobyl, Ukraine and Fukushima, Japan, have slowed the adoption of nuclear power. In the future, nuclear power will likely involve **nuclear fusion**, which is the process of fusing two nuclei to create power.

Keep in mind that nonrenewable resources will, eventually, run out. When they do, we better have perfected a form of renewable energy to sustain ourselves. Remember, for the GED® test, you need to know just the basics about renewable and nonrenewable resources and their respective costs and benefits.

Try out the following question.

Energy Facts about New Hampshire

- About three-fifths (59%) of New Hampshire households use petroleum products as their primary heating fuel, the second-largest share among the states and almost seven times greater than the national average.
- Seabrook, one of only two nuclear power plants in New England and the largest power plant in New Hampshire, provided 58% of New Hampshire's 2022 total in-state electricity net generation.
- In 2022, 14% of New Hampshire's electricity generation came from renewable resources, including small-scale solar installations. Most of the state's renewable generation comes from biomass, hydroelectric power, and wind.
- New Hampshire has the two remaining coal-fired power plants in New England: Schiller at Portsmouth and Merrimack at Bow. Coal-fired plants no longer supply baseload power, but they play an important role in providing electricity on high demand days.
- New Hampshire's residential sector accounted for about one-third of state energy consumption in 2021, even though about 1 in 10 New Hampshire homes are only seasonally or occasionally occupied.

Source: U.S. Energy Information Administration (2022)

1. Based on the provided data on New Hampshire's energy usage, which energy source plays an important role in providing electricity during periods of high demand?

   A. biomass
   B. nuclear
   C. renewable resources
   D. coal

Here's How to Crack It

According to the data, New Hampshire's two remaining coal-fired power plants (Schiller and Merrimack) no longer supply baseload power, but they play an important role in providing electricity on high-demand days. The data does not specifically address the role of (A), (B), or (C) in meeting high-demand electricity needs. Therefore, the correct answer is (D), coal.

Vocabulary

natural resources—resources that exist naturally in the environment and prove beneficial to humans

renewable resources—resources that can be naturally replaced or replenished on a level to meet their consumption and, therefore, are considered inexhaustible. Solar power, wind, and biomass are examples of renewable resources.

biomass—a renewable resource that is comprised of organic materials found in plant and animal materials. Biomass is burned to create electricity or other types of power.

hydroelectric power—a renewable energy source that harnesses the kinetic energy of water moving over a dam to produce electricity

geothermal energy—a renewable resource that is produced by harnessing the Earth's internal heat. Geothermal energy is produced when heat, coming from steam or hot water reservoirs deep in the earth, is transferred through large pipes that drive an electrical generator.

solar power—a form of renewable energy power that involves converting the energy of the Sun's rays into electricity. The most prevalent way of converting sunlight into electricity is through the use of photovoltaic cells.

wind power—a form of renewable energy power that involves harnessing the kinetic energy of wind to generate electrical power. The most prevalent way of converting wind into electricity is by directing wind through turbines.

photovoltaic cells—technology used to convert solar energy to electrical energy

green technology—technology that can be created through environmentally friendly means, including the production of energy that limits environmental harm

nonrenewable resources—resources that exist in limited quantities and cannot be naturally replaced on a level to meet their consumption. Fossil fuels, such as coal, oil, and natural gas, are examples of nonrenewable resources.

fossil fuels—nonrenewable, natural fuels comprised of hydrocarbon deposits that are formed from the remains of living organisms. Coal, oil, and natural gas are examples of fossil fuels.

exploratory well—a deep hole that is drilled into the earth by an oil or gas company in order to determine whether fossil fuels exist in a specific location
proven reserve—a location that is known to house fossil fuel deposits
crude oil—a nonrenewable resource that is composed of hydrocarbon deposits and prehistoric organic matter
fracking—the controversial process of injecting liquid at high pressure into the Earth in order to open existing fissures and extract oil or gas from the Earth
coal—a nonrenewable resource that is comprised of the carbonized remains of prehistoric plant matter
underground mining—a process of making tunnels that is used to gain access to minerals and ores in the ground. There are many detrimental issues associated with underground mining such as worker safety, ventilation, and environmental problems related to extraction.
acid mine drainage—a direct negative environmental effect of the mining process that occurs when sulfides are exposed to air and water, forming sulfuric acid (sulfuric acid that is released can then harm animals and plants)
natural gas—a nonrenewable energy source that is composed mainly of methane gas. Considered the cleanest of the nonrenewable resources, natural gas is extracted from the earth and burned to produce electricity.
nuclear power—energy produced by an atomic reaction. Generally, nuclear fission power plants use uranium, a nonrenewable resource, as fuel.
nuclear fission—the current process used to create nuclear power, during which a nucleus of an atom splits into two smaller nuclei, resulting in the release of energy
nuclear fusion—a process during which the nuclei of atoms fuse together to form a heavier nucleus, resulting in the release of energy. Nuclear fusion is the process that occurs in the Sun, but it has yet to be artificially perfected by scientists.

Now that we've covered information regarding the extraction and use of natural resources, let's try some questions.

Natural Resources Drill

You can check your answers in Part IX: Answer Key to Drills.

Questions 1 through 3 refer to the following information.

> Bashville is looking to reduce its carbon emissions by changing the type of power that's supplied to various parts of the city. Bashville also wants to reduce the amount of organic waste that has been accumulated in the town's landfills. Currently, the majority of the city's power comes from coal, oil, and other fossil fuels. When considering renewable energy sources, such as solar, wind, biomass, and hydroelectric power, Bashville must take into account the geographical limitations of the area. After all, Bashville is located in a large basin surrounded by mountains. Bashville also receives a large amount of rainfall each month and is situated near a system of rivers.

1. [Select... ▼] energy sources
   - Renewable
   - Nonrenewable

   increase [Select... ▼] emissions.
   - carbon
   - oxygen

2. Based on the information provided, which of the following would produce the greatest amount of carbon emissions?

   A. solar power
   B. biomass
   C. coal
   D. hydroelectric power

3. Based on the information in the passage, which of the following renewable energy sources could Bashville potentially adopt? Choose all that apply. (For this drill, write the option letters in the box below.)

Bashville's Renewable Energy Choices

(a) Solar

(b) Wind

(c) Biomass

(d) Hydroelectric

(e) Geothermal

FOSSILS

Much of what we know about both animal and plant life in ancient times comes from studying fossils—the preserved direct or indirect remains of ancient life. Millions of years ago, a tiny insect might have become caught in the mud of a riverbank. Eventually, if conditions were right, that riverbank became sedimentary rock, and although the organic matter of the insect decayed long ago, the rock preserved a perfect impression of that insect, waiting to be found and studied by humans. Sometimes scientists can date the fossil by dating the material that surrounds it. For example, if it is known approximately when a volcanic eruption took place, any fossils found in the volcanic rock formed by the eruption can be assumed to come from the same period. Another method of discovering a fossil's age is to take a small sample of the organic material of the fossil (if any exists) and use a technique called **carbon-14 dating.** Carbon-14 is a mildly radioactive isotope of carbon that occurs naturally in all living things. It decays slowly over time. By measuring how much the isotope has decayed, scientists can date the fossil with a high degree of accuracy.

Let's try an example of a GED® test question on fossils.

Scientists study fossils to learn the conditions of the Earth during certain periods of time. These fossils are found buried in rock layers. According to geological studies, rock layers develop chronologically, so older rocks are found deeper underground than newer rocks. Below is a cross section of rock layers currently being studied by geologists.

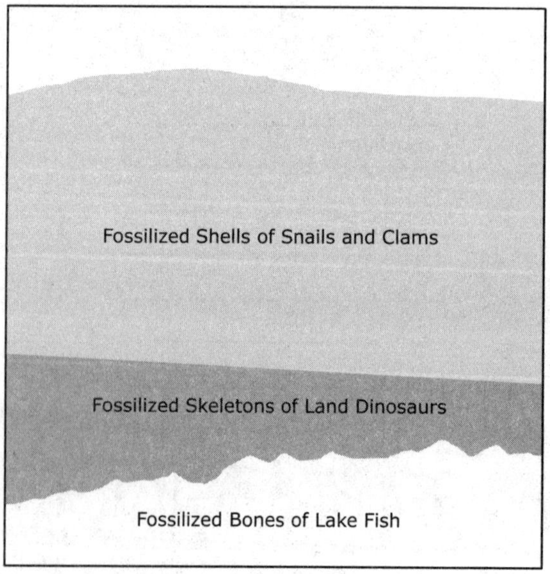

1. Based on the information above, scientists studying this region could infer which of the following?

   A. The region has always been covered by water.
   B. The region was first under an ocean, was later above sea level, and then was under a fresh water source.
   C. This region was first under an ocean, was later above sea level, and then was under an ocean again.
   D. This region was first under a fresh water source, was later above water level, and then was under an ocean.

Here's How to Crack It

According to the information in the passage, older rocks are buried deeper underground than are newer rocks. Therefore, the fossilized bones of lake fish must have appeared earlier than did the fossilized skeletons of land dinosaurs. Lakes are sources of fresh water, so the region must first have been under a fresh water source. Eliminate (B) and (C), since these choices indicate that the region was under an ocean first. Since the next layer of rocks contains fossils of land dinosaurs, the region must have later been above water. Thus, you can eliminate (A). Choice (D) matches the information in the figure, showing that the region was first under a fresh water source, which matches with the fact that the fossilized bones of lake fish were the first fossils to appear; then was above water, which matches with the idea that fossilized bones of land dinosaurs appeared next; and then was under an ocean, which matches up with the idea that fossilized shells of snails and clams appeared next.

Vocabulary

carbon-14 dating—a technique that allows scientists to determine the age of a fossil with a high degree of accuracy and that involves the use of carbon-14, a mildly radioactive isotope that decays over time in living things

Fossils Drill

You can check your answers in Part IX: Answer Key to Drills.

Questions 1 through 3 refer to the following passage.

1 When an organism is buried shortly after its death, it fills with groundwater that contains many minerals. Over time, these minerals precipitate, forming detailed fossils that can reveal fascinating structural information about the organism. Oftentimes, the original remains of the organism dissolve over time so all that remains is the fossil.

2 Over many years, several layers of material can form sediment over the fossilized organism, burying it even further. Each of these layers is representative of a particular time period. Through carbon dating, scientists can determine when a particular layer of sedimentary rock was formed. If a particular organism was fossilized in that layer, the scientists can deduce that that organism most likely lived during that time period.

3 The half-life of carbon-14 (the radioactive isotope of carbon) is approximately 5,000 years. The following diagram depicts several rock layers.

1. The organic material found in rock layer C is probably older than the material found in

Select... ▼ and younger than the

- layer A
- layer E

material found in Select... ▼.

- layer B
- layer D

2. The passage states that the half-life of carbon-14 is about 5,000 years. This means that if you start with a sample of carbon-14 and wait for 5,000 years,

A. you will have double the amount you started with.
B. you will have half the amount you started with.
C. the carbon-14 will have converted into carbon-7.
D. you will have the same amount of carbon.

3. If rock layer D contains fossilized bones from a woolly mammoth, which lived about 200,000 years ago, which of the following statements must also be true?

   A. The rock formed over an area that was once a large ocean.
   B. Rock layer D formed 250,000 years ago.
   C. Rock layer A formed 10,000 years ago.
   D. Rock layer D contained minerals that were capable of fossilization.

ASTRONOMY

Astronomy is the study of the universe beyond the Earth. Astronomers study the Moon, planets, solar system, galaxy, and everything farther away. It is one of the oldest branches of science, dating back to ancient times. In fact, some scientists theorize that the pyramids in Egypt were actually used for astronomical purposes. Thankfully, you won't be asked to know everything about the deepest reaches of space, but here are the basics of the universe.

Earth and the Solar System

We currently live on **Earth**, the third-closest planet to the **Sun**. Earth is a part of the **solar system**, which in turn is part of the **Milky Way Galaxy**. All solar systems are made up of a sun and the objects revolving around it. For a long time, scientists believed that the Earth was the center of the solar system. **Nicolaus Copernicus**, a Polish astronomer, was the first to introduce the idea of a heliocentric, or sun-centered, model of the solar system in the 16th century. It has since been proven that our solar system is indeed heliocentric. The following is a model of our solar system (not to scale):

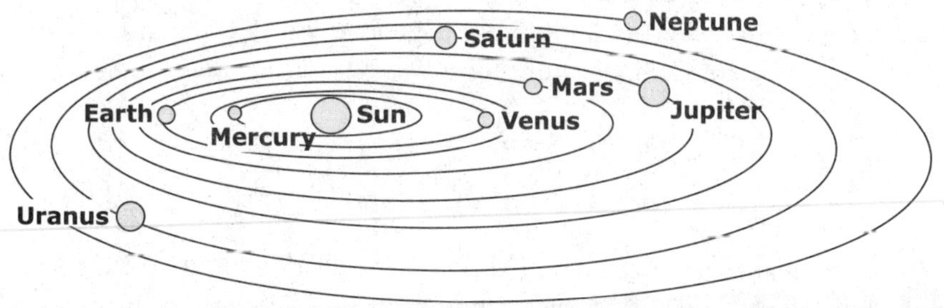

Astronomy Quiz

Q: Earth orbits the Sun. What large body orbits Earth?

Turn the page for the answer.

The four planets closest to the Sun—Mercury, Venus, Earth, and Mars—are called the **inner planets**. They consist mainly of rock with metal cores. They notably do not have rings. Earth and Mars are the only inner planets that have moons; Earth has only one moon and Mars has two (called Phobos and Deimos).

The four planets farthest from the Sun—Jupiter, Saturn, Uranus, and Neptune—are called the **outer planets**. They are also sometimes called the Jovian planets because their structure is similar to that of Jupiter. These planets are the largest in the solar system (with Jupiter being the largest of them all) and are gas giants (meaning that they are not primarily made up of rock or solid matter). They all have numerous moons, ranging at the most recent count from 14 to 83. Also, all of these planets have rings, with Saturn's rings being the most notable and plentiful.

Beyond Neptune we find Pluto, which has been controversial since its discovery in 1930. Although it was once considered the smallest of the planets, in 2006 the International Astronomical Union (IAU) formally downgraded Pluto to a dwarf planet. It has five moons, with the largest, Charon, being roughly half its size, and its elliptical orbit sometimes brings it closer to the Sun than Neptune.

The solar system also contains millions of smaller objects. **Asteroids** are large pieces of rock that orbit the Sun, just as the planets do. Most asteroids are located between Mars and Jupiter in an area that is called the asteroid belt. **Meteoroids** are small pieces of rock and metal. Sometimes meteoroids enter the Earth's atmosphere. When that happens, they are called meteors. Usually the meteor will burn up when passing through the atmosphere. However, on rare occasions, they hit the Earth and are then called meteorites. **Comets** are made up of rock, dust, methane, and ice. Like asteroids, they also orbit the Sun. The Kuiper Belt is a disk-shaped region past the orbit of Neptune that is thought to be the source of the short-period comets.

The Earth's Orbit

Did you know that the Earth is moving, even as you read this book? Right now, the Earth is traveling around the Sun at an average speed of about 106,000 km per hour. The Earth's revolution, or trip around the Sun, takes 365 days (approximately one year). As the Earth revolves around the Sun, it is also spinning on its axis. This spinning is called rotation. It takes the Earth 24 hours (or one day) to make one complete rotation.

The Sun

Ah, the Sun: the center of the solar system. There are two major facts you should know about the Sun: it is very hot and very large. The outer layer (known as the corona) averages 2,000,000 degrees Celsius and the core (or center) is 15,000,000 degrees Celsius! The Sun is about 109 times more massive than the Earth, and it accounts for 99 percent of the total mass of the solar system.

Eclipses

An **eclipse** occurs when a planet or moon passes through the shadow of another. There are two types of eclipses that occur on Earth: solar eclipses and lunar eclipses. During a solar eclipse, the Moon moves between the Sun and the Earth. The Moon blocks the light of the Sun and casts a shadow over a certain part of the Earth. During a lunar eclipse, the Earth moves between the Sun and the Moon. When this happens, the Earth blocks the sunlight and casts a shadow on the Moon.

Solar Eclipse

Astronomy Quiz
A: The Moon orbits Earth.

Lunar Eclipse

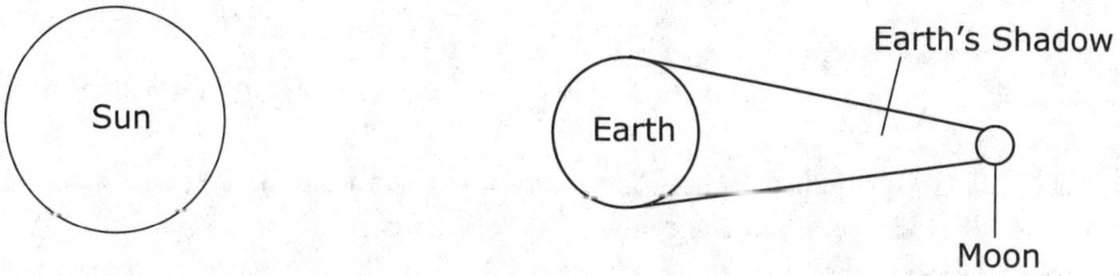

Check out the astronomy question below.

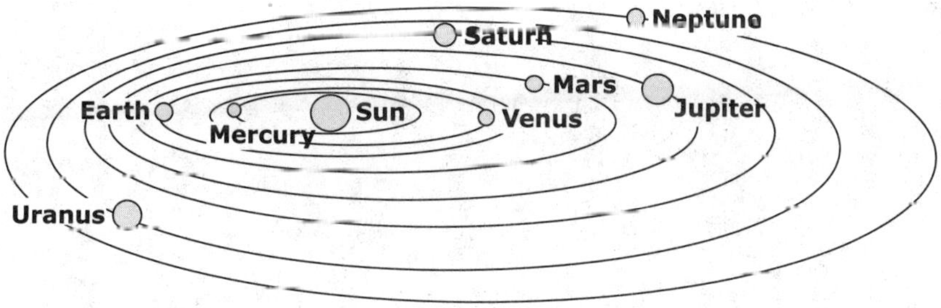

1. A year is the length of time it takes for a planet to complete one entire orbit around the Sun. If each of the planets revolved around the Sun at exactly the same speed, which of these planets would have the shortest year?

   A. Uranus
   B. Earth
   C. Mars
   D. Neptune

Here's How to Crack It

If all of the planets revolved around the Sun at the same speed, then the planet with the smallest orbit would have the shortest year. Since, of the planets listed in the answer choices, Earth, (B), has the smallest orbit, Earth would have the shortest year under those conditions.

Vocabulary

astronomy—the study of celestial objects, phenomena, and the universe beyond Earth's atmosphere

Earth—the third planet from the Sun in the solar system, home to living organisms

Sun—star at the center of the solar system, providing light, heat, and energy to Earth

solar system—a group of planets that orbit a star

galaxy—a group of stars; the galaxy containing our solar system is called the Milky Way

Nicolaus Copernicus—Renaissance astronomer who proposed the heliocentric model, placing the Sun at the center of the solar system

inner planets—the four planets closest to the Sun (Mercury, Venus, Earth, and Mars); consist mainly of rock with metal cores

outer planets—the four planets farthest from the Sun (Jupiter, Saturn, Uranus, and Neptune); gas giants with numerous moons

asteroid—a small, rocky body that orbits the Sun, just like planets do

meteoroids—small pieces of rock and metal

comet—small celestial body consisting of ice, dust, and gas that orbits the Sun, often exhibiting a bright tail

eclipse—event that occurs when a planet or moon passes through the shadow of another

Online Practice Drills

Want more Science practice? Of course you do. Register your book for instant access to the two digital Science drills in your Student Tools.

Astronomy Drill

You can check your answers in Part IX: Answer Key to Drills.

Questions 1 through 3 refer to the following passage.

1 Our solar system includes our Sun, as well as the planets and other objects that orbit it. It was formed approximately 4.5 billion years ago and contains eight planets: Mercury, Venus, Earth, Mars, Jupiter, Saturn, Uranus, and Neptune. Originally, Pluto was classified as the ninth planet and farthest from the Sun; however, in 2006, the International Astronomical Union redefined the necessary characteristics of a planet and in doing so excluded Pluto.

2 The Sun contains 99.9% of the mass of the solar system and thus induces the other planets to orbit around it. The four innermost planets encircling the Sun are relatively small. Immediately beyond them in the solar system is a rocky asteroid belt. Looking farther out in the solar system one can find the largest planets, known as the gas giants. Many of the planets have secondary systems that include moons or planetary ring systems.

3 The following graph indicates the temperatures found on each planet based on its location relative to the Sun. The maximum temperature in Kelvin is reported.

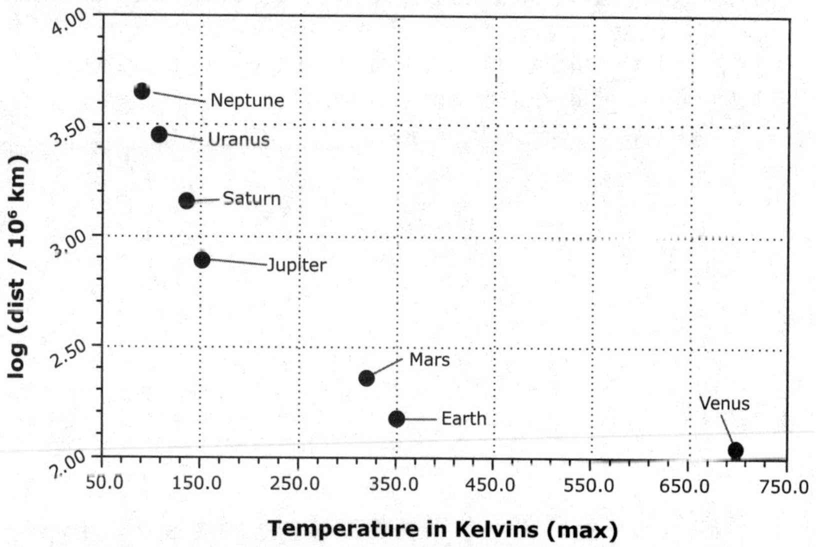

1. Click on the planet above that has the lowest surface temperature. (For this drill, mark the planet with an X.)

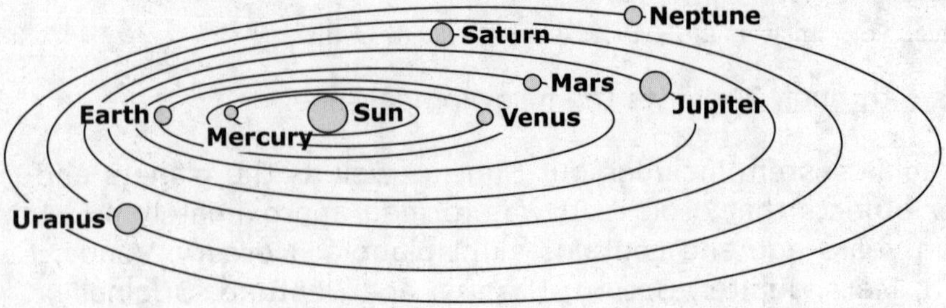

2. A year is the length of time it takes for a planet to complete one entire orbit around the Sun. If each of the planets revolved around the Sun at exactly the same speed, which of these planets would have the longest year?

   A. Mercury
   B. Venus
   C. Earth
   D. Mars

3. Based on the information in the passage, which of the following statements is FALSE?

   A. Jupiter is larger than Earth.
   B. Mars is colder than Venus.
   C. The Sun contains approximately 100 times as much mass as everything else in the solar system.
   D. It's unlikely that life could survive on another planet in our solar system.

Part IX
Chapter Drills: Answers and Explanations

REASONING THROUGH LANGUAGE ARTS

Reading

Informational Passage Drill (Page 191)

1. **C** This is a structure question. Why are the senior executives and directors who crafted and approved this statement publicly dragging employees into the commitments they've made? Using Process of Elimination, (A) is gone quickly—the authors do take responsibility at the end, when they refer readers to the most senior leader, the Chairman and Chief Executive Officer. You can also eliminate (A) because the overall tone of the document is confidence and reassurance, not *worry*. Eliminate (B), because the purpose of the passage is to show that *all* employees are a part of corporate responsibility, not just the ones the stakeholders are *dealing with*. Choice (D) is unsupported by the text and does not answer the question. Only (C) gives a reason that should result in a benefit to the company and to the authors: Now anyone who reads this document knows that meeting these responsibilities is part of everyone's job at Pine Trail Timber and will expect employees to behave accordingly.

2. **D** The context in which "obligations" is used will point the way to the best answer in this language use question. The word occurs in the sentence about suppliers—the companies that provide the products Pine Trail Timber uses in its own manufacturing—and is positioned as the second half of a two-part purchase transaction—specifying its requirements for the products it buys, and then meeting its obligations (i.e., to pay for those products). So while weak arguments could be made for (A), (B), and (C), choice (D) is the most accurate in this context.

3. **A** This question asks you to compare information about Pine Trail Timber given in two different formats—text and figures in a table. However, that information does not portray quite the same company image. The text statement presents a company committed to responsible resource management and concern for employees, including workers' safety. The table tells a rather different story. Even in Pine Trail Timber's largest operations (North America), only 20.8% of the workers have earned safety certification, and the largest percentage of remediation workers (still only 3.8%) is found in Central America, which is only the company's second largest area of activity.

   Now to find the *most significant* difference or similarity, use Process of Elimination. Choice (C) is eliminated because the text statement doesn't say anything about workers controlling their own safety, let alone being able to refuse dangerous work, as the table shows. Read the question carefully—you're comparing topics covered by *both* of the two sources. While (B) has some truth, it's hardly the most significant issue raised in a comparison. Choice (D) is also a weak similarity; having fewer than four percent of the workforce involved in remediation in even the area with the highest percentage isn't much of a commitment to restoring the land. Choice (A) is the correct answer, and you can see it more easily from the percentages than from the absolute numbers. Southeast Asia lags behind the other three areas on all measures of concern for workers' safety, for instance, while Africa has been more successful than the other areas in giving workers a voice in safety (through workers' committees and representatives, and through exercising the right to refuse dangerous work).

4. **B** The question is about the authors' motives for publishing the document, and there is no indication that they are required to do so, nor is there indication about what their competitors have done, so eliminate (A) and (C). Your answer choice should be based *only* on what's in the passage. Choice (D) is eliminated because the CSR statement outlines the company's commitments in carrying out its mission, not the mission itself. That leaves only (B) as the correct answer: Overall, the document is intended to convey a positive public image of the company.

5. **Claim is supported: (a), (c), and (f). Claim is not supported: (b), (d), and (e).** This is an evaluation question that would be presented in an actual test in the drag-and-drop format. You're asked to decide how well the company supports its claims, or whether it supports them at all. The first and third claims—(a) and (c)—are supported by FSC certification and by the invitation to contact the company's Chairman and CEO. The references to a rising stock price and five years of dividend increases support the last claim (f). Since all six claims fit somewhere in the chart, the remaining three must go into the "not supported" column. Indeed, the second and fifth claims—(b) and (e)—are made without any support, and the fourth claim (d) isn't even directly made, let alone supported.

6. **A** In this tricky main idea, or theme, question, you need to find themes not only in the two paragraphs identified, but also in the CSR statement as a whole. Using your critical thinking skills, you'll recognize that the correct answer will identify something inconsistent in those themes. The only choice that does that is (A). If Pine Trail Timber is such a trustworthy custodian, why are there investigations and sufficiently large-scale events to create an impact beyond the company's operations? The need for remediation, mentioned in paragraph 15 of the "Respect for the Environment" section, reinforces the apparent disconnect between the image the company portrays and the actual results of its operations. Each of the other three choices may contain a grain of truth, but does not lead to the significant conclusion with relation to the overall theme of responsible corporate citizenship that (A) does.

7. **D** This is a development question of the building block type. What is the most significant addition to the company's image as a responsible resource manager that is made by the concept of employees planting trees and teaching others how to care for them? Choice (C) can be eliminated quickly; it's doubtful a company in the business of felling trees would be attractive to environmentally conscious recruits. Choices (A) and (B) are true as far as they go, but this is a forestry company, so there's a more direct link than that. Choice (D) provides that direct link to the company's business by pointing out that employees help renew some of the resources the company uses.

Literary Passage Drill (Page 215)

1. **C** To reach the correct answer for this structure question, you need to understand how the passage as a whole is built and then translate that understanding into a graphic shape. Think about the narrators: The passage begins with a first-person ("I") narrator who is talking to the Leopard Man; then the Leopard Man takes over the narration as he tells the story of Wallace and De Ville. It's (C)—a frame (the Leopard Man's story) within a frame (the first-person narrator's story about talking to the Leopard Man). None of the other shapes describes the structural characteristics of the passage. It doesn't begin with a large-scale picture and filter down to particular events or characters, (A). It doesn't lead the reader through a confusing trail of dream sequences or shifts in time periods, (B), and it doesn't keep circling back around the same circumstance, (D).

2. **D** Here we're looking at the author's purpose in giving such a detailed account of the Leopard Man's boredom. The Leopard Man doesn't think taming big cats is exciting or dangerous, he shrugs off his injuries and, for an hour, he can't even think of a thrilling circus story to tell the narrator. His attitude doesn't seem suited to his profession and neither does his small, weak physical build. The author considered that important enough to devote a lot of effort to conveying it. Why?

   Let's start with Process of Elimination. Eliminate (A) because it's not the author's purpose to inform us about any profession; the passage focuses only on this one individual. Eliminate (B) because it's not the author's purpose to blame the Leopard Man's attitude on the result of aging, but rather to contrast that attitude with his profession. Choice (C) has some truth to it: Big, fearless Wallace the lion tamer is gone, and the feeble, bored Leopard Man is still here. That's not the most important goal achieved by the detailed description of the Leopard Man, though.

   The answer is (D). The narrator says, "He was the Leopard Man, but he did not look it" (paragraph 1). In the Leopard Man's story, De Ville hadn't taken his revenge for months, but that didn't mean he wasn't planning to. Things aren't always what they seem—that's one of the main points in the Leopard Man's story and in the narrator's description of the Leopard Man.

3. **C** Look at the context around the quote to find the answer to this language use question. The quote occurs right after the narrator mentions the Leopard Man's right arm, which "looked as though it had gone through a threshing machine" (paragraph 4). The quote doesn't apply to the whole man, as advancing age and boredom with a career would, so (B) and (D) are eliminated. That leaves (A) and (C), and you need to compare them carefully. The reference to "claws and fangs" suggests some type of damage, which both of those choices also suggest. Choice (A) specifies performing with leopards. In the passage, however, the Leopard Man also talks about fighting lions and a tigress. Choice (C), which refers to big cats, is therefore the correct answer.

4. **A** A couple of brief statements in the passage eliminate two choices in this comparison question. The Leopard Man admits, "I was beginning to think it all a scare over nothing" (paragraph 12) when nothing had happened for several months, so he ended up underestimating De Ville, too, eliminating (C). Wallace laughed off the Leopard Man's final warning, but "he did not look so much in Madame de Ville's direction after that" (paragraph 11), so he didn't completely ignore all warnings, eliminating (B). If you're not reading actively in a long passage such as this, it's easy to miss these little clues.

   Now we're down to (A) and (D). Wallace "was afraid of nothing alive or dead" (paragraph 9), but there's no indication that he relied on physical strength for his courage, and the Leopard Man mentions only De Ville's quick temper, not his cleverness, so (D) is out. That leaves (A). The Leopard Man let his guard down after several months passed without any sign of revenge from De Ville, and Wallace let his guard down in the dressing tent; he was "too busy to notice" (paragraph 13) De Ville's look of hatred or De Ville passing close behind him.

5. **Order of events: (d), (g), (a), (b), (e)**
   This plot development question is trickier than most because some of the events didn't happen in the passage. There are eight events and only five spots in the chart, so first try to eliminate the three that didn't occur. Those are the third one (c) (the Leopard Man, not Wallace, notices the hatred), the fifth event (f) (Wallace never tries to talk to De Ville), and the last one (h) (De Ville never reveals his intention to anyone).

Now you're ready to select the order of the five events that do take place in the passage. De Ville's wife looking at Wallace is what starts the whole chain of events, so that's the first one (d). Warnings from several people in the circus follow (g), and then Wallace stops looking at De Ville's wife after the Leopard Man gives his final warning (a)—those are the second and third events, respectively. The fourth event occurs when the Leopard Man watches De Ville walk behind Wallace, to plant the snuff (b). Augustus sneezing is what finishes Wallace off (e), so that's the last one.

6. **B** In this evaluation question, you need to consider whether anything in the plot doesn't "add up."

   There is some question of support in (A). There is no apparent relationship that would prompt the Leopard Man to care enough about Wallace's fate to warn him. On the other hand, there's no reason he wouldn't, either, especially when other people in the circus were giving warnings too. So let's eliminate (A)—we're looking for the *weakest* support. Choice (C) is supported: Wallace isn't afraid of anything. Choice (D) is supported too. Augustus didn't intend to bite Wallace's head off; he simply sneezed.

   So we're left with (B). De Ville's months of hatred followed by his grisly revenge aren't explained in the passage. We're simply told that De Ville is quick to anger, not that he holds a grudge for months despite a correction in the behavior that caused it.

7. **A** This is a version of the main idea or theme question as it applies to a literary passage. After reading all of the details, from your 10,000-foot perch, what moral is the author conveying in this passage?

   Process of Elimination leads smoothly to the correct answer. There's no indication of a struggle with nature in the passage. The only "nature" is indicated by the big cats, who are represented as easy to manage (paragraph 3) or completely trusted (paragraph 8). That eliminates (B). Choice (C) is close: Wallace laughed off warnings about De Ville. However, he didn't see De Ville as an opponent, either, which eliminates this answer. Choice (D) is too general. In being attracted to another man's wife, Wallace may have been thinking the grass would be greener on the other side of the fence—a fatal error, in this case. However, that wouldn't necessarily apply in every situation, eliminating (D).

   So we're left with (A). Wallace has the advantage in size and fearlessness (brawn), but De Ville has the advantage in brains, and that's what defeats Wallace. De Ville waits months before taking his revenge, lulling even the Leopard Man into a sense of false security; then he figures out how to get the trusted Augustus to do the job for him.

Language

Language Drill (Page 239)

The fourth choice is correct for the first drop-down question:

The harsh winter kept people at home more <u>this year, too, which meant fewer customers, even on weekends.</u>

The first answer presents a problem with word choice. "Less" is used for things that can't be counted or for units of measurement (e.g., He has less time than expected to complete the project.); "fewer" for people or things. This answer is also missing the signal word "too." While that's not necessarily a mistake, the signal word does improve clarity by helping the reader understand that the writer is building up points to support his explanation for the loss of business.

The second choice is too wordy. (A harsh winter most likely would have an effect since the beginning of the winter.) The third choice is wrong because there is no reason to capitalize "customers."

The second choice is correct for the second drop-down question.

I participated in a local trade fair, the recent "Home Grown Goodness" food exhibition, and sponsored a booth for a local charity at the fall fair.

The first choice (starting the sentence with "Participating" instead of "I participated," and then beginning a new sentence with "I sponsored") results in a sentence fragment. The third choice fails to set off the apposition with commas. (The trade fair and the "Home Grown Goodness" food exhibition refer to the same thing and perform the same function in the sentence.) This is the only choice that does not have those commas, which suggests that it's incorrect. The fourth choice has a couple of problems: The structure isn't parallel with the first part of the sentence, and the antecedent of "we" isn't clear.

The first choice is correct for the third drop-down question:

I would, of course, welcome any suggestions you can offer.

The second choice is not a complete sentence. (A dependent clause starting with "although" cannot stand alone.) The third choice has a dangling modifier. (The modifier, "Welcoming any suggestions...," does not describe the subject of the sentence, "you." It describes the writer.) The third choice is also wordy. ("Suggestions" and "ideas" refer to the same thing.) The fourth choice is an ugly run-on sentence and is not consistent with the formal tone of the rest of the email.

In the final drop-down question, the third choice is correct:

However, I hope that my excellent credit record and my long business relationship with your bank would make me eligible for special consideration.

The first choice contains two pronoun errors: agreement ("their" is plural and bank is singular) and an unclear antecedent (it's not even clear whether the pronoun is supposed to refer to the bank). Switching from "I" to the third-person pronoun, "their," also creates a lack of parallel structure. The second choice is wordy (of course he was doing business with the bank during a long business relationship). It's also the only choice in which the transition word "however" is missing. That transition word improves clarity by marking a change in direction. The final choice lacks parallel structure again: It changes from a noun (the writer's credit record) to a verb ("I have").

Extended Response Drills

These two drills present different challenges that you might encounter in the Extended Response section. Below you'll find suggested approaches to these challenges, and chains of reasoning you might follow in creating your responses to the prompts.

Electric Vehicles Extended Response Drill (Page 273)

Building the Argument Use active reading to note each side's arguments and support in the charts. That evidence is quite clearly laid out in these passages although, as you'll read below, it's challenging because the authors' purposes are so different. Your chart might look like the one below.

Pro side (government document):

Argument	Support
increased energy security (Paragraph 3)	cars are 70% of U.S. petroleum consumption (Paragraph 2)
better fuel economy (Paragraphs 4 and 5)	lower energy costs (Paragraph 5)
flexible fueling (Paragraph 6)	different charging locations, gas for PHEVs (Paragraph 6)
lower costs (Paragraph 8)	future price reductions, government incentives (Paragraph 8)
lower emissions (Paragraph 9)	none for EVs, lower for HEVs and PHEVs (Paragraph 9)

Con side (father's letter)

Argument	Support
limited range (Paragraph 14)	250 miles (Paragraph 14)
few charging stations (Paragraph 14)	2,000 in Texas (Paragraph 14)
long charging time (Paragraph 14)	8 hours (Paragraph 14)
high costs (Paragraph 15)	parts, batteries (5 years), initial price (2x) (Paragraph 15)
environmentally unfriendly (Paragraph 16)	mining of rare-earth minerals (Paragraph 16)
catch fire (Paragraph 17)	unspecified news reports (Paragraph 17)

Choosing Your Thesis Both sides give several arguments (although Dad has one more than the U.S. government). With one exception (the unspecified news reports of fires), the father also backs up his arguments with specific figures. The government document does in most cases, too, though. The U.S. government has more credibility as an author (one would hope the Department of Energy has professional experts who supplied the data), but the Office of Energy Efficiency and Renewable Energy also has a vested interest in promoting electric vehicles. Dad, on the other hand, has a parent's genuine passion for protecting his child.

One factor that might give the edge to the Department of Energy is the scope of its concern (the well-being of the nation) as opposed to the father's concern for one person. Other factors that weaken the father's case are his reasoning and his assumptions. His visions of Melissa hanging around an isolated charging station all night and sleeping unaware while her car burns outside seem alarmist; he doesn't provide any evidence to justify those leaps from electric vehicles to an endangered daughter. You could add to that the self-interest evident in his remark that, with the concern about safety on the highway, Melissa wouldn't be able to drive home to visit her parents.

If you think you could make a better case for the father's side being better supported, that would not be a wrong choice for a thesis. The Extended Response passages are designed to allow you to argue either side successfully. However, giving the edge to the government does seem an easier thesis to prove.

Organizing Your Argument Organizing specific pieces of evidence is a challenge in this example, since the authors' purposes (and therefore their arguments) don't overlap. Dad isn't the least bit concerned with the government's purpose (fostering energy security), and the government doesn't address the father's goal (safety).

The only minor overlap occurs in the discussion of cost; however, both sides approach that issue from different directions. For the government, the high initial cost of a vehicle is an acknowledged problem. (Any argument that acknowledges an opponent's position gains some credibility.) This cost disadvantage can be offset by lower fuel costs and government subsidies, it argues. The father doesn't mention those offsetting factors, and you have to wonder if he's concerned about having to subsidize repairs or a replacement battery down the road.

Given the general lack of overlap and the fact that cost isn't the main argument for either side, the best approach would be to discuss the evidence that proves your thesis first (the government's arguments) and then point out the alarmist reasoning and unsupported assumptions that weaken the father's case.

Writing the Essay You might take advantage of the two different purposes as an attention-getting opening question for your essay: "Energy security or driver safety: Which goal should decide the choice of a new car?" Your thesis statement and the high-level list of evidence come next: "In these two passages, the U.S. Department of Energy argues that electric vehicles would help protect the nation's energy supply, while a father raises rather alarmist concerns for his daughter's safety. The government's position is better supported by virtue of its credibility and the nationwide scope of its concerns about energy security and lower emissions."

That's the first paragraph. You'd likely end up with a four-paragraph essay here and that's fine, as long as your points are clearly organized in the middle two paragraphs. The second paragraph would discuss the evidence from the government's position, and the third paragraph would outline the evidence from the father's position, pointing out its weaknesses. As always, the final paragraph would restate the thesis in different words and remind readers about the evidence that proves the thesis.

Antibiotics in Farm Animal Feed Extended Response Drill (Page 276)

Building the Argument Here's a different version of the argument/support chart, with the arguments lined up beside each other. Arranging the chart in this way can help you decide which side you could do a better job of arguing.

For the ban (FDA media release)		Against the ban (online forum posting)	
Argument	Support	Argument	Support
contributes to antibiotic resistance; raises the fatality rate for diseases that don't respond to antibiotics (Paragraph 3)	• all uses do (not just agriculture) (Paragraph 3) • world governments consider antibiotic-resistant diseases a major public health threat (Paragraph 3) • may not be preventable but need to slow it down (Paragraph 5) • using drugs that are also used in humans means they won't work in humans (Paragraph 4) • resistant bacteria entering food system can be transferred to people (Paragraph 7) • voluntary ban because it's faster (Paragraph 8) • working with the industry (Paragraph 8) • authority of FDA name (Paragraph 8)	harmful effects not proven (Paragraph 11)	• studies inconclusive (Paragraph 11) • doctors overprescribing and unsafe food handling to blame (Paragraph 11) • hasn't reduced superbugs in Europe (Paragraph 12) • ban would be mandatory if FDA were sure (Paragraph 11)
		cost saving (Paragraph 10)	• cheaper to prevent disease (Paragraph 10)
		faster time to market at lower cost (Paragraph 10)	• faster weight gain using less feed (Paragraph 10)
		meet growing demand for food, lower costs for consumers, make exports competitive (Paragraphs 12, 13, and 14)	• farmer feeds 155 people (6x increase) due to more efficient production (Paragraph 13)

Choosing Your Thesis Breaking these two passages down into an argument/support chart is quite revealing. The FDA has only one main reason for its pro-ban position, and it undercuts even that with statements such as "Antimicrobial resistance may not be completely preventable" (paragraph 5) and "even appropriate therapeutic uses of antibiotics can promote the development of drug-resistant bacteria" (paragraph 7). Its strongest points are the weight of the FDA name and the fact that it has been working with stakeholders across the industry (drug companies, producers, veterinarians, and consumer groups).

On the other hand, the anti-ban side lays out four main reasons for its position. It counters the FDA's argument by pointing to studies that don't prove the link between antibiotic use and superbugs, as well as blaming other culprits (doctors who overprescribe antibiotics and consumers who don't handle food safely). The main argument of the anti-ban side, however, is economic: Adding antibiotics to feed allows farmers to feed more people at a lower cost, keeps food prices low for consumers, and makes agricultural exports competitive. The FDA doesn't even mention, let alone refute, those reasons. It also neglects an argument that would strengthen its own position: It makes only an indirect reference to the high cost (in human lives) of antibiotic-resistant diseases, and makes no mention of high costs to the health care system.

Regardless of your own opinion on the issue, it might be easier, looking at an argument/support analysis of the passage, to claim that the anti-ban side is better supported. Let's call that your "for" side. The writer refutes the FDA's reason for the ban and presents three economic reasons in favor of using antibiotics for growth and feed efficiency, including a specific number for the increase in farmers' productivity (155 people fed). The case would be even better supported if the author had cited specific studies and dollar figures.

Organizing Your Argument It would be ideal if each side's points lined up neatly, so you could discuss why your "for" side's Point A is better supported than your "against" side's Point A. Unfortunately, that doesn't usually happen.

In this example, you would have to include your "against" side's argument in favor of its position, since it makes only one and the prompt tells you to draw evidence from *both* passages. Luckily, your "for" side presents its case about the same point—the increase (proven or unproven) in antibiotic-resistant diseases as a result of antibiotics in farm animal feed. So that would be the first piece of evidence you'd discuss.

Your "for" side makes three more arguments, all of them tied to economic factors. It presents the strongest support for the argument about meeting the growing demand for food through more efficient production, since it gives a specific figure (the increase in the number of people fed per farmer) to support that argument. You'd discuss that point next, then.

The last two arguments can be combined neatly: Lower costs and faster time to market for the farmer mean lower food prices for consumers and more competitive exports. You might point out (if it occurred to you) that the FDA failed to present the economic argument it could have made: higher health care costs as a result of antibiotic-resistant illnesses. That would allow you to draw some more evidence for your thesis from the FDA passage.

Writing the Essay So now you have the thesis—the anti-ban case is better supported—and a plan for organizing your evidence.

It's time to start writing, using the template. The anti-ban author even provides a strong "startling fact" opening for your essay: "Each American farmer today feeds an average of 155 people, *six times* more than in 1960" (paragraph 13). Of course, you'd paraphrase this in your essay ("According to the online farmers' forum posting, each farmer feeds six times more people today than in 1960") or else put it in quotation marks with the paragraph reference.

Then you'd state your thesis (that the anti-ban position is the best supported) and briefly mention the evidence noted in your chart. You might say something like, "That increased productivity is the chief argument in favor of adding antibiotics to farm animal feed. It's the best supported argument, since it explains that the higher productivity leads to meeting ever-increasing demand for food and keeping costs low for both domestic and export customers. The side arguing for a ban on antibiotics doesn't support its one argument with credible evidence that the practice leads to the rise of antibiotic-resistant illnesses. In fact, it even undercuts its own argument by suggesting alternate causes for these illnesses."

The next three paragraphs—each one beginning with a topic sentence—will discuss the arguments you just mentioned (the antibiotic-resistant illnesses in paragraph 11, the higher productivity in paragraph 10, and the cost disadvantages in paragraph 12). In each paragraph, remember to explain *how* that evidence supports your thesis. The final paragraph should restate your thesis in different words and wrap up your argument by summarizing the points you just made in the middle of the essay.

Reviewing Your Work Now, while you're practicing, you have time to ask yourself the questions listed in Chapter 10 (see page 251) to assess your own work. During the test, of course, you won't. Then you'll be reviewing your essay to revise it (Is something not clear? Is there a better way to say it?) and edit it (correcting grammar and spelling errors).

MATHEMATICAL REASONING

Number Line Drill (Page 296)

1. **less than** Just use the values you were given to find the values of points A and B. A is –4 and B is –1, so A is less.

2. **C** To find the distance, count the number of steps between A and B. The answer is 3. Remember that distance must always be a positive number.

3. **C** Count the number of spaces between A and D. You should have counted 9. Half of 9 is $4\frac{1}{2}$. Count over $4\frac{1}{2}$ to the right of point A or $4\frac{1}{2}$ to the left of point D. In either case, the midpoint is between 0 and 1.

Rounding Drill (Page 298)

1. **3,000** In 3,400, the number after the thousands place is 4, so round down.

2. **3.5** In 3.46, the number after the tenths place is 6, so round up.

3. **600** In 565, the number after the hundreds place is 6, so round up.

4. **$433** In $432.70, the number after the dollars is 7, so round up.

5. **4.80** This number already has a zero in the hundredths place.

Adding, Subtracting, Multiplying, and Dividing Positive and Negative Numbers Drill (Page 302)

1. **2** $5 + (-3) = 2$: Adding a positive number and a negative number results in subtraction.

2. **–11** $(-4) + (-7) = -11$: Adding two negative numbers results in a negative sum.

3. **18** $6 \times 3 = 18$: Multiplication of two positive numbers results in a positive product.

4. **–12** $(-2)(6) = -12$. Multiplying a negative by a positive always yields a negative.

5. **1** $(-3) - (2) + (6) = 1$. Subtracting a positive number (2) from a negative number (–3) is the same thing as adding two negative numbers: –5. Add that result to 6 and you get 1.

6. **5** $10 \div 2 = 5$: Division of a positive number by a positive number results in a positive quotient.

7. **10** $(-5)(-2) = 10$. Multiplying a negative by a negative always yields a positive.

8. **3** $-21 \div -7 = 3$. Dividing a negative by a negative always yields a positive.

9. **–4** $12 \div -3 = -4$. Dividing a positive by a negative or a negative by a positive always yields a negative.

10. **–4** $-12 \div 3 = -4$: Division of a negative number by a positive number results in a negative quotient.

Absolute Values Drill (Page 303)

1. **4** The number 4 is four units from the number 0 on the number line, so $|4| = 4$.

2. **7** The number –7 is seven units from the number 0 on the number line, so $|-7| = 7$.

3. **4** The number 6 is four units to the right of 2 on the number line, so $|6 - 2| = 4$. Alternatively, $6 - 2 = 4$, so $|6 - 2| = |4|$. Since 4 is four units from 0 on the number line, $|4| = 4$. Either way, $|6 - 2| = 4$.

4. **2** The number 3 is two units to the left of 5 on the number line, so $|3 - 5| = 2$. Alternatively, $3 - 5 = -2$, so $|3 - 5| = |-2|$. Since –2 is two units from 0 on the number line, $|-2| = 2$. Either way, $|3 - 5| = 2$.

5. **10 or –10** $|x| = 10$, so x is 10 units from 0 on the number line. It cannot be determined whether x is 10 units to the left or 10 units to the right of 0, so consider both possibilities. If x is 10 units to the left of 0, then subtract 10 from 0 to get $x = 0 - 10 = -10$. If x is 10 units to the right of 0, then add 10 to 0 to get $x = 0 + 10 = 10$. Therefore, $x = 10$ or -10.

6. **4 or 14** $|y - 9| = 5$, so y is five units from 9 on the number line. It cannot be determined whether y is five units to the left or five units to the right of 9, so consider both possibilities. If y is five units to the left of 9, then subtract 5 from 9 to get $y = 9 - 5 = 4$. If y is five units to the right of 9, then add 5 to 9 to get $y = 9 + 5 = 14$. Therefore, $y = 4$ or 14.

Order of Operations and Commutative and Distributive Properties Drill (Page 308)

Use **PEMDAS** for these.

1. **–3** $5(3 - 4) + 2 = 5(-1) + 2 = -5 + 2 = -3$: First, solve the expression inside the parentheses, then multiply by 5, and finally add 2.

2. **42** $7 \times 2 \times 3 = 42$: Multiply each number together sequentially.

3. **–12** $3(3 - 1 - 2) + 6(2 - 4) = 3(0) + 6(-2) = 0 - 12 = -12$: First, solve the expressions inside the parentheses, then multiply each expression by the respective coefficient, and finally add the results.

4. **–64** $8(4[3 - 5]) = 8(4[-2]) = 8(-8) = -64$: First, solve the expression inside the innermost parentheses, then multiply by 4, and finally multiply by 8.

5. **3** $\frac{1}{4}(3) + \frac{1}{4}(9) = \frac{1}{4}(3 + 9) = \frac{1}{4}(12) = 3$

Factors and Multiples Drill (Page 311)

1. **1, 2, 3, 4, 6, 9, 12, 18, 36**
Start from the outside and work to the inside. Every number has 1 and itself as factors so 1 and 36 are factors. Now try 2. 36 ÷ 2 = 18, so 2 and 18 are factors. Now try 3. 36 ÷ 3 = 12, so 3 and 12 are factors. Now try 4. 36 ÷ 4 = 9, so 4 and 9 are factors. Now try 5. 36 ÷ 5 is a decimal, so 5 is not a factor. Try 6. 36 ÷ 6 = 6, so 6 is a factor. Since 6 has been repeated, stop here. The factors are 1, 2, 3, 4, 6, 9, 12, 18, and 36.

2. **1, 43**
Start on the outside and work to the inside. Every number has 1 and itself as factors so 1 and 43 are factors. Now try 2. 43 ÷ 2 is a decimal, so 2 is not a factor. 43 ÷ 3 is also a decimal, so 3 is not a factor. 43 ÷ 4 is also a decimal, so 4 is not a factor. 43 ÷ 5 is also a decimal, so 5 is not a factor. 43 ÷ 6 is also a decimal, so 6 is not a factor. Continue through 42 to find that there are no other factors. Therefore, the only factors are 1 and 43.

3. **1, 2, 4, 5, 8, 10, 16, 20, 40, 80**
Start on the outside and work to the inside: 1 and 80, 2 and 40, 4 and 20, 5 and 16, 8 and 10. Since 3, 6, 7, and 9 do not divide 80 evenly, these are not factors. Since the next number after 9 is 10, which is already on the list of factors, there are no other factors. The only factors are 1, 2, 4, 5, 8, 10, 16, 20, 40, and 80.

4. **7, 14, 21, 28, 35, 42, 49, 56, 63, 70**
One way to find the first 10 positive multiples of a number is to multiply the number by all the whole numbers from 1 through 10. 7 × 1 = 7. 7 × 2 = 14. 7 × 3 = 21. 7 × 4 = 28. 7 × 5 = 35. 7 × 6 = 42. 7 × 7 = 49. 7 × 8 = 56. 7 × 9 = 63. 7 × 10 = 70. Therefore, the first 10 positive multiplies of 10 are 7, 14, 21, 28, 35, 42, 49, 56, 63, and 70.

5. **9, 18, 27, 36, 45, 54, 63, 72, 81, 90**
One way to find the first 10 positive multiples of a number is to start with the number itself, and then add the number 9 more times. In this case, start with 9, as 9 is a multiple of itself. Add 9 to get 18. Add 9 to get 27. Add 9 to get 36. Add 9 to get 45. Add 9 to get 54. Add 9 to get 63. Add 9 to get 72. Add 9 to get 81. Add 9 to get 90. Therefore, the first 10 positive multiples of 9 are 9, 18, 27, 36, 45, 54, 63, 72, 81, and 90.

6. **16** Start by finding the factors of 32: 1 and 32, 2 and 16, and 4 and 8. Now, find the factors of 80: 1 and 80, 2 and 40, 4 and 20, 5 and 16, and 8 and 10. The common factors are 1, 2, 4, 8, and 16. The greatest of the common factors is 16. As a shortcut, first get the factors of 32, and then use the outside to inside method for finding factors of 80. The first common factor that is the greater number of a pair of factors must be the GCF. In this case, the first pair is 1 and 80. 80 is not a common factor. The second pair is 2 and 40. 40 is not a common factor. The third pair is 4 and 20. 20 is not a common factor. The fourth pair is 5 and 16. Since 16 is a common factor, 16 is the GCF.

7. **63** List the multiples of 9 until one is also a multiple of 7. The first six positive multiples of 9 are 9, 18, 27, 36, 45, and 54. None of these are multiples of 7. The next multiple, however, is 63, which is a multiple of 7. Therefore, 63 is a common multiple of 7 and 9. Any other common multiple has to be greater, so 63 must be the least common multiple.

8. **24** Find the factors of 24: 1 and 24, 2 and 12, 3 and 8, and 4 and 6. Now begin to use the outside to inside method to find the common factors of 48. The first pair is 1 and 48. Since 48 is not a factor of 24, it is not the GCF. The next pair is 2 and 24. Since 24 is also a factor of 24, it is a common factor. The only greater factor of 48 is 48, which is not a common factor. Therefore, the greatest common factor of 24 and 48 must be 24.

9. **48** List the multiples of 48 until one is also a multiple of 24. 48 is a multiple of itself. 48 ÷ 24 is a whole number, so 48 is a multiple of 24. Therefore, 48 is a common multiple and must be the least common multiple of 24 and 48.

Reducing Fractions Drill (Page 314)

1. $\mathbf{\frac{3}{4}}$ Divide top and bottom by 3.

2. $\mathbf{\frac{1}{3}}$ Divide top and bottom by 11.

3. $\mathbf{\frac{2}{5}}$ Divide top and bottom by 7.

4. $\mathbf{\frac{4}{9}}$ This fraction can't be reduced. If you said $\frac{2}{3}$, you found the square root of top and bottom by mistake.

5. $\mathbf{\frac{15}{8}}$ This fraction can't be reduced.

Adding and Subtracting Fractions Drill (Page 317)

1. $\frac{4}{5}$ Use the Bowtie method.

2. $\frac{48}{35}$ 35 is the common denominator.

3. $\mathbf{\frac{5}{12}}$ 12 is the common denominator.

4. $\frac{5}{9}$ If you use the Bowtie for the first two numbers, you will already have the same denominator as the third number. The answer is $\frac{10}{18}$, which reduces to $\frac{5}{9}$.

5. $-\frac{1}{21}$ 21 is the common denominator. You can have a negative fraction!

Multiplying, Dividing, and Converting Fractions Drill (Page 320)

1. $\frac{3}{10}$ First reduce the 4 on top and the 8 on bottom.

2. $\frac{3}{2}$ Invert and multiply. But before you multiply, divide top and bottom by 3 and then by 5.

3. $\frac{10}{54}$ **or** $\frac{5}{27}$ Invert and multiply, but before you multiply, divide top and bottom by 2.

4. $\frac{2}{5}$ Cancel the 3s and the 4s, and you won't have to multiply at all!

5. $\frac{1}{2}$ First, convert $1\frac{1}{3}$ to an improper fraction: $\frac{4}{3}$. Then cancel the 3s.

Fraction Word Problem Drill (Page 323)

1. **C** Half of the 80 people tested originally had Lyme disease—that's 40 people. Of the other 40 people, one-quarter later developed Lyme disease. One-quarter of 40 is 10. So a total of 50 got Lyme disease out of 80 people: $\frac{50}{80}=\frac{5}{8}$.

2. **August: 110. September: 121.**
One-tenth of 100 is 10, so in August they baked 110 pies. In September they increased production by another tenth. One-tenth of 110 is 11. So in September, they baked 110 + 11 pies, or 121.

3. $\frac{4}{15}$ To work with these fractions, you need to find a common denominator: $\frac{1}{3}=\frac{5}{15}$ and $\frac{2}{5}=\frac{6}{15}$. So if $\frac{5}{15}$ go by public transportation, and $\frac{6}{15}$ go by car, that adds up to $\frac{11}{15}$—which means that $\frac{4}{15}$ walk to work.

Decimals Drill (Page 326)

1. **7.06**

2. **4.36**

3. **8.194** Forget the decimals and just multiply. Then add up the number of digits to the right of the decimals in the original numbers. That is how many places to move the decimal to the left in your new number.

4. **3,200** Set this up like a normal division problem. Then move the decimal place of the divisor as many times as it takes to turn the divisor into an integer. Now move the decimal in the dividend the same number of places, and divide as usual. You end up with 6,400 ÷ 2 = 3,200.

5. **40** Using the same methods you used in question 4, you end up with 320 ÷ 8 = 40.

Percents Drill (Page 331)

1. **16.6** Move the decimal over one place to the left, and then multiply by 2.

2. **4.5** Move the decimal over one place to the left, and then multiply by 3.

3. **288** Move the decimal over one place to the left, and then multiply by 4.

4. **2.1** Move the decimal over two places to the left, and then multiply by 3.

5. **9** Move the decimal over one place to the left (that's 10 percent), and then divide in half.

6. 100 + 15 = **115**

7. 9.8 + 4.9 = **14.7**

8. 3(14) + 7 = **49**

9. $\frac{1}{2}$ of 62 = **31**

10. $\frac{1}{4}$ of 144 = **36**

Percent Word Problems Drill (Page 335)

1. **greater than** Option X is 8% of $650, or $52. Option Y is 3% of $1,500, or $45.

2. **C** Think about what's left over: 40 percent of 1,200. Choice (A) was 60 percent of 1,200, which was a partial answer.

3. **903.61** Add the individual prices to get $120 + $635 + $74 = $829. Next, calculate $829 plus 9 percent of $829, or $74.61, for a total of $903.61.

4. **D** The \$8,437.50 for the year before is a red herring: It doesn't have anything to do with this problem. The best way to do this problem is by working backward. Start with (B). What is 60 percent of \$6,750? It's only \$4,050, which is less than the \$5,400 you're looking for. Go ahead and eliminate (A) and (B). Choice (D) is the next easiest answer to check. What is 80 percent of \$6,750? That's right, it's \$5,400. The answer to this problem is (D).

Basic Arithmetic Drill (Page 337)

1. **0.6 and $\frac{9}{15}$** To get the decimal, just divide 5 into 3, or think "one-fifth = 0.2, so three-fifths = 0.6."

   To get the fraction, multiply the numerator and the denominator by 3 to get the fraction $\frac{9}{15}$.

2. **greater than** The total bill is \$14.65 + \$1.47 = \$16.12, so 20 percent is \$3.22. This is much greater than the amount of the tax, \$1.47.

3. **C** When the boat traveled 30 miles in 2 hours, we can think about it like this: how far does the boat travel in one hour? Divide the total distance (30 miles) by the total time (2 hours). So, the boat travels at a speed of 15 miles per hour. If the boat travels 15 miles in one hour, how many hours will it take to travel 72 miles? Divide the total distance (72 miles) by the speed (15 miles per hour). It takes the boat 4.8 hours to travel 72 miles, (C).

4. **B** Add $\frac{1}{4}$ and $\frac{1}{5}$, but look out for (A): It is a partial answer. We want what is left over, so subtract this from 1.

5. 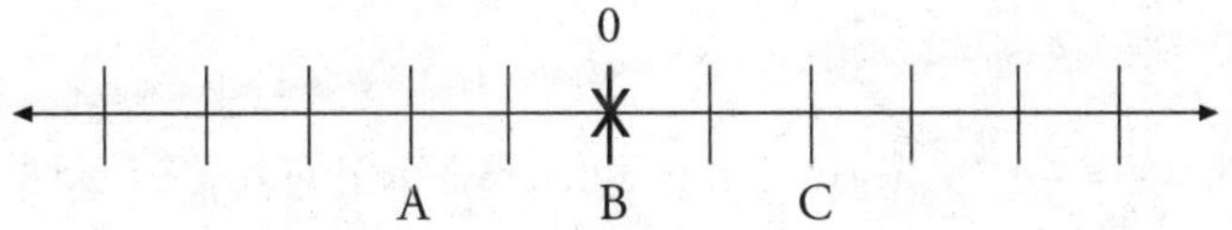

6. **C** 11 percent of \$275 is \$30.25. Add the two amounts (\$275 + \$30.25) to find the total, \$305.25, and then divide by 12. The answer is \$25.43, which rounds to \$25.00, (C).

7. **C** Use the distributive property to get $5(R - S) = 35$. Divide both sides of the equation by 5 to get $R - S = 7$.

8. **–1** Use PEMDAS. Start by simplifying the expressions inside the parentheses:

   Inside the first set of parentheses: 2 – 4 + 1 = –2 + 1 = –1
   Inside the second set of parentheses: 7 – 1 = 6

   Now, substitute these simplified expressions back into the original equation: $5(-1) + \frac{2}{3}(6)$

   Next, perform the multiplications:
   For 5(–1), multiply 5 by –1 to get –5.
   For $\frac{2}{3}(6)$, multiply $\frac{2}{3}$ by 6 to get 4.

Now, substitute these results back into the equation: –5 + 4
Finally, perform the addition: –5 + 4 = –1

So, the solution to the equation $5(2 - 4 + 1) + \frac{2}{3}(7 - 1) = ?$ is –1.

9. **C** $\frac{30}{70} = \frac{3}{7} = 0.4285$, which you can round up to 43 percent. Ballparking shows it will be just under 50 percent.

10. **D** We can eliminate (A) and (B) because they are less than the amount paid. This is a good problem to do backward. Let's start with (D), $12,000. What is 80 percent of $12,000? You guessed it: $9,600.

11. $\mathbf{-\frac{4}{3}, -0.8, -\frac{1}{4}, 0.5, \frac{11}{8}, 2}$

The question asks you to place fractions, decimals, and a whole number on a number line. Since decimals are easier to order than fractions, convert the fractions into decimals. Turn $-\frac{4}{3}$ into a decimal by dividing 4 by 3 to get

$$\begin{array}{r} 1.\overline{33} \\ 3\overline{)4.00} \\ \underline{3\,0} \\ 10 \\ \underline{9} \\ 10 \end{array}$$

Bringing in the negative sign, $-\frac{4}{3} = -1.\overline{33}$. Turn $-\frac{1}{4}$ into a decimal by dividing 1 by 4 to get

$$\begin{array}{r} 0.25 \\ 4\overline{)1.00} \\ \underline{8} \\ 20 \end{array}$$

Bringing in the negative sign, $-\frac{1}{4} = -0.25$. Turn $\frac{11}{8}$ into a decimal by dividing 11 by 8 to get

$$\begin{array}{r} 1.375 \\ 8\overline{)11.00} \\ \underline{8} \\ 30 \\ \underline{24} \\ 60 \\ \underline{56} \\ 40 \end{array}$$

so $\frac{11}{8} = 1.375$. Therefore, in decimal terms, the six numbers are 2, 0.5, $-1.\overline{33}$, –0.8, –0.25, and 1.375.

Put these in order from least to greatest to get $-1.\overline{33}$, –0.8, –0.25, 0.5, 1.375, and 2. Place these in the boxes from left to right. The correct answer is $-\frac{4}{3}$, –0.8, $-\frac{1}{4}$, 0.5, $\frac{11}{8}$, and 2.

12. **A** This question requires a few operations, including absolute value. We need to find the absolute value first.

$$|6 - (-5)| = |11| = 11$$

So this lets us simplify our problem to 14 – 11 × 3.

PEMDAS tells us that we need to multiply before subtracting.

11 × 3 = 33

So that gives us 14 – 33 = –19.

13. **D** The question asks for the sum of the factors of 14. Start on the outside and work inward. 1 and 14 are factors of 14. Since 14 ÷ 2 = 7, 2 and 7 are factors. Since 14 ÷ 3 is a decimal, 3 is not a factor. Since 14 ÷ 4 is a decimal, 4 is not a factor. Since 14 ÷ 5 is a decimal, 5 is not a factor. Since 14 ÷ 6 is a decimal, 6 is not a factor. Since 7 is already on the list, the list is complete. Therefore, the factors are 1, 2, 7, and 14, and the sum of the factors is 1 + 2 + 7 + 14 = 24. The correct answer is (D).

14. **C** The question asks for which choice is NOT a multiple of 4. Divide each choice by 4. Any choice that can be divided evenly by 4 is a multiple. Choice (A) is 4. Since 4 ÷ 4 = 1, then 4 is a multiple of 4. Choice (B) is 12. Since 12 ÷ 4 = 3, then 12 is a multiple of 4. Choice (C) is 34, and 34 ÷ 4 = 8.5. Since this is a decimal, 34 is not a multiple. The correct answer is (C).

Setup Drill (Page 342)

1. **A** 8 times 6 times 4 times $20.

2. **B** The new cost is the old cost ($12,000) plus 0.04 times the old cost.

Mean, Median, Mode, Range, and Weighted Mean Drill (Page 350)

1. **327.60** An average is always equal to the sum of all the elements divided by the number of elements. So $\$23.40 = \frac{x}{14}$. Therefore, x = $23.40 times 14, or $327.60.

Student Test Scores

2.

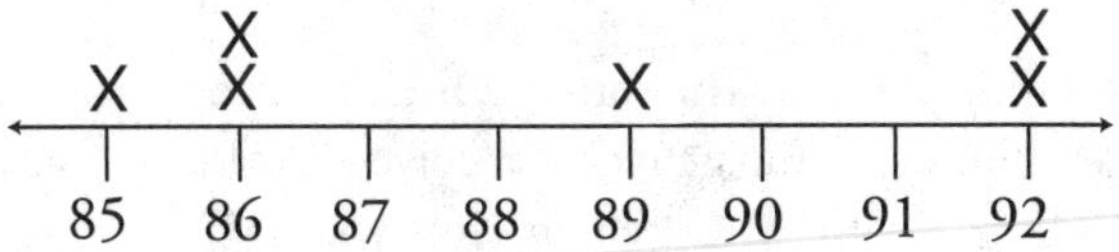

3. **C** Subtract the smallest amount, $35.77, from the largest amount, $73.23, to get $37.46.

4. **D** Add up the total number of cones and divide by the number of days: 595 divided by 5 = 119.

5. **B** Arrange the values in increasing order and then find the middle value.

6. **C** Calculate the total points Olivia earned on the in-class tests:

$$83 + 95 + 93 + 84 + 92 = 447$$

Calculate the average score for the in-class tests:

$$\text{Average score on in-class tests} = \frac{\text{Total points}}{\text{Number of tests}} = \frac{447}{5} = 89.4$$

Next, calculate the weighted average of Olivia's overall grade:

$$\begin{aligned}\text{Weighted average} &= (\text{Average score on in-class tests} \times 0.5) + (\text{Midterm score} \times 0.25) + (\text{Final score} \times 0.25)\\ &= (89.4 \times 0.5) + (84 \times 0.25) + (90 \times 0.25)\\ &= 44.7 + 21 + 22.5\\ &= 88.2\end{aligned}$$

Since Olivia's grade is rounded to the nearest percent, her final grade in math class is 88%, (C).

Ratios and Proportions Drill (Page 355)

1. **B** Given that the shrub is 5 feet tall with a 2-foot shadow, and the tree has a 10-foot shadow, we can plug these values into the proportion:

$$\frac{5\text{ feet}}{2\text{ feet}} = \frac{\text{Height of tree}}{10\text{ feet}}$$

Now, cross-multiply and solve for the height of the tree:

$$5 \times 10 = 2 \times \text{Height of tree}$$

$$50 = 2 \times \text{Height of tree}$$

$$\text{Height of tree} = \frac{50}{2}$$

$$\text{Height of tree} = 25\text{ feet}$$

So, the height of the tree is 25 feet, which corresponds to (B).

2. **B** The ratio is 3 parts for the lyric writer to 2 parts for the music writer, making a total of 3 + 2 = 5 parts. Next, determine the value of each part. Since the music writer receives $2,500 for their 2 parts, you can calculate the value of one part by dividing $2,500 by 2, which gives you $1,250.

Now multiply the value of one part by the number of parts allocated to the lyric writer (which is 3):

Amount received by the lyric writer = $1,250 × 3 = $3,750

3. **D** Not enough information is given. Since we do not know the size of either lawn, we have no method of comparison.

Rate Problems Drill (Page 358)

1. **4** If you set this up in the $R \times T = D$ format, it looks like this: $? \times 3 = 12$. The correct answer is 4 mph.

2. **C** Just divide 5,280 by 4.

3. **D** She drives 20 miles. If we deduct the hour she spent shopping, she drove the 20 miles in one hour.

Scale and Unit Conversion Drill (Page 361)

1. **D** First find 16 percent of 200 pounds, which is 32. Then multiply by 16 to find the number of ounces.

2. **$5\frac{1}{2}$ c. flour; $2\frac{2}{3}$ c. sugar; $1\frac{1}{2}$ c. butter; 2 eggs; 7 t. baking powder; 3 t. vanilla extract**

   If each of the 16 people eats 3 cookies, that is a total of 48 cookies. The original recipe makes 24, so double all the amounts to make 48.

Charts and Graphs Drill (Page 368)

1. **B** Let's say there were 100 telephones in all. If 45 of them were regular, then that number (45) is how many times greater than the number of cellular phones (15)? The answer is 3 times greater.

2. **C** To ballpark this problem, first compare bottles A and B (which have the same number of ounces), and bottles C and D (which also contain the same number of ounces). Bottle A is cheaper than B, and bottle C is cheaper than D, so eliminate B and D. To find the exact price per ounce of each bottle, divide the price by the number of ounces. Bottle A costs 5 cents per ounce. Bottle C costs 3.3 cents per ounce. Bottle E costs 5 cents per ounce. The answer is bottle C.

3. **B** Just ballpark, based on the chart.

Exponents and Radicals Drill (Page 374)

1. **D** $2^3 = 8$. Just try out the answer choices until you find the one that equals 8.

2. **31** $27 + 4 = 31$

3. **D** $4 - 2 = 2$. Try out answers until you find the one that equals 2.

4. **A** Use your calculator! Just be sure to type it in properly:

   .04^(5/2) = .00032

Scientific Notation and Probability Drill (Page 380)

1. **C** Multiply the 2,550 by 3 to get a total lumens of 7,650. Expand the answers until you find the one that matches this.

2. **B** She has two blue dresses, so your numerator will be 2. She has a total of six dresses, so your denominator will be six. The probability is two out of six, or $\frac{1}{3}$.

3. **D** 3,400 + 41,000 = 44,400

Combinations and Permutations Drill (Page 384)

1. **D** Each choice is from a different source, so multiply the number of possibilities from each source. This is $4 \times 5 \times 8 \times 3 = 480$. The correct answer is (D).

2. **C** Each cabinet member is appointed from the same pool of candidates. Since each position is different, the order matters. Look at the number of choices for each position one at a time. There are eight candidates for vice president. After one is selected, seven candidates remain for secretary. After one is selected, six candidates remain for treasurer. Multiply these numbers to get $8 \times 7 \times 6 = 336$. The correct answer is (C).

3. **B** The teacher is choosing three team members from nine candidates. Because no positions or rankings are specified and each candidate is simply selected or not selected, order doesn't matter. Look at the number of choices for each spot on the team, one at a time. There are nine choices for the first spot, leaving eight for the second, and seven for the third. Since order doesn't matter, divide by the number of possible orderings of three team members, $3 \times 2 \times 1$. This leaves $\frac{9}{3} \times \frac{8}{2} \times \frac{7}{1} = \frac{3}{1} \times \frac{4}{1} \times \frac{7}{1} = 84$. The correct answer is (B).

Applied Arithmetic Drill (Page 386)

1. **A** In this setup problem, you need to multiply 0.08 by $5,000 for one year, and then multiply that result by 2 for two years.

2. **B** If you set this up in the rate times time format, you have $5 \times ? = 17.5$. The correct answer is $3\frac{1}{2}$ hours. You could have eliminated (C) and (D) by Ballparking.

3. **D** 50 percent of 200 people is 100 and 40 percent of 200 people is 80. Subtract the two to find the difference.

4. **D** Find the average of each answer with the three test scores given until you get an average of 90. Only (D) works. Add 94 + 88 + 85 + 93 to get 360. Divide 360 by 4 to get 90.

5. **C** Don't bother multiplying further than you have to—it's clear (A) is way too big, for example. Five squared is 25 and the square root of 9 is 3. These values have a difference of 22, which is equivalent to (C).

6. **B** The square root of 9 is 3. This is the closest the answer choices come to the square root of 10.

7. $\frac{2}{7}$ There is a total of 7 possible cars. There are 2 sedans. The probability is 2 out of 7.

8. **12** Rearrange the numbers in ascending order. The middle number is 12.

9. **B** To answer this setup problem, just convert the words into math. She works 40 hours at \$14.50 and 3 hours at one and a half TIMES the \$14.50 rate. The correct answer is (B). Choices (C) and (D) are wrong because we are supposed to add the two numbers, not multiply.

10. **D** Expand out the scientific notation: 23,000 microns versus 32,000 microns. The difference is 9,000 microns.

11. **C** Barb is choosing three shows, so draw three spaces for the shows. There are 5 possible choices for the first show, 4 remaining possible choices for the second show, and 3 remaining choices for the third show. Since she has to choose an order, do not divide, and simply multiply the three numbers: $5 \times 4 \times 3 = 60$.

12. **A** In the numerator, there are two factors with bases of 2. When multiplying numbers with the same base, add the exponents: $(2^{12})(2^5) = 2^{17}$, so the fraction is equal to $\frac{(2^{17})(\sqrt{5})^4}{(2^{16})(5^3)}$. There is a factor with a base of two in the denominator. When dividing numbers with the same base, subtract the exponents: $\frac{2^{17}}{2^{16}} = 2^1 = 2$, so the fraction is equal to $\frac{(2)(\sqrt{5})^4}{(5^3)}$. In the numerator, there is a $\sqrt{5}$, which is equivalent to $5^{\frac{1}{2}}$, so the fraction is equal to $\frac{(2)\left(5^{\frac{1}{2}}\right)^4}{(5^3)}$. When a number with an exponent is raised to another exponent, multiply the exponents: $\left(5^{\frac{1}{2}}\right)^4 = 5^2$, so the fraction is equal to $\frac{(2)(5^2)}{(5^3)}$. Once again, numbers with the same base are divided. Subtract the exponents. Since the denominator is greater, keep the result in the denominator: $\frac{5^2}{5^3} = \frac{1}{5^1} = \frac{1}{5}$. Now don't forget to multiply by 2, so the fraction is equal to $\frac{2}{5}$. The correct answer is (A).

13. **B** This histogram question asks you to interpret the visual distribution of race finishing times. Notice how the data is grouped in the graph: finishing times are grouped by the minute, meaning all seconds are rounded down to the nearest whole minute in each "bin" of the histogram. You also need to notice that the bars represent the number of participants. Choice (A) may seem correct if you add the runners at 18 and 20, but remember that 20 contains everyone who finished under 21 minutes (their finishing times were 20 minutes and possible additional seconds), whereas the answer choice says "under 20 minutes." It is actually easy to see that (B) matches the distribution of the data; 22 to 29 contain most of the runners represented on the graph. To be sure, we can also eliminate (C) by noticing the bulk of the finishers *after* 24 (or over 24 minutes). Choice (D) is also not correct because 45 is the last grouping on the graph, but it contains zero participants (meaning no one finished in the 45-minute range of times). The correct answer is (B).

14. **D** This compound event probability question asks you to find the probability of two events both happening for the desired outcome. Remember that the probability of both happening will be less than that of either one. With compound events like this, we multiply the fraction probabilities of each event together. The first event is one number out of 6 possibilities (6-sided die), so its probability is $\frac{1}{6}$. The second event is one number out of 8 possibilities (8-sided die), so its probability is $\frac{1}{8}$. Multiply these together to get the compound event probability (which will be a smaller fraction): $\frac{1}{6} \times \frac{1}{8} = \frac{1}{48}$. The correct answer is (D).

Simple Equation Drill (Page 392)

1. **C** Add 5 to both sides of the equation, and then divide both sides by 2.
2. **15** Subtract 6 from both sides of the equation, and then divide both sides by 3.
3. **C** Just plug in 2 for x and 3 for y.

Inequalities Drill (Page 397)

1. **C** If the minimum age is five, then anyone five or older can ride the roller coaster.
2. **A** Just solve as if this were an equality.
3. **C** Plug in 4 into each inequality until one is a true statement.

Backsolving Drill (Page 402)

1. **A** First, ballpark. If Onome sees more patients, then she must see more than half of them. The answer must be more than 8, which eliminates every answer choice but (A). If you didn't notice that, how could you have solved the problem? By Backsolving. Try (C) and say that Onome saw 5 patients. If Onome saw 2 more than Lewis, then Lewis saw 3 patients. When you add together Onome and Lewis's patients, you are supposed to have 16. Could this be the right answer? No way. You need a bigger number. Try (B). If Onome had 7 patients, Lewis has 5, and this is still too small. The correct answer must be (A).

2. **D** This is another good backsolve. Just try putting the values in the answer choices into the equation until you find one that works.

3. **B** Ballparking gets rid of (A) because the problem says there are some men workers as well. If you solve this algebraically, watch out for (D), which turns out to be the number of men. However, a good way to avoid any chance of making a mistake is not to use algebra—try Backsolving instead. Start with (B). If there are 60 women and 4 times as many women as men, then the number of men is $\frac{1}{4}$ of 60 or 15. Since $60 + 15 = 75$, you've found your answer.

4. **B** Again, it is much easier to backsolve. Start with (C), 10%. Ten percent of \$45.00 is \$4.50. This is too much, so go down one and find 9 percent of \$45.00. This is the correct answer.

5. **D** You could use algebra, but Backsolving is just as easy. Start with (B), and see whether it makes the equation work. No, we need a bigger number. Choice (C) doesn't work either, so the answer must be (D).

Translation Drill (Page 407)

1. **C** Choice (A) is just Madison's weight alone. The combined weight of both of them is $x + (x + 5)$, which is equivalent to (C).

2. **B** The 2000 figure is just a red herring. It doesn't matter that the number of rabbits doubled in 2000 because by 2001 (the year we are interested in), the population is up five times.

3. **C** Choices (A) and (B) don't multiply Tyler's age by 3. Choices (B) and (D) subtract years instead of adding them.

4. **C** There is a total of nine chips, so set up the equation $B + R = 9$. The blue chips are worth 5 points each, so they're worth $5B$ total. The red chips are worth 3 points each, so they're worth $3R$ total. Since the blue chips and red chips combined are worth 21 points, $5B + 3R = 21$.

Polynomial Drill (Page 414)

1. **A** Add up the total number of *x*s and *y*s.

2. **B** Start by factoring an x out of the first two terms and 3 out of the last two terms. Both leave you with a factor of $(x - 4)$.

3. **B** Even though the coefficients are fractions, follow the same method. The first two terms each have a factor of $\frac{1}{4}x$. Factor this to get $\frac{1}{4}x^2+\frac{2}{4}x=\left(\frac{1}{4}x\right)(x+2)$. The other two terms each have a factor of $-\frac{2}{3}$, so factor this to get $-\frac{2}{3}x-\frac{4}{3}=-\frac{2}{3}(x+2)$. Thus, the original expression factors to $\left(\frac{1}{4}x\right)(x+2)-\frac{2}{3}(x+2)$.

   Notice that the remaining terms both have factors of $(x + 2)$. Factor this to get $\left(\frac{1}{4}x-\frac{2}{3}\right)(x+2)$.

   The correct answer is (B).

4. **C** When multiplying polynomials, use the distributive property: $(x^2 + 2x + 8)(x - 4) = (x^2 + 2x + 8)(x) - (x^2 + 2x + 8)(4)$. Now use the distributive property on the remaining terms: $(x^2 + 2x + 8)(x) = x^3 + 2x^2 + 8x$ and $(x^2 + 2x + 8)(4) = 4x^2 + 8x + 32$. Therefore, the expression is $(x^3 + 2x^2 + 8x) - (4x^2 + 8x + 32)$. Distribute the negative to get $x^3 + 2x^2 + 8x - 4x^2 - 8x - 32$. Group like terms to get $x^3 + (2x^2 - 4x^2) + (8x - 8x) - 32$. Combine like terms to get $x^3 - 2x^2 + 0 + 32 = x^3 - 2x^2 - 32$. The correct answer is (C).

5. **B** Translate the pieces of the question. A player's score is the sum of the squares of the numbers on her cards. Let the two numbers be represented by x and y, respectively. The squares of the two numbers are x^2 and y^2, respectively, so their sum is $x^2 + y^2$. Jennifer's cards have a product of 24, so $xy = 24$. The pairs of factors

of 24 are 1 and 24, 2 and 12, 3 and 8, and 4 and 6. Since the cards cannot have numbers greater than 10, eliminate 1 and 24 and 2 and 12 as possible pairs. The sum of Jennifer's cards is 11, so $x + y = 11$. Since that is the case, the two cards cannot be 4 and 6, since their sum is 10 rather than 11. Therefore, x and y must be 3 and 8. It cannot be determined whether $x = 3$ and $y = 8$ or $x = 8$ and $y = 3$. However, either possibility leads to the same result. Jennifer's score is $x^2 + y^2 = 3^2 + 8^2 = 9 + 64 = 73$. The correct answer is (B).

Quadratic Equations Drill (Page 421)

1. **A** Factor the equation. What two numbers have a sum of –7 and a product of 12? The factors of 12 are 1 and 12, 2 and 6, and 3 and 4. The factors 3 and 4 have a sum of 7. Since 7 is negative, the factors must both be negative, so the equation factors to $(x - 3)(x - 4) = 0$. Set both factors equal to 0. If $x - 3 = 0$, then add three to both sides to get $x = 3$. If $x - 4 = 0$, add four to both sides to get $x = 4$. The correct answer is (A).

2. **B** The answer choices are in square form, so use the complete the square method. In this equation, $b = -10$, so, to have a perfect square, c has to equal $\left(\frac{-10}{2}\right)^2 = 25$. To get $c = 25$, add 9 to both sides to get $x^2 - 10x + 25 = 9$. Factor the left side to get $(x - 5)^2 = 9$. The correct answer is (B).

3. **D** The answer choices are in the form of the quadratic formula, so use $x = \frac{-b \pm \sqrt{b^2 - 4ac}}{2a}$. In the equation $x^2 - 8x + 5 = 0$, $a = 1$, $b = -8$, and $c = 5$. Plug these into the quadratic formula to get $x = \frac{-(-8) \pm \sqrt{(-8)^2 - 4(1)(5)}}{2(1)} = \frac{8 \pm \sqrt{44}}{2}$. The correct answer is (D).

Rational Expressions Drill (Page 427)

1. **C** Find the common denominator for the two fractions. Start by factoring the first denominator. The denominator for the first fraction, $x^2 - 2x - 8$, factors to $(x - 4)(x + 2)$. To get the common denominator, multiply the second fraction by $\frac{x+2}{x+2}$ to get $\frac{2(x+2)}{(x-4)(x+2)} = \frac{2x+4}{x^2-2x-8}$. Since the denominators are the same, subtract the numerators to get $\frac{3-(2x+4)}{x^2-2x-8} = \frac{3-2x-4}{x^2-2x-8} = \frac{-2x-1}{x^2-2x-8}$. The correct answer is (C).

2. **A** To divide fractions (including rational expressions), invert the second and multiply: $\frac{3x-9}{x^2-6x+9} \times \frac{x^2-9}{x^2+8x+15}$. Look to simplify by finding common factors. Factor the numerators and denominators in each fraction to get $\frac{3(x-3)}{(x-3)(x-3)} \times \frac{(x-3)(x+3)}{(x+5)(x+3)}$. Cancel the $(x - 3)$ in the first fraction and the $(x + 3)$ in the second to get $\frac{3}{(x-3)} \times \frac{(x-3)}{(x+5)}$. Don't forget that you can cross-cancel $(x - 3)$ to get $\frac{3}{x+5}$.

   The correct answer is (A).

Simultaneous Equations Drill (Page 430)

1. **C** Since both equations are isolated for x, set the two equal to each other, giving you $2y + 5 = 3y - 6$. Subtract $2y$ from both sides and add 6 to both sides to get $y = 11$. Plug the value back into one of the original equations to get $x = 27$. Notice that (A) is 11, which is the value of y. This is a trap answer. For this question, you are looking for the value of x.

2. **A** Line up the two equations. Since the question asks for the value of y, eliminate x. Multiply the first equation by 2 to get $6x + 8y = -10$ and the second equation by 3 to get $-6x - 15y = 24$. Add the two equations to get $-7y = 14$. Divide by -7 to get $y = -2$.

3. **A** Translate the information into a system of equations. Let A represent the number of apples and B represent the number of bananas that Bill bought. Bill buys a total of 8 apples and bananas, so $A + B = 8$. Each apple costs 25 cents, so the cost of A apples is $0.25A$. Each banana cost 30 cents, so the cost of B bananas is $0.30B$. Since the total cost is $2.15, then $0.25A + 0.30B = 2.15$. Line up these two equations. Multiply the second equation by -4 to get $-A - 1.20B = -8.60$. Add the two equations to get $-0.20B = -0.60$. Divide both sides by -0.20 to get $B = 3$.

Functions Drill (Page 435)

1. **B** A relation is a function if every member of a domain corresponds with a unique member of the range. In the table, 3 corresponds with both -1 and y. In order for $h(x)$ to be a function, these values must be the same, so y must equal -1.

2. **B** Plug in 5 for each value of x, so $g(5) = 5^2 - 6 \times 5 + 9 = 25 - 30 + 9 = 4$.

3. **A** This is a translation problem. "The function of x" translates to $f(x)$. "Is" translates to =. "Three times" translates to 3(   ), with whatever follows filling in the parentheses. What follows translates to "four more than," so fill this in to get 3(+ 4), with whatever follows filling in before the plus sign. Finally, what follows is "the square of x," which translates to x^2. Therefore, the entire function translates to $f(x) = 3(x^2 + 4)$.

Algebra Drill (Page 437)

1. **C** Subtract 9 from both sides, and then divide both sides by 5, or backsolve.

2. **A** "Three times the amount of money Steven has" can be written as $3x$. "$4 more than" this amount means we need to add 4 to $3x$. Combining these two pieces, we get: Laura's money $= 3x + 4$.

3. **29** Just plug in 3 for x and 4 for y.

4. **C** This is a good Backsolving problem. If you start with (B), you'll see it's too small, so go up to the next-biggest answer and try that.

5. **B** Treat this just like an equality and solve for m. Simply subtract 7 from both sides to get $3m < 21$. Then divide both sides by 3 to get $m < 7$. The correct answer is (B).

6. **D** First distribute the 2 in the parentheses to get $2x + 2y$, and then combine like terms.

7. **D** Plug in 4 for x in each of the answer choices until you find the one that is true.

8. **C** You can ballpark this: 30 workers would be one-quarter, or 25 percent. 36 workers would be slightly more. Or work backward: What is 10 percent of the 120 workers? That's right: 12. Twenty percent? 24. Thirty percent? 36. Bingo!

9. **A** Use FOIL.

10. **C** This is a great Backsolving problem. Start with (B). If Lucas is 20, then Erica is 20 – 4 = 16, and Max is 16 + 5 = 21. The sum of their ages is 20 + 16 + 21 = 57. This is too low. Try this with (C) and you'll see that the ages add up to 69. The correct answer is (C).

11. **A** Put the two equations in the same form, so that you can use linear combinations. Take the first equation and subtract 2 from both sides and add $2y$ to both sides to get $3x + 2y = -2$. Now, to cancel x, multiply the second equation by 3 to get $-3x + 9y = -42$. Add the two equations to get $11y = -44$. Divide both sides by 11 to get $y = -4$.

12. **Top right: 9. Bottom left: –3**

To determine the blank space on the top right, plug –2 in for x to get $f(-2) = 2(-2)^2 + 1 = 9$. Select this for this blank space. To determine the blank space on the bottom left, plug in the answer choices to $f(x)$ and select the one for which $f(x) = 19$. Ballpark out 17 and 19, and try the remaining choices. $f(5) = 51$, so the answer has to be smaller. Ballpark out 9, as well. $f(-3) = 19$, so this is the correct answer. Select –3 for this blank.

13. **A** The question involves multiplication of rational expressions, so simplify the expressions by factoring. Factor –2 in the first numerator to get $-2(x - 4)$. Factor the denominator of the first fraction to get $(x - 5)(x + 2)$. The numerator of the second fraction factors to $(x - 5)(x + 4)$. The denominator of the second fraction factors to $(x + 4)(x - 4)$. Therefore, the factored form of the equation is $\frac{-2(x-4)}{(x-5)(x+2)} \times \frac{(x+4)(x-5)}{(x-4)(x+4)} = (x+5)$. Now look to cancel. Cancel $(x + 4)$, $(x - 4)$, and $(x - 5)$ to get $\frac{-2}{(x+2)} = (x+5)$. Get all the variables on one side of the equation by multiplying both sides by $(x + 2)$ to get $-2 = (x + 5)(x + 2)$. Use FOIL on the right side to get $-2 = x^2 + 7x + 10$. Since the right side is now a quadratic, get one side equal to 0 by adding 2 to both sides to get $0 = x^2 + 7x + 12$. Factor the right side to get $0 = (x + 3)(x + 4)$. Set both factors equal to 0 to get $x + 3 = 0$ and $x + 4 = 0$. Subtract 3 from the first equation to get $x = -3$ and 4 from the second to get $x = -4$. Since –4 is one of the choices, the correct answer is (A).

14. **C** For this inequality graph problem, you need to recall how to read the number line, arrow, and circle (open or closed) on this type of graph. Here, the closed circle on the 0 means that 0 is included as a value of x. From here, the arrow goes to the right, meaning we include 0 and all numbers greater than 0. Choice (C) expresses this range of values: x is greater than or equal to 0.

Lines and Angles Drill (Page 443)

1. **40 degrees** 180 – 140 = 40
2. **90 degrees** 180 – 90 = 90
3. **130 degrees** 180 – 50 = 130

Rectangles and Squares Drill (Page 448)

1. **square** All sides are the same length, and all angles are right angles.
2. **rectangle** The sides are different lengths, but all angles are right angles.
3. **9** Multiply length by width: $3 \times 3 = 9$
4. **24** Add the four sides together: $3 + 3 + 9 + 9 = 24$. (The area of Figure B would be 27.)
5. **3** Divide the area of the rectangle by the area of the square: $27 \div 9 = 3$.
6. **5** $3 \times 4 \times ? = 60$
7. **4** The entire volume of the cube equals 8, so halfway is 4.
8. **D** Because you don't know how much the wallpaper costs, there is not enough information given for you to answer the question.

Triangles and Pyramids Drill (Page 457)

1. **B** Area is base times height divided by two. If you picked (A), you forgot to divide by two.
2. **2** This is a 3-4-5 triangle. The answer is 5 – 3 = 2. If you didn't notice the 3-4-5 triangle, you could still solve this problem by using the Pythagorean Theorem.
3. **C** 180 – (27 + 53) = 100.
4. **D** First, use the formula provided on the Mathematics Formula Sheet to find the surface area of the pyramid, 5,068.8. Since one can covers 1,296 square inches, two cans cover 2,592 square inches, 3 cans cover 3,888, and 4 cans cover 5,184. Only (D) is large enough to cover the surface area.
5. **D** Adding up the three angles of the triangle, you get $x + 2x + (x + 20) = 4x + 20 = 180$. Solving for x, you get 40 degrees—but the question is asking for the measure of angle A, which is $2x$ or 80 degrees.

6. **C** The question gives the volume of a pyramid. The formula for volume of a pyramid is $V = \frac{1}{3}Bh$, where B represents the area of the base and h represents the height of the pyramid. The question gives the volume and height, so plug these into the formula to get $320 = \frac{1}{3}B(15)$. Simplify the right side to get $320 = 5B$. Divide both sides by 5 to get $B = 64$. Therefore, the area of the base is 64. Since the question says that it is a square base, use the area formula $A = s^2$. Plug in $A = 64$ to get $64 = s^2$. Take the square root of both sides to get $8 = s$. The question asks for the perimeter of the base. Perimeter is the sum of the lengths of all sides. Since the base is a square, all sides have a length of 8. Therefore, the perimeter is $8 + 8 + 8 + 8 = 4(8) = 32$. The correct answer is (C).

Other Polygons Drill (Page 461)

1. **B** The perimeter is the sum of the sides, so $8 + 10 + x + 14 = 40$. Simplify the left side to get $32 + x = 40$. Subtract 32 from both sides to get $x = 8$. The correct answer is (B).

2. **D** The question asks for the area of the octagon and gives a formula in terms of the side length. Although the side length is not given, the perimeter is given as well as the fact that it is a regular octagon. A regular octagon has eight equal sides, so the perimeter $P = 8s$. Since $P = 56$, $56 = 8s$, and $s = 7$. Plug this into the formula to get $A = 2\left(1 + \sqrt{2}\right)(7)^2 = 2\left(1 + \sqrt{2}\right)(49) = 98\left(1 + \sqrt{2}\right)$. None of the answer choices are in factored form, so distribute the 98 to get $A = 98 + 98\sqrt{2}$. The correct answer is (D).

Circles, Spheres, Cylinders, and Cones Drill (Page 465)

1. **4**

2. **8** Multiply the radius by 2: $4 \times 2 = 8$.

3. **8π** The diameter is 8, so multiply that by π to get the circumference.

4. **16π** Use the formula for area: $\pi 4^2 = 16\pi$.

5. **81π in.³** The area of the circle is 9π. $9\pi \times 9 = 81\pi$.

6. **A** If the diameter is 4, then the radius is 2. Substitute 2 in the formula for the surface area of a sphere: $SA = 4\pi r^2$. Then, $SA = 4\pi 2^2 = 4\pi 2^2 = 16\pi$.

7. **C** The formula for volume of a cone is $V = \frac{1}{3}\pi r^2 h$. The question says that the volume is 100π, so plug this in to get $100\pi = \frac{1}{3}\pi r^2 h$. The question asks for *h*, so you'll need to determine the value of *r*. The question also says that the area of the circular base is 25π. The formula for the area of a circle is $A = \pi r^2$. Plug in $A = 25\pi$ to get $25\pi = \pi r^2$. Divide both sides by π to get $25 = r^2$. Take the square root of both sides to get $5 = r$. Plug $r = 5$ into the volume formula to get $100\pi = \frac{1}{3}\pi(5)^2 h$. Simplify the right side to get $100\pi = \frac{25\pi}{3}h$. (Alternatively, note that $A = \pi r^2$ and plug 25π into the formula directly, by passing the need to find the radius.) Multiply both sides by $\frac{3}{25\pi}$ to get $h = 100\pi \times \frac{3}{25\pi} = \frac{100\pi}{1} \times \frac{3}{25\pi} = \frac{4}{1} \times \frac{3}{1} = 12$.

   The correct answer is (C).

8. **B** The formula for volume of a sphere is $V = \frac{4}{3}\pi r^3$. Plug in $V = 36\pi$ to get $36\pi = \frac{4}{3}\pi r^3$. Divide both sides by π to cancel the πs and get $36 = \frac{4}{3}r^3$. Multiply both sides by $\frac{3}{4}$ to get $r^3 = 36 \times \frac{3}{4} = \frac{36}{1} \times \frac{3}{4} = \frac{9}{1} \times \frac{3}{1} = 27$. Take the cube root of both sides to get $r = 3$, which is (A), but this is not the answer. The question asks for the diameter. Since $d = 2r = 2(3) = 6$, the correct answer is (B).

Graphing Drill (Page 474)

1. **C** To find the slope, take the difference in *y*-values, and put that over the difference in *x*-values. In this case, that is $\frac{2}{4}$ or $\frac{1}{2}$.
2. **C** Did you need the distance formula this time? No way! The *y*-values were the same for both numbers. All we had to do was subtract 5 from 12. If you didn't notice this, you could have sketched it out. Seeing what the problem really looks like almost always makes it easier to solve.

3. To graph point A, count 3 left and 4 down. To graph point B, go right 2 and up 3. For point C, count 3 right and 5 up.

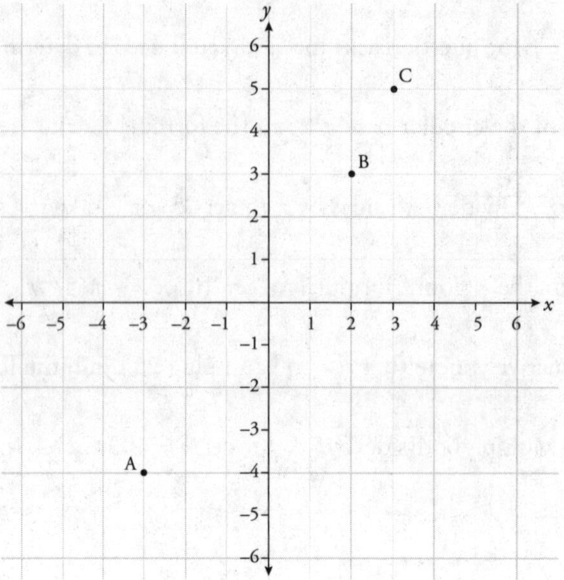

Equation of a Line Drill (Page 483)

1. **A** You want $y = mx + b$ form, in which m is the slope and b is the y-intercept. The question says that the slope is 4, so plug this in for m. Since at the y-intercept, the x-coordinate is 0, the (0, –2) represents the y-intercept, so plug in –2 for b.

2. $\mathbf{y = \frac{1}{2}x + 1}$

   You want $y = mx + b$ form, in which m is the slope and b is the y-intercept. First get the slope. Plug the points you have into the slope formula to get $m = \frac{2-(-1)}{2-(-4)} = \frac{3}{6} = \frac{1}{2}$. Select this for the first box. To get the y-intercept, plug in the slope and one of the points into the slope intercept form to get $2 = \frac{1}{2}(2) + b$. Solve to get $b = \mathbf{1}$. Select this for the second box.

3. **C** You want $y = mx + b$ form, in which m is the slope and b is the y-intercept. Since the slope is –2, the equation is in the form $y = -2x + b$. Eliminate (B) and (D) since they have a slope of 3, not –2. Then plug in the point (–1, 3) to get $3 = -2(-1) + b$. Solve to get $b = 1$, so the equation of the line is $y = -2x + 1$.

4. **A** Get the two equations into $y = mx + b$ form. The first equation, $2x + 8y = -5$, can be put into the form $y = -\frac{1}{4}x - \frac{5}{8}$. The second equation, $3x + 12y = 8$, can be put into the form $y = -\frac{1}{4}x + \frac{2}{3}$. Since the slopes are the same, the lines are parallel.

5.

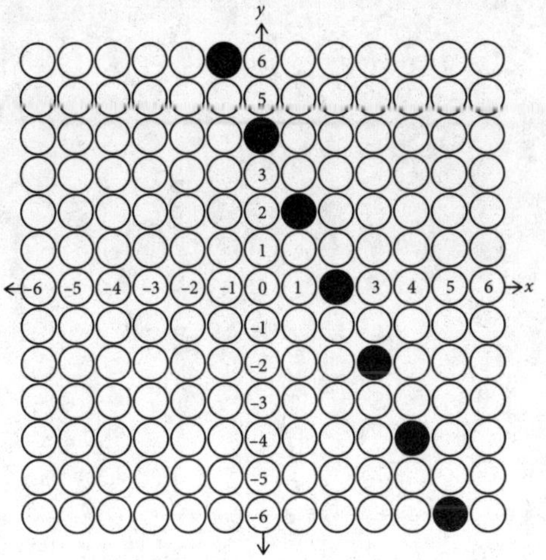

You are given the equation of the line in $y = mx + b$ form: $y = -2x + 4$. Therefore, the slope is –2 and the y-intercept is 4. Mark the point **(0, 4)**, since this is the y-intercept. Since the slope is –2, mark the point that is up 2 and left 1, **(–1, 6)**. Now, go in the other direction and mark the points that are down 2 and right 1: **(1, 2)**, **(2, 0)**, **(3, –2)**, **(4, –4)** and **(5, –6)**.

Proportions and Graphs Drill (Page 487)

1. **12** The speed traveled is equal to the slope of the line. To get the slope, you need two points, so use the points (0, 0) and (5, 60). The speed is $\frac{60-0}{5-0} = 12$.

2. **B** Each box contains 2 red marbles and 5 blue marbles, so the number of red marbles must always be a multiple of 2, and the number of blue marbles must always be a multiple of 5. Start with one box. If a customer buys one box, they will have 2 red marbles and 5 blue marbles. The only graph that has this point is (B).

3. **greater than**
To get Naomi's speed, find the slope of the line. Use the points (0, 0) and (2, 100) to get a speed of $\frac{100-0}{2-0} = 50$.

   To get Ravi's speed, take the coefficient on t, which is 40. Therefore, Naomi's speed is greater.

Interpreting Graphs Drill (Page 493)

1. **C** The y-values of a graph are negative when it is below the x-axis. Look to see where the graph crosses the x-axis. This happens at $x = 3$ and at $x = 9$. Between these points is where the graph is below the x-axis and, therefore, where its y-values are negative.

2.

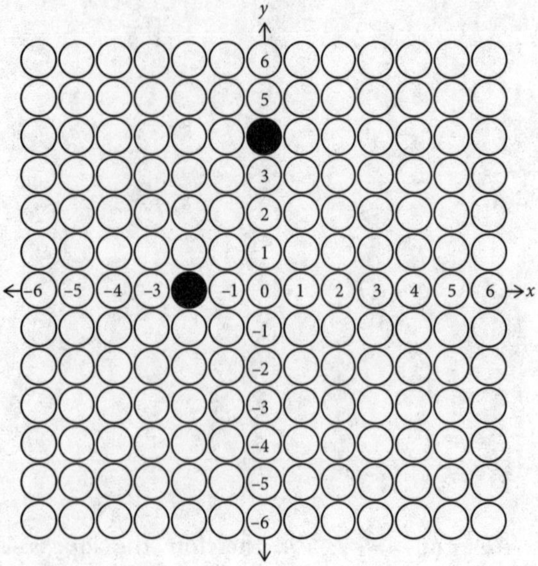

Since the equation of the line is in $y = mx + b$ form, the y-intercept is represented by the b term, in this case 4. Therefore, the y-intercept is the point **(0, 4)**. To get the x-intercept, set $y = 0$ to get $0 = 2x + 4$. Solve for x to get $x = -2$, so the x-intercept is the point **(–2, 0)**.

3. **B** Find the peaks and valleys. In this case, there is only one of each. The graph hits a valley, i.e., a relative minimum, at the point (–3, –4) and a peak, i.e., a relative maximum, at the point (2, 6). The graph is increasing between these two points, so over the interval $-3 < x < 2$.

4. **C** The axis of symmetry is the line that divides the curve into two mirror images. Sketch the graph on scratch paper and draw each line from the answer choices. The only one that divides it into mirror images is $y = 3$.

5. **B** To determine the period, find the peaks in the graph. The graph reaches peaks at (–7, 2), (–1, 2), and (5, 2). Since the distance between each of these peaks is 6, the period is 6.

Geometry Drill (Page 498)

1. **D** The volume of a cylinder is $V = \pi r^2 h$. Given that the diameter of the glass is 3, the radius is 1.5. The height is 6. Substitute these values into the formula.

$$V = \pi(1.5)2 \times 6$$
$$V = 13.5\pi$$

Now, we need to find $\frac{3}{4}$ of the volume:

$$\text{Volume of water} \approx 31.79$$

Rounding to the nearest unit, the volume of water in the glass is approximately 32.

2. **A** Since the answer choices do not include the symbol for pi, use the fraction form $\frac{22}{7}$ to solve. The area is $7^2 \times \frac{22}{7}$, or 154.

3. **B** Each side of the square has the same length, 3. The two sides of an isosceles triangle that are opposite equal angles also have the same length: in this case, 4. The correct answer is 3 + 3 + 3 + 4 + 4 = 17, which is (B).

4. **C** Any three-sided figure is a triangle. If two of the sides have the same length, as the ratio tells you, then it is an isosceles triangle.

5. **A** You could backsolve this. The volume of a cube is the length of a side cubed. Try cubing each answer choice until you find one that gives you the value 27. Obviously, you won't have to go too far to realize you are going to need a pretty small number.

6. **B** The sum of the measures of all three angles must equal 180, so subtract 45 from 180.

7. **D** Divide 168 by 12. The correct answer is 14.

8. **A** The area of a triangle equals the base times the height divided by 2, which is the same as $\frac{1}{2}$ times the base times the height.

9. **D** The diameter of the large circle equals the sum of the diameters of the two small circles, so each small circle has a diameter of 10 and a radius of 5.

10. **D** You need *two* points on a line to find its slope.

11. **B** Get the line in $y = mx + b$ form. Start by getting the slope. The slope is $m = \frac{8-2}{-2-1} = \frac{6}{-3} = -2$. Now plug this in for m and the point (1, 2) in for x and y into the equation to get $2 = -2(1) + b$. Solve for b to get $b = 4$, so the equation is $y = -2x + 4$.

12. **A** To determine where a graph is positive, start with where the value is 0, i.e., the x-intercepts. The x-intercepts are –9.5, 1, and 8. The graph is above the x-axis, and therefore positive, between –9.5 and 1 and to the right of 8. Therefore, it is positive when $-9.5 < x < 1$ and when $x > 8$.

13. **D** Both the area of the hexagon and the formula for area are given, so set $24\sqrt{3} = \frac{3\sqrt{3}}{2}s^2$. Multiply both sides by 2 to get $48\sqrt{3} = 3\sqrt{3}s^2$. Divide both sides by $\sqrt{3}$ to get $48 = 3s^2$. Divide both sides by 3 to get $16 = s^2$. Take the square root of both sides to get $4 = s$. This is (B), but the question asks not for the length of the side but for the perimeter. There are six sides in a regular hexagon and the lengths of all sides are equal; the perimeter is $6s = 6(4) = 24$. The correct answer is (D).

14. **C** To find the surface area of any composite figure, you need to calculate the areas of all faces and add them up, excluding any areas that are shared and not part of the composite figure's surface. In this composite figure, there is a right cylinder with a height of 6 cm and a radius of 5 cm, and on top, a rectangular prism with a height of 8 cm and 2 equal sides of 4 cm. Once you are clear on the dimensions of the composite parts, apply the formulas for finding surface area.

Surface Area of Cylinder: lateral base + area of 2 bases = $2\pi rh + 2\pi r^2$

Plug in the values for radius ($r = 5$), height ($h = 6$), and π (≈ 3.14):

$2(3.14)(5)(6) + 2(3.14)(5^2) = 188.4 + 157 = 345.4$

The surface area of the cylinder is about 345.4 cm^2. Next, we find the surface area of the rectangular prism.

Surface Area of Rectangular Prism: sum of the areas of all 6 faces = $2(wl + hl + hw)$. Plug in the values for length, width, and height:

$2(4)(4) + 2(8)(4) + 2(8)(4) = 32 + 64 + 64 = 160$

The surface area of the rectangular prism is 160 cm^2. Add the surface areas of the cylinder and the rectangular prism to get 345.4 + 160 = 505.4 cm^2. Finally, don't forget that surface area of the composite figure excludes any overlap where the figures are joined. So, we need to subtract the area covered by this overlap. This is the bottom side of the rectangular prism. We remove this area *twice* from the total surface area of the composite figure: $505.4 - 2(4)(4) = 473.4$ cm^2 or the surface area of the composite figure. The correct answer is (C).

15. **C** Identify the figure in this volume question, and get your formula ready. For a triangular prism, we calculate volume as $\frac{1}{2}bhl$. Plug in the values for base ($b = 5$), height ($h = 9$), and prism length ($l = 12$).

Volume of triangular prism: $\frac{1}{2}bhl = \frac{1}{2}(5)(9)(12) = 270$ in.^{3}

Don't forget that with triangular figures, we always end up multiplying by $\frac{1}{2}$! The correct answer is (C).

SOCIAL STUDIES

Colonial America Drill (Page 525)

1. **B** Although the printing is hard to read because some letters were missing, added, or switched by the early technology, an ad trying to sell fruits, (A), would include different information, including the price and type of produce. Celebrating bravery, (C), may make sense with the graphic and the words "exciting" and "fame," but not with "fruites by planting." The same logic goes for (D), raising money for shipbuilding. The ad is offering an exciting opportunity for people to travel to the new colony of Virginia across the Atlantic Ocean, (B).

2. The text at the bottom of the ad tells you that it was printed in **London, England**. But if you figured out its purpose in question 1, you would be able to eliminate people already in the colonies (Jamestown, Virginia; a New England colony) and workers in a shipyard.

American Revolution Drill (Page 528)

1. The preamble includes several action words describing what the Constitution is intended to do, but the final words of the document enact it: "**do ordain and establish.**"

2. **C** Each verb in the preamble is something that the nation will do to live up to its principles, so (C) is the correct answer. You can also eliminate declaring independence, (A), because that action happened earlier in the Declaration of Independence. You should also know that enslaved people were not freed in the American colonies, (B), but much later during the Civil War between the states. Lastly, the Constitution set up the structure of government to which the people elect their representatives; it did not appoint people to positions, (D).

Westward Expansion Drill (Page 531)

1. The passage states that the history of the United States "separates [it] from the past and connects [it] with the future only." This should lead you to select this statement as the one that doesn't belong: "**The greatness of the U.S. is its connection to the past.**" Additionally, the first line of the passage mentions that the American people come from other nations, that is, they are immigrants. You can also find equality as the founding principle of the nation in the first line of the passage.

2. **D** The passage states that the development of the United States will be separate and different from other nations and the past, so you can eliminate (A). There is no mention of either economy or empire in the passage, so neither (B) nor (C) describes the destiny of the United States. The passage presents a "new history" developing the values of democracy, so (D) is the answer.

Civil War Drill (Page 534)

1. **C** This is the key phrase in the document: "all persons held as slaves within any State or designated part of a State, the people whereof shall then be in rebellion against the United States, shall be then, thenceforward, and forever free." From this, you can eliminate (A) and (B) because you know that the Civil War was going on, and the Southern states were already in rebellion or withdrawn from the Union. The document also declares certain enslaved people (in states in rebellion) "forever free," so you can eliminate (D) in favor of (C).

2. The authority of the document is Lincoln's position as president and commander-in-chief of the armed forces; he invokes this authority here: "**the Executive Government of the United States, including the military and naval authority thereof, will recognize and maintain the freedom of such persons.**"

Reconstruction Drill (Page 537)

1. **B** The sign in the back of the drawing names the scene "Great After War Reconstruction." The Civil War, (A), was not a fight between the Republican and Democratic parties, but rather between Northern and Southern states. Deciding how to move the country forward after this war during the Reconstruction was a "partisan fight." World War I, (C), and the American Revolution, (D), also have nothing to do with political parties in the United States.

2. **Skeptical, doubting.** The cartoon depicts an active scene in which no work is getting done. The worker in the background is watching the fight and waiting for these two parties to "get to work." This expresses a skeptical or doubting attitude toward the "work" of Reconstruction.

The Progressive Era Drill (Page 540)

1. **The right to vote.** "Suffrage" means the right to vote, and "ratification" means signing an agreement to pass a law or amendment. These labels lead to the correct selection (the right to vote) and eliminate the other options that are not pictured in any way in the drawing.

2. **A** Ratification involves getting three-fourths of the states to pass an amendment, so the answer is (A). If you didn't know this term, you could try reasoning away the other options: Measurements, (B), don't fit with any political message that you would find in a political cartoon, and if the numbers were years, (D), they would not correspond to the date of the cartoon (1919). Numbers of women may seem possible, (C), but it's not clear how such a small number of individual women might fit in the picture.

World War I Drill (Page 543)

1. **Imperialism**. Nations fight over other lands to grow their own empires; this is called imperialism.

2. **Alliances**. Alliances are what drag countries into wars to defend their allies.

Great Depression Drill (Page 547)

1. **1933** The graph shows the U.S. unemployment rate, so the highest point would indicate the highest number of people unemployed. This would be 1933.

2. **C** When trying to identify the fastest rate of decline, you are looking for the steepest downward slope of the line. This happens from 1940–1942, or (C).

World War II Drill (Page 551)

1. **B** The date of December 7, 1941 is located within the speech, so this should help you identify the event as the attack on Pearl Harbor, (B). Since the president is addressing Japanese aggression on U.S. territory, you can eliminate the other options.

2. The President frames the U.S. response as defensive against Japanese aggression in the following phrases: "**measures be taken for our defense**," "**overcome this premeditated invasion**," "**defend ourselves to the uttermost**," "**unprovoked and dastardly attack by Japan**."

Cold War Drill (Page 555)

1. A proxy war is fought between two parties through others, so the Korean War (**1950**) would be an example of this, since those fighting were supported by the United States and Soviet Union. Launching a satellite into space (**1957**) would be part of the space race. Avoiding nuclear war in the Cuban Missile Crisis (**1962**) demonstrates the stakes of mutually assured destruction.

2. **D** The timeline specifies that the Iron Curtain was "across Europe," so that helps you eliminate (A) and (B). The Cold War had nothing to do with temperature, so you should also be able to rule out (C). The main conflict of the Cold War was between Western capitalist democracies and Communism, so you should select (D).

Civil Rights Movement Drill (Page 559)

1. The numbers of people participating in the Montgomery Bus Boycott support the first statement. There are plenty of documented examples of nonviolent disobedience used to protest, so this statement is also based on evidence. The timing of JFK's push for civil rights legislation in combination with his own official statements support the last statement. Stating that something "would have" been different in history requires speculation, so this statement is based not on fact, but on opinion: **"If the Voting Rights Act had been passed before 1965, the Civil Rights Movement would have ended earlier."**

2. **C** Choices (A), (B), and (D) are actions that violated laws during the time of the Civil Rights Movement, so these would be acts of nonviolent civil disobedience. Choosing not to use a service in a boycott, (C), is not against the law and therefore not nonviolent civil disobedience.

Vietnam War Drill (Page 562)

1. **B** During the Vietnam War, young men protested the draft that randomly selected them for mandatory service, (B). Protests against the war itself used other slogans, so you can reason that (A) and (D) are not correct. Protests about age restrictions had to do with voting, not military service, so (C) also does not align with the picture.

2. **D** The slogan has to do with young men being called to fight when they were not old enough to vote, so these protests pushed for lowering the voting age to 18. The Voting Rights Act, (A), concerned racial discrimination in voting, and universal suffrage, (B), removed the property requirement to extend voting rights to all white men during westward expansion. Poll taxes, (C), charging people to vote, had nothing to do with age, so you can eliminate this answer also.

Globalization and the Information Age Drill (Page 565)

1. **B** The president calls for a "global free trade zone" in which government does "not stand in the way." A regulatory structure, (A), tariffs supporting American businesses, (C), and new laws negotiated between nations, (D), would be stepping in the way of the free market, so you can eliminate these answers and select (B).

2. **Globalization**. Since the speech focuses on encouraging a global free market, isolationism and nationalism do not make sense, since these have to do with promoting U.S. interests only. The president also speaks directly against creating bureaucracy, so you can eliminate this answer also, and select globalization.

War on Terror and Post 9/11 Drill (Page 569)

1. **C** The date September 11 is known for the terrorist attacks crashing hijacked planes into U.S. targets, (C). The 9/11 attacks also prompted the War on Terror declared in this speech.

2. **A** The president states, "Every nation, in every region, now has a decision to make. Either you are with us, or you are with the terrorists." This statement supports (A). He also makes clear that the war will not be one battle or series of airstrikes, so you can rule out (C) and (D). The locations of all terrorist leaders were not known at this time, so (B) does not make sense.

Types of Government Drill (Page 576)

1. **No individual freedom and absolute control by one leader or party with nationalist vision.** Totalitarian rule means no individual freedom to enable absolute control.

2. **Representative democracy.** Direct democracy involves citizens in the decision and law-making process. Since Britain has elected officials representing groups of people, it is a representative democracy. You can also rule out the other two options: communism has to do with state control of the economy, and authoritarian government is about imposing state control over citizens' lives (not representation).

Foundation and Structure of U.S. Government Drill (Page 582)

1. **Sign a bill into law.** The basic power of the executive branch is to sign bills into law. Declaring war requires a vote in Congress. Laws are also introduced in Congress. And it is the power of the judicial branch to review and rule that laws are unconstitutional.

2. **A** The fundamental difference between the Senate and the House is the number of representatives: two senators are elected by each state, while representatives are elected by their home districts, which vary by population.

3. **D** The passage describes what happens to a bill after it has passed in Congress, so you can rule out (C). The bill goes to the president, who signs it into law or vetoes it. The passage is not describing the removal of the president, (A). Laws are declared unconstitutional by the Supreme Court, (B), which is not mentioned here. The correct answer is (D).

Politics in Action and Activism Drill (Page 586)

1. **B** Women gained the right to vote in 1920, so identity as a woman, (A), would no longer prevent someone from voting in 1950. Poll taxes were not abolished until 1962, so it is possible that someone could not afford to vote in 1950, making (B) correct. You can also rule out age of 21 years, (C), since this was the original voting age, and slave ancestry, (D), which was no longer a factor after the 15th Amendment in 1870.

2. **B** The 1st Amendment protects an individual's right to free speech, freedom of the press, and religious expression; the 2nd Amendment protects the right to bear arms.

3. **D** The quote states that "separate schools for white and colored children, has been held to be a valid exercise of legislative power." The words "separation" and "power" make (B) tempting, but this a trap. It cannot be (C), since the quote states that limits to contact "do not necessarily imply the inferiority of either race to the other." On the other hand, the civil rights movement had not gained any influence until the 1960s, so rule out (A). That leaves (D). The quote states that separate schools are "valid," but that this does not imply "inferiority."

Economics Drill (Page 598)

1. **D** For this question, we are interested only in the northeast region, represented by the figure on the left. Just subtract the '09 figure from the '10 figure. Calculate as follows: 9.1 – 7.3 = 1.8, or (D).

2. **A** This is a tough evaluation problem that requires you to make generalizations about the economy based on unemployment figures. If a country's unemployment figures are up, we can make a general assumption that the country's economy is not healthy. Of course, from this chart, we have no idea about the economies of other nations. According to the data in the chart, the unemployment rate in 2010 was higher than it was in 2009. From this data, we can infer that the overall economic situation was worse in 2010 than it was in 2009.

3. **A** Recalling that World War II took place during the 1940s will help you to select (A). Otherwise, use POE. Choice (B) is a trap, since the graph measures employment, not population. The highest level of civilian employment was in the 1940s, but the Great Depression was in the 1930s. You can rule out (C). Choice (D) is not true, since civilian employment was low throughout the early part of the graph. Also, we cannot say what is true of employment in the years not measured by the graph.

4. **D** To answer this question, we need to have a clear understanding of the primary characteristics of capitalism and communism. Capitalism is a system that prioritizes the seeking of profits by individual entrepreneurs and corporations. By contrast, communism seeks to limit private enterprise. Private ownership of property is a fundamental right under capitalism. On the other hand, communist theory supports the idea of citizens jointly owning the rights to the society's land, labor, and capital. Competitive markets are an important component of capitalism. Communist economies are historically based on government control of all aspects of production. Communists also strive for the redistribution of all wealth, the elimination of class distinctions between groups of people, and state ownership of all property. Eliminate (A), since it gets these relationships backwards. Choice (B) is wrong, since communists believe in the state ownership of property. Choice (C) is wrong, since communism is not about maximizing profits. Choice (D) is the best answer.

Statistics Drill (Page 602)

1. **D** The mode of a list is the most frequently occurring number. The most frequently occurring number for females in the chart provided is (D), 83.7.

2. **B** In order to get a median, we must line up all numbers in order from least to greatest and identify the middle number. For females, the numbers are already in numerical order and 83.7 is the middle number. For males, rearrange the numbers in order: 76.7, 76.8, 77.2, 77.8, 78.1, 78.4, 78.6, 78.6, 79. In this list, 78.1 is the middle number, so that is the median. Now, subtract the two medians to get the difference of 5.6. Choice (B) is the correct answer.

Geography (Globe and Maps) Drill (Page 607)

1. **B** The Atlantic Ocean is the continuous body of water, north between the East Coast of North America and Europe, south between South America and Africa.

2. **Australia.** Australia is the only continent that lies completely within one quadrant of the globe. It is both south of the equator (0 degrees latitude) and east of the Prime Meridian (0 degrees longitude).

3. **C** Mountain ranges would not be represented by single lines, and rivers do not run directly North-South. Climate zones correspond to latitude lines, relative to the equator. The lines on this map separate the time zones, (C), from west to east: Pacific, Mountain, Central, Eastern.

Environment Drill (Page 609)

1. **C** This question requires you to select the answer expressed in words that is best supported by the graphical data provided in the map. In other words, you must understand information represented graphically that displays the areas of lowest (lightest) and highest (darkest) imperiled (endangered) biodiversity in the mainland United States. Choice (A) is incorrect, since the map does seem to indicate much higher levels of imperiled biodiversity in the Southwest and Southeast, with much lower levels in the central Plains states. Choice (B) is incorrect, since there are levels of imperiled biodiversity throughout the map, particularly in the Rocky Mountain West, but this does not make (D) a good choice, since both the rates of biodiversity and imperiled biodiversity are still variable. Choice (C) is best supported by the map, since the highest concentrations of shading on the map are in the lower left areas including California.

2. **TRUE**. Biodiversity refers to the number and variety of species of plants and animals in a given geographic area. The map measures concentrations of imperiled or endangered biodiversity. Since we see high concentrations of shading in the lower right portion of the map, it would be accurate to say that many portions of the Southeastern United States are at high risk of losing species diversity.

Human Geography Drill (Page 611)

1. **A** Notice that the arrows are pointing in different directions. An export is a good that a country sends TO another country, not something that it receives. The arrow going from the colonies to Britain lists "tobacco" as one of the exports, so (A) is the best answer. Manufactured goods, (B), are an import from Britain, not an export from the colonies. Enslaved people, (C), are imported from Africa, and sugar, (D), is imported from the West Indies.

2. **Statements (a), (b), and (c) are TRUE.** All of the countries listed on the right side of the map (the East) are European countries, so statement (a) is true. Italy had more than 4,000,000 immigrants, while Ireland had less than 2,000,000, so this ratio is at least "2 to 1" (two times bigger). Therefore, (b) is true. According to the numbers for Japan and France, Japan is slightly higher at 241,000, so statement (c) is true. Statement (d) is deceptive. It certainly looks like Japanese and Chinese immigrants largely landed in the West, but we do not know where they ultimately "settled." Many of them may have migrated East after they landed. **Statement (d) is FALSE.**

SCIENCE

Scientific Method Drill (Page 635)

1. **D** In order for the bird to be found in the lava from the Pompeii eruption, the bird must have lived during that period or it would not have ended up preserved in that rock—(D) is correct. This was an evaluation question. The passage mentions that the bird's species is believed to be extinct, but there is no mention of how this happened, and we cannot assume that the extinction was due to the volcano, so eliminate (A). While it is possible that the bird did not live in Pompeii and was just caught in the wrong place at the wrong time, this is unlikely and cannot be determined from the information in the passage, so eliminate (B). Choice (C) does not define whom it is referring to (no one who lived in Pompeii or no one in general). Obviously the eruption did not kill all humans, or we would not be here today. The passage says that the eruption killed "most of the inhabitants" of Pompeii, which is not strong enough to prove that everyone in the town died: eliminate (C).

2. The only two observations are that **the bird's wings are abnormally long, (d),** and that **Mount Vesuvius erupted in 79 A.D., (a).** The belief that **the bird would have been able to eat more than its competitors, (b),** is a conclusion that the scientists could have made based on its unique beak. Finally, (c) is not supported by the passage (clearly the bird is not alive today) and does not fit into either category.

Cell Theory and the Origins of Life Drill (Page 640)

1. **D** According to the passage, bacteria that keep glowing are still alive so the drug must not be able to kill them. There are two possible explanations for this; first, the drug may not be the correct type (as the passage explains, it is imperative that the correct drug be chosen based on the particular strain) or, secondly, the drug might not have been administered at a high enough dose [(D) is correct, while (A) and (C), which are correct, each do not include the other option and thus are eliminated]. If the cell continues to fluoresce, it must not have been destroyed—eliminate (B).

2. **A** Timing is critical to the test so that the patient can be placed on the correct course of treatment as soon as possible to prevent the spread of infection [(A) is correct]. Choice (B) is a nice feature of the new test but certainly not the most important reason, so eliminate (B). There is not enough information in the passage to know how long the enzyme lasts but, even if (C) were true, it would not support the need for expediency with respect to the test, so eliminate (C). Choice (D) is vague and can be eliminated since the passage does not specifically describe other types of bacteria.

3. The **10,000 mM** point on the x-axis should be clicked on as this represents the dose at which the intensity falls below 20, which the question stem indicates is acceptable.

Genetics Drill (Page 644)

1. 75%

This question wants you to look at the Punnett Square and figure out how often an offspring will have pointy ears. The information in the passage states that the trait will be expressed if the gene is pure or composed of mixed alleles. Accordingly, the probability a cat will have pointy ears is $\frac{3}{4}$ or 75% or 0.75.

2. **A** You need to understand how a Punnett Square works in order to answer this question. You must cross each column with each row in order to find the possibilities; e.g., the first column, which has the allele P, is crossed with the first row, which also has the allele P, to give us the gene PP. Thus, the answer is (A).

3. The genotypic ratio is the pattern of offspring distribution based on genotype. In this example, we have one instance of PP, two instances of Pp, and one instance of pp. Thus, the genotypic ratio is **1:2:1**.

Evolution and Natural Selection Drill (Page 648)

1. **A** In order for some life forms to survive, they would have needed to have the ability to survive despite the conditions described in the passage. One such ability would be to be able to survive without the normal amount of sunlight—(A) is correct. The dinosaurs went extinct; they did not hibernate. If this was true, we would expect to still see dinosaurs, so eliminate (B). As we know, sunlight is critical to the survival of plants, which use it for photosynthesis—eliminate (C). There must have been some food on the planet or else no organisms would have survived, so eliminate (D).

2. **C** This is a good example of a fifty-fifty question because you can probably eliminate two answer choices immediately by thinking about the question. Darwin would very likely agree with this passage because of his belief in natural selection and the conditions under which it occurs. Moreover, he did not believe in destiny—so eliminate (A)—or consider tragedy in his theory, so eliminate (B). Choice (C) closely describes Darwin's views—(C) is correct—while (D) implies that evolution took place at the level of individual organisms, a common misconception about Darwin's theory, which described species and populations but not individuals. Eliminate (D).

Plants Drill (Page 652)

1. **B** The passage states that the tree was cut down at the end of the growing season in 2000, meaning that the outermost ring must correspond to the growth that took place in 2000. You can see that the second-most outer ring has a larger size than this and the next two closest to it, which represent 1998 and 1997, respectively. Therefore, (B), 1999, is the correct answer.

2. **C** Counting the rings reveals that there are 8 complete rings; hence the tree is 8 years old. Choice (C) is correct, so eliminate the other answer choices.

3. The correct answers are, in order, **independent** and **dependent**. The size of the tree ring depends on the amount of rainfall.

Ecosystems and Food Chain Drill (Page 659)

1. **C** Use the arrows to determine which organism is consuming the other. The arrow originates at the organism that is getting eaten and terminates at the organism that is preying on it. The only organism that is eaten by both land and sea creatures is the salmon, which is eaten by both bears and sharks, so (C) is correct. Minnows are eaten only by sea creatures, so eliminate (A). Wolves are eaten only by bears—eliminate (B)—and groupers are eaten only by sharks, so eliminate (D). Note that (B) and (D) could be eliminated immediately because they are each eaten by only one animal.

2. **D** The absence of algae, (D), would have the greatest impact on the rest of the food chain since it is a primary producer.

3. Primary producers: **algae**. Primary consumers: **copepods**, **minnows**. Secondary consumers: **salmon**, **groupers**. Tertiary consumers: **sharks**, **bears**, **barracuda**, **wolves**.

The Human Body and Human Health Drill (Page 663)

1. Based on the passage provided, the **muscular system, (b),** allows the body to move, the **skeletal system, (c),** works in conjunction with the muscular system to enable movement, and the **nervous system, (e),** regulates both voluntary and involuntary motion. Thus, these are the correct answers. Neither the endocrine system, (a), nor the digestive system, (d), is mentioned in the passage and, therefore, these answers are incorrect.

2. We are told that Susan suffered from a heart attack, which would primarily impact the **cardiac**, or heart, muscles within the **muscular** system.

3. **D** According to the passage, the nervous system controls your muscular system and regulates both voluntary and involuntary motions by sending signals to parts of the body. Therefore, prior to the act of running, the nervous system must send signals to the muscular and skeletal systems. Thus, (D) is the correct answer. Don't fall for (B), as this is a trap! The question states that the endocrine system initiates the flight-or-fight response, not the movement itself.

Bacteria and Viruses Drill (Page 668)

1. Based on the passage provided, bacterial infections, unlike viral infections, are living. Therefore, if the disease is alive, it is bacterial. The passage also states that bacterial infections can be treated with antibiotics. Thus, the disease is alive and can be addressed with antibiotics; i.e., **bacterial** and **antibiotics** are correct.

2. According to the passage, the majority of infected individuals drink water from the same well and work with goats. Thus, the likely mode of disease transfer involves drinking **contaminated water, (a),** and exposure to infected animals. Choice (a) includes the contaminated water theory and, therefore, is correct. There is no indication that the disease is airborne, blood-borne, or transferred via human saliva, so eliminate (b), (c), and (e). The only other option is the **bite of an infected animal, (d).** Since we are told that the infected individuals are exposed to goats, which could transfer disease via the bites of infected fleas, (d) is also a potential method of transfer.

3. **C** According to the passage, a viral infection can be prevented via the use of vaccination. Thus, eliminate (A). Quarantining animals and avoiding contact with infected persons can prevent the spread of disease by eliminating contact, so (B) and (D) can be eliminated. The passage also states that *bacterial*, not viral, infections can be treated with antibiotics. Therefore, (C) is correct.

Energy and Heat Drill (Page 675)

1. According to the passage, an exothermic reaction occurs when heat is released in a chemical reaction, while an endothermic reaction occurs when heat is absorbed in the reaction. When Eliz and Kristy started the fire, heat was released into the atmosphere. Thus, an **exothermic** reaction took place because heat was **released**.

2. **B** Based on the passage, conduction occurs when objects are in direct contact with one another. Since Kristy and Eliz were not in direct contact with the fire, conduction did not take place. Therefore, you can eliminate (A) and (C). Choice (B) states that the girls absorbed heat, while (D) states that the campfire absorbed heat. Since Kristy and Eliz were the ones who became warmer and absorbed the heat, the correct answer is (B).

3. Here, you need to determine what happens when Kristy burns her hand. Since she uses a metal pole that is in direct contact with the fire, **heat is transferred, (e),** by means of **conduction, (a),** so select these two choices. While the fire is releasing heat in an exothermic reaction, the question is asking about the reaction that happens when Kristy's hand touches the metal pole. This is **endothermic, (c)**: Kristy's hand burns when her skin absorbs the heat on contact with the metal pole. Select (c) as well.

Physical Laws, Work, and Motion Drill (Page 680)

1. To answer this question, break it up into the three parts. In the original scenario, Bob is the only one pushing on the rock. He is providing a force and so is friction. Note that gravity is supplying a force in all the scenarios. Select **(a)**, **(b)**, and **(d)**. In the second scenario, the first three forces are the same but now there is also the force from Barbara. Select **(a)**, **(b)**, **(c)**, and **(d)**. Finally, when the rock is over the ledge, neither Bob nor Barbara is pushing. Gravity is still a force and so is air resistance, so select **(a)** and **(e)**.

2. **A** Work is defined as the force (F) multiplied by the distance moved (d). Since the rock didn't move, the work done is zero [(A) is correct].

Waves and Radiation Drill (Page 685)

1. According to the passage, electromagnetic waves can pass through empty space, while mechanical waves require a medium. The passage also states that there is an inverse relationship between the frequency of a wave and its period. Therefore, only **electromagnetic** waves can pass through empty space, and the relationship between waves of longer and shorter wavelengths is such that as the **frequency** of a wave increases, the period **decreases**.

2. In order to answer this question, you need to look at the "Applications" section of the provided table and select waves that relate to medical research. According to the chart, **visible light, (e),** is used in physical therapy, **ultraviolet light, (d),** is used in sanitation and air purification, and both **X-rays, (c),** and **gamma rays, (f),** are used to treat cancer. Thus, you should select these four choices.

3. Here, you need to use the table to find the wave type that corresponds to a wavelength size of 1 nm. Make sure you don't fall into the trap of reading the wavelength size as 1 *mm*, as the question asks about nanometers, not millimeters. According to the table, a wavelength size of 60 nm–1×10^{-4} nm is associated with X-rays. Thus, the correct answer is **X-rays**.

Solids, Liquids, and Gases Drill (Page 690)

1. The correct sentence reads as follows: **Increase** the pressure and **decrease** the temperature.

2. **A** Saltwater boils at a higher temperature than freshwater. This is due to a colligative property. The salt dissolves into its constituent ions in the water and the charged ions anchor water molecules down in the liquid. This means that it takes more energy for the water molecules to escape into the gas phase than it would without the salt. As a result, the boiling point is increased—(A) is correct. The water can still boil; it just takes longer, so eliminate (B). Also be wary of extreme wording in answer choices such as this one. Water is already neutral—eliminate (C)—and the fact that salt water is easier to float in has nothing to do with its boiling point, so eliminate (D).

3. **A** This is a difficult question because you have to use the graph and then interpret your findings. Start by finding the first point (–70°C and 70 bar). This corresponds to solid carbon dioxide. If this solid CO_2 is heated and kept at the same pressure, it will become a liquid. A solid-to-liquid phase transition is melting, so (A) is correct. Freezing is the opposite process, so eliminate (B). Boiling and condensing are processes that describe the phase transition that takes place between liquids and gases, so eliminate (C) and (D).

Chemical Reactions Drill (Page 693)

1. **C** In this chemical reaction, $2Ag + H_2S \rightarrow Ag_2S + H_2$, the sulfur atom is originally bonded to the hydrogen atoms. However, after the reaction takes place, the sulfur atom bonds to the silver atoms. Therefore, a single displacement occurs in this reaction; i.e., (C) is the correct answer.

2. **A** In this chemical equation, $2Ag + H_2S \rightarrow Ag_2S + H_2$, two atoms of silver combine with one molecule of hydrogen sulfide to produce one molecule of silver sulfide and one molecule of hydrogen. Therefore, (A) is the correct answer.

3. **6, O**

In order to have a balanced chemical equation, the number of atoms associated with a particular element must be equal in both the reactants and the products. The balanced equation for photosynthesis is $6CO_2 + 6H_2O \rightarrow C_6H_{12}O_6 + 6O_2$. Notice that after the reaction occurs, 1 molecule of glucose is produced, which contains 6 carbon atoms. Since there are 6 carbon atoms after the reaction occurs, there must be 6 carbon atoms prior to the reaction occurring; thus, the first blank is 6. Furthermore, prior to the reaction, there are 12 oxygen atoms associated with carbon dioxide, 6 oxygen atoms associated with the water, and 18 total oxygen atoms. After the reaction, 6 oxygen atoms are associated with the glucose, leaving 12 unaccounted oxygen atoms; thus, the missing element for the second blank is O.

The Changing Earth Drill (Page 697)

1. **B** The figure shows that several earthquakes have taken place along the western coast of the United States—eliminate (C)—and appear to follow a line down below that. Collectively, this suggests that there must be tectonic plates that rub together along this fault line, so (B) is correct. The map shows only the Americas, but there is no reason to suspect that this is the only location on Earth that earthquakes occur—eliminate (A). As the map indicates, more earthquakes occur in the United States than in Canada, so eliminate (D).

2. The correct answer would be to include **tsunamis, (a), tremors, (c), damage to buildings, (d),** and **volcanic activity, (e),** in the drop box. These four outcomes are all mentioned in the passage as being caused by earthquakes, while the others—hurricanes, (b), and tornadoes, (f)—are not.

3. The correct answer is that the earthquake was probably low on the Richter scale (**3**) and **deep**, because it was imperceptible and there was no sign of damage.

Glaciers, Erosion, and the Ice Ages Drill (Page 702)

1. **A** Glaciers are made of ice, which begins to melt once it warms up to slightly above zero degrees Celsius, so (A) is correct. Glaciers were found all over the Earth but predominantly near the poles, not the equator, so eliminate (B). The opposite of (C) is true as well. As glaciers melt, the water that they were comprised of must go somewhere, so it ends up in the oceans and other waterways, which causes their levels to rise—eliminate (C). Finally, while glaciers will certainly feel the gravitational pull of the Moon, they are too large and heavy to be truly affected by it, so eliminate (D).

2. **B** Glaciers move extremely slowly—eliminate (A)—and they are made up of fresh water, just like snow. Choice (B) is correct. Glaciers occur in many geographical locations—eliminate (C)—and there is no evidence to suggest that they will never again cover the Earth, so eliminate (D).

3. You should select the **peaks of the trend line**, as these correspond to the times when the ice was thickest and were likely ice ages.

Natural Resources Drill (Page 708)

1. According to the passage, Bashville uses fossil fuels, which are nonrenewable energy sources, to power the town. Furthermore, the town is looking to decrease carbon emissions, by switching to renewable energy sources. Thus, select **nonrenewable** energy sources, as they increase **carbon** emissions.

2. **C** Based on the passage, Bashville wants to reduce carbon emissions by switching from fossil fuels to renewable energy sources. Therefore, fossil fuels, such as coal, would produce the greatest amount of carbon emissions. Choice (C) is the correct answer.

3. Here, you need to determine which renewable energy sources Bashville could potentially adopt. The passage states that Bashville receives significant rainfall and is located in a basin surrounded by mountains. Thus, solar power, (a), and wind power, (b), are not viable options. Furthermore, the passage does not mention geothermal energy, (e), so this choice is also incorrect. According to the passage, Bashville is located near a number of rivers and receives a significant amount of rainfall each month. Accordingly, **hydroelectric power, (d),** is a viable renewable energy option for the people of Bashville. The passage also states that Bashville wants to reduce the amount of organic waste. Therefore, **biomass, (c),** is also a potential renewable energy choice for Bashville.

Fossils Drill (Page 711)

1. The sentence should read as follows: The organic material found in rock layer C is probably older than the material found in **layer A** and younger than the material found in **layer D**. As the passage describes, the layers form sediment over time, so the oldest material will be on the bottom, while the youngest material will be on the top.

2. **B** After one half-life has transpired, there will be half of the original amount left [(B) is correct and (A) and (D) are incorrect]. The passage does not state what carbon-14 decays into, but you know that only half of it will decay in this time—and carbon-7 does not exist, so (C) is incorrect.

3. **D** There is no evidence that this area was once an ocean; (A) is eliminated. The rock layer could not have formed before the woolly mammoth roamed the Earth, so eliminate (B). There is not enough information to determine when layer A formed, so eliminate (C). There must have been the appropriate conditions for fossilization, so (D) is correct.

Astronomy Drill (Page 716)

1. According to the graph in the passage, the coldest planet is **Neptune**, so the correct answer is to click on Neptune.

2. **D** Of the four choices, Mars is the farthest from the Sun and therefore has the longest orbital distance. If all planets were to travel at the exact same speed, Mars would complete its orbit in the greatest amount of time—(D) is correct. Note that this question asks for an extreme answer. Even if you don't know the right answer, you can eliminate the two answers that are not the extremes (Earth, Venus) right away.

3. **C** The correct answer to this question will be one that is *not* supported by the evidence in the passage. Process of Elimination is a good strategy to use for questions like this one. According to the passage, the outermost planets are the larger ones, so eliminate (A). The graph indicates that the maximum temperature of Mars is less than Venus, so eliminate (B). The passage does not speculate on the likelihood of life on other planets—(D) is neither supported nor contradicted so it is eliminated. The passage states that the Sun contains 99.9% of all mass in the solar system, indicating that it is about 1,000 times as massive as everything else in the solar system, not 100 times—(C) is false and therefore the correct answer.

GED® Test Premium Prep, 32nd Edition
Practice Test 1

The Princeton Review®

YOUR NAME: ______________________________
(Print) Last First M.I.

SIGNATURE: ______________________________ DATE: ___/___/___

HOME ADDRESS: ______________________________
(Print) Number and Street

____
City State Zip Code

PHONE NO.: ______________________________
(Print)

DATE OF BIRTH: ___/___/___
(Print) Month / Day / Year

Section I Reasoning Through Language Arts

1. (A) (B) (C) (D)
2. (A) (B) (C) (D)
3. (A) (B) (C) (D)
4. (A) (B) (C) (D)
5. (A) (B) (C) (D)
6. ☐ → ☐ → ☐ → ☐
7. ________ ________ ________
8. (A) (B) (C) (D)
9. ☐ ☐
10. (A) (B) (C) (D)
11. (A) (B) (C) (D)
12. (A) (B) (C) (D)
13. (A) (B) (C) (D)
14. (A) (B) (C) (D)
15. (A) (B) (C) (D)
16. (A) (B) (C) (D)

Section I Reasoning Through Language Arts

17. For each of the following four menus circle the option that correctly completes the sentence.

neighborhood, just as I do. neighborhood. Just as I do. neighborhood just as I do too. neighborhood; you just as much as I do.
The alarmingly increased burglary incidents, via news reports and social media posts, you must be aware of by now, By now, via news reports and social media posts, you must be aware of the alarming increase in burglary incidents Via news reports and social media posts you must be aware of by now, the alarming increase in burglary incidents The alarming increase in burglary incidents you must be aware of by now, via news reports and social media posts
concerning our community, as we all do as we all were concerned about our community, as we are all concerned about our community, having concern about our community, as were we all,
them it that one

Section II Reasoning Through Language Arts

Write your Extended Response essay on a separate sheet of paper.

Section III Reasoning Through Language Arts

18. (A) (B) (C) (D)
19. (A) (B) (C) (D)
20. (A) (B) (C) (D)
21. (A) (B) (C) (D)
22. (A) (B) (C) (D)
23. (A) (B) (C) (D)
24. ☐ → ☐ → ☐ → ☐
25. (A) (B) (C) (D)
26. ☐ ☐
27. (A) (B) (C) (D)
28. (A) (B) (C) (D)
29. (A) (B) (C) (D)
30. (A) (B) (C) (D)
31. (A) (B) (C) (D)
32. (A) (B) (C) (D)
33. (A) (B) (C) (D)
34. (A) (B) (C) (D)
35. (A) (B) (C) (D)
36. (A) (B) (C) (D)
37. (A) (B) (C) (D)
38. (A) (B) (C) (D)
39. (A) (B) (C) (D)
40. ☐ ☐

Section III Continued

41. (A) (B) (C) (D)
42. (A) (B) (C) (D)
43. (A) (B) (C) (D)
44. (A) (B) (C) (D)
45. (A) (B) (C) (D)
46. (A) (B) (C) (D)
47. ____________ ____________
48. (A) (B) (C) (D)
49. (A) (B) (C) (D)
50. For each of the following four menus circle the option that correctly completes the sentence.

During that period, it is with great pleasure that I see him developing During that period, I had the great pleasure of seeing him develop Seeing him develop during that period, I had great pleasure As I saw him during that period, with great pleasure, he was developing
quickly and effectively, during quickly, effectively, and during quickly and effectively. During quick and effectively. During
worker, able to give guidance and step worker. Just as able to give guidance and step worker, just as able to give guidance and stepping worker, just as able to give guidance as to step
Even a year after his resignation, still, he is remembered here fondly. A year after his resignation, even he is still remembered fondly here. He is remembered here still fondly, even a year after his resignation. He is still remembered fondly here, even a year after his resignation.

Part I Mathematical Reasoning

1. (A) (B) (C) (D)
2. (A) (B) (C) (D)
3. (A) (B) (C) (D)
4. (A) (B) (C) (D)
5. (A) (B) (C) (D)

Part II Mathematical Reasoning

6. (A) (B) (C) (D)
7. (A) (B) (C) (D)

Questions 8 and 9

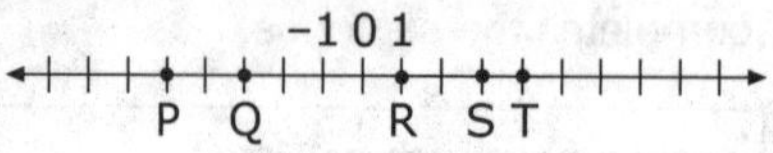

10. (A) (B) (C) (D)
11. (A) (B) (C) (D)
12. (A) (B) (C) (D)
13. (A) (B) (C) (D)
14. ____________
15. ____________ ____________
16. ____________
17. (A) (B) (C) (D)
18. [ ] + [ ] / [ ]
19. (A) (B) (C) (D)
20. (A) (B) (C) (D)
21. (A) (B) (C) (D)
22. (A) (B) (C) (D)
23. ____________ ____________
Action-Adventure Drama
24. (A) (B) (C) (D)
25. (A) (B) (C) (D)
26. ____________
27. (A) (B) (C) (D)
28. (A) (B) (C) (D)

Part II Continued

29.

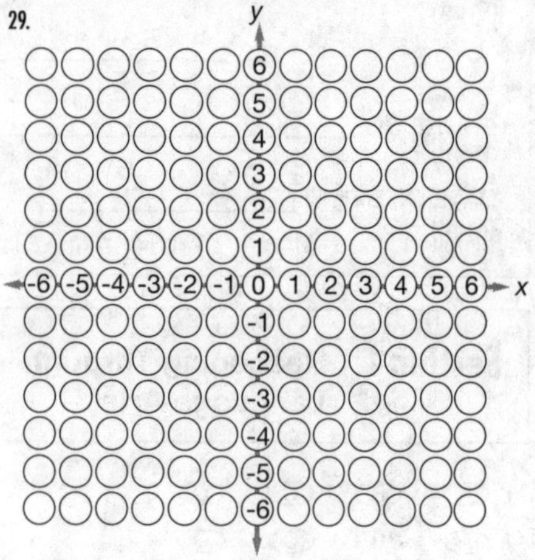

30. (A) (B) (C) (D)
31. (A) (B) (C) (D)
32. (A) (B) (C) (D)
33. (A) (B) (C) (D)
34. (A) (B) (C) (D)
35. (A) (B) (C) (D)
36. ____________
37. (A) (B) (C) (D)
38. ____________
39. (A) (B) (C) (D)
40. (A) (B) (C) (D)

Questions 41 and 42

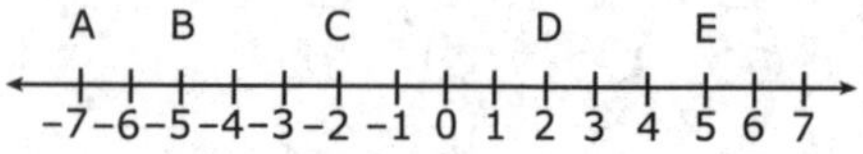

43.

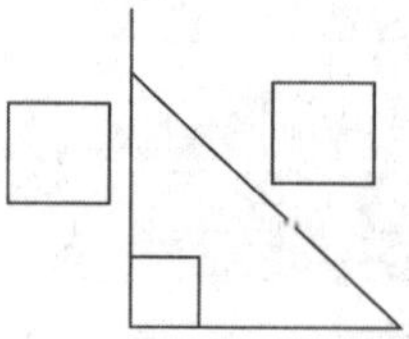

44. ____________
45. (A) (B) (C) (D)
46. (A) (B) (C) (D)

GED® Test Premium Prep, 32nd Edition
Practice Test 1

The Princeton Review®

Social Studies

1. (A) (B) (C) (D)
2. (A) (B) (C) (D)
3. (A) (B) (C) (D)
4. (A) (B) (C) (D)
5. (A) (B) (C) (D)
6. (A) (B) (C) (D)
7. (A) (B) (C) (D)
8. (A) (B) (C) (D)
9. (A) (B) (C) (D)
10. (A) (B) (C) (D)
11. (A) (B) (C) (D)
12. (A) (B) (C) (D)
13. (A) (B) (C) (D)
14. (A) (B) (C) (D)
15. (A) (B) (C) (D)
16. (A) (B) (C) (D)
17. (A) (B) (C) (D)
18. (A) (B) (C) (D)
19. (A) (B) (C) (D)
20. (A) (B) (C) (D)
21. (A) (B) (C) (D)
22. (A) (B) (C) (D)
23. (A) (B) (C) (D)
24. (A) (B) (C) (D)
25. (A) (B) (C) (D)
26. (A) (B) (C) (D)
27. (A) (B) (C) (D)
28. (A) (B) (C) (D)
29. (A) (B) (C) (D)
30. ____________ ____________ ____________
31. (A) (B) (C) (D)
32. (A) (B) (C) (D)
33. (A) (B) (C) (D)
34. (A) (B) (C) (D)
35. (A) (B) (C) (D)

Science

1. (A) (B) (C) (D)
2. (A) (B) (C) (D)
3. ____________________________
4. (A) (B) (C) (D)
5.

The type of coal most likely found closest to the surface of the earth:	The type of coal that contains the greatest amount of carbon per kilogram:

6. (A) (B) (C) (D)
7. (A) (B) (C) (D)
8. (A) (B) (C) (D)
9. (A) (B) (C) (D)
10.

The oldest rock layer:	The newest rock layer:

11. (A) (B) (C) (D)
12. (A) (B) (C) (D)
13. (A) (B) (C) (D)
14. (A) (B) (C) (D)
15. Write your answers in the blanks below:

____________ ____________

16. ____________________________
17. (A) (B) (C) (D)
18. (A) (B) (C) (D)
19. (A) (B) (C) (D)
20. (A) (B) (C) (D)
21. (A) (B) (C) (D)

Science

22. **Waves That Foretell Tidal Waves**

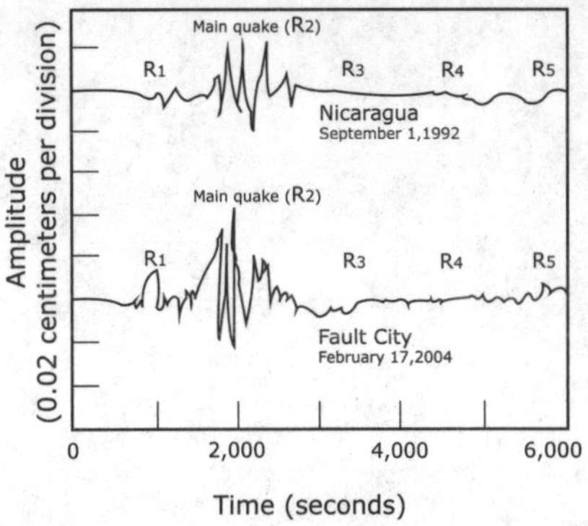

23. (A) (B) (C) (D)
24. (A) (B) (C) (D)
25. (A) (B) (C) (D)
26. (A) (B) (C) (D)
27. (A) (B) (C) (D)
28. (A) (B) (C) (D)
29. (A) (B) (C) (D)
30. (A) (B) (C) (D)
31. (A) (B) (C) (D)
32. (A) (B) (C) (D)
33. (A) (B) (C) (D)
34. **Heat and Temperature of Water**

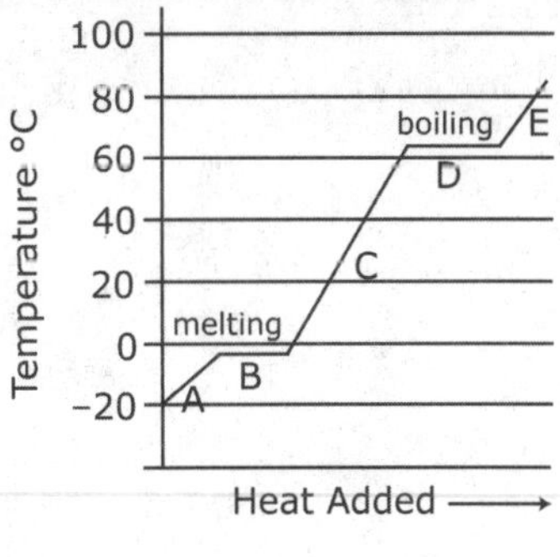

35. (A) (B) (C) (D)

NOTES

NOTES